THE

ECONOMICS OF
THE ENVIRONMENT
AND NATURAL
RESOURCES

THE

ECONOMICS OF THE ENVIRONMENT AND NATURAL RESOURCES

R. QUENTIN GRAFTON
WIKTOR ADAMOWICZ, DIANE DUPONT
HARRY NELSON, ROBERT J. HILL
AND STEVEN RENZETTI

Blackwell
Publishing

350 Main Street, Malden, MA 02148-5018, USA
108 Cowley Road, Oxford OX4 1JF, UK
550 Swanston Street, Carlton, Victoria 3053, Australia

First published 2004 by Blackwell Publishing Ltd

Library of Congress Cataloging-in-Publication Data

The economics of the environment and natural resources/by R. Quentin Grafton
    ... [et al.].
    p. cm.
Includes bibliographical references and index.
    ISBN 0-631-21563-8 (hardcover: alk. paper) – ISBN 0-631-21564-6
(pbk.: alk. paper)
1. Environmental economics. 2. Natural resources. 3. Environmental
policy. I. Grafton, R. Quentin, 1962-

HC79.E5L42 2004
333.7–dc21
                                    2003007539

A catalogue record for this title is available from the British Library.

Set in 10/12 $\frac{1}{2}$; Book Antique
by Newgen Imaging Systems (P) Ltd, Chennai, India
Printed and bound in the United Kingdom
By MPG Books, Bodmin, Cornwall

For further information on
Blackwell Publishing, visit our website:
http://www.blackwellpublishing.com

This book is dedicated to the special people in our lives who share both our joys and sorrows (and everything in between!): Ariana, Brecon, and Carol-Anne; Sharon, Beth, and Kate; Allie and Nicholas; Alex and Joanne; Miriam.

CONTENTS

FIGURES

TABLES

BOXES

PREFACE

Our book is the collective effort of six economists with a great deal of help from their colleagues, teachers, families, and friends and, of course, the publisher (we especially thank Elizabeth Wald at Blackwell). As originally conceived, the book was to have only two authors (Quentin and Rob), but as the scope of the text expanded so did the need to bring in additional expertise for the chapters on non-market valuation (Vic), water (Steven), trade and biodiversity (Diane), and forestry and the global commons (Harry). We view this collective expertise as a major strength of the book.

Although there is a northern connection that links all the authors (four out of six of us work in Canada) and all of us have at least one degree from a Canadian University, the book remains very much an international text. Quentin (grew up in New Zealand and has lived in seven different countries) and Rob (grew up in the United Kingdom) currently live and work in Australia while Harry was born and raised in the United States, but is now a Canadian resident. Vic, a Canadian by birth, completed his Ph.D. at Minnesota and wrote most of his chapters while on sabbatical leave at Resources for the Future in Washington, DC, Diane and Steven, both based in Ontario, finished the final drafts of their chapters while on sabbatical leave at the University of East Anglia. This combined and varied life experience is reflected in the examples in the book that come from many different countries. It means that our book should be as suitable for students in Ames, Iowa, as in Bergen, Norway.

A book, by its very nature, does not provide for two-way communication between the reader and the author. To help overcome this barrier we welcome constructive criticism and feedback. Please direct your comments, in the first instance, to Quentin at qgrafton@cres.anu.edu.au

ACKNOWLEDGMENTS

A large number of people have helped us to write this book. We especially thank our spouses, family and friends who have supported us in ways both large and small. We are also grateful for an understanding and encouraging publisher that had the confidence to stick with us, despite the delays.

We list by name those who helped us directly, mainly by providing us with comments on draft chapters. We especially thank Tom Kompas and Jack Pezzey for help beyond the ordinary call of collegial duty. We also offer our sincere gratitude to Anonymous (for everyone we have inadvertently excluded from this list!), Jeff Bennett, David Campbell, Robin Connor, Brian Copeland, Rob Dyball, Scott Heckbert, Frank Jotzo, Gordon Kubanek, Liz Petersen, Barry Newell, Viktoria Schneider, Dale Squires, Stein Ivar Stenshamn, David Stern, two reviewers who wish to remain anonymous, and our many students.

Quentin also thanks his colleagues at the Center for Resource and Environmental Studies and the Economics and Environment Network at the Australian National University for offering such a stimulating and supportive environment for research and the exploration of ideas. Diane and Steven would like to thank Kerry Turner and the staff at CSERGE (Center for Social and Economic Research on the Global Environment) at the University of East Anglia, UK, for providing a wonderful sabbatical location conducive to thinking deep thoughts. Vic would like to thank his colleagues (staff and students) at the University of Alberta for providing an excellent research environment and he thanks Resources for the Future in Washington, DC, for making his Gilbert White Fellowship year a productive and enlightening experience.

INTRODUCTION

Difficulty is a coin which the learned conjure with so as not to reveal the vanity of their studies and which human stupidity is keen to accept as payment. (Michel de Montaigne, *The Complete Essays* (translated by M. A. Screech), Book II, Essay 12, p. 566)

THE ENVIRONMENTAL CHALLENGE

Our environment and its natural resources provide us with enormous benefits. They sustain life on earth and give us the means to exist and to enjoy the amenities of nature. Despite their importance, we often fail to consider the full costs and benefits of enjoying the environment. We frequently neglect the underlying dynamics of nature, and our institutions and governance structures fall short of what is needed to sustainably manage the environment and its resources.

This book provides the tools, experiences and insights that economists and decision-makers have gained from the management (or mismanagement!) of nature. Whether the challenge is to understand how we can prevent overfishing, develop ways to overcome the institutional barriers to global warming, value a mountain lake, or simply reduce air pollution levels in a cost-effective manner in our neighborhood, this book provides a guide to the study of such issues.

WHAT THIS BOOK OFFERS

Many texts examine environmental, resource, and ecological economics. Most are focused on a narrow set of topics while a few books offer a comprehensive treatment, but at a level that is often unsuitable for advanced undergraduate or graduate-level courses.

Our book covers the essential topics students need to understand environmental problems and their possible solutions. Each chapter is written as the equivalent of 6–8 hours of lectures that would normally be covered in upper-level undergraduate or master's and Ph.D. courses in environmental and natural resource economics. The 15 topics covered in the book could each be of book length, but we have restricted the length to about 30 pages. The chapters are *not* designed to provide every detail of the subject. Instead, our goal is to provide you, the reader, with the fundamental theoretical insights, the major issues of the topic or discipline, and an appreciation of the real-world problems and challenges that motivate the subject. Each chapter has extensive further reading that will enable you to pursue the topic further should you wish.

As is true of all books, we have not included every topic that might be discussed in courses in environmental, resource, and ecological economics. In particular, we do not have a separate chapter on sustainable development, but many aspects of the issues of sustainability appear in various chapters and, in particular, the chapter on growth and the environment and the concluding chapter that focuses on how we can sustain our environment. We also do not have a separate chapter on population growth, but address the importance of demographics in our chapter on growth and the environment. Topics that we have also eschewed from writing are those that focus on a particular technique, such as cost–benefit analysis, as we believe theory, practice, and techniques need to be addressed together and understood in terms of how and why they are applied.

WHAT YOU NEED TO KNOW

We have written the book for readers who have prior training in microeconomics. The assumed background is the equivalent of a third-year course in microeconomics offered in an honors program or a good undergraduate degree in economics. Thus no prior courses or training in environmental or resource economics is required. We expect that most economics students at an advanced undergraduate level, and all graduate students in economics, will have the necessary background to read all the chapters in the book.

HOW THE BOOK IS ORGANIZED

The book covers all of the major topics in environmental and resource economics and is subdivided into four main parts. The first part contains several chapters that provide a more extensive discussion on general theoretical approaches to environmental and natural resources and includes chapters on economic modeling, methods of pollution control, and property rights and incentives. The second part consists of chapters on particular natural resources of the environment including fisheries, forestry, water, and non-renewable resources. The third part covers the theory and practice of environmental valuation and includes chapters on stated preference approaches and indirect methods of environmental valuation. The fourth and final part focuses on larger-scale issues involving the linkages and interaction between human activities and the environment, with chapters on the global commons, economic growth and the environment, trade and the environment, biodiversity, and environmental accounting. Our book also features a glossary that defines specialized terms used in the text and are given in italic the first time they appear in a chapter.

We believe that you will be able to use this book to gain greater insights into the environmental issues facing us today. The concepts, tools and practices you will learn in the following chapters will help you understand the trade-offs and choices we face and the ways in which we might improve the world around us.

CHAPTER ONE

MODELS, SYSTEMS, AND DYNAMICS

We must learn to think in terms of systems. We must learn that in complex systems we cannot do only one thing. Whether we want it to or not, any step we take will affect many other things. We must learn to cope with side effects. We must understand that the effects of our decisions may turn up in places we never expected to see them surface. (Dietrich Dörner, *The Logic of Failure*, p. 198)

1.1 WHAT IS A MODEL?

Our environment is both complex and dynamic. Given this complexity we need a "map" or models to help to understand what processes and interactions are important and to evaluate the outcomes of interest. The first step in modeling is to clearly define what is the problem or problems of interest. For instance, the problem or question to be answered may be, what will be the population of grizzly bears in a national park next year? Any model that adequately addresses this problem must include hypotheses, or statements, about what influences the bear population. By necessity, such statements cannot be a complete representation of the dynamics of the grizzly bear population. For instance, the accumulation of pesticides and other chemicals in the food chain may have an adverse effect on grizzly bear breeding success rate in the *long run*, but incorporating chemical and pesticide build-up in grizzly bears may not help us to improve our prediction of the grizzly bear population for next year. Thus the *purpose* of the model determines the boundary of the model and what we should or should not include within our "map."

A model can be a highly complex system of equations developed in an iterative process that may take months, or even years, to construct. By contrast, it may be as simple as a single statement that represents an underlying process or relationship that can be used to help resolve a particular research problem. For example, "The population of grizzly bears in Banff National Park next breeding season will equal the current population, plus the number of cubs that survive the current season less the number of juvenile and adult bears that die during the season." This statement can be written out as a mathematical model,

$$x_{t+1} = x_t + b_t - d_t$$

where x_{t+1} is the population of grizzly bears in period $t+1$, x_t is the population of grizzly bears in period t, b_t is the number of cubs successfully reared and d_t is the number of juveniles or adult bears that die.

This model provides an understanding, or an interpretation, of the population dynamics of grizzly bears. The formulation of the model may be derived from watching breeding females raise cubs during the breeding season. If data are available on the current population, the number of cubs successfully raised in the first year of their life and the number of juveniles and adults that die, the model can be tested by comparing its predictions to the number of bears observed in next year's breeding season. If subsequent observations and data match our predictions to an appropriately defined level of significance, then the model has achieved its purpose. However, just because a model is useful does *not* imply that a model is "true." Indeed, no single model can be described as being a correct or true representation of reality as it must, by necessity, be an abstraction.

The specified model of the population dynamics of grizzly bears ignores the possibility of the migration of grizzly bears from other populations to Banff National Park, and from grizzly bears in Banff to populations of bears in other locations. However, if net migration of bears is small compared to the birth or death rates, the model may still be a good predictor of next year's breeding population. If the purpose is to predict next year's breeding population, making the model more realistic (and including net migration) is not necessarily desirable. For instance, if including migration in the model increases the prediction error, or the difference between observed and predicted bear numbers, then it may be preferable to leave out net migration from the model. In other words, if the research problem is simply to predict next year's bear population then a model that achieves this purpose with a lower prediction error is preferred to another model, even if the alternative is more realistic and captures more details of the population dynamics. Thus the judgment of a model is not whether it describes reality well or not, but whether it helps address the research problem for which it was built and whether it does so better than alternative models.

A maxim of modeling, known as Occam's razor, is that the simplest logical model that addresses the research problem is preferred over alternative models. Thus the art of modeling is not to include everything that can be incorporated, but rather to make the model as simple and tractable as possible to help answer the question that was posed. Knowing what to leave in, and what to leave out of a model, requires a good understanding of both the processes being modeled and the purpose of the model. For instance, if the purpose of the model of the population dynamics of bears is to understand the relationships between bears and their prey, then the model given above is useless. If, however, its purpose is to simply predict next year's population the model may be very useful. Consequently the judgment on the usefulness of a model is intricately linked to what problem it tries to address, or the questions for which it was devised to answer.

1.2   MODEL BUILDING

Model building often involves both conjectures and hypotheses based on observations of phenomena, and that may be called induction, as well as the specification of a logical and consistent set of statements that purport to explain the phenomena, and that may be called deduction. Good model building requires both induction and deduction. Theories cannot be developed in a vacuum without an understanding of the phenomena being modeled. Similarly, models based purely on observation run the risk of lacking in rigor and logic where "facts" and observations may support a completely wrong model. In other words, just because observations fail to falsify or refute a model, it does *not* mean that the model is correct. Moreover, correlation between variables that conform to a model's hypotheses does *not* necessarily imply causation. Many variables are correlated with each other, but there is not necessarily an underlying causal rela-tionship between them. For instance, in rich countries the average time spent per week watching television is positively correlated with life expectancy, but this does not imply that watching television *causes* us to live longer. A classic example of how observations can support an incorrect model is provided by Apollonius of Perga (265–190 BC) who was one of the greatest mathematicians of antiquity. He developed a geocentric model of the solar system in which the earth was at the center and all other planets, including the sun, orbited around it. The model was supported by observations over many centuries and was able to predict planetary positions to a surprising degree of accuracy.

The testing or disproving of hypotheses is part of the scientific method whereby propositions or models are formulated and are then tested to see whether they conform to empirical observations. The exception, perhaps, is in mathematics, where "truth" is not determined by experimentation but rather by proof. Thus mathematical truths, that are in the form "If A, then B," are results derived by deduction from the initial axioms or statements or rules. In other words, the proofs or propositions derived from the initial axioms are "true" in a *mathematical* sense whether or not the original axioms were correct or whether or not they conform to reality. An axiomatic approach to modeling can be very useful and can provide fundamental insights, but if we seek an understanding of the world around us then, sooner or later, our models (and axioms!) must connect to reality.

If we employ the scientific method, hypotheses that are found lacking, or can be "disproved" in their current formulation, may be modified, or an entirely new model may be devised to test the hypotheses. Any hypothesis that is "scientific" must be falsifiable in the sense that it can be disproved from empirical observations.

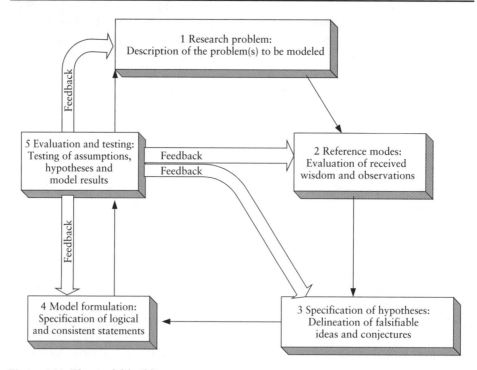

Figure 1.1 The model-building process

Indeed, the falsification process should include the specification in advance of the observations that would falsify the hypothesis. For example, Einstein's theory of relativity (special and general) predicted that light passing through space would be bent when it passed near an object with a massive gravitational field. This prediction was found to be correct in 1919 (14 years after Einstein's special theory was published) when it was observed by British scientists, during a solar eclipse, that distant stars appeared to "move" from a terrestrial perspective as the light they emitted was bent by our sun. Ideally, the falsification of a model should also require that the model being tested make predictions that other models cannot. Sometimes the data or observations may not yet exist to disprove a hypothesis, but provided that such data can be obtained, then the hypothesis is still falsifiable, although it remains untested.

The scientific approach to model building is iterative. It involves a statement of the problem(s) to be addressed, a review of the observed behavior or received wisdom, a formulation of conjectures or statements or equations that purport to explain the processes and relationships, and the subsequent testing and evaluation of the model(s), as illustrated by figure 1.1. The thin black arrows indicate the development, chronology or learning loop of the model-building process that begins first with the research problem and continues through to evaluation and testing. The thick arrows indicate a feedback process that influences all the steps in model building.

The first step in building a model is to establish what is the research problem. The problem must be sufficiently concise and tractable that the model can realistically provide some insight into the question. For example, the problem "What are the costs of climate change?" is so broad that no single model can hope to provide a meaningful answer to the question. This is not to say that the "big" questions should not be asked, but rather that answering such a question requires a research program that will require many models. Indeed, the question regarding the potential consequences of climate change has spawned a huge and multi-disciplinary research program under the auspices of the Intergovernmental Panel on Climate Change (IPCC) that has led to the formulation of many thousands of models. By contrast, the problem "What are the short-term economic costs for Germany from meeting its obligations to reduce its greenhouse gas (GHG) emissions, as specified under the 1997 Kyoto Protocol?" can be investigated (and indeed is currently being investigated) with an appropriate set of economic models.

The second step in modeling is to review the accepted wisdom. This may include a review of the existing theory and evaluation of the results of existing models. This establishes the "reference modes" (Sterman, 2000) or a summary of the fundamentals of what is known. The review should also include an evaluation and assessment of the existing data or observations about the problem or phenomena to be modeled. For example, if the research problem is to predict the future abundance of animal populations, the reference mode should include the history of the population and some measures of its births and deaths. The reference modes, in turn, help shape our initial hypotheses of the relationships, feedbacks, and relative importance of the variables that are to be included in the model.

The third step in the process is to specify conjectures, ideas or a preliminary theory that can be developed into testable hypotheses about the processes for which the model is being built. These hypotheses help dictate the model we ultimately formulate, along with the existing models in the literature. The hypotheses that are to be tested should be sufficiently clear and precise so that they can provide insights into the research problem. The hypotheses to be refuted, and the reference modes, help to formalize the model used to answer the specified research questions. For example, a hypothesis underlying an economic model of climate change could be that reductions in emissions of carbon dioxide reduce real economic growth. Such a hypothesis would require that we build a model that explicitly includes measures of economic activity and carbon dioxide emissions, and their interrelationships.

The fourth, and perhaps hardest, step is to formulate the model. The formal model must be logical, should avoid unnecessary details and be as simple as possible while still being able to help answer the posed research question. What makes a good model is *not* whether it provides an exact description of the phenomena being studied, but whether it can provide real insights and understanding into the research problem. A model should be more than the sum of its parts and should be judged by its ability to provide understanding and insights about the research questions and hypotheses that would otherwise not be possible.

When formulating a model, simplifying assumptions are required about the relationships of the variables under study. For example, we may assume that one variable (such as the price of a good) is unaffected by changes in another variable (such as income). These assumptions, along with the refutable hypotheses, need to be tested if the model is to be of use. In other words, if we assume a certain relationship holds true when formulating a model then for the model to be falsifiable (as it should be!) this assumption should be able to be tested or refuted.

Models may also require us to subsume a set of postulates or assertions that cannot be tested. These assertions presuppose a state of the world, or set of behavior, that cannot be refuted, but may nevertheless be required if the model is to be tractable. For example, we may *assert* that consumers are rational when we are formulating a model of consumer demand that *assumes* that the quantity demanded is a function of the relative price of the good. Without the assertion that consumers are rational (which may or may not be true), it may be difficult to construct a simple model that could, for example, be used to predict future consumption levels of the good. However, the assumption of a functional relationship between the relative price and the consumption of the good in a model, which is used to predict future consumption, must be tested when evaluating the model. Such tests of the model's assumptions are conditional on the assertions or postulates used to formulate the model.

The step that closes the loop in the model-building process is to test and evaluate the model, the results and hypotheses. Testing of the model may involve many different approaches and methods. For example, with econometric or statistical models we can compare our hypotheses with our empirical results. This can be accomplished by tests for misspecification, measurement (and other) errors, influence of different functional forms on the results and whether the assumptions used in estimating the model are valid. In empirical work, care must also be taken to avoid "data mining" in the sense that we select a model that gives the "best" results and levels of significance, but fail to report the many other estimates we discarded to obtain the best model. Such an approach creates a bias in terms of the normal levels of significance we use for testing whether explanatory variables are statistically significant from zero or not.

Empirical models also require tests of robustness to judge their value and should include an analysis of the influence of outliers and influential observations, the effect of the choice of explanatory variables, the selected data series used for the variables and the chosen time period. Further, careful attention should be given to the *economic* significance of the statistical results (McCloskey, 1997). For instance, simulations can be generated from estimated coefficients to help answer "what if?" questions about the effect of changes in the magnitude of one or more of the explanatory variables. Thus, a variable may be statistically significant in the sense that at the 1 percent level of significance we reject the null hypothesis that its estimated coefficient equals zero, but it may have only a small influence on the dependent variable. Conversely, an explanatory variable that may not be statistically significant at the conventional 5 percent level of significance may *potentially* have a very large effect in the sense that a small change in its magnitude could lead to a large change in the dependent variable.

Whatever the form or type of model, "testing" should include a comparison between the results, the initial hypotheses, and the existing literature. Testing of the model also requires that we evaluate competing models or hypotheses that may provide different insights or understanding to the research problem. In other words, the observations may also be consistent with alternative and competing models and not just the model used in the analysis. Moreover, when comparing models that equally fit existing observations, the model that also makes additional and falsifiable predictions is, in general, preferred. The evaluation of the model and competing models should, in turn, stimulate further thinking and inquiry into the original question or problem posed, the accepted or received wisdom and the model that was formulated. Thus, testing and evaluation continue the model-building process and contribute to our understanding of the problems that originally motivated the research.

Parallel to the model-building process is consideration of not only *what* is the research problem, but *who* is the audience for sharing of the insights and results of the model. Too frequently researchers expect that their model and results will "speak for themselves." Unfortunately, even the most brilliant model builder will accomplish little in terms of increasing knowledge and understanding if she fails to present what has been done in a form suitable for the intended audience. If the intended readership is a group of well-trained and knowledgeable researchers then motivating the research problem, describing the model and explaining the results may be sufficient. If, however, the likely audience lacks the training or background to understand the model, or the implications and caveats of the results, then considerable effort is required to explain the model and its implications in a way that is comprehensible to the reader.

1.3   MODEL CHARACTERISTICS

Models can be divided into those that involve optimization, whereby an objective function is optimized over a set of choice or control variables subject to a set of constraints, and models that simulate changes in processes over time. Optimization models are frequently used to answer "what should be"-type questions. For example, what should be the harvest rate in a fishery if we wish to maximize the present value of net profits? Simulation models are often used to answer "what would be" questions such as, what would be the earth's average surface temperature in 2100 if the concentration of carbon dioxide in the atmosphere were to double?

Optimization and simulation

Optimization and simulation models share a number of important characteristics and, indeed, sometimes simulations are used to find an "optimum" strategy while optimization models may be used to simulate possible outcomes under alternative specifications of the objective functions and/or constraints.

In environmental and resource economics we often wish to optimize our rate of discharge or depletion or use of an environmental asset. This requires optimizing an objective function subject to a set of constraints. Most economic models optimize over a particular variable whether it be utility, profits, or some other metric subject to constraints. The appropriate metric is determined by the problem addressed by the model. For instance, if we wish to determine the level of harvest of trees that will generate the highest monetary return over time then an objective function that maximizes the discounted net profits is appropriate. By contrast, if we were concerned with the costs of production for a given level of harvest, then an objective function that minimizes the economic costs of production under a harvest constraint would be appropriate. In such problems, the variables whose values are chosen in the optimization program are called control variables and could include, for example, the harvest rate. Variables whose values are determined within the model, but which depend on the values of the control variables, are called state variables. State variables might include, for example, the resource stock. The potential solution is bounded by constraints that may include dynamic constraints that describe the dynamics of the state variables and boundary conditions that specify any constraints on the starting and ending values of variables.

Simulation models provide predicted values of variables of interest based on specified initial values and parameters of the model. In many cases, the parameters and initial conditions for simulation models are obtained from empirical models or observations of the phenomena under study. Simulation models are enormously useful in helping us understand the interactions and processes of systems. The value of simulation models comes from the analysis of the effects of changes in interactions, parameters, and initial values, called sensitivity analysis. To make such comparisons as easy as possible, several software packages are available. The software Vensim (www.vensim.com), Powersim (www.powersim.com) and Stella (www.hps-inc.com) are widely used and are sophisticated enough to build models of highly complex systems.

Endogenous and exogenous variables

Whatever the purpose, the modeler must decide what variables should be determined within the model (be endogenous), and what variables should be determined from outside (be exogenous), but are included in the model. Variables that are neither exogenous nor endogenous to the model are excluded variables and are not incorporated in the model-building process. All variables that are *critical* in determining future states of the model should be endogenous, whether or not the variables change slowly or rapidly. At the very least, model results should be tested for their robustness to changes in values of those variables treated as exogenous.

To some extent, the decision as to which variables are endogenous, exogenous or are excluded depends on both the purpose and the time-scale of the model.

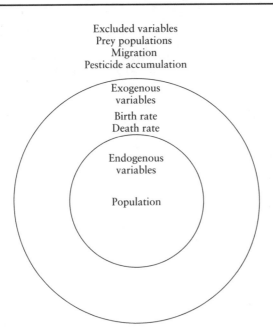

Excluded variables
Prey populations
Migration
Pesticide accumulation

Exogenous
variables

Birth rate
Death rate

Endogenous
variables

Population

Figure 1.2   Boundaries of a model of the grizzly bear population in Banff National Park

For example, a model designed to predict economic growth over the next year could treat population as an exogenous variable and have little effect on the reliability of the predictions. However, if such a model were used to predict economic growth over 25 years or more it would likely suffer from important deficiencies as economic growth and population growth are co-determined and feed back on each other.

To illustrate the boundaries of models, figure 1.2 shows what variables are excluded, exogenous and endogenous in the model used to predict the bear population in Banff National Park. Outside the model boundary are excluded variables (migration, pesticide accumulation, prey effects). The model includes exogenous variables (birth and death rates) that may be varied by the modeler, but are not determined by the model itself. In the core of the model is the endogenous variable (population) that is determined by the model. The initial and past states of the endogenous variable, in turn, help determine future values of the endogenous variable.

Feedback effects

All complex systems are subject to both positive and negative feedback effects. Positive feedbacks reinforce disturbances to a system and move variables further away from their original state while negative feedbacks tend to return systems

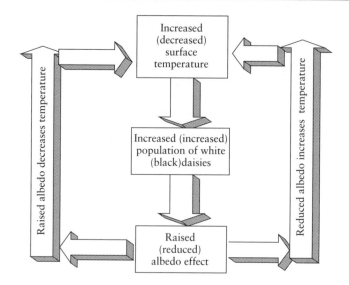

Figure 1.3   Negative feedback effects in Daisyworld

to their former state following disturbance. Negative feedback effects may be illustrated in a simple model of a planet called Daisyworld (Lovelock, 1990). In this world only two plants exist, white and black daisies. White daisies do better at higher temperatures than black daisies, but also have a greater albedo effect and reflect more of the solar radiation reaching the planet's surface. Shocks to the system are provided by changes in solar radiation that affect the planet's surface temperature and the relative abundance of white and black daisies. In turn, the abundance of white and black daisies determines the amount of solar radiation reflected back into space which feeds back to determine the planet's surface temperature and the relative abundance of white and black daisies. This system is presented in figure 1.3.

Both positive and negative feedbacks are important in environmental systems. For instance, the earth's climate includes many different positive and negative feedback effects that contribute to keeping our planet's average surface temperature close to 14 degrees Celsius. These feedbacks are illustrated in figure 1.4. One negative feedback comes from a rising surface temperature that raises the amount of water vapor in the atmosphere that, in turn, increases cloud cover that increases the amount of solar radiation reflected back into space and helps to reduce surface temperature. A positive feedback comes from a rising temperature that increases the melting of the permafrost and wetlands in northern latitudes that, in turn, releases methane (a greenhouse gas) and increases the concentration of greenhouse gases in the atmosphere. An increase in greenhouse gas concentrations increases the ability of the atmosphere to retain heat radiating from the surface and eventually raises surface temperatures.

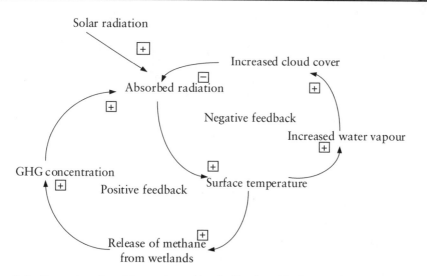

Figure 1.4 Examples of positive and negative feedbacks with climate change

Whatever the model, and whether it be used for optimization or simulation, the fundamental feedbacks of the system should be incorporated. More generally, a failure to incorporate feedback effects into models is likely to result in serious errors in prediction and a failure to understand the important interactions between variables. For example, in a set of models built in the 1970s that were enormously useful in helping people think about the interconnections and dynamics between human activities and environmental outcomes, modelers failed to adequately model the feedbacks between prices, quantity demanded and the supply (proven reserves) for non-renewable resources. In *illustrations* of the possible effects of unlimited economic growth where the demand for resources was assumed to increase exponentially, the model incorrectly predicted that the world's present and known reserves of gold, tin, petroleum, and silver in 1972 would be exhausted by 1990 (Meadows et al., 1974).

Stocks and flows

Common to both optimization and simulation models are stock and flow variables. Stocks, such as the level of capital, can be added to and subtracted from by flows, such as investment and depreciation. In dynamic optimization models, stock and flow relationships are characterized by dynamic constraints that define how a stock changes over time. For example, in an optimization model to maximize the present value of net profits from a fishery, the dynamic constraint that governs the fish stock could be

$$dx/dt = F(x) - h(t)$$

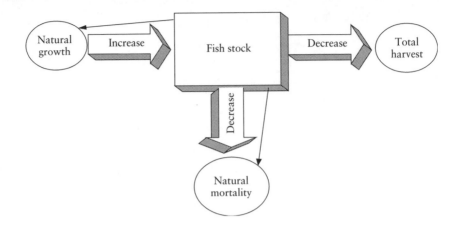

Figure 1.5   Stocks, flows, and feedbacks

where dx/dt is the change in the fish stock with respect to time, $F(x)$ is the natural growth function of the fish stock and $h(t)$ is the harvest per time period. In this case, $F(x)$ is a flow determined by nature and the level of the stock and $h(t)$ is a flow determined by decisions of fishers.

The relationship between stocks and flows can also be visualized in a simulation model, where natural growth is an inflow and natural mortality and the total fishing harvest are outflows represented by large arrows that increase or decrease the stock. A feedback relationship between a flow and a stock is represented by a single-line arrow that indicates the level of the fish stock helps determine both natural growth and natural mortality. A representation of a model in this form in figure 1.5 helps us to understand the relationships, causal connections, and feedbacks in a system.

1.4   MODEL DYNAMICS

The most cursory examination of the world around us reveals that life, our planet, and our universe are continually changing. The fossil record indicates that the earth has suffered from several mass extinctions, and that the earth's biota has changed dramatically in the relatively short period of time that modern humans have been in existence. Thus, researchers who wish to understand environmental challenges, and how to manage natural resources, must recognize that the world is dynamic.

Characteristics of dynamic systems

All natural systems are dynamic in the sense that they change over time, but are able to sustain life despite shocks. For example, the human body is a natural system

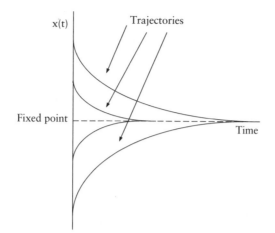

Figure 1.6   Trajectories to a fixed point

whose changes are governed by both underlying processes (such as genetics) and external factors that are partly under our control and predictable (such as our diet) and unpredictable events (such as being struck by lightning). Despite the many changes and shocks that our bodies undergo during our lifetime, they provide us with a blood pressure and a body temperature that vary by surprisingly small amounts despite huge variations and changes in our environment. Such a process that sustains life and that arises from both positive and negative feedbacks is called *homeostasis* and is a common feature in living systems.

Another important feature of dynamic systems is whether they, or variables within the system, tend to converge to a *fixed point* or steady state over time. In other words, is there some point, should it ever be reached, where the variable or system will remain at forever. The existence of fixed points and whether we can ever reach them is of particular importance when managing natural systems. For example, in a fishery we might wish to keep the resource stock within some desirable range and if we are not in this range, we would like to know whether we can arrive at these desirable levels, given sufficient time. This is illustrated in figure 1.6 where the fixed point might represent a desirable level of the resource stock. In this particular example, the fixed point is *globally stable* because whatever the initial value of the variable (be it greater or less than the fixed point) the variable will converge to it over time. The movement or transition of a variable or system from one value to another over time is called a trajectory and is also illustrated in figure 1.6.

A fixed point may or may not be an optimum in the sense that it optimizes a given objective function, but if it is an optimum it provides a point to which we would like the system or variable to converge. Ideally, we would wish for our global optimum (most desirable point) to be a globally stable fixed point in the sense that whatever the initial values of the system the trajectories always converge to the optimum. In reality, dynamic optimization is rarely so straightforward and

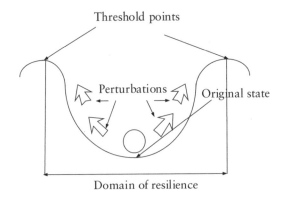

Figure 1.7 Resilience and threshold points

it involves devising a program such that trajectories approach a desired set of values. In some cases, a small change in the trajectories may lead to a radically different (and undesirable) outcome.

Despite the sophistication we can bring to modeling dynamic systems and behavior, our interpretation and prediction of actual systems can be very limited. In part, this arises because system dynamics often arise from both deterministic and stochastic processes and separating the causes, effects, and feedbacks can be very difficult. Fortunately, predicting future values in natural systems is made easier by negative feedbacks. The more able is a system to return to a former state the larger is the magnitude of a shock then the greater is its resilience (Holling, 1973). Unfortunately (for predictive purposes), and no matter how resilient is a system, there is ultimately some threshold point or nonlinearity beyond which the system switches or flips into a fundamentally different state. For example, acid rain over several years may gradually increase the acidity of a fresh-water lake with little apparent effect on the ecosystem, but suddenly at a certain point the environmental system may flip to a fundamentally different state. In the case of acid rain and fresh-water lakes, at a pH threshold point of 5.8 algal mats began to appear along the lake shore disrupting fish breeding and other aspects of the ecosystem.

This system behavior can be visualized in figure 1.7 where movements of the ball represent perturbations to a system and the low point in the "bowl" indicates the system's original state. Provided that the perturbations are not too large the system has a tendency to return to its original state. If, however, the system receives a large shock and is pushed "over the side" the process may become irreversible and the system may never return to its original state.

Discrete time models

Various techniques and approaches have been used to help model the dynamics of the environment and natural resources. Difference equations are used in modeling systems where change occurs at discrete points in time. Difference equations suppose that future values of variables of a system are a function of the current and possibly past values. A first-order difference equation, given below, supposes that the next period value is only a function of the current period value.

$$x_{t+1} = f(x_t)$$

where $f(x_t)$ may be either a linear or nonlinear function.

Difference equations can be used to model both linear and nonlinear behavior. They may also generate fixed points or steady-states (x^*) where x_t is unchanged for all time, i.e.,

$$x^* = f(x_t) \ \forall \ t$$

If the system converges to a fixed point, whatever the initial value of x_t, it is stable or convergent. For example, a system modeled by the difference equation, where a and b are constants,

$$x_{t+1} = a + bx_t$$

will converge to its fixed point of $a/(1-b)$, provided that $|b| < 1$. The fixed point is found by setting $x_{t+1} = x_t$ and then solving for x_t in terms of a and b. If $b < 0$ then the values of x_t will oscillate between positive and negative values. If $b > 1$ then the values of x_t become increasingly large as time progresses and there exists no fixed point or equilibrium. The solution to a difference equation is consistent with the original equation, but contains no lagged values. For this particular difference equation the solution is

$$x_t = a/(1-b) + b^t(x_0 - a/(1-b)).$$

The solution allows us to predict x_t at any time period provided we know the initial value (x_0) and the parameter values (a and b).

Difference equations can also be used to model seemingly very complex system behavior. A commonly used model of the population dynamics of some animal populations is logistic growth,

$$x_{t+1} = a \, x_t(1 - x_t)$$

where a is a constant. Logistic growth characterizes a population that has a low rate of increase when its population level is small and when it is large, and has its highest rates of growth at intermediate levels of the stock. Thus at low population levels a positive feedback exists between the population and growth in the population, but at a high population a negative feedback exists such that further increases in population reduce population growth. Such behavior is

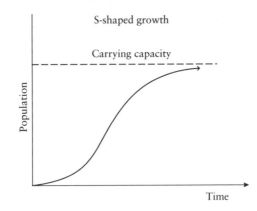

Figure 1.8   S-shaped growth

called density dependent growth. Logistic growth is sometimes referred to as sigmoidal or s-shaped growth, as shown in figure 1.8 because of the shape that it resembles when the total population is plotted against time and begins at a very low level. Because of negative feedback effects the population eventually reaches a carrying capacity beyond which the population cannot be sustained by the environment.

Chaos

To help understand the potential behavior of dynamic but deterministic systems, consider the trajectories or values of x_t over time in a logistic model. Provided that $a<1$ then x_t converges to the fixed point 0 (population becomes extinct) because with each period of time x_t becomes successively smaller. In this case, the parameter a is at a level that extinction of the population is irreversible, whatever the initial population.

If a is greater than 1 but less than 3 then whatever the initial value of x_t the population will converge to the same fixed point or carrying capacity, for a given value of a. As we progressively increase a above 3 then the trajectory (set of points that represent the level of the population at different periods in time) of x_t starts to move towards not one, but two points called *attractors* and will go back and forth between the points. At increasingly higher values of a the number of attractors for the trajectory also rises such that the number of attractors doubles from 2 to 4 when $a \approx 3.45$ and doubles again to 8 points at $a \approx 3.54$, and keeps on doubling at slightly higher values of a. This switch in the qualitative behavior of a system is called a *bifurcation* and, in this case, is called *period doubling* to indicate that a small change in a parameter in the system doubles the number of attractors. As the number of attractors doubles, the time that it takes the system to return to a given attractor also doubles. Thus it takes twice as long to

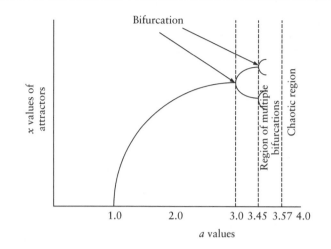

Figure 1.9 Bifurcation to chaos

return to a given attractor when there are four attractors than when there are just two attractors.

For values of a greater than 3.57 and equal to or less than 4, the system exhibits chaos and, depending on the initial value of x_t, the attractor (the points to which the system moves towards over time) may have an infinite number of values. The pattern of attractors for different values of a is illustrated in figure 1.9. Although the system is deterministic such that future values are completely determined, the system is highly sensitive to the initial value of x_t and the parameter a. Moreover, chaos can generate very complex dynamics *without* random shocks or stochastic events and if variables and states of the world are measured imprecisely, we can never predict their long-term values.

In reality, many systems are subject to both deterministic processes and stochastic events. For example, a population that is chaotic (and therefore deterministic) may also be subject to random shocks, such as changes in climate, that also influence its future state. Separating out the effects of shocks from the outcomes of deterministic processes or distinguishing between chaotic systems (which are deterministic) and systems that are not chaotic, but subject to stochastic fluctuations or events, is extremely difficult.

Continuous time models

Another way to model dynamics is to assume that change occurs continuously rather than at discrete points in time. The continuous time analog to difference equations are differential equations that can be written as

$$dx/dt = f(x,t)$$

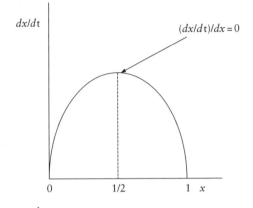

Figure 1.10   Logistic growth curve

where $f(x,t)$ can be a linear or nonlinear function. For comparison, the differential equation and continuous time analog to the difference equation for logistic growth is:

$$dx/dt = ax \, (1 - x)$$

In the case where the differential equation is not a function of time, such as with logistic growth, the equation is said to be autonomous. The population with logistic growth has three fixed points (when $dx/dt = 0$); one when $x = 0$, a second when $x = 1/2$, and a third when $x = 1$. The first case is when the population is extinct, the second case is when the growth in the population is maximized or the point where $(dx/dt)/dx = 0$ and the third point is when the population is at its carrying capacity. The representation of the relationship between dx/dt and x is given in figure 1.10.

As with difference equations, a system of differential equations can be specified to represent the behavior of several and interacting variables over time. Various methods can be used to generate solutions to systems modeled by differential equations. Their solution must be consistent with the original equation, but must not contain any derivative term. Whether or not a system has fixed points and whether the system converges to a fixed point, and from which values, is a fundamental question. Such a question is of particular importance in optimization models where we may be concerned with reaching a target population level (such as a fishery stock) that maximizes our chosen objective function (such as the present value of net profits).

Like difference equations, differential equations can be used to model a range of dynamic behavior. For example, variables in a system may exhibit exponential growth or decay such that the rate of change in the variable over time is proportional to the size of the variable, i.e.,

$$dx/dt = (a - b)x.$$

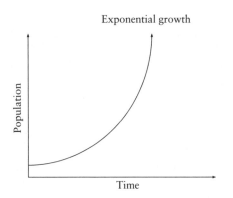

Figure 1.11 Exponential growth

In the case of a population, we can define a as the birth rate and b as the death rate and $(a - b)$ as the net growth rate. If the net growth rate is positive (negative) then the population will continuously grow (decay) over time. The solution to this differential equation can be found by integrating both sides of the equation where the lower and upper limits of integration are 0 and t and is given by,

$$x(t) = x_o e^{(a - b)t}$$

where $x(t)$ is the value of the population in time t, and x_o is the initial value of the population. In this system, future values of the variable or population are completely determined by the net growth rate (parameters a and b) and the initial starting value. The system has only one fixed point (point where $dx/dt = 0$) when $x(t) = 0$. The dynamics of the system for positive net growth are illustrated in figure 1.11. Although some variables may exhibit exponential growth over periods of time, no natural system can have exponential growth in the long run as ultimately energy, space, or other constraints must place a finite limit on the size of the variable or system.

1.5 DYNAMIC OPTIMIZATION

Dynamic optimization is an important method of analysis in environmental and resource economics. For discrete time problems the method called *dynamic programming*, pioneered by the American mathematician Richard Bellman in the 1950s, is often employed. For continuous time problems, economists frequently use a method called *optimal control* first developed by the Russian mathematician L. S. Pontryagin, and his colleagues, about fifty years ago. To be understood properly, both optimal control and dynamic programming require intensive study. Fortunately, the principles and intuition of both methods can be readily understood and applied in environmental and resource economics.

For both methods, the optimization problem must be properly specified. This requires an understanding of what variable(s) are under the control or decision of the person making the optimizing decisions. Such variables are called *control variables* in optimal control and *decision variables* in dynamic programming. The choice of these variables determines the values of *state variables* that are determined within the dynamic optimization model. The constraints to the problem include both *dynamic constraints* that represent how the state variables change over time and *boundary conditions* that specify the initial or starting values of the state variables, and possibly their value at the end of the program. Whether either approach yields a maximum or not also depends on so-called *sufficiency conditions*. For our purposes, this can be satisfied if the objective functional is differentiable and strictly concave in the control variable, no direct constraints are imposed on the value of the control variable, and the functions that govern how the state variables change over time – the *transition equation* in dynamic programming or the *dynamic constraint* in optimal control — are both differentiable and concave.

Dynamic programming

Dynamic programming is an algorithm that allows us to solve optimization problems that can be written as a multi-stage decision process where information about "the state of the world" is completely summarized in the current value of the state variable(s).

The algorithm is derived from the *principle of optimality* that allows us to solve a set of smaller problems for each decision stage, such that the value of the state variable in the next period depends only on the value of the state variable in the current period and the decision in the current period.

If the objective function satisfies certain sufficiency conditions and is also the sum of the net benefit or stage returns at each stage or point where a decision is made, we can define *Bellman's functional recurrence equation* to solve a discrete dynamic optimization problem. Starting with Bellman's functional recurrence equation for the last stage or final period, the algorithm obliges us to work backwards systematically to the initial period. The initial value of the state variable(s) is then used to solve the problem for all values of the decision variables and state variables at every period in the program. To illustrate, take the following problem,

$$\text{Max} \sum_{t=1}^{T} f_t(s(t), d(t)) \tag{1}$$

Subject to:

$$s(t+1) = g_t\left(s(t), d(t)\right) \tag{2}$$

$$s(1) = s_1, \ s(T+1) = s_{T+1} \tag{3}$$

where T is the final period in the program, $f_t(s(t),d(t))$ is the *net benefit* or *stage return function* which depends on the state variable at time t, $s(t)$, and the decision variable at time t, $d(t)$. The function $g_t(s(t),d(t))$ is the *transition* or *transformation function* at time t and determines the value of the state variable in the following stage or time period. An initial value of the state variable (s_1) is *always* required to obtain a solution, but this does not necessarily apply for its final value (s_{T+1}). The functional recurrence equation for this problem is,

$$V_t(s(t)) = \max{}_{d(t)} \left[f_t(s(t),d(t)) + V_{t+1}(s(t+1)) \right] \tag{4}$$

where from (2), $V_{t+1}(s(t+1)) = V_{t+1}(g_t(s(t),d(t)))$.

In general, $V_{T+1}(s(T+1)) = 0$, as it is beyond the final stage or period of the program, T. The method of solution is to first express the problem in the form of the functional recurrence equation for the final stage or time period (T in the problem above) and use the value of the state variable at $T+1$ to obtain an expression for $V_T(s(T))$ solely in terms of $s(T)$. Next, we write the functional recurrence equation for the next to last stage or penultimate period $(T-1)$, substitute $V_T(s(T))$ that we found previously into the expression for $V_{T-1}(s(T-1))$ and use the transition equation to substitute out $s(T)$ for $s(T-1)$ and $d(T-1)$. We then use the first-order condition $(\partial V_{T-1}(s(T)))/(\partial d(T-1)) = 0$ at time $T-1$ to obtain an expression for $d^*(T-1)$ in terms of $s(T-1)$ and then substitute it into $V_{T-1}(s(T-1))$ so that the equation is solely in terms of $s(T-1)$. This backward recursion continues until we reach the first stage (or $t=1$ in the problem above) ensuring that for each stage or time period, t, $V_t(s(t))$ has as its argument only $s(t)$. Using the initial condition, or initial value for the state variable, we can then determine $d^*(1)$ and then $s^*(2)$ and so on until $d^*(T)$ and $s^*(T)$, thus offering a full solution to the problem.

To illustrate the approach we can specify a simple two-period "cake eating" problem where a person receives a "cake" at the start of the first period ($t = 1$), but which must be consumed by the end of the program ($t = 3$). The objective is to maximize utility over time by consuming the cake where utility in each period equals the square root of the amount of the cake consumed, i.e.,

$$\text{Max U} = x_1^{1/2} + x_2^{1/2} \tag{5}$$

Subject to:

$$a_1 = 1 \tag{6}$$
$$a_2 = a_1 - x_1 \tag{7}$$
$$a_3 = 0 \tag{8}$$

where x_i is the amount of the cake consumed in period i and a_i is the amount of cake remaining at period i. For this problem, the sufficiency conditions are satisfied, thus, the approach yields a maximum. The functional recurrence equation in this case is,

$$V_t(a_t) = \max{}_{x(t)} [x_t^{1/2} + V_{t+1}(a_{t+1})] \tag{9}$$

Subject to:

$$a_{t+1} = a_t - x_t \tag{10}$$

where expression (9) or $V_t(a_t)$ is the *return function* and is the maximum value for (5) at time t, given the amount of cake left to be consumed (a_t). Expression (10) is the *transition equation* that determines the value of the next period's state variable.

The functional recurrence equation when $t = 2$ is

$$V_2(a_2) = \max[x_2^{1/2} + V_3(a_3)] \tag{11}$$

Subject to:

$$a_3 = a_2 - x_2 \tag{12}$$
$$a_3 = 0 \tag{13}$$

where $V_3(a_3)$ has the value of zero as it is the value of the return function after the end of the program or optimization period. Combining the constraints (12) and (13) we can obtain an expression for x_2 in terms of a_2 that we can use to rewrite the functional recurrence equation solely in terms of a_2, i.e.,

$$V_2(a_2) = a_2^{1/2} \tag{14}$$

The next step is to write the functional recurrence equation for the previous period, $t = 1$, i.e.,

$$V_1(a_1) = \max[x_1^{1/2} + V_2(a_2)] \tag{15}$$

Subject to:

$$a_2 = a_1 - x_1 \tag{16}$$
$$a_1 = 1 \tag{17}$$

We can substitute in the previously found return function $V_2(a_2)$ and then use (16) to obtain an expression for (15) solely in terms of a_1 and x_1 by substituting out for a_2, i.e.,

$$V_1(a_1) = \max[x_1^{1/2} + (a_1 - x_1)^{1/2}]$$

The necessary condition for a maximum requires that,

$$\partial V_1(a_1)/\partial x_1 = (1/2)x_1^{-1/2} - 1/2(a_1 - x_1)^{-1/2} = 0$$
$$\Rightarrow x_1 = a_1 - x_1$$
$$\Rightarrow x_1^* = (1/2)a_1 \tag{18}$$

Given that $a_1 = 1$, then $(x_1^*, x_2^*, a_2^*) = (0.5, 0.5, 0.5)$. This represents a complete solution to the "cake eating" problem over two periods.

Optimal control

Optimal control provides a set of necessary conditions to help solve dynamic problems in continuous time. These necessary conditions, sometimes called *the maximum principle*, are used to solve for *optimal paths* or trajectories for the control and state variables. The general form of problem that can be solved using optimal control, without discounting the future and where the end of the program T is fixed, can be represented by (19)–(21).

$$\text{Max V} = \int_{t=0}^{T} f[a(t), x(t), t] \, dt \tag{19}$$

Subject to:

$$da/dt = g[a(t), x(t), t] \tag{20}$$
$$a(0) = a_0 \tag{21}$$

In this problem, V is called the *objective functional*, $x(t)$ is the control variable and $a(t)$ is the state variable. All of the variables are functions of time. The dynamic constraint is given by (20) and governs how the state variable changes over time. The minimal boundary condition is the initial value of the state variable and is given by (21). In some problems, the terminal value of the state variable may also be specified as another boundary condition.

The method of solution is to write a function called a *Hamiltonian* that consists of the objective functional plus the dynamic constraint multiplied by a *co-state* or *adjoint variable* that is also a function of time, normally defined by the Greek symbol lambda, or λ. The co-state variable can be interpreted as the shadow or imputed price of the state variable at a given instant in time and, in this sense, is analogous to the notion of a Lagrangian multiplier in static optimization.

At the end of the program, denoted by T, it must be the case that $\lambda(T) = 0$ if $a(T) > 0$, otherwise we would not be on an optimal path and we would not be maximizing the objective functional subject to the constraints. To understand this point, consider the situation if $a(T) > 0$ and $\lambda(T) > 0$. In this case the state variable has a positive value (because $\lambda(T) > 0$), yet we have chosen to leave some of it at the end of the program. This must be sub-optimal because we could reduce the amount of the state variable remaining at the end of the program and simultaneously increase the objective functional.

For the problem specified by (19)–(21), the Hamiltonian function is as follows,

$$H[a(t), x(t), \lambda(t), t] = f[a(t), x(t), t] + \lambda(t)g[a(t), x(t), t] \tag{22}$$

Provided there are no constraints on the control variable and the objective functional is differentiable in the control variable, the necessary conditions for solving (19)–(21) are listed below.

$$\partial H/\partial x(t) = 0 \tag{23}$$
$$d\lambda(t)/dt = -\partial H/\partial a(t) \tag{24}$$
$$da/dt = g[a(t), x(t), t] \tag{25}$$
$$a(0) = a_0 \tag{26}$$
$$\lambda(T) = 0 \quad \text{if } a(T) > 0 \tag{27}$$

Condition (23) states that an optimal path requires that the partial derivative of the Hamiltonian function with respect to the control variable must equal zero at each point in time. Condition (24) states that the change in the co-state variable with respect to time must equal the negative of the partial derivative of the Hamiltonian function with respect to the state variable. Conditions (25) and (26) recover the dynamic constraint given by (20) and the boundary condition given by (21) in the original problem. Condition (27) is called a *transversality condition* that ensures the trajectories are optimal at terminal time T when the program ends.

Given that the conditions (23)–(27) use variables that are functions of time, finding the optimal paths for the control, state, and co-state variables often involves solving differential equations. Sometimes explicit solutions of these differential equations are impossible. In such cases, the "solution" or optimal paths of the variables may be represented qualitatively in terms of phase diagrams provided that the problem is *autonomous* such that time only appears as a function in the control, state, or co-state variables and not explicitly by itself. Phase diagrams trace out the points where the control and state variables are unchanging with respect to time, i.e., the points where $dx(t)/dt = da(t)/dt = 0$. Phase diagrams may also be constructed where explicit solutions are possible as they allow us to visualize and characterize the steady state of the dynamic system and the potential trajectories (if any) to the steady state.

To illustrate the optimal control approach, we can solve the continuous time analog to the "cake eating" problem. In continuous time, the problem can be defined by (28)–(31).

$$\text{Max V} \int_{t=0}^{2} x(t)^{1/2} \, dt \tag{28}$$

Subject to:

$$da/dt = -x(t) \tag{29}$$
$$a(0) = 1 \tag{30}$$
$$a(2) = 0 \tag{31}$$

In this problem, $x(t)$ is the control variable and is the amount of cake eaten at an instant in time and $a(t)$ is the state variable, or the amount of cake remaining at an instant in time. Expression (29) is the dynamic constraint where da/dt is the instantaneous change in the amount of cake remaining with respect to time and equals the negative of the amount of cake consumed at each instant in time. Equation (30) is the initial boundary condition and specifies the initial amount of cake available at $t = 0$. We also have an extra boundary condition, given by constraint (31), that specifies that all the cake must be eaten by the end of the program.

The Hamiltonian for the dynamic problem given by (28)–(31) is,

$$H[x(t), \lambda(t)] = x(t)^{1/2} + \lambda(t)[-x(t)] \tag{32}$$

The necessary conditions that must be satisfied to solve (28)–(31) are given below.

$$\partial H/\partial x(t) = \tfrac{1}{2}x(t)^{-1/2} - \lambda(t) = 0 \tag{33}$$
$$d\lambda(t)/dt = -\partial H/\partial a(t) = 0 \tag{34}$$
$$da/dt = -x(t) \tag{35}$$
$$a(0) = 1 \tag{36}$$
$$a(2) = 0 \tag{37}$$

In this case, we do not specify that $\lambda(T) = 0$ as the transversality condition is superfluous given the boundary condition specified by (37). Simplifying (33), we obtain the following expression for $x(t)$ in terms of $\lambda(t)$, i.e.,

$$x(t) = \frac{1}{4\lambda(t)^2} \tag{33'}$$

Substituting (33′) into (35), or the dynamic constraint, and observing from (34) that $d\lambda(t)/dt = 0$, we can integrate both sides of the resulting expression with respect to time to obtain equation (38), where K is a constant of integration, i.e.,

$$a(t) = K - t/4(\lambda(t))^2 \tag{38}$$

The value of K in (38) can be solved by substituting the initial boundary condition, or (36), into (38) for when $t = 0$, i.e.,

$$1 = K - 0/4(\lambda(0))^2 \quad \Rightarrow K = 1$$

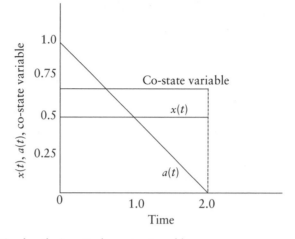

Figure 1.12 Optimal paths in a "cake-eating" problem

Thus, we can rewrite the optimal path for the state variable, $a(t)$, as follows,

$$a(t) = 1 - t/4(\lambda(t))^2 \tag{38'}$$

It now remains to solve for the co-state variable, $\lambda(t)$. Before we do so, we can characterize the solution by noting from (34) that the co-state variable is unchanging with respect to time, i.e., it is a constant. Similarly, from the expression for $x(t)$ in (33'), expression (34) also implies that the control variable is unchanging with respect to time, i.e., $dx(t)/dt = 0$. In other words, both the control and co-state variables will be a constant over the program from $t = 0$ to $t = 2$.

From the boundary condition at the end of the program, condition (37), we can solve out for the value of the co-state variable at $t = 2$ using (38') and thus find the value of $\lambda(2)$, i.e.,

$$0 = 1 - 2/4(\lambda(2))^2 \Rightarrow \lambda(2) = \sqrt{1/2} \tag{39}$$

If $\lambda(t)$ has the value of the $\sqrt{1/2}$ at $t = 2$, it must also have this value at every point in time during the program given condition (34). Substituting the value of $\lambda(t)$ given in (39) into (33'), and also into (38'), we obtain the optimal paths for the control and state variables, i.e.,

$$x(t) = 1/2 \tag{33''}$$
$$a(t) = 1 - t/2 \tag{38''}$$

The optimal paths described by (33") and (38") are illustrated in figure 1.12.

In figure 1.12, the area defined by triangle 0-1-2 equals one, as does the rectangular area defined beneath the $x(t)$ line and the horizontal axis, indicating that the amount consumed over the program exactly equals the amount of cake at the beginning of the program. The slope of the $a(t)$ line is $da(t)/dt$ and equals $-1/2$ (or the negative of $x(t)$) and characterizes the dynamic constraint given by (29) or (35).

If we discount future values and costs, both the Hamiltonian and the necessary conditions need to be modified. In the case of discounting, the objective functional can be specified by (40).

$$\text{Max } V = \int_{t=0}^{\infty} f[a(t),x(t),t]e^{-\delta t}\, dt \tag{40}$$

In (40), $\exp^{-\delta t}$ or $e^{-\delta t}$ is the continuous time discount factor, $e =$ base of the natural logarithm and δ is the instantaneous discount rate. If we use the constraints given by (20) and (21) and the objective functional given by (40), the Hamiltonian with discounting is given by (41).

$$H[a(t),\, x(t),\, \lambda(t),\, \delta,\, t] = f[a(t),\, x(t),\, t]e^{-\delta t} + \lambda(t)g[a(t),\, x(t),\, t] \tag{41}$$

Expression (41) is defined as the *present-value Hamiltonian*. More commonly, the necessary conditions are defined from the *current-value Hamiltonian* defined as $H = \mathrm{H}\, e^{\delta t}$, i.e.,

$$H = f[a(t),\, x(t),\, t] + \mu(t)g[a(t),\, x(t),\, t] \tag{42}$$

where $\mu(t) = e^{\delta t}\lambda(t)$. The only changes to the necessary conditions (now defined in terms of the current-value Hamiltonian) given by (23) to (27) are in terms of the co-state variable. These modified necessary conditions are given by (43)–(47).

$$\partial H/\partial x(t) = 0 \tag{43}$$
$$d\mu(t)/dt - \delta\mu(t) = -\partial H/\partial a(t) \tag{44}$$
$$da/dt = g[a(t),\, x(t),\, t] \tag{45}$$
$$a(0) = a_0 \tag{46}$$
$$\mu(T)e^{-\delta t} = 0 \text{ if } a(T) > 0 \tag{47}$$

If the program has an infinite time horizon and the problem is autonomous then the transversality condition given by (47) only holds true in the limit as $t \to \infty$, provided no constraints are imposed on the value of the state variables. For problems where the terminal time T is chosen by the solution to the program, an additional transversality constraint also applies, namely, $H(T)\, e^{-\delta T} = 0$. In other words, the present-value Hamiltonian must be zero at terminal time.

1.6 DYNAMICS AND ENVIRONMENTAL AND RESOURCE ECONOMICS

An understanding of models, model building, dynamics and systems provides a useful starting point for appreciating the research problems and approaches that predominate in environmental, ecological, and resource economics. In models of fisheries, water, forestry, and other natural resources a fundamental question is, how can we do the best we can given our own and nature's constraints? For such problems, dynamic optimization models are widely employed. Depending upon the nature of the problem, several different approaches can be used for their solution. Such problems can be solved by "pen and paper," but software is also available. For models that are linear in both the objective function and constraints powerful algorithms exist for their solution and several different software packages are available, including GAMS (www.gams.com) that can solve very large mathematical programming problems. However, even quite complex optimization problems can be solved using spreadsheet software, such as Excel (Conrad, 1999). For highly nonlinear objective functions, maxima and minima can be solved for using software packages such as MATHEMATICA (www.wolfram.com) or MAPLE (www.maplesoft.com).

A comprehension of environmental values, environmental accounting, economic growth and the environment, and the interconnections in the global commons also requires that we understand the broad dynamics and feedback effects of the systems we wish to understand. Whatever the question or problem, a systematic and scientific approach to modeling provides us with a framework for increasing our understanding of and, ultimately, improving our environment.

FURTHER READING

This chapter provides an introduction to modeling, systems, and dynamics. Given the importance of modeling in economics, surprisingly very few books explain or discuss how to economically model research problems. A wonderful exception is Blaug (1980) who provides a description of the key methodological issues in economics. Sterman (2000), chapter 3, gives an excellent introduction to the building of simulation models.

A plethora of texts exist on the methods of dynamic analysis. A useful introduction that offers questions and answers in mathematical economics is Grafton and Sargent (1996). A textbook on mathematical economics that is comprehensive and comprehensible is Hoy et al. (2001). Three of the best textbooks on dynamic optimization models, with applications to economics, are Shone (1997), Léonard and Van Long (1992) and Chiang (1992). An excellent book on the solution of dynamic optimization models in natural resource economics is Conrad (1999). Several good texts on building and using simulation models exist including Ford (1999) and Deaton and Winebrake (1999). Williams (1997) is a rigorous but highly accessible book on chaos.

REFERENCES

Blaug, M. (1980). *The Methodology of Economics*, Cambridge University Press: Cambridge.

Chiang, A. C. (1992). *Elements of Dynamic Optimization*, McGraw-Hill Inc.: New York.

Conrad, J. M. (1999). *Resource Economics*, Cambridge University Press: Cambridge.

Deaton, M. L. and Winebrake, J. I. (2000). *Dynamic Modeling of Environmental Systems*, Springer-Verlag: New York.

Dörner, D. (1997). *The Logic of Failure: Recognizing and Avoiding Error in Complex Situations*, Perseus Books: Cambridge, MA.

Ford, A. (1999). *Modeling the Environment: An Introduction to System Dynamics Modeling of Environmental Systems*, Island Press: Washington, DC.

Grafton, R. Q. and Sargent, T. C. (1997). *A Workbook in Mathematical Methods for Economists*, McGraw-Hill: New York.

Holling, C. S. (1973). Resilience and Stability of Ecological Systems, *Annual Review of Ecology and Systematics*, 4: 1–24.

Hoy, M., Livernois, J., McKenna, C., Rees, R., and Stengos, T. (2001). *Mathematics for Economists*, second edition, MIT Press: Cambridge, MA.

Léonard, D. and Long, N. V. (1992). *Optimal Control Theory and Static Optimization in Economics*, Cambridge University Press: Cambridge.

Lovelock, J. E. (1990). Hands Up for the Gaia Hypothesis, *Nature*, 344 (March): 100–102.

McCloskey, D. N. (1997). *The Vices of Economists: The Virtues of the Bourgeoisie*, Amsterdam University Press: Amsterdam.

Meadows, D. H., Meadows, D. L., Randers, J., and Behrens III, W. W. (1974). *The Limits to Growth*, second edition, Signet: New York.

Shone, R. (1979). *Economic Dynamics*, Cambridge University Press, Cambridge.

Sterman, J. D. (2000). *Business Dynamics: Systems Thinking and Modeling for a Complex World*, McGraw-Hill Higher Education: Boston.

Williams, G. P. (1997). *Chaos Theory Tamed*, Joseph Henry Press: Washington, DC.

CHAPTER TWO

PROPERTY RIGHTS

> *But is there nothing recognised as property except what has been produced? Is there not the earth itself, its forests and waters, and all other natural riches, above and below the surface? These are the inheritance of the human race, and there must be regulations for the common enjoyment of it. What rights, and under what conditions, a person shall be allowed to exercise over any portion of this common inheritance cannot be left undecided.* (John Stuart Mill, *Principles of Political Economy*, Book V, Chapter 1, section 2, pp. 161–2)

2.1 WHAT IS A PROPERTY RIGHT?

A property right exists over an asset whenever a recognizable entity (individual, firm, agency, etc.) is able to exclude, at least partially, others from either using it or enjoying a flow of benefits from its use. This may involve legal ownership of the asset, a *de jure* right, but often rights exist in the absence of ownership. For instance, if we manage to find a free seat on a city bus we have a *de facto* "property right" or privilege to that seat until we disembark. The property right exists because all the people on the bus follow the social norm that the first to be seated has the right to sit, despite the fact that passengers neither own the bus nor the seat. Along with this property right comes an obligation to leave fellow passengers undisturbed, such as by avoiding the playing of loud music.

Property rights affect almost every decision we make and are one of the fundamental factors that determine economic performance. These rights include the private ownership over personal assets such as our stereo system, the clothes we wear or our car if we are rich enough to own one! People using or taking these assets without our permission face social sanction and punishment for their actions. The fact that these assets belong to us, and are protected by law, encourages us to look after them because any decline in their value or use to us is a personal cost. Property rights can also be shared between individuals

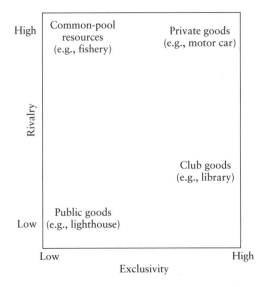

Figure 2.1 Classification of goods by exclusivity and rivalry in use

and groups of individuals. For example, in some societies land is communally controlled, or held in common. Assets may also be owned by the state, such as the land held in a national park, or they may be under the direct control of no one, such as fish in the high seas. Who holds property rights over assets, especially over natural resources and the environment, and the nature of these rights has very important implications in terms of environmental outcomes.

The question of *who* has the property right is intricately linked with *what* is the asset or good over which it is defined. *Private goods* (such as a car, which may or may not be privately owned) share two characteristics. First, private goods are rival in use (one person's use precludes someone else from using it) and second, it is relatively easy to exclude others from using them (for instance, a private good such as a car can be locked and car theft is a punishable offense). By contrast, *public goods* (such as a lighthouse and which may or may not be publicly owned) are inherently non-rival in use (one person's use of the light does not affect its use by anyone else) and non-excludable (the light can be seen by anyone in its vicinity). *Club goods* (such as use of a library or health club which may or may not be owned by a club) are characterized by ease of exclusion and *congestibility* such that beyond a certain number of users increasing usage of the asset reduces the flow of benefits from its use. Many environmental assets are not pure public goods, club goods or private goods. Instead they are *common-pool resources* (such as a fishery) where exclusion is difficult, but not impossible (fishing vessels at sea can be monitored but at a significant cost) and their use is rivalrous (an increased catch for one fisher means less for another). The differences between the four main types of "goods" are presented in figure 2.1. It is worth emphasizing that if a good or asset is highly rivalrous in use (such as a common-pool resource), it means that one person's use of it reduces the ability of the other to either use or enjoy it. Exclusivity refers to the ability to prevent others from using or enjoying a flow of benefits from the good or asset.

Much of the focus of the property rights literature is on understanding the nature of the rights, who has them, and the outcomes associated with these rights. In this chapter we provide a template to analyze the characteristics of property rights, we explore the relationship between efficiency and equity and property rights, examine the importance of legal rights and common law in protecting the environment and investigate the various outcomes associated with different property rights structures.

2.2 CHARACTERISTICS OF PROPERTY RIGHTS

Property rights come in many different forms – private rights held by an individual, agent or firm (*res privatae*), community rights (*res communes*), state rights (*res publicae*) or a mix of all three of these regimes. Property rights regimes can also be described using six characteristics: exclusivity, transferability, duration, quality of title, divisibility, and flexibility (Devlin and Grafton, 1998). These characteristics can be subjectively described using a hexagonal figure where each side of the figure represents a characteristic, as in figure 2.2. The longer is the arrow that points towards a characteristic, the greater is the dimension of that characteristic. Thus, in the figure, the property right has a full dimension in terms of the duration characteristic, but a relatively poor dimension in terms of the quality of title.

Exclusivity (*ius excludendi*) is the most important characteristic. Without some ability to exclude others either using or benefiting from a flow of benefits from a resource or asset, no property right exists. For example, if we had a car that anybody could use and at any time then we would have no property right. Transferability refers to the ability to transfer or alienate (*ius disponendi*) the asset or resource or its flow of benefits. For instance, if we have the right to sell a car that we own to anyone, then we have a highly transferable or alienable asset. Duration represents the time dimension over which we have the right. For example, the right to sit on a bus is of a very limited duration, equal to the validity of a fare from the points we embark and disembark. By contrast, legal title over land held in *fee-simple* and freehold offers virtually unlimited tenure. Quality of title refers to the extent that the right is recognized in law, or in a formal way, such as with a certificate of ownership or title to an asset. Divisibility indicates the ability of the holder of the right to divide up the asset or the flow of benefits from the asset. For instance, a house is not a particularly divisible asset, but water pumped from an aquifer is highly divisible.

The concept of flexibility refers to the limitations and obligations over the use of the rights not covered by the other characteristics. Limitations on the flexibility of the right normally exist as a way of imposing obligations on the holders of property. For example, in many cities planners regulate what owners can and

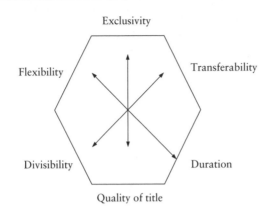

Exclusivity

Flexibility   Transferability

Divisibility   Duration

Quality of title

Figure 2.2   Property rights and their characteristics

Source: Adapted from Devlin and Grafton (1998)

cannot do with respect to additions and renovations on their property. Such regulations limit the flexibility of the owner(s) to do as they might wish.

For common-pool resources, which are the vast majority of natural resources and environmental assets, three other characteristics may be delineated in terms of the flexibility of the right. These characteristics include an access and enjoyment right (*ius utile*), a withdrawal or harvesting right (*ius fruendi* or *usufructus*) and a management right (Ostrom and Schlager, 1996). An access right confers the right to enjoy an asset or resource, but not the right to subtract from the asset or resource. For example, most visitors to conservation areas only have the right of access and cannot interfere or disrupt the flora and fauna in any significant way. A more flexible right exists if the holder can harvest or subtract from the asset or resource. For instance, most fishers with a fishing license have the right to catch and consume fish provided that they meet the defined obligations of the right, such as daily catch limits or minimum size regulations. Even greater flexibility exists if the holder of the right is able to assist in the management decisions about the asset or resource. For example, in artisanal fishing villages, members of the community often help to set the rules about where, when, and how much fish can be caught by villagers. In this sense, community membership confers both a harvesting right to fish and a shared management right over the resource.

2.3   EFFICIENCY AND EXTERNALITIES

The fundamental questions of property rights are, what are the characteristics of the rights? Who has them? And, over what assets or resources are they held? The answers to these questions help determine how *efficiently* the right is used and how *equitably* or fairly the rights are distributed.

Many definitions exist for efficiency, but the benchmark for judging the efficiency of a property rights regime is the concept of *Pareto efficiency*. Simply stated, an outcome is Pareto efficient if it is not possible to make someone better off without making someone else worse off. Thus if a property rights structure is efficient it means that all gains from trade or exchange have been exhausted. In other words, an outcome is efficient if goods and services, assets and resources have been allocated to their highest value in use based on the marginal willingness and ability to pay.

A related notion is the *Pareto criterion* that can be used to compare different states of the world. By this criterion, *unanimity* is needed to move to one state of the world from another. It requires that if one state of the world (A) is *preferred* to another (B) then at A no one is made worse off relative to state B, and at least one person is better off. The criterion is useful when moving from an inefficient to an efficient state, but poses difficulties when two states being compared are both inefficient. To help address such comparisons, the concept of a *potential Pareto improvement* (PPI) was developed whereby one state of the world is preferred to another when those who gain from the change are sufficiently better off to compensate the losers, even if such transfers are *not* undertaken. Thus, according to the PPI, if the aggregate gains exceed the aggregate losses, a change from one state to another is preferred. This notion is frequently used by decision-makers, but is highly controversial because it ignores the issues of equity and income and wealth distribution. In other words, it is possible for a state A to be preferred to state B in terms of the PPI, but state A may also have a much more unequal distribution of income than state B.

A potential problem with the PPI is that it may suffer from a *reversal paradox*: when comparing two inefficient (second-best) states of the world, A and B, it is possible under certain preferences for A to be preferred to B, but also for B to be preferred to A when using the Pareto criterion (Scitovsky, 1941). The paradox can be overcome provided that the gainers can potentially compensate the losers *and* the losers cannot potentially bribe the gainers not to move from one state to another. However, yet another difficulty is that when comparing more than two states of the world that are inefficient, the rankings of the different states can be intransitive, i.e., A is preferred to B and B is preferred to C, but C is preferred to A.

An inefficient outcome arises whenever an individual, agent, or firm undertakes an action that has an external effect, other than through the price system, on the utility function of consumers or production function of producers. This inefficiency is a type of market failure and is called a *technological externality* and may be positive (benefits others) or negative (harms others). Externalities may also be *pecuniary* in the sense that individual actions affect others, but these effects occur only through the price system. For instance, if many people suddenly change their habits and start to drink wine instead of spirits this will have the tendency to initially increase the price of wine, given a fixed short-run supply. The change in drinking habits imposes a cost on all wine drinkers who now have to pay more for their wine. However, because the effect is transmitted exclusively through the price system, wine is still allocated on the basis of marginal willingness to pay, even if it is now more expensive. Thus, with a pecuniary externality, no inefficiency exists provided that all markets are competitive.

Technological externalities lead to inefficiency because they prevent resources from being allocated to their highest value in use. For example, if a person smokes while sharing an elevator, the smoker's actions impose the costs of second-hand smoke on others. If the smoking is permitted (property right exists to smoke) the inefficiency can be resolved if the non-smokers are able to bribe the smoker to desist if his preferences are purely selfish, or if the smoker's preferences are altruistic, it may be possible to inform him that his smoking is hurting others. Whether this takes place or not depends on the *transactions costs* associated with bargaining with the smoker to refrain from smoking. If these costs are high enough, then there may be no bargaining between the smoker and non-smokers, and the inefficiency remains. Namely, both the smoker and non-smokers could all potentially be better off, because the marginal willingness to pay for clean air by non-smokers exceeds the marginal willingness to pay to smoke by the smoker.

In general, the existence of transactions costs – the costs associated with the negotiation, exchange and enforcement of property rights – are a principal reason why externalities remain unresolved. Indeed, the existence of a technological externality implies that transactions costs are either too high, property rights are improperly specified or some other market failure exists, such as imperfect competition, which prevents mutually beneficial trading to an efficient outcome.

2.4 EXTERNALITIES AND PROPERTY RIGHTS

The classic case of where a lack of property rights leads to technological externalities is open access (*res nullius*) where there is free entry and exit and no restrictions on the withdrawal from a common-pool resource. In this case, the *absence* of all property rights leads to the "tragedy of the commons" (Hardin, 1968) where individual users consider only their private costs, but not the costs their actions impose on other resource users. This situation has been aptly described as, "everybody's access is nobody's property" (Bromley, 1989). The end result or "tragedy" is overexploitation or overuse in an economic sense such that a lower overall rate of exploitation has the *potential* to increase the net benefits to all users. It should be emphasized, however, that although open access is wasteful it does not necessarily lead to commercial or biological extinction or complete exhaustion of a resource. This is because at low levels of the resource stock it may no longer be worthwhile to use or exploit the resource.

A special type of open access where the number of resource users is restricted, but the rate of use or withdrawal is not, is called limited-user open access. Such a rights regime might exist for a ground-water aquifer where the number of users equals the number of people with surface rights or use rights to the land above the aquifer. In such a situation, individuals with surface rights can pump out water from the aquifer for their benefit, but the more they pump the less is available to others. Moreover, as the aquifer is lowered the costs of pumping also increase.

In the absence of any property rights over pumping water, or any social or community structure to control individual pumping, the incentive is for each surface

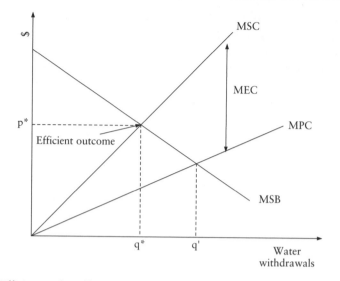

Figure 2.3 Efficient and inefficient water withdrawals

right holder to pump whatever they need without any consideration of the cost imposed on others. The result is over-pumping from the aquifer and, in general, the withdrawn water will not be allocated to its highest value in use.

The limited-user open access outcome is illustrated in figure 2.3. Each holder of a surface right faces a marginal private cost (MPC) of pumping water out of the aquifer, but their actions also impose a marginal external cost (MEC) on others (such as higher pumping costs) that rises with the amount of water withdrawn. To "internalize" the technological externality each surface right holder should incur the marginal social cost (MSC) or the sum of the marginal private cost and the marginal external cost from pumping or withdrawing water. If we assume that the marginal private benefit (MPB) of the water equals its marginal social benefit (MSB) then an efficient withdrawal by an individual with a surface right is q^*, where MSB = MSC. In the absence of property rights over the amount that can be pumped, or any other controls, the individual will pump the inefficient (and greater) amount q', where MPB(= MSB) = MPC.

The need to mitigate or internalize externalities provides an explanation as to how property rights develop over time. Some have argued that rights change in response to a perceived need to better internalize externalities associated with consumption or production (Demsetz, 1967). This "evolutionary" or "induced innovation" explanation to the development of property rights implies that rights become more exclusive for one of two reasons: because of declining monitoring or enforcement costs, or because the holders of the right choose to devote more time and effort to excluding others in response to an increased value of the resource or asset. For example, declining costs of monitoring in fisheries, due to aerial surveillance and other means, have enabled states to exercise control over resources that, in the past, would have been open access. The second way property rights might develop is by an increase in value attributable to the asset or resource. This increase in value may provide the property right holder with a greater incentive to invest more effort in securing greater exclusivity. For example, Demsetz (1967) describes the development of private hunting territories by the Montagnes in Quebec in the eighteenth century that he believes arose because the fur trade made the land over which hunting took place much more valuable. Libecap (1989) also describes the establishment of property rights in the mining camps during the California gold rush, that hitherto did not exist, and that were developed to protect the valuable claims of prospectors and miners.

An evolutionary explanation as to how property rights arise is insightful, but should not be misconstrued to suggest that property rights necessarily evolve to a more desirable regime. Many examples exist of how property rights have been changed in ways that reduce the total flow of benefits from resources, although such changes may have increased the benefits to a particular group or individual. For instance, the designation of exclusive private hunting forests by nobility benefited royalty at the expense of peasants who previously used the forest for firewood, berries and for hunting small game. Further, because property rights have many characteristics and dimensions, an increase in exclusivity for the current holder of the right does *not* necessarily imply a uniform improvement in all characteristics. For instance, increased exclusivity might coincide with reduced divisibility and flexibility that could prevent complementary and non-rival uses of the property rights. Thus, the increased returns associated with greater exclusivity may be more than offset by losses of other uses of the resource or asset. Changes in the characteristics and the property rights regime will also almost always lead to a different, and possibly less desirable, distribution of wealth and income within a society.

2.5 THE COASE THEOREM

Ronald Coase, a Nobel Laureate in Economics, made a pioneering contribution to the understanding of how property rights and transactions costs can mitigate inefficiencies associated with technological externalities. His idea is known as the Coase theorem. It states that if property rights exist then, under certain conditions, *irrespective* of the assignment of property rights, liability, or legal entitlements, the parties affected by a technological externality who negotiate or bargain among themselves will achieve an efficient outcome. The conditions to ensure this result are that parties negotiate or bargain at zero cost, there is no strategic behavior in the bargaining, all parties have complete and full information, and the initial distribution of rights does not affect the marginal valuation of resources or assets. The first three conditions collectively ensure that all the gains from trade are exhausted, while the last condition helps ensure that the efficient outcome is invariant to the distribution of property rights. The Coase theorem implies that parties affected by a technological externality can trade or bargain among themselves to ensure resources or assets are allocated to their highest value in use. Moreover, the efficient outcome of this bargaining or trading is *invariant* to which party has the right to compensation, be it the person(s) causing the externality or the person(s) affected by it.

The Coase theorem is almost tautological in the sense that if there are gains to be made from trade, and trading is costless, trades will be made to everyone's mutual advantage. Moreover, the conditions required to ensure the Coase theorem are almost never satisfied in the real world such that the initial distribution of rights will almost always affect the trading outcome. Nevertheless, the fundamental insight derived from the theorem is important. Namely, the possibility exists to *decentralize* the resolution of technological externalities so that the parties most affected by it are the parties best able to resolve it. In this sense, the Coasian approach is radically different to the traditional methods of legal action, and to the use of regulations and command and control approaches to mitigate externalities. For example, in the case of the ground-water aquifer, a regulatory approach to resolving the overpumping would be to impose maximum rates of withdrawal, coupled with a system of monitoring and penalties for disobeying the regulations. A Coasian approach would be to set a cap on the total amount of water that can be pumped and to allocate (by auction, *gratis*, or other means) transferable, divisible, and durable withdrawal rights among the surface rights owners. By allowing transferability, the persons with a higher marginal value for the withdrawn water will be able to purchase withdrawal rights from persons with lower marginal values. If the market for withdrawal rights is competitive, water trading should ensure that the water withdrawn from the aquifer is allocated on the basis of marginal willingness and ability to pay. Thus the policy intervention for technological externalities implied by the Coase Theorem is to ensure that property rights are well defined, markets are competitive and transactions costs are as low as possible, so that the affected parties can trade rights or bargain to arrive at a more desirable outcome (see box 2.1).

Market-based rights

The Coasian approach to internalizing externalities has inspired economists and regulators to propose and implement market-based rights (MBRs), whereby those most affected by a technological externality can buy and sell property rights to arrive at a more efficient outcome. Such instruments have been introduced for common-pool natural resources, such as fisheries, and for pollution.

To illustrate the outcomes with market-based rights in the presence of technological externalities, assume an industry with n firms where each firm i produces an output (q_i) that has, as a side effect, pollution emissions in the same proportion (one unit of output causes one unit of emissions). Further suppose that firms can regulate their emissions only by controlling their output and that each unit of

BOX 2.1 COASE COMES TO CHESHIRE

In April 2002 the village of Cheshire, Ohio, USA, with a little over 200 residents, agreed to be "bought out" by one of America's largest power companies, American Electric Power (AEP). If the deal goes ahead, AEP will pay about US$20 million (less legal fees) to the property owners and renters in the village. In return, residents will sign a legal agreement not to sue the company over any personal or property damages that may have been caused by emissions from the AEP coal-fired plant nestled right next to the village.

The settlement provides the conclusion to on-going concerns by residents of emissions from the huge plant. Most recently, AEP installed pollution abatement equipment to reduce nitrogen oxide emissions, but this equipment when coupled with scrubbers to reduce sulfur dioxide emissions had an unintended side effect of increasing emissions of sulfur trioxide. Under certain wind conditions, this allegedly caused a visible blue haze to descend over parts of the community.

The AEP payments to the 90 or so property owners reputed to be $150,000 each is well above the market price for Cheshire property, while the 40 or so renters are expected to receive a sum of $25,000 each. The settlement avoids the costs and time involved in suing the company over alleged damages caused by the plant. It also gives property owners and renters the opportunity to leave the pollution problems behind them with money in their pockets. The settlement, if it goes ahead, provides a number of benefits to the company. First, AEP avoids the potential litigation costs from village residents, second, the land they acquire gives the company additional space to expand its plant, and, third, it reduces the likelihood that environmental regulators will force the plant to burn more expensive low-sulfur coal.

Although the settlement is mutually beneficial for residents and AEP, not everyone is happy with the deal. Employees of the village who are not residents will receive no payment and will lose their jobs. Some long-time residents of the village are very sorry to leave the only homes they have ever known. The April 2002 settlement also does not include two schools located very close to the plant, but that lie outside the boundary of the village.

Further reading: Teather (2002), http://www.guardian.co.uk/
international/story/0,3604,715133,00.html
***Cincinnati Enquirer* (text supplied by Associated Press) available at**
http://enquirer.com/editions/ 2002/05/07/loc_cheshire_ohio_no.html
and also *Daily Telegraph* (London), May 14 2002.

emissions produced by a firm imposes a fixed marginal external cost of e. Each firm maximizes profits and faces a competitive market for output where they sell their production at p per unit, and each firm has the same total cost function of cq_i^2 where c is a constant.

In the absence of Coasian bargaining or property rights over emissions or any other controls, firm $i = 1,2,3,\ldots, n$, maximizes the following,

$$\text{Max } A_i = pq_i - cq_i^2.$$

Differentiating profits with respect to q_i and setting the result equal to zero, we find that firm profit is maximized when $q_i = p/2c$.

This result can be compared to the efficient outcome by maximizing the revenue of the firms less the private and external costs of production, i.e.,

$$\text{Max } W = p(q_1 + q_2 + \ldots + q_n) - c(q_1^2 + q_2^2 + \ldots + q_n^2) - e(q_1 + q_2 + \ldots + q_n)$$

Partially differentiating the objective function with respect to q_i where $i = 1,2,3,\ldots, n$, and setting the result equal to zero we obtain the efficient output $q_i^* = (p - e)/2c$. Thus *if* each firm were to fully internalize the costs they impose on other each other, they would produce a lower level of output.

The efficient outcome can be compared to the decentralized outcome if firms were allocated a property right to discharge emissions. In this case firms maximize profits, but also face an extra or implicit cost equal to the cost of owning the right to discharge emissions. Thus, firm $i = 1,2,3,\ldots n$, maximizes the following,

$$\text{Max } A_i = pq_i - cq_i^2 - ∋(m_i + t_i) \tag{1}$$

Subject to:

$$q_i \leq m_i + t_i \tag{2}$$

where $∋$ is the price per unit of marketable rights, here called marketable emission permits, m_i is the initial allocation of emission permits, and t_i is the number of emission permits bought (>0) or sold (<0). Provided that marketable emission permits are scarce and command a positive price and with no uncertainty, the firm's constraint will be strictly binding such that $m_i + t_i$ can be substituted for by q_i in the firm's optimization problem.

Differentiating profits with respect to q_i and setting the result equal to zero we find that with marketable emission permits firm profit is maximized when $q_i^\sim = (p - ∋)/2c$. Thus the efficient and decentralized outcome are identical whenever $e = ∋$, such that the marginal external cost of emissions equals the private or market cost of the marketable emission permits.

We can show that the property rights outcome will be efficient if the allocated number of marketable emission permits equals the *efficient* total level of emissions, and the marginal external cost of emissions for all firms is the same. If we define E as the efficient number of marketable emission permits and remember that one unit of output causes one unit of emissions, the equilibrium in the market for permits is when their total supply (E) equals the total demand ($q_1^\sim + q_2^\sim + \ldots + q_n^\sim$). This is called the market clearing condition and is defined as,

$$E = (q_1^\sim + q_2^\sim + \ldots + q_n^\sim) \tag{3}$$

where we assume a one to one ratio between firm emissions and output.

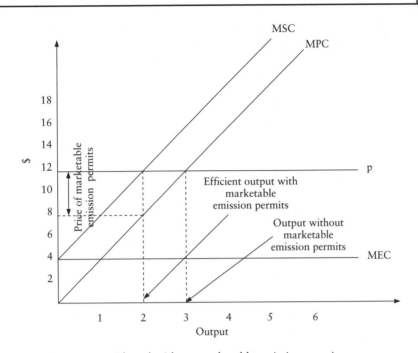

Figure 2.4 Firm output with and without marketable emission permits

From the profit maximization problem for firms with marketable emission permits we know that $q_i^\sim = (p - \ni)/2c$ such that the total demand for emission permits with n identical firms is $n(p - \ni)/2c$. Substituting this expression into the right hand side of (3) and solving for $\ni$, the market price of emission permits, we obtain

$$\ni = p - 2cE/n. \tag{4}$$

Provided that E – the total supply of permits – equals the efficient total level of emissions and the marginal external cost from emissions is the same for all firms then each firm will emit an efficient level of emissions. To illustrate the result, suppose $p = 12$, $c = 2$, $e = 4$ and $n = 2$. In this case, $q_i^* = (p - e)/2c = 2$ such that the efficient total output from the two firms combined is 4 units. Given the ratio between output and emissions, the efficient total level of emissions must also be 4, i.e., $E = 4$. Thus if 4 marketable emission permits are allocated among the two firms, the market price of marketable emission permits will equal $4/unit which is identical to the marginal external cost of emissions for all firms (e).

The efficient outcome is shown in figure 2.4. In this case, the difference between the price of output and the marginal private cost of each firm equals the price of marketable emission permits. This also equals the marginal external cost of emissions that is identical across all firms. Provided the total supply of marketable emission permits equals the efficient level of emissions ($E = 4$) then each firm will produce two units of output and two units of emissions.

In this example, whether firm one or firm two receives all the initial emission permits has no impact on the final distribution or equilibrium allocation of rights, because all the conditions for the Coase Theorem are satisfied. However, the initial allocation does affect the distribution of the benefits from trading. For example, if firm one receives the entire initial allocation of marketable emission permits then it receives all the capital gain or trading profit. Consequently, an efficient outcome is not necessarily a fair or equitable outcome.

Transactions costs

In the previous example, the efficient result arises because we assume no transaction costs, no strategic bargaining, complete information, competitive markets, a fixed and identical marginal external cost of emissions across all firms, and a total supply of permits equal to the efficient level of emissions. In general, transactions costs will reduce the number and size of trades as they increase the costs associated with buying or selling property rights. Positive transactions costs both prevent mutually beneficial trades that would otherwise take place, and also use up scarce resources that could be used in other activities (Stavins, 1995). The presence of trans- actions costs means that, in general, the initial allocation of rights will affect the equilibrium such that who is assigned the property rights will affect the final allocation. In other words, the invariance proposition in the Coase Theorem will, in general, no longer hold.

To illustrate this result, suppose in the previous example that the purchaser (but not the seller) of emission permits incurs a cost of a/unit, in addition to the pur- chase cost of permits. Further, assume that firm one receives all the marketable emission permits and that this equals the efficient level of emissions of 4 units.

Given that firms face the identical and competitive price p for their output, at the market equilibrium for marketable emission permits the marginal operating cost of firm one (the seller) must equal the marginal operating cost of firm two (the buyer) *plus* the marginal transactions costs incurred by firm two, i.e.,

$$2cq_1\tilde{} = 2cq_2\tilde{} + a. \qquad (5)$$

If (5) were *not* an equality it would imply that all the gains from trading emissions permits were not exhausted. For example, if $2cq_1 > 2cq_2 + a$, the marginal value of emission permit for firm one is less than that for firm two implying that both could be better off if firm one sold a marginal amount of emission permits to firm two. From (5), we can express the output of firm one in terms of firm two,

$$q_1\tilde{} = a/2c + q_2\tilde{}. \qquad (5')$$

If we assume, as previously, that $c = 2$ and also $a = 1$, (5') implies

$$q_1\tilde{} = \tfrac{1}{4} + q_2\tilde{}. \qquad (5'')$$

As in (3), the market clearing condition for marketable emission permits requires that,

$$E = 4 = q_1\tilde{\ } + q_2\tilde{\ }$$ (6)

where one unit of output causes one unit of emissions. Substituting in the expression for (5″) into the market clearing condition (6) and solving for q_2, we obtain the following result,

$$q_1\tilde{\ } = \frac{17}{8} \text{ and } q_2\tilde{\ } = \frac{15}{8}.$$

Thus, in this case, positive transactions costs reduce the quantity of marketable emission permits traded from 2 units to 15/8 units.

The equilibrium price for marketable emission permits with positive transactions costs is solved by first noting the equilibrium outputs for the two firms,

$$q_1\tilde{\ } = (p - з)/2c \quad \text{and} \quad q_2\tilde{\ } = (p - з - a)/2c.$$

Substituting into the market clearing condition (6) above and solving for з we obtain,

$$з = p - cE - a/2.$$

Thus, for the specified parameter values, the market price of marketable emission permits is \$3.5/unit. In this case, positive transactions costs reduce the amount of emission permits traded and the price at which they trade. Despite the fact that the total supply of emissions permits equals the efficient total level of emissions (4 units) and each unit of emissions from both firms causes the same marginal external cost (e), the *individual* emissions of each firm are *not* efficient.

2.6 LEGAL RIGHTS

Property rights can exist whether or not they are legally recognized. Nevertheless, legal title over property or assets provides owners, or their leasees, with rights that protect them from the nuisance and interference of others that might infringe upon these rights. These legal or *de jure* rights have a long tradition in English *common law*, and permit owners of property rights to sue or undertake civil action against persons, agencies, or firms that are reducing their flow of benefits from an asset or resource. The basis of judging the claims of such actions is derived from judicial precedent rather than legislation, and underpins the private property rights in the United States and most countries in the British Commonwealth. The underlying feature of common law is that rights are accompanied by obligations and responsibilities, such that the exercise of property rights should not cause injury or nuisance to others in the exercise of their property rights.

BOX 2.2   WESTON PAPER COMPANY VS. POPE ET AL.

More than a century ago in Indiana, USA, plaintiffs undertook a civil suit against a paper mill that was discharging wastes into a stream. The discharges polluted the water and affected the riparian rights of the plaintiffs.

In defending the case, the paper mill argued that the US$90,000 cost of building the plant more than outweighed the material damage to the plaintiffs of $250. In the judgment in favor of the plaintiffs the court noted:

"Before locating the plant the owners were bound to know that every riparian proprietor is entitled to have the waters of the stream that washes his land to come to it without obstruction, diversion, or corruption, subject to only reasonable use of the water … and to take notice of the size, course, and capacity of the stream, and to determine for themselves, and at their own peril, whether they should be able to conduct their business … without injury to their neighbours. "

Source: Brubaker (1995, p. 59)

Common law protection of property rights can be a powerful force in protecting the environment if the exercise of property rights is correlated with environmental quality or the flow of services from nature. For example, an owner of a lake-front cottage could sue a newly established business that rents out motorboats to visitors to the lake if the emissions from the boats materially affect the water quality of the lake. Provided that the cottage owner can establish the legal right to the lake-side property and demonstrate that the boats have materially affected the property right (such as swimming), the suit should result in an injunction. The injunction would forbid the boat hire business from operating until it finds a way to prevent the material damage to the property owner. Under common law tradition, if material damage occurs it represents a "confiscation" or "taking" of the property rights. The intentions of the person(s) causing the material damage, the existence of other material damage from other parties or the size of the costs that an injunction might cause are often deemed irrelevant under common law (see box 2.2). Thus although common law can be a powerful tool in the protection of environmental services it will not, in general, result in an efficient outcome. The possibility always exists, however, for parties to a dispute to negotiate to arrive at a mutually beneficial outcome.

The ability of common law to protect environmental services depends on transactions costs and, in particular, the affordability of litigation and procuring evidence that establishes the defender's responsibility for the material damage. In some jurisdictions plaintiffs may be discouraged from legal action if they are obliged to pay the legal costs of the defender should the plaintiffs lose their case. Where conditions are favorable for common law action, the law can be highly effective in maintaining ecosystem services. For instance, in the United Kingdom the

Anglers' Co-operative Association has played an active role in over six hundred cases to protect the riparian rights of downstream property owners from upstream actions by polluters. With the exception of two cases, the Association has been successful in all its court actions to defend the rights of property owners and protect the quality of rivers and streams for trout and salmon (Brubaker, 1995).

States and government bodies and agencies have enacted many statutes, regulations and acts that have a material influence on property rights. In some cases, such legislation has been enacted to favor the "public" interest whereby planes are allowed to fly over the air space directly above houses even if they create a noise nuisance to property owners. In other cases, governments have legislated to favor the rights of powerful or vested interests. For example, in 1950 the Province of Ontario in Canada passed legislation to allow the continued operations of a pulp and paper mill that was discharging waste into a river. The legislation overturned a court injunction (upheld by a Court of Appeal and the Supreme Court of Canada) to prevent the mill from discharging its wastes into the river and that had upheld the riparian rights of plaintiffs downstream of the plant (Brubaker, 1995).

Legislators have also drafted statutes expressly to protect the environment, even if it may affect the rights of private property owners. For example, the US Endangered Species Act of 1973 has led to actions by federal agencies that have been viewed by some property owners as "takings" that materially damage their property rights. To the extent that the "Just Compensation Clause" of the US Fifth Amendment provides that private property shall not be taken for public use without just compensation, property owners have argued for compensation for the prohibition of otherwise lawful activities (such as logging) that might endanger rare species. Whether preventing otherwise lawful activities to protect endangered species represents a "taking" is a matter of great dispute (see box 2.3). Governments are able to legislate or regulate and infringe upon property rights to *prevent* harm (such as banning use of fireworks on residential property) without compensation. In this sense, the regulation seeks to prevent actions by holders of property rights that might unreasonably impose costs on others (such as increasing the risk of fire on neighbors' properties). Thus the regulation seeks to reduce the possibility of a technological externality from occurring. However, it could be argued that infringements that *promote* the public or common good should not unreasonably be imposed on a few. It is on this premise that land appropriated by the state for the common good, called *eminent domain*, in most jurisdictions requires fair compensation by the state to the previous owners.

The fundamental question from a legal perspective, however, is not whether "takings" prevent harm or whether they promote the common good, but whether changes in regulations "unreasonably" impose a burden on property owners. In part, this requires an understanding of what rights and values regulations take away and what rights and values they leave with property owners. Thus a regulation that prevents *any and all* uses of land rendering it valueless to the owner is most certainly a "taking," but a requirement that the owner build her house according to accepted safety regulations might not be. The former prevents

> ## BOX 2.3   TAHOE-SIERRA PRESERVATION COUNCIL INC. ET AL. VS. TAHOE REGIONAL PLANNING AGENCY ET AL.

In April 2002 the US Supreme Court ruled over the regulatory "takings" imposed by the Tahoe Regional Planning Agency (TRPA) when the latter imposed temporary moratoria in 1981 and 1983 that prevented development on designated property until an environmentally sound plan could be developed to protect the water quality of Lake Tahoe. In response to the moratoria on construction, landowners sued the TRPA for compensation. The landowners, who formed the Tahoe-Sierra Preservation Council (TSPC), argued that they had purchased unimproved land for the express purpose of building single-family homes which they were prohibited from doing under the moratoria.

In a majority opinion (with three Justices dissenting) the court ruled that:

> "Land-use regulations are ubiquitous and most of them impact property values in some tangential way – often in completely unanticipated ways. Treating them all as per se takings would transform government regulation into a luxury few governments could afford" (Supreme Court of the United States 2002, p. 19).

To support their majority opinion, the Justices endorsed the distinguished jurist Oliver Wendell Holmes who noted that "if regulation goes too far it will be recognized as a taking," but made it clear that compensation for every delay in the use of property was not appropriate and again cited Justice Holmes that "[g]overnment hardly could go on if to some extent values incident to property could not be diminished without paying for every such change in the general law."

In upholding a judgment of the Court of Appeals that compensation should not be paid, the Supreme Court emphasized that the judgment of whether a taking has occurred or not requires careful consideration of material evidence on a case-by-case basis.

Source: http://supct.law.cornell.edu/supct/html/00-1167.ZS.html

all actions by the owner, while the latter restricts only a small set of actions and may have little or no impact on the market value of the asset.

2.7   RIGHTS AND WRONGS

The structure of property rights depends on many factors including history, the assets or resources over which they are defined, and the institutional and social structure in which they exist. We explore this diversity by examining the relative merits of private, community, and state rights.

In evaluating different property rights regimes, it should be emphasized that rights vary greatly over space and time: property rights structures are highly diverse. For example, in many Western countries individuals or companies own large amounts of land. By contrast, in some African nations community owner-ship predominates. Even within the same jurisdiction, the property rights can vary greatly such that adjacent land could be publicly owned and controlled by the state (in a national park), be privately owned (nearby ranch) or be commu-nally controlled (aboriginal land or native tenure). Further, legal ownership by one party may not preclude other parties from participating in the management of the resource, or the existence of a mix of all three rights regimes depending upon the flow of the benefits from the land.

Private rights

The diversity of property rights regimes implies that people have been able to craft many different approaches to help resolve conflict over assets and resources. The relative merits of private property stem from the idea that if an asset or resource can be traded, it will end up in the control or ownership of those persons with the highest marginal willingness and ability to pay. In other words, transferability of a divisible and productive asset or resource permits those who can generate a higher marginal net return to acquire a share of the resource from those with a lower value in use. Another advantage of *individually* held and controlled private property rights is that, unlike other rights regimes (such as state rights), the persons making the decisions about the resource reap the full benefits or costs of their decisions. This provides an incentive (but *not* a guaran-tee) that private owners will consider the long-term impact of their resource use decisions.

Private rights have always existed over private goods, but are increasingly being developed and used for common-pool resources (see box 2.4). For example, dozens of fisheries in several different countries have introduced transferable har-vesting rights for fishers where the total number of rights equals a sustainable total harvest (Grafton, Squires, and Fox, 2000). Private rights are also being intro-duced for pollution where firms are allocated tradable pollution rights, also called marketable emission permits, as a proportion of their past emissions, where the total quantity of all emissions is set at a desired level by the regulator (see chapter 3). Such approaches are new ways to internalize the externalities associ-ated with the use of common-pool resources where the market price of the right (harvesting right or emission permit) tries to mimic the external costs that firms impose on others because of their actions.

Although these approaches have not been without their problems, they have often proved effective in changing the incentives faced by firms and internalizing technological externalities.

BOX 2.4   PRIVATE CONSERVATION EFFORTS: "BUYING" A BILBY

Many of Australia's native species, especially its smaller marsupials such as the bilby, are threatened by introduced species, such as the rat. Despite considerable public conservation efforts, 23 percent of Australia's native mammal species are listed either as extinct, endangered, or vulnerable.

To help address the problem of endangered species (especially small marsupials), Earth Sanctuaries Ltd (ESL) in 2000 became Australia's first publicly listed company whose aim is to establish safe habitats for the nation's threatened and endangered native wildlife. ESL achieves its objectives by establishing and maintaining wildlife sanctuaries. As of 2001, it controlled about 90,000 hectares (222,000 acres) of land. This land comprises eight free-hold, one lease-hold, and one managed sanctuary in three Australian states. After acquiring the land for a sanctuary, ESL fences it with a vermin-proof barrier, eliminates all feral animals within the sanctuary and then tries to reintroduce native fauna. Its efforts are funded by revenues from eco-tourism at some of its sanctuaries and by consulting and contractual services it provides to private land holders to help eliminate feral species.

ESL has been successful at increasing the numbers of small native marsupials within its sanctuaries including such animals as the bilby, potoroo, and bandicoot. Its work has also been publicly recognized and it received the 2000 Prime Minister's Environment Award. Although the company continues to increase its revenues, its share price has fallen from its initial offering of AUS$2.50 to $0.75 as of June 30, 2001. In 2000, its sanctuaries received about 25,000 visitors and generated sales of over AUS$700,000.

ESL's principal assets, Australian wildlife in its sanctuaries, cannot be "owned" by the company because under Australian law native wildlife is the property of the state. This restriction has limited its ability to borrow funds that it needs to expand its business. The ability of ESL to achieve its aims of conservation of native wildlife is also limited by its ability to generate revenue. Further, given visitors' inclination to see cute and furry animals, ESL's efforts may have limited value for less photogenic fauna. Finally, since biodiversity almost certainly generates returns in excess of those that can be captured by eco-tourism, it suggests that "private" conservation of biodiversity should complement (as is the case with ESL) rather than substitute for public conservation efforts.

Source: Aretino et al. 2001

Community rights

Many different forms of community rights exist over both private goods and common-pool resources. A common feature of these rights is that access and withdrawal rights to the resource or asset are determined by community norms and rules of behavior. Frequently, persons who are not members of the community are prevented from using, or at least withdrawing or subtracting from

BOX 2.5   COMMUNITY RIGHTS IN FORESTRY

The community or Panchayat forests of Uttar Pradesh in India provide an interesting guide as to the factors that contribute to the success and failure of community rights. Traditional community rights over forests have existed for centuries, but were only officially recognized in 1931 following civil unrest over plans to place the control of forest resources in the hands of the state.

The community rights are limited by the state in terms of their flexibility. For instance, the state still maintains control over timber and resin sales although the net returns from such sales are supposed to go to the communities. The Panchayat's principal management responsibility is over the harvesting of wood litter for fuel-wood and fodder for animals from within the forests. Forest management is determined by a group of individuals elected by village members. These individuals help set the rules of access and withdrawal on behalf of the community. These rules vary considerably across Panchayats.

Successful management of the forests appears to be related to several factors. First, the existence of open and fair elections for the governing body of the forest; second, support by the state to prevent outsiders from using the forest; third, the size of the benefits from the forest that enables the Panchayats to pay for monitoring and enforcement; fourth, effective means for arbitrating disputes between village members; and, fifth, flexible and fair rules for ensuring an equitable distribution of benefits from the forest.

Sources: Arnold (1998) and Agrawal (1994)

the good or resource, while use by members of the community is governed by well-understood rules. Community rights can be highly effective at internalizing the costs imposed on others by resource users, especially where community members are bound by mutual obligations, the number of resource users is small and the resource is important to the livelihood of the community (Wade, 1987).

Many case studies exist of community rights in fisheries, forestry, grazing land, and irrigation schemes (see box 2.5). These studies indicate that community rights over common-pool resources are an integral part of the governance and reciprocity structures of such communities. Indeed, the existence of mutual obligations and reciprocity promote trust and norms of behavior that discourage "free riding" or cheating on fellow users of the common-pool resources managed or controlled by the community.

A pioneer in understanding how community rights can help manage common-pool resources in the collective interest is Elinor Ostrom. Ostrom (1990) identifies eight "design principles" of enduring community rights:

1   well-defined boundaries for the resource and membership of the community;
2   community rules of exploitation accepted by the community that regulate the amount, the location, and timing of withdrawals;
3   the flow of benefits from the resource are commensurate with the costs of users;

4 community rules are well-adapted to the local institutions and particular circumstances of the resource;
5 recognition of community rules by outside authorities;
6 monitoring and enforcement with well-defined, but graduated, penalties for transgressors of community rules;
7 participation by most individuals affected by resource use in both setting and changing community use rules; and
8 effective dispute resolution mechanisms among resource users.

Ostrom's work, and that of others, shows that community rights can be highly effective in internalizing externalities and ensuring the on-going sustainability of common-pool resources. However, the effectiveness of community rights (and indeed all property rights) is, in part, determined by the ability of the state to help protect the exclusivity of these rights. Increasingly, community rights to common-pool resources are being threatened by outside users and sometimes by the state itself. In Indonesia, some tribal groups in Sumatra have been dispossessed of their community lands or have had their land deforested with the connivance of state officials. In India, and elsewhere in south-east Asia, artisanal or traditional community fishing rights are being encroached upon by outsiders with larger vessels and more sophisticated harvesting technology. These encroachments undermine the ability of communities to effectively manage common-pool resources.

State rights

State rights over environmental resources and assets come in many forms. In some countries state regimes have resembled open access, as governments have neither had the institutional capability nor the financial resources to effectively manage or ensure exclusivity. Where this has arisen, especially where states have abrogated pre-existing private or community rights, the end result can be disastrous for the sustainability of common-pool resources. For example, in 1957 Nepal nationalized its state forests in an attempt to reduce deforestation. The result was the opposite to what was intended, as the government undermined long-standing rules and norms governing the use of forests, but failed to provide the personnel or financial resources to adequately monitor or enforce its rights. Thus the state became unable to enforce or make exclusive what it had legislated (Bromley and Chapagain, 1984).

Many poor outcomes exist with state ownership even in countries where the state has considerable capabilities. The state can be captured by special interests and the environment can be used as a capital stock to be depreciated to meet other objectives. These problems are often accentuated in countries without democratic structures or effective resource user associations or organizations. For example, under communism, the former Soviet Union placed production and output targets ahead of the abatement or mitigation of negative environmental impacts. Thus projects that diverted rivers to increase agricultural production were given priority over ensuring environmental services and resulted in environmental disasters, such as the depletion and degradation of the Aral Sea. In democracies, state rights over resources have also been used to undermine resource sustainability. For example, the state may choose to trade off future benefits or to jeopardize the sustainability of resources to meet short-term political goals by setting exploitation rates at too high a level (Grafton and Lane, 1998).

Despite the potential difficulties associated with state ownership, in many countries the state is by far the largest owner of resources and the most important user of assets and resources. Moreover, state ownership continues with apparently broad public support. In part, this may be explained by a view that publicly owned resources are a collective wealth from which all can benefit, to a greater or lesser extent, and that state ownership and control can help in managing the resource or asset in the collective interest. State ownership of unique environmental assets, such as in national parks, also appears to be favored by many. Indeed, without the resources of the state for monitoring and enforcement, it is hard to comprehend how areas in many national parks could be adequately protected or conserved. Thus, where the costs of exclusion are very high, the market returns are relatively low and non-market values are high, state rights can be the most effective property rights regime for the common good. The state also has an important role in supporting the exclusivity of property rights – private, community or otherwise – and in reducing transactions costs by overcoming coordination problems. In this sense, the state's ideal role is more of a facilitator to help ensure desired outcomes rather that of a regulator imposing a given outcome on resource users (Grafton, 2000).

2.8 A RIGHT WAY?

A review of property rights and their effects yields a multitude of examples of how people have been able to "contract" or agree to help resolve conflicts over use, internalize technological externalities, and ensure the sustainability of resources. Such regimes include private rights, community rights and state rights, and a mix of all three. Thus, no particular structure is uniquely favored over any other and the relative merits of any property right is likely to depend on the characteristics of the resource, the institutional structure and many other factors. For instance, individual harvesting rights have been highly successful in some fisheries in some rich countries at increasing the returns from resources, but this does not necessarily imply that their introduction into every fishery in every country is a good idea. Indeed, their introduction into an artisanal fishing community with enduring community rights may be destructive both in terms of the sustainability of the resource and the community.

If there is one common factor shared by successful property rights regimes for environmental resources it is, perhaps, that resource users be actively involved in their management (Grafton, 2000). Participation of resource users in decision-making about resources is also consistent with the Coasian idea that the parties most affected by technological externalities are those best able to resolve them. User involvement in management can take many different forms and provides a way of reducing transactions costs by co-opting information and knowledge about the resource to improve decision-making. The low-cost pooling of information and a forum in which all parties that enjoy benefits from the resource can participate also helps in fostering flexible or adaptable management structures and building social capital. Indeed, property rights regimes that allow the rate and type of resource use to vary in response to changes in circumstances and the environment is a prerequisite for the long-term sustainability of any environmental resource.

FURTHER READING

The number and variety of references on property rights are enormous. Highly recommended books that give the reader a broad understanding of the property rights literature from an economic perspective include Barzel (1989), Eggertsson (1990), Libecap (1989), and Bromley (1991). Scott and Johnson (1985) provide one of the first descriptions of the characteristics of property rights although various authors discuss some of these characteristics, including Posner (1986). Sen (1984) is the definitive reference on collective choice.

The classic reference by Coase on property rights and transactions costs appeared in1960 in *The Journal of Law and Economics* under the title "The Problem of Social Cost." Dales (1968) was one of the very first to propose the use of permits to resolve pollution problems. Posner (1986) is the classic reference of economics and law. Further readings on "takings," from a US perspective, are available in an edited volume by Jacobs (1998). Dwyer et al. (1995) provide a detailed review of case law associated with the US Endangered Species Act. Cole and Grossman (2002) provide a provocative review of the dichotomy between the economic and legal interpretations of property rights.

Several excellent edited volumes on community rights exist including Berkes (1989), Bromley et al. (1992), and Hanna et al. (1996). The book by Baland and Platteau (1996) is highly recommended and offers a carefully reasoned, detailed and insightful exposition of how communities can help to sustain natural resources. Ostrom's work on community rights appears in many different forms. Her 1990 book, *Governing the Commons: The Evolution of Institutions for Collective Action* is a classic text and her co-authored 1994 book *Rules, Games, and Common-Pool Resources* is well worth reading.

REFERENCES

Agrawal, A. (1994). Rules, Rule Making, and Rule Breaking: Examining the Fit between Rule Systems and Resource Use, in E. Ostrom, R. Gardner, and J. Walker, eds, *Rules, Games, and Common-Pool Resources*, University of Michigan Press: Ann Arbor, MI.

Aretino, B., Holland, P., Peterson, D., and Schuele, M. (2001). *Creating Markets for Biodiversity: A Case Study of Earth Sanctuaries Ltd*, Productivity Commission of Australia Staff Research Paper, AusInfo, Canberra.

Arnold, J. E. M. (1998). *Managing Forests as Common Property*, Food and Agriculture Organization of the United Nations: Rome.

Baland, J.-M. and Platteau, J.-P. (1996). *Halting Degradation of Natural Resources: Is There a Role for Rural Communities?*, Clarendon Press: Oxford.

Barzel, Y. (1989). *Economic Analysis of Property Rights*, Cambridge University Press: New York.

Berkes, F. (ed.) (1989). *Common Property Resources: Ecology and Community-Based Sustainable Development*, Belhaven Press: London.

Bromley, D. W. (1989). Property Relations and Economic Development: The Other Land Reform, *World Development*, 17: 867–77.

Bromley, D. W. (1991). *Environment and Economy: Property Rights and Public Policy*, Blackwell: Cambridge, USA.

Bromley, D. W. and Chapagain, D. P. (1984). The Village against the Center: Resource Depletion in South Asia, *American Journal of Agricultural Economics*, 66: 868–73.

Bromley, D. W., Feeny, D., McKean, M. A., Peters, P., Gilles, J. L., Oakerson, R. J., Runge, C. F., and Thomson, J. T. (eds) (1992). *Making the Commons Work: Theory, Practice and Policy*, Institute for Contemporary Policy: San Francisco.

Brubaker, E. (1995). *Property Rights in the Defence of Nature*, Earthscan Publications Limited: Toronto.

Coase, R. N. (1960). The Problem of Social Cost, *Journal of Law and Economics*, 3: 1–44.

Cole, D. H. and Grossman, P. Z. (2002). The Meaning of Property Rights: Law versus Economics?, *Land Economics*, 78 (3): 317–30.

Dales, J. H. (1968). *Pollution, Property and Prices: An Essay in Policy-making and Economics*, University of Toronto Press: Toronto.

Demsetz, H. (1967). Toward a Theory of Property Rights, *American Economic Review*, 57: 347–59.

Devlin, R. A. and Grafton, R. Q. (1998). *Economic Rights and Environmental Wrongs: Property Rights for the Common Good*, Edward Elgar: Cheltenham.

Dwyer, L. E., Murphy, D. D., and Ehrlich, P. R. (1995). Property Rights Case Law and the Challenge to the Endangered Species Act, *Conservation Biology*, 9: 725–41.

Eggertsson, T. (1990). *Economic Behavior and Institutions*, Cambridge University Press: New York.

Grafton, R. Q. (2000). Governance of the Commons: A Role for the State?, *Land Economics*, 76 (4): 504–17.

Grafton, R. Q. and Lane, D. E. (1998). Canadian Fisheries Policy: Challenges and Choices, *Canadian Public Policy*, 24: 133–48.

Grafton, R. Q., Squires, D., and Fox, K. J. (2000). Private Property and Economic Efficiency: A Study of a Common-Pool Resource, *Journal of Law and Economics*, 43 (2): 679–713.

Hanna, S., Folke, C., and Maler, K.-G. (eds) (1996). *Rights to Nature: Ecological, Economics, Cultural and Political Principles of Institutions for the Environment*, Island Press: Washington DC.

Hardin, G. (1968). The Tragedy of the Commons, *Science* 162: 1143–248.

Jacobs, H. M. (ed.) (1998). *Who Owns America? Social Conflict over Property Rights*, University of Wisconsin Press: Madison, WI.

Libecap, G. D. (1989). *Contracting for Property Rights*, Cambridge University Press: New York.

Mill, J. S. (1965). *Principles of Political Economy with Some of Their Applications to Social Philosophy* (with an introduction by V. W. Bladen), Routledge & Kegan Paul, University of Toronto Press: Toronto.

Ostrom, E. (1990). *Governing the Commons: The Evolution of Institutions for Collective Action*, Cambridge University Press: Cambridge, England.

Ostrom, E., Gardner, R., and Walker, J. (1994). *Rules, Games, and Common-Pool Resources*, University of Michigan Press: Ann Arbor, MI.

Ostrom, E. and Schlager, E. (1996). The Formation of Property Rights, in S. Hanna, C. Folke, and K.-G. Maler, eds, *Rights to Nature: Ecological, Economics, Cultural and Political Principles of Institutions for the Environment*, Island Press: Washington DC.

Posner, R. A. (1986). *Economic Analysis of Law*, third edition, Little, Brown and Company: Boston.

Scitovsky, T. (1941). A Note on Welfare Propositions in Economics, *Review of Economic Studies*, 9 (1): 77–88.

Scott, A. D. and Johnson, J. (1985). Property Rights: Developing the Characteristics of Interests in Natural Resources, in A. D. Scott, ed., *Progress in Natural Resource Economics*, Clarendon Press: Oxford.

Sen, A. (1984). *Collective Choice and Social Welfare*, North-Holland: Amsterdam.

Stavins, R. N. (1995). Transactions Costs and Tradeable Permits, *Journal of Environmental Economics and Management*, 29 (2): 133–48.

Supreme Court of the United States, April 23, 2002, No. 00-1167, Opinion of the Court, *Tahoe-Sierra Preservation Council, Inc., et al., Petitioners* v. *Tahoe Regional Planning Agency et al.* On Writ of Certiorari to the United States Court of Appeal for the Ninth Court.

Teather, D. (2002). Smoke, Tears, Anger – Then Emptiness – in the Village Bought by a Power Company, *The Guardian*, May 14, 2002. http://www.guardian.co.uk/international/story/0,3604,715133,00.html

Wade, R. (1987). The Management of Common Property Resources: Collective Action as an Alternative to Privatisation or State Regulation, *Cambridge Journal of Economics*, 11: 95–106.

CHAPTER THREE

ECONOMICS OF POLLUTION CONTROL

Why does an individual pollute? Why does the Los Angeles motorist add his bit to the already smog-laden atmosphere? Why does the family on a picnic dump its litter in the park? ... The individual pollutes, he creates public bad, because it is in his private, personal interest to do so. (James M. Buchanan, *The Limits of Liberty: Between Anarchy and Leviathan*, pp. 102–21)

3.1 INTRODUCTION

Pollution comes in all shapes and sizes. For some pollutants the effects are only felt at the time of discharge and can be readily assimilated by the environment, so they are called *flow pollutants*. For others, their effects accumulate over time and dissipate slowly so they are termed *stock pollutants*. Pollution may also be described in terms of its source. Pollutants that come from an identifiable source that is *mobile* (such as an aircraft) or *stationary* (such as a smokestack) are called *point* sources. They are often easier to identify and control than *non-point* sources (such as fertilizer run-off from farms).

The effects, dispersal, and location of pollutants are important in determining the appropriate method of pollution control. In some cases, the possible effects of pollutants are well understood (such as untreated sewage), while in others considerable uncertainty exists about the impacts (such as persistent organic pollutants). Some emissions quickly become uniformly dispersed while others remain highly concentrated for long periods of time (such as solid waste). Uncertainty may also exist in terms of the costs of abating or mitigating the pollution, and the benefits of reducing emissions. Whether pollution is local, regional, or crosses national boundaries, and the institutional jurisdiction where it occurs also help to determine the preferred method for its control.

Given the huge variation in how, when, and where pollution occurs, different methods of pollution control have been developed for different circumstances. In this chapter, we first explain the notion of an efficient level of pollution then describe the criteria that economists use for comparing methods of pollution control, and investigate the properties of different methods of pollution control.

3.2 AN EFFICIENT LEVEL OF POLLUTION

An efficient level of pollution is defined using the concept of *Pareto efficiency* (see chapter 2). An outcome is efficient if it is not possible to change the allocation of assets and resources to make someone better off without making someone else worse off. An efficient level of pollution does *not* imply pollution is desirable. In an ideal world, we would like to produce what we need at zero cost with no pollution. Unfortunately, we live in a world where reducing or "abating" pollution imposes costs on polluters that use up real resources. Just as there can be too much pollution, there can also be too much pollution abatement if the benefits of reducing pollution are outweighed by its costs. Thus, for many pollutants an efficient level of pollution is positive.

An efficient level of a *flow* pollutant exists when the marginal benefits of pollution control exactly equal the marginal costs of reducing or abating pollution, and is defined as some fixed level of emissions per unit of time. By contrast, the efficient level of pollution for a *stock* pollutant is not, in general, fixed but is rather a function whose values will change over time.

The efficient level of pollution for a flow pollutant, illustrated in figure 3.1, is the point where the marginal cost associated with pollution reduction or abatement exactly equals the marginal benefit of abatement. The marginal benefit represents the reduction in the marginal external costs associated with pollution. For example, a factory may pollute a river, imposing costs on users of the water downstream. The increased costs imposed on downstream users is a negative externality (see chapter 2), and represents expenses external to the factory that negatively affect the utility or production functions of others. Reductions in the discharges by the factory into the river that reduce these downstream costs represent the benefit of abatement. The cost of abatement represents the expenditures incurred by the polluter in reducing its discharges. The possibility also exists that the marginal external cost is greater than the marginal cost of abatement, whatever the level of pollution. In such a situation, the marginal external cost curve would be greater than the marginal cost of abatement for *all* levels of pollution, so that a zero level of pollution is efficient.

The curvatures of the marginal cost of abatement and marginal external cost curves can vary enormously depending on the pollutant and industry. In general, marginal costs of abatement are not smooth or differentiable and may be relatively flat over a range of pollution. However, increasing abatement will often increase costs of pollution reduction. For the first units of pollution reduction a firm may simply employ a relatively cheap "end-of-pipe" treatment, but as more and

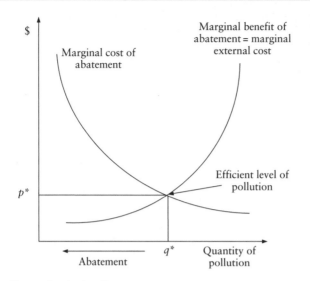

Figure 3.1   An efficient level of pollution

more units of pollution are reduced a completely new production system may be required at very high cost. For some pollutants low levels of discharge may be tolerated quite easily (such as noise pollution), but at higher and higher levels the cost they impose may increase at an increasing rate. Indeed, beyond a threshold, prolonged exposure to noise pollution at very high decibel levels may even cause death.

3.3   COMPARING METHODS OF POLLUTION CONTROL

The objective of an efficient level of pollution is almost never attainable, because we do not have the information to know the marginal cost of abatement or the marginal external cost of all pollution sources. An achievable goal is to ensure that the method of pollution control is cost-effective. In other words, a given amount of pollution reduction or abatement occurs at *least cost*. Using only this criterion, methods of pollution control that give polluters the flexibility to adjust their production and level of emissions in response to a pollution "price" (such as a market price of permits (see chapter 2) or charge per unit of emissions) will, in general, be preferred over regulatory methods that impose a maximum and uniform level of emissions. In the former case, polluters will equate their marginal cost of abatement with the price of pollution. If marginal costs of abatement are increasing and polluters cannot influence the price of emissions, a polluter has an incentive to increase its emissions (reduce its abatement) if its marginal cost of abatement is *greater* than the pollution price.

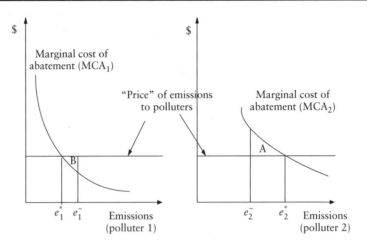

Figure 3.2   Cost-effective pollution control with heterogeneous polluters

The concept of efficiency can be seen in figure 3.2. For polluter 2, the marginal cost of abatement exceeds the pollution price when it discharges $\tilde{e}_2$ units of emissions. Thus if polluter 2 were to increase its emissions from, say, $\tilde{e}_2$ to e_2^*, the *extra cost* from increasing emissions would be the area beneath the price line and the horizontal axis between $\tilde{e}_2$ to e_2^*. This can be compared to the *reduced abatement cost* represented by the area beneath the MCA_2 curve and the horizontal axis between $\tilde{e}_2$ and e_2^*. The net gain or net cost reduction to polluter 2 is given by the triangular area A. Conversely, if the marginal cost of abatement of a firm is *less* than the pollution "price," the firm has an incentive to reduce its emissions (increase its abatement). For example, for polluter 1 in figure 3.2, the net gain or net reduction in costs in reducing emissions from, say, $\tilde{e}_1$ to e_1^* is the triangular area B. Thus provided that all polluters face the same "price" and their abatement cost curves are smooth, the marginal costs of abatement are equalized and emissions are controlled in a cost-effective way.

Polluters will minimize costs of pollution control by equating their marginal cost of abatement to the "price" of emissions. For polluters one and two, respectively, this point in figure 3.2 is shown by e_1^* and e_2^*, where $e_1^* \neq e_2^*$. Thus if polluters' marginal abatement costs differ, the cost-effective level of emissions will, in general, vary across polluters. By contrast, a *uniform* maximum level of emissions will not, in general, ensure least cost pollution abatement with heterogeneous polluters. This is because with heterogeneous polluters identical emissions results in *different* marginal costs of abatement. This is also shown in figure 3.2 for the level of emissions $\tilde{e}_1$ and $\tilde{e}_2$ where $\tilde{e}_1 = \tilde{e}_2$, but $MCA_1 < MCA_2$. Identical emissions with heterogeneous polluters implies that the combined cost of abatement would be *less* if the polluter with the lower marginal cost of abatement reduced its emissions by a marginal amount and the polluter with the higher marginal cost of abatement increased its emissions by the corresponding amount.

Other definitions of efficiency also exist and have also been used to compare methods of pollution control. For example, *dynamic efficiency*, in this context, refers to the ability of a method of pollution control to provide on-going incentives over time to polluters to further reduce their emissions or discharges. A related notion in terms of the dynamic effects of the method of pollution is how *flexible* is the method of pollution control to changes in circumstances. For example, a method of pollution control that automatically adjusts the "price" of pollution based on market forces is flexible. By contrast, a method of pollution control that requires a regulatory review (with appeals) to be changed is not.

The term *economic efficiency* refers to a situation where a firm is both producing maximum output for given level of inputs (*technical efficiency*) and is using its inputs in a way that minimizes costs for a given level of output (*allocative efficiency*). Thus economic efficiency commonly refers to how efficient firms are in terms of their *overall* production and output decisions. Thus it is possible for a firm to be efficient in its pollution abatement, such that the marginal cost of abatement equals the marginal external cost, and still be economically inefficient in the sense that it may not be using the least-cost mix of inputs in its production process.

Although economists place a great deal of attention on efficiency, other criteria are also important in choosing between different methods of pollution control. The notion of *equity* refers to who bears the costs and who enjoys the benefits of pollution control. For instance, some people have argued that it is inequitable for those causing the pollution not to pay at least some of the cost of reducing emissions. This notion of equity is encompassed in the *polluter pays* concept that states that those who pollute should be the ones to bear the costs of abatement and remedial actions (Pezzey, 1988).

Another criterion to evaluate different methods of pollution control is *institution costs*. Some methods are expensive to set up and ensure adequate monitoring and enforcement. Depending on the institutional setting, these costs may be unaffordable in some jurisdictions and in others the capabilities of the institutions to adequately monitor and enforce emissions may be lacking. Thus, a method of pollution control that may be preferred in, say, the United States, may be inappropriate in a poor country with poorly functioning public institutions.

3.4 COMMAND-AND-CONTROL METHODS

"Command-and-control" methods of pollution control refer to a wide range of approaches that impose regulatory standards: standards for maximum permissible emissions, standards for the technology that can be used in a production process, or other controls that might specify the use of inputs and outputs and location of pollution generating activities. As with any method of pollution control, command-and-control approaches require monitoring of polluter behavior, and the use of fines or other sanctions for polluters not in compliance.

Command-and-control methods are particularly useful for location and planning decisions. For example, regulations that separate activities that generate pollution from other activities hindered by emissions are highly desirable. In many situations zoning decisions satisfy the maxim "an ounce of prevention is better than a pound of cure." For instance, a zoning regulation that prevents industrial activity in residential suburbs is a low-cost way of avoiding potentially large negative externalities. Similarly, for some pollutants with threshold effects and very high external costs (highly radioactive wastes), stringent regulations as to where they may be stored or processed can help prevent major environmental costs. In this sense, a rigid control or standard with monitoring and penalties for non-compliance may be preferred to alternative approaches.

Command-and-control approaches also offer a means to address non-point sources of pollution where alternative approaches developed for point sources may be difficult to apply. For example, detecting the source of some pesticides and insecticides can be problematic. Thus, regulations that prohibit or restrict how and when they are used may be the preferred method for their control. Another advantage with command-and-control approaches is that by fixing a maximum permissible level of emissions, they are often the first tier of regulation for transboundary or global pollutants. For example, under the 1997 Kyoto Protocol, most rich countries (a notable exception is the United States) have agreed to reduce their emissions of greenhouse gases (GHGs). Thus a national commitment to not emit beyond a fixed quantity of GHGs is a type of command and control, although it does not prevent a country from using other approaches, such as a carbon tax, as a second-tier instrument within its borders to reduce the cost of meeting the abatement target. Such a combination of instruments can help ensure standards are achieved in a cost-effective way (Baumol and Oates, 1971).

In a world of perfect information and zero transactions costs, standards could be set differentially to ensure Pareto efficiency, by making the marginal external costs of each emission source equal its marginal abatement cost. Unfortunately, such information is almost never available. Thus uniform regulations are often imposed for a whole industry or vintage of equipment. Where there exist differences in the marginal costs of abatement among pollution sources, uniformity of emissions ensures the costs of pollution abatement are *not* minimized and the approach is not cost-effective. This can be shown for n pollution sources where each source has a maximum and identical permissible level of emissions of $e^{\sim}$, and the total cost of pollution abatement for a firm i is $c_i(e_i)$ and this is *decreasing* in the level of emissions, i.e., $c_i{'}(e_i) < 0$. In this case, a uniform standard is a least-cost method of pollution control *if and only if* all pollution sources have the identical marginal costs of abatement for the same level of emissions, i.e., $c_1'(e^{\sim}) = c_2'(e^{\sim}) = \ldots = c_n'(e^{\sim})$.

The greater the heterogeneity in the marginal costs of abatement of pollution sources for a given level of pollution, the larger is the difference between the least-cost abatement and the cost of pollution control with a uniform standard. In a summary table of 20 different studies that compares the least-cost with the command-and-control costs of abatement for air pollution, the US Environmental Protection Agency (2001) finds that the ratio of command-and-control costs to a least-cost method of control ranges from 1.07 (sulfates emissions in Los Angeles) to 22 (particulate matter in the lower Delaware valley). In the same summary table, a total of eight studies had estimated ratios of command-and-control costs to the least-cost alternatives of between 1.1 and 2.0.

Some of the most important emission standards, in terms of air pollution, have been those imposed on US automobile manufacturers (see box 3.1). For a variety

BOX 3.1 US AUTOMOBILE EMISSION STANDARDS

Starting in 1965 with the first amendments to the US Clean Air Act, uniform national emission standards were introduced (starting with model year 1968) for new cars to control carbon monoxide and hydrocarbon emissions. In 1970 much more stringent emissions standards (90 percent reduction in carbon monoxide from 1970 levels) were enacted for new cars beginning in 1975. To help automobile manufacturers, extensions to the deadlines were subsequently permitted until the early 1980s.

The standards were designed to achieve ambient standards in the worst urban air quality areas (Los Angeles) based on air quality measures in 1967. Standards were also imposed on all new vehicles in 1984 for high altitude driving to help address air pollution in low air quality areas such as Denver.

In 1990, further more stringent standards were imposed on all new vehicles. Regulations were also introduced on fuel including the banning of lead additives after 1995 and the use of reformulated (cleaner burning) fuels in areas where air quality standards had not been met. In addition, in areas where air quality standards have not been achieved, all operators with ten or more vehicles will eventually be obliged to use "clean fuel" vehicles with very low emissions for a range of pollutants. Notwithstanding these national standards, California has implemented even more stringent standards for vehicles sold in the state.

Emission standards have been highly successful at reducing the total national emissions of various pollutants from gas or petrol vehicles. For example, in 1970 total lead tail-pipe emissions from vehicles was almost 172,000 tons, but by 1996 the amounts were negligible. Total gasoline-powered vehicle emissions of particulate matter, carbon monoxide, and volatile organic compounds declined to 34 percent, 65 percent, and 45 percent of their levels in 1970 by 1995, despite a large increase in the total number of vehicles on the road over the period.

The emissions standards have raised the cost of new vehicles and led to a "rebound" effect whereby households now own their cars for longer than they used to, which has reduced the expected reductions in emissions. The costs, and especially the benefits, associated with the vehicle emission standards are very difficult to determine. Nevertheless, several cost–benefit studies have been undertaken that indicate that the costs of achieving automobile emissions standards may have exceeded the benefits. In part, this is because national standards that are used to ensure a minimum level of air quality in polluted locations, such as Los Angeles or Denver, impose significant costs on the purchasers of new vehicles who live in areas that enjoy good air quality and where such high emission standards are unnecessary.

Sources: Callan and Thomas (2000); Crandall et al. (1982); Tietenberg (1996)

of reasons, and in particular where high costs are associated with achieving emission standards, regulators have opted for technology-based standards. Such standards often impose a level of technology on new or modified pollution sources that leads to lower level of emissions than the average across all emitting sources. If only imposed on new pollution sources they often provide a competitive advantage to older or existing (and often higher polluting) sources. A possible justification for technology standards is that *if* the costs of installing the required technology are relatively low at the time of construction, the associated costs of pollution abatement will also be relatively small.

The problem with technology standards is that they often only indirectly control the pollutant, and do not allow polluters to determine themselves the least-cost way to achieve a given level of emissions. This lack of flexibility can impose significant costs on polluters and society. For example, a 1979 revision in the US standards governing sulfur dioxide emissions from coal and oil electric utilities eventually forced all sources to install scrubbers to help remove sulfur dioxide, irrespective of the sulfur content of the fuel used by the utilities. Perl and Dunbar (1982) estimate that the net benefit of this particular technology standard, in 1980 dollars, was negative $2.94 billion. In addition, imposing a particular technology on pollution sources, rather than a technology with a particular level of performance, may be distortionary and bias the use of certain factors of production (such as capital) over others (such as labor). Finally, both emission and technology-based standards are dynamically inefficient in the sense that unless standards become progressively more stringent over time, they provide no on-going incentive for further pollution control.

3.5   POLLUTION CHARGES AND SUBSIDIES

One way to control pollution is to levy a charge per unit of emissions or pay a subsidy per unit of emissions abated, either of which creates an incentive for polluters to consider the costs that their emissions impose on others. Before we evaluate the economics of emissions charges and subsidies we first note two reasons why these instruments may not be ideal. First, while they offer theoretical advantages, high monitoring and enforcement costs may make an alternative instrument preferred. For example, if the level of emissions is closely related to the use of inputs (such as the carbon or sulfur content of coal, oil, or gas) or the output (solid waste), it may sometimes be easier to impose the charge on something other than the emissions themselves. This is particularly true in the case of mobile pollution sources (such as cars) where the costs of monitoring and enforcing a tax on the fuel used in vehicles is likely to be several orders of magnitude cheaper, on a national basis, than those of charging for the exhaust pipe emissions for each vehicle. For this reason, fuel taxes have been adopted by several nations to help address the externalities associated with vehicle use.

Another potential problem with emissions charges arises when the timing and the location of the emissions affects the external costs of the pollution. For instance, GHGs rapidly and uniformly disperse such that where and when the emissions occur have no impact on their effect on the environment. By contrast, for some pollutants (such as smoke and whether it occurs upwind or downwind of a community), the timing and location of the pollution affects the external costs it imposes on others. In such situations, a *uniform* charge on the smoke emitted by polluters will *not* result in an efficient outcome. This is because each pollution source imposes a different external cost that cannot be resolved by a uniform price on all pollution sources.

Implementing a charge that differs according to the marginal external costs of emissions by source requires a degree of information that almost never exists. The next best alternative is to impose a charge based on *ambient* measures of the emissions at defined receptor points. In other words, measure the effect of the pollution source by measuring its impact on air or water quality and defined locations. Unfortunately, the information required to implement ambient-based charges renders them difficult to implement in many cases. Thus, often for practical reasons, charges are frequently based on the *level* of emissions or related outputs and inputs rather than directly on the *effects* of emissions. Many examples of such charges exist. For instance, in Germany and the Netherlands charges especially for discharges into water bodies are an important method of controlling water pollution. Provided that charges are set at the appropriate level, they can be highly effective at addressing the externalities associated with pollution in a cost-effective way.

Emissions charges on flow pollutants

Pollution charges and subsidies that are imposed directly on the level of emissions are often called Pigouvian taxes and subsidies, after the economist A. C. Pigou, who argued in the 1920s for their use as a means to rectify pollution that arises from market failures.

The simplest way to represent an emissions charge or subsidy (Mumy, 1980) is as follows:

$$\alpha(e_i - \bar{e}_i) \tag{1}$$

where α is the charge per unit of emissions by polluter i, e_i is the emissions of polluter i over the specified time period and $\bar{e}_i$ is the baseline level of emissions assigned to firm i that allows us to model both charges and subsidies. If $e_i > \bar{e}_i$ then the polluter pays a charge per unit of emissions in excess of the baseline level of emissions, and if $\bar{e}_i = 0$ the amount of tax paid equals αe_i. By contrast, if $e_i < \bar{e}_i$, the polluter receives a per-emission unit subsidy for abatement below the emissions baseline.

If we examine the case with no emissions baseline where $\bar{e}_i = 0$, a cost-minimizing polluter will choose its level of emissions to solve the following problem,

$$\text{Min } c_i(e_i) + \alpha e_i \tag{2}$$

where $c_i(e_i)$ is the total cost of abating or reducing emissions and, as before, is *decreasing* in the level of emissions, i.e., $c_i'(e_i) < 0$. Thus a necessary condition for a cost minimization by the polluter is

$$\alpha = -c_i'(e_i). \tag{3}$$

Provided that all pollution sources face the same charge per unit of emissions (α), all polluters will have the identical marginal cost of abatement despite the fact that, in general, their emissions will differ. Such a result ensures that the emission charge is *cost effective*. In other words, no pollution source has a lower marginal cost of abatement than any other, and for a given *total* level of pollution and technology, abatement occurs at least cost.

The least-cost outcome, however, will be efficient *if and only if* the emissions charge per unit of emissions (α) equals the marginal external cost of emissions at the efficient level of emissions for *all* sources. To illustrate, the efficient level of emissions is found by solving the following minimization problem.

$$\text{Min } \sum_{i=1}^{n} c_i(e_i) + D\left(\sum_{i=1}^{n} e_i\right) \tag{4}$$

where $D \sum_{i=1}^{n} e_i$ is the external cost associated with the flow of uniformly mixed emissions from all sources and is increasing in emissions, i.e., $D'(\sum_{i=1}^{n} e_i) > 0$. Thus a necessary condition for the efficient outcome is,

$$-c_i'(e_i) = D'\left(\sum_{i=1}^{n} e_i\right) \quad \forall i \tag{5}$$

It follows, therefore, that for an emission charge tax to yield the efficient outcome, the marginal external cost of emissions must be identical for all sources and be equal to the marginal abatement cost of each source. For a uniform emissions charge this outcome will only arise under special conditions such as when the per unit emissions charge equals the marginal external cost of emissions which is a constant and the same for all sources. Thus the greater the heterogeneity in the marginal external cost of emissions imposed by polluters, the further away will the emissions charge be from the efficient outcome if all polluters face the same tax per unit of emissions.

Emissions charges on stock pollutants

The appropriate emissions charge is more difficult to derive for a stock pollutant because emissions today impose an external cost in the future. The easiest way to show how to calculate the efficient emissions charge for a stock pollutant is to set up a two-period problem where there is no abatement and the pollutant stock is directly related to the firm's output. The efficient level of pollution is the solution to the following problem:

$$\text{Max } (px_1 - c(x_1) - g(a_1)) + (px_2 - c(x_2) - g(a_2)) \tag{6}$$

Subject to:

$$a_2 = \theta a_1 + x_1 \tag{7}$$
$$a_3 = \theta a_2 + x_2 \tag{8}$$
$$a_1 = \bar{a}_1, \quad a_3 = \bar{a}_3 \tag{9}$$

where p is the price per unit of output for the polluter in both periods, x_t is polluter output in period t, $c(x_t)$ is the firm's private costs in period t, $g(a_t)$ is the external cost from the stock pollutant in period t, a_t is the quantity of the stock pollutant in period t and is measured in the same units as x_t, $\theta \varepsilon (0, 1)$ is the factor by which the pollutant stock decays from one period to the next, and there is no time discounting.

The corresponding Lagrangian function is,

$$\text{Max } L = (px_1 - c(x_1) - g(\bar{a}_1)) + (px_2 - c(x_2) - g(\theta \bar{a}_1 + x_1)) + \lambda(\bar{a}_3 - \theta(\theta \bar{a}_1 + x_1) - x_2)$$

and the necessary conditions for a maximum are,

$$\partial L/\partial x_1 = 0 \quad \Rightarrow \quad p - c'(x_1) - g'(\theta \bar{a}_1 + x_1) = \lambda \theta \tag{10}$$
$$\partial L/\partial x_2 = 0 \quad \Rightarrow \quad p - c'(x_2) = \lambda \tag{11}$$
$$\partial L/\partial \lambda = 0 \quad \Rightarrow \quad \bar{a}_3 - \theta(\theta \bar{a}_1 + x_1) - x_2 = 0 \tag{12}$$

Conditions (10) and (11) require that the marginal net return from production (including the costs imposed on others) equal the shadow price of the stock pollution. To simplify the necessary conditions and to derive a numerical result we assume that $p = 5$, $c(x_t) = x_t^2$, $g(a_t) = a_t$, $\theta = 0.5$, $\bar{a}_1 = 0$ and $\bar{a}_3 = 1.0$. Thus, (10), (11) and (12) become

$$5 - 2x_1 - 1 = 0.5\lambda \tag{10'}$$
$$5 - 2x_2 = \lambda \tag{11'}$$
$$1 - 0.5x_1 - x_2 = 0 \tag{12'}$$

Using (10)' and (11)' to obtain an expression for x_1 in terms of x_2 and substituting this expression into (12)' we obtain the efficient level of output in periods one and two, the value of the Lagrangian multiplier and the terminal value of the stock pollutant, i.e.,

$$(x_1^*, x_2^*, \lambda^*, a_2^*) = (1, 0.5, 4, 1).$$

This problem could also be solved using dynamic programming that uses an algorithm to solve problems in discrete time (see chapter 1, section 1.5). In this method, the output of the pollution source is the *decision* or control variable and the value of the stock pollutant is the *state* variable. The approach is to write a functional recurrence equation that enables us to work backwards in time and solve for outputs and values of the stock pollutant, i.e.,

$$V_t(a_t) = \max_{x(t)} [5x_t - x_t^2 - a_t + V_{t+1}(a_{t+1})] \tag{13}$$

Subject to:

$$a_{t+1} = 0.5 \, a_t + x_t \tag{14}$$

where $V_t(a_t)$ is the *return function* and is the maximum value for (6) at time t, given the value of the stock pollutant a_t and (14) is the *transition equation* that determines the value of the next period's state variable.

The functional recurrence equation when t = 2 is

$$V_2(a_2) = \max [5x_2 - x_2^2 - a_2 + V_3(a_3)] \tag{15}$$

Subject to:

$$a_3 = 0.5a_2 + x_2 \tag{16}$$

$$a_3 = 1 \tag{17}$$

where $V_3(a_3)$ has the value of zero as it is the value of the return function after the end of the program or optimization period. Combining the constraints (16) and (17) we can obtain an expression for x_2 in terms of a_2 that we can use to rewrite the functional recurrence equation solely in terms of a_2, i.e.,

$$V_2(a_2) = 5(1 - 0.5 \, a_2) - (1 - 0.5 \, a_2)^2 - a_2 \tag{18}$$

The next step is to write the functional recurrence equation for the previous period, t = 1, i.e.,

$$V_1(a_1) = \max [5x_1 - x_1^2 - a_1 + V_2(a_2)] \tag{19}$$

Subject to:

$$a_2 = 0.5a_1 + x_1 \tag{20}$$

$$a_1 = 0 \tag{21}$$

We can substitute in the previously found return function $V_2(a_2)$ and then use (20) to obtain an expression for (21) solely in terms of a_1 and x_1, i.e.,

$$V_1(a_1) = \max [5x_1 - x_1^2 - a_1 + 5 - 2.5(0.5a_1 + x_1) - (1 - 0.5(0.5a_1 + x_1))^2 - 0.5a_1 - x_1]$$

The necessary condition for a maximum requires that,

$$\partial V_1(a_1)/\partial x_1 = 5 - 2x_1 - 2.5 + (1 - 0.5(0.5a_1 + x_1)) - 1 = 0$$

This implies that a necessary condition for the return function at $t = 1$ to be at a maximum is,

$$x_1^* = 1 - 0.1\,a_1 \tag{22}$$

Given that $a_1 = 0$, then from (22), (20), and (16) we can obtain $(x_1^*, x_2^*, a_2^*) = (1, 0.5, 1)$ which is identical to the result found by using the method of Lagrange.

By contrast to the efficient level of output in periods $t = 1$ and 2, the pollution source would maximize its profits by ignoring the stock externality and setting its profit maximizing output to $(x_1^\sim, x_2^\sim) = (2.5, 2.5)$. In this particular case, there is a one-to-one correspondence between the firm's output and its contribution to the stock pollutant. Thus a tax on the output is identical to a tax on the source's emissions. The tax on the firms' *output* in period 1 (a_1) and in period 2 (a_2) to achieve the efficient output level can be calculated by solving the polluter's first-order condition, but including the tax on the output for each period , i.e.,

$$5 - 2x_t^* - \alpha_t = 0$$

where if $(x_1^*, x_2^*) = (1, 0.5)$ then $(a_1, a_2) = (3, 4)$. As we might expect, the tax rate that is applied to the firm's output is different for the two periods. The efficient tax in the second period obliges the polluter to pay \$4 per unit of output produced in the second period. This cost per unit is the negative of the value of the Lagrangian multiplier or *co-state* variable found previously when we solved for the efficient level of pollution. This is no coincidence. In general, the tax rate to arrive at an efficient level of emissions per time period should equal the negative (a tax is a cost) of the *shadow price* or *shadow cost* of the dynamic constraint that transforms the current period's stock pollutant and the current period's decision into the next period's stock pollutant. In the case where emissions generate both stock and flow externalities, the optimal tax will exceed the shadow cost of pollution. Moreover, setting the tax at too low a level in the presence of a stock externality or ignoring the flow externality can have effects on both transitory and steady-state output, emissions and tax payments (Sandal et al., 2003).

Other features of emissions charges

In addition to being cost-effective, emissions charges can be described as dynamically efficient in the sense that they provide an on-going incentive to polluters to reduce their pollution. Of course, if the per-unit charge is set at too high a level, the incentive may be such that the level of abatement will exceed the efficient level. In general, however, the opposite is true and emission charges are at set at too low a level and thus do not provide an effective incentive to polluters. Indeed, considerable evidence exists that in some jurisdictions, such as China, the pollution charges imposed are many times below what the efficient level should be. Despite the relatively low level of charges in China, they have been responsible for ensuring that "China's industrial pollution is far less serious than it would have been without the levies" (World Bank, 1999, p. 46).

Another advantage of charges is, to the extent that innovation in reducing emissions is induced by economic incentives, emission charges can spur technological developments in reducing the emissions per unit of output. This notion, in its most optimistic form, is known as the *Porter hypothesis* (Porter and van der Linde, 1995), and suggests that pollution control may even lead to unanticipated technological innovations that may reduce overall production costs, thereby reducing both pollution and total costs. Although serendipitous and unanticipated cost-saving innovations due to pollution controls are possible at a firm level, it seems unlikely that a "free lunch" of such a magnitude is available on an economy-wide basis (see chapter 10).

Pollution charges that tax "bads" also generate revenue that can be used to reduce taxes (such as payroll taxes or income taxes) which can have a negative impact on economic activity. The distortions from traditional taxes that arise from a reallocation of resources can be large, and in the US range from $0.31–0.48 per dollar for payroll tax raised and between $0.40–0.60 per dollar of income tax raised (Morgenstern, 1995). Thus emission charges, and environmental taxes in general, offer the possibility of a *double dividend* whereby environmental quality can improve while at the same time increasing incentives to work (by reducing marginal income tax rates or payroll taxes) and raising productivity.

To what extent a double-dividend exists, and at what level should the environmental tax be set at relative to the social marginal damages of pollution, has provoked a heated debate among economists (Goulder, 1997; Jaeger, 2001). Although most agree that simultaneously reducing tax distortions and correcting environmental externalities can be welfare enhancing, there has been a lively discussion as to the appropriate level to set pollution charges in a "second-best" world and whether they should be higher or lower than the marginal external cost of pollution. The answer depends, in part, on the potential distortions from environmental taxes, especially if they are levied indirectly on outputs or inputs rather than directly on emissions, and the distortions imposed by the taxes they replace. As with any switch from one form of taxation to another, some people will pay more and some will pay less and thus the distributional outcomes with such changes are an important policy consideration.

Emission charges also suffer from some limitations. First, introducing or increasing existing taxes can be politically difficult. Second, in a dynamic world where technologies change rapidly or the overall price level increases at a fast rate, a *fixed* per unit Pigouvian tax may soon become ineffective. Third, a *uniform* Pigouvian tax applied to all polluters where there exist large differences in the marginal

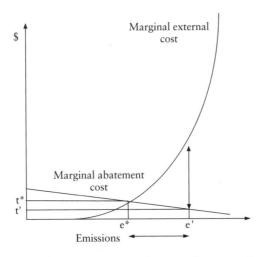

Figure 3.3   Potential error from an emissions charge under uncertainty

external costs per unit of emissions is likely to "underprice" pollution for some sources and "overprice" pollution for other sources. In turn, this could result in pollution "hotspots" in some locations, and more abatement than is desirable in others. Fourth, taxes are a price instrument and only indirectly control the level of pollution. In a world where a regulator has a good knowledge of the costs of pollution abatement this may pose only a small problem, but where such information is lacking the possibility exists that the tax will be set at too high or too low a level resulting in an undesirable level of pollution. Depending on the shape and level of uncertainty of the marginal cost of abatement and marginal external cost curves, it may be preferable to use a quantity instrument that controls the level of emissions directly.

This potential problem of an emissions charge, in a world of uncertainty, is illustrated in figure 3.3. The efficient tax should be set at t* yielding an efficient level of emissions of e*. However, in an uncertain world a relatively small error in setting the tax at t' leads to a much larger level of emissions than is desired, represented by the distance e* to e'.

Weitzman (1974) was the first to show that when setting a tax in a world of uncertainty, the magnitude of the difference between the actual and desired emissions level will be greater the steeper is the marginal external cost curve and the more gently sloped is the marginal cost of abatement curve. In such situations and where uncertainty exists over the slopes of the marginal cost of abatement and marginal external cost curves, it may be better to use a quantity instrument that directly controls the level of emissions than a price instrument (such as a tax) that only does so indirectly. In reference to the type of cases illustrated by figure 3.3, and under uncertainty, Weitzman observes, "it is hard to avoid the impression that there will be many circumstances where the more conservative quantity mode will be preferred by planners because it is better for avoiding very bad planning mistakes" (Weitzman, 1974, p. 486). More recently, Stavins (1996) has shown that if the marginal external cost and marginal abatement costs are positively correlated, in a world of uncertainty, this will also tend to favor quantity instruments over price instruments.

An alternative to a pollution charge is to combine a charge with a standard. In this sense, the charge helps to reduce the costs of abatement while the standard ensures that pollution does not exceed critical levels. Roberts and Weitzman (1993) have proposed such an approach whereby a charge per unit of emissions is imposed in excess of a standard. For polluters with a high marginal cost of abatement the mixed instrument will operate more like a charge, but for most polluters the approach will function more like a standard. Similarly, Roberts and Spence (1976) propose combining marketable emission permits (see chapter 2) with a fee and subsidy. Polluters are allowed to emit above the number of emission permits they own, but must pay a fee per unit of emissions beyond their allowances. Polluters that emit less than the emission permits they own, receive a per unit emissions subsidy, but which is less than the charge. At the same time, polluters are free to trade permits among themselves where the subsidy is set to be equal to or less than the market price of emission permits and the charge is set equal to or greater than the permit price. For both mixed approaches, the charge acts as a "pressure valve" which gives polluters flexibility in deciding on their level of emissions, but only if their marginal costs of abatement are much higher than expected.

Pollution subsidies

Subsidies exist in many forms, and often contribute to pollution as they encourage production or the use of inputs that can lead to pollution. Pollution subsidies, however, represent direct payments to polluters for *reducing* their level of emissions. These subsidies can come in one of two main forms. The subsidy could represent a payment or co-payment for the purchase of capital equipment that reduces emissions by polluter. Alternatively, the subsidy, as shown in equation (1), could represent a payment per unit of emission for reductions in the level of emissions below a defined benchmark ($\bar{e}_i$).

Both emissions and capital or investment subsidies have potential problems. The most practical difficulty in subsidizing polluters with emissions subsidies is that it is politically unpopular to do although capital or investment subsidies for pollution abatement are widely employed. If the government or regulator does not wish to create or enlarge a fiscal deficit, a subsidy also requires that other sectors of the economy be taxed to pay for subsidy payments to polluters. Beyond these practical difficulties, capital or investment subsidies for emissions reduction equipment will be cost-effective *if and only if* the subsidized equipment reduces emissions at least cost for all polluters and the marginal costs of abatement are identical for all polluters. Given heterogeneous polluters, investment subsidies for abatement will not, in general, be cost effective.

The potential problem with an emissions subsidy, or subsidy per unit of emissions abated, is that if the subsidy is paid to any polluter operating in an industry, it might encourage entry of additional firms and may possibly increase *total* emissions, even if emissions per polluter declines. In other words, provided that a polluter's benchmark emissions exceed its current emissions ($\bar{e}_i > e_i$), additional entrants may be attracted by the subsidy, thus increasing total emissions over what is desired. A way to overcome this entry incentive problem is to create a property right over the payment of the subsidy to the polluter. In this situation, only *existing* polluters at the introduction of the emissions subsidy receive the emissions benchmark or allowance of $\bar{e}_i$, and any *new* entrant i receives a zero allowance and faces an emissions charge of αe_i (Pezzey, 1992). Provided that polluters receive the subsidy $\alpha \bar{e}_i$ when it exits or shuts down, the economic profit per time period of an *existing* polluter i that chooses *not* to exit is,

$$\Pi_i = pq_i - c(q_i, e_i) - \alpha(e_i - \bar{e}_i) - \alpha \bar{e}_i$$

where the last term, $\alpha \bar{e}_i$, is the opportunity cost incurred by the polluter when it chooses to *not* exit, and equals the payment it would receive if it were to shut down. In this case, the emissions subsidy is identical to an emissions charge in both its short and long-run effects. Moreover, with perfect information it is theoretically possible to set the baseline emissions ($\bar{e}_i$) for the polluters so that some pay an emissions charge while other are subsidized to reduce emissions and, overall, the scheme is revenue-neutral.

3.6   MARKETABLE EMISSION PERMITS

A marketable or tradable emission permit is a license to emit a certain quantity of a pollutant, where the licence can be bought or sold among polluters and third parties. They were proposed as a method of pollution control in the 1960s (Dales, 1968), but it was not until the 1970s that marketable emission permits were first used. Marketable permits can also be denominated in terms of *ambient* measures of environmental quality for defined sites or receptors. Thus, instead of regulating the emissions of polluters, *ambient permits* regulate the effects of emissions. Whenever the external effects per unit of emissions differs across sources, ambient permits offer an advantage over emissions permits by providing a better price signal to polluters in terms of the costs they impose on others. The major problem with implementing ambient permits, and why they are not used in practice, is the difficulty in tracing the ambient effects to particular sources, and the transactions costs of trading where there are many sources and multiple receptors.

We will focus our attention on marketable emissions permits. They have been employed or are currently used in a number of different countries including the

European Union (ozone depleting substances), Chile (particulate matter), Canada (pilot programs for volatile organic compounds and nitrogen oxides), and the USA, especially for air pollutants (Stavins, 2001a). Such programs are a subset of what may be described as market-based rights that involve the use of tradable quantity instruments to regulate a variety of environmental problems (see chapter 2).

By far the most important marketable emission permit schemes, in terms of their effect and scope, have been in the USA and most have been developed to improve air quality. The broad types are *credit programs* whereby polluters receive tradable emission credits for any reductions in their emissions below an admissible standard and so-called *cap-and-trade programs* where an overall cap or total level of emissions is set by a regulator and sources trade among themselves.

The US emission credit programs grew out of "offsets" instituted by the US Environmental Protection Agency (EPA) designed to ensure new sources of air pollution in areas with less than acceptable air quality both installed technology that had the lowest achievable emission rate, *and* offset their emissions by reducing emissions from existing sources by a greater amount. The scheme has led to more than 10,000 trades in offsets worth about $2 billion (USEPA, 2001). Most of these trades have involved firms shutting down their own existing sources to build new plants.

The offset program contributed to the emergence of emissions reductions credits (ERCs) following 1977 amendments to the US Clean Air Act. The ERCs are administered by states. They are created when a source reduces its emissions below its permitted level, and the state certifies the reduction is permanent and is not required by the state under any other existing regulations. ERCs can be "banked" for a limited period of time and can be traded among sources. Despite the existence of ERCs, the number of trades has been much less than expected in many states. This is explained by limitations and restrictions imposed by some states on trading of ERCs across geographical areas, an administrative reduction in some states of the ERCs available for sale after a source banks its credits so as to reduce overall emissions, and relatively high offset ratios. Combined, these restrictions have raised the transactions or institution costs (see chapter 2) of trading ERCs and reduced the amount traded.

The development of ERCs on a state level has spurred further use of marketable emission permits. One of the most developed state programs is the Regional Clean Air Incentives Market (RECLAIM) in the Los Angeles area. The program began in 1994 with the creation of RECLAIM Trading Credits (RTCs) for nitrogen oxides and sulfur oxides for most stationary sources in the designated area. For each source, the allocated RTCs are scheduled to decline each year until 2003 to improve overall environmental quality. Trades worth over $2 million took place in 1994, and were worth $21 million in 1997 with prices for nitrogen oxides and sulfur oxides averaging $227 and $64 per ton (USEPA, 2001). Other air emissions trading programs also exist on a state basis and have been developed for effluent discharged into water bodies. Unlike their counterparts in terms of air emissions, effluent programs have generated far fewer trades especially in one of the earliest schemes on the Fox River in Wisconsin due to high transactions costs from trading (Devlin and Grafton, 1999).

On a federal level in the US, trading schemes were established in the phase-out of CFCs and lead in gasoline. In the case of CFCs, a marketable emission permit scheme was implemented for producers and importers. Lead tradable credits were allocated to refiners, importers, and blenders of ethanol. The savings associated with these permit schemes, relative to command-and-control approaches, amounted to over $300 million for the CFCs program and over $200 million for the lead program (USEPA, 2001). By far the most important marketable emissions trading scheme anywhere in the world is for sulfur dioxide for US fossil-fueled electric utilities (see box 3.2).

The principle behind marketable emission permits is that each and every pollution source faces the same "price" for their emissions and that the permits represent a durable and exclusive property right (see chapter 2). If markets are competitive and transactions costs are low, a market price per unit of emissions provides an economic signal to polluters similar to an emissions charge. Namely, if a polluter's marginal cost of abatement is *less* than the market price of emissions it pays the polluter to abate and sell the excess permits it no longer needs. Conversely, if a polluter's marginal abatement cost *exceeds* the market price of emissions it pays to buy permits and reduce the level of abatement. Thus the marginal cost of abatement is equalized across all sources, ensuring a cost-effective method of pollution control.

To illustrate, in the absence of uncertainty, but with competitive markets and zero transactions costs, each polluter will minimize the following,

$$\text{Min } c_i(e_i) + \vartheta(m_i + t_i) \tag{23}$$

Subject to:

$$e_i = m_i + t_i \tag{24}$$

where e_i is the polluter's emissions, $c_i(e_i)$ is the cost of abating or reducing emissions where $c_i'(e_i) < 0$, ϑ is the market price of emissions, m_i is the initial allocation of emission permits to polluter i and t_i is the amount of permits bought (>0) or sold (<0) by polluter i. Substituting the compliance constraint (24) into (23) and differentiating with respect to e_i, the necessary condition for cost minimization for firm i is

$$\vartheta = -c_i'(e_i). \tag{25}$$

Provided that a market equilibrium exists for emission permits at the price ϑ (see chapter 2), all polluters will face the same price and the marginal cost of abatement is equalized across all sources. This is the same result we found for an emissions charge and arises whenever polluters face the same per unit "price" of emissions,

BOX 3.2   SULFUR DIOXIDE TRADING BY US ELECTRIC UTILITIES

Following the US Clean Air Act Amendments of 1990, a system of caps on sulfur dioxide emissions were established for coal and oil-fired electric utility boilers, that in aggregate accounted for about two-thirds of national emissions. These caps were in the form of tradable annual emissions allowances that were allocated free to utilities based on their heat input in the period 1985–7. To ensure compliance, emissions in excess of allowances incur a charge of $2,000 per ton, indexed to the inflation rate.

The goal of the program is to reduce sulfur dioxide emissions by about a half from 1980 levels, and thus mitigate the related environmental problems that include acidification of lakes, streams, and soils. On this criterion, the program has been successful as both ambient concentrations of sulfur dioxide and acid rain declined significantly over the 1990s. Phase I of the program from 1995–2000 was restricted to utilities in the mid-western and eastern United States with initial allowances of 2.5 pounds per Btus of heat input in the reference period. Phase II, begun in 2000, has extended the program to almost all electric utilities in the 48 contiguous states, and provides allowances of 1.2 pounds per Btus of heat input in the reference period.

A key characteristic of the allowances is that they are fully transferable to anyone prepared to purchase them. Allowances are denominated in tons of sulfur dioxide emissions, and can also be banked and used in future years, but allowances for future years cannot be used to reconcile emissions for earlier periods. To facilitate trading, each year a small percentage of the allowances (2.8 percent) allocated to utilities is auctioned by the regulatory authority, with the revenue returned to utilities in proportion to the allowances they contributed for sale at the auction. Over time there has been a large decline in the bid and ask spreads at the auctions, and spot auction prices have ranged from $66/ton to $217/ton with a March 2000 price of $130/ton. The amount of allowances traded has increased over time (in the spot auction and private trades). For instance, in the period April 1993 to March 1994 an estimated 400,000 allowances were traded, but for the period April 1996 to March 1997 5.4 million tons were exchanged. By the start of 2000, the program had generated over 9,300 transfers totaling 81.5 million allowances.

The most recent estimates of the long-run gains associated with allowance trading can be compared to a uniform emission standard based on sulfur dioxide emissions per unit of heat input. The cumulative gains from allowance trading by 2010 are estimated to be $784 million in 1995 dollars, or just over 40 percent of the total cost associated with a uniform emission standard. These cost savings are substantial, but are much less than the $2.3–5.9 billion saving estimated by the US Environmental Protection Agency in 1990. Two reasons for the lower gains from trade include a decrease in the marginal cost of abatement over the period due to a decline in the price of low sulfur coal, and technical improvements. Both factors have reduced the costs of compliance that would have occurred with an emission standard. Lower transportation costs to move low sulfur coal from the west to the eastern US have also reduced the *differences* in the marginal costs of abatement across utilities and, thus, the benefits of emissions trading versus an emissions standard.

Sources: Carlson et al. (2000); Joskow et al. (1998); USEPA (2001)

whether it is a tax or a market price for emissions. Key comparative advantages of permits over a charge, however, are that the permit price automatically adjusts to changes in costs and expectations of polluters, and in a world of uncertainty they provide a much greater degree of control over the total level of emissions.

It should be emphasized, however, that the equality of price and quantity instruments in terms of pollution control only exists in very special circumstances. In general, polluters incur transactions costs when trading emission permits (see chapter 2), the emissions market may not be competitive so that not all polluters face the same price, and uncertainty exists over costs and returns for both the polluters and the environmental regulator.

The fact that marketable emission permits can lead to a cost-effective method of pollution control does *not* imply that emission permits lead to an efficient outcome. Even if the marginal external cost per unit of emissions is a constant and the same for *all* sources, the efficient outcome will only result if the cap or total level of emissions equals the efficient level of pollution and the conditions to ensure the Coase theorem occur (see chapter 2).

Practicalities of implementing marketable emission permits

Marketable emission permits, unlike pollution charges, do offer certainty over the level of pollution *provided* there is an adequate system of monitoring and enforcement. Monitoring can be expensive – for example, the start-up cost of establishing continuous environmental monitoring devices in the RECLAIM program was some $13 million (USEPA, 2001) – and enforcement requires a set of institutions that ensure polluters not in compliance are properly sanctioned. Thus, where institutions are not well developed and polluters can flout quantity controls, marketable emission permits may not be appropriate.

A potential problem is that the market for emission permits may not be competitive due to concentration of emissions in the hands of a few polluters (Hahn, 1984). This can pose problems for some polluters and can result in market distortions. Thus when establishing marketable emission permits regulators need to help ensure competitive behavior and that transactions costs for the polluters and regulators are as small as possible.

Marketable emission permits can *potentially* cause two other difficulties. Trading between sources may result in some polluters increasing their emissions, leading to pollution "hotspots." For example, in the US sulfur dioxide trading program some eastern states have been very concerned about trades from east to west, as the prevailing westerly wind may increase acid deposition in the east. In addition, in some circumstances, it may be possible for polluters to substitute from controlled emissions to uncontrolled pollutants thereby reducing the dynamic advantages of emission permits (Devlin and Grafton, 1994).

Such problems may be overcome by imposing ambient limits, in addition to emission permits, as occurs with the US emission reduction credits programs.

Any restrictions on permit trading, however, will tend to increase the costs of abatement for a given level of emissions. Another issue is that setting the initial allocation of permits can be contentious. For example, the initial allocation of permits to polluters proved highly controversial in the RECLAIM program. Not surprisingly, polluters have every incentive to ensure baseline emissions are as high as possible, while environmental groups might wish the total cap on emissions to be as low as possible.

Part of the controversy over assigning baseline emissions is that they often represent a valuable property right. If baseline emissions are given *gratis* or "grandfathered" to polluters based on past emissions rather than auctioned, the initial allocation of emission permits represents an unearned or windfall capital gain. For example, the USEPA allocated CFCs and halon emission permits to only 8 producers and 20 importers based on their market shares in 1986, when it set up a program to ensure the phase-out of their production and import by 2000. The creation of a scarce property right created a windfall gain to the 28 holders of permits that was, in part, taxed back with special excise taxes. This windfall gain is a *scarcity rent* (see chapter 7) associated with emission permits and that arises when a factor of production is constrained in its supply.

Irrespective of any equity issues about who should keep scarcity rents of emission permits, it may be advantageous to combine a charge with the use of permits or simply auction the initial permits. Rent capture or approaches that appropriate the rent but without affecting the economic actions of market participants, reduce permit prices and lower the entry cost of new firms into an industry and thus may make markets more competitive. A lower emissions price may also stimulate trading, as it discourages polluters from holding on to permits for speculative purposes. Finally, some methods of rent capture favor polluters with lower emissions per unit of output, such as a charge based on the price of permits and the holdings of polluters. Thus charges and emission permits can be complementary and collectively provide even greater incentives for adopting "cleaner" technologies (Grafton and Devlin, 1996).

3.7   OTHER APPROACHES

Liability rules

Various legal rules can be used to reduce emissions although they will not, in general, result in a cost-effective method of pollution control. Common law rights (see chapter 2) involve parties affected by pollution suing polluters to prevent further harm. Such approaches can be effective at reducing point sources of pollution, provided that the emissions can be traced to their source, the damage imposed is quantifiable, and those affected by emissions have recognizable property rights (usually defined over water or land). The option also exists for the plaintiff and defender in such cases to arrive at a mutually beneficial outcome or agreement prior to settlement by the court.

The other principal way to control pollution through liability is to create a standard and promote desired behavior via statutes enforced through the courts. In general, enforcement in the courts is initiated by the regulating agency but in some jurisdictions, such as the US, individuals or groups can take violators to court to enforce statutes if they have an interest that is materially affected by the emissions. Citizen suits in the US, however, have been discouraged by strategic lawsuits against public participation (SLAPP), undertaken by polluters who have claimed in court that citizens undertaking actions against them have infringed upon their rights.

The two principal types of liability are *strict liability* and *negligence-based liability*. Strict liability is the most stringent way to encourage polluters to comply with statutes. Under this approach, polluters are liable for all damages their emissions may cause and the costs associated with clean-up and remediation, irrespective of whether or not they were negligent, or in violation of the existing standards and practices. By contrast, liability based on *negligence rules* requires that it be proved the polluter was negligent in its actions in terms of the release of its emissions. Alberini and Austin (2001) have compared the effects of different liability rules using US state data. They find that for uncontrolled releases of pollutants, unintended releases tended to be lower, all else equal, in states with strict liability rules. However, they also find that strict liability reduces the incentives for larger firms to be involved in actions that might result in releases, thereby increasing the specialization in riskier activities by smaller firms. To the extent that smaller firms, in general, have smaller financial resources this reduces the potential payouts in any court settlements for spillages. A shift in economic activity from large to small firms may also be undesirable if the risk of a spill is higher with smaller firms.

Liability rules (especially strict liability) provide incentives for polluters to take into account the potential cost to others of their emissions. To the extent that this promotes a better standard of care and control, especially for pollutants that generate high external costs, liability rules can provide beneficial incentives from a societal perspective. However, such incentives will not, in general, lead to either an efficient or cost-effective method of pollution control. Moreover, the institution costs in the form of legal and administrative costs associated with liability rules can be very large, as has occurred with the clean-up of hazardous waste sites in the US (see box 3.3).

Environmental bonds

Liability rules may be supported on the basis of equity in the sense that polluters who cause harm are obliged to pay for their actions. However, polluters can use a variety of means to avoid their liabilities, such as transferring riskier activities to other and often smaller companies or businesses that have fewer assets. Further, the

BOX 3.3   LIABILITY AND CLEAN-UP UNDER THE US SUPERFUND

The US Comprehensive Environmental Response, Compensation and Liability Act (CERCLA), commonly known as the Superfund Act, was passed in 1980 following widespread concern over the disposal and clean-up of hazardous wastes. The act focuses on identifiable hazardous waste sites and has two important aspects – a superfund to implement clean-up, and a strict and joint liability for any potentially responsible party (PRP) that contributed to the wastes on identified sites.

The superfund was originally financed by taxes on corporate income and oil and chemicals and through government expenditures. The fund is also supplemented by costs recovered by the USEPA from liable parties. By September 1996 the USEPA had collected $1.4 billion in costs from PRPs, while PRPs themselves had spent almost $12 billion in clean-up costs in various agreements with the USEPA. Evidence suggests that clean-up costs are more effectively controlled when PRPs undertake remediation than when it is done directly by the USEPA.

Institution costs associated with cost recoveries have been significant, and have included the legal and associated costs with suits undertaken by the USEPA against PRPs, and also suits by PRPs among themselves to determine the share of the total costs. These institutions' costs have been estimated to be as much as 31 percent of the total expenditures (including clean-up costs) of PRPs.

A key aspect of CERCLA is that liability is retroactive, such that parties can be held responsible for actions that occurred before 1980. This has been highly contentious, especially as some PRPs have argued that their actions at the time of disposal were in compliance with all regulations. The joint and several liability has also cast a "large net" as *any* liable party may be obliged to pay the full costs to clean up a site regardless of its relative responsibility in generating the site.

CERCLA has led to the clean-up of many hazardous waste sites and has been strongly supported by persons living close to such sites. However, by the end of 1996 only about 10 percent of identified sites had actually been cleaned up. Some have also argued that the remediation at sites may have been too effective in the sense that some of the funds allocated to clean-up may have generated higher benefits (in terms of reduced health risks) if they had been spent elsewhere and on other activities.

Sources: Hamilton and Viscusi (1999); Sigman (2001); USEPA (2001)

harm resulting from emissions (especially for stock pollutants) may take years before it can be identified, by which time the polluter may no longer be in business. A way to address this problem is to force firms involved in potentially hazardous activities to post an *environmental bond* that they will forfeit should a pollution event occur. Unfortunately, in the case of hazardous wastes, the costs of a spillage may be many times greater than the profits of a firm engaged in such an activity, so that the bond may only be a small fraction of the potential external costs. To overcome this difficulty, it may be possible to insist that all firms wishing to engage in a hazardous activity tender a bid in the form of a non-refundable bond. The successful firm in the bidding process undertakes the activity and receives the bonds from all bidding firms if no spillage occurs, but in case of a spillage all bonds revert to the regulator and are used to fund those harmed and to pay for remediation (Lewis and Sappington, 2001). In this way, the firm involved in the hazardous activity has a very large incentive to undertake the greatest possible care to avoid a spillage – a highly desirable outcome if the spillage generates very high external costs. Further, the approach is likely to provide much larger funds for remediation and compensation in the case of a spill than an environmental bond that is only provided by the firm that undertakes the activity.

Insurance

An alternative way of controlling environmental risks is to offer insurance to parties who, under certain circumstances, may cause an undesirable environmental outcome such as a spillage of hazardous chemical or agent. The act of offering insurance requires diligence by the insurer to ensure given standards (scientific or regulatory) are maintained so that any pay outs are contingent on some well-specified event. Similarly, the person or firm buying the insurance is contracted to meet appropriate standards or operating procedures or risks not being compensated should the environmental risk occur. Two examples in the United States of such insurance schemes include insurance for firms undertaking asbestos abatement (the risk covered is the release of asbestos fibers above a given level) and for persons purchasing commercial real estate (the risk covered is liability for undetected contamination). For well-quantified risk, with well-defined standards, the approach offers the advantage of lower transactions costs relative to liability rules while still offering incentives for firms to reduce environmental risks (Freeman and Kunreuther, 1996).

Voluntary mechanisms

Voluntary approaches to pollution control can include any unilateral undertaking by a polluter, agreement between pollution sources, or agreement between pollution sources and a regulatory authority, to voluntarily reduce emissions. Given that pollution abatement is costly, the question is why polluters would wish to "voluntarily" abate their emissions? First, the assumption of profit maximization may not be correct and owners, or those in control of pollution sources, may maximize utility. Thus, the "warm glow" from reducing emissions for the decision-maker may more than offset the increased costs associated with abatement. This is likely to be the most important factor for individuals or households who engage in recycling and reuse activities that reduce the amount of solid waste. Second, even if firms maximize profits, polluters may publicize their pollution abatement so as to create a "green" image with their customers and employees. The expected value of such publicity may more than offset the costs of abatement. Similarly, firms may undertake abatement to avoid adverse publicity that might reduce its profits. Third, firms may use pollution abatement to develop technological innovations that they may be able to use to their financial advantage. Fourth, polluters may voluntarily abate their emissions to discourage a regulator from imposing standards or other non-voluntary and more stringent methods of pollution control. Fifth, "voluntary" approaches may involve a *quid pro quo* between polluters and regulators, with incentives for participation such as technical advice about abatement.

Voluntary approaches face a couple of important deficiencies. Given that the external costs of pollution are often borne by a different set of individuals to those who pay the costs of abatement, there is no reason to expect voluntary mechanisms to be either efficient or cost-effective. The greater are the marginal costs of abatement, all else equal, the less we would expect voluntary approaches to be a useful method of pollution control. It is for this reason that voluntary approaches to reduce GHG emissions have been met with considerable skepticism.

Voluntary mechanisms also have some advantages. For instance, a command-and-control approach to pollution control may lead to greater compliance, but if imposed via a technology standard it might be a costly form of pollution control. By contrast, a voluntary approach that involves the provision of information to pollution sources may encourage some polluters to reduce emissions in ways that may be much cheaper. Moreover, because the approach is voluntary, the associated institution costs should be very low as it requires no monitoring or enforcement. Further, in countries with very few financial resources or effective institutions, voluntary approaches may represent the *only* method of pollution control available to regulators.

Even in jurisdictions with well-developed institutions and ample financial resources, voluntary programs offer an alternative approach to address non-point sources of pollution that are not amenable to the use of price and quantity instruments. For example, if fertilizer run-off is a major cause of pollution in a water body, information sessions and extension advice to farmers on the environmental costs of the run-off and ways to reduce fertilizer applications without affecting yields might be quite effective at improving water quality at a low cost (Bosch et al., 1995). In this case, knowledge diffusion and the ability to "shame" individual farmers may provide a way to reduce non-point sources of pollution.

A voluntary program that has been evaluated in detail is the US 33/50 program that was in place from 1991 to 1995 and was designed to reduce manufacturers' emissions of 17 toxic chemicals by 33 percent by 1992 and by 50 percent by 1995, relative to a 1988 baseline for each source. On average, the program is estimated to have reduced emissions per participant by about 20 percent (USGAO, 1997). Aurora and Cason (1995) found that the principal reason why firms participated in the 33/50, and other voluntary programs, was to attract favorable publicity.

Deposit-refund approaches

A commonly used method of pollution control for consumer products is a deposit payable at the time of purchase, combined with a refund upon its return to a suitable disposal or recycling facility. Several countries have introduced such schemes for car batteries and car tires, and in many countries glass bottles attract a refund when returned for recycling.

Deposit-refunds are particularly useful where the product (such as car batteries) is especially hazardous and clean-up costs are expensive, or where the effects are ubiquitous and observation of illegal disposal is difficult (such as broken glass). Such approaches, however, are of limited value for many types of pollutants where the effects arise from the production or consumption process rather than disposal of the depreciated or used product. Further, as with any method of pollution control, the approach is not costless and in some programs the institution costs can be significant (Ackerman et al., 1995).

Labeling and disclosure mechanisms

Labeling and disclosure mechanisms are two approaches that provide signals to investors, consumers, and regulators about the relative and absolute levels of emissions of polluters. The most widely used signaling devices are those that indicate an appliance or a product has achieved some minimum acceptable level of environmental quality. For example, this might be an energy efficiency rating for a major appliance, such as a refrigerator. In some cases, firms and industries have found it worthwhile to develop their own quality standards, so as to command a price premium or to distinguish their products from competitors. In addition to product labeling, some regulators have established environmental awards for exemplary performance over a range of criteria including waste and emissions reduction and promoting environmental awareness. To the extent that such awards provide valuable and positive publicity, they may provide an additional incentive to polluters to further reduce their pollution and may provide a "demonstration effect" for less environmentally friendly polluters.

While labels and awards convey a signal of how environmentally friendly is a product or polluter, disclosure rules normally provide information on how poorly a source or firm is performing. Several countries have initiated public reporting mechanisms on polluters' emissions. In the US, an annual Toxics Release Inventory (TRI) is made publicly available. The TRI names pollution sources that released listed chemicals beyond a certain amount in the previous calendar year. Polluters with an especially poor TRI rating are penalized by investors. For instance, Hamilton (1995) found using 1989 TRI data that polluters that had reported emissions lost on average $4.1 million in the value of the traded stock the day the news was released. Some evidence suggests that polluters have responded to negative signals and total releases have declined by almost half over the period 1988 to 1998, although at least part of this fall may be due to firms substituting to chemicals not listed on the TRI.

Similar approaches have been applied in other jurisdictions, such as Indonesia, where sources are given one of five color-coded ratings that range from black (no attempt at pollution control) to gold (cleanest plant of its type in the world) and the rating is publicly disclosed (Tietenberg and Wheeler, 1998). From June 1995 to September 1996 the number of polluters designated as black fell from six to just one, and the number of polluters in the red category (some pollution control, but not in compliance with regulatory standards) fell from 115 to 87, indicating the program may have given incentives for the worst sources to improve their performance.

The particular advantage of disclosure mechanisms is their relatively low institution costs. Thus they are particularly well suited where few resources are available for monitoring and enforcement. Disclosure also promotes flexible responses because pollution sources that choose to improve their public image are able to reduce their emissions in the cheapest way available to them.

3.8   PUTTING IT ALL TOGETHER

Our review of the various methods of pollution control makes it clear that no one approach is preferred in every situation. A method of pollution control in one jurisdiction may not be appropriate in another, even if the pollutant is the same and external effects are similar. Where minimizing the costs of abatement is an important criterion, approaches that equalize the "price" of pollution across sources (emission charges and marketable emission permits) will be favored, provided there exists adequate monitoring and enforcement. If equity is the over-riding concern, such that those responsible for pollution end up paying to abate it or pay for remediation, then approaches that require polluters to pay (liability rules and emissions charges) may be the instruments of choice of regulators. In a second-best world with inter-temporal and economy-wide effects, however, the choice of the appropriate method(s) of pollution control and the desired level of pollution reduction is a very difficult problem to resolve.

In situations where the level of emissions must not be exceeded due to threshold effects, quantity instruments (permits and standards) may be favored. In jurisdictions where financial resources are very limited and institutions do not exist to monitor and enforce, less direct methods (voluntary approaches and information disclosure) may be the best approach. Different methods of pollution control may also be preferred depending on the type of pollutant. Voluntary approaches, and even standards, can be effective approaches for types of non-point pollution, while deposit-refund systems are suitable for waste that can be recycled or that requires special disposal. In sum, a mixed approach that selects the appropriate instrument for the circumstances while considering the goals of emissions control, and uses mixed instruments where possible to complement the strengths of the different methods (charges and standards, charges and emission permits), is probably the best way to regulate pollution.

FURTHER READING

A huge literature exists on the economics of pollution and the methods of pollution control. A classic reference is Baumol and Oates (1988) while an excellent presentation on static and dynamic pollution models, with and without uncertainty, is given by Førsund and Strøm (1988).

The classic reference on marketable emission permits is Montgomery (1972). A well-written description and overview of different methods of pollution control worldwide is given by Stavins (2001a). The World Bank (1999) provides a useful review of successful methods of pollution control in newly industrializing countries. The US Environmental Protection Agency (2001) report on the US experience is highly recommended, as is Stavins (2001b) and Callan and Thomas (2000). Segerson and Li (1999) give a useful review of the literature on voluntary approaches, while Shortle and Abler (1998) provide a nice overview of the economics of non-point pollution. Goulder (1997) gives an insightful description of the tax interaction effects and the double dividend.

As a balance to the focus on efficiency in the economics of pollution control, Bromley (1990) provides a thought-provoking piece on the application of efficiency to policy analysis. A compendium of some of the most influential articles on the economics of the environment and pollution control is Dorfman and Dorfman (1993).

REFERENCES

Ackerman, F., Cavander, D., Stutz, J., and Zukerman, B. (1995). *Preliminary Analysis: The Cost and Benefits of Bottle Bills*, Tellus Institute: Boston.

Alberini, A. and Austin, D. (2001). Liability Policy and Toxic Pollution Releases, in A. Heyes, ed., *The Law and Economics*, Edward Elgar: Cheltenham.

Aurora, S. and Cason, T. N. (1995). Why Do Firms Overcomply with Environmental Regulations? Understanding Participation in EPA's 33/50 Program. Discussion Paper No. 95-38, Resources for the Future: Washington DC.

Baumol, W. J. and Oates, W. E. (1971). The Use of Standards and Prices for Protection of the Environment, *Swedish Journal of Economics*, 73: 42–54.

Baumol, W. J. and Oates, W. E. (1988). *The Theory of Environmental Policy*, Cambridge University Press: New York.

Bosch, D. J., Cook, Z. L., and Fuglie, K. O. (1995). Voluntary versus Mandatory Agricultural Policies to Protect Water Quality: Adoption of Nitrogen Testing in Nebraska, *Review of Agricultural Economics*, 17 (1): 13–24.

Bromley, D. W. (1990). The Ideology of Efficiency: Searching for a Theory of Policy Analysis, *Journal of Environmental Economics and Management*, 19: 86–107.

Buchanan, J. M. (1975). *The Limits of Liberty: Between Anarchy and Leviathan*, University of Chicago Press: Chicago.

Callan, S. J. and Thomas, J. M. (2000). *Environmental Economics and Management: Theory, Policy, and Applications*, second edition, Dryden Press: Orlando, FL.

Carlson, C., Burtraw, D. Cropper, M., and Palmer, K. L. (2000). Sulfur Dioxide Control by Electric Utilities: What Are the Gains from Trade? *Journal of Political Economy*, 108 (6): 1292–326.

Crandall, R. W., Keeler, T. E., and Lave, L. B. (1982). The Cost of Automobile Safety and Emissions Regulation to the Consumers: Some Preliminary Results, *American Economic Review*, 72 (2): 324–7.

Dales, J. H. (1968). *Pollution, Property and Prices: An Essay in Policy-making and Economics*, University of Toronto Press: Toronto.

Devlin, R. A. and Grafton, R. Q. (1999). *Economic Rights and Environmental Wrongs: Property Rights for the Common Good*, Edward Elgar: Cheltenham.

Devlin, R. A. and Grafton, R. Q. (1994). Tradeable Permits, Missing Markets, and Technology, *Environmental and Resource Economics*, 4: 171–86.

Dorfman, R. and Dorfman, N. S. (1993). *Economics of the Environment: Selected Readings*, W. W. Norton and Company: New York.

Førsund, F. R. and Strøm, S. (1988). *Environmental Economics and Management: Pollution and Natural Resources*, Croom Helm: London.

Freeman, P. K. and Kunreuther, H. (1996). The Roles of Insurance and Well-specified Standards in Dealing with Environmental Risks, *Managerial and Decision Economics*, 17 (5): 517–30.

Goulder, L. H. (1997). Environmental Taxation in a Second-best World, in H. Folmer and T. Tietenberg, eds, *The International Yearbook of Environmental and Resource Economics 1997/1998*, Edward Elgar: Cheltenham.

Grafton, R. Q. and Devlin, R. A. (1996). Paying for Pollution: Permits and Charges, *Scandinavian Journal of Economics*, 98 (2): 275–88.

Hahn, R. W. (1984). Market Power and Transferable Property Rights, *Quarterly Journal of Economics*, 99: 753–65.

Hamilton, J. T. (1995). Pollution as News: Media and Stock Market Reactions to the Toxics Release Inventory Data, *Journal of Environmental Economics and Management*, 28 (1): 98–113.

Hamilton, J. T. and Viscusi, W. K. (1999). How Costly Is "Clean"? An Analysis of the Benefits and Costs of Superfund Site Remediations, *Journal of Policy Analysis and Management*, 18: 2–27.

Jaeger, W. K. (2001). Double Dividend Reconsidered. *AERE Newsletter*, 21 (2): 11–20.

Joskow, P. L., Schmalensee, R., and Bailey, E. M. (1998). The Market for Sulfur Dioxide Emissions, *American Economic Review*, 88 (4): 669–85.

Lewis, T. R. and Sappington, D. E. M. (2001). Horizontal Vicarious Liability, in A. Heyes, ed., *The Law and Economics*, Edward Elgar: Cheltenham.

Montgomery, W. D. (1972). Markets in Licences and Efficient Pollution Control Programs, *Journal of Economic Theory*, 5 (3): 395–418.

Morgenstern, R. (1985). Environmental Taxes: Dead or Alive? Resources for the Future. Discussion Paper 96-03, Resources for the Future: Washington, DC,//www.rff.org./disc_papers/PDF_files/9603.pdf

Mumy, G. E. (1980). Long-run Efficiency and Property Rights Sharing for Pollution Control, *Public Choice*, 35: 59–74.

Perl, L. J. and Dunbar, F. C. (1982). Cost-effectiveness and Cost–Benefit Analysis of Air Quality Regulations, *American Economic Review*, 72 (2): 208–13.

Pezzey, J. (1988). Market Mechanisms of Pollution Control: "Polluter Pays," Economic and Practical Aspects, in R. K. Turner, ed., *Sustainable Environmental Management: Principles and Practice*, Belhaven Press: London.

Pezzey, J. (1992). The Symmetry between Controlling Pollution by Price and Controlling it by Quantity, *Canadian Journal of Economics*, 25 (4): 983–91.

Pigou, A. C. (1952) [1920]. *The Economics of Welfare*, Macmillan and Co. Ltd: London.

Porter, M. E. and van der Linde, C. (1995). Toward a New Conception of the Environment–Competitiveness Relationship, *Journal of Economic Perspectives*, 9: 97–118.

Roberts, M. J. and Spence, M. (1976). Effluent Charges and Licences under Uncertainty, *Journal of Public Economics*, 5: 193–208.

Roberts, M. J. and Weitzman, M. L. (1993). Regulatory Strategies for Pollution Control, in R. Dorfman and N. S. Dorfman, eds, *Economics of the Environment: Selected Readings*, third edition, W. W. Norton and Company: New York.

Sandal, L. K., Steinshamn, S. I., and Grafton, R. Q. (2003). "More is Less": The Tax Effects of Ignoring Flow Externalities, *Resource and Energy Economics*, 25: 239–54.

Segerson, K. and Li, N. (1999). Voluntary Approaches to Environmental Regulation, in H. Folmer and T. Tietenberg, eds, *The International Yearbook of Environmental and Resource Economics 1999/2000*, Edward Elgar: Cheltenham.

Shortle, J. S. and Abler, D. G. (1998). Nonpoint Pollution, in H. Folmer and T. Tietenberg, eds, *The International Yearbook of Environmental and Resource Economics 1997/1998*, Edward Elgar: Cheltenham.

Sigman, H. (2001). Environmental Liability in Practice: Liability for Clean-up of Contaminated Sites under Superfund, in A. Heyes, ed., *The Law and Economics*, Edward Elgar: Cheltenham.

Stavins, R. N. (1996). Correlated Uncertainty and Policy Instrument Choice, *Journal of Environmental Economics and Management*, 29 (2): 218–32.

Stavins, R. N. (2001a). Experience with Market-based Environmental Policy Instruments. Discussion paper 01-58, Resources for the Future.

Stavins, R. N. (2001b). Lessons from the American Experiment with Market-Based Environmental Policies, John F. Kennedy School of Government Faculty Research Working Paper Series 01-032, Harvard University.

Stegman, H. (2001). Environmental Liability in Practice: Liability for Clean-up of Contaminated Sites under Superfund, in A. Heyes, ed., *The Law and Economics*, Edward Elgar: Cheltenham.

Tietenberg, T. (1996). *Environmental and Natural Resource Economics*, HarperCollins: New York.

Tietenberg, T. and Wheeler, D. (1998). Empowering the Community: Information Strategies for Pollution Control, http://www.colby.edu/personal/t/thtieten/

United States Environmental Protection Agency (EPA) (2001). *The United States Experience with Economic Incentives for Protecting the Environment*, Washington DC: EPA.

United States General Accounting Office (GAO) (1997). *Environmental Protection: Challenges facing EPA's Efforts to Reinvent Environmental Regulation*, Washington DC.

Weitzman, M. L. (1974). Prices vs. Quantities, *Review of Economic Studies*, 41 (1): 477–91.

World Bank (1999). *Greening Industry: New Roles for Communities, Markets, and Governments*, Oxford University Press: New York.

PART TWO

RESOURCE ECONOMICS

CHAPTER FOUR

BIOECONOMICS OF FISHERIES

The basic economic choice to be made with respect to living resources such as fish stocks is how intensively they should be exploited. Fishing requires the application of manpower, fuel and various implements, all of which could be used for some other purpose. The question we must consider is whether we are getting as much value in return for our efforts when fishing as we would be getting otherwise. (Rögnvaldur Hannesson, *Bioeconomic Analysis of Fisheries*, p. 1).

4.1 INTRODUCTION

Catching fish from the sea is a tradition that goes back tens of thousands of years when people hunted animals and gathered plants for their survival. Over the millennia we have transformed our "hunting" culture to one of cultivation of plants and domestication of animals. The great exception is *capture fisheries*, which are the focus of this chapter. Despite large increases in aquaculture production in the recent past, most of the world's fish protein is still harvested by ships at sea. Although the technology for catching fish has changed immensely over time, the fundamental process remains the same as it did 100,000 years ago – first find, then catch, and then enjoy the "fruits" of the hunt.

The reason why most of the fish in the sea are not farmed is that, unlike land resources, most fish are highly mobile, cannot be domesticated in a terrestrial sense and inhabit a world where boundaries are difficult and expensive to enforce. The difficulty in creating property rights (see chapter 2) over a resource that inhabits an alien world has prevented its "cultivation" in a way that has occurred for all major food sources on land. As a result, many fisheries are over-exploited from both a biological and economic perspective.

The consequences of overexploitation have a profound impact on millions of people. Often the poorest of the poor are artisanal fishers in developing countries who have no surpluses, or other resources, to draw upon should fish stocks decline (Squires et al., 2003). For an even greater number, especially in Asia, fish represents the major source of animal protein. Even in rich countries where commercial fishing is a relatively small economic activity, it sustains many coastal communities and is an important recreational activity.

In this chapter we review the evidence of overfishing, describe the essential characteristics of population dynamics, analyze economic models that explain and predict the stylized facts about capture fisheries and present approaches that have been used to help overcome the "tragedy of the commons" (see chapter 2).

4.2   WHEN THE BOAT COMES IN

Many examples exist of how overfishing has brought about the collapse of fisheries such as Canada's northern cod fishery, innumerable salmon fisheries, many shell-fish fisheries, and important sardine and herring fisheries. Where fish stocks have not declined precipitously, fishing has reduced the resource stock or biomass (measured as the total weight of all fish species in the sea) of some fisheries to such a level that they are vulnerable to environmental shocks. Degradation of habitats, especially important spawning grounds, by fishing and other activities has also had negative impacts on several important stocks, especially salmon fisheries.

According to one estimate, a substantial part of the world's fisheries are biolog-ically overexploited in the sense that if stocks were allowed to recover they would generate a higher yield or catch (Hilborn and Walters, 1992). Despite this obser-vation, the world's catch has continued to increase. As shown in figure 4.1, the world harvest (capture fisheries and aquaculture) continues to rise, as does the world catch (capture fisheries) because existing and previously underex-ploited stocks are coming under increased fishing pressure.

Increased fishing pressure in capture fisheries can also be measured in terms of fishing inputs. These include the vessels and engines, the gear used to find and harvest fish, the labor, fuel, and bait used up when catching fish and the process-ing facilities to render the fish into a consumable product. Combined, these inputs represent total *fishing effort*.

A frequently used single measure of fishing effort is the gross registered tonnage (GRT) of fishing vessels that indicates both a boat's size and its ability to catch fish. Often larger vessels can stay longer at sea, fish in more difficult weather conditions, have more sophisticated search gear for finding fish, and more effec-tive fishing gear. A worrying trend over the past twenty years or so, given the assessment of biological overexploitation for many fisheries, is that the GRT of all fishing vessels has increased in every region except Europe, as shown in figure 4.2. Regional growth in GRT has ranged from 94 percent for the former Soviet Union (FSU) to 230 percent for Oceania over the period 1970–92. By contrast, over the same period, the world fish catch has increased by a little over 50 percent while the world's GRT has almost doubled. This is an indication that, as of ten years ago, capture fisheries were somewhere between points A and B (and certainly closer to

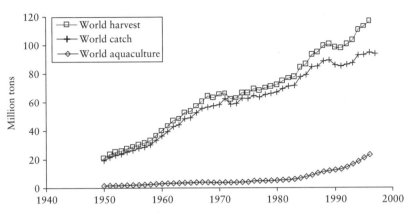

Figure 4.1   World fisheries catch and aquaculture production

Source: Worldwatch Institute Database Disk (2000)

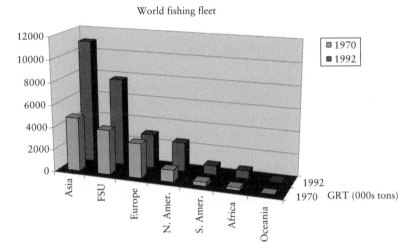

Figure 4.2   Gross vessel tonnage of the world's fishing fleet, by region

Source: Worldwatch Institute Datadisk (2000)

B than A) of a hypothetical curve that plots the relationship between catch and aggregate fishing effort, as shown in figure 4.3. In other words, as of 1992, world fishing was at the point of diminishing returns where one percent increase in fishing effort resulted in a smaller than one percent increase in catch. Further increases in fishing effort may even result in a decline in the world catch of fish.

Increasing fishing effort and declines in the catch and stocks of some important fisheries can be analyzed using both biological and economic models. We introduce the important characteristics of fish species, describe the models used to describe

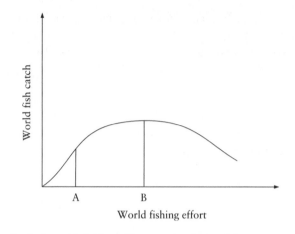

Figure 4.3   Hypothetical world fishing effort–catch relationship

fish populations and understand the economic behavior of fishers, and evaluate the implications of these models for fisheries management.

4.3   BIOLOGY AND DYNAMICS OF FISHERIES

Despite a huge variation in the habitats, size, and shape of fish, most species share a number of similarities. Many fish ensure their survival by producing enormous quantities of eggs (for some species a single female may produce hundreds of millions of eggs), but only a tiny proportion mature to larval fish, to juvenile fish, and eventually adults of spawning age. To help reduce predation, some species will spawn in shallower water or relatively protected areas (such as mangroves or reefs) where the likelihood of being eaten by larger fish is reduced.

In the early part of a fish's life, eggs and larval fish often drift with ocean currents and, because of their small size, are prey to a large number of fish, including adults of their own species. Thus the spawning grounds, the nursery grounds, and feeding grounds of a species may differ and can be separated by large distances. At some point in their lifecycle, which may be as short as a few months or as long as several years, the fish reach a sufficient size that they are "recruited" into the fishery in the sense that they become vulnerable to being caught by fishing gear. From this point on fish numbers decline due to both natural and environmental factors and fishing mortality.

Fish species and fishing methods

Depending on where fish are located in the water column, their feeding and migration habits and how they are caught, fish have been classified into three broad categories. *Pelagic* species that include tuna, sardines, herring, and anchoveta can travel large distances as adults and are commonly caught near the surface in schools. A favored method of fishing for larger pelagics is with baited hooks and lines or *longlines* and with *purse seines* that are employed for both small and large fish that enclose schools of fish with a net which is then drawn together from underneath to capture the fish.

Anadromous species, such as salmon, are often classified as pelagics, but have a very special lifecycle that involves spawning in streams and rivers and subsequent migration by the juveniles to the sea. Salmonids are caught by purse seines and traps and gillnets that entangle the fish, but also with *troll* gear where lines and hooks with lures and bait are set to lines and rods attached to fishing boats.

Demersal species such as cod, plaice, pollock, snapper, haddock, whiting are often caught in mid-water or at or towards the sea bottom. *Bottom trawls* (that are dragged along or near the bottom) and *mid-water trawls* (dragged in mid-water between the surface and the sea bottom) are favored methods for catching demersal species. Bottom trawls are only suitable where the sea bottom is relatively free of reefs and corals that would otherwise damage the nets. Whether a bottom or mid-water trawl is used, the method of fishing involves the towing of a cone shaped net through the water column where the catch depends, in part, on the "swept area," or the area of sea that has come in contact with the trawl opening in a given period of time. In addition to trawl gear, both demersal and pelagic species may also be caught closer to inshore with traps, and also *gillnets* that entangle the fish.

Shellfish species include molluscs (mussels, clams, scallops, oysters, abalone) and crustaceans (lobsters, crabs, and shrimp) and are often much more sedentary at maturity than either pelagic or demersal species, and are often caught close to shore. An exception includes some shrimp that can be caught using trawl gear a considerable distance offshore. Crustaceans are often caught with pots or traps (especially lobsters and crabs) where bait is used to lure the animals into a pot from which they cannot escape. *Dredging*, which involves running a heavy steel frame across the sea floor is commonly used for harvesting non-cultivated clams, scallops and oysters. Finally, for some highly valued species such as abalone, geoduck, sea urchins and sea cucumbers, *sea diving* is the principal form of harvesting.

Biological models of fish populations

To better understand the dynamics of fish populations we review three broad classes of models: stock–recruitment models, dynamic pool models and surplus production models. Such models are used to both estimate the current and desired levels of fish stocks and to determine the preferred harvest levels. After describing these biological models and the economics of fishing, we shall use the insights of these two approaches to develop a better understanding of fisheries management.

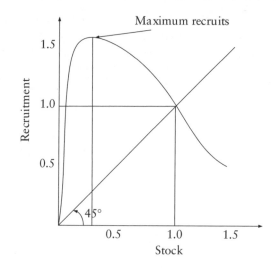

Figure 4.4   Hypothetical stock–recruitment relationships in fisheries

Stock–recruitment models

One of the most important relationships in fisheries is that which relates the future recruitment into a fishery to the current stock of fish. One of the earliest estimated stock–recruitment relationships was developed for Pacific salmon and is given in a modified form as,

$$R = \alpha S_t\, e^{-\beta\, S_t} \tag{1}$$

where R is the number of recruits into the fishery, α and β are parameters and S_t is the size of the adult fish stock which determines the number of eggs produced.

A typical stock–recruitment relationship is given in figure 4.4 and is sometimes called the Ricker curve after the originator of equation (1). The point where the curve intersects the 45° line is an "equilibrium" stock level that ensures recruitment exactly equals the current stock level. A higher value of β implies a lower "peak" in terms of the stock–recruitment relationship.

Figure 4.4 implies there is a density-dependent relationship between the number of recruits and the current stock. In other words, higher levels of stock do *not* necessarily imply higher levels of recruitment. This arises from density-dependent mortality where, for example, higher levels of the stock increase the predation on larval and juvenile fish due to cannibalism. Figure 4.4 also indicates that just to the left of the stock that maximizes recruitment, recruitment declines rapidly. This part of the curve where R/S_t is *increasing* in the stock is called *depensation*. Depensation can potentially pose major problems for fishery managers because small changes in the stock can lead to large changes in recruitment. For example, in figure 4.4 if the stock is mistakenly set at a level slightly below that which maximizes recruitment the effect on the level of recruits would be substantial. In the case of *critical depensation*, the stock recruitment curve may even cross the horizontal or stock axis at a point greater than zero, implying that below a minimum or threshold stock there will be no more recruitment.

Dynamic pool models

An important set of biological models, sometimes called Beverton–Holt or age-class models, can be used to separate and analyze a fishery into distinct age or size classes of cohorts. This allows for greater understanding of the fishery as often harvesting takes place on a small number of cohorts, and sizeable differences in the relative strengths of cohorts are important determinants that affect the total catch. Such models were originally developed for temperate marine waters where fish can be accurately aged and there exists considerable variation in the number and weight of fish per cohort.

Dynamic pool models are used to develop estimates of yield or harvest-per-recruit relationships that will depend on, among other things, fishing mortality, natural mortality and the age or size at which fish from a given cohort or age class become vulnerable to fishing. A key component in determining the yield or harvest per age class or cohort is the relationship between weight and age of fish. A commonly used growth function is the von Bertalanffy growth equation that can be expressed in terms of either the length or the weight of the fish, and that gives a good fit for most marine species. A von Bertalanffy growth equation in terms of weight is given by (2),

$$W_t = W_\infty \left(1 - e^{-K(t-t_0)}\right)^3 \tag{2}$$

where W_t is the weight of a fish at time t, W_∞ is the asymptotic weight of the fish that it approaches given sufficient time, K is the Brody growth coefficient and determines the rate at which fish gains weight and t_0 is the hypothetical age at which the fish has zero weight. A typical weight-at-age relationship is sigmoidal shaped (see chapter 1), as illustrated in figure 4.5. From the figure it can be seen that that weight gain is positive throughout the life of the fish, but the greatest weight gain per time period is greatest at an intermediate age. At near the end of the animal's lifecycle it is almost at its maximum weight or very close to the asymptote.

The other important aspect to determining yield-per-recruit is mortality: fishing mortality (F) from harvesting fish and natural mortality (M) that occurs from causes other than fishing. Thus at any point in time the instantaneous change in the number of fish is defined by (3),

$$dN/dt = -[F + M]N_t \tag{3}$$

where N_t is the number of fish at time t and F and M are coefficients of fishing and natural mortality. Equation (3) is a linear first-order differential equation

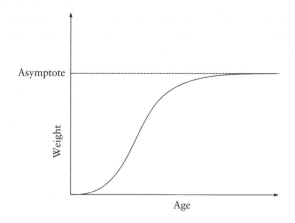

Figure 4.5   Typical weight-at-age relationship

(see chapter 1) that can be solved to obtain a definite solution provided we know the number of fish at $t = 0$, N_0, i.e.,

$$N_t = (N_0)e^{-[F + M]t} \tag{4}$$

Equation (4) can also be used to derive a survival rate between any two periods defined as (4'), i.e.,

$$N_{t+1}/N_t = e^{-[F + M]} \quad \text{or} \quad N_{t+1} = N_t e^{-[F + M]} \tag{4'}$$

A quick calculation using (4') indicates that an instantaneous total mortality rate equal to 1.0 does *not* imply that all fish die in a single time period. For example, if $F + M = 1.0$ then the survival rate after one period of time (0 to 1) is about 37 percent which implies that about 63 percent of the fish die either by natural causes or are harvested.

   If we assume that instantaneous natural mortality is constant and independent of fishing mortality, we can calculate the total harvest of fish over one time period as the total number of fish that were present at the start of the period, but not at the end, multiplied by the *exploitation ratio* or proportion of this total that were taken because of fishing, i.e.,

$$\text{Total number of fish harvested} = (N_t - N_{t+1}) (F/ [F + M]) \tag{5}$$

where $N_t - N_{t+1}$ equals the total number of fish that died over the period t to t + 1 and $F/ [F + M]$ is the exploitation ratio. Substituting (4') into (5) we obtain,

$$\text{Total number of fish harvested} = N_t (1 - e^{-[F + M]})(F/ [F + M]) \tag{5'}$$

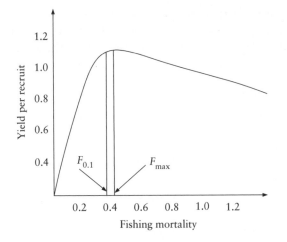

Figure 4.6 Hypothetical yield per recruit and fishing mortality

The total yield or catch over the time period can be determined by multiplying (5′) by the mean weight of fish for each cohort.

In general, the total yield or harvest from a particular cohort or recruit that "enters" or becomes vulnerable to fishing at time t_c and completely disappears by time t_{max} is

$$\text{Total yield or catch (weight)} = \int_{t_c}^{t_{max}} FN_t W_t \, dt$$

where F is the constant fishing mortality, N_t is the number of fish at time t and W_t is the mean weight of the fish at time t and which can be substituted for by the growth equation given in (2). The yield per recruit is calculated as the total yield divided by the number of fish (recruits) that entered the fishery at time t_c.

A hypothetical yield-per-recruit relationship in figure 4.6 relates the yield (or catch) in tonnes of fish to the level of fishing mortality, for a constant t_c. Another common representation is to graph yield-per-recruit against the age of first capture keeping fishing mortality constant. To help understand the relationship between the age of first capture and fishing mortality, *isopleth* plots can also be calculated that join points of equal yield-per-recruit values as a function of both t_c and F.

The age at first capture can be affected by changes in fishing gear, such as mesh sizes, the start date of the fishing season, the location of fishing or other controls on fisher behavior. Regulations that affect the fishing gear and the size that fish become vulnerable to fishing determine *gear selectivity* or the ability to discriminate between different sized fish. Typically, in most fisheries fish do not suddenly become vulnerable to fishing as soon as they reach a certain size so-called *knife-edge selection* – but start to become vulnerable at a certain size or age, and become increasingly vulnerable to fishing mortality as they increase in age or size.

In figure 4.6, the older or larger is the recruit or cohort when it becomes vulnerable to fishing (higher t_c), the lower the natural mortality (M) and the higher the Brody coefficient (K), the higher will be the yield-per-recruit curve. Thus a desirable feature of a fishery, from the perspective of fishers, is to have as low a (M/K) ratio as possible so that as many fish and as large as possible are recruited, or become vulnerable to fishing, at t_c.

Figure 4.6 can also be used to illustrate the constant fishing mortality that max-imizes yield per recruit or F_{max}. An *ad hoc*, but a common target fishing mortality rate is $F_{0.1}$, which is the mortality where the slope of the yield-per-recruit curve is one tenth of its initial slope when fishing mortality is very close to zero. A $F_{0.1}$ is more conservative (has a lower harvest) than F_{max} and thus has been viewed (incorrectly!) by some fishery managers as an exploitation rate that will ensure the sustainability of a fishery.

It should be clear that using a dynamic pool model requires reliable estimates of both fishing and natural mortality. The best way to separate total mortality into its two categories is to tag fish and determine the proportion of tagged fish that are harvested. To be reliable, this requires that tagging does not change the fish-ing mortality of tagged fish and that all tagged fish that are harvested have their tags returned.

More commonly, fishing mortality is calculated by assuming a linear relationship between it and a measure of fishing effort, E, defined as vessel days at sea, fuel consumption, total area of the ocean swept by the fishing gear, or some other meas-ure, i.e., $F = qE$, where q is unknown and is called the *catchability coefficient*. Provided that total mortality (Z) and the fishing effort is known between the two time peri-ods of interest, such that at t_1 fishing effort is E_1 and at t_2 fishing effort is E_2, then

$$Z_1 = qE_1 + M \tag{6}$$
$$Z_2 = qE_2 + M \tag{7}$$

Equations (6) and (7) can easily be solved to find the unknowns q and M and thus fishing mortality F (Gulland, 1983, p. 108). Unfortunately, such an approach to estimating fishing mortality suffers from a number of problems. First, a single or even composite measure of fishing effort is unlikely to properly represent the fishing power exerted in a fishing season. Second, fishing mortality is unlikely to be related to fishing effort in a linear way. Third, an accurate measure of fishing mortality requires an accurate measure of total mortality that is obtained *independ-ently* from the measure of fishing effort, such as through regular surveys.

In many fisheries, surveys of stock abundance are not undertaken due to the costs involved and measures of abundance, from which total mortality rates are calculated, are obtained by the following relationship,

$$N_{mean} = (1/q)(Y/E) \tag{8}$$

where N_{mean} is mean number of fish over the defined period, Y is the total yield or catch and E is the level of fishing effort and (Y/E) is the catch per unit of effort (c.p.u.e). Equation (8) is often used by fishery managers to obtain an index of stock abundance. If the catchability coefficient is *constant*, the size of the resource stock is proportional to c.p.u.e such that a 10 percent decline in c.p.u.e results in a 10 percent decline in mean stock abundance. Unfortunately, in some fisheries and in particular pelagic species (such as tunas and sardines), the c.p.u.e may be invariant to or even inversely proportional to stock abundance. This is because school size often determines the ability of fishers to capture fish, but not necessarily overall abundance. Fishers may also exhibit a "learning curve" such that over time they become much better at catching fish per unit of fishing effort and that may more than compensate for declines in stock abundance.

Surplus yield models

An important class of biological models that are widely applied in fisheries, and elsewhere, are surplus yield or production models. Surplus production models ignore the issues of differences in cohorts and mortalities and simply analyze the interaction effects of the biomass and growth in the biomass on the fishery.

Surplus production models can take on a variety of functional forms, but all assume density-dependent growth. This assumption accords with observations of most fisheries that the biomass has a tendency (in the absence of fishing) to approach its maximum level or *carrying capacity*, but at a rate that depends on the size of the biomass. The fastest growth is when the biomass is at an intermediate level and its slowest growth is when the biomass is either close to zero or close to its carrying capacity. Growth in the biomass is zero when there are no fish, or when the biomass is at its carrying capacity.

A commonly estimated model that has these characteristics is a logistic growth equation (see chapter 1), commonly called the Schaefer model in fisheries, and is given below,

$$dx/dt = rx(1 - x/k) \qquad (9)$$

where x is the biomass, r is called the *intrinsic growth rate*, and k is the maximum carrying capacity for the fishery. A more general form of the Schaefer model, identical to (9) if $\alpha = 2$, is given by (10).

$$dx/dt = rx - rx^{\alpha}/k \qquad (10)$$

Figure 4.7 illustrates the relationship between growth in the biomass (dx/dt) and the biomass (x) where $\alpha = 2$. If α were less than two, the curve would be skewed to the left and if α were greater than two, the curve would be skewed to the right. For an $\alpha < 1$ then the fishery could exhibit critical depensation.

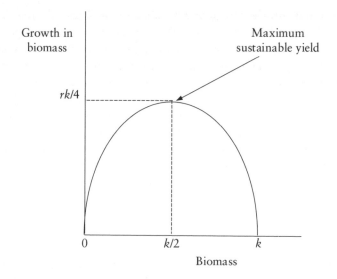

Figure 4.7   Schaefer model of a fishery

If we differentiate the growth in the biomass given by (9) by the biomass, and set the result equal to zero, we can determine the biomass level that maximizes its growth, i.e.,

$$(dx/dt) / dx = r - 2xr/k = 0 \quad \Rightarrow \quad x^* = k/2 \tag{11}$$

where x^* is commonly called the *maximum sustainable yield*. Thus $k/2$ is the biomass level that yields the highest yield or harvest of fish without reducing the biomass. By substituting (11) into (9), the yield at this level of the biomass can be shown to equal $rk/4$.

The biomass that coincides with the maximum sustainable yield (MSY) is commonly referred to as x_{MSY}. If fishers were only concerned about how much fish they caught, x_{MSY} would be the optimal level of the biomass as it corresponds to the greatest surplus yield or sustainable harvest from the fishery. This harvest level is called a *surplus yield* because it can be taken from the fishery without changing the level of the biomass. The harvest level at x_{MSY} is the counterpart of the F_{max} in the dynamic pool models, or the fishing mortality that maximizes yield per recruit, provided that recruitment into the fishery is unaffected by harvesting. In the absence of fishing, the biomass would converge to its carrying capacity at K which generates a zero surplus yield.

Many fishery managers have tried to regulate fisheries to be at x_{MSY} under the belief that the largest sustainable harvest from a fishery is desirable. Such an approach to management is problematic for several reasons. First, fisheries, like any natural population, are subject to random shocks and trying to manage a fishery to be always at a given biomass level will almost certainly fail. Moreover, in the face of uncertainty, an important management goal is likely to include a lower variance in the catch from year to year, and which may not coincide with trying to be at the biomass level x_{MSY}. Second, measuring the parameters of the surplus yield model is prone to both error and bias such that estimates of r and k with any reasonable degree of precision require data on the biomass at, or near to, the point that growth in the biomass is close to zero (Hilborn and Walters, 1992). Third, and as we will shortly demonstrate, the biomass that maximizes the total harvest will, in general, not maximize the net economic returns from the fishery.

4.4   ECONOMICS OF FISHING

Economists have known for a long time that a maximization of a harvest or a yield from a renewable resource does not coincide with the maximization of the resource rent. This is because neither costs nor revenues are proportional to harvests. One of the first to show this result in a formal way using a biological and economic (or bioeconomic) model of a fishery was Scott Gordon in 1954, who also modeled the fish population as a surplus production or Schaefer model. Thus, his analysis of the fishery is commonly called the Gordon–Schaefer model.

Gordon–Schaefer (or static economic) model

In Gordon's original paper, he assumed that the harvest of fishers was proportional to both the level of the biomass (x) and the level of fishing effort (E), i.e.,

$$h = qEx \tag{12}$$

where q is a catchability coefficient that is independent of either fishing effort or the biomass.

Using (9) and (12) the effort required to harvest the surplus yield which leaves x unchanged can be calculated as follows:

$$qEx = rx(1 - x/k) \quad \Rightarrow \quad E = r/q(1 - x/k) \tag{13}$$

The maximization problem that will solve for the biomass level that will give the highest net return (revenue minus cost) from the fishery on a sustained yield basis is, therefore,

$$\text{Max } \pi = ph - cE \tag{14}$$

where p is the competitive price of fish and c is the competitive price per unit of fishing effort. Given that the harvest equals the surplus yield, we can substitute (13) into (14) to obtain,

$$\text{Max } \pi = p[rx(1 - x/k)] - c[r/q(1 - x/k)], \tag{14'}$$

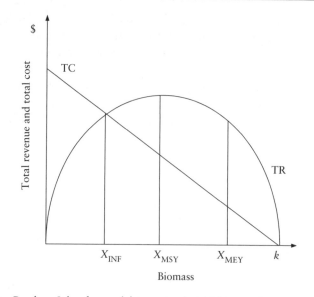

Figure 4.8   The Gordon–Schaefer model (sustained yield-biomass)

such that,

$$d\pi/dx = pr(1 - 2x/k) + cr/qk = 0 \quad \Rightarrow \quad x^* = c/2qp + k/2 \tag{15}$$

If (14′) is positive then fishers are earning resource rents or *super-normal profits* (where if total revenue equals total cost fishers earn normal profits). The biomass that maximizes the resource rent or sustainable economic yield from the fishery, x^*, is commonly called x_{MEY} or the biomass that gives the *maximum economic yield*. Provided that q, c, and p are greater than zero it follows from (15) and (11) that the biomass that maximizes the resource rent or sustainable economic yield from the fishery is *greater* than the maximum sustainable yield, i.e., $x_{MEY} > x_{MSY}$. This can be seen in figure 4.8 where the total revenue curve is the Schaefer model multiplied by the price p and x_{MEY} represents the point where the marginal revenue from a change in the biomass exactly equals the marginal cost in harvesting this quantity of fish. The maximum economic yield gives a higher level of the biomass than x_{MSY} because the total cost of harvesting is *decreasing* in the biomass. In this sense, the biomass is like an input into the harvesting function of fishers – the more fish available, the more fish that can be caught for the same level of fishing effort.

Although x_{MEY} is the biomass level that maximizes the resource rents, in the absence of any control on entry into the fishery, positive rents would attract further fishing effort reducing the biomass below x_{MEY}. In fact, if fishers can only earn normal profits in alternative employment, and so long as resource rents are positive in the fishery, additional fishing effort will continue to increase until eventually the resource rents are completely dissipated. This point is represented by $x_{INF}(x$ infinity) and is called the *bionomic equilibrium* because if the biomass were greater than x_{INF}, additional fishing effort and entry would move it towards x_{INF}, while exploitation with a biomass less than x_{INF} generates a negative return that reduces effort and exit. The time it would take to reach the bionomic equilibrium in an open access fishery depends on the rate of entry, the size of the resource rents, the initial rate of exploitation, and other factors.

The tendency for a common-pool resource, where yields are rivalrous and exclusion is difficult (see chapter 2), to move towards x_{INF} has been called the "tragedy of the commons" (Hardin, 1968). The tragedy arises because the resource is overexploited economically because no property rights exist. Thus, although fishers would be better off if the fishery were at x_{MEY}, the lack of any property rights precludes the possibility of staying at such a point, or at any other biomass with positive resource rents. This is because positive rents attract additional fishing effort that reduces the biomass and moves it towards the bionomic equilibrium.

The Gordon–Schaefer model may also be represented directly in terms of the level of fishing effort rather than the level of biomass. This can be done by solving (14), but substituting out for x rather than e. Thus the maximization problem becomes,

$$\text{Max } \pi = pqEk(r - qE)/r - cE \tag{16}$$

such that,

$$d\pi/dE = pqk - (2pq^2Ek)/r - c = 0 \quad \Rightarrow \quad E^* = r\,(1/2q - c/2q^2pk) \tag{17}$$

The level of effort that maximizes the economic yield is given by E^* or E_{MEY} and can also be found directly by substituting (15) into (13). The levels of fishing effort that correspond to x_{MEY}, x_{MSY} and x_{INF} are E_{MEY}, E_{MSY} and E_{INF} and are given in figure 4.9. From (12), we note that a higher x implies a *lower* level of fishing effort. Thus if $x_{MEY} > x_{MSY} > x_{INF}$ then it follows that $E_{MEY} < E_{MSY} < E_{INF}$. In other words, the level of fishing effort that gives the maximum economic yield is *less* than the level of fishing effort that ensures the maximum sustainable yield. Thus, in the Gordon–Schaefer or static economic model of the fishery, rent maximization is more conservative with lower fishing effort than the maximization of the sustained yield from the fishery.

The implication that fishery managers have drawn from figure 4.9 is that *if* fishing effort could be controlled at E_{MEY} (or at any point less than E_{INF}) then complete rent dissipation can be avoided. The first step is to restrict access to the fishery or limit entry in terms of the number of fishers or vessels. The second step is to control the fishing effort of fishers who have access to the fishery. The former has proved much easier than the latter, as we shall discuss in section 4.5.

The results from the Gordon–Schaefer model have proved very insightful in understanding fisheries and fisher behavior. However, the model fails to consider what is the *optimal path* to get to the rent maximizing level of the biomass, a point

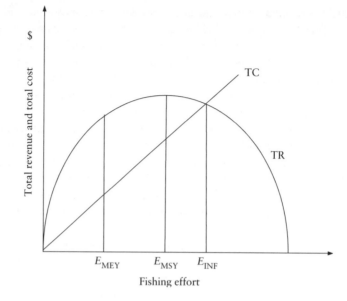

Figure 4.9   The Gordon–Schaefer model (sustained yield-effort)

recognized by Gordon himself (Gordon, 1956). Nor does the model consider the consequences of discounting (see box 4.1), or how a dollar is valued today versus the future, on the optimum harvest and biomass level.

Fishing dynamics

Discounting has important implications in terms of both the optimal level of harvest and biomass. The greater the discount rate, the less valuable are returns in the future relative to the present, and the greater the incentive not to "invest" in the resource by reducing the current harvest. This result can be shown formally, but first we need to determine the optimal level of the biomass given a positive discount rate.

Optimal biomass

To better understand how the discount rate influences the optimal level of the biomass we will derive an important result in fisheries economics and renewable resources – the *fundamental equation of renewable resources*. To obtain the result, we first specify the dynamic problem of a fishery where we wish to maximize the present value of resource rents (V), i.e.,

$$\text{Max } V = \int_{t=0}^{\infty} e^{-\delta t}\{(p-c(x)h\}dt \qquad (18)$$

BOX 4.1   INTRODUCTION TO DISCOUNTING

Discounting converts the future value (FV) of costs and benefits into a present value (PV). The higher the discount rate, i, or the lower the discount factor $1/(1+i)$, the lower is the present value of costs and benefits that occur in the future. For a positive discount rate the further into the future we go, *ceteris paribus*, the lower is the present value of a future value of a cost or benefit.

For a lump sum $\$A$, discounted n discrete periods into the future with a discount rate i, its present value is:

$$PV = \$A/(1+i)^n \tag{1}$$

In continuous time, the present value on an annual basis can be calculated as follows:

$$PV = \$A\,e^{-\delta n} \tag{2}$$

where $e =$ base of the natural logarithm, δ is the instantaneous discount rate such that $\ln(1+i) = \delta$ and $e^{-\delta n}$ is the continuous time discount factor.

The choice of the discount rate can have a large impact on the present value of a stream of costs and benefits especially values that occur many years in the future. For this reason, *hyperbolic discount rates* have been proposed that have a higher discount rate close to the present and a lower discount rate further into the future.

The *social discount rate* may be defined as i, where $i = mg + n$ and m is the elasticity of the social marginal utility of consumption per person, g is society's growth rate in real per capita consumption and n is positive time preference. The positive time preference is *not* the marginal rate of substitution between consumption in two periods, but is the willingness to pay a positive interest rate to raise present consumption at the expense of future consumption, even if society endowments for consumption are identical across the two periods.

If all markets are competitive and there are no taxes and no market failures, the discount rate used by society between periods t_1 and t_2 should equal i. In this case, $-(1+i)$ is the slope of the tangency point where the "social" indifference curve is tangent to the economy's production possibility curve between the two periods, i.e., where the marginal rate of substitution in consumption between t_1 and t_2 (incorporating positive time preference) = marginal rate of transformation in economy-wide production between t_1 and t_2. The more skewed is the production possibility frontier towards the future (more than can be produced in the future than in the present), the greater will be the social discount rate. The less willing society is to trade off consumption today for consumption tomorrow, the greater will be the social discount rate.

Sources: Olson and Bailey (1981); Pearce and Turner (1990); Rao (2000); Just et al. (1982)

Subject to:

$$dx/dt = F(x) - h \tag{19}$$
$$x_0 = x(0) \tag{20}$$

In this problem, the choice or *control variable* is the level of harvest (h) as it determines, along with the initial condition, the present and future values of the resource stock. $F(x)$ is the growth in the biomass in the absence of fishing.

This particular problem is said to be linear in the control because the level of harvest enters the objective function and the constraints in a linear way. Harvesting costs are defined by $c(x)h$, where $c'(x) < 0$, to indicate that an increase in the biomass for a given harvest level, *reduces* the costs of fishing. The instantaneous resource rent or net returns in the fishery is $(p - c(x))h$ which can be more concisely written as $\pi(x, h)$.

Time enters the problem only through the discount factor $e^{-\delta t}$(see box 4.1) and provided that $\delta > 0$, a dollar net return from the fishery in the future is worth less than a dollar today. Equation (19) is the dynamic or biological constraint that states the change in the biomass over time must equal the growth in the biomass less the harvest. If $dx/dt = 0$ the resource is being harvested sustainably, if $dx/dt < 0$ the harvest exceeds the growth in the biomass and we are "disinvesting" or reducing the resource stock, and if $dx/dt > 0$ we are "investing" in the resource stock. Equation (20) is the initial condition or initial value of the *state variable* – the resource stock or biomass – that describes the "state of the system" in terms of the fishery.

From (18), at any point in time, the instantaneous marginal return from harvesting is,

$$(p - c(x))$$

If this marginal return were invested in an alternative asset that paid a rate of return equal to the prevailing discount rate (δ), the marginal instantaneous rate of return from harvesting, or "disinvesting" in the fishery, becomes

$$\delta(p - c(x)) \tag{21}$$

The instantaneous return from "disinvesting" in the resource can now be compared to the return from "investing" in the fishery.

If we only wish to determine the effect of the discount rate on the optimal steady-state level of the biomass – the biomass level at we wish to remain – it must be true that $dx/dt = 0$ or $F(x) = h$. Thus, at this optimum level of the biomass the instantaneous net returns from fishing can be written as,

$$(p - c(x))h = (p - c(x))F(x) \tag{22}$$

Equation (22) can be interpreted as the instantaneous return from "investing" in the fishery and allowing the biomass to reach its optimal level. The *marginal* value of "investing" in the fishery, at the optimal level of the biomass, is the derivative of the instantaneous net returns with respect to the biomass, i.e.,

$$d[(p - c(x))F(x)]/dx = F'(x)(p - c(x)) - c'(x)F(x) \tag{23}$$

The marginal benefits from "investing" in the fishery are composed of two parts: the instantaneous change in the biomass ($F'(x)(p - c(x))$) and the reduction in the future value of harvesting costs weighted by the optimal harvest level ($- c'(x)F(x)$), where

$$-c'(x) > 0$$

If we assume that $F(x)$ is a Schaefer model then $F'(x)$ is at its highest (and positive) value when the biomass is at its lowest possible level, is zero when the biomass is at the maximum sustainable yield and has its lowest (and negative) value when the biomass is at its carrying capacity.

Setting (21) and (23) equal ensures that at the optimal biomass the instantaneous marginal return from "disinvesting" in the fishery equals the instantaneous marginal return from "investing" in the fishery in terms of its biomass, i.e.,

$$\delta(p - c(x)) = F'(x)(p - c(x)) - c'(x)F(x) \tag{24}$$

Equation (23) can be rewritten as follows,

$$\delta = F'(x) + (-c'(x)F(x))/(p - c(x)) \tag{24'}$$

In turn, equation (24') can be rewritten in a more general form as in (25), given that $F(x) = h$. Equation (25) is the fundamental equation of renewable resources.

$$\delta = F'(x) + (\partial\pi/\partial x)/(\partial\pi/\partial h) \quad \text{(given } F(x) = h) \tag{25}$$

The left-hand side of (24) represents the discount rate or the *external rate of return* on assets outside of the fishery while the right-hand side represents the instantaneous *internal rate of return* in the fishery. The right-hand side consists of two parts: the instantaneous "biological" return or the change (which can be zero, negative or positive) in the growth in the biomass from change in the biomass ($F'(x)$) and the "marginal stock effect" ($\partial\pi/\partial x/\partial\pi/\partial h$).

The marginal stock effect itself consists of two components: the numerator and denominator. The numerator is the partial derivative of the instantaneous resource rent in the fishery with respect to the biomass, given the biomass is at its optimal level ($F(x) = h$), i.e., $\partial\pi/\partial x$. To ensure the fundamental equation is satisfied at the optimal level of the biomass and harvest rate, the *larger* is the numerator ($\partial\pi/\partial x$), which is positive, the *smaller* must be $F'(x)$ and the *larger* must be the optimal biomass. In other words, the more sensitive are the instantaneous resource rents to changes in the biomass, the greater will be the optimal level of the biomass. This is because the more sensitive are harvesting costs to changes in the biomass (higher biomass implies lower costs for a given harvest rate) the more advantageous it is to have a larger biomass. The denominator is the partial derivative of the instantaneous resource rent with respect to the harvest level at the optimal level of the biomass, i.e., $\partial\pi/\partial h$. To ensure that (25) holds as an equality at the optimal level of the biomass, the larger is the denominator, and which is positive, the *larger* must be $F'(x)$ and the *smaller* must be the optimal biomass. In other words, the greater is the instantaneous marginal resource rent from harvesting, the smaller will be the optimal biomass. This is because if the harvesting costs at any given level of the biomass are lower (the smaller is $c(x)$), the more profitable it is to increase the harvest and reduce the optimal biomass.

Optimal paths

The fundamental equation of renewable resources provides a condition that must be satisfied at the optimal level of the biomass, but it does not tell us how we get there. The optimal harvesting strategy from moving from the current biomass to the optimal biomass is called the *optimal path* or *approach path* of the state variable.

To determine the optimal path we can set up a function that incorporates the objective functional in (18) and the dynamic constraint given by (19), i.e.,

$$H = e^{-\delta t}[(p - c(x))h] + \lambda(F(x) - h) \tag{26}$$

where both h and λ are functions of time and λ is the present value of the shadow price of the resource stock. The shadow price is often called the *co-state* or *adjoint* variable and represents the sensitivity of the instantaneous resource rent $((p - c(x))h)$ to changes in the biomass at any point in time, discounted back into a present value.

If we differentiate the function H – the *present value Hamiltonian* – with respect to our control variable, the harvest rate h, and set the result equal to zero we obtain an equation that must be satisfied at each point in time along the optimal path to the optimal biomass, i.e.,

$$\partial H/\partial h = e^{-\delta t}[p - c(x)] - \lambda = 0 \quad \Rightarrow \quad \lambda = [p - c(x)]\,e^{-\delta t} \tag{27}$$

Equation (27) may be interpreted as a portfolio condition in the sense that the left hand side represents the instantaneous value from "investing" in the biomass and the right hand side is the instantaneous marginal return from "disinvesting" in the resource.

For this particular problem, the instantaneous resource rent is linear in the control variable or harvest rate such that the instantaneous marginal resource rent only depends on the level of the biomass and *not* the harvest rate. In other words, there is no penalty associated with harvesting at a small or high rate in terms of either the price received for fish or the cost of harvesting fish. Thus, should we not be on the optimal path – such that $\lambda < [p - c(x)]\,e^{-\delta t}$ meaning that we are "investing" too much in the resource or biomass – we could increase the present value of the resource rents from the fishery by increasing the harvest rate to its highest possible rate to get onto the optimal path, i.e., set $h = h_{max}$. Conversely, if $\lambda > [p - c(x)]\, e^{-\delta t}$, we are "disinvesting" too much and we could be better off by reducing the harvest rate and setting the harvest rate to its lowest possible level, i.e., $h = 0$. By the same logic, if the current level of the biomass *exceeds* the optimal biomass we should harvest at h_{max} to get there as quickly as possible. Similarly, if the current level of the biomass is *less than* the optimal biomass we should set the harvest rate equal to 0. This approach path to the optimal biomass has been called a "bang-bang" or *most rapid approach path* in that we try to get to the optimal biomass as quickly as possible, whether or not the current biomass is greater than or less than the optimal level.

If either the price of fish or the cost of harvesting vary with the change in the harvest rate or control variable, such that (18) is no longer linear in the harvest rate, the most rapid approach path to the optimal biomass will no longer be desirable. This is because harvesting at the maximum possible rate reduces the instantaneous marginal resource rent. For instance, if the price of fish is *decreasing* in the harvest rate, or if the cost of harvesting is *increasing* in the harvest rate, a higher harvest rate will reduce the instantaneous marginal resource rent. In this situation, if the current level of the biomass exceeds the optimal biomass, the approach path will be more gradual to its optimal level and the harvest rate will change over time. Another argument in favor of a more gradual approach path and not setting $h = 0$ is that fishing vessels and fishing capital are not perfectly malleable and cannot be shifted from fishing to alternative activities at zero cost (Munro, 1992). High transitional costs may also apply to the labor employed in fishing, especially if located in isolated coastal regions.

Comparison of the static and dynamic fishing models

To understand the differences between the Gordon–Schaefer, or static economic model, and the dynamic economic model of fishing, it is useful to calculate the optimal steady-state biomass using (25), or the fundamental equation of renewable resources. As with the static model we assume a surplus yield function given by (9), a harvest function given by (12), and a fishery resource rent given by (14). Thus, at the optimal biomass,

$$F(x) = rx(1 - x/k) \quad \Rightarrow \quad F'(x) = r(1 - 2x/k) \tag{28}$$
$$E = h/qx \tag{29}$$
$$\pi = ph - c(h/qx) \quad \Rightarrow \quad \partial\pi/\partial x = ch/qx^2 \tag{30a}$$
$$\Rightarrow \quad \partial\pi/\partial h = p - c/qx. \tag{30b}$$

Substituting (28), (30a), and (30b) into (25) we obtain,

$$\delta = r(1 - 2x/k) + (ch/qx^2)/(p - c/qx) \tag{31}$$

At the optimal biomass, $h = rx(1 - x/k)$, which can be substituted into (31) to derive an equation that is only a function of the biomass, i.e.,

$$\delta = r(1 - 2x/k) + (cr(1 - x/k))/(pqx - c) \tag{31'}$$

Equation (31') is a quadratic equation that has the following positive root (Conrad, 1999, p. 46),

$$x^* = k/4\{(c/pqk + 1 - \delta/r) + [(c/pqk + 1 - \delta/r)^2 + (8c\delta)/(pqkr)]^{1/2}\} \tag{32}$$

where it can be shown that,

$\partial x^*/\partial\delta < 0$ (increase in discount rate *reduces* optimal biomass)

$\partial x^*/\partial c > 0$ (increase in cost per unit of effort *increases* optimal biomass)

$\partial x^*/\partial p < 0$ (increase in price of fish *reduces* the optimal biomass)

In the case where the discount rate is zero ($\delta = 0$) the optimal biomass (x^*) given in (32) simplifies to the following,

$$x^* = k/4\{c/pqk + 1 + c/pqk + 1\} = c/2qp + k/2 \tag{33}$$

where (33) is identical to (15) or x_{MEY} – the biomass that maximizes the economic yield in the static or Gordon–Schaefer model. This result should be not be surprising if we realize that x_{MEY} is the biomass that gives the highest single period net return. Thus if we value the future as much as the present, x_{MEY} must give the highest resource rent of any level of the biomass. By contrast, if the discount rate is as large as possible so that it approaches infinity the optimal level of the biomass approaches x_{INF} – the bionomic equilibrium – a level of the biomass where there is no value from "investing" in the resource.

"Optimal" extinction

In most fisheries, the optimal biomass that satisfies the fundamental equation for renewable resources is positive. However, in a few fisheries where the harvesting costs are insensitive to changes in the biomass the marginal stock effect may be very small, or in the extreme case, even zero. In the extreme case, the fundamental equation of renewable resources is satisfied if and only if,

$$\delta = F'(x) \tag{34}$$

If $F(x)$ is the Schaefer model then (34) implies,

$$\delta = r(1 - 2x/k) \tag{35}$$

It follows, therefore, that if the discount rate (δ) is greater than the intrinsic growth rate (r) then (35) *cannot* be satisfied for any positive level of the biomass if $r, k > 0$. This result implies that the optimal biomass is as small as possible, or $x^* = 0$.

An example that satisfies the conditions for "optimal" extinction is that of Antarctic baleen whales that have a very low intrinsic growth rate such that $F'(x)$ is less than 0.05 (Clark, 1999). Thus if harvesting were undertaken to maximize the present value of resource rents, it might be profitable under reasonable discount rates to harvest them to extinction and invest the returns in faster-growing assets.

The problem with the "optimal" extinction result for whales, or any renewable resource, is that it is derived from the assumption that resources should be exploited to maximize the present value of resource rents. It also ignores the *equity* issue between the current generation and future generations of fishers. In the models we have so far examined the fish have no other value except the growth they can contribute to the biomass and their harvested value. In reality, species have a worth beyond their market price in terms of their contribution to ecological integrity, biological diversity (see chapter 15) and their non-market value (see chapter 9). For example, the blue whale – the world's largest animal – likely has a value in the sea other than just its market value in terms of meat and oil. If these non-market values are sufficiently high enough, it implies a lower rate of exploitation and in some cases, a zero rate of exploitation.

4.5   FISHERIES MANAGEMENT

The two most critical aspects of fisheries management are, one, an understanding that fish populations are dynamic, such that they change over time and the magnitude of the change is difficult to predict and two, "managing" fish is about managing fisher behavior to ensure individual interests coincide with the collective interest.

Managing uncertainty

If fish populations were well behaved and could be reliably predicted with an acceptable degree of accuracy, many of the problems (but not all!) associated with fisheries management would be overcome. In such an ideal world, fisheries managers could set a total allowable catch (TAC) at a desired level to arrive at an optimal level of the biomass and could remain at this level (with fluctuations) by judicious adjustments of the TAC. Such an approach could be described as "steady-state" management in that predictable shocks would allow the regulator to adjust the current harvests to return to a desired equilibrium or steady state.

Unfortunately, in many fisheries the overexploitation of resource stocks is diffi-cult to detect, the total catch is poorly measured, understanding of the underlying dynamics is missing and predictions about future levels of the biomass are subject to a great deal of error (Ludwig et al., 1993). Thus fishery managers find them-selves in the unenviable situation of trying to manage a resource where they may not even know the correct model to explain its dynamics, let alone have reliable estimates of the model's coefficients. In the face of this uncertainty, pretending the world is in a steady state and managing according to this belief can be disastrous. Many examples exist of fisheries that have collapsed because managers have grossly overestimated the biomass or failed to adopt strategies to address unex-pected shocks (Hannesson, 1996; Berrill, 1997).

To incorporate uncertainty into fisheries management requires an appreciation that no matter how much research is undertaken, fish populations fluctuate in ways that are not fully predictable. It also requires developing strategies, from a range of alternatives, to explicitly account for uncertainty. For example, if a fish population is subject to unpredictable fluctuations and may exhibit critical depen-sation, it would be unwise to solely manage the fishery with a total harvesting limit. Instead, management should also include other strategies, such as closed exploited areas, to help ensure a minimum viable population regardless of the level of exploitation. However, as with any management tool, closed exploitation areas and marine reserves are not without problems of their own (Smith and Wilen, 2002).

Hilborn and Walters (1992) have proposed an *active adaptive* approach to management whereby uncertainty is managed by constructing different models or explanations for the same phenomena and simulating the effects of alterna-tive strategies and policies. Adaptive management helps managers prepare for uncertain events and suggests those strategies that may be better able to cope with uncertainty while achieving desired goals. An economic example of an adaptive management approach to fisheries management is the use of optimal feedback rules. Optimal feedback rules link information about the resource stock, harvest rate and desired level of the biomass, compare payoffs of alternative strategies using different models and parameter values, and continuously update the optimal strategy based on the latest information about the fishery. In an application, Grafton, Sandal, and Steinshamn (2000) evaluate one of the most spectacular declines in resource abundance of the twentieth century – the collapse of the northern cod fishery off the east coast of Canada in the late 1980s and early 1990s. Using the same information that was available to fishery managers when they made their decisions, the optimal harvest rate with the feedback rule would have been less than actual in every year, but one, from 1962 to 1991 and would have generated much higher resource rents. For example, figure 4.10 compares the undiscounted net revenue in the fishery using actual harvest and stock levels with the optimal harvest using the optimal feedback rule and predicted stock levels.

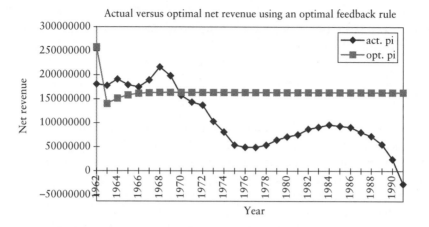

Figure 4.10 Actual vs. optimal net revenue in Canada's northern cod fishery

Source: Grafton, Sandal, and Steinshamn (2000)

A more difficult problem is what fishery managers should do if they neither have an appropriate model of the population nor the data to distinguish between competing models. Such a situation may arise if populations are chaotic (see chapter 1) such that fluctuations are deterministic in that they are generated by the underlying population dynamics, but are non-periodic, and even the smallest errors in estimating the coefficients of such a model will soon lead to large errors in prediction. In such an environment, emphasis should be placed on how and when fish are caught rather than on how much is caught, and research should focus on understanding ecosystems rather than predicting populations (Wilson et al., 1994). A chaotic population also requires the use of a mix of strategies to provide a management option whatever the underlying dynamics (Grafton and Silva-Echenique, 1997).

Managing fishers

Fisheries management has often developed in an *ad hoc* way in response to challenges or crises. Managers have often responded to problems without a great deal of thought as to their potential consequences. In particular, many fishery managers have focused on understanding fish – a complicated task enough in itself – rather than understanding fisher behavior.

The key to understanding fishers is almost tautological, namely, they will do the best they can, given the constraints they face. It implies that a management strategy that constrains the actions of fishers, but does not change the underlying incentives, is likely to be less effective than a strategy that tries to ensure individual and collective interests coincide. We assess three broad types of approaches to the economic management of fisheries: limited-entry that restricts access of fishers and their use of inputs, rights-based approaches that try to change the incentives of fishers, and marine reserves.

Limited-entry management

The Gordon–Schaefer model shows that in the absence of any controls or property rights the bionomic equilibrium of fishing effort exceeds the level of fishing effort that maximizes the resource rent. This arises because there is a negative externality whereby each fisher optimizes without considering the negative impact of his or her actions on others. In general, these negative consequences can occur in two main ways: a stock externality and a congestion externality. A *stock externality* stems from the common-pool nature of a fishery whereby one fisher's harvest reduces the amount of fish available to be harvested by others. A *congestion externality* can occur where fishers are severely constrained by either time or space so that the act of fishing increases the harvesting cost of others, regardless of the catch (Smith, 1969).

The most obvious way to control the stock externality in a fishery is to limit both the number of fishers and to control their level of fishing effort. Such forms of management transform an open access fishery to what has been called a limited-user open access fishery (Wilen, 1993). If both can be accomplished perfectly, and at zero cost, it is possible to arrive at a level of fishing effort that maximizes the resource rent. Unfortunately, the experience of limited-entry is that although fishery managers can easily restrict access to fisheries, this is often done *after* there are already too many vessels.

The other aspect of limited-entry is to control the level of fishing effort of vessels given access to the fishery. If the harvesting technology required inputs to be used in fixed proportions such an approach would control fishing effort provided that at least one input was adequately controlled. In reality, fishers are able to substitute among some inputs and can switch from regulated to unregulated inputs (see box 4.2). Indeed, the experience of many limited-entry fisheries is that fishers are often better at devising ways to increase their fishing effort than are regulators at controlling fishing effort (Townsend, 1990). The end result is "capital stuffing" and a low rate of input (especially capital) utilization.

This limited-entry outcome is illustrated in figure 4.11. We assume N identical fishers harvesting a given total allowable catch (TAC) with a given biomass. The minimum capital *per vessel* (assuming N vessels) required to harvest the total catch is K_0, and that coincides with the maximum vessel capital constraint imposed by the regulator. If fishers are able to substitute from regulated to unregulated inputs at the same and constant price, they would *prefer* to be at the capital level K_i, or the point where the value of their marginal product equals the marginal cost of capital, i.e., where $ph'(K_i) = c$. The *actual* capital for each fisher

BOX 4.2 RENT DISSIPATION IN A FISHERY

The British Columbia (BC) salmon fisheries provide a good example of the ability of fishers to substitute to unregulated inputs and overcome restrictions on fishing effort imposed by the regulator. The fishery includes four types of vessels: purse-seiners, gill-net vessels, troll vessels and gillnet-troll vessels that collectively harvest five main species of salmon.

Starting in 1969 the number of fishing vessels was restricted to 5,800 by the issuance of fishing licenses by the regulator. Restrictions on the number of licenses, however, failed to prevent further increases in fishing effort such that by 1971 the tonnage of each vessel was restricted to a maximum level. Subsequently, additional controls were placed on their fishing inputs that fishers, in turn, have tried to circumvent by substituting to unregulated inputs.

A study of rent dissipation in the BC salmon fisheries was undertaken using 1982 data on 245 vessels (21 seine, 80 gillnet, 84 troll and 60 gillnet-troll), or about 5 percent of the fleet. In the study, an estimate of the rent dissipation in the fishery was calculated by measuring the difference between potential rent using optimal tonnage less the actual rent in 1982. For the four classes of vessels in the sample the status quo and potential annual rent in 1982 Canadian dollars were:

	Status quo rent	Potential rent
Purse-seiners	919,000	3,012,000
Gillnet	−128,000	484,000
Troll	−238,000	−117,000
Gillnet-troll	510,000	1,027,700
All vessels	1,062,600	4,406,700

Simulations using the data reveal that for the industry as a whole the status quo rent in 1982 was −$38,695,000, indicating complete rent dissipation and an unsustainable return. A substantial part of this rent dissipation is attributable to vessel redundancy that represented about 22 percent of the total fleet in 1982. Using the actual tonnage of vessels, but with the minimum number of vessels, the potential rent would have been $14,129,000, and if the minimum number of vessels were at their optimal tonnage the potential rent would have been $35,486,000. The potential rent would be even higher if only one type of vessel (purse-seiners) participated in the fishery. In this case, the estimated potential rent would have been almost $70 million, or over $100 million/year more than what the rent actually was in 1982.

Source: Dupont (1990)

at the given TAC and biomass would, however, be somewhere between K_0 and K_i because if all fishers substitute to unregulated inputs the individual harvest function ($h(K_i)$) will shift inwards reflecting the fact less fish can be caught for the same amount of fishing capital.

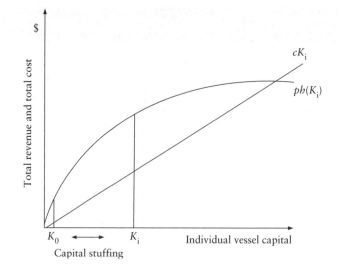

Figure 4.11 Capital stuffing in a limited-entry fishery

Rights-based management

Rights-based management refers to approaches that try to affect the incentives of fishers rather than control their behavior through regulations. Broadly defined, rights-based approaches include both private property rights and incentives, and community rights (see chapter 2).

Community rights most commonly exist in inshore fisheries where a well-defined area of the coast or sea is managed and controlled by a community. Typically, access to the fishery is limited to only community members who are expected to abide by accepted rules of behavior. Members of the community who fail to abide by the rules face a number of community sanctions. Community-based management exists in many different forms and numerous examples exist of fisheries that have been both sustainably managed and have provided positive resource rents to members (see box 4.3).

A private property approach that mimics some of the characteristics of community rights creates a property right over an area of sea or ocean. These rights are called territorial user rights in fisheries (TURFs) and can allow the owner to enhance the area's productivity (such as by creating artificial reefs) and optimize the harvest level to maximize resource rents. A major drawback of TURFs is that most fish are migratory and thus investments made in a TURF may end up benefiting persons other than the TURF owner.

Another private property approach to managing fisheries is to create individual tradable harvesting rights denominated as shares of the TAC called individual transferable quotas (ITQs). Provided that ITQs are a durable and exclusive property right and are a binding constraint on fishers, they change the incentives faced by fishers.

BOX 4.3   LOCAL-LEVEL MANAGEMENT OF FISHERIES IN TURKEY

Numerous examples exist of successful community management of fisheries. Most of these cases are artisanal fisheries (traditional and small-scale) where there exists a history of long-standing community participation. An exception is the lagoon fishery of the Ayvalik-Haylazli on the Turkish Mediterranean coast near the town of Adana. The community management of the fishery began in 1974 with the formation of a cooperative to which fishers must belong. To restrict access, membership is limited to persons with at least six months residency in one of the three local villages and who do not have wage employment income. The residency rule helps bind fishers to the collective interest and makes it easier to police individual behavior.

The cooperative has a little over a hundred members and fishing costs are kept low by the mode of fishing. Fishers harvest in groups of four where each has equal share to the gears and boats and to the returns from fishing. Policing of the lagoon fishery is undertaken by the cooperative with few problems from cooperative members, but encroachment from outsiders (especially sports fishers) is difficult to control. Enforcement by the cooperative is recognized by the state as the lagoon fishery is leased from the government.

The local-level management of the lagoon fishery has been viewed as successful in that the fishers land per person almost as much as the larger trawl vessels operating in the Turkish Mediterranean, but employ a fraction of the fuel and capital used by trawlers.

Source: Berkes (1986)

This is because the price of ITQs is either an explicit or an opportunity cost to fishers that can help fishers internalize the externality that their harvest imposes on others. Moreover, by providing fishers with a much greater assurance that they can harvest a given quantity of fish in a period of time, there is less incentive for fishers to "race to fish" (Grafton, 1996). In addition, ITQs may make certain forms of regulation superfluous, such as a limited fishing season, thus permitting fishers to market all their fish as a higher priced fresh product rather than marketing as a lower priced frozen product, and to focus on quality and higher valued landings (see box 4.4).

ITQs are not without problems, especially *quota busting*, or the harvesting of fish without quota, and *highgrading*, the dumping of smaller or lesser-valued fish at sea so as to maximize the return per quota unit. Quota trading may also lead to market power and lead to an undesirable concentration of quota in the hands of a few. The experience is that with adequate monitoring and enforcement ITQs offer a much superior form of management relative to limited entry. The relative success of ITQs in such countries as New Zealand and Canada has encouraged their introduction in other countries including Australia and Iceland, among others. In fact, the success of ITQs in some fisheries at increasing the resource rents has led

BOX 4.4   "PRIVATIZING" A FISHERY

In 1990, within just a six-day fishing season, fishers in the British Columbia halibut fishery on Canada's Pacific coast caught the entire allowable catch of almost 4,000 metric tonnes. Just 10 years earlier, the fleet had needed 65 days to catch a third less amount of fish. In response to increased investments in vessel and gear by fishers that led to this increased fishing effort the owner of the resource (Government of Canada) introduced individual harvesting rights in 1991.

Initially, the rights had only limited transferability, but transfers were allowed after 1993. The immediate impact of the harvesting rights was to enforce the limited total harvest for the fishery through the use of individual harvesting rights assigned to fishers, rather than by limiting the harvest through a very short fishing season. Thus with the introduction of individual harvesting rights the fishing season greatly increased to 214 days in 1991 and increased again to 245 days in 1992. The individual harvesting rights removed the incentive to invest in the gear or vessel to simply out-compete other fishers. Instead, fishers with individual harvesting rights were now obliged to purchase or lease rights to expand their operations.

The biggest economic benefit from the introduction of harvesting rights has been an increase in the price received per quantity of fish landed. Under a much longer fishing season due to harvesting rights, fishers can now land and market halibut as a much higher priced fresh, rather than as a frozen product. In addition, the longer fishing season has provided fishers with greater time and opportunity to care for the harvested fish, further increasing its quality and price. These factors contributed to a price premium of over 30 percent directly attributable to the longer fishing season and raised the producer surplus per kilogram by over 80 percent between 1988 and 1994. A longer season has also made fishing safer and reduced the loss of gear as fishers now have the luxury of not being obliged to fish in bad weather. Coupled with these benefits, for the period 1991–4 which coincided with an improvement in the characteristics of the harvesting rights in terms of duration, divisibility, and transferability, evidence also exists of improvements in short-run cost efficiency within the fishing fleet. In addition, the period 1988–94 has coincided with a statistically significant reduction in capacity per day per vessel for small and large vessels by 28 percent and 24 percent.

Sources: Grafton, Squires, and Fox (2000); Squires, Jeon, Grafton, and Kirkley (2002)

to heated debates as to who should reap the benefits of ITQs, and whether a share of these rents should also be captured by the resource owner, which is often the state (Grafton, 1995).

Marine reserves

An increasingly popular approach to fisheries management is to establish marine reserves or defined locations where fishing is prohibited or severely restricted.

The value of marine reserves to achieve biological objectives has long been realized. This is because risks of catastrophic collapse are often greater for exploited rather than unexploited populations. Thus, the reserve provides a "safe haven" to restock a fishery should a negative shock be realized (Grafton et al., 2003). In addition, multiple stocks in different locations or reserves hedge against shocks by helping to ensure that not all subpopulations are affected by a localized event.

Marine reserves may also be used to achieve economic objectives. In the work to date reserves have been compared to a total harvest limit under the assumption of restricted open access. Depending on the assumptions used in such models, optimally set TACs alone may generate greater or lower resource rents than a mix of reserves and a TAC. Pezzey, Roberts, and Urdal (2000), however, have shown in simulations assuming open access and by calibrating their models with stock, catch, and fish price data from three Caribbean coral reefs, that reserves could increase catches in the range from 10 percent to 80 percent. Generalizing for coral reef fisheries worldwide, they suggest that reserves could increase equilibrium catches that could be worth as much as US$ one billion.

4.6 FISHING FOR THE FUTURE

Much of the history of fisheries regulations can be characterized by missed opportunities and mismanagement. Fortunately, since the 1970s there has been a virtual revolution in our understanding about fish populations and how to manage fishers. Some of this thinking is reflected in this chapter.

The economics of fisheries is related to forestry, water, and even non-renewable resources by the notion of optimal investment and disinvestments, or when and how much to subtract or harvest. This connection to capital theory, a broader realization of the importance of natural capital, recent developments in the Law of the Sea and much more detailed empirical analysis of productivity, efficiency, and capacity in fisheries is leading to improved management. These initiatives are beginning to yield substantial benefits in the returns fisheries yield and in helping to ensure the sustainability of marine resources. These positive developments offer hope that the past history of mismanagement of fisheries will not be a predictor of the future of fishing.

FURTHER READING

There is a rich and vast literature on fisheries. Two classic papers that developed the static economic model of the fishery are Gordon (1954) and Scott (1955). The classic reference on the dynamics of fisheries management is Clark and Munro (1975) that derived (but did not solve) the fundamental equations of renewable resources. Munro and Scott (1985) forms the basis of much of the discussion in 4.4 on the economics of fishing while Flaaten (2002) inspired the heuristic derivation of equations (21) and (23). Van Kooten and Bulte (2000, chapter 6) provide an excellent discussion on the choice of the social rate of discount and the use of discounting in cost-benefit analysis.

Two highly recommended texts on the bioeconomics of fisheries are Clark (1985) and Clark (1990). A more accessible text is Hannesson (1993). An advanced, but still accessible, discourse on the economics of fishing is provided by Munro and Scott (1985). Another excellent and more recent survey article on fisheries economics is Bjørndal and Munro (1999). Two very good texts on the economics of fishing and renewable resources are Conrad and Clark (1987) and Conrad (1999). A useful, but more general, presentation on fisheries and the economics of renewable resources is offered by Brown (2000).

Four classic texts on fisheries from the biological perspective are Ricker (1975), Cushing (1981), Gulland (1983) and Hilborn and Walters (1992). A review and analysis of the factors that contributed to the decline of the northern cod is given by Myers et al. (1996). Sainsbury (1986) is a good book that describes different commercial methods of catching fish. Two useful books on ITQs are Kaufmann, Geen, and Sen (1999) and the National Science Foundation (1999). Detailed case-studies on ITQ fisheries worldwide are provided in Shotton (2001a) and a comprehensive survey in terms of multi-species ITQs is provided by Squires et al. (1998). Kirkley and Squires (1999) is already a "classic" and is the definitive reference on overcapacity and its measurement in fisheries. Case-studies of overcapacity in fisheries are provided in Shotton (2001b).

REFERENCES

Berkes, F. (1986). Local-level Management and the Commons Problem: A Comparative Study of Turkish Coastal Fisheries, *Marine Policy*, July: 215–29.

Berrill, M. (1997). *The Plundered Seas*, Greystone Books: Vancouver.

Bjørndal, T. and Munro, G. R. (1999). The Economics of Fisheries Management: A Survey, in T. Tietenberg and H. Folmer, eds, *The International Yearbook of Environmental and Resource Economics*, Edward Elgar: Cheltenham.

Brown, G. M. (2000). Renewable Natural Resource Management and Use Without Markets, *Journal of Economic Literature*, 38: 875–914.

Clark, C. W. (1985). *Bioeconomic Modelling and Fisheries Management*, John Wiley and Sons: New York.

Clark, C. W. (1990). *Mathematical Bioeconomics: The Optimal Management of Renewable Resources*, second edition, John Wiley and Sons: New York.

Clark, C. W. (1999). Renewable Resources: Fisheries, in J. C. J. M. van den Bergh, ed., *Handbook of Environmental and Resource Economics*, Edward Elgar: Cheltenham, England.

Clark, C. W. and Munro, G. R. (1975). The Economics of Fishing and Modern Capital Theory: A Simplified Approach, *Journal of Environmental Economics and Management*, 2: 92–106.

Conrad, J. M. (1999). *Resource Economics*, Cambridge University Press: Cambridge, England.

Conrad, J. M. and Clark, C. W. (1987). *Natural Resource Economics: Notes and Problems*, Cambridge University Press: New York.

Cushing, D. H. (1981). *Fisheries Biology: A Study in Population Dynamics*, second edition, University of Wisconsin Press: Madison, WI.

Dupont, D. P. (1990). Rent Dissipation in a Restricted Access Fisheries, *Journal of Environmental Economics and Management*, 19(1): 26–44.

Flaaten, O. (2002). A Lecture Note on the Economics of Fish Stock Investment. Paper presented at the 2002 International Institute for Fisheries Economics and Trade (IIFET), August, Wellington, New Zealand.

Gordon, H. S. (1954). The Economic History of a Common Property Resource: The Fishery, *Journal of Political Economy*, 62: 124–42.

Gordon, H. S. (1956). Obstacles to Agreement on Control in the Fishing Industry, in R. Turvey and J. Wiseman, eds, *The Economics of Fisheries*, Food and Agricultural Organization: Rome.

Grafton, R. Q. (1995). Rent Capture in a Rights-Based Fishery, *Journal of Environmental Economics and Management*, 28: 48–67.

Grafton, R. Q. (1996). Individual Transferable Quotas: Theory and Practice, *Reviews in Fish Biology and Fisheries*, 6: 5–20.

Grafton, R. Q. and Lane, D. E. (1998). Canadian Fisheries Policy: Challenges and Choices, *Canadian Public Policy*, 24: 133–48.

Grafton, R. Q., Sandal, L. K., and Steinshamn, S. I. (2000). How to Improve the Management of Renewable Resources: The Case of Canada's Northern Cod Fishery, *American Journal of Agricultural Economics*, 82: 570–80.

Grafton, R. Q. and Silva-Echenique, J. (1997). How to Manage Nature? Strategies, Predator–Prey Models, and Chaos, *Marine Resource Economics*, 12: 127–43.

Grafton, R. Q., Ha, P. V., and Kompas, T. (2003). On Reserves and Uncertainty, mimeograph.

Grafton, R. Q., Squires, D., and Fox, K. J. (2000). Private Property and Economic Efficiency: A Study of a Common-Pool Resource, *The Journal of Law and Economics*, 43(2): 679–713.

Gulland, J. A. (1983). *Fish Stock Assessment: A Manual of Basic Methods*, John Wiley and Sons: New York.

Hannesson, R. (1993). *Bioeconomic Analysis of Fisheries*, Fishing News Books: Oxford.

Hannesson, R. (1996). *Fisheries Mismanagement: The Case of the North Atlantic Cod*, Fishing News Books: Oxford.

Hardin, G. (1968). The Tragedy of the Commons, *Science*, 162: 1243–8.

Hilborn, R. and Walters, C. J. (1992). *Quantitative Fisheries Stock Assessment: Choice, Dynamics and Uncertainty*, Chapman and Hall: London.

Just, R. E., Hueth D. L., and Schmitz, A. (1982). *Applied Welfare Economics and Public Policy*, Prentice-Hall: Englewood Cliffs, New Jersey.

Kaufmann, B., Geen, G., and Sen, S. (1999). *Fish Futures: Individual Transferable Quotas in Fisheries*, Fisheries Economics, Research and Management Ltd: Kiama, Australia.

Kirkley, J. and Squires, D. (1999). Measuring Capacity and Capacity Utilization in Fisheries, in Dominique Gréboval, ed., *Managing Fishing Capacity: Selected Papers on Underlying Concepts and Issues*, FAO: Rome.

Ludwig, D., Hilborn, R., and Walters, C. (1993). Uncertainty, Resource Exploitation, and Conservation: Lessons from History, *Science*, 260: 7–36.

Munro, G. R. (1992). Mathematical Bioeconomics and the Evolution of Modern Fisheries Economics, *Journal of Mathematical Biology*, 54: 163–84.

Munro, G. R. and Scott, A. D. (1985). The Economics of Fisheries Management, in A. V. Kneese and J. L. Sweeny, eds, *Handbook of Natural Resource and Energy Economics Vol. 2*, North Holland: Amsterdam.

Myers, R. A., Hutchings, J. A., and Barrowman, N. J. (1996). Hypotheses for the Decline of the Cod in the North Atalantic, *Marine Ecology Progress Series*, 138: 293–308.

National Research Council (1999). *Sharing the Fish: Toward a National Policy on Individual Fishing Quotas*, National Academy Press: Washington, DC.

Olson, M. and Bailey, M. J. (1981). Positive Time Preference, *Journal of Political Economy*, 89: 1–25.

Pearce, D. W. and Turner, R. K. (1990). *Economics of Natural Resources and the Environment*, Johns Hopkins University Press: Baltimore, MD.

Pezzey, J. C. V., Roberts, C. M., and Urdal, B. T. (2000). A Simple Bioeconomic Model of a Marine Reserve, *Ecological Economics*, 33: 77–91.

Rao, P. K. (2000). *Sustainable Development*, Basil Blackwell: Malden, MA.

Ricker, W. E. (1975). *Computation and Interpretation of Biological Statistics of Fish Populations*, Fisheries and Oceans Canada: Ottawa.

Sainsbury, J. C. (1986). *Commercial Fishing Methods: An Introduction to Vessels and Gears*, second edition, Fishing News Books: Farnham, Surrey.

Scott, A. (1955). The Fishery: The Objective of Sole Ownership, *Journal of Political Economy*, 63: 116–34.

Shotton, R. (2001a). *Case Studies on the Allocation of Transferable Quota Rights in Fisheries*, FAO Technical Paper 411: Rome.

Shotton, R. (2001b). *Case Studies on the Effects of Transferable Fishing Rights on Fleet Capacity and Concentration of Quota Ownership*, FAO Technical Paper 412: Rome.

Smith, V. L. (1969). On Models of Commercial Fishing, *Journal of Political Economy*, 77: 181–98.

Smith, M. D. and Wilen, J. E. (2002). The Marine Environment: Fencing the Last Frontier, *Review of Agricultural Economics*, 24(1): 31–42.

Squires, D., Campbell, H., Cunningham, S., Dewees, C., Grafton, R. Q., Herrick Jr., S. F., Kirkley, J., Pascoe, S., Salvanes, K., Shallard, B., Turris, B., and Vestergaard, N. (1998). Individual Transferable Quotas in Multispecies Fisheries, *Marine Policy* 22: 135–59.

Squires, D., Grafton, R. Q., Alam, M. F., and Omar, I. H. (2003). Technical Efficiency in the Malaysian Gill Net Artisanal Fishery, *Environment and Development Economics*, 8: 481–504

Squires, D., Jeon, Y., Grafton, R. Q., and Kirkley, J. (2002). Capacity and Capacity Utilization in Common-Pool Resources: The Transition from Input to Output Controls, mimeograph.

Townsend, R. E. (1990). Entry Restrictions in the Fishery: A Survey of the Evidence, *Land Economics*, 66: 359–78.

Van Kooten, G. C. and Bulte, E. H. (2000). *The Economics of Nature: Managing Biological Assets*, Basil Blackwell: Oxford.

Wilen, J. E. (1993). Enhancing Economic Analysis for Fisheries Management: Discussion, *American Journal of Agricultural Economics*, 75: 1198–9.

Wilson, J. A., Acheson, J. M., Metcalfe, M., and Kleban, P. (1994). Chaos, Complexity and Community Management of Fisheries, *Marine Policy*, 18: 291–305.

CHAPTER FIVE

FORESTRY ECONOMICS

The time for felling the great oaks was one of the chief problems of the timber grower. There was a "psychological" moment for cutting, when the tree would yield a greater profit than at any other time. Oaks, it will be remembered, grow very slowly. The period of maturity is reached between the ages of eighty and a hundred and twenty years ... [u]p to that time it was not profitable to cut oaks for ship timber because of the additional value of a large-sized tree. Beyond that period of maturity, the risk of decay was great ... [the] results of a century of patience might be wasted in attempting to grow great stern-posts or beams. (Robert Albion, *Forests and Sea Power* (1965), describing the key problem facing the British Navy in encouraging land owners to grow timber for the fleet)

5.1 INTRODUCTION

Forests have been a fundamental part of the natural landscape through human history. They have provided fuel, foodstuffs, building materials, and have even been considered a strategic resource, providing the timbers to build the great ships through which some countries asserted their power for over three centuries. Throughout early European history, forests were considered at best a nuisance and barrier to development, and at worst, symbolized barbarism, far different from modern western attitudes that now see them as valuable repositories of cultural values and social significance.

Today, interest in forests covers the wide spectrum of goods and uses they provide, ranging from commercial timber production to environmental services, to their social and cultural significance for forest-dwelling indigenous groups as well as society as a whole. Forestry economics has also broadened its focus from the study of the production of timber or forest products to more complex problems involving the important environmental amenities forests can provide as well as the critical role they play in sustaining ecosystems and rural communities.

The timber that is harvested, as is the case of other renewable resources, replenishes itself over time. The key problem in forestry is to determine the best time to harvest that timber and indeed, to what extent management of the forest should emphasize timber production. Several distinctive characteristics of forestry distinguish it from other renewable resources, such as fisheries, and these differences continue to shape both the research direction and questions in the area of forest economics.

The principal difference is the long time span associated with forest growth. Some forests may not produce commercial timber until the trees are eighty years or older; some old growth forests contain trees over five hundred years old. Time also plays a role in the second difference. Trees are both a capital input as well as output because tree growth is a function of the age of the trees and hence of the standing biomass, much as is the case in fisheries. Decision-makers face the choice each year as to whether to hold the trees for another year (treat them as a capital stock) or harvest the entire biomass (output). Complicating the decision is the fact that a forest is capable of producing other goods and services that may also be dependent upon the age of the trees.

Finally, there is the pervasiveness of multiple outputs from forests and the positive and negative externalities associated with different uses of the forest. Many of these externalities involve environmental services and amenities that have no market values or price, further complicating the decision-maker's problem.

A subject that has received growing attention in forestry has been the institutional arrangements under which forests are used. Such issues range from the divergence between practice and theory in public forest management, to land use policies and deforestation. Indeed, much of the research involving forests hinges on not only the economic circumstances surrounding a particular forest, the host of biophysical factors associated with it, but also the social and economic context under which the forest is utilized. In this chapter, we will review the biological and economic aspects of forestry that contribute to these distinctive characteristics, the economic models used in forestry, and provide an overview of the current issues involving forestry and how institutions can influence their use.

5.2   THE WORLD'S FORESTS

The Food and Agriculture Organization (FAO) of the UN defines forests as areas where the tree canopy covers 10 percent of the area. Forests cover 30 percent of the world's landmass, with nearly one-third of that found in Europe, including Russia (table 5.1). The distribution of forests across the different continents differs significantly: forests cover less than one-fifth of Asia, while over half of South America is forested. Measured in per capita terms, Asia is the poorest in forest resources, while Oceania is the richest (reflecting Australia and New Zealand's large forest areas relative to their populations).

Table 5.1   The world's forest cover, 2000

Country/area	Total land area (000 ha)	Forest cover		
		Total forest area (000 ha)	% of land area	Area per capita (ha/person)
Africa	2,978,394	649,866	21.8	0.85
Asia	3,084,746	547,793	17.8	0.15
Oceania	849,096	197,623	23.3	6.58
Europe	2,259,957	1,039,251	46.0	1.43
North and Central America	2,136,966	549,304	25.7	1.15
South America	1,754,741	885,618	50.5	2.60
Total world	13,063,900	3,869,455	29.6	0.65

Source: FAO 2001a

Table 5.2   World's forests, by ecozone

Ecozone	Tropical	Sub-tropical	Temperate	Boreal
% of all forest cover	49	9	13	25

Source: FAO 2001b

Just under half of the world's forests are found within the tropical regions (table 5.2). These forests are dominated by *hardwood* species and are characterized by mild temperatures and growing conditions that permit growth year round. The tropical rain forests found predominantly in South America, Africa, and Asia sustain the highest levels of biodiversity found in the world. Temperate forests include *softwood* and *hardwood* species and characterize the forests found in the US and Central and Northern Europe that have historically provided most of the wood used to produce lumber, pulp, and paper. The *boreal* forest, the second largest type, occupies a broad swathe of land extending across Alaska, Canada, and northern Russia.

Despite the wide distribution of forests, just five countries account for over half of the world's forests (table 5.3). Forests account for over half of the area of the Russian Federation and Brazil, while these two countries, along with Canada, are the most abundant in terms of forest resources measured on a per capita basis.

Natural and plantation forests

Humans have planted trees throughout human history, and sometimes in great quantities, for a variety of ends. Today there are plantations that have been established for environmental objectives, to control erosion and halt desertification;

Table 5.3   The five largest forested countries, 2000

Country	Total land area (000 ha)	Total forest area (000 ha)	Forest as % of land area	Forest area per capita (ha)
Russian Federation	1,688,851	851,392	50.4	5.8
Brazil	845,651	543,905	64.3	3.2
Canada	922,097	244,571	26.5	7.9
United States	915,895	225,993	24.7	0.8
China	932,743	163,480	17.5	0.1
Total 5 countries	5,305,237	2,029,341	38.3	n.a.

Source: FAO 2001a

Table 5.4   Representative rotation length and growth rates for different forest types around the world

Forest type	Country or region	Typical rotation (years)	Mean annual increment (m^3/ha/yr)
Tropical plantation hardwoods			
Acacia mangium	Indonesia	10	20
Eucalyptus	Brazil	5–20	30–70
Teak	Tropics	40–60	14
Temperate plantation softwoods			
Pinus radiata	New Zealand, Chile	25–30	20–24
Pinus elliotti, other pine species	US South	25	10
Natural forests			
Tropical hardwood	South America		3
Temperate softwood	British Columbia		1.5–5.3
Boreal softwood	Finland, Siberia	60–200	1–2.5

Source: Various in Tomberlin and Buongiorno 2001

social objectives, the provision of fuelwood and building materials for rural communities; and economic objectives, the production of fiber for industrial purposes. In 2000, plantations covered 186.7 million ha or just under 5 percent of the world's forest area. In some countries, such as India and China, they account for over 25 percent of the area classified as forest. In New Zealand, commercial plantations now provide virtually all the timber for the country's forest products industry.

Commercial plantations are commonly established with fast growing species such as eucalyptus, acacia, and certain pine species. Under suitable growing conditions some species can be harvested in as little as seven years. On shorter rotations they can provide fiber suitable for pulp and papermaking and fiberboard, while longer-term rotations are required if they are to provide fiber for lumber and other solid wood products. Table 5.4 shows some representative rotation and growth rates for some commonly grown plantation species and compares them to the growth rates for natural forests found in different regions of the world. The growth rates can differ by an order of magnitude or more between natural forests and plantations. In part, this reflects the more favorable growing conditions associated with plantations in tropical and temperate areas, but also the application of additional inputs such as fertilizer and the use of selected *cultivars*.

5.3   BIOLOGICAL AND ECONOMIC ASPECTS OF FORESTS

One of the main issues involved in modeling forestry problems is that of choosing the appropriate scale. The forest may be as small as a five-hectare private wood-lot or span two continents (as is the case for the boreal forest covering the northern part of Europe and North America). It may contain a diverse mix of tree species, or in the case of a plantation, homogeneous timber stands distinguished only by age.

The most common unit of analysis used in investigating forestry issues is the timber stand. In general, a timber stand consists of trees within a contiguous area that share similar characteristics such as age, species composition, or *site quality*. A forest can then be made up of a number of stands that are commonly managed as individual units.

The fact that trees are fixed in location has several important implications. First, it is possible to gather relatively precise information about certain aspects of the resource, such as existing timber volumes and expected future timber volumes. Second, the economic and environmental benefits associated with timber stands can vary directly with their location. Third, it is possible to specify property rights (see chapter 2) that can be assigned to the trees alone or extend to the land on which they stand that has important implications for how forests are managed.

In general, a stand becomes more valuable with age as the standing volume increases. In addition, it is also often assumed that the per unit volume value of trees also increases with age, reflecting the higher prices associated with older and larger trees. At the same time, the environmental amenities associated change as a timber stand matures. There are a number of different variables, including but not limited to: forage for both domestic grazing stock and wildlife; wildlife habitat; water flow; and recreation opportunities. The flow of these benefits from a timber stand changes over time as trees mature. Some of these may vary inversely with the age of the trees; for example, forage opportunities and water flows will decrease as trees grow and their canopies close while recreational values may increase. The abundance of different plant and animal species will change as the habitat changes; some species such as spotted owls or woodland caribou prefer mature timber, while others such as deer are better adapted to the more open conditions commonly associated with younger forests. The ability of trees to sequester carbon is also dependent upon the size and age of the trees.

A forest can contain a diverse mix of stands, where local factors such as the average temperature; precipitation patterns; and soil fertility; and local variations in topography favor particular tree species over others. The location of the forest or stand also influences the economic value of the trees; the costs involved in transporting the timber to processing facilities and eventually to markets, and the harvesting costs associated with the terrain (again influenced by local factors) determine the ultimate value of the standing timber.

Within a forest, these costs may be such that standing timber has no commercial value (since the price of the forest products that can be derived from the wood, net of all processing costs, just equals these transportation and harvesting costs). This limit marks the *extensive margin*, beyond which trees have no commercial value. These timber stands may consist of the forest that lies in remote areas, far from any transportation system or processing facilities, or timber stands found in rugged terrain. Other land uses, such as agriculture, may also compete with forestland. Where the economic returns to forestland equal those of competing land uses, this delineates the *intensive margin*. The intensive margin is also used to sometimes describe the level of economic utilization within a timber stand; certain species or smaller trees may be uneconomic and therefore be left behind, depending upon harvesting policies.

Choosing when to harvest

The typical relationship between the age of a timber stand (or tree) and volume is shown in figure 5.1. The growth rate increases over time to a maximum, then declines and eventually becomes zero when trees cease growing as they reach maturity (and may actually become negative when trees are lost to rot and decay).

The *average* annual increase in tree or timber stand volume is known as the Mean Annual Increment, or MAI, while the annual increase in timber volume (the change in volume from year to year) is known as the Current Annual Increment or CAI. A common management approach has been to choose the harvest age at which the MAI of the trees in the timber stand is maximized (which is sometimes called the Culmination of the MAI or CMAI). In a forest where the number of even-aged stands equals the rotation age, harvesting a stand each year and replanting that stand will yield the maximum harvest by volume that can be sustained over time (since each stand advances in age and the trees that are T_{m-1} mature will become available for harvest in the succeeding year). The problem is formulated as then choosing the time to harvest, T, that maximizes harvest volumes over time.

$$\text{Maximize } W = \frac{V(T)}{T} \tag{1}$$

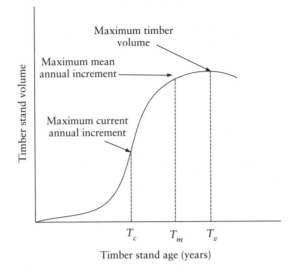

Figure 5.1 Relationship between timber stand volume and age

Taking the derivative with respect to the time to cut down the trees (T) we obtain

$$dW/dT = V'(T)/T - V(T)/T^2 = 0$$

$$\Rightarrow \quad \frac{V(T)}{T} = V'(T) \tag{2}$$

Figure 5.2 shows the MAI (which corresponds to the average product curve or V(T)/T) and the CAI (the marginal product curve or V'(T)) based on the growth function depicted in figure 5.1. The CMAI is reached where the CAI crosses the MAI curve at T_m. This is equivalent to choosing the stock and harvesting effort that will maximize the sustained yield in fisheries (MSY). Under this approach each year $1/T_m$ of the forest would be harvested (assuming all stands are identical). This is otherwise known as the fully managed forest and in the past has been the basis for calculations used in determining sustainable harvest levels on public lands in North America and Europe.

Economic models

Much as in the case in fisheries, a maximization of total production has been the focus of public resource managers. This approach based on biological criteria has been criticized because it does not take economic criteria into account, and we now turn to economic models of timber management that have been focused on identifying the optimal age to harvest trees. The problem is phrased as choosing the optimal rotation age for a forest stand, given a set of exogenous variables

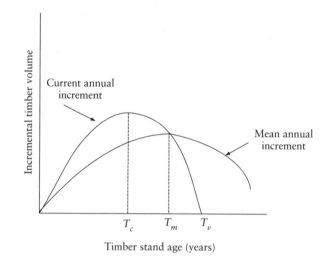

Figure 5.2   Mean annual increment, current annual increment, and the CMAI

describing the growth of trees, the outputs they produce, and the discount rate, δ, to maximize the value from harvesting the trees.

The single stand, one rotation problem

In the most basic formulation of the problem, it is assumed that the stand has been established and that there are no costs involved in tending the stand, and that a new stand will not be established after harvest. Expressing the value of the tree at time t as the constant price net of harvesting, P, times the volume V(t), the net present value of a harvest at time T is then:

$$\pi = ((P)(V(T))e^{-\delta T} \tag{3}$$

The one period optimal rotation problem can then be written as choosing the optimal harvest age, T_s, that maximizes the net present value:

$$\frac{d\pi}{dT} = ((P)(V(T)))e^{-\delta T}(-\delta) + (P)V'(T)e^{-\delta T} = 0 \tag{4}$$

The first order condition can be rewritten as:

$$PV'(T) = \delta PV(T) \quad \text{or} \quad \frac{V'(T)}{V(T)} = \delta \tag{5}$$

The left-hand side of (5) is the instantaneous increase in value of standing timber from waiting (the net revenue accruing from the increase in growth) to harvest the trees while the right-hand side is the return if all the trees were harvested and the money put in a bank to receive a rate of interest equal to the discount rate. When the net price (P) is constant, this is equivalent to choosing the rotation length where the growth rate (expressed in percentage terms) is equal to the discount rate. The example in box 5.1 shows how the economically optimum time to harvest is chosen when actual data on growth rates and timber values are used to weigh the benefits of postponing the harvest one more year against the forgone income.

BOX 5.1 CHOOSING WHEN TO HARVEST

The growth function in figure 5.1 was drawn from actual data for Douglas fir trees growing in the Pacific northwest in the US (Clawson, 1977). The fitted curve is $V = 40t + 3.1t^2 - 0.016t^3$ where volume is expressed in cubic feet per acre. The table below shows the standing volume, mean annual increment, and current annual increment at 10 year intervals and selected years. The reported values in the two right-hand columns are based on an estimated stumpage rate of $10 per cubic metre starting at age 30 and rising by $2 every 10 years until age 80 and then remaining constant at $20 per cubic metre. The values are then converted into cubic feet per acre. They show the mean annual increment reaches its maximum between ages 90 and 100; however, discounting the value shortens the optimal harvest age in the case of a 3 percent discount rate to age 70, and in the case of a 9 percent discount rate to age 30 – the moment it becomes profitable to harvest. This illustrates the power of discounting, where the longer timespan associated with timber production typically reduces future values significantly, a problem explored later in the discussion on public land management.

Age	Volume (ft³/acre)	Current annual increment (ft³/acre)	Mean annual increment (ft³/acre)	Current annual increment as % of volume	Value discounted at 3% ($)	Value discounted at 9% ($)
1	43	43	43	99.8	0	0
10	694	95	69	13.6	0	0
20	1,912	143	96	7.5	0	0
30	3,558	181	119	5.1	415	76
40	5,536	210	138	3.8	577	60
50	7,750	229	155	3.0	701	41
60	10,104	239	168	2.4	777	26
70	12,502	239	179	1.9	805	15
80	14,848	230	186	1.5	791	9
90	17,046	210	189	1.2	675	4
100	19,000	182	190	1.0	560	2
125	22,188	68	178	0.3	312	0
149	21,856	−98	147	−0.4	151	0
150	21,750	−106	145	−0.5	146	0

The single stand, continuous forestry problem

If we assume that the land will be dedicated to forestry we then need to incorporate the effect of growing subsequent crops of trees on the same site. Martin Faustmann in 1849 was the first to identify the problem correctly as choosing the harvest period to maximize the net present value of a series of future harvests, or using the previous terminology, the optimal rotation age T_f for a series of sequential harvests of a timber stand on the same site. We now introduce c as the replanting cost associated with establishing the next stand of trees immediately following harvest but again assume that the first stand has already been established:

$$\pi = (PV(T) - c)e^{-\delta T}\{1 + e^{-\delta T} + e^{-\delta 2T} + e^{-\delta 3T} \dots\} \tag{6}$$

which can be rewritten as

$$\frac{(PV(T) - c)e^{-\delta T}}{1 - e^{-\delta T}} \quad \text{or} \quad \frac{PV(T) - c}{e^{-\delta T} - 1} \tag{7}$$

so setting

$$\frac{d\pi}{dT} = 0$$

yields

$$\frac{d\pi}{dT} = \frac{(PV(T) - c)(-e^{\delta T}\delta)}{(e^{\delta T} - 1)^2} + \frac{PV'(T)}{(e^{\delta T} - 1)} = 0 \tag{8}$$

rewriting the above equation as

$$PV'(T) = \frac{\delta(PV(T) - c)e^{\delta T}}{e^{\delta T} - 1} = \frac{\delta(PV(T) - c)}{1 - e^{-\delta T}}$$

and multiplying both sides by $(1 - e^{-\delta T})$ yields

$$PV'(T) = \delta(PV(T) - c) + PV'(T)e^{-\delta T} \tag{9}$$

The equation again equates the marginal benefits of harvesting against the marginal cost of waiting. It now includes a second term on the right-hand side that reflects the opportunity cost in delaying the establishment of new trees that can grow faster. This additional increase in cost attributed to waiting therefore reduces the optimum rotation age compared to the single stand case (this is easiest to see by setting $c = 0$ as it is in the single stand, one rotation case and seeing that the right-hand side is now greater. For the equality to be re-established the forest owner must harvest sooner where $V'(T)$ is greater at an earlier age).

We can express this new factor in another way. The second term on the right-hand side can be rewritten where T_f or T^* has been chosen to optimize the problem as:

$$PV'(T^*)e^{-\delta T} = \frac{\delta(PV(T^*) - c)e^{\delta T}}{(e^{\delta T} - 1)e^{\delta T}} = \delta\left\{\frac{(PV(T^*) - c)}{e^{\delta T} - 1}\right\} = \delta\pi^* \tag{10}$$

The term π^* is then the capitalized value of the land from growing trees in perpetuity on that site. The term $\delta\pi^*$ has been called the site or land rent, and reflects the flow of that value per period of time associated with the use of that land dedicated to forestry. It can also be thought of as the opportunity cost associated with using the land to grow trees.

Comparison of rotation ages

Each of these rules provides a different harvest age. We can compare how the optimal harvest age changes when we use economic criteria rather than biological criteria, using the logistic growth function from our earlier example. Doing so enables us to plot the optimum rotation ages yielded by different formulations of the problem.

If we are using biological criteria, we are interested in maximizing volume. Figure 5.2 expresses the average annual growth $(V(T)/T)$ and incremental annual growth of timber $V'(T)$ as a function of the timber age T. We can express both the average annual growth and incremental growth as a function of total timber

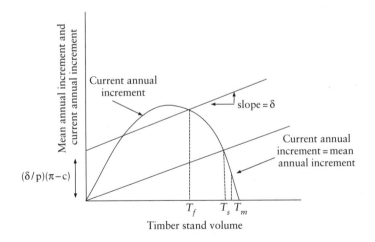

Figure 5.3   Comparison of optimal rotation ages

volume $(V(T))$ since timber volume increases directly with age. The relationship looks the same with the only difference that the horizontal axis now shows timber volume, not age, in figure 5.3. The rotation length that maximizes the average timber volume over time is when the mean annual growth rate equals the average annual growth rate, given by T_m in figure 5.2.[1]

Under the single stand, one time harvest problem, the optimal rotation length is given by equation 5. This can be rewritten as:

$$V'(T) = \delta V(T) \tag{11}$$

This gives a line with slope delta through the origin; the optimal harvest age is then given by T_s where the line intersects $V'(T)$. In this case the trees are harvested earlier when we use economic criteria rather than physical criteria.

If we are looking at practicing continuous forestry, we then use the Faustmann rule. In order to do so, we need to express the relationship derived under the Faustmann formulation as a function of the growth rate. Rewriting

$$PV'(T) = \delta(PV(T) - c) + PV'(T)e^{-\delta T} \tag{12}$$

by substituting $\delta \pi$ into the equation and dividing by P yields:

$$V'(T) = \delta V(T) + \frac{\delta}{P}(\pi - c) \tag{13}$$

This yields a line with slope δ and intercept $\delta/P\,(\pi-c)$ that can be plotted against volume $V(T)$. If forestry yields positive economic values such that the capitalized value of the land exceeds the replanting cost (so that $\pi > c$) then the line is shifted up and the optimal rotation length will be T_f, less than that in case of the one period model. If $\pi = c$, then the cost of replanting exactly offsets the value expected from future harvests (which also take into account the cost of replanting in the future). In this case, there is no value associated with future harvests and the solution is the same as in the single stand case. If $\pi < c$, then the land expectation value is negative, suggesting that the land will not remain in forestry since after harvest the replanting cost will exceed the expected value if the land is reforested (so that one would not expect a rational decision-maker to replant).

Changes in exogenous factors

Both the single stand, single period and Faustmann models can be used to investigate the influence of different exogenous variables upon the optimal rotation length. Examples include changes in the discount rate; changes in net price; and changes in the cost of replanting. Other factors that can be modeled include: changes in the growth rate; changes in the productivity of the timber stand; and the impacts of different types of taxes. The Faustmann model is most commonly used since it can provide the short- and long-run effects from these changes. Using the first order conditions and comparative statics, one can show that an increase in the discount rate will shorten the optimal harvest, while a decrease in the net price would lengthen the optimal rotation. This can be seen in figure 5.3; increases in δ, the discount rate, will steepen the slope and shift the intercept up, shortening the optimal rotation age, while increases in the net price, P, will shift the intercept up (which makes intuitive sense since the land will now be worth more).

However, one cannot establish a general rule regarding the optimal rotation if more than one variable changes unless one specifies the relationship between the parameters. For example, if the discount rate increases but the price decreases, the change in rotation depends upon the relative magnitude of the two opposing effects.

Incorporating environmental amenities

The major extension of the Faustmann model has been the incorporation of environmental amenities into the harvest decision (Hartman, 1976). Positive environmental values can lengthen or shorten the rotation age and may even lead to optima where harvest does not take place. The results depend on how the amenities are modeled; whether or not they increase with stand or tree age, and their value relative to other values (timber and non-timber products).

For the *single period rotation*, the equation can be rewritten so that:

$$\max \pi(T) = \int_0^t e^{-\delta t} F(t) dt + e^{-\delta T} PV(t) \tag{14}$$

Where $PV(t)$ equals the value of the trees at harvest and $F(t)$ is the value of the amenities flowing from the timber stand over time. In this case, maximizing social welfare requires us to maximize the discounted sum of environmental benefits generated by the timber stand over time and the discounted timber value at the time of harvest. This yields the first order conditions for an interior maximum:

$$F(T) + PV'(T) = \delta PV(T) \tag{15}$$

or

$$\frac{V'(T)}{V(T)} = \delta - \frac{F(T)}{PV(T)} \tag{16}$$

and where the second order condition for an interior maximum is:

$$F'(T) + PV''(T) < \delta PV'(T) \tag{17}$$

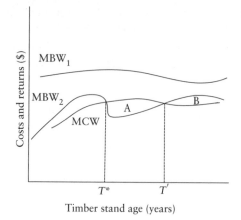

Figure 5.4   Whether or not to harvest in the presence of environmental amenities

The optimal rotation involves choosing the harvest period at which the marginal benefit of delaying the harvest (the increase in the value of the trees and the flow of amenities from the standing timber for the period) just equals the opportunity cost of waiting (the forgone interest on the value of the trees for the period) as in equation (15). Where $F(t)$ is zero (no amenities), equation (16) collapses to the standard condition under the single period rule – the harvest should take place when growth equals the discount rate. The presence of environmental amenities, however, means that $F(T)$ will be positive so the optimal rotation will be longer (since the growth rate will be lower for equation (16) to hold).

The second order conditions in equation (17) are important because they show that harvest will take place only if the value of the timber exceeds the flow of environmental benefits at some age T. It may be the case that the amenities are significant enough to delay the harvest so that it takes place when the growth rate is negative (so that the right-hand side term in equation (16) is greater than the discount rate). Finally, it may be possible that the value of the environmental amenities exceeds the value of timber such that it is optimal to never harvest (in which case there is no interior maximum).

We can see how the level of environmental amenities can determine whether or not harvest will take place by looking at equation (15). The terms on the left-hand side represent the marginal benefit of waiting (MBW) – letting the timber stand remain (grow) for another year means we enjoy the flow of environmental amenities $(F(T))$ and the increase in stumpage value $(PV'(T))$. The right-hand side of the equation represents the cost from waiting another year (MCW) – the forgone interest we could earn from depositing the money in the bank $(\delta PV(T))$. The first order conditions tell us that we want to harvest when the marginal benefit of waiting just equals the cost of waiting (or MBW = MCW).

Figure 5.4 shows how the level of environmental amenities can change the marginal benefit and the decision to harvest. If the flow of environmental amenities is given by MBW_1 the optimal decision is to never harvest because MBW_1 is always greater than MCW. Where the level of environmental amenities is given by MBW_2 the stand may or may not be cut. The decision will depend upon the value to be gained from never cutting the stand (represented by area B discounted as the stand age goes to the limit).

Harvest will take place at T^* if the discounted opportunity cost from forgone interest on stumpage (area A) exceeds the discounted flow of environmental amenities and gain in stumpage values (area B) from never harvesting. In that case, T^* is not only an interior maximum but also a global maximum (note that T' is a local minimum). If, however, the discounted flow of environmental services from letting the trees grow is greater than the forgone interest (area B is greater than area A) then the forest should never be harvested.

Swallow et al. (1990) introduce the idea of nonconvexities into the forest benefits function; in other words, MBW may have multiple peaks and troughs because $F(T)$ seesaws up and down with the age of the timber stand. This may reflect the fact that some environmental benefits decrease as trees grow, some may display a concave relationship first increasing and then decreasing, while some may only be associated with older stands so that the overall flow of environmental amenities might change considerably over time as the stand ages. They use examples from national forests in Montana: water flow and grazing opportunities decrease directly with stand age; ruffed grouse habitat peaks when trees are 20 years old; while wilderness and old growth species values are associated with mature timber. In this case, the marginal benefit line may cross the marginal opportunity cost in more than one place; the decision-maker then has to check the interior maximum against one another as well as the case of not harvesting to determine the global maximum.

Finally, the continuous rotation problem incorporating environmental amenities is expressed as

$$\max_t \pi(T) = \frac{\int_0^t e^{-\delta t}F(t) + e^{-\delta_T}pV(t)}{1 - e^{-\delta_T}} \tag{19}$$

The harvest age, T, that solves this problem depends not only on the flow of environmental amenities over time associated with a timber stand, but also whether the decision-maker starts with an existing stand on the site or bare land which influence the timing of those environmental benefits. The decision-maker will practice continuous forestry (planting and subsequently harvesting the trees on an ongoing basis) if they start with bare land and the environmental benefits to be gained from delaying or forgoing harvest are outweighed by the marginal opportunity cost of forgone future stumpage values gained from practicing commercial forestry on that site. However, if the decision-maker starts with an existing timber stand on the site, they may or may not harvest depending upon the age of the trees. The presence of trees on the site can reduce both the marginal opportunity cost (since a portion of the forgone stumpage values may already be sunk into the standing trees) and increase the marginal benefits of waiting since the decision-maker may already be enjoying environmental amenities. If the trees are old enough, the combination of sunk costs and high enough level of environmental amenities may be such that it is optimal to never harvest (Strang, 1983).

Why rotations under market conditions may differ from the social optimum

The optimum rotation age achieved through private markets may differ significantly from the socially optimal age for several reasons. First, there may be environmental benefits associated with the timber stand that are not taken into account by the decision-maker. These externalities can lead to rotation ages that are too short or may even lead a private manager to harvest where a public manager would not. Second, where the private discount rate is higher than the social discount rate, this will lead to shorter rotation ages. Finally, imperfect markets may also yield incorrect prices that then lead to incorrect rotation ages.

Timber supply models

One area of research interest is in modeling the timber supply function. Depending upon the research question, this can take place at two different scales. One involves the determination of timber outputs from a particular forest or location, or the optimal sequence of harvesting a series of different timber stands. The second exercise takes place at a larger scale and involves modeling aggregate supply from a number of different sources.

Forest level modeling

The Faustmann model can be used to generate the optimal harvest age for a timber stand. This harvest rule can be applied to a series of otherwise identical stands that differ only in age (the fully managed forest described earlier in the chapter). Aggregating across these stands yields the supply curve where each stand is cut when it reaches the optimal age with a constant amount supplied each year. The model can then be used to investigate short- and long-run changes in timber supply assuming that the forestland base is fixed and that the forest will continue to be managed on an even-age basis. Therefore, any changes that shorten the optimal rotation will decrease the long-run annual harvest from that forest (since the trees that will be harvested will be younger and smaller) while in the short run, supply would actually increase as managers harvest those trees older than the optimal harvest age.

The model can be modified to determine the optimal harvesting schedule for a forest, based on the initial starting conditions where one can either assume that the forest is made up of stands of a similar age or it may be comprised of stands of different maturity in which case harvesting would be staggered. In some cases, it can be shown that the supply curve for an area would be backwards bending as increases in price reduce the rotation age sufficiently such that the volume harvested falls on an annual basis. In these models, the price is exogenously given so that any variation in timber supplied over time does not influence the price and land is fixed. However, the Faustmann model has been criticized for not meeting the normal neoclassical criteria of maximizing a profit function nor does it expressly include land as a factor of production. Theoretical models that explicitly incorporate land into the production function can generate timber supply curves that are upward sloping as more land is used to grow trees (the extensive margin shifts out) or capital is substituted for timber to increase output (a shift in of the intensive margin).

Most timber supply models for specific forests are not derived on a theoretical basis. Instead, the models rely on the introduction of constraints that link timber stands together over time in the production of different outputs. These constraints, and the weight given different outputs, create a number of possible paths for timber supply over time. The optimal path chosen is dependent upon the values and assumptions embodied in the model, which require the use of data applicable to the particular forest under investigation. These constraints might be requirements that the annual harvest remain constant over time, that a certain proportion of the forest be maintained in various age classes, or that a timber stand adjacent to a previously harvested area cannot be harvested until the trees on that site reach a certain age or size.

Optimal land allocation

The relationship between location and the ability of the forest to supply multiple outputs (as we shall see in the section on public land use issues) have led economists to investigate how heterogeneous land quality may influence forest management. It is possible to construct models that show that providing both timber and non-timber outputs (e.g. recreational opportunities, environmental amenities) from the same unit of land is inefficient and that allowing different units of land to specialize in different types of production may lead to increased welfare as shown by Vincent and Binkley (1993). Swallow et al. (1997) show that the temporal and spatial interaction between timber stands can lead to different management practices (such as different rotation periods) on otherwise identical units of land. The relative efficiency gains upon specialization depend upon the extent to which different outputs are competing vs. complementary. Again, it is not possible to specify any general rules without again identifying the parameters of interest and applying them to a particular forest. The problem is considerably complicated when some of the outputs have considerable non-market values and compete with timber production, as is the case for preservation values associated with valuable old growth timber.

Issues in forest level modeling

The problem of modeling a forest becomes considerably more complex when we allow for interactions and feedback effects between timber stands within the forest. These interactions may take place over time or spatially. The interactions may involve complementarities or substitution effects between different uses, and where the magnitude may depend upon the relative proximity of the stands (either in time or location). One timber stand might be managed to produce timber while an adjacent timber stand is managed for wildlife habitat; however, two otherwise identical timber stands might be managed differently where a river divides the two stands. As is the case in determining the optimal rotation where more than one variable is changing, it turns out that determining the optimal management strategy depends on using data specific to the forest in question. Swallow et al. (1997) show that identical timber stands may be managed in significantly different ways with just small changes in exogenous variables such as site productivity and price. The investigation of these kinds of models has relied mainly on empirical approaches, using data gleaned from different forests to examine the optimal management strategy for a particular set of circumstances.

Although the Faustmann model, because of its tractability, has been the most widely used, there is no single unique model used in forestry. The problem of integrating stand into forest level models, the choice of scale, the specification of spatial relationships, and the number of different variables of interest besides simply timber outputs, have led to the development of problem-specific models designed to address a particular research issue. In general, the approach has been to use either linear programming or Markov-style models (in which timber stands progress through predictable states) and simulate either outcomes under different management approaches or use goal-seeking algorithms. These models require actual data and will necessitate the use of non-market valuation techniques for many of the variables of interest. These empirical requirements have to be kept in mind in the analysis of large-scale, forest-level issues since missing data, as well as any limitations of the model, may limit the conclusions that can be drawn.

Forest-sector models

There is a second set of models that are best characterized as forest-sector models. These larger-scale models aggregate timber supply from different forests and attempt to explain the demand and supply of wood products at the macroeconomic scale. One of the principal goals of policy-makers in modeling (aside from investigating optimal management strategies for different forests) is to develop long-term projections about future timber supply and demand to identify any potential gaps. Because of the long time span associated with timber production, a long-standing concern has been the identification and prevention of future timber shortages.

Table 5.5 Annual harvest by ownership in the US in 2001 (million ft^3)

	Volume	% of total
National forest	819.4	5.1
Other public	929.2	5.8
Forest industry	4,677.9	29.4
Non-industrial private	9,506.8	59.7
Total	15,933.3	100.0

Source: USDA 2002

These models use several different methods. One approach involves the construction of supply curves in different regions based on the physical availability of timber and cost of accessing that timber. Given different assumptions about demand, equilibrium prices are then determined in these timber markets. These markets may be explicitly linked through trade in the model (this can be intra-regional trade or international trade). Another approach has been to use historical data to estimate timber supply curves based on different characteristics, including biological as well as economic criteria such as ownership. There are two principal sources of timber, public forests and private forests, and their supply responsiveness depends in part upon institutional constraints, which are determined by ownership.

Two main groups own private forests: non-industrial private landowners (forest land held by individuals that may not be held for commercial reasons) and industrial forest landowners (held by forest products companies and other institutions expressly for the purpose of growing and selling timber). Table 5.5 shows the importance of these different groups in terms of US timber supply (*National forest* refers to federally owned land in the national forest system while *Other public* includes other federally-owned land as well as land owned by states and other levels of government).

These models have been used to project global timber demand and supply to smaller models examining the effect of different government policies on timber markets, such as the impacts of restricting timber harvests on US public lands and the impact of tariffs on Canadian lumber exports to the US.

5.4 CURRENT FOREST ISSUES

The high degree of diversity of the world's forests contributes to the complexity of the modeling problem described above. Not only do the biophysical factors underlying the forest vary, there is a wide range of institutional arrangements that govern forests around the world and help determine outcomes. Public ownership of forests continues to remain extremely important. Table 5.6 shows the percentage of forestland that is publicly or privately owned (measured in terms of area) for the five largest forested countries. Two of these countries, the US and Canada,

Table 5.6   Forest ownership for selected countries (based on area)

Country	% publicly owned	% privately owned
Russian Federation	100	0
Brazil	90	10
Canada	93.5	6.5
United States	43.7	56.3
China	45	55
Sweden	30	70
Finland	20	80

Source: World Trends

are the first and second largest producers of forest products; Sweden and Finland (included in the table) are the third and fourth. The variation between countries is striking; public ownership is dominant in Russia, Brazil, and Canada, while private ownership is larger for the other four countries.

This adds another dimension to forestry, as governments grapple with the (at times) competing uses of forestland and the trade-off between the economic and environmental aspects of commercial forestry. This becomes considerably more complex in some regions, where forestland is owned under a mix of institutions, ranging from small landowners with woodlots and rural communities with traditional rights over neighboring land to forest products companies with their own commercial woodlands and state institutions.

These differing patterns of ownership and institutional arrangements have yielded a variety of different patterns in terms of how forests are used. In Canada, forest product companies rely on long-term leases with provincial governments for their timber that incorporate not only economic but also environmental and social objectives; while in the US, companies gain access to public timber through auctions but mainly rely on timber from private lands (see table 5.5).

In rich countries, the focus has been on the management of public forests and the appropriate mix of outputs from public land, with a growing emphasis on preservation and the provision of environmental amenities. For poor countries, issues center on the conversion of forestland to other uses.

Public forest management policies

Increasing attention in forestry is now being paid to the multiple aspects of forestlands, and in particular the wide range of environmental amenities associated with forests, including the role they provide in habitat for different species, their role in regulating water run-off, in sequestering carbon, and providing non-timber goods to local communities. This has occurred at the same time as there has been a shift in the public debate centered on ideas of sustainability and on how we use

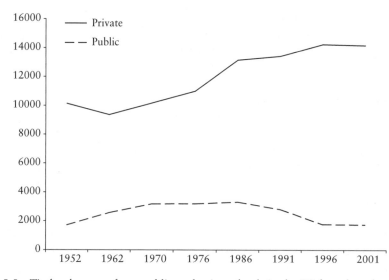

Figure 5.5   Timber harvests from public and private lands in the US for selected years (millions of cubic feet)

Source: USDA 2002

existing forests, as shown by changes in the management of national forests in the US described below.

National forests in the US

National forests in the US account for 147 million acres of the 747 million acres of the total forest area (this excludes other public forest land held outside of the national forest system). National forests were established in response to fears of a timber shortage as the US expanded westward in the nineteenth century and were meant to overcome the problem of "cut and run" associated with early settlers that would mine the forest, logging the timber without reforesting. Over time, the purpose of these national forests has shifted from the provision of timber to the forest products industry to that of multiple use – the attempts to provide a range of outputs including timber, recreational opportunities, and environmental values from the forest resource. This shift has been accompanied by a rancorous debate over the use of public lands and repeated lawsuits from both environmental groups and industrial users over what constitutes the appropriate mix of outputs. The effective outcome of this debate has been a shift towards greater preservation of public lands in recent years and an increased reliance on private lands (and imports) to supply domestic demand for forest products as seen in figure 5.5. In the eastern US, public ownership accounts for 17.4 percent of forestlands, while in the west, public ownership accounts for 68.9 percent (USDA 2002).

The regional impacts of this policy were quite distinct as the western US forest products industry had to adjust to a sharp reduction in available timber supply; at the same time, increased demand led to sustained price increases that led to sharply increased harvesting on private lands across the US and a higher level of imports.

This debate is taking place in other countries as well, as they attempt to determine what mix of outputs to produce and how to best achieve them. In many countries, the debate is taking place under the larger debate about sustainable development and the long-run impact of timber harvesting on forest ecosystems. Increased values are being placed upon natural forests, but different values and goals held by various forest stakeholders – rural communities, indigenous groups, environmentalists, governments, and forest industry firms and workers – make it difficult to agree on common definitions let alone management approaches.

One idea under consideration is zoning, under which land would be allocated to three zones. Commercial forestry activities would be intensified on land deemed suitable for timber production, while the second zone would permit less intensive harvesting; and the third zone would consist of land set aside for preservation. The success of this approach depends upon the economic feasibility of practicing more intensive forestry coupled with the ability to reach a consensus on what land falls into what zone and the suitable mix of outputs from the intermediate zone providing both timber and environmental outputs. One ambitious suggestion has been to preserve all natural forests and to rely on plantations for all our forest products (see box 5.2).

Critiques of public management

A common approach to the management of forest on public lands has been to manage for maximum sustained yield, or the greatest volume of timber that can be removed on an annual basis in perpetuity. This has led to the idea of the fully managed forest, where the forest is divided into T equal-sized areas, where T represents the rotation age (assuming all areas are equally productive). Each year, one of the areas is harvested so that over time the forest will be made up of a series of different timber stands, each representing an age class of T-1, T-2, T-3 ... This timber volume, which can be sustained in perpetuity, has often been called the Allowable Annual Cut (AAC) in North America. This constraint can be modified such that it provides a series of equal harvest volumes on an annual basis (even flow) or may be expressed such that long-term harvest levels do not drop below a specified level (non-declining even flow).

Where a component of the harvest consists of mature trees (beyond the rotation age), as has commonly been the case for public forests in North America, this approach has been modified to permit higher harvest levels because of the larger wood volumes associated with older trees. One example of this is the *Hanzlick rule*, in which the volume that can be harvested annually equals the sustained yield

BOX 5.2   PARK OR PLANTATION?

Victor and Ausubel (2000) have suggested a concerted policy effort to preserve the world's forests through improving crop yields (to reduce pressures to convert forestland to agricultural production), developing better technology to improve wood utilization (including recycling), and concentrating forestry in intensive plantations. They argue such a policy would permit 3 billion hectares of natural forests to be set aside while 400 million hectares of intensively managed plantations could provide all of our future forest product needs. Otherwise, they predict that total forest area will be reduced by 200 million hectares by mid-century, while 40 percent of the 3 billion hectares of natural forest will be managed as industrial forests with an emphasis on fiber production. Such a change would require that the current area of forest plantations more than double from just under 190 million hectares today. While it may be biologically feasible to produce sufficient timber from a smaller landbase, the economic feasibility of expanding the area of plantations depends upon two key variables. First, plantations will have to compete against other land uses – principally agricultural uses that currently account for a third of the world's land area – and where the demand for land to supply food can be expected to increase with population growth. Second, the cost of establishing plantations can be considerable, especially given the length of time capital can be tied up in the standing trees. If timber prices are not high enough to overcome these two hurdles, firms and individuals will be unlikely to engage in plantation forestry voluntarily, thereby requiring a government role. An additional problem is that the highest potential for such plantations is often found in developing countries where land is already intensively used and there are limited government funds for such investments.

(based on what the forest is theoretically capable of producing managed on an even-age basis) plus the additional volume of timber associated with the mature timber that will be harvested as the forest is converted into an even-age forest. This additional volume is divided equally over the rotation period of the forest so that harvest levels will be initially higher through the first rotation; there will then be a *fall down effect* when all the mature timber is harvested and the forest becomes a fully managed forest.

Economists have criticized the use of rules like these because they ignore the opportunity cost associated with the longer rotation periods by holding mature timber that may no longer be growing and instead emphasize harvest levels that remain relatively constant (or change in a gradual manner). The imposition of sustained yield policies on public lands in Canada and the US and the presence of mature trees has also led to what has been termed the allowable cut effect (ACE) that has also been critiqued on economic grounds. A proposed silvicultural project, such as tree pruning or thinning designed to increase either the volume or the value of timber at harvest time may fail standard cost–benefit tests. On public lands in North America, however, the harvest level is determined based on biological criteria such as growth rates and requirements that trees cannot be harvested before they reach a certain age. If the proposed treatment does yield a future increase in timber volumes, or reduce the harvest age, this then raises the steady long-run harvest level on public lands since more will be available to be harvested in the future. The ACE describes in general what happens when a change in policies relaxes the even flow constraint and permits the harvest of more timber volume. The ability of firms to harvest more *now* resulting from the proposed treatment makes silvicultural investments much more attractive since firms immediately receive the benefits through a permanent increase in ACE, rather than having to wait fifty years or more.

ACE will only work if there is excess inventory (such as old-growth timber that is characteristic of public forests in North America) so that the government can increase annual harvest levels. In an even-aged forest, where there is an age class for each stand, any silvicultural treatment would be evaluated on its effect when the treated stand reached harvest age.

The ACE arises because of the institutional constraints imposed by even-flow principles (or some kind of general volume regulation). Economists have criticized it because the decision to engage in a silvicultural treatment that will affect future timber yields and values – based on the ability to increase current harvest levels today – is based on the way regulatory constraints imposed by even-flow timber scheduling are relaxed rather than on the fundamental economics of such a decision, although some have argued that, given these constraints, it can be used to positive effect (Haley and Luckert, 1995). The example in box 5.3 shows how the relaxation of a regulatory constraint can change the apparent profitability of an investment, leading to the ACE effect.

BOX 5.3   AN EXAMPLE OF THE ALLOWABLE CUT EFFECT AT WORK

A firm may look at fertilizing a one-hectare timber stand to increase the yield at maturity. If the increase in yield was an additional 10 cubic meters per hectare in 50 years, and the trees are worth $20 per cubic meter at harvest, the discounted value of that $200 in 50 years time based on a 10 percent interest rate would be $1.70 today (10 cubic meters of increased volume × $20 in 50 years discounted back to the present). The firm would likely be unwilling to invest any money in fertilizing. If, however, the firm is harvesting public timber, the annual harvest is determined based on what the forest is physically capable of supplying. In this case, the public landowner may determine that the annual harvest can now be higher (so long as the silvicultural activity continues); the firm can then see an increase in its harvest today. The value to the firm from fertilizing the timber stand is no longer $1.70 but now $200 – the increase in the *current* AAC attributable to the increase in the long-run timber supply – making the investment much more likely.

Deforestation

The principal conversion of forestland to other uses has been for agricultural land; it has been estimated that between 1850 and 1990, 250 million hectares of forests in temperate and boreal zones and 600 million hectares in the tropics were transformed into agricultural land (Houghton, 2002). More recent changes in forest cover are shown in table 5.7. Northern countries have generally shown an increase in forest cover since the 1980s, while forest cover in the majority of developing countries has declined. There are concerns that this deforestation, which

Table 5.7   Forest areas and rates of deforestation, 1981–1990, 1990–1995, 1990–2000

| Region/country | Forest cover, 2000[a] (10^6 ha) | Average annual change in forest cover | | | | | |
| | | 1981–90 | | 1990–95 | | 1990–2000 | |
		Area (10^3 ha)	Rate (%)	Area (10^3 ha)	Rate (%)	Area (10^3 ha)	Rate (%)
Africa	649.9	−4,100	−0.7	−3,748	−0.7	−5,264	−0.7
Tropical	634.2	a	−0.7	−3,695	−0.7	−5,295	−0.8
Non-tropical	15.7	a	−0.8	−53	−0.3	+31	+0.2
Asia	524.1	a	a	−3,328	−0.7	−651	−0.1
Tropical	288.6	−3,791	−1.2	−3,055	−1.1	−2,427	−0.8
South Asia	76.7	−551	−0.8	−141	−0.2	−98	−0.1
SE Asia	211.9	−3,240	−1.4	−2,914	−1.3	−2,329	−1.0
Europe	161.6	a	a	+389	+0.3	+424	+0.3
Northern	58.0	a	a	+8	+0.0	+40	+0.1
Western	67.8	a	a	+358	+0.6	+311	+0.5
Eastern	35.8	a	a	+23	+0.1	+73	+0.2
Former USSR	901.4	a	a	+557	+0.1	+739	+0.1
Canada	244.6	a	a	+175	+0.1	0	0.0
USA	226.0	a	a	+589	+0.3	+388	+0.2
Central America							
and Mexico	73.0	−1,112	−1.5	−959	−1.2	−971	−1.2
Caribbean	5.7	−122	−0.3	−78	−1.7	+13	+0.2
South America	885.6	a	a	−4,774	−0.5	−3,711	−0.4
Tropical	834.1	−6,173	−0.7	−4,655	−0.6	−3,456	−0.4
Brazil	543.9	−3,671	− 0.6	−2,554	−0.5	−2,309	−0.4
Temperate	51.5	a	a	−119	−0.3	−255	−0.5
Oceania	197.6	a	a	−91	−0.1	−365	−0.2
Tropical	35.1	−113	−0.3	−151	−0.4	−122	−0.3
Temperate	162.5	a	a	+60	+0.1	−243	−0.1
Global total[b]	3,869.5	a	a	−11,269	−0.3	−9,397	−0.2

[a]Not available or not applicable;
[b]Totals may not tally due to rounding.

Source: FAO (2001b, 1993, 1997); table compiled by Meyer and Van Kooten 2002

Table 5.8 Annual change in forest area, 1990–2000 (10^6 ha)

Region	Natural forest					Forest plantations			Total forest
	Loss			Gain		Gain			
	Deforestation	Conversion to forest plantations	Total loss	Natural expansion of forest	Net change	Conversion from natural forest	Afforestation	Net change	Net change
Tropical areas	−14.2	−1.0	−15.2	+1.0	−14.2	+1.0	+0.9	+1.9	−12.3
Non-tropical areas	−0.4	−0.5	−0.9	+2.6	+1.7	+0.5	+0.7	+1.2	+2.9
Global total	−14.6	−1.5	−16.1	+3.6	−12.5	+1.5	+1.6	+3.1	−9.4

Source: FAO (2001b)

happens when forest canopy cover is reduced to 10 percent or less, represents a permanent reduction in forest in these areas. Tropical forests show the greatest loss (tables 5.7 and 5.8), a source of great concern since they account for most of the globe's biodiversity (see chapter 15), with over half of the earth's 10–30 million species (Lovejoy, 1997).

Deforestation can also have other consequences. Countries may lose valuable timber species, which are difficult to re-establish; soil fertility can be severely diminished or even lost; and indigenous and rural communities may face social and economic disruption. There have been a number of studies to ascertain causes of deforestation to examine the relative importance of factors such as population pressure and demand for agricultural land (Barbier and Burgess, 1997). Research results suggest that while these may contribute to the conversion of forestland to other uses, there are a number of other institutional factors at work that can create perverse incentive structures that encourage deforestation. Insecure or absent property rights can lead to overexploitation. This may be due to inadequate enforcement or even the lack of political stability (Deacon, 1995). Government policies may promote other land use activities through subsidizing agricultural practices (Southgate et al., 2000). The example in box 5.4 shows how a number of different factors can combine to create unsustainable harvesting patterns.

Adding to the complexity of the problem is the fact that there may be a number of factors at work. Weak institutions, effective open access to timber, limited alternative economic opportunities, and markets for the illegally harvested timber can all contribute to the problem. Government policies to combat deforestation, depending upon their design and especially if they lack any enforcement mechanisms. Policies may also may be ineffective if there are fundamental problems of poverty, and growing population pressure increases the demand on forests for fuel, short-term economic gains from harvesting timber, or even the conversion of forestland into farm plots.

A new dimension to forestry issues

How countries manage their forests is increasingly taking on an international aspect for several reasons. First, many of the important environmental characteristics associated with forests such as biodiversity and their potential to sequester carbon have an international dimension, recognized in two international environmental agreements, the Convention on Biodiversity and the Framework Convention on Climate Change (Kyoto Protocol). Second, the shift towards sustainable development espoused within many western countries has taken place at the same time trade in forest products has also grown and the environmental aspects of how goods are produced has become increasingly important. This means that the impact from changes in one country's policies designed to satisfy broader environmental objectives cannot be examined without the indirect effect such changes might have elsewhere: for example, setting aside a greater proportion

BOX 5.4   HERE TODAY AND GONE TOMORROW! INDONESIA'S TROPICAL FORESTS

Indonesian government officials estimate today that Indonesian forests are being cleared at the rate of 1.6 million hectares per year, an area the size of Connecticut. It has been estimated that the lowland natural forests on Sumatra, home of the endangered Sumatran orang-utan and rare Sumatran tiger will disappear within five years, while those in neighboring Kalimantan will vanish in ten years. The problem has been well documented but continues. Why? A professor of forestry at Bogor Agricultural University in Indonesia answers succinctly: money, power, and politics. Illegal loggers supply unlicensed sawmills that ship wood products to brokers in Malaysia that then sell to markets in China, Taiwan, the US and Europe. It can be highly profitable, especially so given widespread economic stagnation and high unemployment. Sawmills can buy logs for $90 per cubic meter, saw them into boards, sand, and sell the boards for $280 per cubic meter. The Secretary General of the Ministry of Forestry says stopping illegal logging is a priority; however, people in positions of power control many of the unlicensed sawmills. In an effort to curtail overharvesting, Indonesia imposed a log ban in 2001. Firms simply shaved off part of the log so that it was no longer subject to the ban and continued exporting. Wood products are a major export from Malaysia, which, in response to environmental pressure several years ago, enacted strong regulations and protected much of its forests and is now dependent on timber from Indonesia to help sustain its industry. In June, Malaysia banned all imports of logs from Indonesia over concerns that it was becoming a transit point for illegally harvested logs but did not ban cut timber so that squared-off logs are free to enter. As one port worker says: "It is the same wood coming through but in different shapes." European buyers are now saying that they will not buy Malaysian wood products unless the sellers can demonstrate that it was harvested in a sustainable manner. As one Malaysian official notes, "How do you tell if it is legal or not? If you ask the Indonesians to provide you with documents, they will provide you with all the documents you need." The documents are either forgeries or have been obtained through bribes.

Source: Bonner (2002)

of protected land may reduce domestic production but shift demand to other regions where forests are managed in an unsustainable manner. Efforts to combat deforestation through measures such as log export bans may be counterproductive. Maestad (2001) argues that timber trade restrictions, designed to reduce deforestation, may not reduce but actually increase logging and induce the conversion of forestland to other uses by depressing the value of timber, a point echoed by Braga (1992) in looking at the experience of Brazil and Indonesia.

Efforts to develop an international consensus through an international environmental agreement on how to manage forests have so far failed (Wang, 2001). There are a number of ongoing efforts between countries to identify and measure the different components of sustainability, which in many ways reprise the debate over multiple use: how do policy-makers reconcile environmental, economic, and social objectives when some of these objectives compete with one another? How are public values recognized under systems of private ownership and how can policy-makers create incentives for sustainable forestry?

One attempt to answer some of these questions has been through forest product certification, which identifies forest products produced in a sustainable manner. This is the first major attempt to use private markets to provide public goods and was initiated by non-government organizations (NGOs) that have developed an international label based on the manner in which timber is produced. The aim was to create new markets that would provide a premium over traditional markets; this would provide firms with an incentive to practice sustainable forestry. Competing systems have emerged, some sponsored by domestic forest products industries, and while certified forestland has grown rapidly, it has done so principally in developed countries. To date, a significant premium has yet to emerge in the marketplace and much of the impetus for certification appears to be about retaining access to export markets, and developing countries have voiced concerns that certification may emerge as a trade barrier meant to protect domestic industries in developed countries.

The increasing attention paid to certification will link countries' domestic forest management policies even more firmly to the international marketplace. This will reinforce the attention paid to international issues in forest management; especially the role forests play in sustaining biodiversity and the potential role they may serve in addressing climate change (see chapter 14). Increasingly, forest management decisions will involve issues of land use that have traditionally been decided at either national or sub-national levels, especially in developed countries. This means that policy-makers will have yet another question to consider: how can non-market values that have a global dimension be captured in a system where traditionally countries make their own choices on how to utilize their forests?

FURTHER READING

There are a number of different models that have been employed in studying forestry-related problems. Reed (1986) and Kallio et al. (1987) provide excellent surveys of both forest level and forest sector models. Binkley (1993) shows how the Faustmann model can be used to generate a timber supply model. Yin et al. (1997) provide an argument as to why the emphasis on Faustmann models is incorrect and lay out an alternative specification. Van Kooten et al. (1995) show the durability and flexibility of the Faustmann model in showing how carbon sequestration can influence the optimal rotation length.

Bowes and Krutilla (1989) provide a detailed exploration of multiple use policies. Calish et al. (1978) use data to examine to what extent rotation ages may differ when various environmental amenities are incorporated into forest planning in the Pacific Northwest. A good example of a forest sector model used to project global timber supply is the FAO's global fibre supply model described in Bull et al. (1998). Other well-known forest sector models include TAMM (Adams and Haynes, 1980) and CINTRAFOR's model described in Kallio et al. (1987). Nilsson (2002) provides a synthesis on the current projections of the adequacy of timber supply over the next few decades.

Gibson et al. (2000) look at the relationship between institutions, land use, and deforestation. Barbier and Burgess (1997) develop a model of competing land use to investigate deforestation. Tomberlin et al. (1998) provide an excellent survey of the existing literature on the impact of trade on forestry. There are a number of international efforts, most organized around particular forest types or regions, to develop criteria and indicators of sustainable forestry: examples include the Montreal Process for temperate and boreal forests in North and South America, Australia and New Zealand; the Taropoto Process for tropical forests in South America, and the African Timber Organization Initiative for tropical forests in Africa. The FAO is the best source for current developments. Certification is also a rapidly evolving area. The Forest Stewardship Council, supported by NGOs, is the longest operating certification scheme. Other systems include those in Canada, the US, and several different European systems, as well as a Pan European Forest Certification (PEFC) system. Again, the FAO is a good source for recent developments, as are the various websites maintained by each of the certification systems and NGO groups; one example is www.sfms.com.

Osmaston (1968) provides an overview of the history of forest management. There have been a number of excellent books written about the interaction of human society with nature, and forests, because of their prominence, constitute important sections of these books. Good references include Thomas (1983) and Schama (1995); Albion (1965) provides an interesting view of the historical importance of timber supply as a determinant of British foreign policy (and suggests that the American Revolution was lost by Britain, in part, due to poor timber supply planning!).

NOTE

1   The relationship between growth rate and timber volume is given by the biological function for the particular timber stand. In this example, maximizing the MAI for the logistic curve yields a longer rotation compared to the single stand, single rotation, and Faustmann cases. This may change depending upon the nature of the growth function; for particularly fast growing species, it may be the case that this rule would yield a shorter rotation.

REFERENCES

Adams, D. and Haynes, R. (1980). The 1980 Timber Asset Market Model: Structure, Projections, and Policy Simulations, *Forest Science*, 33 (1): 164–73.
Albion, R. (1965). *Forests and Sea Power*, Harvard University Press: Cambridge, MA.
Barbier, E., and Burgess, J. C. (1997). The Economics of Tropical Forest Land Use Options. *Land Economics*, 73 (2): 174–95.
Binkley, C. (1993). Long-run Timber Supply: Price Elasticity, Inventory Elasticity, and the Use of Capital in Timber Production. *Natural Resources Modeling*, 7 (2): 163–80.

Bonner, R. (2002). Indonesia's Forests Go Under the Ax for Flooring, *New York Times*, Friday, September 13, page A3.

Bowes, M. D. and Krutilla, J. V. (1989). *Multiple-use Management: The Economics of Public Forestlands*. Resources for the Future: Washington, DC.

Braga (1992). In *Trade and the Environment*, World Bank: Washington, DC.

Bull, G., Mabee, W., and Scharpenburg, R. (1998). *Global Fibre Supply Model*. FAO: Rome.

Calish, S., Fight, R., and Teeguarden, D. E. (1978). How Do Nontimber Values Affect Douglas-Fir Rotations? *Journal of Forestry*, 76: 217–21.

Clawson, M. (1977). Decision-making in Timber Production, Harvest, and Marketing. Research Paper R-4, Resources for the Future: Washington, DC.

Deacon, R. T., (1995). Assessing the Relationship between Government Policy and Deforestation, *Journal of Environmental Economics and Management*, 28: 1–18.

Food and Agriculture Organization (FAO) (2001a). FAOSTAT online statistical database http://apps.fao.org/default.htm

Food and Agriculture Organization (FAO) (2001b). *State of the World's Forests 2001*, Rome: Food and Agriculture Organization.

Food and Agriculture Organization (FAO) (1997). *State of the World's Forests 1997*, Rome: Food and Agriculture Organization.

Food and Agriculture Organization (FAO) (1993). *State of the World's Forests 1993*, Rome: Food and Agriculture Organization.

Forest Trends (2002). *Who Owns the World's Forests?* Washington, DC.

Gibson, C., McKean, M., and Ostrom, E. (eds) (2000). *People and Forests: Communities, Institutions, and Governance*. MIT Press: Cambridge, MA.

Haley, D. and Luckert, M. (1995). The Allowable Cut Effect as a Policy Instrument in Canadian Forestry, *Canadian Journal of Forest Research*, 25: 1821–9.

Hartman, R. (1976). The Harvesting Decision When a Standing Forest Has Value, *Economic Inquiry*, 14: 52–8.

Houghton, R. (2002). Forests and Agriculture, in G. Woodwell, ed., *Forests in a Full World*, Yale University Press: New Haven, CT, pp. 36–50.

Kallio, M., Dykstra, D., and Binkley, C. (eds) (1987). *The Global Forest Sector: An Analytical Perspective*, John Wiley: New York.

Lovejoy, T. E. (1997). Biodiversity: What Is It?, in M. L. Reaka-Kudla et al., eds, *Biodiversity II: Understanding and Protecting Our Natural Resources*. Joseph Henry Press: Washington, DC.

Maestad, O. (2001). Timber Trade Restrictions and Tropical Deforestation: A Forest Mining Approach, *Resource and Energy Economics*, 23: 111–32.

Meyer, A. L. and Van Kooten, G. C. (2002). Social and Cultural Roots of Deforestation: A Cross-country Comparison. Unpublished Master's dissertation, University of Nevada. Reno.

Nilsson, S. (2002). Global Wood and Forest Balances, in G. Woodwell, ed., *Forests in a Full World*, Yale University Press: New Haven, CT, pp. 86–96.

Osmaston, F. C. (1968). *The Management of Forests*, George Allen and Unwin: London.

Reed, W. (1986). Optimal Harvesting Models in Forest Management: A Survey, *Natural Resource Modeling*, 1 (1): 55–79.

Schama, S. (1995). *Landscape and Memory*. Alfred Knopf: New York.

Southgate, D., Salazar-Canelos, P., Camacho-Saa, C., and Rigoberto, S. (2000). Markets, Institutions, and Forestry: The Consequences of Timber Trade Liberalization in Ecuador, *World Development*, 28 (11): 2005–12.

Strang, W. J. (1983). On the Optimal Forest Harvesting Decision, *Economic Inquiry*, 21: 576–83.

Swallow, S., Parks, P., and Wear, D. (1990). Policy-relevant Nonconvexities in the Production of Multiple Forest Benefits.

Swallow, S., Talukdar, P., and Wear, D. (1997). Spatial and Temporal Specialization in Forest Ecosystem Management under Sole Ownership, *American Journal of Agricultural Economics*, 79 (May): 311–26.

Thomas, K. (1983). *Man and the Natural World: A History of the Modern Sensibility*. Pantheon Books, New York.

Tomberlin, D., Buongiorno, J., and Brooks, D. (1998). Trade, Forestry, and the Environment: A Review, *Journal of Forest Economics*, 4 (3): 177–206.

Tomberlin, D. and Buongiorno, J. (2001). Timber Plantations, Timber Supply, and Conservation, in M. Palo, J. Uusivori, and G. Mery (eds), *World Forests, Markets, and Policies*, Kluwer Academic Publishers: London, pp. 207–17.

US Department of Agriculture (2002). *US Forest Facts and Historical Trends*: http://fia.fs.fed.us

Van Kooten, G. C., Binkley, C., and Delcourt, G. (1995). Effect of Carbon Taxes and Subsidies on Optimal Forest Rotation Ages and Supply of Carbon Services, *American Journal of Agricultural Economics*, 77: 365–74.

Victor, D. and Ausubel, J. (2002). Restoring the Forests. *Foreign Affairs*, Nov.–Dec.: 127–144.

Vincent, J. and Binkley, C. (1993). Efficient Multiple-use Forestry May Require Land-use Specialization, *Land Economics*, 69: 370–6.

Wang, S. (2001). Towards an International Convention on Forests: Building Blocks Versus Stumbling blocks, *International Forestry Review*, 3 (4): 251–64.

Yin, R. and Newman, D. (1997). Long-run Timber Supply and the Economics of Timber Production, *Forest Science*, 43 (1): 113–20.

CHAPTER SIX

WATER ECONOMICS

When the Well's dry, we know the Worth of Water.
(Benjamin Franklin *Poor Richard's Almanac*, 1745, p. 2)

6.1 INTRODUCTION

The purpose of this chapter is to examine the economic issues surrounding the allocation of water. This analysis of the allocation of water, however, is complicated by a number of factors. First, most uses of water have an impact on its quality. As a result, there are strong opportunities for water use to lead to negative externalities. Second, different analytic models are required to consider the allocation of water in different situations. This is because, depending on the context and physical circumstances, water can be considered renewable (subject to the hydrologic cycle), depletable (that is, renewable but at a fixed rate and subject to exhaustion) or exhaustible (that is, finite in supply – such as deep aquifers). Third, water is a fugitive resource: its movements are governed by the laws of hydrology rather than the laws of any country. This last feature means that establishing property rights in water is, in many instances, quite difficult. These features provide another reason to expect that one agent's use of water may reduce the welfare of other users.

The remainder of this chapter is organized as follows. The next section provides some background data regarding water use and research that has been directed at estimating the structure of water demands. Section 3 examines the issues surrounding the allocation of water in a static context. Section 4 extends the analysis by examining water allocation in a dynamic context. An important issue in these two sections is the identification of the conditions necessary for an efficient allocation of water. Section 5 compares and contrasts real-world institutions that govern the allocation of water with the theoretical prescriptions derived in the preceding sections. Section 6 shifts the focus towards the determination of the efficient level of water quality and briefly examines the alternative regulatory methods available for achieving that goal. Section 7 concludes the chapter.

6.2 WATER DEMAND AND SUPPLY

The annually sustainable supply of potable water for the globe is approximately 14,000 km^3 (Gleick, 2000). This is 3–4 times the current level of all recorded water withdrawals by society. However, this global figure hides dramatic differences in regional supply–demand balances. For example, the annual amount of water available on a sustainable basis per person in 1990 ranged from 100,000 m^3 in Canada to 400 m^3 in Israel (Dinar and Subramanian, 1997). In fact, there are many countries where domestic water use is even less than Israel's estimated 1 m^3/day. Approximately 2,200 million people live in 62 countries that report average domestic water use below 50 liters per capita per day in 1990 (Gleick, 2000). What is surprising about these countries, however, is that not all of them face absolute shortages of water. In fact, only 12 of the 62 countries have less than 1 m^3 per person per day of water available on average. This observation raises the question of whether observed water shortages are the result of absolute water scarcity, problems with the management and allocation of water, or some combination of the two.

Water use figures reported for a specific year also do not inform us of trends in water use. Biswas (1997) reports that total global water use has increased almost ten-fold during the twentieth century (while population increased by a factor of 3.5). This trend is expected to continue and perhaps even accelerate as global climate change, growing population, spreading use of irrigation technologies and rising real incomes exert greater pressure on global water resources (Easter et al., 1993). It is important to also remember that the amount of water available on a sustainable basis fulfills many environmental functions besides potentially satisfying human needs. These other functions include groundwater recharge, nutrient cycling, weather modification, and the provision of habitat for innumerable aquatic species.

A significant amount of research has been conducted into the structure of water demands (Renzetti, 2002). Much of this research has been directed at examining the relative importance of the variables predicted by economic theory to influence water demands. In the case of residential water use, those variables include the price of water, the price of sewage treatment, prices of other goods, the stock of water-using capital owned by a household, household income, and demographic characteristics of the household. In the case of commercial, industrial, and agricultural water use, those variables include the price of water (intake and discharge), the prices of other inputs, the price of output and the state of the firm's technology. In addition, most sectors' water demands are influenced by climatic conditions.

The agricultural sector is the largest user of water in many regions and countries and, as a result, agricultural water use has received a significant amount of attention from economists (Zilberman, Chakravorty, and Shah, 1997). Agricultural water use has been demonstrated to be sensitive to its own price, the prices of other inputs, and the price of output. For example, Edwards, Howitt, and Flaim (1996) examine the impact of changes to electricity prices on groundwater use by farmers in the American southwest. The authors find that a 10 percent increase in the price of electricity leads to decreases of approximately 7 percent in farmers' withdrawals of groundwater. In addition, choices regarding irrigation technologies and the demand for irrigation water have been found to be strongly influenced by climatic conditions and soil quality (Dinar and Zilberman, 1991). Indeed, investment in irrigation technology can be thought of as a substitute for poor-quality soil and uncertain surface water supplies.

The estimation of residential water demands is made difficult by the fact that many households and firms face a price schedule in which the marginal price for water is a function of the quantity consumed (Dinar and Subramanian, 1997). For example, in an "increasing *block rate* structure," the marginal price rises at discrete intervals as the quantity consumed increases. The presence of these nonlinear price schedules can introduce a simultaneity bias into the estimation of the demand equation (this is because the price, an important explanatory variable, cannot be considered exogenous as it is determined by the quantity consumed). Researchers have confronted this problem by using a two-part specification for the price of water. The first part is the marginal price for the observed level of consumption and the second is the "difference variable." The latter is calculated as the difference between the household's actual water bill and what it would have been had all the units of consumption been charged at the marginal price (Howe, 1982). Most empirical models of residential water demands indicate that households' use of water is inelastic with respect to price and income. There is also some evidence that summer outdoor water use is more responsive to price changes than indoor water use (Espey, Espey, and Shaw, 1997).

Industrial water use has not received as much attention as agricultural or residential water use. This may be because the bulk of water used by industrial facilities is self-supplied rather than being supplied by a water utility. This situation means that, in many jurisdictions, firms face little or no external price of intake water. Nonetheless, firms must pay for pumping, treating, and discharging water and it is these costs to which an optimizing firm can be expected to be sensitive. For example, Dupont and Renzetti (2001) estimate that the Canadian manufacturing sector's water intake price elasticity is -0.775. Another important feature of industrial water use is the possibility of in-plant recirculation of water. The same study finds that water intake and recirculation are substitutes.

Not all water uses require water to be withdrawn from a river, lake, or *aquifer*. In-stream water uses include commercial navigation, waste assimilation, hydroelectric power generation, recreation, and the provision of habitat and other ecological functions. Estimating the demand for these water uses is particularly challenging as it is difficult to determine the quantity of water used and many of the uses do not have market prices. The latter feature implies that non-market valuation techniques may have to be employed. Duffield, Neher, and Brown (1992) investigate fishers' valuation of changes in stream-flow and fish populations at several popular fishing sites in Montana. The authors find that these groups have a positive but declining marginal valuation of increases in stream-flow. Specifically, the marginal value of a 100 cubic feet per second (cfs) increase in stream-flow ranges from $10.31 at 100 cfs to $4.51 at 1000 cfs (1988 US$). Another area of research has applied non-market valuation methods to the outputs and services provided by wetlands. These services include flood regulation, nutrient cycling, habitat for commercially valuable species, and recreation (Turner, Adger, and Brouwer, 1998).

6.3 THE STATIC ALLOCATION OF WATER

Most households, firms, and farms rely on rivers and lakes for their supply of potable water. An individual river or body of water may be the source for thousands or even millions of individual users. The hydrologic cycle ensures that these rivers and lakes have a sustainable (if cyclical) rate of flow or level. Given the potentially large number of users who share (or compete for) a common body of water, an important issue concerns the allocation of that resource across competing demands. This may be considered as a static allocation problem because, in most cases, the current period's allocation of surface water does not have any implication for future periods' allocations. Thus, a single time period may be considered in isolation from other time periods.

In order to consider the problem of allocating a given supply of potable water across competing users, begin by assuming that there are N agents who each draw water from a shared source. Each user has a demand for water of $p_i = f_i(x_i)$ where x_i is the quantity of water used in each time period (within the water resources literature, there is a debate as to the best method to define and measure the "use" of water in this context – see Renzetti (2002), chapter 2). In order to keep this initial case straightforward, assume that each user's application of the water is entirely consumptive; that is, none of the water withdrawn is returned to the shared source (for example, this might be true of firms withdrawing water for the production of beer). With this assumption, we can avoid having to be concerned with return flows and with changes in water quality in the shared water source. The total sustainable supply of water per time period is X. Finally, assume that the cost of acquiring water is zero. Under these assumptions, each user will choose a quantity of water to withdraw to maximize his/her own benefit:

$$\max_{x_i} \int f_i(x_i)dx_i \quad \Rightarrow \quad f_i(x_i^*) = p_i^* = 0$$

Since $f(x)$ is the inverse demand curve, its height at each level of x indicates the marginal benefit of consumption. Integrating under the demand curve, then, provides the total benefit associated with any consumption level. This area is maximized when the decision-maker chooses a consumption level at which the marginal unit provides no further additional benefit. That is, each user seeks to withdraw water to the point where his/her marginal valuation is zero.

Now consider the case of a social planner whose task is to allocate water amongst competing users. The planner is assumed to choose the allocation that maximizes the sum of the users' benefits subject to the constraint that the sum of withdrawals does not exceed the sustainable supply:

$$\max_{x_i} \sum_i^N \left(\int f_i(x_i)dx_i \right) s.t. \sum_i^N x_i \leq X$$

$$\Rightarrow \quad f_i(x_i^{**}) = p_i^{**} = \lambda$$

$$\Rightarrow \quad \sum_i^N x_i^{**} \leq X$$

In this case water is allocated according to users' respective marginal valuation of the resource. At the optimal allocation, users have a common marginal valuation of water given by the shadow value on the resource constraint. This shadow value represents the opportunity cost (i.e. the forgone net benefits) of any user's withdrawal of water. It should be noted that this opportunity cost could be the value associated with another extractive use or it could be the value of in-stream water use such as maintaining river flows for fish spawning. One implication of this result is that, if there is a change in relative valuations in the applications to which water is put, then efficiency requires a reallocation of water towards the now more highly valued uses. This might occur in an arid region where water has been used historically for irrigation but the growth of urban centers raises the demand for (and value of) water for residential uses. Of course, if the sum of the optimal allocations is less than the amount of water available on a sustainable basis, then there is no opportunity cost associated with withdrawals and the shadow value (λ) will be zero. In this case, the two solutions will be identical.

6.4   DYNAMIC ALLOCATION OF WATER

The previous section considers the efficient allocation of a given quantity of surface water resources that is made available on a sustainable basis by the earth's hydrologic cycle. However, as the competition for surface water intensifies and as the quality of many sources of surface water declines, users are increasingly turning to groundwater as a source of water. In fact, groundwater is now the primary source of drinking water for 1.5–2.0 billion people worldwide and a mainstay of irrigated agriculture for much of southern and eastern Asia (Postel, 2000; Sampat, 2001). While this growing reliance on groundwater has made possible significant improvements in agricultural output and residential water consumption, it has also raised very serious concerns regarding the sustainability of continuing groundwater use in some locations. For example, Vajpeyi (1998) points out that the groundwater underlying Beijing was only 5 meters below the surface in 1950 but by 1989 its average depth was 50 meters. In cases where use rates exceed natural recharge rates, declines in aquifer depths are being observed (Gleick, 2000).

These declines in groundwater stocks have the potential to lead to increased pumping costs, land subsidence, contamination of aquifers, seawater intrusion in coastal areas, and diminished recharging of surface water bodies.

When modeling the allocation of surface water resources, it is assumed that the hydrologic cycle will provide a specific rate of flow (or lake-level) on a sustainable basis. However, a different situation arises when the use of groundwater resources is considered. In the case of very deep aquifers, there may be effectively no recharge (that is, infiltration from the surface) of the stock of groundwater. As a result, the stock of water is a non-renewable resource – once it is withdrawn it will not be renewed (at least not during any time period that is relevant for our analysis). In the case of more shallow aquifers, there may be infiltration (or recharge) and, thus, some increase in the stock of water available for use. Changes in the volume of the aquifer over time in these cases will be a function of withdrawals and infiltration.

In addition to the need to understand the physical workings of groundwater supplies, a separate set of issues concerns the regulation of groundwater. Aquifers may extend over surface property boundaries and even political boundaries. This feature, combined with the fact that it is often difficult to monitor withdrawals from an aquifer, suggests that the exploitation of aquifers may suffer from the problems often associated with common property resources.

These features of groundwater have a number of implications. The first implication is that withdrawal from an aquifer by one user in the current period has the potential to impose costs on others both in the current and future periods. Costs may be imposed in the current period when one user's withdrawals lower the level of the aquifer thereby increasing pumping costs for others or when one user's withdrawals reduce water quality in the aquifer thereby reducing its value to other users (see chapter 2). Costs are imposed on future water users because a unit of groundwater removed in the current period is unavailable for use in future periods just as in the case of oil and gas reserves (see chapter 7). Provencher and Burt (1993) refer to these two types of costs as depth costs and stock costs, respectively. The authors also identify a third source of cost when aquifers are used to supplement stochastic surface water supplies. Assuming that water users (such as farmers) are *risk averse*, then any reduction in the size of the aquifer will impose a cost on users because their incomes are now more likely to be tied to uncertain surface water supplies rather than being tied to the certain groundwater supply. Provencher and Burt refer to this externality as a risk cost. The second implication is that the difficulties associated with observing withdrawals from an aquifer, combined with limited scientific information regarding the physical properties of many groundwater stocks, imply that agencies tasked with regulating aquifer withdrawals face formidable challenges.

Let us now consider groundwater use more formally. Because of the importance of recharges (either natural or artificial) to the volume of the aquifer and of the possibility of externalities across time periods, it is necessary to consider groundwater use from a dynamic perspective. Fortunately, the apparatus for this approach is presented in chapter 1 and we will make use of those tools (the interested reader can also consult Kamien and Schwartz, 1991; Neher, 1990). We begin by examining the socially optimal extraction profile (that is, the optimal plan for groundwater withdrawals over time). Assume that the volume of the groundwater stock at time is x_t and its recharge rate is r (assumed to be constant). The ith user's withdrawal in time t is y_{it} and aggregate withdrawals are Y_t. The groundwater stock's dynamics depend on the relative magnitude of aggregate withdrawals and recharge:

$$\dot{x}_t = r - Y_t$$

Each user enjoys private benefits $b(y_{it})$ while aggregate benefits are $B(Y_t)$. Each user faces pumping costs $c(y_{it}, x_t)$ while aggregate pumping costs are $C(Y_t, x_t)$. It is assumed that pumping costs rise as the size of the groundwater stock declines

$$\partial c(y_{it}, x_t)/\partial x_t < 0 \quad \text{and} \quad \partial C(Y_{it}, x_t)/\partial x_t < 0$$

Thus, it is possible for one user's withdrawals of groundwater to raise the costs of other water users in the current and/or future time periods. Finally, assume that all users share a common rate of time preference δ and planning horizon T. The social planner's problem, then, is to choose a time path for aggregate extractions that maximizes the present value of the future stream of net benefits while satisfying the hydrologic constraints

$$\max_{Y_t} \int_o^T [B(Y_t) - C(Y_t, x_t)]e^{-\delta t}\, dt$$

$$s.t.$$

$$(1) \quad \dot{x}_t = r - Y_t$$

$$(2) \quad x(0) = x_0$$

The present-value Hamiltonian (see chapter 1) associated with this problem is the following

$$H = [B(Y_t) - C(Y_t, x_t)]e^{-\delta t} + \lambda_t(r - Y_t)$$

In solving this type of problem, it is often more convenient to construct the current-value Hamiltonian

$$\overline{H} = e^{\delta t}H$$

$$= e^{\delta t}\{[B(Y_t) - C(Y_t, x_t)]e^{-\delta t} + \lambda_t(r - Y_t)\}$$

$$= [B(Y_t) - C(Y_t, x_t)] + e^{\delta t}\lambda_t(r - Y_t)$$

$$= [B(Y_t) - C(Y_t, x_t)] + \mu_t(r - Y_t)$$

Where $\mu_t = e^{\delta t}\lambda_t$. The necessary conditions for optimizing the intertemporal problem may be expressed in terms of the current value Hamiltonian

$$\frac{\partial \overline{H}}{\partial Y_t} = 0 = \frac{\partial B(Y_t)}{\partial Y_t} - \frac{\partial C(Y_t, x_t)}{\partial Y_t} - \mu_t \tag{1}$$

$$-\frac{\partial \overline{H}}{\partial x_t} = \dot{\mu}_t - \delta \mu_t = \frac{\partial C(Y_t, x_t)}{\partial x_t} \tag{2}$$

$$\dot{x}_t = r - Y_t \tag{3}$$

$$x(0) = x_0 \tag{4}$$

$$\mu_T x_T = 0 \tag{5}$$

The last condition indicates that, at the end of the planning horizon, either the stock is exhausted or its shadow value is zero (due to rapidly escalating pumping costs, for example). If we suppress the time index and use subscripts to denote partial derivatives, these conditions may be rewritten in more compact form

$$B_Y = C_Y + \mu \tag{1'}$$

$$\frac{\dot{\mu}}{\mu} = \delta + \frac{C_x}{\mu} \tag{2'}$$

$$\dot{x}_t = r - Y \tag{3'}$$

while equations (4) and (5) remain the same. Let us consider the economic interpretation of these necessary conditions. Equation (1') indicates that the time profile of extractions from the aquifer must be characterized by the equality of marginal benefits and marginal costs of withdrawals at every point in time. If this were not the case, then withdrawals could be re-scheduled in order to increase the present value of discounted net benefits. It is clear from the right-hand side of (1') that the marginal cost of withdrawals contains two components. The first of these is the private marginal cost of extraction experienced by the water user. The second of these is the marginal shadow price of the stock of groundwater. This represents the present value of the future increase in pumping costs brought on by the reduction in aquifer size in the current period. Efficiency, then, requires users to consider not only their private costs of groundwater use but also the costs imposed upon others.

Equation (2') describes the evolution of the groundwater shadow price. It can be seen that, if the second term on the right-hand side were zero (that is, current period pumping did not lower the stock and, thus, raise costs), the rate of change of the shadow price would equal the rate of *social discount*. In the presence of the effect of the changing stock size on extraction costs, we are left with a modified

Hotelling rule where the behavior of the shadow price is determined by two, conflicting, forces (see chapter 7). On the one hand, the presence of the discount factor indicates a rising shadow price – indicating growing scarcity of the stock. On the other hand, the presence of the stock effect term leads the shadow price to decrease because successive withdrawals reduce the stock, increase extraction costs, and thereby reduce the value of the remaining water in storage. It can be shown that the time path of μ depends, in part, on the size of the initial stock relative to the optimum. Brown and Deacon (1972) show, for example, that if the initial stock exceeds the optimal stock, then the shadow value declines as withdrawals occur.

In the case of a steady-state equilibrium, $\dot{x} = \dot{\mu} = 0$, it is possible to use equations (1′–3′) to solve for the steady-state values of y and μ:

$$Y^* = r$$

$$\mu^* = \frac{C_x}{\rho}$$

Thus, the efficient steady-state extraction rate from the aquifer equals the rate of recharge and the shadow price on the stock equals the present value of the stock effect that is described above.

Comparison of the socially optimal solution to a competitive outcome is complicated by the difficulty of specifying competitive firms' behavior in a dynamic common-property setting. Intuition tells us that the two should diverge as individual users will plan withdrawals so as to maximize only the present value of private net benefits. Thus, individual users will take account of any change in pumping costs brought on by the change in aquifer depth related to their own pumping but they will not consider the same change in costs imposed on others. Provencher and Burt (1993) demonstrate that the unregulated competitive extractions from an aquifer will exceed the social optimum under a number of behavioral assumptions. This result has also been demonstrated by Brown and McGuire (1967) and Worthington, Burt, and Brustkern (1985). Despite these findings of the sub-optimal nature of competitive groundwater withdrawals, there is less agreement in the literature regarding the magnitude of the welfare gains associated with the movement from competitive to managed withdrawals. On the one hand, Gisser and Sancez (1980) argue that the divergence between competitive and socially optimal withdrawals may be relatively small in cases where withdrawals are small relative to the size of the aquifer and where property rights to groundwater use are already clearly defined. On the other hand, Provencher and Burt (1993) and Tsur and Graham-Tomasi (1991) argue that welfare losses can be large when surface supplies are stochastic or when stock effects are important.

There are a number of extensions to the above model that have been considered in the economics literature. In some settings, groundwater withdrawals can have effects on surface water supplies. As a result, a number of authors have considered the problem of jointly managing ground and surface water supplies (Tsur and Graham-Tomasi, 1991; Knapp and Olson, 1995). In terms of the model presented above, considering the interaction between surface and groundwater supplies implies that there is potentially an additional source of cost associated with groundwater withdrawals. Reducing groundwater levels may affect surface water users in two ways. First, surface water supplies may be tied physically to groundwater levels and, as a result, decreases in the depth of the aquifer may mean decreases in lake levels or river flows. Second, decreases in aquifer depth may compel users to increase their reliance on surface water sources whose supply and quality may be less certain than the aquifer. If water users are *risk averse*, this increased reliance on a more uncertain source of water will lower their welfare. Another line of research examines how the use of groundwater (both in terms of withdrawals and depositions of waste products) can influence the quality of groundwater (Hellegers, Zilberman, and van Ierland, 2001). This is an important extension but it requires more complex optimization models that can incorporate the spatial distribution and diffusion of contaminants in groundwater. Finally, because of concerns regarding the declining quality of groundwater, there has been a significant effort recently to establish users' valuations of groundwater resources. For example, Poe (1998) employs a contingent valuation survey (see chapter 9) to assess the way in which households' understanding of the risks associated with exposure to nitrates in their groundwater drinking supplies influences their willingness to pay for water quality improvements. Poe finds that

> reliance on subjective perceptions of exposure and health risks may not provide a reliable reference point for valuing groundwater protection policies. People simply do not have well-informed reference conditions, and thus it is unlikely that values collected under these conditions would reliably predict WTP values for a population actually experiencing groundwater contamination. (p. 3627)

6.5   WATER ALLOCATION IN PRACTICE

The previous sections in this chapter have presented stylized theoretical models that describe the efficient allocation of surface and groundwater resources. Important characteristics of these models include balancing the costs of supply and benefits from consumption, the need to consider social (as opposed to private) costs and benefits, and the need to consider costs and benefits over different time periods. The results of these models demonstrate the importance of information regarding the relative valuation of water users in different applications and different time periods. Furthermore, the models point to the need for an institutional mechanism (perhaps the government or the private market) to implement that allocation.

This section briefly describes how water is actually allocated in much of the world and considers the efficiency properties of those allocations. Regional allocations of water are considered first, followed by allocations at the local or municipal level. Overall, the finding is that, with few exceptions, water allocations have been and continue to be highly inefficient. Historically, most agencies concerned with the provision of water have been concerned with supplying what were perceived to be exogenously specified water "needs" rather than balancing the costs of supply with the benefits of consumption (Easter et al., 1993). As a result, this section concludes with a brief discussion of alternative allocative mechanisms that hold the promise of more efficient outcomes.

Regional water allocation

In North America and Europe, there have been two historically common sets of rules for the allocation of water (Scott and Coustalin, 1995, provide a comprehensive overview of the evolution of water rights). These are *riparian rights* and the *doctrine of prior appropriation*. Riparian rights were one of the earliest rules for water use and applied only to those landowners close to water bodies. Specifically, a riparian right confers to the owner of land adjacent to a water body the right to use that water. This right is tied to the ownership of land and cannot be transferred, for example, to the owner of land that is not adjacent to a water body. It is important to note that this right is for the use but not ownership of water and that the right was not unlimited – it is only for use that does not reduce the availability of water (in quantity or quality) to other riparian users.

The inadequacies of the riparian doctrine became apparent as population growth and economic development increased the demand for water in areas that were not immediately adjacent to bodies of water. As a result, a new set of rules, the doctrine of prior appropriation, emerged (particularly in the American west). Under this allocation rule, the priority or ranking of a claim to water use was based on the time at which it was first made (relative to other claims). Thus, claims that were more senior had a higher priority to water use. An important difference between this rule and that under riparian rights was that the right to water use was no longer tied to the ownership of riparian lands. As a result, the doctrine of prior appropriation broke the link between water rights and the ownership of riparian property but still hampered transfers of water to higher valued uses. This is because holders of senior water rights could maintain their hold on water despite the existence of alternative applications with potentially higher values. In many jurisdictions, private rights (riparian and prior appropriation) to water use were at one time or another constrained by governments asserting their ownership over water. For example, in many parts of the United Kingdom, Canada, and the United States, governments retain ownership of water and grant users *usufructuary rights*. That is, the right to use but not own water.

In order for any mechanism or institution to allocate water efficiently, it must ensure that certain conditions are satisfied. First, it must base allocations on the relative value of water in different uses. Second, it must provide some security of tenure. That is, rights must be clearly defined and enforced (see chapter 2). Third, it must allow for the transfer of water from relatively low-valued to high-valued applications. Finally, it must protect in-stream water needs and it must ensure that water use and the trading of water rights do not generate negative externalities (or, if they do, that those externalities are internalized by decision-makers). Not surprisingly, no real-world allocation mechanism for water meets all of these requirements although the markets for water rights that are emerging in a number of arid regions are proving to be potentially attractive options. The features of water markets are discussed below. Riparian rights lack transferability and restrict water use to owners of riparian properties. The doctrine of prior appropriation is an advance over riparian rights in so far as the right to use water is no longer tied to the ownership of land adjacent to water. Nonetheless, the doctrine establishes different priorities to water use according to the seniority of the user's claim and these priorities will not necessarily be correlated to the value of water use. In fact, it is not uncommon in a number of arid jurisdictions operating under this doctrine to observe agricultural operations holding "senior" water rights and applying this water to produce relatively low-valued crops while growing cities and industries with "junior" water rights must search for distant and costly water supplies (Postel, 2000).

In principle, government issuance of private water rights could address many of the shortcomings of other rules. This would require government auctioning transferable water rights while regulating water quality to protect in-stream water needs as well as third parties. In practice, governments' distribution of water rights have rarely come close to these requirements. Most governments establish classes of water uses with arbitrarily determined priority of access to water resources. For example, the Boundary Waters Treaty between Canada and the United States directs the International Joint Commission to regulate water levels on the Great Lakes and to consider only the interests of domestic water users, commercial navigation, and hydroelectric power generation to the exclusion of all other water users (Allee, 1993). Furthermore, government-created water rights are frequently not transferable and are not designed to avoid the generation of negative externalities from diminished water quality (Dupont and Renzetti, 1999).

International water allocation

An additional set of challenges arises when the efficient allocation of *transboundary* waters (those that are shared by more than one state or that form a part of the boundary between states) is considered. Examples of these water bodies include the Great Lakes in North America, the Rhine River in Europe and the Indus River in Asia. The allocation of transboundary water resources presents special challenges because no "super-government" can impose a settlement on the parties involved in a dispute (that is, define and enforce property rights) and because international law in the area of water resources is still evolving (Utton, 1996).

Governments who share transboundary waters have often asserted particular forms of property rights over those resources (Frederick, 1996). For example, the doctrine of unlimited territorial sovereignty specifies that a nation has exclusive rights to any water in its territory. At the other end of the spectrum, an alternative doctrine, unlimited territorial integrity, asserts that one country may not alter the quantity or quality of water flowing to another country. It is fairly easy to see that these two opposing doctrines resemble the extreme positions usually set out in Coase's description of the externality problem: a party may either be free to pollute in unlimited quantities or may be completely protected from any harm due to pollution (see chapter 2). Furthermore, as Coase's analysis indicated, there are potential welfare gains to be enjoyed through negotiation towards an efficient allocation of *transboundary* water resources. This has, indeed, been the case in a number of instances with the doctrine of equitable and reasonable use – perhaps based more on equity concerns than efficiency principles – often being used in determining allocations (Utton, 1996).

Given this context, economists have demonstrated the value of using game-theoretic models to understand the structure of disputes over water resources (Frisvold and Caswell, 1997). From a different perspective, Becker, Zeitouni, and Schecter (1997) illustrate how, under a cooperative environment, markets can be extended across international boundaries to promote efficient allocation of water.

Municipal water allocation

In addition to regional rules for water allocation, it is important also to consider the allocation of water at the local level. This is because most of the world's population relies upon water supplied by a municipal water authority. Furthermore, in many low-income countries, large cities' urban water systems (such as Mexico City, Manila, Karachi, and Cairo) are unreliable and fail to serve a sizeable fraction of the city's inhabitants. Municipal water utilities undertake a number of activities in order to provide for their residential, commercial, and institutional customers. Water must be removed from the natural environment, treated to remove impurities, pressurized, stored, and transported. Water utilities are capital-intensive operations with many of the features of natural monopolies. A water utility's annual costs are typically recorded as operations and maintenance expenditures and capital costs. The latter usually reflect the current principal and interest owed on investments made in the past. Water utilities then set prices in order to meet these costs (and a regulated rate of return if the utility is investor owned). The price of water can take a number of forms depending, in part, on whether the consumer's water use is metered. Many North American cities charge residential consumers either a constant price per unit or a declining block rate price structure. However, Tate and Lacelle (1995) report that close to half of all Canadian cities (including 25 percent of those with populations over 100,000) levy only a flat rate for residential customers (this involves a connection fee but no marginal price for water consumed). Furthermore, in contrast to suppliers of natural gas, electricity, and telephone service, very few water utilities charge water prices that vary by distance or time of use.

Most municipal water prices are inefficient for a number of reasons. First, there is strong evidence that they have little relationship with the marginal costs of supply. For utilities that charge only a connection fee to their unmetered customers, there is obviously a gap between price and marginal cost. Furthermore, in a study of water utilities in Canada, Renzetti (1999) finds that "Prices charged to residential and commercial customers are found to be only a third and a sixth of the estimated marginal cost for water supply and sewage treatment, respectively. For example, the average price to residential customers is $0.32/m^3$ while the estimated marginal cost is $0.87/m^3$" (p. 688). Second, water prices are based on the utilities' accounting of their historical investment expenditures rather than current period capital costs. Third, as mentioned above, water prices rarely vary by distance or time of use despite evidence that these factors play a significant role in the marginal cost of supply (Renzetti, 1999). Fourth, utilities may understate their capital costs. This may occur if current period prices are based on historical capital costs rather than the capital costs of the utility's next planned expansion. Alternatively, capital costs may be understated if utilities fail to impute a competitive rate of return in their calculation of the opportunity cost of capital. Finally, water utilities cost accounting may understate the full social costs of water supply if they neglect the costs of negative externalities arising from diminished water quality and from the value of the raw water input.

There is empirical evidence that moving to efficient prices may raise welfare. The principal reason for this finding is that increased prices lead to decreases in aggregate consumption. For each unit of water whose marginal cost of supply exceeds society's aggregate willingness to pay, avoiding consumption leads to a net gain to society. In the long run, further efficiency gains are possible if the increased prices lead to slowed demand growth and, thus, delayed capital investment by the water utility. Box 6.1 considers the application of these principles.

Water markets

Given the shortcomings of most regional and local water allocation mechanisms and the specter of growing water demands, it is not surprising that researchers have examined alternative means of securing an efficient allocation of water. At the regional level, the emphasis in the research literature has been directed at examining the efficacy of more market-orientated allocation institutions (Easter, Dinar, and Rosegrant, 1998). *Water markets* usually involve users in a specific geographic region or who share a common source of water supply. These markets can be established formally (through government legislation) or may work informally within a group of water users (for example, farmers sharing an irrigation canal). In order for water markets to function, rights to use water must be well defined,

BOX 6.1 THE WELFARE EFFECTS OF REFORMING MUNICIPAL WATER PRICES

A number of researchers have found that municipal water utilities often set prices in an inefficient manner. In particular, water prices rarely reflect how the marginal cost of supply is influenced by differences in distance from the water source or the time at which consumption occurs. This is in stark contrast to the pricing practices of firms providing telephone services and electricity. In these cases, prices commonly vary with time and distance. Renzetti (1992) examines the case of Vancouver, Canada (a city that, while not short of water, faces a rapidly growing population) and simulates the impact of introducing residential water metering and moving to peak-load pricing. This is a pricing method where prices are higher in "peak" or high demand time periods and lower in "off-peak" or low-demand periods. This method of pricing is efficient when demand fluctuates and capacity is fixed (Brown and Sibley, 1986). This case was complicated by the fact that the gaps between estimated marginal cost and water prices differed across user groups. Nonetheless, the attendant increases in prices were seen to delay planned capital expenditures by the water utility as well as to encourage conservation and substitution by water users. Aggregate welfare is estimated to increase by approximately 4–5 percent.

One of the main reasons why people oppose reforming water prices is a genuine concern that low-income households may be harmed by price increases. Hall and Hanemann (1996) examine the move to efficient water prices in Los Angeles and consider how that transition may need to be modified to account for concerns regarding impacts on low-income households and the utility's budgetary position. The authors are able to demonstrate that it is possible for the water utility to alter the structure of price schedules in a way that encouraged conservation while protecting low-income households and maintaining a balanced budget.

The issue of municipal water pricing is also critically important for large urban centers in low-income countries. The water supply systems in cities such as Mexico City, Manila, and Dhaka have been fiercely criticized for failing to provide potable water to all citizens. Indeed, it is often the case that the poorest citizens must purchase water from private vendors at prices many times those paid by households connected to the municipal system (Munasinghe, 1992). In situations such as these, reforming water prices (when combined with institutional reforms to improve water utility performance) may provide the needed financial resources to improve system reliability and to extend service to poor neighborhoods.

enforced, and must be transferable. Sales may be permanent (that is, allowing for a transfer of the right in perpetuity) or temporary (for example, allowing the transfer of a certain amount of water for a single growing season). Finally, governments or water allocation agencies may retain the right to block trades due to potential impacts on third parties or on in-stream requirements.

There is a growing body of empirical evidence that demonstrates the ability of well-defined water markets to improve the efficiency of water allocations and to encourage water conservation (Easter, Dinar, and Rosegrant, 1998). These gains appear to be largest in arid environments characterized by rapid growth in demand, an initial distribution of water rights that was not representative of relative water values, and where water markets can be easily grafted onto existing legal institutions. Another important feature of water markets is that they may remove (or diminish) the incentive for water users to manipulate the political system to achieve a desired water allocation or to avoid price increases.

An example of the empirical analysis of water markets is Horbulyk and Lo (1998). The authors consider the welfare effects of relying more heavily upon market-based water allocation mechanisms. As a result of regulatory changes, the province of Alberta, Canada, is moving away from unpriced and untradable water withdrawal licenses and towards a market-based system for surface water allocation. The authors develop a programming model that simulates the efficient water allocation. The market is assumed to work costlessly. Demand curves are calibrated using data for Alberta and published elasticity estimates for irrigation, municipal, and industrial water uses. The program seeks a static allocation of water that maximizes the sum of producer and consumer surpluses while meeting any exogenous hydrologic, in-stream, and inter-provincial transfer constraints.

The simulations indicate that the broadest definition of allowable trades yields both significant intersectoral shifts in water consumption and significant welfare gains. Specifically, 23 percent of irrigation water consumption is shifted to municipal and industrial uses and this represents almost a doubling of the latter's water use. The welfare gain from this shift is approximately $530 million (Canadian). Interestingly, a more limited market arrangement that allows trades only within river sub-basins achieves more than 85 percent of the potential welfare gains and 75 percent of the volume of trades. This may be due to the fact that the model assumes that all of the farms (and cities) are basically the same in terms of their water demands (except for their scale).

Despite the potential for markets to improve the efficiency of the allocation of water, there remain concerns regarding their operation. Perhaps the most important challenges are to protect third parties and in-stream needs from the impacts of transactions in water markets and to ensure that the structure of water markets is consistent with the country's existing legal framework. In principle, both of these issues can be dealt with through some degree of government scrutiny of proposed trades.

6.6   WATER QUALITY

Much of the discussion in this chapter has been concerned with allocating a specific quantity of water amongst competing users. However, almost all water uses (with the exception of commercial navigation and hydroelectric generation) are functions of the quality of water as well. That is, the value that users assign to their applications of water is usually a function of not just of the quantity of water but also of its physical, biological, and chemical properties. Physical properties include the presence of suspended solids as well as the odor and temperature of water. Biological properties refer to the presence of life forms such as algae, bacteria, and viruses in water. Chemical properties relate to the presence of organic and inorganic substances in water. Examples of organic materials are hydrocarbons and many pesticides while examples of inorganic substances include nitrogen, phosphorus, and metals.

There is a strong relationship between water quality and the value of water (Renzetti, 2002, chapters 8 and 9). Irrigation water that is highly saline is less valuable to farmers because it damages their crops. Lakes that are warm and abundant with algae are less valuable to recreational users because of odor and taste problems. Drinking water that contains any one of a number of viral, bacterial, or chemical contaminants is significantly less valuable to households because of health concerns. In fact, the consumption of contaminated water remains a leading public health problem for many parts of the world. As the World Bank (see box 6.2) recently expressed "The challenge is enormous: one billion people still lack access to safe water, two billion lack safe sanitation. Slow progress is not acceptable, as more than three million children still die every year from avoidable water-related disease" (World Bank Water Supply and Sanitation website, September 30, 2002, http://www.worldbank.org/html/fpd/water/).

Most water uses are not only a function of the quality of water but also have an impact upon water quality. Industrial operations emit a variety of chemical substances, sewage treatment plants emit organic contaminants such as bacteria, and agricultural operations deposit fertilizers and pesticides. Aside from the specific types of contaminants released into the environment, there is an important difference between the first two and the third sources of pollution. Industrial and sewage treatment plant-related emissions are examples of *point source* pollution: the location and activity of the polluter are known and may in principle be measured. Furthermore, it is usually possible to link the polluter's activities (e.g. the quantity of a contaminant released) and ambient environmental quality. Agricultural operations, by way of contrast, are examples of *nonpoint sources* of pollution. This is because it is very difficult to monitor emissions and to link emissions and ambient environmental quality. A farmer, for example, may apply nitrogen to her crops. The amount of nitrogen that eventually finds its way into a neighboring water course and the impact of that nitrogen on water quality can be expected to be a complex (and, most likely, stochastic) function of physical parameters (soil type, weather conditions, and groundwater mobility) as well as behavioral factors such as the farmer's cropping and tilling practices. We will deal consider the efficient level of pollution and policies to achieve this goal for point and nonpoint sources separately (also consult chapter 3).

BOX 6.2   WATER POLLUTION

It is commonly said that the single most common cause of premature death globally is not warfare, smoking, or even AIDS. Rather, it is consuming contaminated water (Cosgrove and Rijsberman, 2000). There is an almost bewildering array of contaminants that find their way into water. Some of these are relatively benign nuisances as they affect only the taste, color, and odor of drinking water supplies. Indeed, it has been suggested that the chemicals introduced into drinking water supplies (especially chlorine) to combat these problems may lead to greater risks than those posed by the substances they are designed to combat.

Other contaminants are more serious. Viral and microbiological contaminants such as *Escherichia coli* (more commonly known as E. coli) can cause immediate discomfort and, in cases of people with weakened immune systems, organ damage, and even death. Outbreaks of waterborne E. coli are often linked to contamination of water supplies by animal wastes. Ingestion of other waterborne contaminants such as metals, nitrates, arsenic, and mercury can have significant long-run health consequences (Tchobanoglous and Schroeder, 1997).

Governments have usually responded to the threats posed by these substances by specifying maximum concentrations that may be found in drinking water supplies. Water utilities are then responsible for testing and treating raw water supplies to ensure compliance. In Ontario, Canada, for example, the Drinking Water Surveillance Program requires water utilities to test for several dozen contaminants and report their findings to their customers (Ontario, 1998). The challenge for the social scientist, however, is to assess whether the cost of the resources devoted to reducing the threats of waterborne contaminants is exceeded by society's valuation of that reduced risk. While it is usually a straightforward matter to measure the costs of improving water quality, measuring the benefits is more difficult. Economists have employed a number of "nonmarket" valuation methods such as contingent valuation surveys to do this – these are reviewed in Renzetti (2002).

Point source water pollution

Pollution-generating activities have the potential to lower the welfare (or raise costs) of other water users. If water users do not take these impacts into account, then externalities may arise. In order to see this result, consider the following situation. Two competitive firms (which operate in the same output market and share the same technology) are situated on a river. Both withdraw water, employ it in the production of their output, and discharge it (diminished in quality) back to the river. The downstream firm has higher costs because it must treat its intake water to remove the contaminants deposited by the upstream firm. As indicated above, this is an example of a point-source water pollution problem as the sources of effluents are known and it is in principle possible to monitor the quantities of effluents being emitted.

For simplicity, assume that water (w_i) is the only productive input. Private maximization of profits implies the following first-order conditions:

$$\max_{w_1} \pi_1 = pf(w_1) - c_1(w_1) \quad \rightarrow \quad pf'(w_1) - c_1'(w_1) = 0$$
$$\max_{w_2} \pi_2 = pf(w_2) - c_2(w_1, w_2) \quad \rightarrow \quad pf'(w_2) - c_2'(w_1, w_2) = 0$$

where subscripts denote the firm and the prime denotes the first derivative. The firms' first-order conditions only differ in that the second firm's costs are a function of not only its own water use but also the water use of its upstream competitor. By assumption,

$$\partial c_2(w_1, w_2)/\partial w_1 > 0$$

The socially optimal allocation of water is achieved by jointly maximizing both firms' profits:

$$\max_{w_1, w_2} \pi_1 + \pi_2 \quad \rightarrow \quad pf'(w_1) - c_1'(w_1) - c_2'(w_1, w_2) = 0$$
$$\rightarrow \quad pf'(w_2) - c_2'(w_2) = 0$$

Under the socially optimal allocation of water use, the first firm must now confront not only its own water-use costs but also the externality it imposes on the second firm in the form of higher costs. As a result, the first firm uses less water than it does in the privately optimal allocation. This simple model can be extended in a variety of directions. For example, researchers have considered the spatial distribution of pollutants (Tomasi and Weise, 1994); the interaction between surface and groundwater quality (Fleming and Adams, 1997); issues arising from transboundary pollutants (see chapter 14 of this volume) and the presence of stock pollutants (see chapter 3 and Neher, 1990).

A dynamic model of water pollution

Consider, for example, the case of identifying the efficient level of a stock pollutant. Stock pollutants are different from flow pollutants in that they persist in the environment for a number of time periods. Examples of stock pollutants include mercury and radioactive substances. An important implication of the persistent nature of stock pollutants is that the quantity of the pollutant that is present in the environment at any point in time (or, more accurately, in a state in which it may have an impact on human welfare) will depend on the previous period's stock, the rate at which it is being deposited into the environment (through industrial processes) and the rate at which it degrades or becomes unavailable to affect humans (through sedimentation of a lake, for example). Thus, if we denote the stock of pollutant at any point in time as S_t, the rate of deposition as e_t and the rate at which the pollutant decays or becomes unavailable as θ_t, then the equation describing the size of the stock is the following:

$$S_t = S_{t-1} + e_t - \theta_t$$

The socially optimal stock of pollutant is then determined by finding the level at which marginal costs and benefits are equated. Assume that benefits are a function of deposition, $B(e_t)$, while damages are a function of deposition and the size of the stock, $D(e_t, S_t)$. Unlike the previous analysis of a flow pollutant, we must consider the impacts of decisions made in one time period on the benefits and damages experienced in other time periods. This is because an increase in depositions in the current period not only changes benefits and damages in this time period but, by changing the size of the stock for a number of time periods in the future, also influences damages in other time periods. This means that the determination of the efficient level of a stock pollutant is inherently a dynamic problem. If we continue to use δ to denote the discount rate, then the dynamic optimization problem becomes the following:

$$\max_{e_t} \int_0^T [B(e_t) - D(S_t, e_t)]e^{-\delta t}\, dt$$

$$s.t.$$

$$\dot{S}_t = e_t - \theta_t$$

$$S(0) = S_0$$

Aside from differences in notation, this problem is the same as the one presented earlier for the dynamically efficient depletion of a stock of groundwater where costs are a function of withdrawals and the remaining stock.

Regulation of point source water pollution

Let us return to the static *point source* externality model and consider how the privately optimal allocation could be made to mimic the socially optimal allocation through the implementation of a pollution policy. This topic is discussed more generally in chapter 3 and, as a result, is only briefly considered here. Further, it is important to be mindful that the policies discussed here are appropriate for point source pollutants. The problem of nonpoint pollutants provides its own challenges for the design of efficient policy instruments, as discussed below.

There are essentially two ways that this can be done: create a shadow price for the negative externality or extend property rights to include either the right to pollute or the right to be free from pollution. The first measure is based on the idea that private decision-makers are making socially sub-optimal decisions regarding their water discharge because they lack full information regarding the social costs and benefits of their decisions. Thus, in order for the decision-maker to internalize the externality an effluent fee or charge must be created and levied against the firm discharging the effluent. In the point source water pollution example the appropriate level for the charge is $c_2'(w_1, w_2)$ evaluated at the social optima.

The second approach is based on the premise that the fundamental cause of the externality is the lack of clearly defined rights to water use. The solution, then, lies in creating the necessary property rights. One option is to provide the upstream polluter with unconditional rights to use (and degrade) the water. In this case, the downstream water user would have to bear the costs of the reduced water quality or would perhaps have to compensate the upstream polluter for any pollution control measures undertaken. Alternatively, the downstream user could be given the right to water that is undiminished in quality. In this case, the upstream user would have to eliminate its effluent or perhaps compensate the downstream user for any reduction in water quality caused by a positive amount of pollution. However, which of the two options will lead to an efficient level of externality being generated?

The answer is that, under certain circumstances, the socially optimal allocation of water use and production of pollution will occur independent of which party is provided the property right. As Ronald Coase argued, so long as the property right is clearly defined and enforced and transactions costs are low, the social optimum will be attained (see chapter 2 for a more detailed discussion of the *Coase theorem*). The choice of who receives the property right will influence only the distribution of wealth and not the level of externality produced. It is important to remember, of course, that this result is a function of the assumptions and limitations of Coase's analysis. For example, Coase's analysis is partial and, thus, does not consider economy-wide implications of the allocation of property rights. In addition, Coase's analysis assumes that "income effects" are absent – that is, the allocation of wealth (between polluter and the harmed part, for example, will not affect expenditure patterns and, thus, resource allocation, throughout the economy).

In the case of multiple water polluters, the idea of providing property rights naturally leads to consideration of creating a market in tradable pollution permits (Hoag and Hughes-Popp, 1997). This involves the government determining the allowable level of pollution (presumably below current recorded levels) and then allocating each firm the right to pollute a specified amount (see chapter 3). This allocation can involve a simple transfer or an auction where firms must purchase the permits. Any firm that is allocated fewer pollution units than it is currently emitting would have to either abate or purchase permit units from another firm. In principle, this scheme should lead to a reduction in emissions at least cost to society as firms with the lowest cost of abatement will be the most willing to sell off their pollution rights. While there has been considerable interest expressed in markets for tradable air pollution permits, there has been less interest in their use to address *point sources* of water pollution. This is most likely due to the fact that there are relatively few water bodies that are sufficiently large to include a substantial number of firms emitting the same pollutants. In the case of air pollution, the nature of the atmosphere means that the pollution from firms hundreds of kilometers from each other may be considered as having the same environmental impact. In contrast, water pollution's effects are usually much more localized and this reduces the possible scope for a market in tradable permits. Nonetheless, recent simulation analysis suggests that these markets may lead to significant cost savings in cases where there are a sufficient number of firms (such as a large inland lake or coastal estuary – cf. Hanley et al., 1998)

These two policy measures hold considerable theoretical appeal. Their real-world application, however, faces a number of challenges. These include determining shadow prices for a wide range of industrial and agricultural effluents and the difficulty of establishing property rights for transboundary pollutants. These challenges may partially explain why North American governments have relied almost exclusively on other approaches to control water quality.

The regulation of *point source* threats to water quality in North American jurisdictions has shared a number of features (Freeman, 1990). In most cases, uniform performance standards are imposed on all polluters in a given jurisdiction. These standards may be specified as quantitative limits to outflows (either as a specific quantity of contaminant per time period or as a maximum concentration of the contaminant in the polluter's discharge stream). Alternatively, these standards may be specified in terms of the types of technologies that must be adopted by polluters. These technologies, in turn, are based on notions such as the "*best available technology*," "best practicable technology," or "best available technology economically achievable."

These regulations have been responsible for considerable water quality improvements in a number of North American jurisdictions. Nonetheless, they can still be criticized on economic grounds. First, in setting the water quality goals that determine allowable discharges, regulators have rarely compared the costs and benefits of alternative levels of water quality. Thus, it is unlikely that they have found the socially optimal level of water quality. Second, these regulations did not achieve water quality improvements at least cost to society. This is because they failed to take account of differences in polluters' *marginal abatement costs*. Since efficiency dictates that abatement requirements should be allocated so that marginal abatement costs are equalized, dissimilar marginal abatement cost functions will lead to unequal abatement requirements. Third, the regulations fail to provide incentives for polluters to innovate and find more environmentally benign production technologies. This is because, once a firm is in compliance with the regulation (that is, discharging less than its allowed maximum), it has little or no incentive to invest in technologies that reduce discharges even further. These features mean that *command and control regulations* achieve water quality goals at significantly higher costs than necessary. Tietenberg (1985) reviews a number of studies that have examined the cost of compliance under US regulations aimed at curbing bio-oxygen demand emissions and finds that the estimates of the ratio of costs under command and control regulations to costs under "least-cost" regulatory approaches range from 1.19 to 3.13.

A significant part of economists' criticisms regarding the North American approach to improving water quality stems from the absence of economic instruments. As Howe (1994) points out, with the exception of a small number of experiments with tradable discharge permits, North American regulators have preferred using command and control regulations rather than effluent charges or other market-based incentives. In contrast, a number of European and Asian countries have experimented with economic instruments to achieve water quality goals. Brown and Johnson (1984) describe and assess Germany's water quality regulations. Under Germany's effluent charge law, the national government established a series of permits that detailed the allowable effluent levels and a set of charges based on effluent quantities and the quality of the receiving waters. On the whole, the authors contend that the charges were set too low to induce significant changes in firms' behavior. Nonetheless, the authors note that there were apparent increases in investment in abatement equipment at municipal sewage treatment facilities and in some industries. Zhang (1999) echoes this criticism in his recent study of the costs of effluent reductions in China. The author finds that effluent charges must be increased to 8–10 times their current level if they are to accurately reflect treatment costs and environmental damages. Despite these concerns, there are indications that a number of European and Asian countries are moving in the direction of relying more heavily on market-based instruments to achieve water quality improvements (Tao, Yang, and Zhou, 1998; OECD, 1999; Chave, 2002).

Nonpoint source water pollution

The preceding discussion of the efficient level of pollution and of policies to achieve this level of pollution assumes that measuring emissions and ambient environmental quality are costless. This is certainly not the case when we consider the problem of nonpoint pollution. Thus, we now turn our attention to the problem of defining the optimal level of nonpoint pollution and identifying the policies needed to achieve it.

As indicated above, *nonpoint source* pollution (whether it is from a mobile source such as an automobile or a fixed source such as a farm) exhibits several characteristics which present daunting challenges to regulators. These characteristics may include uncertainty regarding the source of emissions, the quantity of emissions from each source, the relationship between actions of polluters and emissions and between emissions and ambient environmental quality. In addition, because of the crucial importance in physical conditions (such as local soil types, groundwater–surface water interactions, and weather conditions), the analysis of *nonpoint source* pollution and the design of policies aimed at controlling it are likely to be quite case specific.

Despite these challenges, economists have made progress in developing theoretical models that identify the optimal level of *nonpoint source* pollution and the features of the regulatory instruments needed to achieve that goal. Important features of these models include the role played by parameters describing the physical environment (such as the rate at which pollutants disperse in a body of water) and the level of information regarding individual polluter's technology and risk preferences. In order to understand these and other factors influencing the efficient level of *nonpoint source* pollution, Shortle, Horan, and Abler (1998) present a model of a large number of competitive polluters (e.g. farmers within the same watershed). Surface water quality, a, is a function of each farmer's emissions, r_i, stochastic environmental variables that influence transport of the emissions, w, and watershed characteristics, λ:

$$a = a(r_1, r_2 \ldots r_n, w, \lambda)$$

In addition, each farmer's emissions are a function of input choices, x_i, environmental conditions, v_i, and farm-specific characteristics such as soil type, α_i:

$$r_i = r_i(x_i, v_i, \alpha_i)$$

The regulator's task is to find the level of emissions that maximizes social welfare. Since emissions are not directly controllable, however, the regulator targets input use. Thus, the regulator chooses the levels of the x_{ij} to maximize the difference between industry profits and expected damages:

$$\max_{x_{ij}} NB = \sum_{i=1}^{n} \pi_i(x_i) - E[D(a)]$$

Where the first term on the right-hand side is industry profit and the second is expected damages. The expectation is taken over the distributions of the stochastic environmental and characteristic variables' distributions. The efficient level of input use (and, thus, emissions) is governed by the first order condition:[1]

$$\frac{\partial \pi_i}{\partial x_{ij}} = E\left\{ D'(a)\frac{\partial a}{\partial r_i}\frac{\partial r_i}{\partial x_{ij}} \right\} \quad \forall\, i, j$$

This equation dictates that the efficient choice of input use equates marginal net benefits (the left-hand side) and marginal expected damages (the right-hand side). This model demonstrates that, in theory, it is possible to characterize the efficient level of polluting activity for each nonpoint source. As an empirical matter, the reader should note that the right-hand side is based on three potentially stochastic and difficult to observe relationships: the relationship between ambient water quality and damages; the relationship between polluters' emissions and ambient water quality; and the relationship between input use and polluters' emissions.

Regulation of nonpoint source water pollution

Having identified the theoretically efficient level of *nonpoint source* pollution, the challenge then becomes to find a regulatory instrument that will decentralize this outcome (that is, induce polluters to regard the efficient level of input use as the profit-maximizing choice). As is the case with most other forms of pollution, policies can be broadly divided into regulations and economic instruments. Regulatory approaches include design standards such as specifications of the types of pollution control equipment that may be used and performance standards such as limiting the number of livestock per hectare in a farming operation. Economic instruments include taxes, subsidies, and tradable permits. As we discussed earlier in the case of *point source* pollutants, economists have generally favored economic instruments over regulatory approaches. This preference holds for nonpoint source pollutants, as well (Ribaudo, Horan, and Smith, 1999). This position largely derives from the finding that regulations do not account for differences across polluters (such as their respective costs of abatement or the relative impact of a given quantity of emissions on different parts of a water body) and do not provide polluters with an ongoing incentive to innovate and reduce pollution beyond the mandated standard.

Economists have considered a number of economic instruments for the control of nonpoint source water pollution including input-based taxes/subsidies and ambient quality-based taxes/subsidies (Segerson, 1988; Ribaudo, Horan, and Smith, 1999). Emissions-based taxes and subsidies – the most commonly considered instruments in the case of point source pollutants – cannot really be applied here as emissions cannot be measured and cannot be linked directly to either ambient water quality or actions taken by polluters. Researchers have demonstrated that, in theory, input-based or ambient quality-based instruments can be designed to achieve a first-best outcome – that is, the efficient level of *nonpoint source* pollution. The difficulty with these models is the information that is required in order to implement them. For example, input-based taxes and subsidies exploit the fact that increasing the use of some inputs (such as fertilizers) increases emissions while increasing the use of other inputs (such as using climate data to improve the timing of fertilizer applications) decreases emissions. In order to make use of these relationships, the regulator must know not only the relationship between each polluter's emissions and ambient water quality but also have complete information regarding the polluters production technology (specifically, the regulator must know the substitution possibilities between all inputs). Possessing this information would allow the regulator, in principle, to design first-best firm-specific and input-specific taxes and subsidies.

In addition to the interest in taxes and subsidies, economists have considered the application of tradable permit programs to the control of *nonpoint source* pollution. For example, farmers within a watershed could be allotted (or sold) permits for the application of nitrogen on their crops. The total allotment of nitrogen would be some quantity less than previously deposited within the watershed and would be based on a model of the watershed's assimilative capacity and the costs and benefits of nitrogen application. Farmers desiring to apply more than their allotment would be required to purchase permits from another farmer. In this manner, nitrogen use would be allocated to those applications with the highest value or, equivalently, the reduction in nitrogen use would be achieved at the lowest possible opportunity cost (in the form of raised costs or forgone output). The challenge in implementing trading schemes for nonpoint pollution is two-fold. First, as discussed above, the damage caused by a given quantity of emissions will depend on a variety of factors. As a result, regulators will not, in general, be indifferent to the time, location, and manner that the nitrogen is applied. These concerns will necessarily narrow the range of possible trades and, as a result, restrict the potential efficiency gains from trading. Second, it must be possible for regulators to monitor and measure nitrogen use to ensure that farmers are not employing more than they are allotted.

Researchers have turned their attention to the design of second-best instruments because of the informational requirements of first-best economic instruments. In a *second best* environment, the goal may be either to find the policy instrument that achieves a given improvement of ambient water quality at least cost ("cost-effectiveness") or to the design of policy instruments under a specific constraint (such as a tax that is common across all firms in a given region). While these types of policy instruments do not yield the same potential efficiency gain as first-best instruments, they do not have the same informational requirements.

Given the informational difficulties surrounding the regulation of *nonpoint sources*, it is not surprising that governments first sought to control *point source* pollutants. Ribaudo, Horan, and Smith (1999) discuss efforts by American regulators to control nonpoint source pollution with an emphasis on efforts to address the agricultural sector's emissions. The authors point out that a variety of policies have been adopted including design and performance standards (e.g. for waste-handling practices and pesticide application), subsidies and cost-sharing for pollution-abatement equipment, technical assistance (educational programs and development of best management practices) and research. A common challenge in assessing the efficacy of these programs is compiling the needed water quality data and estimating the analytic models that relate emissions to ambient water quality. In addition, some researchers have modeled the technology of polluting agricultural operations and argued that the small input and output price elasticities that they observe will mean farmers are relatively unresponsive to changes in input and output prices. As a result, this type of observation, would suggest that economic instruments would be relatively ineffective (Weersink and Livernois, 1996).

It is clear, then, that regulation of nonpoint source pollution will remain an active area of research and experimentation.

6.7 SUMMARY

The earth is a water-rich planet. Nonetheless, the vast majority of water is highly saline, frozen or deep underground. Furthermore, much of the world's potable surface water is located far from population centers. These supply-side concerns are re-enforced by a variety of features that are increasing the demand for water. These features include rising population, increasing per capita income levels, urbanization, and global climate change. Taken together, then, the forces leading to the growing scarcity of low-cost potable water provide a strong motivation for considering the allocation of water resources.

In particular, the purpose of this chapter has been to outline a number of the economic issues associated with the efficient allocation of water. The static and dynamic theoretical models have demonstrated the derivation of conditions necessary for the efficient allocation of water and the efficient level of water quality. Not surprisingly, these models have in common the need to account for, and balance, social benefits and costs to achieve the efficient outcome. This feature points out the importance of acquiring the data needed to estimate these relationships.

This chapter has also discussed the features of real-world water allocation mechanisms and has considered their efficiency properties. Many of these mechanisms and institutions do not produce efficient outcomes as a result of improper and incomplete cost accounting, failure to weigh costs and benefits, and a reliance on command and control style quantitative regulations. Nonetheless, there are indications that the growing reliance on pricing and markets to allocate water and on economic instruments to regulate the quality of water may lead to increased efficiency in the use of water resources.

NOTE

1   Shortle, Horan, and Abler (1998) also note that an additional first-order condition is required to ensure the optimal number of firms is present in the industry.

FURTHER READING

Aside from a remarkable public lecture by Alfred Marshall (1925) during which he considers the extent to which water contributes to national wealth, economists have turned their attention to water only relatively recently. In the 1960s, a number of important studies were completed. Hirshleifer, De Haven, and Milliman (1960) is a classic reference that demonstrates the application of economic principles to the management of municipal water systems. Burt (1967) provides an early application of dynamic optimization techniques to the analysis of the optimal exploitation of an aquifer. Headley and Ruttan (1964) is an early example of the valuation of water use in agriculture. Howe and Linaweaver (1967) is the first significant econometric effort to characterize residential water demands. At the same time, large water-research projects were undertaken at Harvard and Johns Hopkins Universities and Resources for the Future. These resulted in important work on the valuation of recreational water use (Clawson and Knetsch, 1966) and water's role in regional economies (Eckstein, 1958) and in production technologies (Bower, 1966).

Since that time, the economic analysis of water resources has proceeded along several streams. The examination of the structure of water demands has used increasingly sophisticated econometric methods to cope with the price of complex price schedules. This literature is surveyed in Renzetti (2002). Water use in agriculture has received a significant amount of attention because it is the largest water-using sector in many countries. Boggess, Lacewell, and Zilberman (1993) review developments in this area. A significant amount of effort has been directed at developing methods to value water resources and changes to water quality. Bergstrom, Boyle, and Poe (2001) provide an excellent review of methods and findings regarding the valuation of water resources. Easter, Feder, Le Moigne, and Duda (1993) is a comprehensive review of the challenges facing water management with a strong emphasis on water allocation in low-income countries and Easter, Dinar, and Rosegrant (1998) is an excellent collection of articles concerned with the design and operation of water markets. Finally, Baumann, Boland, and Hanemann (1998) provide a comprehensive review of issues related to the management of municipal water supply systems.

REFERENCES

Allee, D. (1993). Subnational Governance and the International Joint Commission: Local Management of United States and Canadian Boundary Waters, *Natural Resources Journal*, 33 (1): 133–51.

Baumann, D., Boland, J., and Hanemann, W. M. (1998). *Urban Water Demand Management and Planning*, McGraw-Hill: New York.

Becker, N., Zeitouni, N., and Schecter, M. (1997). Employing Market Mechanisms to Encourage Efficient Use of Water in the Middle East, in D. Parker and Y. Tsur, eds, *Decentralization and Coordination of Water Resources Management*, Kluwer Academic Press: Boston, pp. 199–221.

Bergstrom, J., Boyle, K., and Poe, G., eds (2001). *The Economic Value of Water Quality*, Edward Elgar: Cheltenham.

Biswas, A. K. (1997). Water Development and Environment, in Asit K. Biswas, ed., *Water Resources, Environmental Planning, Management and Development*, McGraw-Hill: New York, pp. 1–37.

Boggess, W., Lacewell, R., and Zilberman, D. (1993). The Economics of Water Use in Agriculture, in G. Carlson, D. Zilberman, and J. Miranowski, eds, *Agricultural and Environmental Resource Economics*, Oxford University Press: New York, pp. 319–84.

Bower, B. (1966). The Economics of Industrial Water Utilization, in A. Kneese and S. Smith, eds, *Water Research*, Resources for the Future: Baltimore, pp. 143–73.

Brown, G. and Deacon, R. (1972). Economic Optimization of a Single-Cell Aquifer, *Water Resources Research*, 8 (3): 557–64.

Brown, G. and Johnson, R. (1984). Pollution Control by Effluent Charges: It Works in the Federal Republic of Germany, Why Not in the US, *Natural Resources Journal*, 24 (October): 929–66.

Brown, G. and McGuire, C. (1967). A Socially Optimal Pricing Policy for a Public Water Agency, *Water Resources Research*, 3 (1): 33–43.

Brown, S. and Sibley, D. (1986). *The Theory of Public Utility Pricing*, Cambridge University Press: Cambridge.

Burt, O. (1967). Temporal Allocation of Groundwater, *Water Resources Research*, 3 (1): 45–56.

Chave, P. (2002). *The EU Water Framework Directive: An Introduction*, IWA Publishing: Colchester.

Clawson, M. and Knetsch, J. (1966). *Economics of Outdoor Recreation*, Johns Hopkins University Press: Baltimore.

Cosgrove, W. and Rijsberman, F. (2000). *World Water Vision: Making Water Everybody's Business*, Earthscan Publishers for the World Water Council: London.

Dinar, A. and Subramanian, A., eds (1997). *Water Pricing Experiences: An International Perspective*, World Bank Technical Paper No. 386, The World Bank: Washington, DC.

Dinar, A. and Zilberman, D. (1991). Effects of Input Quality and Environmental Conditions on Selection of Irrigation Technologies, in A. Dinar and D. Zilberman, eds, *The Economics and Management of Water and Drainage in Agriculture*, Kluwer Academic: Boston, pp. 229–50.

Duffield, J. W., Neher, C. J., and Brown, T. C. (1992). Recreation Benefits of Instream Flow: Application to Montana's Big Hole and Bitterroot Rivers, *Water Resources Research*, 28 (9): 2169–81.

Dupont, D. and Renzetti, S. (1999). An Assessment of the Impact of a Provincial Water Charge, *Canadian Public Policy*, 25 (3): 361–78.

Dupont, D. and Renzetti, S. (2001). Water's Role in Manufacturing, *Environmental and Resource Economics*, 18 (4): 411–32.

Easter, K. W., Dinar, A., and Rosegrant, M. (1998). Water Markets: Transactions Costs and Institutional Options, in K. W. Easter, M. Rosegrant, and A. Dinar, eds, *Markets for Water: Potential and Performance*, Kluwer Academic Press: Boston, pp. 1–19.

Easter, K. W., Feder, G., Le Moigne, G., and Duda, A. (1993). *Water Resources Management: A World Bank Policy Paper*, The World Bank: Washington, DC.

Eckstein, O. (1958). *Water Resources Development: The Economics of Project Evaluation*, Harvard University Press: Cambridge, MA.

Edwards, B., Howitt, R., and Flaim, S. (1996). Fuel, Crop and Water Substitution in Irrigated Agriculture, *Resource and Energy Economics*, 18: 311–31.

Espey, M., Espey, J., and Shaw, W. D. (1997). Price Elasticity of Residential Demand for Water: A Meta-Analysis, *Water Resources Research*, 33: 1369–74.

Fleming, R. and Adams, R. (1997). The Importance of Site-specific Information in the Design of Policies to Control Pollution, *Journal of Environmental Economics and Management*, 33: 347–58.

Frederick, K. (1996). Water as a Source of International Conflict, *Resources* v. 123, Resources for the Future: Washington, DC.

Freeman, A. M. III (1990). Water Pollution Policy, in P. Portney, ed., *Public Policies for Environmental Protection*, Resources for the Future: Washington, DC, pp. 97–149.

Frisvold, G. and Caswell, M. (1997). Transboundary Water Agreements and Development Assistance, in D. Parker and Y. Tsur, eds, *Decentralization and Coordination of Water Resources Management*, Kluwer Academic Press: Boston, pp. 115–33.

Gisser, M. and Sanchez, D. (1980). Competition Versus Optimal Control in Groundwater Pumping, *Water Resources Research*, 16 (4): 638–42.

Gleick, P. (2000). *The World's Water 2000–2001*, Island Press: Washington, DC.

Hall, D. and Hanemann, M. (1996). Urban Water Rate Design Based on Marginal Costs, in D. Hall, ed., *Advances in the Economics of Environmental Resources: Marginal Cost Rate Design and Wholesale Water Markets* vol. 1, JAI Press: Greenwich, CT.

Hanley, N., Faichney, R., Munro, A., and Shortle, J. (1998). Economic and Environmental Modeling for Pollution Control in an Estuary, *Journal of Environmental Economics and Management*, 52 (2): 211–25.

Headley, J. and Ruttan, V. (1964). Regional Differences in the Impact of Irrigation on Farm Output, in S. Smith and E. Castle, eds, *Economics and Public Policy in Water Resources Development*, Iowa State University Press: Ames, pp. 127–49.

Hellegers, P., Zilberman, D., and van Ierland, E. (2001). Dynamics of Agricultural Groundwater Extraction, *Ecological Economics*, 37 (2): 303–11.

Hirshleifer, J., De Haven, J., and Milliman, J. (1960). *Water Supply: Economics, Technology and Policy*, University of Chicago Press: Chicago.

Hoag, D. and Hughes-Popp, J. (1997). Theory and Practice of Pollution Credit Trading in Water Quality Management, *Review of Agricultural Economics*, 19 (2): 252–62.

Horbulyk, T. and Lo, L. (1998). Welfare Gains from Potential Water Markets in Alberta, Canada, in K. W. Easter, M. Rosegrant, and A. Dinar, eds, *Markets for Water: Potential and Performance*, Kluwer Academic Press: Boston, pp. 241–57.

Howe, C. (1982). The Impact of Price on Residential Water Demand: Some New Insights, *Water Resources Research*, 18 (4): 713–16.

Howe, C. (1994). Taxes *Versus* Tradable Discharge Permits: A Review in the Light of the US and European Experience, *Environmental and Resource Economics*, 4: 151–69.

Howe, C. and Linaweaver, F. (1967). The Impact of Price on Residential Water Demand and Its Relation to System Design and Price Structure, *Water Resources Research*, 3 (1): 13–31.

Kamien, M. and Schwartz, N. (1991). *Dynamic Optimization*, New York: North Holland.

Knapp, K. and Olson, L. (1995). The Economics of Conjunctive Groundwater Management with Stochastic Surface Supplies, *Journal of Environmental Economics and Management*, 28 (3): 340–56.

Marshall, A. (1925). Water as an Element of National Wealth, in A. Pigou, ed., *Memorials of Alfred Marshall*, Kelley and Millman: New York, pp. 134–41.

Munasinghe, M. (1992). *Water Supply and Environmental Management: Developing World Applications*. Studies in Water Policy and Management, Westview Press: Boulder, CO.

Neher, P. (1990). *Natural Resource Economics: Conservation and Exploitation*, Cambridge University Press: Cambridge.

OECD (1999). *Economic Instruments for Pollution Control and Natural Resources Management in OECD Countries: A Survey*, Organization for Economic Cooperation and Development: Paris.

Ontario Ministry of the Environment (1998). *The Drinking Water Surveillance Program*, The Queen's Printer: Toronto.

Poe, G. (1998). Valuation of Groundwater Quality Using a Contingent Valuation-damage Function Approach, *Water Resources Research*, 34 (12): 3627–33.

Postel, S. (2000). Redesigning Irrigated Agriculture, in L. Brown, ed., *State of the World 2000*, WorldWatch Institute: Washington, DC, pp. 39–58.

Provencher, B. and Burt, O. (1993). The Externalities Associated with the Common Property Exploitation of Groundwater, *Journal of Environmental Economics and Management*, 24 (2): 139–58.

Renzetti, S. (1992). Evaluating the Welfare Effects of Reforming Municipal Water Prices, *Journal of Environmental Economics and Management*, 22 (2): 147–63.

Renzetti, S. (1999). Municipal Water Supply and Sewage Treatment: Costs, Prices and Distortions, *Canadian Journal of Economics*, 32 (3): 688–705.

Renzetti, S. (2002). *The Economics of Water Demands*, Kluwer Academic Press: Boston.

Ribaudo, M., Horan, R., and Smith, M. (1999). *Economics of Water Quality Protection from Nonpoint Sources: Theory and Practice*, Economic Research Service Agricultural Research Report 782, United States Department of Agriculture: Washington, DC.

Sampat, P. (2001). Uncovering Groundwater Pollution, in L. Brown, ed., *State of the World 2001*, WorldWatch Institute: Washington, DC, pp. 21–42.

Scott, A. and Coustalin, G. (1995). The Evolution of Water Rights, *Natural Resources Journal*, 35 (4): 821–979.

Shortle, J., Horan, R., and Abler, D. (1998). Research Issues in Nonpoint Pollution Control, *Environmental and Resource Economics*, 11 (3–4): 571–85.

Segerson, K. (1988). Uncertainty and Incentives for Nonpoint Pollution Control, *Journal of Environmental Economics and Management*, 15 (1): 88–98.

Tao, W., Yang, W., and Zhou, B. (1998). Tradable Discharge Permits System for Water Pollution of the Upper Napan River, China, Research Report for the Economy and Environment Program for South East Asia: http://www.eepsea.org

Tate, D. and Lacelle, D. (1995). Municipal Water Rates in Canada, 1991: Current Practices and Prices, Social Science Series 30, Ottawa: Inland Waters Directorate, Environment Canada.

Tchobanoglous, G. and Schroeder, E. (1997). *Water Quality*, Addison Wesley: New York.

Tietenberg, T. (1985) *Emissions Trading: An Exercise in Reforming Pollution Policy*, Resources for the Future: Washington, DC.

Tomasi, T. and Weise, A. (1994). Water Pollution Regulation in a Spatial Model, in C. Dosi and T. Tomasi, eds, *Nonpoint Source Pollution Regulation: Issues and Analysis*, Kluwer: Dordrecht and Boston, pp. 151–74.

Tsur, Y. and Graham-Tomasi, T. (1991). The Buffer Value of Groundwater with Stochastic Surface Water Supplies, *Journal of Environmental Economics and Management*, 21 (2): 201–24.

Turner, R. K., Adger, W. N., and Brouwer, R. (1998). Ecosystem Services Value, Research Needs and Policy Relevance: A Commentary. Special section: Forum on Valuation of Ecosystem Services, *Ecological Economics*, 25: 61–5.

Utton, A. (1996). Which Rule Should Prevail in International Water Disputes: That of Reasonableness or That of No Harm?, *Natural Resource Journal*, 36 (3): 635–41.

Vajpeyi, D. K. (1998). Introduction, in D. K. Vajpeyi, ed., *Water Resources Management: A Comparative Perspective*, Praeger: Westport, CT, pp. 1–18.

Weersink, A. and Livernois, J. (1996). The Use of Economic Instruments to Resolve Water Quality Problems from Agriculture, *Canadian Journal of Agricultural Economics*, 44: 345–53.

Worthington, V., Burt, O., and Brustkern, R. (1985). Optimal Management of a Confined Groundwater System, *Journal of Environmental Economics and Management*, 12: 229–45.

Zhang, F. (1999). Marginal Opportunity Cost Pricing for Wastewater Disposal: A Case Study of Wuxi, China, Research Report for the Economy and Environment Program for South East Asia: http://www.eepsea.org

Zilberman, D., Chakravorty, U., and Shah, F. (1997). Efficient Management of Water in Agriculture, in D. Parker and Y. Tsur, eds, *Decentralization and Coordination of Water Resource Management*, Kluwer Academic Press: Boston, pp. 221–46.

CHAPTER SEVEN

ECONOMICS OF NON-RENEWABLE RESOURCES

If the old mines are insufficient to supply the quantity of coal required, the price of coal will rise, and will continue rising till the owner of a new and inferior mine finds that he can obtain the usual profits of stock by working his mine. If his mine be tolerably fertile, the rise will not be great before it becomes his interest so to employ his capital; but if it be not tolerably fertile, it is evident that the price must continue to rise till it will afford him the means of paying his expenses, and obtaining the ordinary profits of stock. (David Ricardo, *On the Principles of Political Economy and Taxation*, Chapter 24, paragraph 9, p. 317)

7.1 INTRODUCTION

From the earliest periods, the making of tools with stone and eventually metals such as copper, bronze, and iron has played a fundamental role in human development. Conflicts over access to non-renewable resources, whether it be gold or precious minerals at the height of the Egyptian civilization, or oil in modern times, have helped shape human history. Today, non-renewable resources form the basis of our modern economy. Without metals and fossil fuels, modern industrial society would, as we know it, be very different.

In this chapter we address the fundamental challenges of resource economics: what is the optimal rate of extraction of non-renewable resources? Are we as a society using them at too fast a rate? And, are there sufficient non-renewable resources to maintain our economic well-being for the foreseeable future? The answers to these questions revolve around how mineral prices and the costs of mineral production change over time. Thus, much of the chapter examines the dynamics of extraction costs and mineral prices under various assumptions. An empirical review of the trends in prices and reserves is also provided to examine what measures can be used as indicators of resource scarcity. The chapter concludes with a review of policy issues and particularly the capture of rents from the mining industry.

7.2 ECONOMICS OF MINING

The fundamental difference between the economics of the mine and that of renewable resources, such as fisheries or forests, is that other than on a geological timescale a mineral is a sterile asset. In other words, the resource stock of minerals can, at best, remain constant but can never increase. Thus in the economics of mining the only steady state is one where there is no extraction.

In the following section we examine the economics of extracting a non-renewable resource. In particular, we derive the extraction path (the set of period-by-period extraction rates) that maximizes the present value rents from a mine. We first examine this problem from the perspective of an individual mine operating in a competitive market with costless extraction.

Individual competitive mine

We illustrate the simplest mining problem assuming zero extraction costs, a competitive market for the mineral, perfect information in terms of the resource stock and prices, and all of the extracted mineral is sold in the period it is mined. Such a problem is given by equations (1) to (3) where x, the extraction rate, is chosen to maximize the present value of rents from extraction,

$$\text{Max } V = \int_{t=0}^{T} e^{-\delta t} px \, dt \tag{1}$$

Subject to:

$$db/dt = -x \tag{2}$$

$$b_0 \geq \int_{t=0}^{T} x \, dt \tag{3}$$

In this problem, the choice or *control variable* is the rate of extraction (x) and is defined as some quantity per time period. The price of the mineral is denoted by p and the discount rate used by the firm is δ. The rate of extraction on the right-hand-side of (2) determines the rate as which the remaining reserves (b) given on the left-hand-side of (2) change with respect to time. The greater is the extraction rate the faster will be the decline in the remaining reserves. The initial reserves of the mineral equal b_0 and are a known quantity. Equation (3) ensures that cumulative extraction can never exceed this quantity. For the moment, we assume the time horizon for the mine is given such that T is known.

To determine the optimal extraction path we can set up a function that incorporates the objective functional in (1) and the dynamic constraint given by (2), i.e.,

$$H = e^{-\delta t} px + \lambda(-x) \tag{4}$$

where p, x, and λ are functions of time, p is the unit resource price for a given quantity of the mineral, λ is the present value of the shadow price of the resource stock and H is the present-value Hamiltonian.

If the firm is maximizing the present value of its rents over time then at any instant in time it must be that

$$\partial H/\partial x = e^{-\delta t}p - \lambda = 0 \Rightarrow \lambda = pe^{-\delta t} \tag{5}$$

In this special case, where costs of extraction are zero, the shadow price of the resource equals the present value of the resource price and there is no benefit on the *cost side* from delaying extraction. For the competitive mine, the price it receives for its production is given. Thus the optimal rate of extraction is determined solely by the rate at which the resource price changes over time and the discount rate δ. If the resource price were constant, it would be optimal to extract *all* of the remaining reserves of the mineral at the earliest possible moment (provided $\delta > 0$) because any delay in extraction would lower the present value of the rents from the mine.

If the price of the mineral were increasing over time such that $p = e^{\gamma t}p(0)$ where $p(0)$ is the price at t = 0, but $\gamma < \delta$, it would still be optimal to extract all of the mineral at the earliest possible moment because any delay in extraction would reduce the present value of the returns from extraction as the present value of the resource price would be declining over time. By contrast, if $\gamma > \delta$, the present value of the resource price would be increasing over time and it would be optimal to wait to the last possible moment (just before T) to extract the remaining reserves of the mineral. In this case, although the mineral is a sterile asset, it would pay to keep it in the ground for as long as possible because delaying extraction allows the firm to sell the mineral at the highest possible price.

If $\gamma = \delta$, the present value of the resource price would be the same at any point in time and the firm would be *indifferent* between extracting now or later provided that all the resource would be extracted by time T. In this particular case, the rate of increase in the mineral price would be exactly equal to the discount rate, i.e.,

$$(dp/dt)/p = \delta \tag{6}$$

For non-renewable resources, the terminal time or *transversality conditions* also play an important role in determining the optimal rate of extraction. In the problem above, it will *always* pay to extract and sell the mineral reserves because extraction costs are zero. In reality, the costs of extraction are positive and it is possible at the terminal time, T, for some of the mineral to be left in the mine because it is not profitable to extract it. The other possibility is that at the terminal time the mineral is completely exhausted. The transversality conditions, given by (7) and (8), help ensure optimal extraction and determine whether the mine is completely exhausted or not at T.

$$H = e^{-\delta T}px + \lambda(-x) = 0 \tag{7}$$

$$e^{\delta T}\lambda b(T) = 0 \tag{8}$$

Condition (7) can be called a "performance test" (Neher, 1990) and requires that at the terminal time T it is no longer profitable to extract the mineral. If this were *not* the case ($H > 0$), it would imply that mineral had been left in the ground while it was still profitable to extract it. In other words, the extraction path would not be optimal.

Condition (8) is the so-called "asset test" (Neher, 1990) and requires that the product of the current value of the shadow price ($e^{\delta T}\lambda$) of the resource and the remaining reserves denoted by $b(T)$, be zero at T. This can be satisfied if either the current value of the shadow price is zero, or if the mineral has been completely exhausted ($b = 0$). In the first case, it is no longer worthwhile to extract the mineral, and in the second, the mine has been exhausted and there is no more mineral left to extract.

Competitive mining industry

The problem of the individual competitive mine can be expanded to examine the implications of optimal extraction on the rate of extraction for the industry as a whole. We examine this problem by assuming the industry inverse demand for the mineral is given by (9), where the time subscripts on the market price (p) and the industry level of extraction (x) have been dropped for convenience and a and g are parameters,

$$p = a - gx \tag{9}$$

At terminal time, when the mineral from all mines has been extracted, it has to be the case that $p = a$ where a is called the *choke price*. The choke price is the price at which the quantity demanded is zero. It may be explained by the existence of readily available substitutes at the choke price. Such substitutes may arise from a readily available technology, often called a *back-stop technology*, that can supply a perfect substitute at the choke price (Nordhaus, 1979).

If the value to society from extracting the mineral is the present value of the area under the inverse demand curve, then the rate of extraction that maximizes this value is the solution to the following problem.

$$\text{Max } V = \int_{t=0}^{T} \left\{ \int_{0}^{x(0)} (a - gx)dx \right\} e^{-\delta t} \, dt \tag{10}$$

Subject to:

$$db/dt = -x \tag{11}$$

$$b_0 \geq \int_{t=0}^{T} x \, dt \tag{12}$$

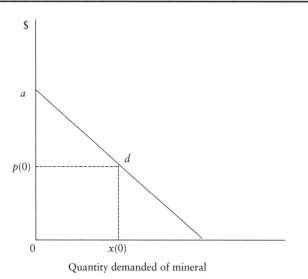

Quantity demanded of mineral

Figure 7.1   Area under the inverse demand curve

The expression in the curly brackets in (10) represents the area under the industry inverse demand curve. The lower limit of integration is the industry demand at the choke price and the upper limit of integration is $x(0)$, the initial industry demand at the initial price of the mineral $p(0)$. This is illustrated in figure 7.1 where the area under the inverse demand curve is defined by the area bounded by the vertices 0, a, d, and $x(0)$.

The present-value Hamiltonian for the problem defined by (10)–(12) is

$$H = \left\{ \int_{0}^{x(0)} (a - gx)dx \right\} e^{-\delta t} + \lambda(-x) \tag{13}$$

As with the individual competitive mine, the optimal rate of extraction must ensure that the present-value Hamiltonian is maximized at each point in time, i.e.,

$$\partial H / \partial x = (a - gx)e^{-\delta t} - \lambda = 0 \Rightarrow \lambda = (a - gx)e^{-\delta t} \Rightarrow \lambda = p \, e^{-\delta t} \tag{14}$$

Condition (14) must be satisfied at each moment in time and is identical to the optimal rate of extraction for the individual mine in (5) with the exception that x now refers to the industry demand for the mineral supplied by all mines. Unlike the individual mine problem, however, we cannot treat the price of the mineral as given because it is determined by the amount extracted by all mines.

To understand how the price of the mineral must change to maximize (10), we can examine a number of possible price paths. Suppose that the industry price path is defined by,

$$p = e^{\gamma t} p(0) \tag{15}$$

If $\gamma \neq \delta$, the mineral price path *cannot* maximize the present value of the consumer surplus. To understand this point, consider the following. If the growth rate of the resource price were rising at *less* than the discount rate, it would be possible to increase the present value of the consumer surplus by *increasing* the industry extraction rate because extracting more today would give a greater return than leaving a marginal unit of the resource in the ground. Similarly, if the growth rate of the mineral price were rising at *greater* than the discount rate, it would be possible to increase the present value of the consumer surplus by *decreasing* the industry rate of extraction because extracting marginally less of the mineral would generate a greater return.

The only growth rate at which the resource price can rise that ensures both the present value of the consumer surplus is maximized and *all* mine owners are indifferent from extracting today versus in the future is the discount rate, δ. This result, given in equation (6), is commonly called the *Hotelling rule*, after Harold Hotelling who first derived this result. The Hotelling rule can come in different forms, as we shall see, depending on the assumptions about the costs of extraction. The Hotelling rule is an *equilibrium condition* in that at each point in time the industry demand for the mineral at the prevailing price exactly equals the amount supplied or extracted.

To determine the industry rate of extraction of the mineral at each point in time we can substitute (15) into (9), given that $\gamma = \delta$, to derive the industry demand (which equals supply) as follows:

$$x = (a - e^{\delta t}p(0)\,)/g \tag{16}$$

We may also observe that the mineral is exhausted by the terminal time (or when the price reaches its choke price) because extraction is costless. This can be represented by the following constraint,

$$\int_{t=0}^{T} x \, dt = b_0 \tag{17}$$

From the Hotelling rule given by (6), we can solve for how the rate of extraction changes over time. First, we differentiate the inverse demand (9) with respect to time,

$$dp/dt = -g \, dx/dt \tag{18}$$

Substituting (18) into (6) where x is now defined as the industry demand (and supply) we obtain,

$$dx/dt = (p\delta)/-g \tag{19}$$

To solve for the optimal extraction path for x, all that remains is to solve for the initial and terminal conditions given by the initial price $p(0)$ and the terminal time T. To do so, we can substitute (16) into (17) and then do the necessary integration, i.e.,

$$b_0 = (a/g)T - (p(0)/g\delta)(e^{\delta T} - 1) \qquad (20)$$

We also know that the initial price must rise at the discount rate to eventually equal the choke price at terminal time, i.e.,

$$e^{\delta T}p(0) = a \qquad (21)$$

Equations (20) and (21) combined have two unknowns and can be solved to obtain $p(0)$ and T for specific values of δ, b_0, a, and g. The easiest way to make these calculations is to use (21) to solve out for T by taking the natural logarithm of both sides of the equation to obtain, $T = \ln[a/p(0)]/\delta$. This expression for T can be substituted into (20) to numerically solve for the value of $p(0)$ that satisfies the equation and the optimal extraction path. For example, if we define $\delta = 0.05$, $b_0 = 100$, $a = 10$, and $g = 1$, we can use a spreadsheet program or simulation software with trial and error to find an *approximation* for two unknowns, i.e., $p(0) = 3.03$ and $T = 23.88$. The extraction profile is characterized by a decreasing extraction rate over time that converges to 0 at T. Sensitivity analysis shows that a rise in the initial reserves (b_0) increases T but decreases $p(0)$, while a rise in the discount rate (δ) lowers both T and $p(0)$.

Provided that all of the conditions for perfect competition are met, such that all mines have perfect knowledge about current and future prices and remaining reserves, their private rate of discount equals the social rate of discount (see chapter 4), no externalities exist in production or consumption of the mineral, and all buyers and sellers are price takers, then the rate of extraction will ensure the price of the mineral rises according to the Hotelling rule.

The monopoly mine

The most cursory observation of the mining industry indicates that the market structure is frequently not competitive. For many minerals, there are a relatively small number of large suppliers that are either state-owned enterprises or large multinational corporations. For instance, almost the entire output of bauxite, copper, iron ore, manganese, molybdenum, and nickel come from just a few very large mines (Mikesell and Whitney, 1987). To appreciate the effect of market structure on the rate of extraction, we can compare the extraction rate under a competitive market structure to that of a monopolist.

The problem for the monopolist miner is given by (22)–(24). The principal difference with the competitive mine is that the monopolist's extraction rate affects the resource price it receives for the mineral it sells.

$$\text{Max } V = \int_{t=0}^{T} e^{-\delta t}p(x)x\,dt \qquad (22)$$

Subject to:

$$db/dt = -x \tag{23}$$

$$b_0 \geq \int_{t=0}^{T} x \, dt \tag{24}$$

The present-value Hamiltonian for the monopolist's problem is,

$$H = e^{-\delta t} p(x)x + \lambda(-x) \tag{25}$$

At each point in time, for the monopolist to maximize the present value of its rents, it must be the case that,

$$\partial H/\partial x = [p(x) + (dp/dx)x] \, e^{-\delta t} - \lambda = 0 \Rightarrow \lambda = [p(x) + (dp/dx)x] \, e^{-\delta t} \tag{26}$$

where $[p(x) + (dp/dx)x]$ is the marginal revenue (MR) of the monopolist. This result is very similar to that of the competitive mine except that the growth rate of the *marginal revenue* of the monopolist must rise at the rate of discount if the present value of the returns from extraction are to be maximized, i.e.,

$$(dMR/dt)/MR = \delta \tag{27}$$

In the case of the monopolist, it practices *intertemporal price discrimination* and ensures that the present value of its marginal revenue is the same at each point in time. By contrast, the competitive industry in equilibrium ensures that the present value of the resource price is the same at any point in time.

The effect of market structure on the rate of extraction depends on the industry demand for the mineral. If the price elasticity of demand varies with the rate of extraction, as it does with the inverse industry demand given by (9), then it will pay the monopolist to set its extraction profile so as to maximize the marginal revenue it receives. This results in the tendency to lengthen the extraction profile and to reduce the initial rate of extraction at $t = 0$ of the monopolist relative to the competitive industry.

To better understand this result, it is useful to rewrite the monopolist's marginal revenue as follows,

$$MR = p[1 - 1/|\epsilon|] \tag{28}$$

where $\epsilon = (dx/dp)(p/x)$ is the price elasticity of demand. It can be shown that a monopolist will *never* operate on the inelastic part of the demand curve because $|\epsilon| < 1$ implies that a marginal increase in the rate of extraction will *reduce* total revenue. Thus, for a linear demand where the absolute value of the price elasticity of demand varies from 0 when $p = 0$, to ∞ when $p = a$, the monopolist can

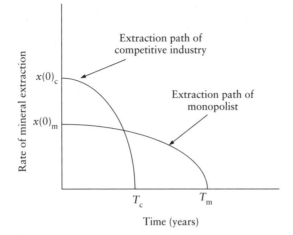

Figure 7.2 Optimal extraction paths of competitive industry and monopolist with a linear demand

increase the present value of its rents by establishing a different extraction profile to the competitive industry. In particular, the monopolist will supply relatively *less* on the least elastic portion of the demand curve, and supply relatively *more* on the most elastic part of the demand (thus receiving a higher price) in comparison to the competitive industry. In this sense, the monopolist "stretches out" the extraction profile in comparison to the competitive industry by supplying very small amounts of the mineral over a longer period of time when the demand is most elastic. As a result, for the same linear inverse industry demand and initial reserves, a monopolist will exhaust the mine at a later date than a competitive industry. This is illustrated in figure 7.2. In the figure, $x(0)_m$ and $x(0)_c$ are the initial rates of extraction of the monopolist and competitive industry and T_c and T_m are the corresponding shut-down points.

It should be emphasized that the extraction profile of a competitive industry and a monopolist will *not* always be different as it depends critically on the inverse industry demand. If the inverse demand is *isoelastic*, such as an inverse demand given by $p = ax^{-8}$, the price elasticity is the same whatever the price and the extraction profiles of the monopolist and competitive industry will be identical (Stiglitz, 1976). In this case, the monopolist is unable to practice price discrimination by changing its rate of extraction.

Costly extraction (constant marginal extraction cost)

For tractability, we have so far assumed that the mineral can be extracted at zero cost. In reality, the total costs of extraction will *increase* with the rate of extraction (increasing marginal cost of extraction) and, for a given level of extraction, costs will be higher the lower are the remaining reserves, a so-called a *stock* or *depletion effect*. Offsetting these factors is technical change that may reduce the costs of production in the future for a given level of extraction and remaining reserves. Combined, these factors have important implications for the optimal extraction of non-renewable resources.

Unlike the previous examples where the present value of the shadow price equals the price of the mineral, positive marginal extraction costs place a "wedge" between the two prices. In this case, the shadow price (more precisely the current value of the shadow price, or $\lambda e^{\delta t}$) is called the *net price*, rent or the marginal *user cost*. It represents the marginal value of the mineral *in situ*, or in the ground.

For the moment, we will assume that the marginal cost of extraction is a constant so the stock effect is zero and there is no technological change. Thus the maximization problem for a competitive mine in this case is,

$$\text{Max } V = \int_{t=0}^{T} e^{-\delta t}(p(x) - cx)\, dt \tag{29}$$

Subject to:

$$db/dt = -x \tag{30}$$

$$b_0 \geq \int_{t=0}^{T} x\, dt \tag{31}$$

where c is the constant marginal cost of extraction, measured in dollars per unit of mineral extracted. The present-value Hamiltonian for this problem is,

$$H = e^{-\delta t}(px - cx) + \lambda(-x) \tag{32}$$

A necessary condition to maximize the present value of rents is, therefore,

$$\partial H/\partial x = (p - c)e^{-\delta t} - \lambda = 0 \Rightarrow \lambda = (p - c)e^{-\delta t} \tag{33}$$

In keeping with convention, we can rewrite (33) by multiplying both sides of the equation by $e^{\delta t}$ and define

$$\lambda e^{\delta t} = q = (p - c) \tag{34}$$

where q is the net price of the resource. Equation (34) can also be derived directly from a current-value Hamiltonian defined as $H = H e^{\delta t}$ (see chapter 1). For the firm to be indifferent between extracting the mineral today versus the future, equation (34) implies that the growth rate in the net price must increase at the discount rate, i.e.,

$$(dq/dt)/q = \delta \tag{35}$$

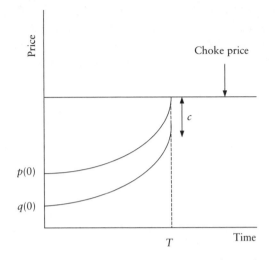

Figure 7.3   Resource and net price paths with linear inverse demand

Equation (35) is equivalent to the Hotelling rule we found previously in equation (6), except that the growth rate of the *net price* equals the discount rate. Indeed, in this special case where the marginal cost of extraction is unaffected by either the rate of extraction, the remaining reserves or technological progress, the growth rate in the resource price will also equal the discount rate. This is illustrated in figure 7.3 for an inverse linear demand and can be shown by rewriting (34) and differentiating with respect to time, noting that both p and q are a function of time (but c is not), i.e.,

$$dp/dt = dq/dt + dc/dt, \quad \text{where } dc/dt = 0$$

This result is illustrated in figure 7.3 where the initial net and resource prices are defined as $q(0)$ and $p(0)$. At terminal time, T, the resource price equals the choke price and the net price equals the choke price less that constant marginal cost of extraction, c.

Provided that all markets are competitive, all mines have the same private rate of discount that equals the social rate of discount and all mine owners have perfect information about current and future prices and reserves, then (35) is an *equilibrium condition*. In other words, a growth rate of the net price equal to the discount rate will ensure that the supply of the mineral exactly equals the demand for the mineral at all points in time. A key assumption to obtain this result is that mine owners have perfect information regarding reserves and future prices. In reality, even with futures markets and long-term mineral supply contracts, prices are known with uncertainty and thus expectation about future prices has an important effect on current and future supply of non-renewable resources.

If extraction is costly, the possibility exists that not all the reserves will be exhausted by terminal time, T. In this case, however, provided it is worthwhile to exploit the first unit of the resource it will also be worthwhile to exploit the very last unit. In other words, if $q(0) > 0$ it has to be the case that $q(T) > 0$, which from the "asset test" given in (8) implies that at T the reserves are exhausted. The "performance test" is automatically satisfied provided that the growth in the net price equals the discount rate, i.e.,

$$H = e^{-\delta T} (px - cx) + \lambda(-x) \Rightarrow (px - cx) + q(-x) = 0$$

Equation (35) also has an important economic interpretation when rewritten as follows,

$$dq/dt = \delta q \tag{36}$$

The left-hand side represents the instantaneous return from leaving a marginal amount of the mineral in the ground – the increase in the net price of the resource. The right-hand side represents the instantaneous return from extracting a marginal amount of the mineral and the returns were placed in a bank and earned an interest rate equal to the rate of discount. Provided the left-hand side (the instantaneous return from "investing" in the resource) equals the right-hand side (the instantaneous return from "disinvesting" or extracting the resource) the firm's extraction rate maximizes the present value of rents from the mine.

Costly extraction (with stock effect)

If the costs of extraction rise with a decline in the remaining stock of reserves, this "stock effect" represents an additional return from investing (or not extracting) a marginal amount of the resource. This extra return represents the cost savings from having a larger amount of the resource in the future that will result in a lower marginal extraction cost. Thus if we were to write the total cost of extraction as $c(x,b)$ then the marginal cost of extraction (MC) would be $\partial c(x,b)/\partial x$, or written equivalently as $c_x(x,b)$, and if the costs of extraction were increasing as the remaining reserves declined then $\partial c(x,b)/\partial b < 0$, or written equivalently as $c_b(x,b) < 0$. This last term represents the "stock effect," or the additional return (lower extraction costs in the future) from not extracting a marginal unit of the resource. It can be shown that with a stock effect for a firm to be indifferent from extracting or not extracting a marginal amount of the resource the following condition must be true,

$$dq/dt + c_b(x,b) = \delta q \tag{37}$$

where (37) is called the *modified Hotelling rule*.

In the presence of a stock effect, it is possible to have the mine shut down before all the remaining reserves are exhausted. To understand this point, note that as the reserve stock b approaches 0, the marginal costs of extraction may become so high that the net price q also approaches 0. When the net price is zero, it is no longer profitable to extract the resource, and this is the so-called *shut-down* point. Thus, whether or not the mine shuts down depends on the characteristics of the cost function $c(x,b)$.

If the mine does shut down with incomplete extraction then the net price must be *decreasing* over time. Moreover, the rate of extraction is *declining* over time until the shut-down point. To show this, we can use two necessary conditions that must be satisfied along the optimal extraction path: the "performance test" at terminal time (38) and the partial derivative of the current-value Hamiltonian with respect to the rate of extraction set equal to zero (39), i.e.,

$$(px - c(x,b)) + q(-x) = 0 \quad \text{at } T \tag{38}$$

$$p - c_x(x,b) = q \quad \text{for all t} \tag{39}$$

At the shut-down point $q = 0$ (and $b > 0$), thus from (38) $p = c(x,b)/x$, or the average cost (AC) of extraction equals the resource price. From (39), at T, $q = 0$ such that $p = c_x(x,b)$, such that the marginal cost of production equals the resource price. Thus (38) and (39) imply that AC = MC. Prior to the shut-down point, however, $(px - c(x,b)) + q(-x) > 0$ so that AC is *not* at its minimum point and thus MC > AC. For well-behaved cost functions with monotonically increasing marginal cost this implies the rate of extraction is highest when recovery of the mine begins, and as q declines, MC converges to AC, thus implying the rate of extraction declines.

Costly extraction (stock effects and technical change)

We can now examine what may happen with the net price and the resource price if there is both technological progress (that tends to reduce costs over time) and an offsetting stock effect. In this case, we assume the following extraction cost function,

$c(x,b;t)$ where $c_x(x,b;t) > 0$, $c_{xx}(x,b;t) > 0$, $c_{xb}(x,b;t) < 0$ and $c_{xt}(x,b;t) < 0$

The associated present-value Hamiltonian for a competitive firm with such a cost function is,

$$H = e^{-\delta T}[px - c(x,b;t)] + \lambda(-x)$$

A necessary condition for the firm to maximize the present value of its rents from extraction is, therefore,

$$\partial H/\partial x = e^{-\delta T}(p - c_x(x,b;t)) - \lambda = 0 \Rightarrow p - c_x(x,b;t) = q \ (= \lambda e^{-\delta T}) \tag{38}$$

where $MC = c_x(x,b;t)$. Rewriting (38) and differentiating with respect to time we obtain the following expression,

$$dp/dt = dq/dt + dMC/dt \tag{39}$$

where

$$dMC/dt = c_{xx}(x,b;t)dx/dt + c_{xb}(x,b;t)db/dt + c_{xt}(x,b;t)$$

Rewriting (37), the modified Hotelling rule, which must also hold true along the optimal extraction path in terms of dq/dt and substituting into (39), we obtain

$$dp/dt = \delta q - c_b(x,b) + dMC/dt$$
$$\Rightarrow dp/dt + c_b(x,b) - dMC/dt = \delta q \tag{40}$$

Equation (40) is a portfolio balance equation and may be called the *fundamental equation of non-renewable resources*. The left-hand side of (40) is the instantaneous return from "investing" in the resource or not extracting a marginal amount of the resource. It consists of any rise in the resource price, lower marginal costs of extraction in the future from having marginally greater remaining reserves, and lower marginal costs in the future associated with technological progress. The right-hand side is the instantaneous return from extracting a marginal amount of the resource and placing the returns in a bank to receive a rate of return equal to the discount rate.

Depending on the relative magnitudes of $c_b(x,b)$ and the terms that comprise dMC/dt, the resource and net price may be rising or falling over time. This has been shown formally by Farzin (1995) where, depending on the form of technical change, the resource price, the extraction cost, and the user cost may move in different directions over time.

Variable quality of reserves

Up to this point we have assumed that mines all have the same quality of ore. In reality, the quality of ore varies across mines and over time for any given mine. Moreover, in many mines the quality or grade of the ore extracted at any point in time is partly determined by the mine owner. Thus when choosing an optimal extraction path a mine owner faces two decisions: the rate of extraction (how much of the resource to be removed) and quality of the ore (the proportion of the mineral in the ore) to be extracted.

We would expect that the highest-grade ore with the highest user cost be extracted first, and the more marginal deposits be extracted later if the present-value of the resource price is rising over time. This is because the rising resource price will eventually make the marginal deposits profitable to extract – an insight first made by David Ricardo around two hundred years ago. Indeed, and as we would expect, the trend for most minerals is for the quality of ore to *decline* over time. However, if different grades of ore are *joint products* then different grades of ore will be extracted at the same time. This may also be true if the marginal cost of extraction of a lower grade ore is *declining* over some range in the rate of extraction of a higher-grade ore. This may arise, for example, where the ore bodies are in close proximity to each other. In this case, the mining of higher-grade ore may make it profitable to also extract low-grade ore simultaneously – a not infrequent occurrence in mineral mining (Carlisle, 1954).

The simultaneous mining of various grades of ore with different marginal extraction costs is also possible provided that the user costs in all the operating mines are positive. In this case, the mines with the higher user costs generate the highest rents, but all mines may enjoy positive rents. However, changes in the resource price will have the greatest impact on the most marginal mines located at the *extensive margin* – the point beyond which a mine with higher costs would not find it profitable to extract the mineral.

7.3   RUNNING ON EMPTY?

The economics of mining indicate a potential relationship between the costs of extraction, the resource price, the net price of non-renewable resources and the level of remaining reserves. These, and other variables, have been used to provide measures of *scarcity* of non-renewable resources. Such indexes of scarcity have generated a very large literature and have been motivated by the concern that the world may soon "run out" of key resources that have few or very expensive substitutes. These concerns have been labeled "scarcity controversies" as some have argued that the availability of key non-renewable resources (such as oil) will impose limits on growth (Meadows et al., 1974), while others have argued that few, if any, limits exist (Simon, 1995).

When comparing various notions of scarcity, it should be clear that *absolute* scarcity is increasing as our planet only has a finite amount of non-renewable resources. Thus any scarcity index that we use is a *relative* measure of scarcity. These indexes can be separated into physical or resource indexes and price or economic measures.

Resource measures

Before evaluating resource measures of scarcity it is worth observing that the mere existence of a non-renewable resource in the earth's crust does *not* imply that it is available for extraction. This is because for the vast majority of the earth's minerals (but not hydrocarbons) there exists a hypothesized *mineralogical barrier* (see box 7.1). All current mining of minerals takes place on the "favorable side" of this barrier, beyond which mineral extraction is required at the atomic level rather than physical separation currently used in mining operations. This is illustrated in figure 7.4.

BOX 7.1   "INFERENCE AND PROOF"
FOR MINERAL RESOURCES
AND RESERVES

Only a tiny fraction (between 0.01 and 0.001 percent) of the total amount of minerals in the earth's crust lie above a *mineralogical barrier*, below which minerals are only found as trace elements. Geologists have developed terms to describe mineral deposits that lie above this barrier. These terms, summarized below, were agreed to by a number of countries in Geneva in October 1998 in a joint collaboration between the United Nations Commission for Europe (UN-ECE) and the Council of Mining and Metallurgical Institutes (CMMI).

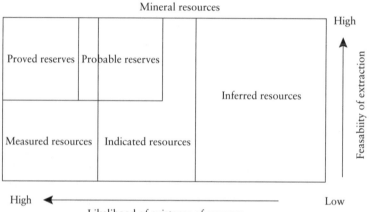

A *mineral resource* is defined as a concentration of material of intrinsic economic interest where there exists a reasonable prospect for eventual economic extraction. Mineral resources can be further divided into *inferred, indicated,* and *measured* resources where the quality and quantity of the mineral resource can be estimated with a low, reasonable, or a high level of confidence.

A *mineral reserve* is the economically extractable part of a measured or indicated mineral resource. Mineral reserves can also be divided into probable and proved reserves. A *probable reserve* is the economically extractable part of an indicated (and in some cases measured mineral resource) and a *proved reserve* is the economically extractable part of a measured resource.

Sources: Institute of Mining and Metallurgy (2002); Skinner (2001)

At present, global mining is in the favorable part of the density function of mineral abundance given in figure 7.4, but the grades of ore above the mineralogical barrier are likely to be a tiny fraction of the total amount available in the earth's crust (Skinner, 2001). Extraction of minerals beyond the barrier is technically possible, but is of several orders of magnitude times greater in cost than current

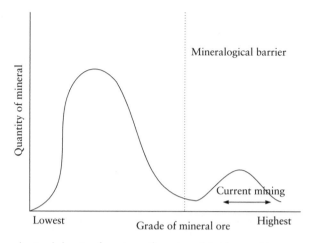

Figure 7.4 Hypothesized density function of a mineral in the earth's crust
Source: Adapted from Skinner (2001)

methods of mining. Thus, beyond the mineralogical barrier there will almost certainly be a large discontinuity in terms of relative scarcity of minerals despite the fact only a small proportion of the total amount of mineral will have been extracted when the hypothesized barrier is reached. Thus, physical indexes of minerals in terms of their absolute abundance in the earth's crust are worthless as measures of relative scarcity. An alternative physical measure to crustal abundance is the size of reserves, or the economically extractable part of mineral resources (see box 7.1). Such measures include reserve-to-use ratios and have frequently been used as indicators of scarcity of non-renewable resources, as given in table 7.1.

Although superficially appealing, reserve-to-use ratios of the type given in table 7.1. can be very misleading. First, reserves (by definition) do not include

Table 7.1 World mineral reserves and production

Mineral	Production	Reserves	Reserves/production
Iron	560	240,000	428
Copper	12.1	320	26
Gold	0.0023	0.045	20
Zinc	7.75	190	25
Nickel	1.13	40	35
Silver	0.0161	0.28	17
Tin	0.208	7.7	37

[a] Annual production and reserves given in million tons. [b] Annual production is 1997–99 annual world average taken from table 3.2, p. III-22 of Tilton (2001). [c] Reserves are taken from table 2, p. 139 of Lomborg (2001)

measured, indicated, or inferred resources that will provide a potential source of supply should the net price or user cost of the resource rise sufficiently. Second, if increasing relative scarcity increases the resource price, it provides an incentive to explore for new mineral sources that are undiscovered. Third, an increasing resource price stimulates the development and search for substitutes that may be renewable. For example, rising energy prices of hydrocarbons have stimulated research and development into photovoltaic cells that generate electricity from solar radiation. Fourth, a rising real price of a resource will, all other things equal, tend to reduce the demand thus extending the remaining life of the reserve.

These four issues mean that a reserve-to-use ratio such as 20 years for gold, as given in table 7.1, should *not* be interpreted to mean that all gold reserves will be exhausted 20 years hence. For example, the world reserve-to-use ratio for petroleum in 1950 was 20 years, but rose to 29 years in 1980 (Randall, 1987) despite the fact that annual world consumption increased almost six-fold over the intervening 30 years! Moreover, reserve-to-use ratios are based simply on current estimates of resource use and do not consider any trends in production (increasing or decreasing) over time.

Price measures

Three broad price measures have been employed to assess the relative scarcity of non-renewable resources: the real price of the resource, the real extraction costs, and the user cost or net price. It should be emphasized, however, that these three price measures are not independent as we have shown in the Hotelling rule and the modified Hotelling rule. As we might expect with the interplay of changes in demand, stock effects, and technological change, real prices may be rising over some period and then declining over others. This is illustrated by the real price of oil given in figure 7.5.

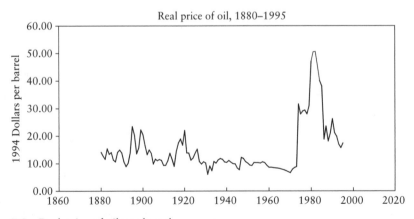

Figure 7.5   Real price of oil per barrel

Source: World Watch Database Disk 2000

One of the most cited studies of real non-renewable resource prices is by Barnett and Morse (1963), which has been updated. The evidence indicates that for the period 1870 to 1973 an index of mineral prices, relative to non-extractive commodities, has varied considerably, but there has been no discernible long-term upward trend. This has not prevented some people testing for the existence of an upward linear and quadratic trend in non-renewable prices that have (incorrectly) predicted rising mineral prices (Slade, 1982). In fact, looking back, the real price of major minerals and energy sources (aluminium, coal, copper, iron, lead, natural gas, nickel, petroleum, silver, tin, and zinc) tended to rise during the 1970s, but many declined in price during the 1980s and 1990s (Krautkraemer, 1998).

Despite the lack of resource-price evidence to support increasing relative scarcity, price spikes in key non-renewables, such as petroleum, have triggered widespread concern over the rate of depletion. In reality, the first oil price shock, and its aftermath (often called "the energy crisis") that began in 1973, was caused by the exercise of market power by the Organization of Petroleum Exporting Countries (OPEC) triggered by conflict in the Middle East, and *not* by a sudden depletion in oil reserves (see box 7.2). OPEC's market power enabled it to reduce its supply, increase the price of oil and also increase its revenues.

BOX 7.2   THE "OIL WARS"

In Baghdad in September 1960 representatives of five countries – Iraq, Saudi Arabia, Kuwait, Iran, and Venezuela – met and formed the Organization of Petroleum Exporting Countries (OPEC) that has subsequently been enlarged to 13 members. Their aim was to increase their influence over the price of oil relative to the major and foreign-owned oil companies of Exxon, Chevron, Mobil, Shell, Texaco, Gulf, and BP – known as the "seven sisters." Although none of its members were directly involved in the 1967 "Six Day War" between Israel against Egypt, Syria, and Jordan, it led to the adoption of oil exports as a weapon. All Arab members of OPEC agreed to an oil embargo on the United States and Britain, and Saudi Arabia, Kuwait, Libya, and Iraq immediately stopped all exports. Given the short duration of the war, and frictions between Egypt and Saudi Arabia, the embargo was lifted shortly after the cessation of hostilities.

The "oil weapon" was to be used with much more impact following the 1973 Egypt/Syria–Israel conflict known as the "Yom Kippur war." The war began on October 6 and 10 days later the six Gulf members of OPEC unilaterally increased their crude oil prices by 70 percent from around US$3/barrel. Following the cessation of hostilities on October 23, the Arab members of OPEC agreed to a 25 percent reduction in production and imposed an embargo on "enemy" countries that had helped Israel in the conflict, including the United States. Following peace negotiations initiated by the United States, oil sanctions were finally dropped by July 1974, but by this time the price of oil had quadrupled.

The second oil price shock began with the Iranian Islamic Revolution and the over-throw of the Shah of Iran in January 1979. Prices had already begun to rise before the end of 1978 due to strikes in the Iranian oil industry, but prices jumped even further as all Iranian exports were halted by the chaos after the Shah's departure. World supplies fell only marginally because of increased production by Saudi Arabia and other OPEC members, but the price increased significantly as some major importing countries, such as the United States, increased their demand by enlarging their strategic reserves. By the time Iran recommenced oil exports in March 1979, spot oil prices were about $20/barrel and the official OPEC price was $13.30/barrel that was subsequently raised to $14.50/barrel and then to $18.50/barrel (base price). By the start of the Iran–Iraq war in September 1980, official prices had more than doubled in 18 months to $30/barrel and spot prices reached as high as $42/barrel at the start of hostilities. At the beginning of 1983 official OPEC prices began to fall as increased supply from non-OPEC sources (the North Sea and Mexico in particular) came onto the market. By 1985, oil was trading as low as $10/barrel.

Sources: Terzian (1985); Wheelwright (1991)

An alternative price measure is the marginal user cost or net price of non-renewable resources. The *higher* the user cost or *in situ* value of a resource, the *greater* is its relative scarcity. Whether the user cost is rising or falling depends on the interplay of stock effects, demand (existence of substitutes) and technological change. Thus it is perfectly possible to have a *declining* user cost and decreasing relative scarcity due to stock effects, but for the absolute level of abundance of the resource to decline over time as the remaining reserves are extracted.

The other "price" that has been used to signal relative scarcity is real extraction costs. Barnett and Morse (1963) found a declining trend in real unit cost of extraction for the period 1870 to 1958, and which continued until 1970 (Johnson, Bell, and Bennett, 1980). For some minerals, the downward trend in extraction costs continued in the 1970s (Hall and Hall, 1984), although for most oil and gas fields that came into production in the 1970s and later (especially offshore deposits), the real costs of exploration and extraction were several times greater than for some of the highest-quality pre-existing reserves (such as in Saudi Arabia).

Prices, substitutes, and public policy

As we have shown, "prices" (resource price, user cost, and extraction costs) may be declining or falling over time. The implication is that measures of relative scarcity may move in the *opposite* direction of measures of absolute scarcity. For some observers, the lack of a discernible upward trend in "prices" is a cause of concern because they believe without it the market will not give an appropriate signal or incentive to firms to develop substitutes. In this pessimistic, sometimes called "Malthusian" perspective, prices will eventually rise due to a stock effect, and may do so suddenly, thereby causing a major negative economic shock. This is illustrated in figure 7.6.

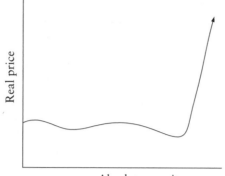

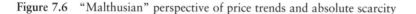

Absolute scarcity

Figure 7.6   "Malthusian" perspective of price trends and absolute scarcity

The scenario given in figure 7.6 is possible, but unlike the oil supply shocks of 1973 and 1979, a rapidly rising price due to cumulative extraction will almost certainly be anticipated. Consequently, expectations of a soon-to-be rapidly rising resource price should, in turn, spur research and development for substitutes *before* a rapid rise in its "price." Technological change may also render some resources superfluous long before any rapid increase in "price" implied by figure 7.6. For example, in nineteenth-century Britain the two major sources of energy in transportation and industrial production were coal and horses. The former provided the energy used by steam engines in a multitude of tasks, and for heating, while horses were widely used for transportation and delivery, and also in agricultural production. Technological change has rendered "horsepower" redundant while the demand for coal, because of the availability of cleaner substitutes (such as North Sea gas), has declined despite the fact that abundant deposits of coal still remain in the ground.

Concerns over running out of non-renewable resources have led some policy-makers to provide public incentives for developing substitutes and exploring for undiscovered resources. At a local level, efforts have also been made to increase the recycling of metals. Following the first oil price shock, various governments also offered research and development support to develop alternative energy sources, such as solar energy and wind power. The developments from these public and private research efforts are already being enjoyed in some countries. For example, wind power in especially windy locations and close to areas of electricity demand is now price competitive with some non-renewables (such as coal) in terms of electricity generation.

Another set of government or state initiatives has been to impose rental charges on non-renewable resource extraction. Such charges are often called royalties and are paid by firms to the owner of the mineral or energy deposit, which in many countries is the state itself. These charges are legitimate payments for the right to exploit a resource that belongs to someone else, just as we pay a rental for the use of land that we do not own. These royalties have also been used to generate "trust funds" such as in the province of Alberta, Canada – a major oil producer – so as to provide benefits for Albertans into the future. Indeed, investing *all* the rents from non-renewable resources to create a stream of benefits today and into the future has been called *Hartwick's rule* (Hartwick, 1977). It represents an important way to help sustainable development (see chapter 11) by ensuring that future generations can also benefit from resource extraction.

The most frequently applied charge is a so-called depletion or *severance tax* τ based on the amount extracted and the resource price. Thus, if p is the resource price and x is the amount extracted in a given period of time, the severance tax collects τpx. A potential problem with a severance tax is that it reduces the total amount of the resource that is extracted, if there are stock effects. This can be shown using equations (38) and (39), suitably modified for the existence of the severance tax, that must be satisfied for an optimal extraction path, i.e.,

$$(1 - \tau)px - c(x,b) + q(-x) = 0 \quad \text{at } T \tag{38*}$$

$$(1 - \tau)p - c_x(x,b) = q \quad \text{for all t} \tag{39*}$$

Equation (38*) is the "performance test" that must be satisfied at terminal time T, or when the mine shuts down. Given the stock effect, or rising marginal extraction costs due to declining remaining reserves (b), the user cost (q) is declining over time and at T, $qb = 0$, where $q = 0$ and $b > 0$.

Without the severance tax, the shut-down point is where the resource price equals the average cost of extraction (from (38)) and the marginal cost of extraction (from (39)), such that $p = c_x(x,b) = c(x,b)/x$. *With* a severance tax, the resource price net of the tax equals the average cost of extraction (from (38*)) and the marginal cost of extraction (from (39*)), i.e., $(1 - \tau) p = c(x,b)/x = c_x(x,b)$. For well-behaved cost functions (monotonically increasing marginal cost of extraction) this implies that with a severance tax the user cost reaches zero at a level of cumulative extraction that is *less* than without the tax. In other words, the shut-down point with a severance tax occurs when there is more of the resource left in the ground.

Alternative methods of rent capture have been proposed that, in theory, do not change the optimal rate of extraction or amount extracted. The *resource rent tax*, suggested by Garnaut and Clunies Ross (1975), levies a charge on mines in excess of extraction and exploration costs, including a return on the capital employed. Other methods of rent capture that have been proposed include the auction of mineral leases and charges imposed in excess of a defined rate of return of capital employed by mines.

7.4 RESOURCES AND RENTS

We have loosely defined *rent* as the net return after all costs of production. Not surprisingly, rents provide the principal incentive for the extraction of non-renewable

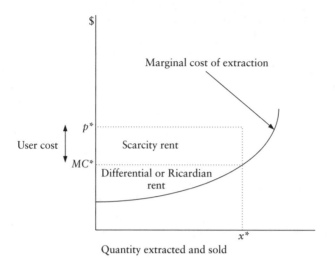

Figure 7.7   Rents and non-renewable resources

resources. Thus, an understanding of the factors that contribute to rents provides insights into the extraction of non-renewable resources.

The term *economic rent* refers to those returns that exceed those required to ensure the supply of a factor of production. In the case of non-renewable resources, economic rent exists whenever user cost is positive. The user cost multiplied by the amount of mineral extracted is sometimes defined as *scarcity rent*, indicating that it is a "payment" or return to the owner of the resource that arises from its limited supply. In this case, although marginal extraction of the resource would generate a positive return (user cost is positive), additional supply is constrained because miners are intertemporally better off by satisfying the fundamental equation of non-renewable resources and ensuring the instantaneous rate of return from not extracting exactly equals the rate of return of competing assets.

Another rent that may be enjoyed by owners of non-renewable resources is a *differential rent*, sometimes called *Ricardian rent* after the originator of the term, David Ricardo. Differential rent arises from the fact that for a factor of production fixed in supply (such as a mineral reserve) the marginal output from the addition of successive units of variable factors (such as labor and capital) must eventually fall. If the marginal cost of extraction were constant, there would be no differential rent. The returns from the sale of units of the output (such as the mineral) that exceed both the variable costs of production and the return to the fixed factor in an alternative use is differential rent.

The concepts of resource rent and differential rent are illustrated in figure 7.7 for an individual mine supplying x^* at point in time t for a price p^*. The scarcity rent is the difference between the resource price and the marginal cost of extraction multiplied by the amount of mineral extracted. The units of mineral extracted at a cost *less* the marginal cost of extraction (MC^*) associated with x^*, enjoy a differential rent or Ricardian rent that arises from the quality of resource, such as its accessibility or location or other factors. The combination of the resource and differential rent constitutes the firm's economic rent from selling x^* units of the resource at price p^*.

In addition to resource and differential rents, mine owners may also enjoy *quasi-rents* that arise from managerial skills of employees or owners and judicious investments in technology and capital that generate a return in excess of the payments received by the factors of production. This interpretation differs to the classical or standard definition of a quasi-rent that is simply returns in excess of variable costs. Our interpretation reflects the idea that rents can arise from both the "the gifts of nature" (economic rent) and the "judicious use" (quasi-rents) of labor and capital (physical, human, and social). In a competitive market quasi-rents should, for a given firm, decline over time as the price of factors of production that generate them will be bid up by competitors, or because cost-savings innovations are eventually copied by competitors.

Separating out quasi-rents from differential rent is difficult because it is not easy to distinguish between lower costs of production due to good fortune (easily accessible and higher-grade deposits) and lower costs due to superior methods of production and extraction. It also imposes an important policy dilemma. The capture of economic rent such as differential rent should, in theory, not affect the extraction profile of mines as it represents an "unearned gift of nature." By contrast, capture of quasi-rents that arise from innovations and judicious investments may affect long-run extraction as it reduces the incentive to innovate that, in turn, reduces marginal extraction costs in the future.

7.5   BETWEEN A ROCK AND A HARD PLACE

The question of whether we face a crisis in terms of the scarcity of non-renewable resources is a perennial issue. In the nineteenth century, some politicians (and some economists) worried about looming shortages of coal. Today, people are preoccupied about dwindling stocks of petroleum. Such worries are magnified by any unexpected price rise in an important non-renewable, such as when the spot price of oil rose by about half when Iraq invaded Kuwait in August 1990.

Notwithstanding such concerns, and the possibility of oil or other non-renewable shocks due to temporary and unexpected supply disruptions, the trend of the past few decades suggests that measures of relative scarcity of many non-renewables are *not* increasing. Thus for the foreseeable future (for the next one or two generations), and before the mineralogical barrier is reached, non-renewable relative resource scarcity should not be a major concern. By contrast, a major issue of concern for non-renewables in the foreseeable future is likely to be the negative externalities that their extraction and consumption generate. For example, the use of fossil fuels results in emissions of carbon dioxide that contributes to an enhanced greenhouse effect that may, in turn, lead to climate change. How we manage such issues, that involve both inter- and intragenerational trade-offs, will have a large impact on how we use and extract non-renewable resources today and in the future.

FURTHER READING

A rich and varied literature exists on non-renewable resources. Two of the classic articles on the subject are Gray (1914), who introduced the concept of user cost, and Hotelling (1931). Barnett and Morse (1963), who examine the scarcity of non-renewable resources, is worth reading and still offers valuable insights 40 years after it was written. A definitive reference on non-renewable resources is Dasgupta and Heal (1979). More recent and highly recommended texts on non-renewable resource use are Conrad (1999, chapter 5) and Neher (1990, chapters 15–18).

For those interested in learning more about the costs of extraction, Livernois and Uhler (1987) is one of the best empirical studies in terms of oil extraction. Cairns (1990) provides a good review of the economics of non-renewable resource exploration. Anderson (1991) is a useful introduction to the methods of rent capture. Cleveland and Stern (1999) is a helpful starting point into the scarcity literature. They emphasize the importance of incorporating measures of scarcity into an overall understanding of the economy. A review of the literature regarding tests of the Hotelling rule and measures of scarcity is provided by Krautkraemer (1998). Berck (1995) also provides an informative review of tests of the Hotelling rule.

Tilton (2001) provides a nice economic overview of the history and issues associated with mineral scarcity and use, while Skinner (2001) gives a geologist's perspective. Van Kooten and Bulte (2000, chapter 4) present an insightful discussion on rents in natural resources.

REFERENCES

Anderson, F. J. (1991). *Natural Resources in Canada*, Nelson Canada: Scarborough, Ontario.

Barnett, H. J. and Morse, C. (1963). *Scarcity and Growth: The Economics of Natural Resource Availability*, Johns Hopkins Press for Resources for the Future, Inc.: Baltimore, MD.

Berck, P. (1995). Empirical Consequences of the Hotelling Principle, in D. W. Bromley, ed., *The Handbook of Environmental Economics*, Blackwell Publishing: Cambridge, USA.

Cairns, R. D. (1990). The Economics of Exploration for Nonrenewable Resources, *Journal of Economic Surveys*, 4: 361–95.

Carlisle, D. (1954). The Economics of a Fund Resource with a Particular Reference to Mining, *American Economic Review*, 44: 595–616.

Cleveland, C. J. and Stern, D. I. (1999). Indicators of Natural Resource Scarcity: A Review and Synthesis, in J. C. J. M. van den Bergh, ed., *Handbook of Environmental and Resource Economics*, Edward Elgar: Cheltenham.

Conrad, J. M. (1999). *Resource Economics*, Cambridge University Press: Cambridge.

Dasgupta, P. S. and Heal, G. M. (1979). *Economic Theory and Exhaustible Resources*, Cambridge University Press: Cambridge.

Farzin, Y. H. (1995). Technological Change and the Dynamics of Resource Scarcity Measures, *Journal of Environmental Economics and Management*, 29: 105–20.

Garnaut, R. and Clunies Ross, A. (1979). The Neutrality of the Resource Rent Tax, *Economic Record*, 55: 193–201.

Gray, L. C. (1914). Rent Under the Assumption of Exhaustibility, *Quarterly Journal of Economics*, 28: 466–89.

Hall, D. C. and Hall, J. V. (1984). Concepts and Measures of Natural Resource Scarcity with a Summary of Recent Trends, *Journal of Environmental Economics and Management*, 11: 363–79.

Hartwick, J. M. (1977). International Equity and the Investing of Rents from Exhaustible Resources, *American Economic Review*, 66: 972–4.

Hotelling, H. (1931). The Economics of Exhaustible Resources, *Journal of Political Economy*, 39: 137–75.

Institute of Mining and Metallurgy (2002). Joint CMMI/UNECE Definitions for Mineral Resources and Reserves: http://www.imm.org.uk/genevadef.htm

Johnson, M. H., Bell, F. W., and Bennett, J. T. (1980). Natural Resource Scarcity: Empirical Evidence and the Public Policy, *Journal of Environmental Economics and Management*, 7: 256–71.

Krautkraemer, J. A. (1998). Nonrenewable Resource Scarcity, *Journal of Economic Literature*, 36 (4): 2065–107.

Livernois, J. R. and Uhler, R. S. (1987). Extraction Costs and the Economics of Nonrenewable Resources, *Journal of Political Economy*, 95: 195–203.

Lomborg, B. (2001). *The Skeptical Environmentalist: Measuring the Real State of the World*, Cambridge University Press: Cambridge, England.

Meadows, D. H., Meadows, D. L., Randers, J. and Behrens III, W. W. (1974). *The Limits to Growth*, second edition, Signet: New York.

Mikesell. R. F. and J. W. Whitney (1987). *The World Mining Industry: Investment Strategy and Public Policy*, Allen and Unwin: Boston.

Neher, P. A. (1990). *Natural Resource Economics: Conservation and Exploitation*, Cambridge University Press: Cambridge.

Nordhaus, W. (1979). *The Efficient Use of Energy Resources*, Yale University: New Haven, CT.

Randall, A. (1987). *Resource Economics: An Economic Approach to Natural Resource and Environmental Policy*, John Wiley and Sons: New York.

Ricardo, D. (1891) [1817]. *Principles of Political Economy and Taxation*, edited and introductory notes by E. C. K Gonner, George Bell and Sons: London.

Simon, J. L. (1995). Introduction, in J. L. Simon, ed., *The State of Humanity*, Blackwell Publishing: Cambridge, USA.

Skinner, B. J. (2001). Exploring the Resource Base, Mimeograph, Resources for the Future: Washington, DC.

Slade, M. E. (1982). Trends in Natural Resource Commodity Prices: An Analysis of the Time Domain, *Journal of Environmental Economics and Management*, 9: 122–37.

Stiglitz, J. E. (1976). Monopoly and the Rate of Extraction of Exhaustible Resources, *American Economic Review*, 66: 655–61.

Terzian, P. (1985). *OPEC: The Inside Story*, translated by Michael Pallis, Zed Books: London.

Tilton, J. E. (2001). *Depletion and the Long-Run Availability of Mineral Commodities*: http://www.mines.edu/Academic/econbus/faculty/tilton.htm

Van Kooten, G. C. and Bulte, E. H. (2000). *The Economics of Nature: Managing Biological Assets*, Blackwell Publishing: Malden, MA.

Wheelwright, T. (1991). *Oil & World Politics: From Rockefeller to the Gulf War*, Left Book Club Co-operative: Sydney.

PART THREE

ENVIRONMENTAL VALUATION

CHAPTER EIGHT

ENVIRONMENTAL VALUATION: INTRODUCTION AND THEORY

Nowadays people know the price of everything and the value of nothing. Oscar Wilde (1854–1900), in *The Picture of Dorian Gray*, Chapter 4 (1891)

8.1 INTRODUCTION

All students of natural resource and environmental economics are taught about the importance of externalities and public goods. In understanding externalities they are presented with cases of emissions of smoke from factories that have uncompensated effects on laundry owners, or emissions of water pollution from industrial facilities that have uncompensated effects on brewery owners. The externality problem is often corrected by identifying the impact of the emitter on the receptor and engaging the two parties in a bargaining process through which the externality is internalized (Coase, 1960). The standard analytical technique used is a characterization of marginal damage costs and marginal abatement costs. However, imagine a case where there are hundreds (or millions) of affected parties, as is the case with air emissions affecting human health. Not only will a bargaining process be difficult to construct, but any attempt to have a neutral party (perhaps the government) bargain on behalf of the affected individuals will require some form of measurement and aggregation of the impacts on health.

Conversely, consider the case of the creation of public goods. Economic theory shows that public goods will be underprovided unless demand-revealing mechanisms are employed. Suppose that the public good in question is a wilderness area that will benefit all members of society and a government is deciding whether to establish this protected area or allocate the area to a forestry company for harvesting. The vertical summation of demand curves should provide the aggregate demand for the wilderness area, but can these demands actually be measured? Can the benefit–cost analysis on the protected area versus the forest harvesting be carried out?

Both of the cases outlined above are common in the sense that decision-makers need more than conceptual models of externalities and public goods, they need measures of value and benefit in order to develop regulations or make decisions. Environmental valuation is a necessity in such cases. Environmental valuation is by its nature a "practical" and empirical component of environmental economics. Environmental valuation is used to construct measures (usually monetary measures, but not always) of welfare arising from changes in the environment. Since most environmental goods and services are not traded in markets, valuation requires that we go beyond simply measuring market demand functions. We must identify links between market goods and environmental goods and use these links in evaluating the welfare changes associated with changes in environmental quality, changes in the stock of natural resources or changes in ecosystem services. Alternately, we may create synthetic or hypothetical markets that include environmental goods and evaluate change using these hypothetical markets. In either case, a mixture of theory and empirical methods is required to identify and construct measures of the value of environmental quality change. In this chapter two case studies of policy decisions that involve environmental valuation are presented to motivate the analysis. Then, a typology of environmental value is presented. Finally, the theoretical framework upon which environmental valuation is based is presented. This provides a review of consumer and welfare theory that is necessary for the development of valuation techniques. Two chapters that examine the major approaches to valuation follow this chapter: approaches based on observed market or near market behavior, and approaches based on non-market or political behavior.

CASE STUDY 1: SETTING REGULATORY LEVELS FOR AIR QUALITY

A standard regulatory exercise is the establishment of regulations or standards that balance the marginal benefits and marginal costs of the situation. Suppose we are attempting to develop ambient quality standards for particulate matter (PM). PM is now recognized as "toxic" in many jurisdictions as high levels of PM have been linked to premature death, chronic bronchitis attacks, etc. (for a detailed discussion of the effects of PM, see *Report of the Royal Society of Canada Expert Panel* to Review the Socioeconomic Models and Related Components Supporting the Development of Canada-wide Standards for Particulate Matter and Ozone. The Royal Society of Canada. June 2001. Ottawa, Ontario. 240 pp.). Fine particles, those about 2.5 microns in size or $PM_{2.5}$, are hypothesized to be responsible for significant health effects. In Canada a process was initiated through which the costs of implementing regulation to reduce PM emissions were to be evaluated against the benefits of reducing PM levels in the air. This is a perfectly rational, economically oriented approach to the development of standards. However, the challenge involved in such an approach is the development of empirical estimates of the benefits and costs of changes in PM emissions and ambient levels.

In order to evaluate various levels of PM standards, the effect of changing PM levels on human health had to be evaluated (other "endpoints" beyond human health were evaluated as well – but we will not dwell on those endpoints here). Then, these changes in human health status had to be "valued" in monetary terms in order to compare the effects against the costs faced by industry associated with the new standard. The valuation measures included the benefits of reduced morbidity (or reduced health effects such as cardiac arrest and bronchitis) and the benefits of reduced risk of death. The latter is particularly challenging as the value of changing the risk of dying, in particular the risk of dying a year sooner than expected, is being evaluated in the valuation process (see box 8.1).

These types of measures that convert changes in human health risks into monetary values are emotionally and ethically charged. However, this type of analysis is critical to the formation of policy based on sound rational process. As the Royal Society of Canada expert panel report describes, the process of cost–benefit analysis (CBA) including environmental value "provides the decision-maker with a systematic identification, estimation, and measure of uncertainty of monetary values for the relevant costs and benefits of interest to decision-makers and stakeholders." The panel concluded "The Panel recommends that CBA be used to inform decision-makers about the projected costs and anticipated benefits of Canada Wide Standards."

BOX 8.1   THE VALUE OF REDUCING HEALTH RISKS

Individuals often make choices that reflect consideration of health risks. They may purchase automobiles with enhanced safety equipment. They may purchase air purifiers because of concerns over air quality and the potential for illness. Purchases of bicycle helmets, sunscreen, or carbon monoxide detectors are all indicators of the choices that consumers make that reflect concerns over health and safety risks. The trade-offs that individuals make in the marketplace relating to health risks provide information on the amount that people would be willing to exchange for a reduction in the risk of illness or death. Workers also have the opportunity to make choices about activities in the workplace and part of that choice may reflect considerations about relative safety risks and the relative wages in different jobs. Economists sometimes rely on data from occupational choices to calculate the value of reducing health risks. In addition, highly structured surveys can be used to identify trade-offs that people would make in response to small changes in health risks. All of these approaches provide information on the value to an individual of reductions in mortality or morbidity risks.

Imagine that we observe two occupational categories, and we are able to control statistically for all the non-safety related differences between these jobs to find the difference in wage associated with differences in safety. We find the difference to be $500 per year and to be associated with an increase in the risk of a fatal accident of 1 in 10,000 per year. This indicates that individuals are willing to trade off $500 in income for a 1 in 10,000 reduction in mortality risk. A program that reduced mortality risks by this amount for 10,000 people would generate benefits of $5 Million ($10,000 \times $500). Knowing the value of small risk reductions for individuals leads to the calculation of the benefits of a risk reduction program for the affected population. Note that reducing mortality risks by 1 in 10,000 for a population of 10,000 people is statistically equivalent to reducing 1 mortality or 1 *statistical life*. Thus, the estimate of $5 Million has been referred to as the *value of statistical life (VSL)*. VSL is a misleading label and is better represented as a *value of reducing risk of death*.

Though conceptually simple, this type of calculation has plenty of practical problems when used as a measure of preferences for reducing mortality risks. In the labor market, workers may not have the economic freedom to choose among occupational alternatives. Further, it is not easy to control for all the differences in occupational categories unrelated to safety that may be contributing to differences in wages. Also, one must account for the risk of injury separately from accounting for the risk of mortality. If products like bottled water or organic food are used to assess willingness to pay for reductions in risk there are difficulties in separating out the risk reduction aspects from the other benefits arising from the product (taste, convenience, etc.), and questions arise regarding the quantitative measurement of the risk reduction arising from such products versus the range of beliefs that may be determining willingness to pay. Survey methods, including contingent valuation methods, can control for many of these issues, but other concerns associated with the survey approach arise. Note also that the discussion above does not consider the dimension of time. The concept that is more relevant to most discussions of environmental policy is the trade-off individuals make to increase the probability of living for an additional specified period of time (e.g. 1 year of life beyond expected values). In the jargon of the literature this is referred to as the *value of a statistical life year* but again it should be thought of as the value of reducing risks of premature mortality, where premature is defined relative to population life expectancy. Researchers continue to develop methods to refine the estimates of how individuals make trade-off decisions relating to health and safety risks.

Source: Report of the Royal Society of Canada Expert Panel to Review the Socioeconomic Models and Related Components Supporting the Development of Canada-wide Standards for Particulate Matter and Ozone. The Royal Society of Canada, June 2001, Ottawa, Ontario, 240 pp.

CASE STUDY 2: DETERMINING COMPENSATION FOR ENVIRONMENTAL DAMAGES

When a private entity (individual, firm) is responsible for damage to property, that entity may be liable for compensation to the owner of the property. Such a principle is common in law and is evident in traffic accidents and other cases of damage to property. What happens when a private entity damages a public good, a good that by definition is "owned" by the collective or the state? If the tradition of compensation exists, then the responsible party should compensate the "public" or somehow make the public "whole" again. This is exactly the type of logic used in Natural Resource Damage Assessments or NRDA cases. Figure 8.1 illustrates the case of damage taking place at a specific point in time.

An "incident" is assumed to have occurred at a specific time, before which the state of the environment was at its "baseline" or original level. The incident (an oil spill or chemical spill) shifts the state of the environment (an abstract measure of environmental quality) down. Under US regulations, the responsible party is required to bring the environmental system back to the baseline condition. This is required essentially regardless of the cost (although there is clearly some room for debate about appropriate baselines and restoration goals). However, returning the system to baseline (in 3–5 years in figure 8.1) leaves a period of time during which the service flow of the public good was reduced. The area between the baseline (original state) and the actual level of environmental quality before restoration is complete is a measure of the loss of services to the public. NRDA cases involve the measurement, in monetary terms, of this area. The amounts, once discussion (and potentially a court case) has ceased, are paid to "trustees" who are responsible for the wise use of these compensation payments in order to "make the public whole."

The most famous NRDA case is the *Exxon Valdez* oil spill. In that case the loss in service flow was not only considered to be the losses associated with recreational fishing and commercial fishing, but a host of values including so-called passive use values. The latter are values that people hold for a good without consuming it (also called existence values). Passive use values for the environment in Prince William Sound were the source of considerable controversy in the Exxon case.

Even when only use values (values associated with recreation, for example) are considered to be "damaged" by the incident, there can be significant challenges in the measurement of the actual monetary value of the impact. The availability of substitute recreation sites, the impact on recreation site choice versus the frequency of recreation trips, the impact of dynamics of recreation demand-like habits all need to be evaluated and quantified within an economic context. Naturally, assumptions are made and limitations of data and budgets affect the degree of analysis that can take place. However, some of the most detailed micro-econometric studies for specific goods or services have been conducted in the attempt to value natural resource damages.

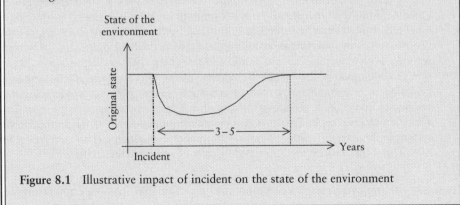

Figure 8.1 Illustrative impact of incident on the state of the environment

8.2   WHY VALUE ENVIRONMENTAL AMENITIES?

The case studies above present only two of the reasons that economists engage in the practice of environmental valuation. A more structured list of reasons for environmental valuation is presented below.

1   *Cost–Benefit Analysis (CBA)*: Economists are engaged in CBA for a variety of projects and policies. CBA for irrigation projects, water resource development projects, transportation infrastructure, and many other public or private projects often involve significant non-market benefits (or costs). These non-market values arise because the good or service is not traded in a market and thus the price system cannot signal its value.

2   *Damage assessment*: As described above, the determination of compensation from environmental damages is an important use of environmental valuation. This activity in the US has probably had the largest influence on the development of environmental valuation and on the profile of valuation efforts and techniques.

3   *Regulatory analysis*: Developing standards for environmental quality require the valuation of environmental amenities for at least part of the process. Without information on the monetary values associated with changes in the standards the process of balancing marginal benefits and marginal costs cannot take place. It is noteworthy that in the US, such a process is often prohibited. Analysis of the costs and benefits of regulation, especially after the regulation has been put in place, are common. However, analysis of environmental standards relating to human health is expected to be based on the consideration of human health impacts alone.

4   *Land use planning*: In exercises such as forest management planning or transportation planning environmental issues often arise. In forest management the issue may be the optimal timing and location of forest harvesting given that benefits arise from both forestry and recreation. Since recreation quality (and thus value) may be affected by forest management the optimal management strategy would consider both of these sources of benefits when evaluating management plans.

5   *Natural resource accounting*: It has been recognized that traditional measures of economic well-being (GNP based measures) do not capture the depreciation of environmental or natural resource stocks, or changes in the values of non-market values arising from the environment. New approaches to national accounting, often called green accounting or natural resource accounting, are being developed to attempt to take into account such omissions to traditional GNP and in many cases require the use of environmental valuation techniques. (For a detailed discussion of natural resource accounting, see Nordhaus and Kokkelenberg, 1999 and also chapter 12.)

6   A recent discussion by Bishop (2003) suggests another important use of environmental valuation. Bishop examines the concept of *economic sustainability* in considerable detail and shows that in order to achieve sustainability it will be necessary to impose sustainability constraints, typically constraints on industrial development, on our economic system. In this context he suggests that environmental valuation will have an important role to play in evaluating the "opportunity costs of sustainability constraints."

These are the major categories of policy and practice that involve environmental valuation. There has been an increasing demand for environmental valuation as the importance of environmental services increases, but there has also been increasing scrutiny placed on valuation cases. In the following sections, a typology of environmental values is presented, followed by a discussion of the conceptual foundation of valuation.

8.3   A TYPOLOGY OF ENVIRONMENTAL VALUES

Value typologies are difficult to construct because values arise in different ways and in different contexts. Most categorizations of value are based on the methods that are used to measure the value, and that is essentially the approach that will be followed here.

The key point is that value measures always encompass a *change* in something – typically a change in environmental quality in the cases examined in this chapter. An improvement (change) in air quality, for example, may generate changes in various "values" including:

- values arising from improved human health state;
- values from improved recreation experiences because of improved visibility;
- values accruing to homeowners because of improved views of scenery; and/or
- values arising from knowledge that an endangered species has had its probability of survival increased by the air quality improvement.

Any individual may experience some or all of these categories of value change ranging from direct effects on their health through to values the individual has for things that they may never see (endangered species). While values could be categorized according to how they affect the person, they are more easily categorized in the way that behaviors, of various kinds, help illustrate the type of value.

Values expressed through market/near-market behavior

Values associated with changes in environmental quality may be expressed through changes in market behavior. This market behavior may be the purchases of specific goods or the purchases of combinations of goods that are jointly related to the environmental change. This type of environmental value is often referred to as "use value" as the value is commonly observed through changes in the "use" of specific goods or services. Some categories of valuation by observing market behavior include:

1   Variation in the price of housing or residential rental markets arising in part from change in environmental quality. Methods used to evaluate such variation are referred to as "*hedonic methods.*" These methods can also be used to evaluate the response of wage rates to changes in environmental/health characteristics of the employment and are called hedonic wage methods.

2   Attributes or characteristics of goods/services explain the demand for the good/service and include environmental quality attributes. Recreation sites, for example, can be considered bundles of attributes including natural (environmental) attributes and human-made attributes. Changes in the environmental attributes that generate changes in the demand for the recreation site can be captured using "*Random utility models*." Similarly these methods can be used to capture the impact of an attribute like "pesticide free" on a food product.

3   The value of recreation sites is typically not revealed through an entrance or access fee. Therefore, *Travel cost methods* have been developed that employ the cost of traveling to the site as a proxy for the price/access fee. These methods typically examine the response of the quantity of visits to levels of the travel cost but they can be linked with random utility models to evaluate the frequency of visits as well as the site visited.

4   Changes in environmental conditions may affect industrial production and cost. Values arising from changes in production can be considered as responding to changes in ecological service flows. For example, changes in water quality or quantity may affect agricultural output that may in turn affect profit levels. Models that examine such changes range from simple production function analyses to complex models of industrial behavior in response to changes in the environmental factors. Such models are referred to as "*Ecosystem Service Models*." In addition, models of *averting behavior* have also been employed to examine such values. These approaches examine expenditures on goods and services that allow the consumer to avoid the damages associated with environmental change (also known as *defensive behavior models*). It is necessary to point out that "costs" and "benefits" are symmetric in the sense that "costs" associated with production can measure negative impacts (increased costs) as well as positive impacts or "benefits" (reduced costs). Similarly, positive changes in compensating variation for consumers may reflect "benefits" while negative changes in compensating variation reflect "costs."

Values expressed through non-market, latent or political behavior

In some cases responses to environmental change can be observed through market behavior. However, in other cases there are either no easily observable behaviors that arise in response to the environmental quality change, or the responses that do arise are not easily identified in observable behavior. An example of the former is a case in which individuals would like to support the development of an ecological reserve but there is no mechanism through which they can pay for, or directly vote to be taxed for, the creation of such a reserve. They value the existence of the ecological reserve, and thus such a value has often been referred to as "*existence value*." A person's change in utility associated with only the knowledge that this ecosystem has been damaged would be a form of existence value. In addition, an individual may have value for the ecological reserve because in the future they would like to visit it, or they would like it to be available for their children to visit and thus the value is related to potential future use values. That has led to the use of the term "*passive use value*" to refer to such values. In general if the value associated with an environmental good or service is not associated with any market purchases or behavioral trail the value falls into the category of non-use values.

Because observed behavior cannot be used to measure non-use values *stated preference methods* have been developed. These methods employ "conversations" with individuals through structured surveys. A wide range of stated preference methods have been employed in environmental economics. Some of these are described below.

1 *Contingent valuation*: Contingent valuation is probably the most commonly used stated preference technique in environmental economics. This method constructs a market for an environmental good and elicits the economic welfare change associated with the change in the environmental good or service. It is commonly structured as a hypothetical referendum in which respondents vote on accepting an environmental improvement (or not) in exchange for an increase in tax payments (or no increase).

2 *Attribute based methods*: In contrast to contingent valuation methods, attribute based methods divide the situation or valuation context into attributes and elicit responses on choices of different bundles of attributes. These attribute bundles are designed to contain the levels of environmental quality involved in the change, as well as different levels of monetary outlays by the respondent. This method focuses on eliciting choices over many attributes, including monetary attributes, while contingent valuation tends to focus on the monetary factors.

Accounting for uncertainty

The value categories described above are all based on deterministic or "certain" values of environmental quality, income, etc. Changes in environmental quality, and the impacts of these changes on human systems, are seldom perfectly certain. The attempt to incorporate uncertainty into environmental values led some researchers to suggest that values associated with uncertainty would add to the deterministic values. However, a more careful development of the literature has resulted in two major categories of value.

1 *Option prices*: When states of nature are uncertain the value (economic welfare measure) may be state dependent. When uncertainty is included in the determination of welfare measures a number of welfare measures can be generated including *ex ante* welfare measures, *ex post* welfare measures, state-dependent welfare measures or state-independent welfare measures. Only in very specific circumstances does adding uncertainty in such contexts result in a premium to be added to the deterministic welfare measure. This premium, sometimes referred to as option value, is in general not a measure of value but an artifact of a specific restrictive situation. A more general measure of welfare, option price, or a state-independent *ex ante* measure of value, is a relevant measure of value and arises from the incorporation of uncertainty into a model of welfare calculation (Freeman, 1993; Graham, 1981).

2 *Quasi option value*: In cases where benefits are uncertain, irreversibilities exist and where learning can occur, there may be a value premium associated with avoiding the irreversibility or maintaining flexibility while learning about the situation.

This premium, referred to as quasi option value, is essentially the value of keeping one's options open. In some cases this premium may be added to deterministic environmental values, but models of learning and information are complex and the results are dependent on the structure of the learning and information flow (Hanemann, 1989; Fisher and Hanemann, 1986).

This completes the summary of types of value. Chapters 9 and 10 expand on these descriptions and provide more formal discussion of the theory and methods used in each of these cases. However, in order to employ these methods the theoretical foundation of environmental valuation must be presented. That is the objective of the remainder of this chapter.

8.4   THEORETICAL UNDERPINNINGS OF ENVIRONMENTAL VALUATION

Environmental valuation is based on individual-level welfare economics. In order to construct measures of economic value associated with changes in environmental quality, the relationships between utility, environmental quality, and monetary welfare measures must be defined. At this point it is necessary to note that environmental values in an economic context are *anthropocentric* as the values ascribed to changes in the environment are assumed to arise from human preferences. *Non-anthropocentric* or *biocentric* value systems have been discussed in the literature; however, these are generally not consistent with the economic notion of values and preferences arising from individuals. That does not suggest that economic approaches are the only approaches that are valid. However, in exploring environmental valuation in an economic context it is necessary to remain consistent with economic theory. Environmental values are also *utilitarian* or based on utility theory. Once again there are other theories of value that are not utilitarian, but these are outside of the purview of traditional microeconomics and are left to the interested reader to examine on their own.

In beginning our discussion of economic welfare measures we must also consider that we are "building from the ground up." Aggregate welfare change, or social welfare, is assumed to be the sum of the individual welfare changes. This arises from the difficulty in making any other approach to social welfare measurement practical and defensible. The Pareto principle (see chapter 2), that only changes in which no one is made worse off and at least one person is made better off be considered social welfare enhancing, is not practical in policy analysis as in most cases at least one person is made worse off by a change. The Compensation principle (see chapter 2) that states that the gainers must be able to compensate the losers and still be better off, suffers from a variety of difficulties, but remains the basis for benefit–cost analysis. In order to operationalize the compensation principle, individual level measures of "gain" and/or "loss" are required. This necessitates our analysis of individual-level welfare.

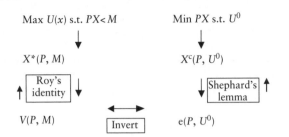

Figure 8.2   Schematic of duality theory

Duality theory[1]

Duality theory is essential for the understanding of individual welfare measures and for empirical estimation of welfare measures. A schematic map of duality theory is provided in figure 8.2 in which the results of maximizing utility and minimizing expenditures are outlined. Let x be a vector of goods $(x_1 ... x_n)$, U be a utility function that maps goods into utility, P be a price vector $(P_1 ... P_n)$, M be income. Maximizing utility subject to an income constraint yields X^* or the Marshallian demand for each good. Recall that the Marshallian demand is a function of prices and income. If the Marshallian demand is inserted into the utility function, utility can be expressed as a function of prices and income, i.e., $V(P, M)$. This is referred to as the indirect utility function. The indirect utility function can be used to recover the Marshallian demand by employing Roy's identity, or:

$$x_i^* = -\frac{\partial V}{\partial p_i} \bigg/ \frac{\partial V}{\partial M} \tag{1}$$

Now instead of maximizing utility let us minimize expenditures $(P*X)$ on goods subject to holding utility at some level U^0. The result of this minimization problem is X^c or the Hicksian demand. Note that the Hicksian demand is a function of prices and utility and not income. Inserting the Hicksian demands into the expenditure calculation (multiplying them by price) yields the expenditure function (a function of prices and utility). The relationship between the expenditure function and Hicksian demand is captured in Shephard's lemma that states

$$x_i^c = \frac{\partial e}{\partial p_i} \tag{2}$$

Finally, the indirect utility function can be recovered from the expenditure function by simply inverting the expenditure function and solving for utility, and the expenditure function can be recovered from the indirect utility function by reversing the process and solving the indirect utility function for expenditure.[2]

Individual welfare measures[3]

There are many approaches to constructing individual welfare measures. The following is an intuitive approach to understanding welfare measures. Begin by totally differentiating an indirect utility function $V(p,M)$ to produce

$$dV = \sum \frac{\partial V}{\partial p_i} dp_i + \frac{\partial V}{\partial M} dM \qquad (3)$$

Let $\lambda = \partial V/\partial M$ and recall Roy's identity:

$$x_i = -\frac{\partial V}{\partial p_i} \Big/ \frac{\partial V}{\partial M} \qquad (4)$$

Divide both sides of the totally differentiated indirect utility function and rearrange to yield:

$$\frac{dV}{\lambda} = -\sum x_i(p, M) \, dp_i + dM \qquad (5)$$

The expression on the left-hand side is a change in utility divided by the marginal utility of income and can be loosely considered a "change in money." The right-hand side is the change in prices times the Marshallian demand, plus the change in income. Note that this is for "small" changes. To evaluate this over non-marginal changes we must evaluate the integral over the range of the change, or

$$dW = \frac{dV}{\lambda} = -\sum \int_{p^1}^{p^2} x_i(p, M) \, dp_i + dM \qquad (6)$$

The first term on the right-hand side is the sum of consumer surpluses (Marshallian demands) evaluated from the initial price (P^1) to the final price (P^2). This can be evaluated graphically by observing figure 8.3. The area under the

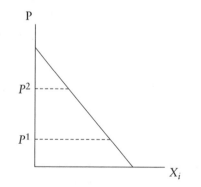

Figure 8.3   Welfare change associated with price change

Marshallian demand curve, between the two price levels, is the measure of welfare change arising from the price change.

The welfare measure in (6) is called consumer surplus and provides us with
a method of calculating welfare effects from observed demand function
(Marshallian demand). However, this welfare measure has some unfortunate properties. Suppose that we are interested in examining a case where the price of one
commodity increases, but a lump sum amount is paid to consumers. This is a case
of one price change and an income change. The welfare measure is not necessarily
unique. This situation is displayed in figure 8.4 (based on Just, Hueth, and Schmitz,
1982). If consumer surplus is evaluated at M1, the welfare change = area X, if
evaluated at M2, welfare = area X + Y. Therefore, the *order* of the evaluation of the
price and income change will affect the welfare measure.

This is referred to as path dependence. In figure 8.4 various paths from P^1 M1 to P^2
M2 are displayed. Any path from M1, P^1 to M2, P^2 can be followed (changing prices
and income) and will not necessarily yield the same outcome (path dependence).

Similarly, if two prices change, the welfare measure is not necessarily unique.
Multiple price changes involve the sum of integrals from the expression

$$dW = \frac{dV}{\lambda} = -\sum \int_{p^1}^{p^2} x_i(p,M)\, dp_i + dM \tag{7}$$

and if the demand for one good depends on the price of the other good, then the
order of integration will affect the outcome. In other words, if the two goods being
evaluated are substitutes or complements for each other, then the welfare measures will not necessarily be unique.

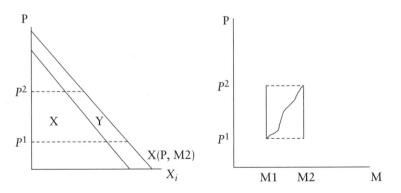

Figure 8.4   Welfare change associated with price and income changes

Source: Based on Just, Hueth, and Schmitz (1982)

Under some conditions these welfare measures will be unique. A mathematical theorem states that a function will be *path-independent* if the cross-partials of "*x*" are symmetric.

$$\frac{\partial x_i}{\partial p_j} = \frac{\partial x_j}{\partial p_i} \tag{8}$$

In the case of a Marshallian demand function, cross-partials need not be symmetric since there is no restriction on "cross-elasticities" being equal.

Compensating variation

Consider an alternative approach to defining welfare changes. Define M^1 as initial income (before a change), and M^2 as income after the change. Similarly, let U^1 and U^2 be utility before and after the change. Define a welfare measure as the amount of money it takes to make a person as well off as they were before the change. Express this using expenditure functions as:

$$e(p^2, U^1) = e(p^2, U^2) - CV \tag{9}$$

where CV = *compensating variation*. Recall that $x_i^c = \partial e / \partial p_i$, $M^1 = e(p^1, U^1)$, $M^2 = e(p^2, U^2)$ and $dM = M^1 - M^2$. Rearrange expression (9) to yield $CV = M^2 - e(p^2, U^1)$. Add and subtract M^1 to create:

$$CV = e(p^1, U^1) - e(p^2, U^1) + dM \tag{10}$$

in the case of marginal changes or,

$$CV = -\sum \int_{p^1}^{p^2} x_i(p, U^1)\, dp_i + dM \tag{11}$$

in the case of non-marginal changes. These expressions are the area under the Hicksian demand curve with utility evaluated at the level "before" the change (plus any change in income or dM). Are these measures path-independent? Yes, because the restrictions on utility functions (that they be continuous, differentiable, concave, etc.) result in the condition that expenditure functions are continuous and differentiable. Another theorem (Young's theorem) states that a function that is twice differentiable and continuous has symmetric cross-partial derivatives (Boadway and Bruce, 1984).

Equivalent variation

Define a welfare measure as the amount of money it takes to make a person as well off as they would be after a change. Express this using expenditure functions:

$$e(p^1, U^2) = e(p^1, U^1) - EV \tag{12}$$

where EV = *equivalent variation*.

Rearrange $EV = e(p^1, U^2) - M^1$ and add and subtract M^2 to create

$$EV = e(p^1, U^2) - e(p^2, U^2) + dM \tag{13}$$

for marginal changes or

$$EV = -\sum \int_{p^1}^{p^2} x_i(p, U^2) \, dp_i + dM \tag{14}$$

for non-marginal changes. This is the area under the Hicksian demand curve but with utility held at the "after" level rather than the "before" level. This measure is also *path-independent* (Boadway and Bruce, 1984).

Equivalent variation and compensation variation can be defined either as areas under the Hicksian demand curve or as the difference between expenditure functions, evaluated at the appropriate utility level. These measures are the basis for most applied welfare economics and will be the basis for environmental valuation. The welfare measures described above, however, focus on price and income changes. In environmental valuation we are most often interested in changes in environmental quality and these effects typically do not appear as changes in price and income directly. In the measures defined above one can consider environmental quality as a "fixed" or exogenous quantity in the utility and/or demand functions. The most common way to examine welfare changes in environmental quality is to examine discrete changes in quality levels. We now turn to such an analysis.

Compensating and equivalent variation measures for environmental quality changes

The indirect utility function can also be used to evaluate welfare impacts. Let $V^1(P^1, M^1)$ be the initial level of utility. Now let prices rise to P^2. The amount of money required to make the individual as well off as they were before the change is the amount CV in the expression below:

$$V^1(P^1, M^1) = V(P^2, M^1 - CV) \tag{15}$$

Note that "$-CV$" in this expression is exactly the amount of income given to the person to offset the price increase (CV is negative as a price increase reduces welfare, but $-CV$ is positive). In the case of a price decrease the CV would be positive ($-CV$ would reduce overall income to offset the price decrease). Now let us extend this analysis to include environmental goods. Suppose that environmental quality enters the indirect utility function. Let Q^1 represent the initial level of environmental quality. Now let Q^2 be some new improved level of quality. The expression for compensating variation for a quality change is

$$V^1(P^1, M^1, Q^1) = V(P^1, M^1 - CV, Q^2) \tag{16}$$

In this case CV is a positive because income is taken away from the person so that when coupled with the increase in environmental quality associated with Q^2, it makes the person as well off as they were before the change. However, in the case of a decrease of environmental quality, CV would be negative. The quantities of CV and EV can be either positive or negative depending on the change involved. A similar definition for EV is:

$$V^1(P^1, M^1 + EV, Q^1) = V(P^1, M^1, Q^2) \tag{17}$$

Determination of CV and EV using indirect utility functions is illustrated in figure 8.5. Isoutility curves (in income and environmental quality space) are depicted for two levels of utility. Consider V1 as the initial utility level and M1, Q1 as initial levels of income and quality. Suppose a change to Q2 is being evaluated. The isoutility curve V2 shows the level of utility experienced for income M1 and quality Q2. To return the individual to the original level of utility (V1) the amount of income removed would be CV, illustrated on the graph as the amount of income required to move from utility level V2 down to V1, but holding quality at Q2. Alternately EV can be depicted as the amount of income require to make the person at V1 as well off as they would be with the change (V2) by adding to income.

Welfare measures for environmental quality can also be derived using expenditure functions. Let the expenditure function include an argument for quality (Q),

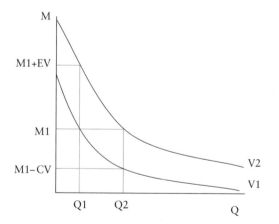

Figure 8.5   Graphical representation of CV and EV associated with a quality change

arising from including of Q in the utility function. Changes in environmental quality can be expressed as

$$CV = e(p^1, U^1, Q^1) - e(p^1, U^1, Q^2) + dM \qquad (18)$$

For compensating variation and

$$EV = e(p^1, U^2, Q^1) - e(p^1, U^2, Q^2) + dM \qquad (19)$$

for equivalent variation. The only difference in the expressions is the base level of utility in the expenditure functions; U^1 for CV and U^2 for EV.

Marshallian vs. Hicksian welfare measures

It should be clear from the discussion above that Marshallian welfare measures have some properties that are undesirable, especially non-uniqueness. However, Marshallian measures are relatively easily derivable from observable information (prices, quantities, income). Hicksian measures rely on being able to identify concepts of utility, since utility is an element in the Hicksian demands. For many years the fact that utility is unobservable kept applied economists from using the theoretically defensible Hicksian measures. There was also considerable discussion of the difference between Hicksian and Marshallian measures and under what conditions one could be confident that the Marshallian measure was a good approximation of the Hicksian measure. However, duality theory illustrates that once a functional form for the demand function is "assumed," the structure of the utility function (and all other components of the individual's preference structure) is at least in part revealed. In other words, when we engage in econometric analysis to estimate a Marshallian demand function and we choose a specific functional form for the demand function (or system), we are implicitly assuming a structure for the utility function, indirect utility function, and other structures of demand theory. Integrability theory in microeconomics provides us with the necessary restrictions on the parameters of the demand function that will result in it being consistent with the properties we require of utility functions. More formally, given a Marshallian demand function (or system) $x_i(P, M)$, we can integrate this demand system to yield the direct utility function. Given a direct utility function the indirect utility function can be derived, and so on (Boadway and Bruce, 1984).

A somewhat different approach to this issue has been used in the literature that employs indirect utility functions in empirical research. If one observes a choice of one good over another (available) good then one can assume that the individual's indirect utility associated with the first good must have been greater than the utility they could have gained from the second good. If one assumes a functional form for the indirect utility function, and makes appropriate statistical assumptions, these choices can reveal the parameters of the indirect utility function.

Observations of choices reveal information about preferences and the structure of the utility function. This approach is what has come to be known as random utility theory, or discrete choice analysis. The key element is that the structure of the indirect utility function is assumed, and observations on choices are used to identify parameters of this function that best explain the choices. Therefore, reliance on Marshallian measures has to a great degree disappeared with the increased use of random utility models. Researchers still employ Marshallian measures in some cases but many either transform their demand functions into Hicksian demands, or they begin applied research with assumptions of the structure of the indirect utility function or expenditure function. Those who continue to employ Marshallian measures are supported by the research of Willig (1976) who illustrates that under certain plausible conditions the difference between Hicksian and Marshallian measures will be relatively small.

Willingness to pay and willingness to accept compensation

Hicksian and Marshallian measures of welfare allow for the assessment of willingness to pay for a good/service/level of quality that the consumer desires as well as the willingness to accept compensation for giving up a good/service/level of quality. However, considerable empirical and some theoretical research has shown that the relationship between willingness to pay and willingness to accept is more complex than simply adjusting one measure for income effects. There appear to be endowment effects associated with goods/services that individuals feel they currently own or have rights to (Knetsch, 1989). There are systematic differences between willingness to accept and willingness to pay depending on the structure of the indifference curves and the degree of substitution facing the individual (Hanemann, 1991). While most valuation exercises employ willingness to pay measures, or implicitly assume that willingness to pay is equal to willingness to accept it is clear that in many cases willingness to accept is a more appropriate measure than willingness to pay. Empirical assessments have revealed that these two measures may differ by an order of magnitude, depending on the context.

Using information from market goods to assess value for environmental goods

If one had knowledge about the expenditure function or the indirect utility function it would be possible to construct welfare measures for environmental quality change directly. However, often we only observe changes in purchases in market goods that are related to changes in the environmental good. The welfare measures arising in this case require some assumptions, and the development of the welfare measures also reveals important issues regarding *passive use values* (Flores, 2003).

Begin with the definition of compensating variation (ignoring the change in income component):[4]

$$CV = e(p^1, U^1, Q^1) - e(p^1, U^1, Q^2) \tag{20}$$

Suppose that the demand curve for the market good is affected by the level of environmental quality. For example, increases in environmental quality shift the demand for the market good to the right. Define the choke price for the market good as $\hat{p}$ (the choke price is the price at which quantity demanded is zero). Add and subtract expenditure functions (to maintain the equality in expression (20) above) as follows:

$$CV = [e(\hat{p}^1, U^1, Q^2) - e(p^1, U^1, Q^2)] - [e(\hat{p}^1, U^1, Q^1) - e(p^1, U^1, Q^1)]$$

$$+ [e(\hat{p}^1, U^1, Q^1) - e(\hat{p}^1, U^1, Q^2)] \tag{21}$$

The first and sixth terms in this expression cancel out, and the third and fifth terms cancel out, leaving the original expression for CV. However, as shown by Flores (2003) the expression above provides a way to interpret CV using market goods changes. The first terms in square brackets represent the compensating variation for a change from the original price to the choke price or the welfare measure for the "removal" of the good at the new environmental quality levels. The second term in square brackets reflects the same type of welfare change except the "removal" of the good is evaluated at the original environmental quality level. The last term in square brackets is the difference between expenditure functions evaluated at the choke prices and at different levels of environmental quality. If we assume that quality affects the demand for the market good, and that the value of a change in quality is zero if the good is not consumed (at the choke price) then the expression above, with the last term in square brackets now set to zero, becomes the welfare measure for a quality change. Examining the first two elements in square brackets we see that they are simply the difference between area under the (Hicksian) demand curve evaluated at one quality level minus the area evaluated under the other quality level. The area between the demand curves, where the shift in the demand curve arises from the change in environmental quality, is the welfare measure. The assumptions of market links to environmental quality and zero value when no market good is consumed are jointly referred to as *weak complementarity* (Flores, 2003).[5]

The last term in expression (21) has an interesting interpretation. This term can be viewed as *passive use value* (Flores, 2003). It represents the change in expenditure function values relating to a change in environmental quality when the market good is held at the choke price (or not consumed). Clearly the value of the quality change cannot be captured through observations of market purchases since no market good is being consumed. Thus if there is value arising from the change other methods must be used to estimate it. Another interpretation is that if passive use values are positive for the quality change and one uses market behavior to estimate the value, then the estimate based on weak complementarity will only provide a lower-bound estimate of the value. The passive use value component is assumed to be zero in weak complementarity and thus the value measure will underestimate the total value by the amount of the last term in expression (21). In chapter 9 a graphical version of weak complementarity will be presented in the context of recreation valuation.

8.5   UNCERTAINTY AND WELFARE ESTIMATES

The welfare measures described above assume perfect certainty. If there is uncertainty about the state of the world, then the welfare measures must be adjusted to account for this uncertainty. Graham (1981) developed welfare measures that account for uncertainty and the following presentation and example is based on his work. Different states of the world may affect preferences, income, or other aspects of the situation. For example, consider a case in which there are two states of the world, with the probability of being in these states summarized as π_1 and π_2. These two states of the world could be purely exogenous (rain or shine, etc.) or they could be more complex and endogenous probabilities (today is a fishing day or not). Preferences for an umbrella will depend on whether it is raining or not. In terms of welfare measures, a person's compensating variation for an umbrella will probably be higher on rainy days than on sunny days. Alternately, as described in the classic article by Graham (1981), a farmer's willingness to pay for irrigation water will differ if it has been a dry year versus a wet year. But what is the "correct" welfare measure to use? One could wait until the uncertainty has been "realized" and construct an *ex post* welfare measure. The *CV* for the umbrella will be higher if evaluated after a rainy day. However, an *ex post* welfare measure in this case does not tell us much that can help in planning. That is, suppose the individual is deciding whether or not to spend $20 for an umbrella. They must evaluate the value of the umbrella on rainy days, as well as the probability that there will be rainy days. If that probability is low, then they may not be willing to pay $20. A more interesting case is that of the farmer and the irrigation water. What should the farmer be willing to pay for an irrigation dam to be constructed, or how should a benefit–cost analysis of an irrigation dam be constructed given that there will be dry years and wet years and the value of the dam will change depending on the states of nature?

One could simply take the weighted average of the two welfare measures. Or $W_1 = \pi_1 \, CV_1 + \pi_2 \, CV_2$. This is an average of the *ex post* welfare measures and is called the expected *CV* (Graham, 1981; Freeman, 1993). However, one could also construct a welfare measure that is *ex ante* or is based on willingness to pay before the uncertainty is realized. This welfare measure is constructed by initially assuming that the individual uses expected utility to make choices. That is, the expected utility for the situation can be written as:

$$E(U) = \pi_1 \, V_1(\cdot) + \pi_2 \, V_2(\cdot) \tag{22}$$

where V is an indirect utility function and the subscripts represent the two states of nature.[6] Let the indirect utility function in this case take the following form:

$$V_i(\cdot) = V_i(M_i, \delta) \tag{23}$$

where M is income and is subscripted by state to indicate that income varies by state, and δ is an indicator for the presence or absence of a "project" (dam or umbrella, for example). Let the two states be A and B, or $i = A, B$ and let δ be 0 when there is no project and 1 for a project. The state-dependent CV can be calculated as:

$$V_i(M_i, 0) = V_i(M_i - CV_i, 1) \quad i = A, B \tag{24}$$

where CV_i is the compensating variation (or willingness to pay) for the project in each state of nature (Graham, 1981).

Using this structure, a new type of welfare measure can be constructed using expected utility. Rather than equating utility in the base and changed cases, a measure that equates *expected* utility in the base and changed cases is created.

$$\pi_A \, V_A(M_A, 0) + \pi_B \, V_B(M_B, 0) = \pi_A \, V_A(M_A - \chi_A, 1) + \pi_B \, V_B(M_B - \chi_B, 1) \tag{25}$$

The left-hand side of the equation is the base expected utility (no project) while the right-hand side is the expected utility after the change. The welfare measures are *pairs* of values (χ_A, χ_B) that equate the two expected utilities (Graham, 1981). Note that these values can be different. In fact, one pair that satisfies this expression is (CV_A, CV_B) from expression (24) above. The challenge created by incorporating uncertainty into the welfare measure is that there are now an infinite number of different "welfare measures" that can be constructed. Some, like (CV_A, CV_B), are *state-dependent*. That is, the willingness to pay is constructed from measures that depend on what state one is in (Graham, 1981). One can also construct a *state-independent* welfare measure. Such a measure is the willingness to pay for the project, regardless of the state of nature that is realized. This measure is called *option price* (Graham, 1981) and is determined by:

$$\pi_A \, V_A(M_A, 0) + \pi_B \, V_B(M_B, 0) = \pi_A \, V_A(M_A - OP, 1) + \pi_B \, V_B(M_B - OP, 1) \tag{26}$$

Note that in expression (26) only one welfare amount is calculated, the value for OP.

The welfare measures (pairs of values) can be graphed in terms of the monetary measures in each of the two states of nature. This is illustrated in figure 8.6 for the

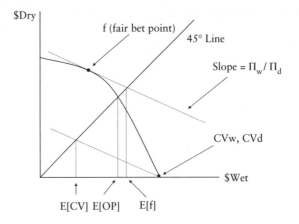

Figure 8.6 Welfare measures under uncertainty

case of the value of an umbrella. The value for option price (*OP*) is along the 45 degree line since it is equal in the two states of nature. The *CV* for the umbrella in the sunny state is zero while the *CV* in the rainy state is $25. The remaining points in this expression could be found if an explicit form for the utility function was known. However, we can assess the general shape of the graph of these pairs of values. The set of values is commonly termed the *willingness-to-pay locus* (Graham, 1981; Freeman, 1993). The shape of the locus depends on the utility function. If we write the expected utility as

$$E(U) = \pi_A \, V_A(M_A - \chi_A, 1) + \pi_B \, V_B(M_B - \chi_B, 1) \tag{27}$$

and differentiate this to obtain

$$dE(U) = \pi_A \, d\chi_A \, \partial V_A / \partial M_A + \pi_B \, d\chi_B \, \partial V_B / \partial M_B \tag{28}$$

Setting $dE(U)$ to zero we can solve for $d\chi_A / d\chi_B$ as

$$-\frac{d\chi_A}{d\chi_B} = \frac{\pi_B \, \partial V_B / \partial M_B}{\pi_A \, \partial V_A / \partial M_A} \tag{29}$$

If the marginal utility of income is constant and identical between the two states, the slope of the willingness to pay locus is constant at the ratio of probabilities. If, as one normally expects, that the marginal utility of income is positive but decreasing, or $\partial V_i / \partial M_i > 0$, $\partial 2 V_i / \partial M_i^2 < 0$, then the locus takes a form of being concave to the origin as in figure 8.6 (see Freeman, 1993). Note that such a relationship between income and utility is also the definition of *risk aversion*. That is, a risk averse individual is one who is defined as having:

$$\pi_A \, V(M_A) + \pi_B \, V(M_B) < V(\pi_A \, M_A + \pi_B \, M_B) \tag{30}$$

This is also a definition of concavity of the utility function in income. The risk averse individual would rather take $\pi_A M_A + \pi_B M_B$ with certainty than gamble on the chance of $\pi_A V(M_A)$ or $+ \pi_B V(M_B)$.

The expected value of any point on the willingness to pay locus can be found by running a line with a slope as the negative of the ratio of the probabilities of the two states through the 45-degree line. In figure 8.6 the expected value of the CV is shown as E(CV). Another welfare measure that can be constructed is the pair (χ_A, χ_B) that maximizes the expected willingness to pay, or maximizes $\pi_A\chi_A + \pi_B\chi_B$. This is referred to as the *fair bet point* (Graham, 1981; Freeman, 1993). This point can be found by sliding a line with slope of the ratio of probabilities out until it is tangent to the willingness to pay locus (Freeman, 1993). This point is illustrated in figure 8.6 as f and its expected value is E(f).

The incorporation of uncertainty has given us a richer analysis of welfare measures, but it has also left us with a problem of choosing the "correct" welfare measure. It turns out that there is no *perfect* welfare measure in this case. In a benefit–cost context, the objective is to be able to construct a measure of the benefits (under uncertainty) to compare them to the costs (also potentially under uncertainty) to evaluate whether the benefits exceed costs (or the case passes the compensation test and is potentially Pareto improving). Here a variety of issues affect the analysis (see Freeman, 1993):

- Are the risks affecting the beneficiaries the same? If so, they may be aggregated to form a collective willingness to pay locus. If not, there will be additional difficulties evaluating the benefits.
- Are the costs subject to risks? If so, a similar state-dependent analysis will have to be done to develop a *willingness to accept locus*.
- Are the risks affecting costs and benefits identical? If they are then the willingness to pay and willingness to accept loci can be examined in the same space.

Freeman (1993) provides a detailed analysis of the possibility of different welfare measures leading to accurate descriptions of potential Pareto improvements. Freeman (1993) provides the following summary of welfare measures under uncertainty:

- Showing that the E(CV) for beneficiaries is greater than the E(CV) (from the willingness to accept locus) for those bearing the costs is neither necessary nor sufficient to indicate a potential Pareto improvement.
- Showing that the option price for beneficiaries is greater than the option price for cost-bearers is sufficient (but not necessary) for potential Pareto improvements.
- Showing that the fair bet point for beneficiaries is greater than the equivalent point for cost-bearers is necessary but not sufficient for potential Pareto improvements.

The result of this analysis is that simply using the *average* welfare measure could be quite misleading in applied benefit–cost work. Using option price measures at least has the advantage that it is sufficient for potential Pareto improvements and it is a single state independent welfare measure. The average welfare measure

(E(CV)) and the option price are measures that could be determined in empirical analysis. The fair bet point, while having some desirable properties, cannot be easily developed without complete knowledge of the willingness to pay (or accept) locus and thus will probably have limited empirical application.

A different type of welfare under uncertainty: quasi-option value

An alternative form of welfare analysis under uncertainty considers the case that future benefits (and/or costs) are uncertain and that decisions made today will be affected by this uncertainty. This becomes a more challenging issue when the decision to be made is to some degree irreversible. For example, if a decision regarding the draining of a wetland is being considered the action is to a large degree irreversible. If the benefits of this irreversible action are uncertain, then the decision-maker must attempt to factor in the expected benefits plus consider that some degree of learning about the benefits may occur over time. Decomposing the decision into benefits "today" and benefits in the "future" after learning has occurred allows one to examine the value of information about the wetland benefits and the impact that information flow has on the development decision. As shown in Hanemann (1989) and Fisher and Hanemann (1990), a simple two-period model with passive learning can be used to show that there are fewer chances that the development decision will be undertaken if information on the uncertain wetland benefits is forthcoming. This does not imply that the development decision is never made. It simply states that the conservation decision is more likely when conservation benefits are uncertain, irreversible, and learning about these benefits will occur. This outcome has also been referred to as the value associated with maintaining flexibility.

The analysis developed by Hanemann (1989) and Fisher and Hanemann (1990) proceeds as follows. Let P indicate a preservation decision and D be a development decision. Let $B_t(P)$ be the net benefit of preservation in time period t (not draining the wetland) and $B_t(D)$ the net benefits of development (drainage). In period 1 the comparison of the benefits of development vs. preservation are identical as there is no uncertainty. In period 2 the benefits of preservation are uncertain and are represented by a probability distribution. Learning can be represented in the model by examining the expected benefits of preservation in a case where information is expected to arise, versus a situation where no information will be forthcoming. The value arising in period 2 of choosing not to develop (avoiding the irreversibility) in the case of no information can be represented as $\max\{E[B_2(P), B_2(D)]\}$. In this case the decision-maker employs the maximum of the expected value of the uncertain benefit amounts. The maximum of the expected value is chosen because the uncertainty will not be resolved in period 2. If information will arise in period 2, the value expression is $E\{\max[B_2(P), B_2(D)]\}$. In this case the decision-maker employs the expected value of the maximum because it is expected that the uncertainty will be resolved in period two. The difference between these two measures is the value of information, conditional on avoiding the irreversible development (if the irreversible development is chosen in period 1, then the benefits in period two are the certain development benefits). The expression of the value of information, or quasi-option value, is

$$VOI \mid \text{non-irreversible choice} = E\{\max[B_2(P), B_2(D)]\}$$
$$- \max\{E[B_2(P), B_2(D)]\} \qquad (31)$$

This expression is always greater than or equal to zero (by Jensen's inequality and the convexity of the maximum operator) (Fisher and Hanemann, 1990). This implies that the value of information, conditional on not choosing the irreversible option, is non-negative. The likelihood of choosing the non-development option (irreversible option) is greater in the case where information is forthcoming than in the case where no learning occurs.

While this simple analysis shows the value of flexibility, cases with additional complexity are not always clear-cut. The basic analysis can be extended to multiple-period cases, cases where learning does not occur without investment, cases where uncertainty is not completely revealed in the future, and other variation on the initial situation. The intuition this simple case provides however is useful.

8.6 VALUING THE ENVIRONMENT

This chapter has introduced the concept of environmental valuation through the discussion of a set of case studies. The use of environmental valuation estimates has grown dramatically since the 1970s, in part because of the US legislative framework that requires the payment of compensation for damages to ecological systems. The case studies outlined in this chapter illustrate the range of economic policy issues that require empirical assessments of environmental values. As awareness of the linkages between human systems and environmental systems increases the use of environmental valuation will undoubtedly increase.

While valuation efforts and research on valuation will increase, it must also be realized that there is still considerable skepticism regarding valuation. Some economists question the validity of stated preference estimates of any kind and prefer to rely on revealed preference information. This, of course, rules out passive use value estimation entirely. Non-economists often question the use of monetary measures of environmental service flows and criticize the use of cost–benefit analysis as a method of decision-making. However, in order to assess items that are incommensurable such as water quality and costs of effluent treatment, or forestry output and songbird populations, some method that provides a mechanism for creating commensurability between outcomes is necessary.

Valuation measures are employed because in our current institutional structure these "public goods" have no effective economic value. Valuation is an attempt to provide estimates of value for goods and services that would otherwise be ascribed zero value. There are also concerns that valuing environmental amenities will create markets for them and turn goods that are public goods into private or commercial goods. Valuation estimation will probably not cause commercialization since that requires changes in institutions and property rights. Nevertheless, the degree of skepticism necessitates that practitioners adhere to theory and sound empirical methods as closely as possible.

FURTHER READING

An excellent overview of environmental valuation can be found in Freeman (1993). Other excellent discussions of valuation include Braden and Kolstad (1991), Smith (1990) and McFadden (1996). The debate on contingent valuation and passive use values (*Journal of Economics Perspectives*, 1994) is a *must read* for anyone involved in valuation, especially the measurement of passive use values. Navrud and Pruckner provide an overview of the necessity, and the challenges of valuation. Smith (2000) provides a discussion on the importance of environmental valuation in environmental economics. For details on the *Exxon Valdez* case and a discussion of the valuation effort, see Carson et al., 1994. Readers interested in theories of choice that are not utilitarian should consult Hargreaves-Heap et al., 1992.

Welfare economics has been presented and discussed in many volumes including Boadway and Bruce (1984), Just, Hueth, and Schmitz (1982), and Freeman (1993). These discussions present overviews from individual welfare measures through potential Pareto improvement tests and the challenges of making interpersonal comparisons. An excellent article by Slesnick examines the link between theory and empirical practice of welfare economics. Flores (2003) provides a modern overview of the elements of welfare economics necessary for environmental valuation and includes a presentation of weak complementarity for multiple goods. The concept of weak complementarity was originally developed by Maler (1974).

Discussions of option price and related concepts associated with benefit measurement under uncertainty include Graham (1981) and Freeman (1993). An early attempt to empirically assess the difference between various measures of welfare under uncertainty can be found in Cameron and Englin (1987). Quasi-option value is illustrated in Hanemann (1989) and Fisher and Hanemann (1990). The latter includes some empirical estimates of quasi-option value and provides concrete examples of quasi-option value. Graham-Tomasi (1995) and Freeman (1993) provide overviews of the concept and implications.

On the topic of benefit cost analysis involving health, safety, and environmental values an excellent summary of economic arguments can be found in Arrow et al., 1996. Many of these arguments are again summarized and focused in a recent *AMICI CURIAE* regarding the case of the American Trucking Association versus the US Environmental Protection Agency. Note, however, that even with a set of signatories that included several Noble laureates and other eminent economists, the US Supreme Court rejected the argument. (http://www.aei.brookings.org/publications/related/amici_brief.pdf).

NOTES

1 A review of duality theory and welfare measures at the individual level can be found in Boadway and Bruce (1984).

2 The description of duality presented here is rather cursory and has omitted many details and proofs. For additional detail see Boadway and Bruce, 1984 or Flores, 2003.

3 This derivation of individual welfare measures and the presentation of compensating and equivalent variation is based on Boadway and Bruce (1984). Other good presentations can be found in Flores (2003), Freeman (1993), and Just, Hueth, and Schmitz (1982).

4 Flores (2003) provides a more detailed analysis of these issues. The approach presented here is based on Flores (2003) but develops a simplified version of the analysis.

5 More detail on weak complementarity is presented in chapter 10.

6 Note that there is considerable controversy regarding whether individuals actually make decisions in a fashion consistent with expected utility maximization. Nevertheless, expected utility provides a convenient and flexible approach to outlining the problem at hand. See Machina (1987) for a discussion of expected utility and variants.

REFERENCES

Arrow, K. J., Cropper, M., Eads, G. C., Hahn, R. W., Lave, L. B., Noll, R. G., Portney, P. R., Russell, M., Schmalensee, R., Smith, V. K., and Stavins, R. N. (1996). Is There a Role for Benefit–Cost Analysis in Environmental, Health and Safety Regulation?, *Science*, 272: 221–2.

Bishop, R. (2003). Where To From Here? In P. Champ, T. Brown, and K. Boyle, eds, *A Primer on the Economic Valuation of the Environment*, Kluwer: Dordrecht.

Boadway, R. W. and Bruce, N. (1984). *Welfare Economics*, Basil Blackwell: London.

Braden, J. B. and Kolstad, C. D. (1991). *Measuring the Demand for Environmental Quality*, North Holland: New York.

Cameron, T. A. and Englin, J. (1987). Welfare Effects of Changes in Environmental Quality under Individual Uncertainty About Use, *Rand Journal of Economics*, 28: S45–S70.

Carson, R. T., Mitchell, R. C., Haneman, W. M., Kopp, R. J., Presser, S., and Rand, P. A. (1994). Contingent Valuation and Lost Passive Use: Damages from the Exxon Valdez. Resources for the Future Discussion Paper 94-18, Washington, DC.

Coase, R. H. (1960). The Problem of Social Cost, *Journal of Law and Economics*, 3: 1–44.

Diamond, P. and Hausman, J. (1994). Contingent Valuation: Is Some Number Better Than No Number?, *Journal of Economics Perspectives*, 8: 45–64.

Fisher, A. C. and Hanemann, W. M. (1986). Environmental Damages and Option Values, *Natural Resources Modelling*, 1: 111–24.

Flores, N. (2003). Conceptual Issues in Non-market Valuation, in P. A. Champ, K. J. Boyle, and T. C. Brown, eds, *A Primer on Nonmarket Valuation*, Kluwer.

Freeman, A. M. (1993). *The Measurement of Environmental and Resource Values*, Resources for the Future Press: Baltimore.

Graham, D. H. (1981). Cost–Benefit Analysis Under Uncertainty, *American Economic Review*, 71: 715–25.

Graham-Tomasi, T. (1995). Quasi-Option Value, in D. W. Bromley, ed., *The Handbook of Environmental Economics*, Blackwell: London, pp. 594–614.

Hanemann, W. M. (1989). Information and the Concept of Option Value, *Journal of Environmental Economics and Management*, 16: 23–37.

Hanemann, W. M. (1991). Willingness to Pay and Willingness to Accept: How Much Can They Differ? *American Economic Review*, 81: 635–47.

Hanemann, W. M. (1994). Valuing the Environment through Contingent Valuation, *Journal of Economics Perspectives*, 8: 19–44.

Hargreaves-Heap, S., Hollis, M., Lyons, B., Sugden, R., and Weale, A. (1992). *The Theory of Choice: A Critical Guide*, Blackwell: Cambridge.

Just, R., Hueth, D., and Schmitz, A. (1982). *Applied Welfare Economics and Public Policy*, Prentice-Hall: New Jersey.

Knetsch, J. L. (1989). The Endowment Effect and Evidence of Nonreversible Indifference Curves, *American Economic Review*, 79 (5): 1277–84.

Machina, M. J. (1987). Choice under Uncertainty: Problems Solved and Unsolved, *Journal of Economic Perspectives*, 1: 121–54.

Maler, K.-G. (1974). *Environmental Economics: A Theoretical Inquiry*, Baltimore: Johns Hopkins Press for Resources for the Future.

McFadden, D. (1996). Why Is Natural Resource Damage Assessment So Hard? Hibbard Lecture, April 12. Presented at the Department of Agricultural and Resource Economics, University of Wisconsin, Madison: http://elsa.berkeley.edu/wp/mcfadden0496/readme.html

Navrud, S. and Pruckner, G. J. (1997). Environmental Valuation: To Use or Not to Use? *Environmental and Resource Economics*, 10: 1–26.

Nordhaus, W. D. and Kokkelenberg, E. C. (eds) (1999). *Nature's Numbers: Expanding the National Economic Accounts to Include the Environment*, Washington DC: National Academy Press.

Portnoy, P. (1994). The Contingent Valuation Debate: Why Economists Should Care, *Journal of Economics Perspectives*, 8: 3–18.

Report of the Royal Society of Canada Expert Panel to Review the Socioeconomic Models and Related Components Supporting the Development of Canada-wide Standards for Particulate Matter and Ozone (2001), The Royal Society of Canada, June, Ottawa, Ontario, 240 pp.: www.rsc.ca

Slesnick, D. T. (1998). Empirical Approaches to the Measurement of Welfare, *Journal of Economic Literature*, 36: 2108–65

Smith, V. K. (1990). Can We Measure the Economic Value of Environmental Amenities?, *Southern Economic Journal*, 56: 865–78.

Smith, V. K. (2000). JEEM and Non-Market Valuation, *Journal of Environmental Economics and Management*, 39: 351–74.

Willig, R. D. (1976). Consumer's Surplus Without Apology, *The American Economic Review*, 66: 589–97.

CHAPTER NINE

ENVIRONMENTAL VALUATION: STATED PREFERENCE METHODS

We have been too prone, on the one hand, to overstate the difficulties of introspection and communication, and on the other, to underestimate the problems of studying preferences revealed by observed behavior. (A. K. Sen (1973), Behavior and the Concept of Preference, *Economica* 40: p. 258)

9.1 INTRODUCTION

The most common objective of environmental valuation is to determine the "value" of a change in environmental quality or the provision of some public good, as measured by compensating or equivalent variation. In an ideal economic world there would be no need to measure these values because a set of institutional arrangements would exist that would reveal their value. In a somewhat less ideal world it might be possible to identify the values of environmental quality changes through market transactions (the topic of chapter 10). But in many cases there are no markets to rely on to provide information on the value of environmental goods. In these cases we must rely on stated preference methods or methods that reveal values through non-market or political behavior. The values may be revealed through voting or referenda in which constituents agree to increase their own taxes to provide a public good. Or they may be revealed through mechanisms that currently do not exist in the actual market, but which could be accurately described to individuals using surveys. In these cases economists resort to methods that involve conversations with individuals in an attempt to elicit their trade-offs or values. These methods have been called conversational, direct, expressed preference, or stated preference. While there are several variants of these methods they all share the basic traits of developing scenarios and asking individuals to provide a response that indicates their willingness to trade off money against other goods/services/environmental conditions.

There are several examples of cases that require the use of stated preference methods. Any attempt to assess passive use value, or the values that are not associated with any observable behavior (visiting a wilderness area, etc.), requires stated preference methods. By definition there is no market behavior that can be used to identify the trade-off involved. The amount that the public is willing to pay to protect coastal wilderness areas from oil spills is an example of such value. Stated preference methods may also be used in cases where revealed preference methods could operate, but for a variety of reasons may not accurately reflect preferences. In assessing the value of reduced risks of mortality, examinations of wages across jobs with different levels of mortality risk can reveal the implicit value of risk reduction. However, this assumes that workers accurately perceive the risk levels and are informed about the risk levels. Such analysis also requires a significant degree of variation in the risks. Finally, wage-risk studies are useful for identifying the risk trade-offs made by individuals in the labor force, but they may not be accurate in identifying the risk trade-offs for retired individuals or children. In these cases, stated preference methods can be used to elicit the value of risk reductions.

Stated preference valuation involves a blending of economic theory, econometrics, survey design (psychology, social-psychology), and other disciplines. It involves issues that economists do not typically deal with including administering focus groups, designing and administering surveys, and employing experimental designs to elicit trade-offs. To deal with these issues effectively requires an entire volume of its own (see Further reading for some suggestions). In this chapter we examine the basic economic and econometric issues associated with stated preference methods and we focus on two major stated preference variants: contingent valuation and choice experiments.

Figure 9.1 illustrates the variety of stated preference methods. There is a considerable amount of confusion regarding the names of these approaches. In figure 9.1 the approaches are categorized according to whether they involve rating, ranking, or choice, and then within choice whether the approach involves a choice

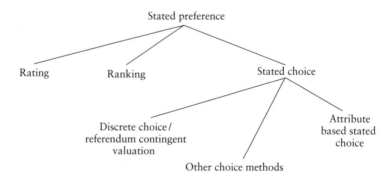

Figure 9.1   Stated preference methods

Source: Adamowicz, Louviere, and Swait (1998)

of yes or no between scenarios (as in a referendum) or a choice between options described by attributes (attribute based methods). Simple "open-ended" contingent valuation approaches – approaches that ask individuals to state how much they would be willing to pay for a good/service or quality change, can be thought of as a form of rating approach. However, the rating scale used is not a numerical score but a very specific form of preference indicator – money.

9.2 THE CONTINGENT VALUATION METHOD

The contingent valuation method is the most common stated preference valuation method. It involves careful structuring of a scenario in which an individual is offered a good (improved environmental quality, new public good, etc.) and is requested to identify whether he/she would be willing to trade off money for the offered public good. The value of the good is elicited contingent on there being a market for the good (where the market is described by the researcher).

A contingent valuation survey typically involves a series of 6 steps (based on Carson, 2000). These are

1   identification of the issue in general;
2   specific description of the current situation and the proposed alternative regarding the public good or environmental quality change in question;
3   description of the payment mechanism including the institutions surrounding the payment (e.g. annual property taxes and government provisions);
4   elicitation of the willingness to pay or choice decision in a discrete choice framework;
5   a set of debriefing questions to identify how certain the individual is about their choice, why they chose a particular option and elicit other information about the individual's reaction to the valuation task; and
6   elicitation of demographic characteristics and attitudinal information from the individual.

Step 1 provides a "warm-up" for the respondent and begins framing the issue for them to consider. Step 2 typically contains a considerable amount of descriptive material, often biological in nature, regarding the current situation and the proposal for the improvement. This component often requires considerable effort with focus groups to develop descriptions that are understandable and objective yet not burdensome. Step 3 outlines the mechanism by which the improvement will be funded. This step also requires the development of credible realistic payment institutions. Step 4 is relatively straightforward if the open-ended approach is used. However, within the discrete choice approach there are several alternatives, each with its own merits and difficulties. These are discussed below. Step 5 is important for analysis of the responses to the valuation question and allows the researcher to assess the degree to which the respondent understood the task and their confidence in their responses. Step 6 is a relatively standard component of survey design and development although it will be fine-tuned to the specific application.

Table 9.1 outlines the major variants of the actual valuation question or the variants of step 4. These include open-ended approaches in which the individual is asked to state the amount that they would be willing to pay (a single question) or auctions in which the individual participates in an auction for the good. Individuals may also be presented with discrete choice questions that identify if their true value is less than or more than the bid that is presented to them. Note that these discrete choice approaches do not identify the actual willingness to pay, rather, they bound the willingness to pay.

The simplest form of discrete choice response is a single presented offer and a request for a Yes (pay the amount and receive the public good) or No response. This can also be framed as a referendum in which the program will only be approved if 50 percent of the population votes Yes in which case all households/ individuals will be required to pay. The latter is a useful framing in that it identifies what obligations other members of the community will have in funding the program and in many cases makes the situation more realistic. Such a question is also often incentive compatible (discussed below).

In order to increase efficiency in the elicitation of the willingness to pay amount, the respondent could be asked repeated questions. If they voted Yes the respondent could be asked if they would also vote Yes if the price was higher. If they voted No they could be asked if they would vote Yes for a lower amount. This is a double-bounded approach, which can be generalized to a N-bounded approach with a series of N questions (see Hanemann and Kanninen, 1999). A variant on double-bounded questions is the "spike model" in which individuals are given an option to say if they would pay anything ($CV > 0$) and then they are asked to vote yes or no to specific bid amounts. This helps identify those who would pay positive amounts (but not necessarily pay the amount requested of them) from those who would not pay anything (Hanemann and Kanninen, 1989). Finally, in response to some challenges arising in the double-bounded approaches the one and a half bounded approach has been suggested (Cooper et al., 2002; Hanemann and Kanninen, 1999). Double-bounded approaches often generate "irrational" responses to the second bid. Individuals may perceive the good offered in the second bid to be somehow different from the good offered in the first bid (perhaps

Table 9.1 Forms of contingent valuation questions (based on Mitchell and Carson, 1989)

	Actual WTP	Discrete choice
Single question	Open ended	Referendum
	Payment card	Take-it-or-leave-it
	Sealed bid	
Iterated or series	Bidding game	Take-it-or-leave-it with follow up
of questions	Auctions	Double-bounded CVM
		N-bounded CVM
		Spike CVM
		$1\frac{1}{2}$ bounded CVM

because price is perceived as an indicator of quality). They may also imagine that the situation has changed into a bargaining game. For these reasons the one and a half bounded approach has been suggested. In this case the individual is first told that two bids have been prepared because uncertainties about the situation preclude the development of single bid. The respondent is then offered the choice with the first bid (randomly selected from the two). The second bid is presented to the respondent if it is consistent with the respondent's answer. For example, if the respondent voted Yes to the first bid, and the remaining bid is higher than the first bid, the interviewer would ask about the second bid. If the remaining bid is lower no further questions are asked, as it is clear that the respondent would pay at least that amount (Cooper et al., 2002).

Discrete choice contingent valuation[1]

In this section the basic structure of random utility theory and the fundamental versions of the discrete choice contingent valuation approach are presented. Contingent valuation involves a combination of economic theory associated with the structure of the utility function, and econometric theory associated with the way that randomness enters into the process. This means that economic theory is not separable from econometrics for these types of models (thus this chapter and chapter 10 contain a significant amount of econometric presentation). The choice of distribution for the random component will affect the structure of the utility function. In principle, respondents are assumed to know their preferences but researchers only observe a portion of the elements that explain these preferences. The researcher can only explain in probabilistic terms the decision that the respondent makes.

Let us begin with a simple case of utility arising from a yes or no response to a referendum contingent valuation question. In this case utility is assumed to arise from income (M), the presence or absence of the public program. This is an indirect utility function since utility is a function of income and not goods. Also, it is often referred to as a conditional indirect utility function as the utility received is conditional on the choice of Yes or No. For the moment we will ignore demographic factors and other elements in the utility function. Utility is made up of a systematic component (V) and a random component (ε). The subscript i indexes the alternatives Yes and No ($i = 1$(Yes), 0 (No)). If the individual votes Yes they receive the program or public good and their income is reduced by the amount of the bid $\$B$. If they vote No they do not receive the program and their income is not reduced. The second argument in V_i indicates the presence or absence of the program.

$$U_i = V_i + \varepsilon_i \tag{1}$$
$$V_1 = V(M - \$B, 1) \tag{2}$$
$$V_0 = V(M, 0) \tag{3}$$

The probability that the individual says Yes to the bid amount (the probability that the utility of yes is greater than the utility of no) is:

$$\Pr\{Yes\} = \Pr\{V_1 + \varepsilon_1 > V_0 + \varepsilon_0\} \tag{4}$$

Rearranging terms this becomes:

$$\Pr\{Yes\} = \Pr\{\varepsilon_0 - \varepsilon_1 \leq V_1 - V_0\} \tag{5}$$

Equation (5) is a cumulative distribution function where the left-hand side of the inequality is a random variable and the right-hand side is the utility difference (a function of observable elements). We can make assumptions about the errors in this expression and statistically derive estimates of the parameters of the indirect utility functions. To understand the decision to say Yes we need to examine the utility difference between the Yes and No states. This utility difference will depend on the bid amount and the utility from the program being voted on. This logic forms the basis of random utility models and discrete choice analysis. The analyst is examining the probability of a certain response (Yes or No) as a function of the differences in the utilities in the options.

Let us examine this issue in a slightly more general fashion. Rather than examine the probability of saying Yes in terms of utility differences, we can also think of the probability that the individual's actual willingness to pay is greater than the amount they are presented as the bid. Consider a version of the indirect utility function that includes the random element associated with choice (elements not observed by the researcher). In addition to the notation above, let Q^1 be the quality level associated with the program or public good and Q^0 the quality level without the program. Let M represent income and B the bid or price presented to the respondent. The probability of saying Yes is:

$$\Pr(Yes) = \Pr(V(Q^1, M - B, \varepsilon) > V(Q^0, M, \varepsilon)) \tag{6}$$

C defines compensating variation in the expression:

$$V(Q^1, M - C, \varepsilon) = V(Q^0, M, \varepsilon) \tag{7}$$

A variation function (Hanemann and Kanninen, 1999) that describes the compensating variation for any chosen quality difference is defined as:

$$C(Q^1, Q^0, M, \varepsilon) \tag{8}$$

An alternate way to express the probability of saying Yes is based on the compensation function, or the notion that the respondent will say Yes if the willingness to pay (defined by compensating variation) is greater than the bid, or;

$$\Pr(Yes) = \Pr(C(Q^1, Q^0, M, \varepsilon) > B) = 1 - \Pr(C(Q^1, Q^0, M, \varepsilon) \leq B) \tag{9}$$

Define F as the investigator's assumption of a cumulative distribution function. The probability of saying Yes can now be stated as a function of the bid B, or:

$$Pr(Yes) = 1 - F(B) \tag{10}$$

Suppose the indirect utility function V is linear. An expression for compensating variation can be formed as follows where the information on the quality change (Q^0 to Q^1) is captured in the elements superscripted by 1 and 0 (the intercept and error components):

$$V^1 = \alpha^1 + \beta(M - C) + \varepsilon^1 = \alpha^0 + \beta(M) + \varepsilon^0 = V^0 \tag{11}$$

or, after re-arranging terms,

$$C = \frac{(\alpha^1 - \alpha^0) - (\varepsilon^1 - \varepsilon^0)}{\beta} \tag{12}$$

The compensation function in this case is the utility difference set equal to zero and solved for C. Note that in this case compensating variation depends on the random terms and therefore is itself a random variable. Given assumptions about the distribution of ε^i we can estimate the parameters α^i and β.

Quality in equation (11) is reflected in the parameter α^i. The compensating variation depends on the difference in the α^i parameters (with the program versus without), however, we will normalize this difference by assigning the utility without the program a value of zero (since only relative utility matters) or we will redefine the difference in α^i values as simply α.

Define delta V, or the utility difference as:

$$\Delta V = V^0 - V^1 = \alpha^0 + \beta(M) - (\alpha^1 + \beta(M - B)) \tag{13}$$

and normalize the α values to a single α. The change in utility between having the program and not having the program is

$$\Delta V = V^0 - V^1 = -\alpha + \beta(B) \tag{14}$$

When set equal to zero this provides a measure of the bid B that would make the individual indifferent between having the program and not having the program, or it forms an expression of the compensating variation function (7).

The probability of saying Yes can be defined based on equation (7) and (9) for this case of a linear utility function. The probability of saying Yes is the probability that the willingness to pay or compensation function (the utility difference expression) is greater than or equal to the bid amount B. This is also 1 minus the probability that the willingness to pay is less than or equal to the bid amount B, one minus the cdf of the compensation function (Hanemann and Kanninen, 1999).

Since F reflects our assumption of the form of the cdf, the probability of saying Yes becomes:

$$\Pr(\text{Yes}) = 1 - F(-\alpha + \beta B) \tag{15}$$

If we assume a type I extreme value distribution for the error terms, or a logistic distribution for the difference in the error terms, the following closed form expression results for the probability of saying Yes.

$$\Pr(\text{Yes}) = 1 - \frac{e^{(-\alpha + \beta B)}}{1 + e^{(-\alpha + \beta B)}} = \frac{1}{1 + e^{(-\alpha + \beta B)}} \tag{16}$$

If a normal distribution is assumed, the probability of saying Yes becomes

$$\Pr(\text{Yes}) = 1 - \Phi(-\alpha + \beta B) \tag{17}$$

where Φ is the cdf of the normal distribution. One can make other assumptions about the shape of the utility function and corresponding assumptions about the shape of the cdf, including a logarithmic, log-normal, Weibull (see Hanemann and Kanninen, 1999).

The parameters of these indirect utility functions are typically estimated by maximum likelihood where the likelihood function is the product across respondents of the probability of their response, or

$$L = \prod_{n=1}^{N} \Pr_n(\text{Yes})^\delta \Pr_n(\text{No})^{1-\delta} \tag{18}$$

where the probability of saying No is simply 1 minus the probability of saying yes, and δ is an indicator variable that equals 1 for those who voted Yes. Note that this simple model assumes that everyone has the same preferences. There has been considerable advance on the representation of heterogeneity in random utility models (see Haab and McConnell, 2002, and the discussion below).

Welfare measures in the contingent valuation model

Given the definition of the probability of Yes the expected value of the random variable compensating variation is (Hanemann and Kanninen, 1999):

$$C = \int_{-\infty}^{0} F(B)\, dB + \int_{0}^{\infty} (1 - F(B))\, dB \tag{19}$$

A graphical depiction is presented in figure 9.2. The measure in equation (19) assumes that willingness to pay for this program can be either positive or negative.

In some cases researchers limit the measure of willingness to pay to include only the positive component, ruling out negative willingness to pay for programs that are welfare improving. This results in a measure of expected compensating variation of:

$$C = \int_0^\infty (1 - F(B))\, dB \tag{20}$$

Graphically this is illustrated in figure 9.3. In addition, one can also define the median welfare measure by the value of B that solves the expression (Hanemann and Kanninen, 1999):

$$1 - F(B) = 0.5 \tag{21}$$

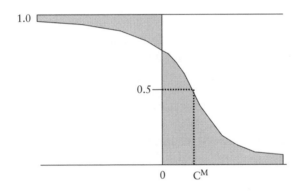

Figure 9.2   Welfare measures in a discrete choice model

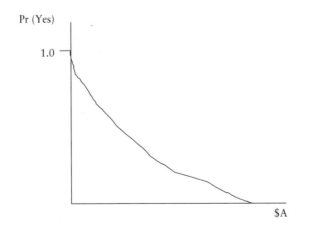

Figure 9.3   Expected value of willingness to pay assuming no non-positive WTP

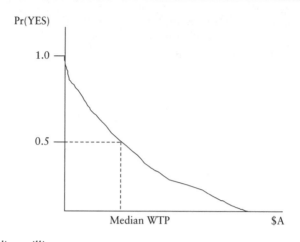

Figure 9.4   Median willingness to pay

or the value that makes the probability of saying Yes equal 0.5. The median is illustrated in figure 9.4 and in figure 9.2 as C^m.

Double-bounded contingent valuation

In the case of double-bounded contingent valuation the respondent is asked two questions. They are first asked if they would be willing to pay a specified amount (B). If they say Yes they are asked if they would pay a higher amount (B_U). If they say no they are asked if they would pay a lower amount (B_L). Four discrete outcomes are possible, {Yes, Yes}, {Yes, No}, {No, Yes}, and {No, No}. Using the notation above, the probability expressions for each of the four cases are:

$$\Pr\{\text{Yes, Yes}\} = P^{YY} = 1 - F(B_U)$$
$$\Pr\{\text{Yes, No}\} = P^{YN} = F(B_U) - F(B) \tag{22}$$
$$\Pr\{\text{No, Yes}\} = P^{NY} = F(B) - F(B_L)$$
$$\Pr\{\text{No, No}\} = P^{NN} = F(B_L)$$

The logic behind equation (22) can be illustrated using a distribution of bids as presented in figure 9.5. The initial bid, upper bid, and lower bid are illustrated on the graph. The areas corresponding to the probabilities are also illustrated. For example, a person who answers Yes and Yes falls into the right hand tail of the distribution and thus the probability of saying Yes is identified by examining the distribution relative to B_U or Bid upper.

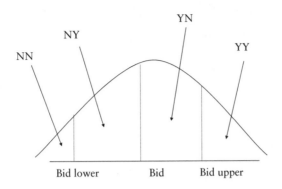

Figure 9.5   Illustration of double-bounded contingent valuation

These probabilities are employed in a likelihood function of the form:

$$L = \Pi_n\{I_{YY}\, \mathrm{Pr}_n{}^{YY} * I_{YN}\, \mathrm{Pr}_n{}^{YN} * I_{NY}\, \mathrm{Pr}_n{}^{NY} * I_{NN}\, \mathrm{Pr}_n{}^{NN}\} \tag{23}$$

where I_{jk} is an indicator of the response (Y or N) to the first (j) and the second (k) questions and n indexes individuals. For example, I_{YY} equals one if the person answered Yes, Yes, and 0 otherwise (Hanemann and Kanninen, 1999).

Design issues in contingent valuation

While considerable effort has been spent on the economic and econometric structure of contingent valuation, there are several issues that the practitioner or reviewer must be aware of. The first of these is the issue of *Strategic Behavior*, or the potential that the respondent is behaving strategically when responding. Strategic behavior depends on two elements, the perceived payment obligation and the expectations about the actual provision of the program. For example, if an individual perceives that they will never have to actually pay the amount they offer, but they expect that high reported bids will result in provision of the program, they will report a high (untruthful) value. Conversely, if they think that they may actually have to pay the amount they report, but they don't think that the amount that they report will affect the actual provision of the good, they will under-report their value. This suggests that in order to accurately elicit truthful responses a contingent valuation question must be credible in the sense that the respondent should believe that they will actually have to pay and they should expect that the amounts they report will affect the provision of the public good. In other words they should believe that the contingent valuation task is "consequential" or will have consequences regarding the provision of the program and the collection of funds. There is still considerable debate in the literature regarding strategic behavior, but it appears that binary choice, referendum contingent valuation questions have the potential to be incentive compatible (or elicit a truthful response) when they are consequential. Conversely, open-ended contingent valuation questions or questions that elicit payments as donations or as voluntary contributions (not binding referenda) will probably not be incentive compatible (see Carson, Groves, and Machina, 2000). Further discussion of preference revelation mechanisms as a way of avoiding strategic behavior can be found in Johansson (1991)

A second and somewhat related issue is the degree to which there is a difference between *hypothetical and real valuations*. A number of experiments have been conducted comparing hypothetical valuations and "real" payments. Some of these have been conducted by comparing actual sales with hypothetical sales. Other experiments have been in the form of hypothetical and real auctions. It appears that individuals can provide values in contingent valuation tasks that approximate values in actual transactions when they are dealing with familiar goods or transactions they have had some experience with. There is also some evidence that adding "cheap talk" scripts aids in obtaining accurate valuations (Cummings and Taylor, 1999; List, 2001). Cheap talk is a statement that explains to the respondent that this is a hypothetical valuation question, and that individuals often don't treat hypothetical valuations as they would an actual transaction. The script then encourages the respondent to choose as if this was an actual transaction. These relatively innocuous scripts appear to have a significant impact on valuation elicitation. A further addition to surveys that can improve elicitation is to ask the respondent how certain they are of their decision (or value). This information helps identify those individuals who are unsure of their valuation and reflects a high variance in the valuation response.

A phenomenon discovered by contingent valuation practitioners referred to as *scoping and sequencing* or by some as the *embedding effect* (Kahneman and Knetsch, 1992) is best illustrated by an example. Imagine that three groups of respondents, A, B, and C are asked contingent valuation questions. The first group is asked to value program 1 as well as a program that is a subset of program 1, called program 2. They are also asked to value program 3, a subset of program 2. The value of program 1 should exceed program 2 which should exceed program 3. The second respondent group is only asked to value programs 2 and 3 and the third respondent group is asked to value program 3. Results of the following form have been discovered (Kahneman and Knetsch, 1992).

	Respondent groups		
Program	A	B	C
1	$150		
2	$30	$150	
3	$15	$40	$140

The values expressed by the groups on their first choice indicate that across the samples the respondents are not sensitive to the scope of the program. This illustrates a lack of sensitivity to *scope* (see Carson, 2000; Carson and Mitchell, 1995). Within a respondent group the valuation declines with program as one would expect. However, in this case it appears that question order makes a difference in the valuation. If the survey began with program 2, it would be worth $150 to group B. However, it would only appear to be worth $30 to group A. Placing the program lower in the list of items to be valued appears to reduce the value of the good. This is referred to as the *sequencing* effect (Carson and Mitchell, 1995; Carson, 2000).

Of these two issues *scope* has received the most attention. That is because a good survey instrument should show sensitivity to scope. In most cases contingent valuation practitioners now include tests of scope within their survey designs. The *sequencing* effect presents a different problem. Economic theory suggests that compensating variation elicited in a sequence will result in decreasing values because of income and substitution effects (Carson and Mitchell, 1995). However, the amount of the decrease is an empirical question and will not in general be resolved in a general sense. This is a kind of context effect and the degree of difference within the sequence depends on the specifics of the case in question.

A phenomenon known as *warm glow* arises in contingent valuation responses (Kahneman and Knetsch, 1992; Andreoni, 1990). The respondent appears to be voting Yes (or providing a large willingness to pay amount) because of the general "cause" associated with the program rather than the specifics of the program itself. The respondent appears to be purchasing moral satisfaction rather than a specific public good. In environmental cases this occurs when respondents wish to pay for anything that is good for the environment, rather than considering the specific circumstances of the program being offered and the other available uses for their funds. This phenomenon can be identified to a certain degree using debriefing questions and by probing individuals during interviews. It is often also confounded with scoping and sequencing effects.

Another way to view the issue of "bias" in response to contingent valuation or stated preference questions is to assess the *validity* of the response (Mitchell and Carson, 1989). There are several forms of validity. *Construct validity* assesses the degree to which the responses conform to predictions from theory. Contingent valuation responses, for example, should be sensitive to changes in income and should vary with the price or bid. *Content validity* examines whether the survey as presented accurately captures the description of the environmental change and other associated components of the valuation context. *Criterion validity* examines whether the response corresponds to other similar measures derived using different approaches. For example, a contingent valuation case may be comparable to an experimental auction providing some support for the results on the basis of criterion validity.

A challenging issue arising in valuation is the difference between willingness to pay and willingness to accept compensation (Knetsch, 1989; Kahneman et al.,

1990; Mitchell and Carson, 1989). Almost all contingent valuation tasks are structured as willingness to pay questions, implying a property rights situation with the respondent not the current owner of the good/service. Willingness to accept questions are much more difficult to frame and ask because of the implied property right. Furthermore, these values will not, in general, be the same. The difference between willingness to pay and willingness to accept can be substantial and has been found in experiments with market goods as well as hypothetical experiments. One should expect these values to be different if there are limited substitutes for the good being valued (Hanemann, 1991). This suggests that in many cases contingent valuation researchers are eliciting willingness to pay values while they should be eliciting willingness to accept values. In a case of determining compensation for environmental damage, for example, the willingness to pay valuation results will underestimate the "true" value. The difference between willingness to pay and willingness to accept has substantial ramifications for valuation researchers, as well as for economists in general. Figure 9.6 illustrates the willingness to pay versus willingness to pay difference. This figure examines preferences for "income" versus a single public good. The initial position is at income level M0 and public good X0. Suppose the public good level was increased to X1. The individual would move to a higher indifference curve. We can examine the amount of money that the individual would give up to get to this utility level (U1) by determining the amount of money it would take to move from U0 to U1 at public good level X1. This is illustrated on the right-hand side of figure 9.6 as the WTP. Conversely, if the amount of the public good dropped to X2, utility would decrease and be reflected by indifference curve U2. The amount of money required to compensate the individual for this loss is illustrated by WTA on the graph. Notice the significant difference between WTP and WTA.

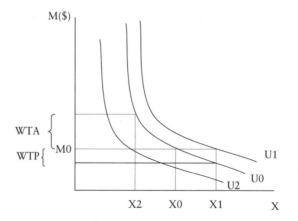

Figure 9.6   Illustration of the difference between willingness to pay and willingness to accept

Table 9.2 NOAA panel recommendations: a selected shortlist

1 Use unbiased/probability sampling
2 Minimize non-response
3 Employ personal interviews
4 Pre-test for interviewer effects
5 Report: the sampling scheme, non-response rates, item non-response rates,
 the actual questions
6 Pre-test the CV question
7 Employ a conservative design
8 Use a willingness to pay format
9 Use a referendum format
10 Pre-test the photographs/description.
11 Remind respondents of substitutes
12 Allow for adequate time lapse from the incident
13 Average responses from several time periods
14 Include a no-answer (don't know) option
15 Include debriefing questions
16 Present simple crosstabulations
17 Include checks on the respondent's understanding
18 Remind respondents of alternative expenditure possibilities
19 Reduce the warm glow effect
20 Burden of proof on survey designers

Summary

Contingent valuation has evolved significantly since the 1970s. It has been rigorously tested on a number of different dimensions and substantial improvements in the protocols and methods have been developed. The current standards for a contingent valuation task are outlined in the NOAA Panels Recommendations (Arrow et al., 1993). These are summarized in table 9.2. There is some debate about specific elements in the NOAA recommendations, but in general they provide sound guidelines on the collection of values.

9.3 ATTRIBUTE BASED STATED CHOICE METHODS

An alternative to contingent valuation that has emerged over the past few years is Attribute Based Stated Choice Methods (ABSCM). These methods present a set of alternatives (not just two as in the discrete choice contingent valuation case) where the alternatives are defined by attributes (including the price or payment). The choice sets or sets of alternatives are constructed from specific experimental designs that allow the attributes to be uncorrelated and thereby yield un-confounded estimates of the parameters of the conditional indirect utility function. Most applications of ABSCMs also elicit several responses from each individual.

ABSCMs will not be applicable to all valuation cases. However, ABSCMs will be useful for cases in which the investigator is interested in the valuation of the attributes of the situation, or cases in which the decision lends itself to a case of respondents choosing from a set of alternatives. ABSCMs arose from the marketing and transportation literature where they were used to measure the demands for market goods or services, especially new goods and services. The technique also has its roots in conjoint analysis ("consider jointly") in which individuals are asked to provide ratings of products with different profiles. Design and analysis of modern ABSCMs is based on random utility theory and thus is consistent with the theoretical underpinnings of contingent valuation.

ABSCMs can be used to identify values in passive use cases or for use values. These methods can also be used to provide data to mix with data from actual markets and help identify preference parameters. Most practitioners in the field recognize the advantages of ABSCM as: (1) the control of the stimuli is in the experimenter's hand, as opposed to the low level of control generally afforded by observing the real marketplace; (2) the control of the design matrix yields greater statistical efficiency and eliminates collinearity (unless explicitly built into the design); (3) the development of more robust models because wider attribute ranges can be applied than are found in real markets; and (4) the introduction and/or removal of products and services is straightforwardly accomplished, as is the introduction of new attributes (see Adamowicz, Louviere, and Swait, 1998; Holmes and Adamowicz, 2003).

Applications of ABSCMs generally follow the seven steps outlined below (see Adamowicz, Louviere, and Swait, 1998; Holmes and Adamowicz, 2003):

(1) *Characterization of the decision problem*: This involves the identification of the problem at hand (change in environmental quality affecting recreation behavior, change in provision of public goods that requires a social choice mechanism to be specified for this issue, etc.). The researcher may decide to frame the decision problem as a referendum with multiple alternatives, or as a choice of a set of hypothetical recreation sites, depending on the context.

(2) *Attribute-level selection*: The number of attributes and value of the levels for each attribute is defined in this stage, as appropriate for the decision problem at hand. The attributes of the situation are generally determined by the research problem (definitions of the program or public good) and the interpretation of the respondents. The attributes must be presented in a fashion that is understandable to the respondent and meaningful in terms of the policy problem. Some examples of ABSCMs employ large numbers of attributes (6 or more) while more tend to simplify the problem to 4 or 5 attributes, each with 3 or 4 levels. An example is presented in figure 9.7. The attributes considered in this case were the population levels of important wildlife species, the size of wilderness area, the degree to which recreation was restricted, the employment status of the forest industry and the tax paid by the household. Each of these attributes had four levels that spanned the historical range of the attributes.

(3) *Experimental design development*: Once attributes and levels have been determined, experimental design procedures are used to construct the choice tasks,
alternatives, or profiles that will be presented to the respondents. There is a large
literature on experimental design that provides many options for designing choice
tasks. The main problem is that the universe of all possible combinations of attributes and levels is usually very large. In the example in figure 9.7 there are
5 attributes and each has 4 levels. The number of combinations of these attributes
and levels is 4^5. If two alternatives are presented at a time (two different combinations of attributes) the number of possible combinations (the full-factorial)
is $4^5 \times 4^5$ or over 1 million combinations. There are several ways to generate
combinations of attributes that are useful in statistical analysis and provide a set
of alternatives that will elicit trade-offs from respondents. The first is to randomly
sample from the universe of all possible combinations of attributes and levels.
In the limit this random sample will be orthogonal (no correlation between attributes) and will allow for estimation of the utility parameters. However, it is
not clear how large the sample should be to be satisfactory and one cannot ask

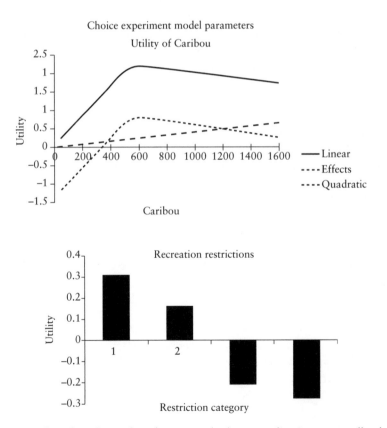

Figure 9.7 Attribute based stated preference methods: an application to woodland caribou
conservation in Alberta

respondents an unlimited number of questions. An alternative is to use experimental design principles. A main effects fraction of the full factorial can be employed. This is a fraction or subset of the full factorial that allows for the estimation of main effects of attributes (but not interactions between attributes). In the case presented in figure 9.7 the main effects orthogonal design generated 32 choice pairs to be presented to respondents (see Adamowicz, Louviere, and Swait, 1998; Holmes and Adamowicz, 2003; Louviere, Hensher, and Swait, 2000).

(4) *Questionnaire development*: The questionnaire can vary from paper and pencil tasks to computer aided surveys. As in any survey-based research, pre-testing of the questionnaire is a necessary component of the research program. The issues raised in the discussion of contingent valuation also apply here – focus groups and pre-tests are necessary elements of a good ABSCM application.

(5) *Sample size and data collection*: The usual considerations of desired accuracy levels versus data collection costs must guide definition of sample sizes.

(6) *Model estimation*: ABSCMs are based on random utility theory. The most common estimation approach has been the use of multinomial logit (MNL), and the most common estimation method has been maximum likelihood, although the most appropriate method will depend on the issues being examined. These methods are extensions of the methods presented for contingent valuation.

Random utility theory poses the notion that individual consumers choose alternatives that provide them with the greatest utility. Therefore, the probability of selecting an alternative increases as the utility associated with it increases. The utility that an individual derives from an alternative is considered to be associated with the attributes of the alternative, and her utility function is composed of a deterministic component (V) and an unobservable or stochastic component (ε):

$$U = V + \varepsilon \tag{24}$$

where V is the indirect utility function in which the attributes are arguments. Therefore, V can be characterized as:

$$V_i = \beta_k X_i \tag{25}$$

where X is a vector of k attributes associated with alternative i and β is a coefficient vector. If the stochastic component or error term, is distributed as a type-I extreme value random variable, McFadden (1981) shows that the conditional choice probability of selecting alternative i is:

$$\Pr{ob}(i) = e^{(\mu \, \beta_k X_i)} / \sum_{j \in c} e^{(\mu \beta_k X_j)} \tag{26}$$

where μ is a scale parameter and C is the choice set. Note, however, that μ is confounded with the parameter vector β and cannot be identified. Normally, μ is set equal to 1.0 and the parameters are estimated using maximum likelihood methods.

An individual application of the method involves the generation of a number of bundles of attributes, and these are presented to respondents in series of choice tasks. Thus, the attributes of each alternative offered in a task comprise the X vector and the sets of alternatives in each task comprise C, the choice set. If a respondent was required to answer eight choice tasks, each consisting of three alternatives, the common method of analysis would consider this information as eight individual choices from a trinary universe. The econometric analysis (maximization of the likelihood employing the probabilities derived in (26)) provides the estimates of the marginal utilities associated with the attributes and allows for their use in welfare measures.

(7) *Policy Analysis and Decision Support System (DSS) development*: Most ABSCM applications are targeted to generating welfare measures, or predictions of behavior, or both. Thus, the models are used to simulate outcomes that can be used in policy analysis or as components of decision support tools.

In a linear form of the conditional indirect utility function V, the β coefficients are the marginal utilities of the attributes. The ratio of the coefficients provides a measure of the marginal rate of substitution between the attributes. The ratio of any attribute and the price parameter provides a measure of the marginal value of an attribute. For example, if the β coefficient estimated for the tax or price attribute was -0.01 and the β coefficient for an attribute describing the number of caribou present (as in figure 9.7) was 0.05, then the implicit value of an additional caribou would be $5.00. It is important to note that these ratios of coefficients are not welfare measures like compensating variation but are only marginal value measures.

There are two main categories of welfare measures that arise from the use of ABSCMs. The first is the "state of the world" approach in which one compares the utility in the base case with the utility in a "changed" case. In these state of the world models the welfare comparison is between two states of the world even though the choice task may ask respondents to choose from several states. In contrast, in ABSCMs that involve choice from several alternatives that can all exist simultaneously (such as multiple brands for products, or multiple recreation sites), the welfare measure must take into account the probability of choosing each alternative when developing the estimate. In these latter cases, the base situation contains multiple alternatives and so also does the improved situation, thus the welfare measure must examine the utilities with and without the improvements, as well as the probabilities of choosing each alternative. If there is an improvement at a site that has little chance of being chosen, then the welfare impact will be small.

Welfare measures in "state of the world" models

Assessment of economic welfare involves an investigation of the difference between the well-being (or utility) achieved by the individual under the status quo (or constant base) alternative and some other alternative. It is therefore a matter of considering the value of a change away from the status quo. Let V_0 be the base situation and V_1 be the improved situation. Compensating variation can be expressed as

$$CV = (1/\beta_\$)(V_1 - V_0) \tag{27}$$

Where $\beta_\$$ is an estimate of the marginal utility of money. More complex expressions will result from non-linear functional forms of the utility function but the concept of evaluating the amount of money it will take to make V_1 equal V_0 remains.

Models with multiple alternatives

If there are multiple alternatives available, as in the case of recreation sites or product choice, the welfare measure involves the expected value of the maximum of utility (or utility for each alternative and the probability of choosing each alternative) arising from the multiple alternatives. The expected value of the base case is compared to the expected value of the "changed" case and again, in the case of linear models, the difference is multiplied by 1 over the marginal utility of income to convert the utility difference into monetary values. For multinomial logit models (MNL) with no income effects, the expected value across the alternatives can be expressed as the "log-sum" or $\ln \Sigma \exp(V_i)$ where "ln" indicates natural logarithm, "exp" is the mathematical constant "e", the summation is over all of the alternatives, and V_i is the conditional indirect utility associated with alternative i. The expression for welfare in these cases is:

$$\frac{1}{\beta_\$}\left(\ln \sum_{i=1}^{C} e^{V_i^1} - \ln \sum_{i=1}^{C} e^{V_i^0} \right) \tag{28}$$

where the superscript 0 indicates the base situation and the superscript 1 indicates the "changed" situation. The alternatives are indexed by $i = 1, \ldots, C$. Note that instead of quality changes this measure can also be used to assess the impact of the addition of a new alternative as:

$$\frac{1}{\beta_\$}\left(\ln \sum_{i=1}^{C+1} e^{V_i^1} - \ln \sum_{i=1}^{C} e^{V_i^0} \right) \tag{29}$$

or the removal of an alternative, for example the removal of alternative 1:

$$\frac{1}{\beta_\$}\left(\ln \sum_{i=2}^{C} e^{V_i^1} - \ln \sum_{i=1}^{C} e^{V_i^0} \right) \tag{30}$$

Design issues in attribute based stated choice methods

Practitioners employing ABSCMs must be concerned with many of the same issues as those using contingent valuation. Is the scenario accurately specified? Do the respondents understand the choices and the payment vehicles? Is the task "consequential" or does it appear to be entirely hypothetical? Issues of strategic behavior in response apply to choice experiments just as they do to contingent valuation (Carson et al., 2000) although the more complex nature of choice tasks may limit this behavior. Issues of scope are addressed internally by ABSCMs (via changing attribute levels) but there remain questions about attribute range – a form of scope effect. ABSCMs have also elicited differences in willingness to pay and willingness to accept, just as other mechanisms have. However, a number of other design issues arise in ABSCMs. First the researcher must decide on the number of attributes, the number of levels and the number of replications that each respondent will face. This is a difficult task involving a combination of judgment arising from focus groups and pre-testing to considerations of fatigue and learning. It is now relatively commonplace to provide one or two "warm-up" tasks for respondents. These tasks familiarize the respondent with the process and result in reduced "noise" throughout the remainder of the tasks. Most practitioners suggest using no more than eight replications per person, although this depends on the context being considered.

Econometric considerations also apply in ABSCMs. There is less debate regarding the choice of error distribution as most researchers have adopted the logit framework. However, there are concerns regarding the limitations on preferences arising from the simple logit specification. For example, the simple logit structure implies that the independence of irrelevant alternative assumptions holds. In terms of the probabilities of choice this implies that the ratio of probabilities of any two alternatives is independent of any other alternative (equation (31)).

$$\frac{P_r(i)}{P_r(j)} = \frac{e^{(V(i))}}{e^{(V(j))}} \tag{31}$$

This also implies that the cross-elasticities for the alternatives are all identical. This is a relatively severe restriction of preferences. As an alternative some have proposed the use of nested logit models that involve a type of grouping of alternatives into similar classes (or groups with positive correlations in the unobserved component). For example, the utility of choosing alternative jm, where j indicates the elemental alternative and m indicates a non-status quo choice, can be decomposed into the utility of making a non-status quo choice (U_m) and the utility of choosing alternative j, conditional on making a non-status quo choice.

$$U_{jm} = U_{j|m} + U_m = V_{j|m} + V_m + e_{j|m} + e_m \tag{32}$$

This type of model results in the estimation of utility parameters as well as the estimation of the degree of similarity between alternatives in a group.

Another econometric issue that has received considerable attention in the ABSCM literature is the treatment of heterogeneity. Since these models are estimated on the basis of the difference in utility levels between alternatives, elements that are not different between alternatives cannot be included directly in the estimation. Income, age and other demographic elements cannot be included in estimation directly. They can be included as interactions with attributes of the model or they can be included in latent class or finite mixture models. A finite mixture model assumes that there exists some finite number of classes of preference parameters, indicated by the subscript s in (33) (see Holmes and Adamowicz, 2003). The number of classes is unknown to the researcher but is estimated by examining the probability of choices, as a function of classes of preference parameters, with a secondary function estimating the probability of being in a particular preference class as a function of demographic and other factors (e.g. income, age, etc.).

$$Pr_{n/s}(i) = \frac{e^{(\mu_s)}(\beta_s X_i)}{\sum_{k \in C} e^{(\mu_s)}(\beta_s X_k)} \qquad (33)$$

This model allows for the inclusion of demographic elements in explaining preference differences. Another model that allows for preference heterogeneity is the random parameters logit model, or the mixed logit model (Train, 1999). This approach begins with the simple logit model as an expression of the probability of choice. Then, a distributional assumption about the preference parameters (β) over the sample is made and the probability of choice is examined using equation (34) to incorporate variability of preferences over the sample.

$$Pr(j) = \int \pi_j(\beta) g(\beta) \, d(\beta) \qquad (34)$$

The random parameters logit approach allows for parameter heterogeneity and essentially permits the estimation of individual parameters, conditional on the overall sample estimates. These models also, in general, do not suffer from the independence of irrelevant alternatives assumption (Train, 1999).

ABSCMs can be considered a "data generating mechanism" just as the market is a data generating mechanism. In some cases, the data from these two mechanisms can be combined. For example, if limited variation in environmental quality currently exists across recreation sites, but a policy to increased quality at one specific site is being considered, actual behavioral data (revealed preference data) cannot be used to identify the benefits. That is because the lack of variation limits the ability of the analyst to identify the impact of quality changes. An ABSCM however, can identify quality effects by asking individuals about changing quality levels and their behavioral response. While these data could be analyzed separately from revealed preference data, they can also be combined with the revealed preference data to increase the data scope and variability, while not relying entirely on hypothetical question responses. There is some evidence that the forecasts from these combined approaches are superior to individual approaches.

Contingent valuation and ABSCMs

ABSCMs, in contrast to contingent valuation methods, have not been tested as rigorously in the process associated with a Natural Resource Damage Assessment context. However, recent cases including (Breffle et al., 1999 (http://www.fws.gov/r3pao/nrda/recfish.pdf) and the case in Lavaca Bay Texas (Texas General Land Office, 1999, http://www.darp.noaa.gov/pdf/lavacbaydarp.pdf) illustrate the use of ABSCMs in NRDA cases and the potential for use of ABSCMs in resource compensation cases (see Adamowicz, Louviere, and Swait, 1998).

Other stated preference approaches

While contingent valuation and ABSCMs have risen to be the most commonly used stated preference approaches, other methods are also being employed. Preference evaluations using ratings (traditional conjoint) or rankings have been used in environmental valuation (see Layton, 2000). Rated pair approaches have been used to identify preferences or rankings of environmental (and non-environmental goods) (see Brown and Petersen, 2003). In the health economics literature QALYs (quality adjusted life years) elicit preferences between different health states using a type of rating scale. Standard gambles are also used in which the individual is asked to choose between a reduced health state (with certainty) and a gamble between perfect health (with probability p) and death (with probability $1 - p$). The probability p at which the person is indifferent between the two reflects the preferences over the reduced health state. Details on these methods can be found in Gold et al. (1996).

APPENDIX 9.1: ECONOMETRICS 101 – MAXIMUM LIKELIHOOD ESTIMATION

Many modern valuation methods rely on random utility models that employ maximum likelihood techniques to estimate the parameters of the (conditional indirect) utility function. Maximum likelihood is simply an approach to find the "best fitting" parameter estimates given some amount of data from a survey or set of behavioral data.

Students who have studied some econometrics or statistics will be familiar with methods of parameter estimation that minimize the sum of squared errors (SSE). Minimizing the SSE involves comparing the actual data to some estimate or prediction. The actual data minus the predicted values are the errors. These errors are squared and summed to create the sum of squared errors. A set of parameters that minimizes the sum of squared errors (or results in the smallest sum of square error) can be considered a form of "best fitting" model. Random utility models, however, do not have dependent variables that are observable. Thus it is not possible to construct a set of errors as the difference between the actual and predicted utility levels – because utility levels are unknown. In a binary choice contingent valuation model, for example, all the researcher observes is whether a person chooses to vote yes or no and the bid value associated with that choice. In such cases the researcher often makes an assumption about the probability distribution that underlies the choice process and finds parameters that best fit this probability distribution. This approach is referred to as maximum likelihood estimation.

Maximum likelihood estimation involves finding the parameters that provide the highest probability of obtaining the observed data. In other words, once one has chosen the form of the probability distribution, one can search for the parameters that result in the best fit between the data and the distribution. An example may help illustrate the concept (this example is based on Greene, 2000, pp. 123–4). Suppose that a researcher has 10 data points {5, 0, 1, 1, 0, 3, 2, 3, 4, 1} and the researcher knows that these points are generated by a Poisson distribution. The Poisson probability density function is:

$$f(x_i, \theta) = \frac{e^{-\theta}\theta^{x_i}}{x_i!}$$

where θ is a parameter and x_i represents the data points, $i = 1, \ldots, 10$. The parameter that describes the distribution, θ, is also the expected value. The likelihood function is the joint probability over the 10 values or the product of the probabilities (assuming that the 10 values are all independent). Thus, the likelihood function is:

$$L(x_i, \theta) = \prod_{i=1}^{10} f(x_i, \theta)$$

or

$$L(x_i, \theta) = \frac{e^{-10\theta}\theta^{\Sigma x_i}}{\Pi x_i!}$$

Most often the likelihood is not used for evaluation; rather, the logarithm of the likelihood (or log-likelihood) is used for analysis since it is usually easier to work with and provides the same optimum values. The logarithm of the likelihood in this case is:

$$\text{Log } L = -10\ 2 + 20\ \ln(2) - 12.242$$

Maximization of the likelihood involves taking the derivative the log-likelihood function with respect to θ and setting the derivative equal to zero. This provides the value of θ that maximizes the joint probability of the occurrence of the 10 values. The derivative is:

$$d\text{Log } L\ /\ d2 = -10 + 20/2$$

Setting this expression equal to zero returns the result that $\theta = 2$. Thus, the best estimate of the parameter of the Poisson distribution that generated these values is 2.

A more typical example is the use of the normal distribution. A univariate normal distribution has two parameters, the mean (μ) and the variance (δ^2). The probability density function multiplied n times results in a log-likelihood function (LogL) that takes the form:

$$\text{LogL}\,(\mu, \sigma^2) = -\frac{n}{2}\,\ln\,(2\pi) - \frac{n}{2}\,\ln\sigma^2 - \frac{1}{2}\sum\frac{(x_i - \mu)^2}{\sigma}$$

Taking the derivative of the log-likelihood function with respect to μ and setting this equal to zero results in

$$\mu = (1/n)\,\Sigma\,x_i$$

in other words, the maximum likelihood estimate of the mean of a normal distribution is the "average" x value in the sample.

In the case of random utility models the probability of choosing a particular alternative is often expressed as

$$\Pr(i) = \frac{e^{(X_i\beta)}}{\sum_{j=1}^{J} e^{(X_j\beta))}}$$

This expression arises from the assumption of a Type I extreme value distribution as the error in the random utility model. Assuming independence between choices the likelihood function is formed as the product of the probabilities of observing each alternative over the sample of individuals. For the case of two alternatives "Yes" and "No" the likelihood function is

$$L = \prod_{n=1}^{N} \Pr(\text{Yes})^{\delta_n}\,\Pr(\text{No})^{1-\delta_n}$$

where the indicator δ_n equals 1 if person n responded "Yes" and 0 otherwise. The log-likelihood based on this expression is maximized to find the values of β that provide the best fit for the data. These values of β are the best estimates of the parameters of the conditional indirect utility function.

NOTE

1   This section is modeled on Hanemann and Kanninen (1999) where additional detail can be found.

FURTHER READING

Contingent Valuation

A major reference on the practice of contingent valuation continues to be Mitchell and Carson (1989). The debate published in the *Journal of Economic Perspectives* 1994 continues to be an excellent outline of the issues involved in Contingent Valuations (Hanemann, 1994; Portney, 1994; Diamond and Hausman, 1994). An excellent overview of the technical issues involved in contingent valuation is Hanemann and Kanninen (1999). Other overviews of the method include Carson (2000), Boyle (2003) in Champ, Boyle, and Brown (2003) and sections of Freeman (1993). Econometric issues are concisely examined in Haab and McConnell (2002).

Attribute Based Stated Choice Methods

Overviews of ABSCMs can be found in Adamowicz et al. (1998) or Holmes and Adamowicz (2003). Bennett and Blamey (2001) provides an introduction to choice experiment methods with several case studies. An excellent overview of ABSCMs in general is Louviere et al. (2000).

REFERENCES

Adamowicz, W., Boxall, P., Williams, M., and Louviere, J. (1998). Stated Preference Approaches for Measuring Passive Use Values: Choice Experiments and Contingent Valuation, *American Journal of Agricultural Economics*, 80 (1 February): 64–75.

Adamowicz, W., Louviere, J., and Swait, J. (1998). Introduction to Attribute-based Stated Choice Methods. Final Report to Resource Valuation Branch, Damage Assessment Center, NOAA, US Department of Commerce. January. 44 pp.

Adamowicz, W. L., Louviere, J., and Williams, M. (1994). Combining Stated and Revealed Preference Methods for Valuing Environmental Amenities, *Journal of Environmental Economics and Management*, 26: 271–92.

Adamowicz, W. L. (2000). Environmental Valuation, in J. Louviere, D. Hensher, and J. Swait (eds) (2000). *Stated Choice Methods: Analysis and Application*, Cambridge: Cambridge University Press.

Andreoni, J. (1990). Impure Altruism and Donations to Public Goods: A Theory of Warm Glow Giving, *Economic Journal*, 100: 464–77.

Arrow, K., Solow, R., Portnoy, P., Leamer, E., Radner, R., and Schuman, H. (1993). Report of the NOAA Panel on Contingent Valuation, *Federal Register*, 4601–14.

Bennett, J. and Adamowicz, W. (2001). Some Fundamentals of Environmental Choice Modelling, in J. Bennett and R. Blamey, eds, *The Choice Modelling Approach to Environmental Valuation*, Edward Elgar: Northampton, pp. 37–69.

Bennett, J. and Blamey, R. (eds) (2001). *The Choice Modelling Approach to Environmental Valuation*, Edward Elgar: Northampton.

Breffle, W. S., Morey, E. R., Rowe, R. D., Waldman, D. M., and Wytinck, S. M. (1999). Recreational Fishing Damages from Fish Consumption Advisories in the Waters of Green Bay: http://www.fws.gov/r3pao/nrda/recfish.pdf

Boyle, K. J. (2003). Contingent Valuation in Practice, in P. A. Champ, K. J. Boyle, and T. C. Brown, eds, *A Primer on Nonmarket Valuation*, Kluwer.

Brown, T. C. and Peterson, G. (2003). Multiple Goods Valuation, in P. A. Champ, K. J. Boyle, and T. C. Brown, eds, *A Primer on Nonmarket Valuation*, Kluwer.

Carson, R. T. (2000). Contingent Valuation: A User's Guide, *Environmental Science and Technology*, 34 (8); 1413–18.

Carson, R. T. and Mitchell, R. C. (1995). Sequencing and Nesting in Contingent Valuation Surveys, *Journal of Environmental Economics and Management*, 28: 155–74.

Carson, R., Groves, T. and Machina, M. (2000). Incentive and Informational Properties of Preference Questions. Paper presented at the Japan Forum of Environmental Valuation, January, 2000.

Champ, P. A., Boyle, K. J., and Brown, T. C. (2003). *A Primer on Nonmarket Valuation*, Kluwer.

Cooper, J. C., Hanemann, M., and Signorello, G. (2002). One-and-One-Half-Bound Dichotomous Choice Contingent Valuation, *Review of Economics and Statistics*, 84: 742–50.

Cummings, R. and Taylor, L. (1999). Unbiased Value Estimates for Environmental Goods: A Cheap Talk Design for the Contingent Valuation Method, *American Economic Review*, 89 (3): 649–65.

Diamond, P. and Hausman, J. (1994). Contingent Valuation: Is Some Number Better Than No Number?, *Journal of Economics Perspectives*, 8: 45–64.

Freeman, A. M. (1993). *The Measurement of Environmental and Resource Values*, Resources for the Future Press: Baltimore.

Gold, M. R., Siegel, J. E., Russell, L. B., and Weinstein, M. C. (1996). *Cost-effectiveness in Health and Medicine*, Oxford University Press: Oxford.

Greene, W. (2000). *Econometric Analysis*, fourth edition, Prentice Hall: New Jersey.

Haab, T. C. and McConnell, K. E. (2002). *Valuing Environmental and Natural Resources: The Econometrics of Non-market Valuation*, Edward Elgar: Cheltenham.

Hanemann, W. M. (1991). Willingness to Pay and Willingness to Accept: How Much Can They Differ?, *American Economic Review*, 81: 635–47.

Hanemann, W. M. and Kanninen, B. (1999). The Statistical Analysis of Discrete Response Data, in I. Bateman and K. Willis, eds, Valuing Environmental Preferences, Oxford University Press: Oxford.

Hanemann, W. M. (1994). Valuing the Environment through Contingent Valuation, *Journal of Economics Perspectives*, 8: 19–44.

Holmes, T. and Adamowicz, W. (2003). Attribute Based Methods, in P. A. Champ, K. J. Boyle, and T. C. Brown, eds, *A Primer on Nonmarket Valuation*, Kluwer.

Johansson, P.-O. (1991). *An Introduction to Model Welfare Economics*, Cambridge University Press: Cambridge.

Kahneman, D. and Knetsch, J. (1992). Valuing Public Goods: The Purchase of Moral Satisfaction, *Journal of Environmental Economics and Management*, 22: 57–70.

Kahneman, D., Knetsch, J. L., and Thaler, R. (1990). Experimental Tests of the Endowment Effect and the Coase Theorem, *Journal of Political Economy*, 98 (6): 1325–48.

Knetsch, J. L. (1989). The Endowment Effect and Evidence of Nonreversible Indifference Curves, *American Economic Review*, 79 (5), 1277–84.

Layton, D. (2000). Random Coefficient Models for Stated Preference Surveys, *Journal of Environmental Economics and Management*, 40: 21–36.

List, J. A. (2001). Do Explicit Warnings Eliminate the Hypothetical Bias in Elicitation Procedures? Evidence from Field Auctions for Sportscards, *American Economic Review*, 91 (5): 1498–1507.

Louviere, J., Hensher, D., and Swait, J. (2000). *Stated Choice Methods: Analysis and Application*, Cambridge University Press: Cambridge.

McFadden, D. (1981). Econometric Models of Probabilistic Choice, in C. Manski and D. McFadden, eds, *Structural Analysis of Discrete Data with Econometric Applications*, Cambridge: MIT Press, pp. 198–272.

Mitchell, R. C. and Carson, R. T. (1989). *Using Surveys to Value Public Goods*. Resources for the Future Press: Washington, DC.

Portnoy, P. (1994). The Contingent Valuation Debate: Why Economists Should Care, *Journal of Economics Perspectives*, 8: 3–18.

Sen, A. K. (1973). Behavior and the Concept of Preference, *Economica*, 40: 241–59.

Texas General Land Office et al. (1999). http://www.darp.noaa.gov/pdf/lavacbaydarp.pdf

Train, K. E. (1999). Mixed Logit Models for Recreation Demand, in *Valuing Recreation and the Environment: Revealed Preference Methods in Theory and Practice*, Edward Elgar: Northampton MA, pp. 33–64.

CHAPTER TEN

ENVIRONMENTAL VALUES EXPRESSED THROUGH MARKET BEHAVIOR

The market is not an invention of capitalism. It has existed for centuries. It is an invention of civilization. (Mikhail Gorbachev, June 8, 1990)

10.1 INTRODUCTION

Chapter 8 introduced the concept of *use value* and the notion that the value of environmental goods and services, even when they are not freely traded in a marketplace, can be inferred from market transactions. These approaches are often referred to as "revealed preference" methods. Examples of these values include:

1 the values exhibited by home purchasers for environmental quality when they pay higher prices for homes in areas with better air quality, less noise, or better scenic amenities,
2 value illustrated by recreationists choosing to travel further (and spend more) to visit sites with better scenery, less congestion, or more wildlife to view,
3 values for mortality risk reduction evident in individuals accepting employment in higher-risk jobs only when wages are higher (everything else remaining constant),
4 recognition of the value of environmental quality changes on crops by examining the impact of the environmental change on production, supply, and demand.

In each of these cases there are no markets for the environmental goods, but the changes affect economic behavior. Note that environmental quality in these cases enters individual utility functions (e.g. noise and homeowner's utility) or production relationships and implicitly profit functions (agricultural effects). In this chapter several approaches for identifying the value of environmental amenities through market behavior are presented. We begin with a discussion of the welfare analytics associated with revealed preference methods and then move to discussion of simple demand models, hedonic models, and random utility models associated with environmental quality effects on individual utility. We complete the chapter with a discussion of environmental quality measurement in production systems.

10.2   MARKET BEHAVIOR AND WELFARE MEASURES

Market behavior will not be useful as a method for assessing environmental quality in all cases. There may be no link between changes in the environment and
behavior because people do not recognize or perceive the environmental impacts,
or the impacts are below some threshold level. For example, if individuals are not
aware that a certain pollutant is in water, and this pollutant has no observable
impact on water quality in terms of smell, taste, etc., then behavioral changes will
not be observed over of a range of pollution levels. If information is disseminated
about the pollutant, its effects and occurrence, then it is possible that behavioral models could be used. A somewhat different condition under which behavioral models
will have limited value is a case where there is no variation in the level of environmental quality, although in this case it may be possible to use stated preference
methods to introduce variability into the data. Finally, the structure of the utility
function may be such that environmental quality effects will not arise. Suppose
that utility is a linearly separable function of goods and environmental quality as
in equation (1), where U is utility, x represents goods, and q represents environmental quality.

$$U(x, q) = G(x) + F(q) \tag{1}$$

This is a strongly separable utility function meaning that maximization of this utility
function with respect to a budget constraint $M = p_x x$ will yield demand functions
for the goods in x that are independent of q (see Phlips, 1983, for a discussion of
separability). Freeman (1993, p. 123) refers to this as a "hopeless case." It will be
impossible to identify environmental values that arise from such a structure using
market observations. The concept of passive use value is in principle derived from
this notion. In equation (1) it is clear that environmental quality does affect utility
and therefore should be considered in economic assessment; however, there is no
observable behavioral trail that can be used to assess this impact on utility.

   If utility functions are such that market demands do include the level of
environmental quality then we can employ the welfare measures presented in
chapter 8. One of the key concepts presented in chapter 8 is the notion of weak
complementarity. This concept relies on the link between environmental quality
and a market good to derive welfare measures. An alternative presentation of the
weak complementarity assumption is presented below.

   Weak complementarity can be described in the following way:

1   The demand for a good x_i is a function of prices, income, and environmental quality
     where increases in environmental quality increase the demand for x_i.
2   There is a price associated with market good x_i such that at that price the demand for
     the good is zero (or, there is a choke price for good x_i).
3   When at the choke price, the change in the expenditure function for a change in the
     level of environmental quality is zero.

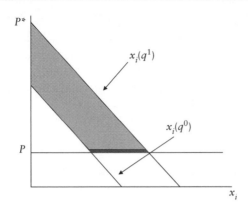

Figure 10.1 Illustration of weak complementarity

These conditions generate a situation where the demand for x_i is increased when environmental quality increases. The welfare change associated with this environmental quality increase can be evaluated as the difference in the area under the demand curves and above price with the change versus without the change. Since the demand curves have choke prices these areas can be evaluated. Freeman (1993) provides a graphical interpretation that is presented in figure 10.1. The current price is represented as P while the choke price is P^*. The demand for good x_i at lower environmental quality levels is $x_i(q^0)$ while the demand shifts out when quality is at level q^1. The area under the demand curve $x_i(q^0)$ and above price reflects the value of $x_i(q^0)$ (consumer surplus for a Marshallian measure or compensating variation for a Hicksian demand curve: see chapter 8 for a definition of compensating variation and consumer surplus) or the amount that the individual would have to be compensated to accept a movement to the choke price. Once at the choke price the level of environmental quality could be increased, shifting the individual to the demand curve $x_i(q^1)$, but still at zero quantity demanded. If the price is now returned to its original level, the value of $x_i(q^1)$ is the area under the new demand curve and above price. Therefore, the value of the quality change is the (shaded) area between the two demand curves (Freeman, 1993). This logic, and the measures of welfare presented in chapter 8 will form the basis for the evaluation of welfare from revealed preference data.

10.3 VALUES REVEALED THROUGH TRAVEL BEHAVIOR: TRADITIONAL TRAVEL COST MODELS

One of the oldest, and probably most common models of environmental valuation is the travel cost model. The model has its origins in Harold Hotelling's insights regarding the value of parks being reflected in travel costs (Hotelling, 1947). This model arises because of the link between purchases of market goods (fuel, etc.)

and environmental quality that is found in recreation behavior. It also has been widely used because of the importance of recreation values as an environmental issue. While the model discussed here is applied to recreation demand, other applications have been conducted, including the application of the model to measure demand for hospital services and veterinary services.

The basic model[1]

Consider a recreationist, labeled n, who obtains utility from visits to recreation sites (V_j) and purchases of other market goods (x). Price for the composite market good is p while the "price" of the recreation visit is the travel cost c_{nj}. The cost is indexed by the individual and the destinations since the distance from each individual's home to the recreation site makes up the individual specific price. There are many recreation sites, referred to as a choice set S_n. The choice set is also indexed by n because each individual may have a different choice set. Let M be income. Thus, this simple utility maximization problem takes the form

$$\text{Max } U_n(x_n, V_{nj})$$
$$\text{subject to } px_n + c_{nj}V_{nj} \leq M \qquad (2)$$

This maximization problem will generate a simple set of demand functions for trips to each site as:

$$V_{nj} = f(c_{nj}, p, M) \qquad (3)$$

In this case observations of the number of visits to each site in the individual's choice set, and observations on other prices will allow the estimation of a demand system for trips to recreation sites. Welfare measures for price changes or for the "removal" of any of the recreation sites can be calculated using standard techniques. However, in order to make this model tractable we must simplify some components of the system. Also, in order to make the model more realistic with respect to recreation we must increase the complexity of some components.

First, the model in (3) contains the prices of all goods. It is unlikely that the prices of all other goods that a consumer purchases will affect the demand for recreation visits directly. Thus, some form of separability over goods will likely be assumed. In fact, in most travel cost demand models the prices of all other goods are not present, implying separability between the recreation sector and all other purchases. Second, the system of demand outlined in (3) could be quite large. It could include a large number of possible sites and it could be differentiated on the basis of types of trips (long, short, type of activity, etc.). Thus, separability assumptions will also likely be made regarding the recreation activities to be included. The time domain must also be specified. That is, the time over which recreation trips are made must be ascertained, e.g. trips per year, per season, etc.

In this simple form of model the consumer determines the number of trips in the relevant time period and information gained on one trip will not affect future trips within this time domain. The simplest possible demand model will involve only one site, no prices of other goods, and income.

It also requires time to access the recreation sites; therefore, we must incorporate time into the set of constraints. Let the budget constraint be defined by income (M) which is a function of time spent working (T_w), expenditures on market goods and expenditures on recreation trips. There will be a total time constraint that requires that the amount of time spent working, on recreation trips and in other activities to not exceed a total time constraint. These time constraints may also be quite complex as time available for work may be limited by regulations or labor market constraints. Time spent in recreation and other activities may also have complex constraints. Imagine a simplified model in which only one recreation site is considered and a simple time constraint is included. The time constraint specifies that total time available for work and recreation (T) limits the sum of time spent working (T_w) and time spent on recreation visits (T_v). Income is the time spent working times the wage rate (W).

$$\text{Max } U\,(x,\,V)$$
$$\text{subject to } px + cV \le M = wT_w \tag{4}$$
$$\text{and } T_w + T_v \le T$$

This simple specification can be rearranged (assuming equality in the constraints) to

$$\text{Max } U\,(x,\,V)$$
$$\text{subject to } px + cV \le M = w(T_w + T_v) \tag{5}$$

This shows that the opportunity cost of time in this basic model is the wage rate. An hour spent engaged in recreation will reduce income by the hourly wage, therefore, the wage rate should be included in the calculation of the price of accessing the site. This is a very simplistic model, however, and more realistic analyses have revealed that the opportunity cost of time is likely a non-linear function of the wage rate. The opportunity cost of time in recreation could be zero, some amount less than the wage or even an amount more than the wage. For a review of these issues see Parsons (2003) or Feather and Shaw (1999). Specific models of value of time can also be found in Bockstael, Strand, and Hanemann (1987) and Smith, Desvousges, and McGivney (1983). Bockstael, Strand, and Hanemann, for example, discuss the implications of various labor market conditions on the value of time and examine empirical methods to identify individual differences in the value of time. Feather and Shaw examine the situation where some individuals may have opportunity costs of time that are greater than the wage rate because they would rather be involved in recreation but constraints prohibit them from releasing work time. Similarly they discuss cases where individuals cannot work extra hours and therefore have values of time lower than their wage. In any event, the key issue for assessing the demand for recreation trips is that assumptions must be made about the opportunity cost of time in the construction of the travel cost variable. In the model in (5), if T_v is replaced by t_v*V, where t_v is the per trip time requirement to access the site, then the "full cost" of each trip to site V is $(c + w*t_v)$ or the out-of-pocket costs plus the time per trip valued at the wage rate.

Econometric considerations

To estimate the simple model may seem relatively straightforward. The quantity of visits over a sample of individuals can be regressed on the travel cost and income to provide an estimate of the demand equation. Demographic characteristics could be added as modifiers of the demand function. However, several econometric issues arise in the specification of the model.

If recreation demand data are available for the general population, then these data can be used to estimate a demand curve. However, it is often the case that the data are collected "on-site." This means that all the members of the sample have taken at least one trip to the recreation site, or the data are "truncated." There is no information about those individuals who have not gone to the site (those with zero trips). Truncation can induce significant bias into the estimation of the demand equation. Estimators that account for truncation have been employed in some recreation demand analyses (see Parsons, 2003). A similar condition arises when one knows something about those who do not participate in visits to the site ("zeros" in the data). This is referred to as censoring in the data. The number of visits is only known for those who visit but demographic information is available for all individuals (Greene, 2000). Censored data give rise to "hurdle" models. Consider the following breakdown of a decision on the number of trips to take to a given recreation site. An individual may never recreate at this site, regardless of the circumstances, or they may choose to recreate only in certain circumstances. A set of variables available to the researcher may help define these decisions. Conditional on choosing to recreate the individual determines the number of trips they make based another set of variables (travel cost, etc.) that may include some or all of the variables in the participation decision. This is referred to as a hurdle model as the individual first passes a hurdle assessing if they ever participate, they then pass a hurdle assessing if they choose a non-zero number of trips, assuming that they are potential participants. Finally, given participation and the decision to choose a non-zero number of trips, the number of trips is determined (Greene, 2000; Parsons, 2003).

While much of the early literature on travel cost modeling employed simple regression models or ordinary least squares, it has been recognized that models of counts or frequencies are more appropriate for such microeconometric analyses. A count data model assumes that observations of the dependent variable (trips to a site) are integers $(0, 1, 2, \dots, N)$. The model is specified to predict the probability that the observed number of trips (V) equals $v_i = 0, 1, 2, \dots, N$. This probability is specified as a Poisson distribution:

$$\Pr(V = v_i) = \frac{e^{-\lambda_i} \lambda_i^{y_i}}{y_i!} \tag{6}$$

where $\Pr(V = v_i)$ is the probability that the number of visits equals an integer $(0, 1, 2, \dots)$ and λ_i captures the independent variables in the model. Typically λ_i is parameterized as $e^{(\beta' x_i)}$. The expected value of this probability expression (or the expected number of trips given the independent variables and parameter estimates) is $e^{(\beta' x_i)}$ (see Greene, 2000; Parsons, 2003).

A difficulty associated with the simple Poisson distribution is that the expected value is equal to the variance and implicitly the model contains no error component. An alternative is to specify the probability as a negative binomial with $\lambda_i = e^{(\beta' x_i + \varepsilon_i)}$ or $\ln \lambda_i = \beta' x_i + \varepsilon_i$ with $e^{(\varepsilon_i)}$ following a gamma distribution with mean 1 and variance α. This generates a modification of the Poisson model that contains an additional parameter, α, that captures the variance (see Cameron and Trivedi, 1998 for econometric details).

Just as censoring and truncation affect continuous demand models these issues will also affect count models. A truncated Poisson model can be derived such that the probability expression in (6) is replaced by

$$\Pr(V = v_i | v_i > 0) = \frac{e^{-\lambda_i} \lambda_i^{y_i} / (y_i)}{1 - e^{[-\lambda_i]}} \tag{7}$$

where the probability is now the probability that the random variable is an integer, conditional on the integer being greater than zero. The right-hand side of the expression "scales" the standard Poisson expression by an expression for the probability that $y_i > 0$. A similar adjustment can be made to the negative binomial model.

The models described above provide estimates for single demand equations (a single site). These approaches have been modified to account for multiple sites using a count data framework (Englin, Boxall, and Watson, 1998) or using a demand systems framework (Phaneuf, Kling, and Herriges, 2000).

Welfare measures

Welfare measurement in the single site demand framework is relatively straightforward. The models estimated are Marshallian demand equations. The choice of functional form specifies the form of the welfare measure for the value of a site or the value per trip (the more commonly reported measure). For example, if a linear demand function is assumed ($V = \alpha + \beta c$; where c is travel cost) then the value per trip is simply $(V/(-2\beta))$ and if a semi-log form of demand is specified

$(\ln V = \alpha + \beta c)$ then the value per trip is simply $(1/-\beta)$ (see Adamowicz, Fletcher, and Graham-Tomasi, 1989). Note that these are values for accessing the site and are not values associated with quality changes. The traditional travel cost model cannot provide measures of the value of quality changes unless there is variation in quality over time (time-series data) or a systems model has estimates that allow for spatial variation in quality to affect demand. We now turn to models that do provide measures of the value of quality changes.

ATTRIBUTE BASED MODELS – RANDOM UTILITY MODELS

Traditional demand models assume that utility is derived from goods. An alternative view, initially presented by Lancaster (1996) is that utility is derived from attributes of goods. That is, people do not purchase houses *per se*, they purchase a bundle that provides bedrooms, kitchen facilities, a yard, a neighborhood, etc. This view of consumer demand is very convenient for the assessment of environmental quality as another attribute or set of attributes. In the housing example this means consideration of local air quality, scenery, or level of traffic noise as attributes of the housing choice. In a recreation demand context the attributes could be the number of camping sites at a recreation destination and the water quality.

Attribute based models can be classified into two main categories, random utility models and hedonic price models. The former assume specifications for the utility function and examine choice based on these assumed structures. Hedonic price methods examine prices of goods arising as market equilibria and decompose these prices into attribute components. In this section we review random utility models with hedonic price analysis to follow in later sections.

The random utility model (or RUM) assumes that individuals choose from a discrete set of goods (houses, recreation sites, etc). Let these goods be labeled $y_1, ..., y_J$. Each good has a quality vector associated with it denoted by $q_1, ..., q_J$ as well as prices $p_1, ..., p_J$. The numeraire good representing all other goods is z and its price is normalized to one. The budget constraint is $\sum_{i=1}^{J} p_i y_i + z \leq M$ where $i = 1, ..., J$ indexes the alternatives available (or the choice set) and M is income. In this discrete choice problem it must also be the case that choice is mutually exclusive. That is, a consumer can choose only one of the alternatives on a given "choice occasion." A utility maximization problem that provides for this mutually exclusive choice is presented below (based on Hanemann 1982)

$$\text{Max } U(y_1 \ldots y_J, q_1 \ldots q_J; z)$$

subject to

$$\sum_{i=1}^{J} p_i y_i + z \leq M$$

$$y_i \cdot y_j = 0 \quad \forall i \neq j \tag{8}$$

$$y_i = y_i^* \quad \forall i$$

The second constraint requires that the product of quantities of goods be zero, thereby requiring that only one y_i can be positive. The third constraint sets the quantity of the goods to an optimal level, y_i^*, a single house or a single trip to a recreation site, for example. The last two constraints together generate a mutually exclusive choice (Hanemann, 1982). Maximization of this utility function subject to the constraints yields an indirect utility function that depends on which alternative is chosen. This is referred to as a conditional indirect utility function that describes the utility realized by the individual – conditional on choosing that alternative. The conditional indirect utility function is specified as:

$$V_{in} = V_{in}(M, P_i, q_i) \quad \text{or} \quad V_{in}(M - P_i, q_i) \tag{9}$$

Note that this indirect utility function contains only those elements relevant to alternative i. Therefore, conditional on choosing alternative i the individual experiences the utility associated with attributes of alternative i and no other alternative. This is an assumption that is analogous to the weak complementarity assumption. If an alternative is not chosen, changes in the quality levels at that alternative do not enter the utility of the alternative chosen (Hanemann, 1982).

The conditional indirect utility function presented in (9) is deterministic in the sense that it would be observed by the researcher if there were no uncertainties associated with demand. In fact, there may be several reasons that the utility is random or stochastic. Ben-Akiva and Lerman (1985) suggest that the individual may have random preferences or that the researcher only observes certain elements of the utility function while the individual knows all the components. Therefore, to the researcher choice of a specific option is uncertain because they do not have all the information that the individual making the choices does. Uncertainty can be added by augmenting the conditional indirect utility function with an error component. A general form is:

$$U_{in} = V_{in}^*(M, P_i, q_i, \varepsilon_{in}) \tag{10}$$

or, assuming that the random component is additive to the observed or systematic component:

$$U_{in} = V_{in}(M, P_i, q_i) + \varepsilon_{in} \tag{11}$$

Let C_n describe the choice set or set of alternatives individual n faces. The probability that individual n chooses alternative $i \in C_n$ is given by

$$P_{in} = \Pr\{U_{in} > U_{jn}, \quad \forall j \neq i, \ i, j \in C_n\}$$
$$= \Pr\{V_{in} + \varepsilon_{in} > V_{jn} + \varepsilon_{jn}, \quad \forall j \neq i, \ i, j \in C_n\} \tag{12}$$

The probability of choosing an alternative depends on the information in the systematic component (data) as well as the choice of the error component. The most common choice for an error component distribution is the Gumbel distribution. If one assumes that all of the ε_{in}'s are identically and independently Gumbel distributed, the probability of choosing alternative i is the closed-form expression:

$$P_{in} = \frac{e^{[\mu \cdot V_{in}]}}{\sum_{j \in C_n} e^{[\mu \cdot V_{jn}]}} \tag{13}$$

where μ is a scale factor that is inversely related to the variance of the error component[2] (see Ben-Akiva and Lerman, 1985, chapter 5). Expanding expression (13) to provide more detail on the conditional indirect utility function we obtain:

$$P_{in} = \frac{e^{[\mu \cdot V_{in}(M - P_i, q_i)]}}{\sum_{j \in C_n} e^{[\mu \cdot V_{jn}(M - P_j, q_j)]}} \tag{14}$$

or, assuming a linear functional form for the conditional indirect utility function:

$$P_{in} = \frac{e^{[\mu \cdot (\beta_1(M - P_i) + \beta_2(q_i))]}}{\sum_{j \in C_n} e^{[\mu \cdot (\beta_1(M - P_j) + \beta_2(q_j))]}} \tag{15}$$

More generally, if there are many quality attributes (q_i), we can let x_i be a vector of attributes associated with alternative i, including the price term, and write:

$$P_{in} = \frac{e^{[\mu \cdot (\beta' x_i)]}}{\sum_{j \in C_n} e^{[\mu \cdot (\beta' x_j)]}} \tag{16}$$

This is only one of many possible specifications for the probability (based on the assumption of the Gumbel distribution). Other distributional assumptions can be made. In addition, this version of the probability expression does not contain any information on demographic characteristics. Because demographic characteristics (including income) do not vary across alternatives, if they were entered in the indirect utility function as linear terms they would drop out of the utility difference expression (12). Therefore, accounting for heterogeneity requires advanced analysis (discussed below).

Given an expression for the probability of choosing an alternative, maximum likelihood can be used to estimate parameters of the conditional indirect utility function (Ben-Akiva and Lerman, 1985; Louviere, Hensher, and Swait, 2000). Data on the choices made by individuals and the attributes that the individuals face are the independent variables in the probability expressions. The fact that the parameters estimated are elements of the conditional indirect utility function facilitates welfare measurement.

Welfare measures in the random utility model

The basic structure of welfare measures in the RUM arises from the definition of compensating variation that is based on indirect utility functions or:

$$V(M, P^0, q^0) = V(M - CV, P^1, q^1) \tag{17}$$

where P^0 and q^0 are base prices and quality while P^1 and q^1 are "changed" prices and quality. CV represents the compensating variation or the amount of money it will take to make the person as well off as they were before the change. Note that this expression for CV is deterministic. In order to estimate welfare effects in the RUM we will need to define a welfare measure that incorporates the randomness in the utility. Thus, CV itself will be a random variable (Hanemann, 1999). An expression that captures this notion is:

$$V(M, P^0, q^0, \varepsilon) = V(M - CV, P^1, q^1, \varepsilon) \tag{18}$$

where the stochastic nature of the utility function is now included in the definition of CV. In other words we must examine the unconditional utility rather than the conditional indirect utility function. The expected value of the maximum of the utility functions provides an approach for this. The expected value of the maximum of the utilities can be written in general form as (Morey, 1999):

$$E(U) \int_{\varepsilon_1 = -\infty}^{\infty} \cdots \int_{\varepsilon_j = -\infty}^{\infty} \max(v_1 + \varepsilon_1, \ldots, v_j + \varepsilon_j) f(\varepsilon_1, \ldots, \varepsilon_j) d\varepsilon_1 \cdots d\varepsilon_j \tag{19}$$

where v_i represents the conditional indirect utility function for alternative i and, i $(i = 1, \ldots, J)$ is the random component. This expression provides a measure of the "expected utility" arising from the alternatives and random component. The choice of error distribution and functional form of the utility function will specify the final form for utility; however, if we once again choose a Gumbel distribution and assume that the indirect utility function is linear in income (implying no income effects) then the expression for the expected value of the maximum reduces to

$$E(U) = \ln\left(\sum_{j=1}^{J} e^{(V_j)}\right) + D \tag{20}$$

where D is Euler's constant. This is also known as the "log sum" expression. The estimate of CV becomes (Morey, 1999; Hanemann, 1999)

$$CV = \frac{1}{\lambda_M}\left[\ln\left(\sum_{j \in C_n} e^{(V_j^1)}\right) - \ln\left(\sum_{j \in C_n} e^{(V_j^0)}\right)\right] \tag{21}$$

where λ_M is the marginal utility of income or the parameter on $(M-P_i)$ in the conditional utility indirect function. This is a very convenient representation of CV but it must be recognized that this expression assumes that there are no income effects and that the errors follow the Gumbel distribution. This commonly used expression can describe the welfare associated with changes in attribute levels for some or all of the alternatives, removal or addition of alternatives, or combinations of the two.

If the functional form of the indirect utility function is not linear in income then expression (18) will likely have to be evaluated numerically to find the value for CV that solves to equate expected maximum utilities before and after the change. Morey et al. (1993) present some results using such a numerical simulation approach. Further discussion can be found in McFadden (1998, 1999).

A simple example

As a simple example of a random utility model using revealed preference data consider the case reported by Adamowicz, Louviere, and Williams (1994). In this paper actual water-based recreation trips for a sample of households are examined. The choice set is specified as 22 different water-based recreation sites (lakes, reservoirs, streams, and river sites). The relevant attributes include distance to the site (translated into travel cost), fishing catch rates per unit time, ability to swim at the site, presence of a beach, a water quality rating, whether boat use is unrestricted (or not) and whether power boats are allowed (or not). The econometric estimation provides the following estimates of the parameters of the conditional indirect utility function (for standing water sites; lakes and reservoirs).

$V(i) = -0.028$ (Travel cost) $+ 2.03$ (Fish catch rate) $+ 2.75$ (Swimming)
$+ 0.99$ (Beach) $- 0.82$ (Water quality index) $+ 6.66$ (Unrestricted boating)
$+ 7.25$ (Power boating)

All of the coefficients (parameters of the indirect utility function) are statistically significant except the water quality index parameter. To interpret the model consider that the travel cost parameter is negative (the marginal utility of price is negative, marginal utility of money is positive) while all other attributes (fish catch, etc.) are positive. Increasing fish catch at a single site will increase the probability of visiting that particular site. Removing beaches or swimming will reduce the probability that a site is visited. This model (and others presented in the paper) were used to assess the welfare measures for a water resource improvement program (building infrastructure and controlling water flows). The results differ depending on where the people live relative to the areas where the infrastructure affects the water flows. For the 24 different residence regions defined, the values of the program ranged from $0.46 / trip (1994 Canadian $) to $3.99 per trip. Note that this simple model assumes that all people have the same preferences.

Furthermore, the alternatives in this model are assumed to satisfy the independence of irrelevant alternative assumptions (discussed below).

Econometric issues

In the presentation above we have relied almost entirely on the Gumbel distribution as the representation of the error component. However, there are significant drawbacks to this assumption. First, this form assumes independence of irrelevant alternatives (IIA). That is, the ratio of probabilities of choices between two alternatives is independent of any other alternatives. This implies, among other things, that the cross-elasticities between alternatives are equal (see Louviere, Hensher, and Swait, 2000; Ben-Akiva and Lerman, 1985). This is a rather strict restriction on preferences. In addition, we have not yet explored how demographic factors can be included in the model.

One method of relaxing the IIA assumption is to construct a nested model in which the alternatives are grouped into similar classes and the probability of choosing a class is estimated as well as the probability of choosing an alternative from a specific class conditional on choosing the class. This product of conditional and unconditional probabilities provides for a richer set of cross-elasticities and fewer restrictions on preferences (see chapter 10 for further discussion of IIA and nested logit as an approach for treating IIA and see Louviere, Hensher, and Swait for additional details). Morey (1999) provides an excellent example and explanation of nested logit in the recreation demand context.

An alternative approach to increasing flexibility in the model is to employ a mixed logit specification. Train (1998, 1999) expresses the conditional indirect utility function as

$$V_j = \beta \, x_j + \eta S_j + \varepsilon_j \tag{22}$$

where the first term in the conditional indirect utility function is the standard set of attributes, the second term is an additional stochastic component in the utility function and the final term is the standard IID Gumbel error. If η is assumed to be mean zero then S can take the form of various stochastic components. For example, if $x = S$ then the model is interpreted as a random parameters model with β as the mean and η capturing the variance. If S_j is defined as a dummy variable equaling one for a subset of the alternatives, the variance on η provides a measure of the error correlation between this subset (equivalent to the correlation parameter arising in nested logit models).

The estimation of a mixed-logit model begins by representing the probability of a particular alternative being chosen with the standard logit expression:

$$P_{in} = \frac{e^{(\beta' x_i)}}{\sum_{j \in C_n} e^{(\beta' x_i)}} \tag{23}$$

However, the coefficients (β) are assumed to have a predetermined distribution rather than being fixed. An additional step is required to express the probability as the integral over the form of the distribution chosen, or

$$\pi_{in} = \int P_{in}(\beta)g(\beta)d\beta \tag{24}$$

Given a choice of distribution the original logit expression is "weighted" or "mixed" with the distribution chosen (e.g. normal) (Train, 1998, 1999).

Heterogeneity, or assessment of the degree to which individual specific factors affect preferences, is also discussed briefly in chapter 9. Among the main issues are the choices between modeling heterogeneous preferences using observed factors (demographic variables) as interaction effects with attributes, as explanatory variables in a finite-mixture or latent-class model, or in a random parameters framework. Econometric approaches to heterogeneity are discussed in Train (1998), Train (2002), Louviere, Hensher, and Swait (2000). Applications in environmental economics include Train (1998 – mixed logit) and Boxall and Adamowicz (2002 – latent class).

Defining the choice set

In any random utility model a key component is the set of alternatives defined as being available (and being considered) by the consumer. In the case of recreation sites this is the set of places that the individual considers on each choice occasion. In the context of housing choice the choice set will be varying over time and may be influenced by real estate agents. The researcher must define a choice set for the RUM to be operational. This is often one of the most challenging aspects of RUM modeling. Discussions of the influence of choice set definition on the parameters and welfare measures from RUMs include Parsons and Hauber (1998), Parsons et al. (2000), and Peters, Adamowicz, and Boxall (1995). Some researchers have chosen to define choice set boundaries based on distance (e.g. sites close enough for a one day trip) while others have used more elaborate rules or even used information from the respondent. Swait (1987 and 2001) provides more in-depth analysis of the choice set issue.

10.5   COMBINING TRADITIONAL AND ATTRIBUTE BASED MODELS

One of the difficulties associated with random utility models is that the simple model accounts well for the choice of a particular alternative on a specific occasion, but does not account for the frequency or quantity demanded (recall that the quantity in the simple RUM model is exogenous). Therefore, RUMs capture which fishing site will be chosen, but not the number of trips to that alternative. A change in an attribute, perhaps as a policy change, can induce impacts on the probability of choice as well as the frequency choice.

Two RUM-based approaches have been explored to address such issues. A simple approach, given data availability, is to include non-participation as an alternative. This model can be assumed to operate on a specific time period (per week or per day) and is referred to as a repeated logit model (see Morey et al., 1993; Parsons, 2003). The second approach is a modification of the standard RUM to account for frequency. Consider a frequency-based model (quantity demanded). This model can be adjusted so that the expected utility of the set of alternatives is one of the explanatory variables. The expected utility expression can be derived from the RUM within a time period. In this model the quantity of trips in any given period (e.g. a season) is examined as a function of demographic characteristics as well as the inclusive value (log-sum) from a RUM model over the alternative destinations. There are several variants of this linked frequency-choice model. Parsons, Jakus, and Tomasi (1999) and Parsons (2003) provide additional discussion on this form of model.

While the repeated discrete-choice model examines choices partitioned into specific choice occasions (weeks, days) a model introduced by Phaneuf (1999) and Phaneuf, Kling, and Herriges (2000) approaches the problem from the standpoint of an optimization problem with corner solutions. This approach specifies the utility function over a longer time horizon (a season for example) and maximizes this utility subject to a budget constraint. Corner solutions are possible since some alternatives will have zero quantity demanded over the season. This means that solving the optimization problem will involve Kuhn–Tucker conditions (inequalities that provide necessary conditions for the optimization). Given the careful choice of a structure for the utility function (that includes a random component) the Kuhn–Tucker conditions can be treated as an econometric problem, estimating parameters for the utility function that best fit these conditions. This technique provides a utility-consistent approach to the problem of quantity demanded and choice of alternatives.

10.6 ATTRIBUTE BASED MODELS: HEDONIC PRICE METHODS

The random utility model examines consumer choice from a finite set of alternatives and characterizes their choice in terms of the attribute trade-offs made. The hedonic price method[3] examines prices rather than choices and attempts to assess the contribution of various attributes to prices. The prices are market-clearing prices and thus are observations where buyers and sellers reach some agreement. The objective of hedonic price analysis in environmental valuation is to "untangle" the contribution of environmental attributes from other components of price.

Let the consumer's optimization problem be characterized by:

$$\text{Max } U(z, q_1 \ldots q_J)$$
$$\text{subject to } \sum_{i=1}^{J} p_i q_i + z \leq M \tag{25}$$

where q_i are characteristics (or attributes) z is the numeraire good and M is income. The consumer maximizes utility over attributes, subject to a budget constraint that contains prices for attributes. This maximization will yield a bid function,

$$\Theta(q, U, M) \tag{26}$$

that contains the consumer's willingness to pay for attribute q at defined levels of income and utility. This bid function arises from the marginal rates of substitution derived in the optimization problem. The optimization problem states that the marginal rates of substitution between attributes and the numeraire good must be equal, and this in turn defines that the derivative of the bid function for attribute i must equal the marginal rate of substitution between i and the numeraire.

$$\frac{\partial U/\partial q_i}{\partial U/\partial z} = \frac{\partial \Theta}{q_i} \tag{27}$$

This expression also reveals that the consumer's willingness to pay (or bid) for an additional unit of the attribute i must equal the implicit price of the attribute in the marketplace. While these attributes include typical components of houses, they also include environmental attributes like air quality, surrounding scenery, and other aesthetic characteristics. This defines the consumer's component of the equilibrium, but we must also define the producer's component.

The producer can generate various combinations of attributes. In the case of housing, builders can construct houses with various levels of attributes (sizes of homes, number of rooms, quality of appliances, etc.). They may also be able to affect the levels of environmental amenities (trees, landscaping, etc.). Individuals selling their homes also provide an array of attribute combinations for various asking prices. Considering the suppliers as firms, one can specify an offer function as:

$$\Psi(q, \pi, \tau) \tag{28}$$

where q is the vector of attributes, π is profit, and τ identifies the technology available to firms. This offer function captures what the sellers will accept for various levels of attributes, holding profits constant at given levels of technology. Figure 10.2 illustrates the basic hedonic relationship (figures 10.2 and 10.3 present the relationships for a single attribute, labeled as "q;" this relationship can be described for any of the attributes q_i in the hedonic price function). The price–attribute relationship $(P(q))$ is identified through exchanges between buyers and sellers. This hedonic price function is an envelope of the equilibria between demanders and suppliers. Three bid functions $(\Theta^k, k = a, b, c)$ are illustrated in figure 10.2. Θ^b and Θ^c are tangent to the hedonic price function and tangent to supply (or offer) functions Ψ^j and Ψ^l. Θ^a is not tangent to the price function nor is Ψ^k, indicating

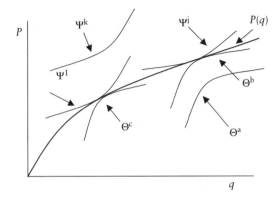

Figure 10.2   Hedonic price function with bid and offer functions

that no observed transaction occurred as a result of an agreement between buyers and sellers. Bid functions Θ^b and Θ^c can be considered to be the bid functions for two different consumers who differ in terms of income or preferences. Θ^a and Θ^b reflect the bid functions for a single consumer but at different levels of utility where the curve lower on the vertical axis reflects a higher utility level (lower price at constant attribute levels). Similarly, supply functions Ψ^k and Ψ^l reflect a single supplier and two different levels of profit while Ψ^j and Ψ^l represent two different firms, perhaps with different technologies. The transactions resulting from supply and demand interactions generate data on prices and attribute levels that can be assessed in a regression framework. Examining these data over all attributes produces the hedonic price function as

$$P = f(q_1, \ldots, q_J) \tag{29}$$

From this expression the marginal value of an attribute can be assessed as $\partial P / \partial q_i$. While this development of the hedonic price function has been in the context of housing choice, a similar approach can be used to derive a hedonic wage relationship in which individuals trade off different attributes associated with employment options. The hedonic wage relationship is one of the main mechanisms through which values associated with risk reduction have been derived (Freeman, 1993).

Welfare measurement

Measures of willingness to pay for a quality improvement in a hedonic model depend on the assumptions implicit in the welfare change situation. If only marginal changes in attributes are being considered then the implicit price (or derivative of the hedonic price function with respect to the attribute) provides

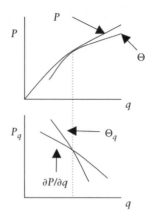

Figure 10.3   Marginal bid values and hedonic price function

a measure of the marginal willingness to pay. Nonmarginal changes can be evaluated by examining the impact of the change on price levels. The difference in price levels can be a measure of welfare change. However, issues such as transactions costs associated with moving (to enjoy the benefits of improved quality) and whether the effect is local or regional also affect the measurement of welfare (see Taylor, 2003). The local or regional issue is important because a larger-scale change may affect the shape and position of the original hedonic price function.

Welfare measures can also be determined by solving for a derived demand for characteristics. The marginal bid function (the derivative of the bid function with respect to a specific attribute) is equivalent to a Hicksian demand function for attributes. The marginal bid function is

$$\frac{\partial \Theta}{\partial q} = \Theta_q(q, U) \tag{30}$$

and can be integrated over the change in attribute levels to provide measures of welfare. The marginal bid function crosses the implicit price line (derivative of the hedonic price function) at the point of tangency between the bid function and the hedonic price function. This is illustrated in figure 10.3.

Consumer surplus can be derived from an expression that is analogous to a Marshallian demand curve for characteristics, or

$$q_i(P_i, \ldots, P_J, M) \tag{31}$$

where P_i, $i = 1, \ldots, J$ are implicit prices of the attributes and M is income. The area under this demand curve evaluated at two different attribute levels provides a measure of welfare associated with a change. These measures could also be evaluated in a fashion consistent with Hicksian measures by integrating the demand functions and obtaining exact welfare measures (Boadway and Bruce, 1984).

Econometric issues

- *Functional form*: As in most cases theory provides relatively little guidance about functional form of the hedonic price function. One would expect that flexible forms and non-linear forms would fit the data better as it is likely that the implicit prices will decrease as the level of the attribute increases. Additional discussion on functional form can be found in Palmquist (1991); Taylor (2003).
- *Multicollinearity*: Many attributes can be included in a hedonic regression. However, it may be difficult to identify the contribution of any particular attribute if it is strongly correlated with other attributes. Treatment of this issue ranges from the standard econometric/statistical tests and treatments for multicollinearity (Greene, 2000), to the use of attribute-based stated preference data to help condition the data matrix. The use of stated preference data improves the situation as the stated preference data can be designed to be orthogonal and thus not suffer from collinearity.
- *Identification*: The estimation of the hedonic price function only identifies a single point on any individual's bid function. Therefore, it is not clear that bid functions are actually being identified accurately. Variation in hedonic price functions, likely across markets, is required to identify more than one point on bid functions (see Taylor, 2003).
- *Exogeneity/instrumental variables*: The implicit prices may be endogenous. That is, consumers can choose to influence the level of implicit price by making different choices of attribute levels. This will only occur if the hedonic price function is non-linear and implicit prices are non-constant. Under these conditions instrumental variable techniques must be used to estimate consistent hedonic price functions (Taylor, 2003).
- *Information, perceptions, objective measures*: The development of the hedonic price method assumes that individuals perceive and have accurate information about the attributes of the good. One would expect individuals to base their behavior on perceived measures of attributes but if these perceptions differ from the objective or "real" levels of attributes then welfare measurement becomes complex. In the case of environmental goods like air quality or water quality, perceptions may be quite different than objective measures and may be more important in driving choice behavior.
- *Spatial econometric issues*: In most cases of housing market hedonic price analyses, there is likely to be spatial autocorrelation, or some other form of spatial relationship between the properties. In other words, neighboring property values will affect the property value of a specific house or the error terms arising from a regression model will have systematic spatial relationships. See Anselin (1988) for a discussion of spatial relationships in econometrics and Taylor (2003) for a discussion of applications to hedonic price methods.

Hedonic wage analysis

The principles developed for hedonic property value models also apply to analysis of wages. Decomposing wage outcomes into bid functions (employees) and supply functions (employer) over the attributes of the employment results in the hedonic wage relationship. Hedonic wage analysis has been instrumental in developing estimates of the monetary value of risk reductions. These estimates have been very important in policy analysis including the analysis of the US Clean Air Act Amendments (US EPA, 1999; see also box 10.1). Hedonic wage analysis, however, suffers from a number of assumptions or challenges (see Freeman, 1993; Taylor, 2003, for details).

- Wage risk studies are often based on a limited range of occupations where mortality risks vary significantly.
- Wage risk studies rely on "accurate" worker perception of risks. If workers do not perceive risks then wage variation will reveal no information on the value of risk reductions.
- As in any hedonic study, issues of identification of the demand for attributes function arise.
- The basic wage risk model assumes that workers have information on the available occupations and they can choose between various offers of wage–risk trade-offs. In reality workers may be uninformed about the options for employment available.
- Characteristics of the location of the employment may be important in the hedonic wage relationship. The attributes of the location of the job may influence employee choice at least as much as the attributes of the job.
- The workers are assumed to be able to move without cost to other opportunities. In reality there are transactions costs associated with changing jobs, just as there are transactions costs associated with changing residences.

10.7   A DIGRESSION ON THE VALUATION OF HEALTH EFFECTS

Hedonic wage analysis is used to assess the value of mortality risk reductions and as such is very commonly used in policy analysis involving mortality health risks (see box 10.1). While the relationship between wages and risk reductions can readily be observed in the context of hedonic wage analysis, other health-risk valuation models also exist. The following is an overview of the theory associated with health-risk valuation.

Values of health effects are most often classified as mortality values and morbidity values. Mortality values are clearly associated with value of reducing the probability of death. Morbidity values are associated with the value of reducing the probability of suffering an illness. Morbidity values may be affected by the type of illness (symptoms), the length of the illness, as well as characteristics of the individual. Mortality values will also probably be affected by the cause of

BOX 10.1   A SURVEY OF VALUES OF RISK REDUCTION FROM LABOR MARKET STUDIES

Mrozek and Taylor (2002) examined 33 studies of the value of risk reduction estimated using labor market/wage risk studies. These studies are summarized by calculating the "value of statistical life" (VSL) or the implicit value that would be derived if mortality risks were increased for by 1 percent per year for 100 individuals. A summary histogram of 31 of these studies is presented below (removing two studies that did not report the range of their results). Mrozek and Taylor analyzed the studies to account for differences in mortality risk estimates that arise from the characteristics of a sample of individuals in each study, the baseline level of risk used in the study, and the statistical methods employed by the researchers. They then derive an estimate of the VSL that would arise from using "best practices." The value they derive is approximately $0.5 m to $1.3 m (1998 US$). This range is substantially lower than the $4.8 m (1990 US$) used in the evaluation of the US Clean Air Act Amendments (US EPA, 1999) and is lower than many VSL estimates used in policy analysis. The measure of the VSL is very important for policy analysis. For example, in the analysis of the US Clean Air Act Amendments the mortality risk reduction benefits accounted for approximately 90 percent of the overall benefits of pollution control. Similarly, in examples presented in the Royal Society of Canada Expert Panel on Ozone and Particulate Matter (Royal Society, 2001) the mortality reduction benefits were about 80 percent of the total monetary value of benefits.

Source: Mrozek and Taylor (2002)

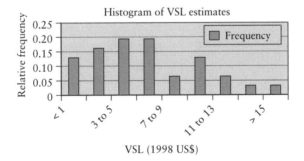

mortality (cancer, auto accident, etc.) and the characteristics of the individual. Note that valuation is most often conducted in an "*ex ante*" fashion. That is, the values are identified as the individual's willingness to pay to reduce the health risks, given that they currently do not have the illness. These values would be quite different if they were examined in an *ex post* framework. The *ex post* value associated with mortality is likely infinite (or all of the resources that the person can collect) while the *ex post* value of reducing morbidity risks depends on the experience of the individual in that health state (see Freeman, 1993).

Conceptual models

An early conceptual framework for the value of health risks, particularly those associated with mortality, was the human capital approach. This valued mortality risk reductions as the expected value of lifetime labor-market earnings that would be gained from an increase in life expectancy. This approach suffers from a number of difficulties. First, it is not a utility consistent welfare measure as it does not assess an individual's willingness to pay for risk reductions. Second, it is problematic in terms of a measure for individuals not in the labor market, particularly the elderly. These individuals are often more likely to be affected by change in environmental quality and thus accurate measures are required for this demographic sub-group. The human capital approach also precludes considerations of altruism; however, in practice most other approaches do as well. In any event there is relatively little use of human capital approaches in the literature today.

A second approach, outlined by Freeman (1993), is one based on individual preferences. Suppose an individual maximizes the expected utility of consumption (C) where consumption is multiplied by the probability of survival (π). The expected utility is $E(U) = \pi\, U(C)$. Let the endowment of consumption be C_0 and the initial survival probability be π_0. Suppose further that the individual can trade consumption to "purchase" increased probabilities of survival. Then the individual optimizes expected utility subject to a budget constraint that allows them to trade consumption for survival probabilities, or $M = (C_0 - C) + p\,(\pi_0 - \pi)$ where p is the relative price of survival probabilities to consumption. Maximizing expected utility subject to this constraint provides the first-order conditions (where λ is the Lagrange multiplier):

$$\pi\frac{\partial U}{\partial C} - \lambda = 0$$
$$U(C) - \lambda p = 0$$
$$M - [C_0 - C + p(\pi_0 - \pi)] = 0 \tag{32}$$

Further decomposition of these first-order conditions produces the relation:

$$p = \frac{U(C)}{\pi(\partial U/\partial C)} \tag{33}$$

This expression describes the "price" of risk reduction as a function of the utility of consumption, marginal utility of consumption and the risk level (Freeman, 1993). The individual will be willing to pay to reduce mortality risk by trading consumption for risk reduction. This relationship exemplifies the type of analysis that occurs in hedonic wage models (trading wage benefits for risk reductions), averting behavior models (where individuals give up consumption by choosing

risk-reducing goods like smoke alarms, bicycle helmets, etc.) and stated preference models in which individuals are asked to trade money for risk reductions.
This model has been extended to include changes over time as well as various
sources of risk reduction. However, the basic notion that individuals are willing to
pay to increase survival probabilities remains.

An alternate formulation that better fits the case of morbidity related values is
based on the same construct that was used to develop a measure of the option
price in chapter 8 (see Freeman, 1993, for more detailed development of these
approaches). Recall that the expected utility associated with being in two different
states of nature can be written as:

$$E(U) = \pi_S V_S(M, S) + \pi_H V_H(M, 0) \tag{34}$$

where S reflects "sickness" and π_S and π_H reflect the probabilities of being in sick
or healthy states. Let π represent sickness and $(1 - \pi)$ represent healthy status.
Differentiating this expression yields

$$\pi \frac{\partial V}{\partial M} dM + \pi \frac{\partial V}{\partial S} dS + (1 - \pi) \frac{\partial V}{\partial M} dM = 0 \tag{35}$$

Rearranging this expression to solve for dM/dS, or the marginal willingness to
pay for changes in "sickness" results in (approximately)

$$\frac{dM}{dS} = \frac{\pi(\partial V/\partial S)}{\partial V/\partial M} \tag{36}$$

An individual's willingness to pay to avoid sickness will depend on the marginal
(dis)utility associated with illness, the probability of illness, and the marginal utility of money. A welfare measure for risk reduction can be written as:

$$\pi_S V_S(M, S) + \pi_H V_H(M, 0) = r_S V_S(M - OPr, S) + r_H V_H(M - OPr, 0) \tag{37}$$

where the probability of illness is reduced from π_S to r_S ($\pi_S > r_S$). OPr provides
a state independent measure of willingness to pay to reduce this risk.
Alternately, the health effects associated with illness could be examined. A welfare
measure associated with the reduction in severity of illness from S to S' can
be written as

$$\pi_S V_S(M, S) + \pi_H V_H(M, 0) = \pi_S V_S(M - OP', S') + \pi_H V_H(M - OP', 0) \tag{38}$$

These models also suggest that methods of valuation that examine expenditures
to reduce risks of illness or to reduce severity of illness (pharmaceuticals, for
example) could be used to measure the willingness to pay for morbidity effects.
Stated preference methods could also be used to assess these values.

A common method of examining morbidity values, however, is not based on observations of behavior or stated preference but is based on the costs associated with treating the illness. While this measure is not consistent with utility theory it is often used because of the availability of data. Cost of illness methods may seem to be relatively straightforward, but these methods are actually quite complex. Apportioning costs for specific illnesses, difficulties involved in valuing work loss time, costs in a system with health care insurance, marginal costs where there are fixed cost aspects and other complexities make cost of illness analysis challenging (see Dickie, 2003, for a detailed discussion of cost of illness methods). Cost of illness methods often understate utility consistent willingness to pay because the latter include "pain and suffering" components of illness value. Nevertheless, cost of illness methods have been used in many policy analyses.

A summary of values of health effects is summarized in box 10.2. This table provides estimates in 1990 dollars employed in some of the common policy models that are used for environmental regulatory analysis. The table reveals a great deal of similarity across the models and the dominance of the value of mortality risk reduction.

The values presented in box 10.2 are commonly used in a technique referred to as *benefits transfer*. This technique uses benefit estimates from primary data studies and transfers them to a new policy setting. The new setting may be geographically distinct from the original study site. Researchers have engaged in simple transfer of unit values (e.g. transferring the value of statistical life estimates from one country to another) or they have attempted to transfer "functions" (e.g. hedonic price functions or random utility models). Clearly the more information that is available in the original study on the environmental/health aspects and the demographic aspects, the better the opportunity to transfer the values. For a summary of benefits transfer see Rosenberger and Loomis (2003).

BOX 10.2   HEALTH RISK VALUATION

Assessments of environmental policy often rely on measures of the value of health improvements associated with improved environmental quality. The analysis of the US Clean Air Act Amendments is a case in point (US EPA, 1999). The human health and non-health benefits from pollution reductions expected by the regulations were examined against the costs. The net effect suggests a substantial benefit arising from the reduction of some pollution emissions in terms of health benefits. The values in table 10.1 are examples of the monetary estimates per unit per year that are used in such policy assessments. Some estimates are based on behavioral analysis (wage-risk studies), some are contingent valuation studies, and some are derived using cost of illness estimates. In many cases the values used are a blend or weighted average of the values appearing in the literature.

Table 10.1 Comparison of unit values used in several major health risk valuation models (US$ 1990)

Values	US EPA[a]			US TAF[b]			Canada AQVM[c]			Europe Extreme E[d]
	Low	Central	High	Low	Central	High	Low	Central	High	Central
Mortality	1,560,000	4,800,000	8,040,000	1,584,000	3,100,000	6,148,000	1,680,000	2,870,000	5,740,000	3,031,000
Chronic bronchitis – cases	—	260,000	—	59,400	260,000	523,100	122,500	186,200	325,500	102,700
Chronic bronchitis – episodes	—	—	—	—	—	—	—	—	—	—
Cardiac hosp. admissions	—	9,500	—	—	9,300	—	2,940	5,880	8,820	7,696
Resp. hosp. admissions	—	6,900	—	—	6,647	—	2,310	4,620	6,860	7,696
ER visits	144	194	269	—	188	—	203	399	602	218
Work loss days	—	83	—	—	—	—	—	—	—	—
Acute bronchitis	13	45	77	—	—	—	—	—	—	—
Restricted activity days	16	38	61	—	54	—	26	51	77	73
Resp. symptoms	5	15	33	—	12	—	5	11	15	7
Shortness of breath	0	5.3	10.6	—	—	—	—	—	—	7
Asthma	12	32	54	—	33	—	12	32	53	36
Child bronchitis	—	—	—	—	45	—	105	217	322	36

[a] The benefits and costs of the Clean Air Act 1990 to 2010 (US EPA, 1999). Low and high estimates are estimated to be 1 standard deviation below and above the mean of the Weibull distribution for mortality. For other health outcomes they are the minimums and maximums of a judgmental uniform distribution.

[b] Tracking and analysis framework (www.lumina.com/taf/index.html), developed by a consortium of US institutions, including Resources for the Future. Low and high estimates are the 5% and 95% tails of the distribution.

[c] Air Quality Valuation Model Documentation (Stratus Consulting Inc., 1999) for Health Canada. Low, central, and high estimates are given respective probabilities of 33%, 34%, and 33%.

[d] ExternE report, 1999. Uncertainty bounds are set by dividing (low) and multiplying (high) the mean by the geometric standard deviation (2).

Source: Royal Society of Canada Expert Panel (2001, p. 174) and Alberini and Krupnick (2002, p. 238)

10.8   MODELS OF CHANGES IN PRODUCTION/ COST/ PROFIT

Environmental values may also be reflected in changes in production systems. Changes in water quality may be reflected in higher production costs for firms who use water in their production processes. Changes in air quality may affect forest growth. Changes in ground-level ozone, for example, are found to affect crop yields and profitability (Royal Society of Canada, 2001). These values are at times referred to as measures of the value of ecosystem services. While there has been considerable interest in valuing ecosystem services, in fact, these values are quite complex and challenging to identify. First, the specific linkage between the impact on the ecosystem and the production system must be identified. This often involves detailed analysis of the biology and ecology of a system and the linkages with the production unit. This investigation is also often site-specific because of the unique conditions associated with a specific geographical region. For example, consider the evaluation of the impact of increased water pollution on soft drink production. The linkages between water quality and production in two different geographical regions may be quite distinct. One region may have a higher buffering capacity and may be able to assimilate more, or one region may experience higher rainfall amounts resulting in very different relationships between pollution emissions and the quality of water entering the soft drink plant. This highlights the need for careful analysis of the biological and ecological relationships. In addition, the economic and behavioral elements must be examined. Some physical impacts (e.g. changes in water quality) will only affect production functions or technical relationships while other impacts will induce behavioral change. In the following discussion we focus on the economic/behavioral impacts, recognizing that the biological impacts are also important in such analysis.

Conceptual approach to valuation

Changes in environmental quality that affect production systems will shift the supply functions. In figure 10.4 two cases of supply shifts are illustrated. The first case illustrates the situation with a downward sloping demand curve. The supply shift reduces consumer surplus (the area under the demand curve above price) but the effect on producer surplus is ambiguous. In the right-hand case the demand is elastic and the shift in the supply function generates a loss to producers. This loss is equivalent to an increase in costs that generates the shift in the supply function. In the right-hand case the valuation of the effects is relatively straightforward – they are simply the losses in producer surplus. On the left-hand case the losses are more complex and involve the evaluation of the producer and consumer surplus changes. It is possible, if the supply and demand curves have certain elasticities, to obtain a situation where the reduction in environmental quality actually increases producer surplus because the supply shift generates a

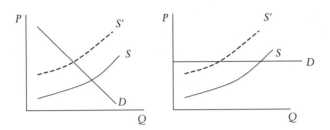

Figure 10.4   Impacts of environmental quality change on production systems

large price increase and a relatively small change in the equilibrium quantity. The structure of market (e.g. monopoly power) will play a large role in affecting these elasticities and the response to quality changes. Therefore, it is very important to assess the behavioral/market response as well as the production/technology response to changes in environmental quality.

Adams and Crocker (1991) provide an overview of the approaches for valuing changes in production systems. They outline three components in the analysis as:

1   Evaluate the change in environmental quality and the resulting impact on production technology.
2   Examine the response of the firm in terms of substitution and adaptation. A firm may not respond to changes in the environment by simply accepting a change in production. They may respond by changing input mixtures or changing production strategies. These adaptive responses may lessen the effect of the environmental quality change on production and profits. For example, ozone may reduce forest yield resulting in a reduction in wood yield. However, forest managers may respond by fertilizing, thinning, or changing the rotation age in response to the change in yield. If reductions in ozone increase production of agricultural crops and prices drop, it is possible that farmers will switch crops in response to the price drop. These types of behavioral responses should be captured if the environmental quality change in question has wide-ranging effects. Note that this implies that the valuation exercise must have a temporal dimension to capture adaptation effects and technological innovation.
3   Assess the response of input and output markets to the changes in production. The responses may include a change in input prices/quantities, output prices/quantities, or both. These responses capture the market effects of a change in production due to a change in environmental quality.

As a formalization of the problem of firm response to environmental quality change, consider the following intertemporal profit maximization problem (based on Adams and Crocker, 1991). The firm maximizes profit over time from selling output (Y_t) at prices p_t while incurring costs of production ($C(X_t, K_t)$) as well as investment costs (I_t). The output is produced by combinations of inputs and capital, or $Y(X_t, K_t)$. The cost function is a function of inputs X_t as well as capital, K_t.

Capital, in this case, includes natural capital such as forests, soil stocks, water, etc. The constraint is an equation of motion of the rate of change of capital. Capital can appreciate by investments (including investments in the natural capital stock) and can depreciate through production (output generation and input use) as well as exogenous pollution effects (A_t). The firm maximizes profits over time by choosing levels of input and investment.

$$\text{Max} \sum_{t=1}^{T} p_t Y(X_t, K_t) - C(X_t, K_t) - I_t$$
$$\text{subject to } K_{t+1} - K_t = I_t - D(Y_t, X_t, A_t) \tag{39}$$

In valuation we may be most interested in the effects of changes in pollution (A_t) on capital, costs, and profits. The impact of pollution (A_t) may affect profit by requiring offsetting investment in the natural capital or by adjusting levels of input. Of course it is possible that the optimal adjustment involves no change in inputs or capital but the firm simply suffers a loss of profit associated with the increased pollution. The optimal response of the firm depends on the production technology and the substitution relationships between inputs, outputs, and pollution. Equation (39) tends to simplify the situation somewhat. There are no market structure effects considered in (39). This could be included by making output price a function of output or input price a function of input use. Furthermore, there are no natural appreciation effects for the capital stock. It is possible that the optimal response to pollution is to allow natural assimilative capacity to offset the effect. Equation (39) does help to outline the complexity involved in the assessment of the impact of environmental quality change on firms and helps identify the information required to measure such impacts.

The methods used to assess the impact of changes in environmental quality on economic production systems range from simply examining the production function for a single firm to examining the input and output market effects associated with multiple firms and consumers. The simplest method involves examining the change in the production function associated with the change in environmental quality, multiplying this change by output price and subtracting the marginal costs. This yields a single firm assessment of the change in profits and corresponds to a simplification of equation (39) that only examines the production function response. However, it assumes that there are no changes in input or output markets. This will only be the case if a single small producer is being examined. An analogous case is one in which the change in environmental quality changes costs (rather than production) but the impact on costs can be easily measured through factor input markets (Freeman, 1993). In this case a perfect substitute in the input mix for the environmental quality factor can be used to value the change. Again, if no market effects occur, the change in costs required to return to the pre-environmental quality change levels can be viewed as the monetary impact of the change.

A more elaborate approach, as outlined in Adams and Crocker (1991), involves the development of a mathematical programming model that describes the optimal response to changes in environmental quality. Such models have been used extensively to examine the effects of air quality changes on agricultural systems. For example, Adams et al. (1986), use a multi-sector mathematical programming model of the agricultural sector to assess the consumer and producer surplus changes arising from changes in ozone. Econometric approaches can also be used, but they depend on sufficient variability in the levels of environmental quality to identify effects.

10.9   CONCLUSIONS

Values associated with environmental goods and services can be observed through market behavior. The market is not always an ideal "data generating mechanism"; therefore, methods to identify values in market behavior can be quite complex. Nevertheless, economists have been very creative in developing conceptual models and empirical tools to capture environmental values as expressed through market behavior. The discussion in this chapter illustrates the inseparable nature of theoretical and empirical issues in environmental valuation. The nature of the exercise requires that both empirical and theoretical issues be considered throughout the analysis. While there are many topics that require further research, the examination of preferences, values, and economic decision-making associated with environmental goods and services has developed rapidly and made impressive strides in its short history. The demand for this type of information will likely increase given the importance of environmental issues in society. Continued research effort will be necessary to enhance the quality of information in this controversial and challenging area.

APPENDIX 10.1   ECONOMETRICS 102 – THE LOGIT MODEL

A popular model for examining discrete choice outcomes is the logit model (also referred to as the conditional logit model). The model is derived from the random utility maximization structure and the assumption of a type I extreme value distribution for the error component. Suppose utility is expressed as

$$U_{in} = V_{in}(X_i) + \varepsilon_{in} \qquad (1)$$

where X captures the deterministic components of the alternative i that individual n faces. The variable X is indexed by i since it is specific to the alternative. The error component, ε_{in}, captures the elements that are not observed by the researcher but are known to the individual. Note that embedded in $V_{in}(X_i)$ are parameters (β) that the researcher wishes to estimate based on the data and assumed model structure. The probability that alternative i

is chosen can be expressed as:

$$
\begin{aligned}
P_{in} &= \Pr\{U_{in} > U_{jn}, \quad \forall j \neq i, \, i, \, j \in C_n\} \\
&= \Pr\{V_{in} + \varepsilon_{in} > V_{jn} + \varepsilon_{jn}, \quad \forall j \neq i, \, i, \, j \in C_n\}
\end{aligned} \tag{2}
$$

where the choice set, or set of all alternatives is identified by C. We can re-express the probability statement above to compare alternative 1 with the maximum of all the other alternatives, $j = 2, \ldots, J$, or,

$$
\begin{aligned}
P_{1n} &= \Pr\{U_{1n} > U^*_{jn}, \quad \forall j \neq 1, \, 1, \, j \in C_n\} \\
&= \Pr\{V_{1n} + \varepsilon_{1n} > \max(V_{jn} + \varepsilon_{jn}), \quad \forall j \neq 1, \, 1, \, j \in C_n\} \\
&= \Pr\{\max(V_{jn} + \varepsilon_{jn}) - (V_{1n} + \varepsilon_{1n}) \leq 0\}
\end{aligned} \tag{3}
$$

where the last expression is a CDF (cumulative distribution function) in terms of the errors ε_j. To derive the probability expression for the logit we will use this formulation comparing the utility of alternative 1 to the maximum over the other alternatives $j = 2, \ldots, J$.

A common assumption is that the error terms follow a Type I extreme value (or Gumbel) distribution. The CDF of a Gumbel variable with location parameter η and scale parameter μ is:

$$
\begin{aligned}
F(\varepsilon) &= e^{-e(-\mu(\varepsilon - \eta))} \\
\text{or } F(\varepsilon) &= 1/e^{e(\mu(\eta - \varepsilon))}
\end{aligned}
$$

Some properties of the Gumbel distribution are (Ben Akiva and Lerman, 1985) as follows.

Property A: If ε is distributed Gumbel $G(\eta, \mu)$, where η is the location parameter (a measure of central tendency like a "mean") and μ is the scale (inversely related to the variance), and V and α are constants, then $\alpha \varepsilon + V$ is distributed $G(\alpha \eta + V, \mu/\alpha)$. This means that the "mean zero" Gumbel distribution can be shifted by adding V to have a location parameter equal to V. This is important as the random utility specification can be thought of as a deterministic component V added to a random component ε.

Property B: ε_1 and ε_2 are independent and distributed Type I extreme value with location parameters η_1 and η_2 respectively, and scale parameter μ, then $\varepsilon_1 - \varepsilon_2$ is logistically distributed (see Ben Akiva and Lerman, 1985 for a discussion of theorems and proofs of the logit model):

$$
F(\varepsilon_1 - \varepsilon_2) = F(\varepsilon^*) = \frac{1}{1 + e^{\mu(\eta_2 - \eta_1 - \varepsilon^*)}} \tag{4}
$$

Property C: If Type I extreme value ε_j's are independent, each with their own location parameter η_j and common scale μ, then the maximum over the set is distributed (location, scale):

$$
\max(\varepsilon_2, \ldots, \varepsilon_J) \to \left(\frac{1}{\mu} \ln \sum_{j=2}^{J} e^{\mu \eta_j}, \mu \right) \tag{5}
$$

Note that the index in the expression above runs from 2 to J. This specific series is used below when we derive the probability for choosing alternative 1 given the set of other alternatives 2, ..., J. All other probabilities are derived in a similar fashion.

Taking the expression from $\max(V_{jn} + \varepsilon_{jn})$ as the location η_2, and V_1 as the location for η_1 and substituting the expressions for the individual location parameters (5) into (4) and simplifying, we obtain:

$$P_{1n} = \frac{e^{\mu V_1}}{\sum_1^J e^{\mu V_{jn}}}$$

(6)

The likelihood function is formed by multiplying the probability of each alternative over the individuals in the sample, or,

$$L = \prod_{n=1}^{N} \left(\frac{e^{\mu V_{1n}}}{\sum_1^J e^{\mu V_{jn}}}\right)^{Y1n} \left(\frac{e^{\mu V_{2n}}}{\sum_1^J e^{\mu V_{jn}}}\right)^{Y2n} \cdots \left(\frac{e^{\mu V_{jn}}}{\sum_1^J e^{\mu V_{jn}}}\right)^{YJn}$$

(7)

where Y_{in} is 1 if alternative i is chosen by individual n and zero otherwise. The log-likelihood function is:

$$\text{Log } L = \sum_{n=1}^{N} \sum_{j=1}^{J} Y_{jn} \ln (P_{jn})$$

(8)

The expression for the probability of choosing an alternative makes simulation of the impact of changing attributes very simple. The following example is provided as a numerical exercise. Suppose three parks are available to an individual. The travel costs to each park and the values of the only attribute that differs between the parks, the number of trees, are reported in the table below. The individual has a conditional indirect utility function of the form:

$$Vi = a_i + b\ (M - P_i) + c(T_i)$$

where a_i, b and c are parameters, M is income, P_i is travel cost, and T_i is the number of trees. The parameter b is the marginal utility of money, parameter c is the marginal utility of trees, and the a_1 parameters are alternative specific constants.

Alternative parks and attribute values

	Park 1	Park 2	Park3
Travel costs	$10	$15	$20
Trees	6	12	18

Assuming a conditional logit random utility structure for this problem (expression (6) with a scale set to 1), with estimates of the parameters as: $a_1 = 1$, $a_2 = 2$, $a_3 = 0$, $b = -0.2$, $c = 0.4$, the probability of the individual choosing parks 1, 2, and 3 is $P(1) = 0.055$, $P(2) = 0.61$, $P(3) = 0.335$. The probability of choosing park 2 is the highest as it has a very high "alternative specific constant" (parameter a_2) as well as mid-range travel costs and numbers of trees. The alternative specific constant captures elements of the utility function that are independent of trees and travel costs. This site has some features that are unobserved to the researcher that result in the utility associated with it being higher than the utility for the other parks if all attributes were identical.

Suppose that the number of trees at park 1 was increased to 20. The new probabilities of choosing each park are $P(1) = 0.941$, $P(2) = 0.038$, $P(3) = 0.021$. Note that the probability of choosing park 1 is now much higher while the probability of choosing the other parks is reduced. The welfare impact of the increased number of trees at park 1 can be calculated using expression (21). This yields a value of $13.85 per individual per choice occasion or a willingness to pay $13.85 to experience the additional trees planted at park 1.

Suppose that instead of adding trees to park 1, park 3 was eliminated as an alternative. The welfare impact of this change can be calculated by using expression (21) with the "new" utility level removing alternative 3 from the summation. The result is a welfare loss of $2. Note that the welfare gain by adding trees is substantial relative to the welfare loss from removing park 3. That is because park 3 is a low probability choice and thus the loss of this site has little welfare impact.

Finally, note that in this model it is assumed that the people always visit one of the three parks. Not visiting a park is not included as an alternative in the model. Therefore, welfare measures from this type of model should either be interpreted as impacts on those who visit parks, or they should be interpreted as welfare measures that are biased upwards because the "substitute" of not visiting any parks is excluded from the set of alternatives.

NOTES

1   Reviews of the travel cost model include Fletcher, Adamowicz, and Graham-Tomasi (1990), Parsons (2003) and Phaneuf and Smith (2002).
2   The scale factor cannot be identified separately from the parameters in the utility function; thus the model always provides estimates of relative parameters (parameters of V relative to the scale). However, one can examine the relative scale between two subsets of data (the ratio of two scale terms) using the techniques outlined in Louviere, Hensher, and Swait (2000).
3   Palmquist (1991) and Taylor (2003) provide overviews of hedonic price methods and are the basis for this presentation.

FURTHER READING

There are several excellent reviews of travel cost modeling. Parsons (2003) and Phaneuf and Smith (2002) provide superb overviews of the issues and challenges involved in travel cost models of recreation demand. Reviews of hedonic price methods can be found in Taylor (2003), Freeman (1993), and Palmquist (1991). Random utility models are described in detail in Louviere, Hensher, and Swait (2000), Morey (1999), Hanemann (1999). Econometric consideration in random utility models can be found in Ben-Akiva and Lerman (1985), Louviere, Hensher, and Swait (2000), Haab and McConnell (2002), and Train (2002). Dickie (2003) provides a detailed overview of cost of illness and averting behavior models. Champ et al. (2003) contains overviews of various valuation methods and is designed for individuals undertaking their first valuation study. Adams and Crocker (1989) outline materials damage models and examine methods that assess the impact of changes in environmental quality firms and industry.

REFERENCES

Adamowicz, W. L., Fletcher, J. J., and Graham-Tomasi, T. (1989). Functional Form and the Statistical Properties of Welfare Measures, *American Journal of Agricultural Economics*, 71: 414–21.

Adamowicz, W. L., Louviere, J., and Williams, M. (1994). Combining Stated and Revealed Preference Methods for Valuing Environmental Amenities, *Journal of Environmental Economics and Management*, 26: 271–92.

Adams, R. M. and Crocker, T. D. (1991). Materials Damages, in J. B. Braden and C. D. Kolstad, eds, *Measuring the Demand for Environmental Quality*, North-Holland: Amsterdam.

Adams, R. M., Hamilton, S. A., and McCarl, B. A. (1986). The Benefits of Pollution Control: The Case of Ozone and US Agriculture, *American Journal of Agricultural Economics*, 68: 886–93.

Alberini, A. and Krupnick, A. (2002). Valuing the Health Effects of Pollution, in T. Tietenberg and H. Folmer, eds, *The International Yearbook of Environmental and Resource Economics*, 2002/2003, Edward Elgar, Cheltenham.

Anselin, L. (1988). *Spatial Econometrics: Methods and Models*, Kluwer: Dordrecht.

Ben-Akiva, M. and Lerman, S. (1985). *Discrete Choice Analysis: Theory and Application to Travel Demand*, MIT Press: Cambridge, MA.

Boadway, R. W. and Bruce, N. (1984). *Welfare Economics*, Basil Blackwell: London.

Bockstael, N. E., Strand, I. E., and Hanemann, W. M. (1987). Time and the Recreational Demand Model, *American Journal of Agricultural Economics*, 69: 293–302.

Boxall, P. C. and Adamowicz, W. (2002). Understanding Heterogeneous Preferences in Random Utility Models: The Use of Latent Class Analysis, *Environmental and Resource Economics*, 23: 421–46.

Cameron, A. C. and Trivedi, P. K. (1998). *Regression Analysis of Count Data*, Cambridge University Press: New York.

Champ, P., Brown, T., and Boyle, K. (2003). *A Primer on the Economic Valuation of the Environment*. Kluwer: Dordrecht.

Dickie, M. (2003). Defensive Behavior and Damage Cost Methods, in P. Champ, T. Brown, and K. Boyle, eds, *A Primer on the Economic Valuation of the Environment*, Kluwer: Dordrecht.

Englin, J., Boxall, P. C., and Watson, D. O. (1998). Modeling Recreation Demand in a Poisson System of Equations: An Analysis of the Impact of International Exchange Rates, *American Journal of Agricultural Economics*, 80 (2): 255–63.

Feather, P. and Shaw, W. D. (1999). Estimating the Cost of Leisure Time for Recreation Demand Models, *Journal of Environmental Economics and Management*, 38: 49–65.

Fletcher, J. J., Adamowicz, W. L., and Graham-Tomasi, T. (1990). An Overview of Travel Cost Models: Problems and Potential Improvements, *Leisure Science*, 12 (Jan.–March): 119–47.

Freeman, A. M. (1993). *The Measurement of Environmental and Resource Values*, Resources for the Future Press: Baltimore.

Greene, W. (2000). *Econometric Analysis*, fourth edn, Prentice Hall: New York.

Haab, T. C. and McConnell, K. E. (2002). *Valuing Environmental and Natural Resources: The Econometrics of Non-Market Valuation*, Edward Elgar: Cheltenham.

Hanemann, W. M. (1999). Welfare Analysis with Discrete Choice Models, in J. Herriges and C. Kling, eds, *Valuing Recreation and the Environment*, Edward Elgar: Cheltenham.

Hanemann, W. M. (1982). Applied Welfare Analysis with Qualitative Response Models. Working Paper No. 241, Giannini Foundation of Agricultural Economics, University of California: Berkeley.

Hotelling, H. (1947). Letter to the Director of the National Parks Service, US Department of the Interior. Appearing in Prewitt (1949) *The Economics of Public Recreation: The Prewitt Report*, Department of the Interior: Washington DC.

Lancaster, K. J. (1966). A New Approach to Consumer Theory, *Journal of Political Economy*, 74: 132–57.

Louviere, J. J., Hensher, D., and Swait, J. (2000). *Stated Choice Methods: Analysis and Applications in Marketing, Transportation and Environmental Valuation*, Cambridge University Press: Cambridge.

McFadden, D. (1998). Measuring Willingness-to-pay for Transportation Improvements, in T. Gärling, T. Laitila, and K. Westin, eds, *Theoretical Foundations of Travel Choice Modeling*, Elsevier Science: Amsterdam, pp. 339–64.

McFadden, D. (1999). Computing Willingness-to-pay in Random Utility Models, in J. Moore, R. Riezman, and J. Melvin, eds, *Trade Theory, Theory and Econometrics: Essays in Honour of John S. Chipman*, Routledge: London.

Morey, E., Rowe, R., and Watson, M. (1993). A Repeated Nested-logit Model of Atlantic Salmon Fishing, *American Journal of Agricultural Economics*, 75: 578–92.

Morey, E. R. (1999). Two RUMs Uncloaked: Nested Logit Models of Site Choice and Nested Logit Models of Participation and Site Choice, in J. A. Herriges and C. L. Kling, eds, *Valuing Recreation and the Environment: Revealed Preference Methods in Theory and Practice*, Northampton MA: Edward Elgar.

Mrozek, J. R. and Taylor, L. O. (2002). What Determines the Value of Life: A Meta Analysis, *Journal of Policy Analysis and Management*, 21 (spring): 253–70.

Palmquist, R. B. (1991). Hedonic Methods, in J. B. Braden and C. D. Kolstad, eds, *Measuring the Demand for Environmental Quality*, North Holland: Amsterdam, pp. 77–120.

Parsons, G. (2003). The Travel Cost Model, in P. Champ, T. Brown, and K. Boyle, eds, *A Primer on the Economic Valuation of the Environment*, Kluwer: Dordrecht.

Parsons, G. R. and Hauber, A. B. (1998). Spatial Boundaries and Choice Set Definition in a Random Utility Model of Recreation Demand, *Land Economics*, 74 (1): 32–48.

Parsons, G. R., Plantinga, A. J., and Boyle, K. J. (2000). Narrow Choice Sets in a Random Utility Model of Recreation Demand, *Land Economics*, 76 (1): 86–99.

Parsons, G. R., Jakus, P. M., and Tomasi, T. (1999). A Comparison of Welfare Estimates from Four Models for Linking Seasonal Recreational Trips to Multinomial Logit Models of Site Choice, *Journal of Environmental Economics and Management*, 38: 143–57.

Peters, T., Adamowicz, W. L., and Boxall, P. C. (1995). Influence of Choice Set Considerations in Modeling the Benefits from Improved Water Quality, *Water Resources Research*, 31 (7): 1781–7.

Phaneuf, D. and Smith, V. K. (2002). Recreation Demand Models. Manuscript, North Carolina State University.

Phaneuf, D. J., Kling, C. L., and Herriges, J. (2000). Estimation and Welfare Calculation in a Generalized Corner Solution Model With an Application to Recreation Demand, *Review of Economics and Statistics*, 82: 83–92.

Phaneuf, D. J. (1999). A Dual Approach to Modeling Corner Solutions in Recreation Demand, *Journal of Environmental Economics and Management*, 37: 85–105.

Phlips, L. (1983). *Applied Consumption Analysis*, North-Holland: Amsterdam.

Rosenberger, R. S. and Loomis, J. B. (2003). Benefit Transfer, in P. Champ, K. Boyle, and T. Brown, eds, *A Primer on Non-Market Valuation*, Kluwer: Dordrecht.

Royal Society of Canada (2001). *Report of the Expert Panel to Review the Socioeconomic Models and Related Components Supporting the Development of Canada-wide Standards for Particulate Matter and Ozone*, The Royal Society of Canada. Ottawa, Ontario. 240 pp.: www.rsc.ca

Smith, V. K., Desvousges, W. H., and McGivney, M. P. (1983). The Opportunity Cost of Travel Time in Recreation Demand Models, *Land Economics*, 59 (3): 259–77.

Swait, J. (2001). Choice Set Generation within the Generalized Extreme Value Family of Discrete Choice Models. *Transportation Research B*, 35 (7): 643–67.

Swait, J. and Ben-Akiva, M. (1987). Incorporating Random Constraints in Discrete Models of Choice Set Generation. *Transportation Research B*, 21B, (2).

Taylor, L. O. (2003). The Hedonic Method, in P. Champ, T. Brown, and K. Boyle, eds, *A Primer on the Economic Valuation of the Environment*, Kluwer: Dordrecht.

Train, K. (1998). Recreation Demand Models with Taste Differences over People, *Land Economics*, 74 (2): 230–9.

Train, K. (1999). Mixed Logit Models for Recreation Demand, in J. A. Herriges and C. L. Kling, eds, *Valuing Recreation and the Environment: Revealed Preference Methods in Theory and Practice*, Edward Elgar: Northampton, MA, pp. 33–64.

Train, K. (2002). *Discrete Choice Methods with Simulation*, Cambridge University Press: Cambridge.

US EPA (1999). The Benefits and Costs of the Clean Air Act 1990 to 2010. Prepared for US Congress. November.

PART FOUR

GLOBAL ENVIRONMENT

CHAPTER ELEVEN

GROWTH AND THE ENVIRONMENT

Ecology and economy are becoming ever more interwoven – locally, regionally, nationally, and globally – into a seamless net of causes and effects. (The World Commission on Environment and Development, *Our Common Future*, p. 5)

11.1 INTRODUCTION

For the past hundred thousand years or so our modern ancestors (*Homo sapiens sapiens*) have used natural resources to improve their quality of life. In the earliest times, consumption consisted of the killing of game animals, the harvesting of plants and fruits, and the foraging of wood for fire and stones for the manufacture of tools. Probably in response to a rising population, climate change, and the scarcity of wild game, our ancestors were able to use their knowledge of plants and animals to gradually domesticate food sources. Over time, they became increasingly reliant on agriculture and/or pastoral practices. The domestication of plants and animals, the labor inputs they required, and the surpluses they generated led to the development of the first permanent settlements some ten thousand years ago and eventually to towns and cities. Increased population density and a food surplus that could be securely stored provided for greater specialization of labor and developments beyond food production. For example, the earliest writing that originated more than five thousand years ago had its antecedents in symbols and signs that were developed for use in trade and commerce. Over time, and at a much more rapid rate in the past three centuries, the human population has increased along with our technological sophistication. This growth, coupled with rising incomes, has placed an increasing burden on our natural resources and the environment's ability to assimilate the wastes of our production and consumption.

In this chapter we examine the interrelationships between economic growth, population growth, and environmental performance. We compare and contrast improving and worsening environmental trends, address the issues of sustainability, evaluate economic models of economic growth and the environment, and explore the issues of population and resource abundance. We close with a review of the ways forward to ensure that critical aspects of our environment are maintained in the face of increases in both income and population.

11.2   THE ENVIRONMENT: DOOM OR BOON?

Most reviews on the state of the environment indicate that many ecosystems are highly stressed. For example, the inhabitants of cities in poor countries often suffer from levels of air and water pollution injurious to their health. Indeed, consuming untreated and contaminated water is one of the leading causes of infant mortality in low-income nations. Even in rural areas where industry is limited, farming practices and increased population are contributing to soil erosion and salinization that reduce yields. Important aspects of natural capital including fisheries and forests are also being depleted, especially in poor countries. Transportation of pollutants is occurring over great distances and is responsible for the build-up of polychlorinated biphenyls (PCBs) in large mammals (including humans) in the Arctic. Other persistent organic pollutants (POPs) that disrupt our hormonal or endocrine system are of increasing health concern with their links, even at very small levels of contamination, to physical abnormalities and cancers (Colborn et al., 1997).

Globally, emissions of chlorofluorocarbons (CFCs) have led to a 50 percent depletion over Antarctica of stratospheric ozone that protects us from ultraviolet radiation (Somerville, 1996). Anthropogenic emissions of greenhouse gases (GHGs) are likely to result in climate change and warming of the global average surface temperature from between 1.4 to 5.8 degrees Celsius, with an even greater warming at high latitudes (IPPC, 2001). Destruction of habitat in biodiversity "hotspots," especially tropical rain forests, is also an issue of growing concern in terms of its potential effects on genetic diversity (see chapter 15). These environmental challenges are occurring from a backdrop of past environmental disasters that have occurred from time to time when ecosystems have been stressed to a point that human populations and civilizations have "crashed" (Ponting, 1991).

Despite the abundant evidence of environmental stresses, there also exist a number of encouraging trends. For example, in response to the destruction of stratospheric ozone by CFCs all rich countries agreed to stop their production in the London and Copenhagen Amendments to the 1987 Montreal Protocol. These agreements have drastically reduced global emissions. More recently, there has been agreement to restrict trade and production of POPs in the May 2001 United Nations Treaty on Chemicals. In terms of concentrations in urban areas of particulate matter, carbon monoxide and sulfur dioxide, a significant downward trend exists in many rich countries. For instance, in the US between 1976 and 1997 urban ambient concentrations of carbon monoxide fell by 61 percent, nitrogen oxides fell by 27 percent, and sulfur dioxides by 58 percent (Moore and Simon, 2000, p. 184).

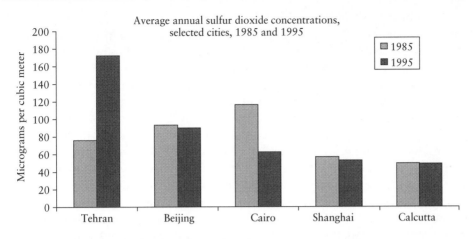

Figure 11.1 Trends in sulfur dioxide in selected cities in poor countries

Source: Worldwatch Database Disk (2000)

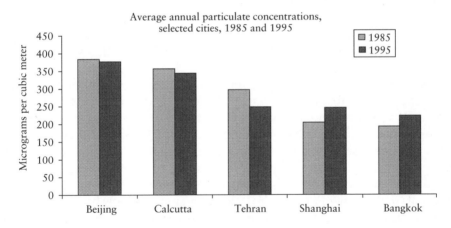

Figure 11.2 Trends in particulate matter in selected cities in poor countries

Source: Worldwatch Database Disk (2000)

In some cases the improvements have been spectacular. For instance, the smog of December 1952 in the city of London may have led to over 4,000 premature deaths (Ponting, 1991, p. 359). Thanks to controls on the use of coal and other measures, some fifty years later Londoners breathe a very much cleaner air. Significant changes have also occurred in other cities such as Los Angeles, where the number of poor air quality days fell by a half from 1978 to 1992, and Pittsburgh where improvements have been even more dramatic. Unfortunately such rapid declines are not uniformly repeated in many poorer countries over the period 1985–95, as indicated by figures 11.1 and 11.2. Moreover, declines in poor countries are beginning from much higher levels than the current concentrations in rich countries. For instance, average urban particulate concentration in the USA in 1995 was less than 40 micrograms per cubic meter, or smaller by a factor of four or more than the levels in the most polluted cities in poor countries.

Measures of organic pollution (dissolved oxygen and fecal coliform) and some contaminants (heavy metals) have also declined (for some rivers and pollutants the decline has been dramatic) since the 1970s in major rivers of wealthy countries. For instance, in the US the proportion of streams usable for fishing and swimming more than doubled between 1972 and 1994. Moreover, in some countries, such as Canada and the United States, an increasing proportion of land has been set aside for national parks and conservation purposes. These beneficial trends have led some to suppose that rising incomes will, eventually, lead to similar improvements when poorer countries reach a sufficiently high level of income. Whatever the explanation, the trends do represent feedback effects between the state of the environment and how we care for the environment. Thus increased production generates pollution feedbacks to reduce environmental quality, but also a poor state of the environment may provide feedbacks and incentives for people to improve environmental quality.

11.3   HUMAN ACTIVITIES AND THE ENVIRONMENT

The environment is often used to represent all the chemical, biological, and geological systems that exist on a local, national, and global scale. They can be degraded by many different factors, but human activities are responsible for many environmental changes, either directly or indirectly. Human impact varies from place to place and over time. For example, considerable evidence exists that prehistoric hunters were responsible for hunting to extinction north American megafauna, such as woolly mammoths, giant sloths, and up to 30 other large mammals in the upper Palaeolithic (Williams and Nowak, 1993). Such extinctions have occurred repeatedly whenever hunters have discovered animals that provide a large food source and are relatively easy to catch or kill. Transformation of the environment through hunting, burning practices to promote particular plant and animal species, farming practices, land conversion (forest or grassland to agriculture), depletion of natural resources (such as fish stocks and water resources) have all contributed to environmental disasters over the millennia. For example, a contributing factor to the decline of successive city-states in Mesopotamia from 4,000–3,000 years before present (BP) was increasing salinization of soils due to irrigation practices. More recently, technological developments and industrialization have increased our ability to influence natural systems and some environments are contaminated in ways that would have been impossible in the past. In the US alone, 34,000 potentially hazardous landfill sites have been identified. Moreover, global industrial processes are at such a level that we are capable of transforming our environment on a planetary scale.

In response to anthropogenic, or other induced environmental change, people have modified their individual behavior, institutions, and technology to adapt. These interrelationships have had a profound effect on human culture and belief systems, and the success or failure of human populations. For instance, it has been argued that the progressive adoption of agriculture arose from the need to feed a population that could not be supported by hunting and gathering alone, possibly in response to climate change. In turn, agriculture promoted technological developments (such as metallurgy) and practices (such as living in villages or towns) that contributed to other changes, such as deforestation. Much later, and in part due to a scarcity of timber, alternative energy forms, such as coal, were developed that spurred on further innovation such as the development of the steam engine that was crucial in the development of the first industrial revolution.

The principal factors that determine the influence of human activities on the environment are the size of the human population, technology, culture and institutions, and the distribution and level of income. These factors help determine (and are determined by) the major environmental challenges – global change (such as climate change and stratospheric ozone depletion), ecosystem integrity (such as species loss), degradation of natural resources (such as deforestation) and increased incidence of death and diseases due to a poor environment (Day and Grafton, 2001).

Another way of describing the effects of human activity on the environment is through stock and flow relationships (see chapter 1). In this representation, the environment provides four major benefits: ecological services and natural resources into the production process and an assimilative capacity to break down wastes and regenerate renewable resources. Human activity can be aggregated into production that uses natural resources in the production process to produce a flow of outputs and services that are delivered to consumers. Feedbacks exist in each of these processes, including recycling of consumer wastes into the production process, and also in how they relate to the state of the environment. Each stage of the flow from natural resources to final consumption generates wastes or emissions that are absorbed by the environment. Figure 11.3 shows a simplified representation of these relationships. Feedbacks are represented by thin arrows and flows of material (including wastes and dissipated heat) are represented by large arrows.

Figure 11.3 illustrates the materials balance in the economy–environment relationship in that the sum of material taken from the environment must equal the mass of residuals returned to the environment plus the mass converted into energy and the net investment in capital goods and durable goods. Waste occurs in terms of both materials and dissipated heat. Degradation of the environment does not occur provided that the environment's assimilative capacity is not exceeded and the extraction of renewable resources does not exceed their rates of regeneration. The system "adds up" and sustains life because low entropy material (such as hydrocarbons) is converted into energy (such as to heat our homes) and materials (such as plastics) with higher entropy. Solar radiation provides the energy for the biogeochemical cycles that renew and regenerate the low entropy materials in our environment that sustain life.

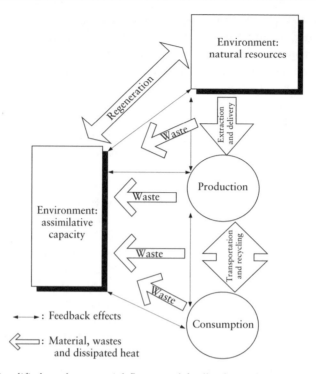

Figure 11.3   Simplified stocks, material flows, and feedbacks in economy–environment

A useful reduced form of the human–environment relationship is provided by the Holdren–Ehrlich (1974) decomposition:

$$ED = P \cdot Y \cdot I$$

where ED is gross or aggregate environmental degradation, P is total human population, Y is real output or income per capita and I is an aggregate environmental impact coefficient per unit of aggregate economic activity. In this simple representation, human-induced changes to the environment arise from changes in the population level, per capita income and the environmental impact coefficient. The magnitude of the negative effects on the environment that stem from gross economic activity $(P \cdot Y)$ are determined by the aggregate environmental impact coefficient. This coefficient, in turn, is a proxy for the effects of changes in *technical efficiency* (ratio of outputs to inputs), the *composition of inputs* (such as the amount of electricity generated by coal or other means), the *composition of outputs* (such as the proportion of total output produced by service industries and amount spent on pollution abatement) and the *emissions and waste* generated from both production (such as sulfur dioxide emissions) and consumption (such as solid waste).

A rise in either income or population does *not* inevitably result in a worse state of the environment, but to prevent environmental degradation offsetting reductions in their per unit impact on the environment are required. However, the greater the increase in population and output the larger must be the offsetting declines in their impacts on the environment to prevent environmental degradation. Drawing upon the materials balance argument Common (1995) argued that for ever increasing levels of $(P \cdot Y)$ there must be a point beyond which the environmental impact coefficient cannot fall (however small it may be) and thus environmental degradation must eventually increase. In fact, the material balance condition does not necessarily require that environmental degradation rise even with continued increases in $(P \cdot Y)$ *provided* that we have the energy inputs (such as from solar energy or possibly nuclear fusion) to either remove (such as into space) or render harmless the wastes and residuals of our outputs. Given that we have not yet reached (and may never reach!) a nirvana of cheaply harnessing the almost limitless energy from our sun we remain bound to a material throughput (wastes and residuals) that can threaten our environment.

11.4   SUSTAINING THE ENVIRONMENT

As a first step in exploring the economic growth–environment relationship, we can plot a measure of environmental quality with per capita income for 115 countries, as given in figure 11.4. On the vertical axis is an aggregate environmental quality measure that has been given the somewhat misleading name, the environmental sustainability index (ESI). The ESI is derived from 22 core environmental indicators compiled by the Yale Center for Environmental Law and Policy and the Center for International Earth Science Information Network at Columbia University. As with any single measure for environmental quality, the index has its limitations.

The value of the ESI ranges from a low of 24.7 for Haiti to a high 80.5 for Finland where a higher number indicates a better overall level of environmental performance. Plotting the ESI against per capita income measured by real GDP per capita in purchasing power parity dollars (US$ 1995) indicates a positive relationship although there exists a large variation in environmental performance for countries at similar levels of per capita income. The relationship indicates that *some* aspects of the environment need not permanently decline with increases in per capita income. It also suggests the *possibility* that increases in per capita income in today's poor countries need not result in permanent declines in overall environmental quality.

A simple cross-sectional comparison and a positive correlation between the ESI and per capita income, however, does not necessarily imply a causal relationship between the variables, and neither does it explain the dynamics of the interrelationships. For instance, increases in per capita income of all poor countries, where most of the world's population resides (from an average of some $2,000/year) to the levels currently enjoyed by people in the richest countries (over $20,000/year) may stress ecosystems beyond their capacity and lead to undesirable thresholds. In other words, the assimilative and regenerative capacity of the environment may be insufficient to sustain the world's population at income levels enjoyed by affluent nations.

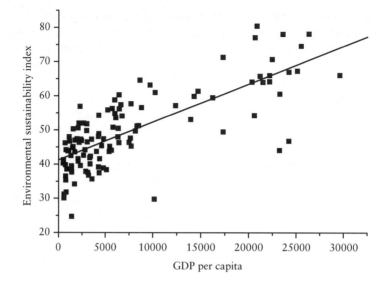

Figure 11.4   National environmental quality and GDP per capita

The question of whether our planet can sustain humanity is, perhaps, the fundamental question of environmental economics. Given the uncertainty that surrounds what the future might bring and whether we can improve both our living standards and our environment, much of the literature on the conditions for sustainability is theoretical. Two widely used concepts are that of *weak sustainability* and *strong sustainability*. Weak sustainability is commonly interpreted as maintaining the total stock of capital (reproducible and natural) at such a level that the welfare of today's and all future generations is non-declining. An implication of weak sustainability is that the possibility exists for the current generation to draw down the natural capital stock *provided* there is a corresponding net investment in reproducible capital to ensure non-declining average welfare across generations. Thus, weak sustainability implies there is some degree of substitutability between human-produced capital and natural capital in production. Given that reproducible and natural capital produce different "goods and services," weak sustainability may also be viewed as implying a degree of substitution between the flow of benefits from natural capital and mass consumption.

Strong sustainability is commonly interpreted as maintaining the natural capital stock (or some critical subset thereof) undiminished in terms of its resilience (see chapter 1) and ability to assimilate wastes and regenerate renewable resources. Even under this strict interpretation, it may still be possible to deplete aspects of natural capital, such as draw-down reserves of oil and natural gas, provided that this does not impinge on the ability of natural capital to provide its critical environmental services.

To date, most of human development has involved using natural capital both for consumption purposes and also to create reproducible capital. The fact that most people today enjoy a far higher standard of living compared with our ancestors of ten thousand years ago indicates that (so far!), as a species, we have been able to both draw down the natural capital stock and increase our standard of living. Such a desirable trend, however, is by no means assured for the future. Evidence exists that several civilizations, such as the Maya, may have succumbed to steep declines in welfare after drawing down their natural capital or stressing it to such a point that it was unable to sustain the human population at a level that it had been accustomed. The proponents of strong sustainability believe that maintaining the natural capital stock at a sufficiently high level is necessary to avoid a similar fate. Their ideas provide a salutary warning to those who are fixated on increasing economic growth as a means to increasing prosperity and welfare. For instance, elements of our environment, such as an "optimum" climate and an atmosphere that protects us from harmful ultraviolet radiation, are critical to our long-term welfare. Thus economic growth that compromises critically important natural capital stocks (CINCS) places at risk future generations, and other species, with whom we share this planet.

The problem we face in implementing any policy to ensure non-declining per capita welfare over time is in determining the desirable level of production and net investment in reproducible and natural capital. It should be clear that markets in which only the current generation can participate, where information is imperfect and stochastic and unpredictable shocks may arise will not, in general, lead to a desirable development path if we consider future generations as much as we do our own. To help address what is essentially *the* policy issue, a number of *ad hoc* rules have been proposed. One of the earliest rules developed for species preservation is the notion of a *safe minimum standard* (SMS) proposed by Ciraicy-Wantrup (1952). As originally proposed the SMS could, depending on the circumstances, involve complete conservation or simply a change in how aspects of the environment were managed. The idea is that by acting today with appropriate management tools society can guard against the potential of very high costs in the future.

A related concept is a *minmax* strategy whereby the decision rule is to *minimize* the maximum possible damage associated with a decision. In other words, maximize the outcome or gain (or minimize the loss) in the worst possible state of the world. For example, the table below presents the payoffs associated with two possible plans (A and B) in two possible states of the world (I and II).

Plan A	Plan B
10,000 (State I)	0 (State I)
−100 (State II)	−90 (State II)

If we apply the minmax rule then we choose plan B because it gives the highest payout in the worse state of the world (state II). Thus, despite the fact that plan A provides a much higher expected payoff, even when state II is highly likely, plan B is still preferred on the basis of the minmax rule. This approach does offer a potentially risk-averse decision rule on development, but poses some problems in terms of its implementation. For example, it may not always be clear what is the basis of comparison for states of the world. Further, development decisions often involve multiple and tiered decisions that can conflict when using a simple decision rule. Moreover, in many development decisions not all the states of the world are known and neither are the values associated with known states of the world. The minmax rule also says nothing about *who* bears the costs associated with decisions. For instance, a cost imposed on a very poor person imposes much greater disutility than if it were imposed on a billionaire.

An alternative rule to help ensure sustainability is the precautionary principle (PP). It explicitly recognizes that many decisions, such as what to do about possible climate change, involve uncertainty about costs and benefits. The PP states that uncertainty, or a lack of a scientific consensus about future outcomes, are *not* sufficient reasons to allow a development or action that may harm the environment. In practice, the PP has been reinterpreted to mean that the burden of proof for an action, or continuing business as usual, is on the agents undertaking the potential harm to show that their actions will not degrade the environment by an unacceptable degree. In other words, if persons cannot show that their actions will *not* threaten the environment, even if this threat is uncertain, then their actions should not be permitted. The problem with this interpretation is that *any* development imposes some degree of risk on ecosystems, but the PP rule provides little guidance to the question, is the risk worth it?

A much better approach to using *ad hoc* rules to ensure sustainability is to adopt the approach of active adaptive management (Walters and Hilborn, 1976). Current (and future) generations must set their priorities, but developments should be undertaken only after considering the possible environmental consequences and feedbacks using different and competing models of how the world changes over time. If a decision in favor of development is made then the effects should be measured, compared and evaluated with the models at hand, and wherever possible, experimentation and testing should occur to learn, verify, and check whether the development decision was appropriate. To this end, environmental accounting (see chapter 12) and other ways of quantifying environmental performance are very useful in improving environmental management. Although active adaptive management is highly useful in improving decision-making it may still lead to less than optimal management, especially in situations where the environment gives very little information or time to improve our decisions and where our decisions lead to irreversible consequences, such as species extinction.

Irreversibilities and uncertainties suggest that, wherever possible, mixed strategies should be encouraged so that some degree of management control and options exist whatever the state of the world (Grafton and Silva-Echenique, 1997). For example, uncertainties about the costs and benefits of climate change have led to bitter disputes about the appropriate level of mitigation of emissions today and in the future. In a mixed strategy approach, whatever the chosen level of mitigation, resources should be invested in adapting to climate change so, whatever the state of the world, we still have options to help address uncertain problems in the future.

11.5 MODELING ECONOMIC GROWTH AND THE ENVIRONMENT

Economic growth is commonly defined as an increase in real per capita GDP over time. Clearly this does not necessarily coincide with increases in overall welfare as GDP includes "bads," such as expenditures on crime prevention or cigarettes, does not include non-market services, such as unpaid labor, and fails to consider depreciation in human-produced or natural capital stock, or value changes in intangibles, such as social capital, but which can have a large impact on our well-being. Alternative measures, such as net national product that does account for depreciation in capital stocks, are not as widely used, but are receiving increasing attention (see chapter 12 on environmental accounting). For our purposes, we simply use real GDP per capita as an indicator of economic activity.

Understanding the economy–environment relationships requires us to make assumptions and simplifications so as to capture the important linkages and processes in a tractable way. We review three broad approaches to modeling economic growth and the environment.

Reduced form models

To help determine what relationships might exist between economic growth and environmental quality, a number of researchers have estimated a variety of reduced form models using both panel and cross-sectional data. These models are in "reduced form" in the sense they posit a relationship between a variable (environmental degradation) and various exogenous variables (such as per capita income), but without a theoretical model of the underlying relationship. By contrast, structural models are underpinned with a theory, such as demand and supply functions derived from consumer or producer theory. Despite their inability to *explain* relationships, reduced form models can quantify both direct and indirect aggregate effects of the explanatory variables on the dependent variable.

Reduced form regressions often suppose that a measure of environmental degradation depends on levels of per capita income, time, and potentially other variables such as population density. Some of the earliest work provided evidence that for some measures, environmental degradation initially increases with rises in per capita income, but reaches a turning point and then declines, as illustrated in figure 11.5. The resulting curve resembles an inverted U that was made famous by Kuznets (1955) in a study comparing inequality with income where he suggested that inequality rises with increasing income and then eventually declines. Consequently, the inverted Us in growth–environment relationships have become known as *environmental Kuznets curves* (EKCs) despite the fact that Simon Kuznets had nothing to do with their development.

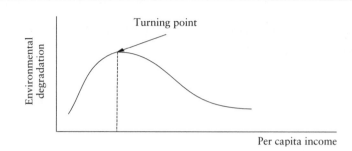

Figure 11.5   The environmental Kuznets curve

Various explanations have been offered as to why an inverted U relationship might exist. First, the upward sloping part of the curve could be the result of changes in the composition of outputs. For instance, the switch from agriculture to industrial output could increase environmental degradation, while the downward sloping part could arise from the increasing importance of services as an economy develops. Second, the growth in income is, in part, determined by technological progress that can increase technical efficiency and reduce the emissions or waste per unit of output that might more than offset increased production. Third, rising living standards may induce a change in priorities in consumption. For instance, as people get richer, they might become more concerned about the environment and be able to exert pressure on politicians to introduce environmental regulations and improve environmental quality. Such pressure is more likely to translate into a concerted program of pollution abatement in a country rich enough to have the means to adequately monitor and enforce environmental regulations and where there exists a democratic government, the rule of law, a free press and effective institutions to improve environmental quality. Finally, an EKC may arise from polluting industries and wastes migrating from rich to poorer countries. Whatever the explanation for an EKC, if the results of reduced form models are taken at face value for most measures of environmental degradation, they imply a *worsening* of environmental quality. This is because for most countries the reported turning points are at a level greater than their current per capita income (Ekins, 2000).

To obtain an EKC from a reduced form model, a quadratic term in per capita income must also appear as an independent variable in the estimation. Many authors have also included a cubic term for per capita income, a variable to account for the existence of an underlying trend separate from income, exogenous variables and intercepts to account for individual country or regional fixed effects. A typical reduced form model, that may be estimated in either log-log form or in levels, is given by the following equation:

$$ED_{it} = \alpha_1 + \alpha_2 Y_{it} + \alpha_3 Y^2_{it} + \alpha_4 Y^3_{it} + \alpha_5 t + \alpha_6 X_{it} + e_{it}$$

where ED_{it} is a measure of environmental degradation in country i at time t, Y_{it} is per capita income of country i at time t, t is a linear time trend, X_{it} represents exogenous variables that may affect environmental quality in country i at time t, and e_{it} is an error term assumed to be independently and normally distributed. Exogenous variables that have been included in such models and assumed to be independent of per capita income include population density, trade intensity, energy prices, economic, spatial intensity of economic activity, and income inequality, among others.

The "classic" EKC, or inverted U relationship, arises if $\alpha_2 > 0$, $\alpha_3 < 0$, and $\alpha_4 = 0$, provided that $|\alpha_3|$ is strictly less than $|\alpha_2|$, but several other potential relationships may exist. For example, environmental degradation may be monotonically increasing ($\alpha_2 > 0$, $\alpha_3 = \alpha_4 = 0$) or decreasing ($\alpha_2 < 0$, $\alpha_3 = \alpha_4 = 0$) with per capita income, or it may be a U shape ($\alpha_2 < 0$, $\alpha_3 > 0$, and $\alpha_4 = 0$, provided that $|\alpha_3|$ is strictly less than $|\alpha_2|$).

Two other turning points may also exist. Environmental degradation may at first rise with income and then fall and then rise again such that $\alpha_2 > 0$, $\alpha_3 < 0$, and $\alpha_4 > 0$, provided that $|\alpha_4|$ is strictly less than $|\alpha_3|$ and $|\alpha_3|$ is strictly less than $|\alpha_2|$. By contrast, environmental degradation may at first fall with income and then rise and then fall again such that $\alpha_2 < 0$, $\alpha_3 > 0$, and $\alpha_4 < 0$, provided that $|\alpha_4|$ is strictly less than $|\alpha_3|$ and $|\alpha_3|$ is strictly less than $|\alpha_2|$. The latter case gives the same long-run result as an inverted U in that increasing per capita income eventually reduces environmental degradation. A problem that arises in determining the shape of the relationship and whether one or more turning points exist is the potential *multicollinearity* that arises because of correlation between the variables for per capita income, per capita income squared and per capita income cubed. Such correlation makes it difficult to interpret the tests of significance for the individual coefficients α_2, α_3, and α_4.

Several reviews of reduced form models have been undertaken. Stern, Common, and Barbier (1996) compare five different studies and emphasize the inability of the EKC approach to lead to informed policy in the sense that it does not *explain* why the inverted U curve arises. A number of important econometric critiques also exist. For instance, depending upon the chosen measure of environmental degradation and sample of countries, the possibility exists that GDP per capita and environmental quality are co-determined, thus rendering the estimates biased and inconsistent (Stern, 1998).

Another major problem is that EKCs estimated using time-series data may exhibit spurious regression results. In particular, if the data are *non-stationary* such that the variance of per capita income and environmental degradation are increasing with respect to time, then one of the key assumptions for ordinary least squares (OLS) estimation is violated. If this is the case, standard tests of significance are no longer valid and if a significant relationship between per capita income and environmental degradation is found, the result may be spurious. Thus reduced form models that use time-series data must test whether the variables are stationary or not, which requires the use of *unit root* tests. If unit roots are found in the data such that the variables are non-stationary, OLS might still be appropriate, but only *if* income and environmental degradation are *co-integrated* such that the variables move together and a linear combination of the two is stationary.

Most EKC studies that use panel or time-series data report neither unit root or co-integration tests. An exception is Day and Grafton (2003) who use Canadian data for several measures of environmental degradation. They find that estimates from a standard reduced form model with a linear time trend may be spurious for environmental degradation measures that include carbon monoxide, carbon dioxide, and total suspended particulate matter. In their study, causality tests also indicate that the hypothesis that environmental degradation does *not* influence per capita income is rejected. This indicates a bi-directional causality, rather than a unidirectional causality from income to the environment.

In a recent survey of EKC studies, de Bruyn (2000) observes that an inverted U-shaped curve occurs in only 12 of the 23 cases. In another review of past work, Ekins (2000) finds 20 out of 43 models estimated an EKC while 14 of the studies found that rising per capita income eventually leads to increases in environmental degradation. These reviews suggest that the strongest evidence for an inverted U exists for some measures of air pollution. These measures represent aspects of environmental degradation whose effects can be observed locally and where control is relatively straightforward, such as emissions of sulfur dioxide, carbon monoxide, nitrogen oxides, and particulate matter. Nevertheless, the most recent study that uses a sample that includes both OECD and non-OECD national emissions of sulfur finds that the estimated turning point of US$101,166 is at such a high level as to render the relationship monotonic (Stern and Common, 2001). The Stern and Common study is also noteworthy for the testing of the robustness and reliability of the results – a quality lacking in some of the previous EKC studies.

For other measures of environmental degradation, such as water pollution and land use change, little evidence exists for an inverted U shape. For instance, Grossman and Krueger (1995) and also Beede and Bloom (1995) find that municipal solid waste (MSW) increases with per capita income. In terms of biodiversity, Naidoo and Adamowicz (2001) show that increases in per capita income in poor countries is likely to threaten or reduce the abundance of invertebrates, plants, amphibians, and reptiles. Thus, even if one accepts the reduced form approach, the results do *not* imply that increasing income will, past some turning point, improve all aspects of environmental quality. Finally, without further analysis, EKC studies fail to enlighten us as to what policies or actions lead to improvements in environmental quality.

Structural models and decompositions

To explain the growth–environment relationships, we must understand *why* environmental degradation may rise or fall with per capita income. This requires that we explicitly model the economy–environment linkages and/or decompose trends in technical efficiency, emissions per unit of output, the composition of outputs, and composition of inputs. For example, an understanding of the links between the economy and concentrations of sulfur dioxide requires explanations for why sulfur dioxide emissions from sources such as automobiles, mineral smelting, and coal-fired electricity generating plants change over time. In particular, sulfur dioxide emissions may decline due to fuel switching (from high- to low-sulfur coal), increased energy efficiency (less fuel used per unit of output produced) or because of the use of emissions-control devices that are, in turn, influenced by environmental regulations (Day and Grafton, 2001, p. 303).

In an informative study that *explains* declines in sulfur dioxide emissions in the United Kingdom (UK), Ekins (2000, p. 286) decomposes sulfur dioxide emissions in the following way:

$$SO_2 = (SO_2 \text{ output/S input}) \cdot (S \text{ input/energy input}).$$
$$(\text{energy input/output}) \cdot \text{output}$$

The decomposition helps to determine whether sulfur dioxide emissions have declined in the UK, due to increased abatement (SO_2 output/S input), reduced sulfur intensity (S input/energy input), reduced energy intensity (energy input/output) or reduced output. If abatement is an important factor for the decline it suggests that environmental regulations may be important, while if decline in energy intensity is the principal cause, it suggests technological factors may predominate. In a model that decomposes 12 fuel users and 10 fuel sources (ultimate source of domestic emissions) in the UK, Ekins (2000, p. 294) finds that, despite a rise of 62 percent in the value-added of the sectors over the period 1970–90, total emissions fell by 38 percent. The decline arose because of a fall in sulfur intensity (33 percent) and energy intensity (43 percent) over the same period. Not surprisingly, the greatest declines in sulfur emissions per energy input were in those sectors that made the most substitution away from coal (a high-sulfur fuel) to other energy inputs such as electricity and natural gas.

Similar decompositions and sectoral analyses can be used for a number of different pollutants where there are identified point sources of emissions. In particular, decompositions are well suited to understanding the links between carbon dioxide emissions, carbon intensity, energy intensity, and output growth in various sectors of the economy and across countries (Hamilton and Turton, 2002).

Macroenvironomic models

Given the interrelationships between the environment and the economy, economic decisions and policies invariably affect environmental outcomes. To evaluate policies, and to simulate possible outcomes under a range of scenarios, a variety of macroeconomic models have been developed. These models include environmental components or separate models for the environment and, thus, may be called *macroenvironomic* models.

Some of the earliest macroenvironomic models were simulation models used to predict environmental impacts under various scenarios. The most famous set of models undertaken for the Club of Rome (Meadows et al., 1972) were not developed by economists and failed to include the appropriate feedbacks in terms of supply and demand of natural resources from changes in prices. Despite their limitations, the Club of Rome models were helpful in focusing attention on the important environment–economy linkages. Their work, in turn, has helped stimulate a huge range of macroenvironomic models.

Models developed from an economic perspective, such as input–output models, have been expanded and adapted to include environmental components. In traditional input–output models the economy is divided into industries where purchases and supply between sectors are measured in a money metric. A tableau of the economy can be constructed with n sectors where the element in the ith row and jth column of the tableau represents the value of purchases from the ith industry by the jth industry. By varying the final demands in each industry, which are treated as exogenous, the effect (purchases and supply) on the various sectors of the economy can be evaluated. Further, incorporating environmental sectors into the input–output table, such as the level of extraction of natural resources and the residuals produced in each sector, the framework also provides a means to assess the effects of changes in the economy on the environment. For example, input–output models are helpful in assessing how economic shocks, such as a change in demand for automobiles, affect emissions and waste by using emission coefficients for a range of pollutants over various economic sectors.

Increasingly, economists (and policy-makers) are using computable general equilibrium (CGE) models that include environmental components to assess a range of policy alternatives. CGE models are particularly good at evaluating the costs and benefits of different environmental policies, but are not appropriate for economic forecasts. Many variants of CGE models exist depending on how or why they were built. All CGE models, however, mimic a competitive equilibrium and share a common feature whereby inter-industry transfers and intermediate deliveries within the economy are determined by an input–output structure. Their value is in their modeling of the interrelationships within an economy in a way that accords with neoclassical theory – producer supply and demand functions are derived from profit maximization subject to feasibility constraints and household demand and supply functions are derived from utility maximization subject to budget constraints.

One of the motivations for incorporating the environment in macroeconomic models is the need to assess the costs and benefits associated with climate change (see box 11.1). One of the earliest economic models, the dynamic integrated climate economy (DICE) model (Nordhaus, 1992), adds an emissions factor and an endogenous emissions reduction function for greenhouse gases (GHG) to a neoclassical aggregate production function for the world economy. The entire model is optimized to maximize the discounted sum of the utilities from per capita consumption multiplied by the world population. Consumer preferences are given by a logarithmic utility function that is a function of per capita consumption where consumption is equal to total world output less investment in

BOX 11.1   INTRODUCTION TO CLIMATE CHANGE

Climate change may refer to a number of factors, but it commonly refers to changes associated with increases in the concentration of greenhouse gases in the atmosphere. The principal greenhouse gases (GHGs) include carbon dioxide, methane, nitrous oxide, chlorofluorocarbons, ozone, and water vapor.

Greenhouse gases act as a "radiation blanket" in the sense that they emit less thermal radiation into space than they absorb from the earth's surface. Increases in concentrations of GHGs create an imbalance in the earth's radiation budget as more energy is being absorbed than emitted. This imbalance increases surface temperatures until a new equilibrium is reached. Climate modelers predict that, with feedback effects, the average surface temperature will rise at least 2.5 degrees Celsius following a doubling of the carbon dioxide concentration in the atmosphere.

GHGs are often measured in terms of global warming potential (GWP) of one kilogram of carbon dioxide. The higher the GWP, the greater is the difference between a GHG's ability to absorb thermal radiation from the surface and emit it into space. Although other GHGs have GWP much greater than one (for example, methane and nitrous oxide have a GWP of 24.5 and 320 over 100 years), carbon dioxide is the most important anthropogenic (of human origin) GHG because of the size of emissions. Human activity is responsible for almost all the recent increase in the atmospheric concentration of carbon dioxide. The concentration has risen from around 280 parts per million 250 years ago to 360 parts per million today, and is expected to reach over 550 parts per million before the end of the century. The principal source of anthropogenic emissions of carbon dioxide is fossil fuel combustion, which accounts for about three-quarters of total emissions.

The potential consequences of climate change will vary greatly by the income level, location, and topography of nations. Some sectors of some countries may even benefit from a higher average surface temperature. The biggest losers will be densely populated, low-lying, and poor countries such as Egypt or Bangladesh. The negative consequences of climate change include increased morbidity and mortality, species loss, increased extreme events (hurricanes, etc.), increased sea level (through thermal expansion), changes in precipitation, among others. Rapid climate change may also increase the possibility of catastrophic events, such as rapid melting of the Greenland ice-sheets. Responding to climate change involves reducing increases (or even the absolute levels) of GHG emissions and adapting to its potential effects.

Sources: IPCC (1997); Houghton (1997)

reproducible capital. Output, or gross world product (GWP), comes from an aggregate Cobb–Douglas production function defined by:

$$Y(t) = \Omega(t)A(t)K(t)\gamma P(t)^{1-\gamma}$$

where $\Omega(t)$ is the fractional costs and damages associated with climate change at time t, $A(t)$ is total factor productivity at time t, $K(t)$ is reproducible capital at time t,

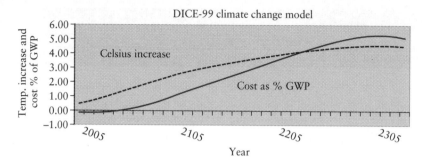

Figure 11.6   Climate change predictions from the DICE-99 model

Source: Nordhaus (1999)

$P(t)$ is population at time t and γ is the elasticity of output with respect to reproducible capital.

The climate change and economy linkage comes through the function $\Omega(t)$ that
is a function of the emission control rate at time t (that reflects GHG emissions
control policies and regulation) and the average surface temperature (that
depends on a simplified climate change model). In this specification the lower the
emission controls associated with reducing GHG emissions the higher is GWP, but
the greater the average surface temperature the lower is GWP.

The model has been updated and revised (Nordhaus, 1999) and "optimum"
time paths for all variables can be calculated. The time paths from 2005 to 2335 for
average surface temperature increase and loss in GWP using the base case of the
DICE-99 model are given in figure 11.6.

The DICE-99 results suggest a relatively small percentage cost in terms of world
output due to climate change (although such costs are likely to be very unevenly
distributed) despite a large increase in average surface temperature of over
4 degrees Celsius. However, the costs associated with climate change would still
be the equivalent of 36 percent of GWP in 1995 as the model projects a seven-fold
increase in output over the 330-year period. As with any model, the "optimal"
time paths projected by DICE-99 are open to criticisms. For example, not discounting future utility leads to greater abatement in GHG emissions as would
increases in the damage function associated with climate change. Thus an evaluation of the results of DICE-99, or any other macroenvironomic model, requires
careful assessment of the underlying assumptions, the feedbacks, the robustness
of the results to changes in parameters, and comparisons to alternative models.

11.6   POPULATION AND THE ENVIRONMENT

The world's population rose from a few dozen individuals to reach an estimated
three million or so about 20,000 BP. Two thousand years ago the world's population
was below 200 million – less than the current population of Indonesia. In the

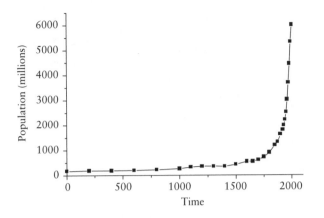

Figure 11.7 World population in the Common Era

Source: Kremer (1993)

following 18 centuries the population increased at a small, but positive rate, apart from the decades that coincided with the "Black Death" or bubonic plague in the fourteenth century. Only in the past two centuries or so has the rate of population growth increased substantially. Today the world's population numbers over six billion and is expected to increase, barring unforeseen catastrophes, to a level between 8 billion and 12 billion.

The recent rapid increase in population gives the *appearance* of exponential growth, as shown in figure 11.7. The primary reason for the rise has been a large fall in the death rate (especially among infants and children) primarily due to better hygiene and public sanitation, and improvements in public health and nutrition. As a result, average life expectancy, the age or older to which half of all children at birth are expected to reach, has grown rapidly and continues to increase, as shown by figure 11.8.

Improvements in public infrastructure, nutrition, and medicine may also feed back to increase labor productivity and further rises in per capita income at low levels of income. For example, Fogel (1994) estimates that 30 percent of the growth in per capita income in Britain between 1790 and 1980 was caused by improved nutrition that increased labor productivity.

Increased economic opportunities for women have also empowered them in terms of their fertility decisions and reshaped cultural attitudes and expectations about families and child rearing. These changes, especially in middle-income and rich countries, have dramatically increased the costs of leaving the workforce for child rearing and have reduced the "demand" for children as women postpone giving birth until much later in their lives and lowered the number of children they wish to have. Trends to reduce family size have been further enhanced by opportunities in rich countries to save for retirement that have greatly diminished the need (as still exists in poor countries) to have children as a form of "savings"

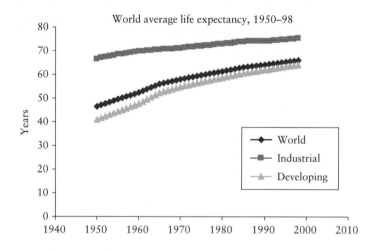

Figure 11.8   World average life expectancy

Source: Worldwatch Database Disk (2000)

for old age. Thus rises in per capita income, especially if they create educational and employment opportunities for women, and declines in infant and child mortality, provide positive feedbacks to further reduce birth rates.

These feedbacks have reached a point in some countries that the fertility rate (total births per woman) is less than that required for replacement. This implies, in the absence of positive net migration, an eventual decline in the total population. For instance, the 1999 fertility rate in Germany of 1.35 and in the United Kingdom of 1.71 are both below their replacement level and have declined by 6 percent and 10 percent from their 1980 levels (Svejnar, 2002).

Declining fertility rates have led to a decline in the world's *rate* of population growth. This trend is presented in figure 11.9. The sharp decline in the late 1950s is attributed to the great Chinese famine of 1959–61 that may have contributed to the early deaths of up to 30 million people. The declining trend in population growth has led some demographers to predict that the world's population may even start to decline before the end of the twenty-first century, but from a predicted level significantly higher than the current population of over 6.2 billion. The level at which the earth's population peaks (barring a collision with a comet!) will primarily be determined by the relative importance of increasing life expectancy due to continuing improvements in health care and nutrition and offsetting factors such as AIDS, pandemic diseases, and environmental stresses.

Overshoot and collapse?

The recent and rapid increase in the world's population has led some to predict an imminent population catastrophe. The most extreme prediction is that

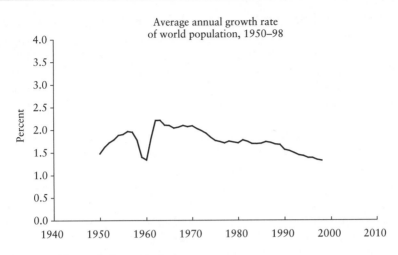

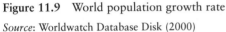

Figure 11.9   World population growth rate

Source: Worldwatch Database Disk (2000)

environmental stresses will be such that mass starvation, especially in poor countries, will happen soon (Ehrlich, 1968). This concern, on a global scale, has its
origins in the writings of the Reverend Thomas Malthus at the end of the
eighteenth and the early nineteenth century. Malthus argued that population had
a tendency to increase at a fixed rate such that the change in the population is
proportional to population size, i.e., $dL/dt = aL$ where $a > 0$ and L is the population. This represents exponential growth (see chapter 1) such that the population
at time t, $L(t)$, only depends on the initial population at $t = 0$, L_0, the rate of
growth a and the period, t.

$$L(t) = L_0 e^{at}$$

According to Malthus the population faced only two constraints on its growth:
moral restraint to offset "irrational passion" and misery and vice that arise from
insufficient food and resources for survival. As already discussed, the world's
population is *not* increasingly exponentially, as hypothesized by Malthus, but the
concern remains that the current population is too high to prevent environmental
catastrophes, especially in poor countries. For example, Paul Ehrlich, an entomol-
ogist, predicted in a book published in 1968 that an imminent population collapse
would arise because of mass starvation. Similar, if not so extreme, predictions have
been made for the future using sophisticated models of resource availability and
demographic projections. By contrast, others argue that such predictions are wrong
and that population growth is an important force for the benefit of humankind
(Simon, 1980). Indeed, there is both theoretical and empirical evidence to support
the hypothesis that a higher population density promotes faster technological
change (Kremer, 1993).

The fact that the world's population has not collapsed in recorded history, although it declined in the fourteenth century due to the bubonic plague, does not provide a guarantee that it may not happen. There is abundant evidence that local human populations, in response to both anthropogenic and natural disturbances, have "overshot" their environment's capacity to feed them and this has resulted in starvation or mass migration. One of the earliest recorded was the migration of the so-called sea peoples some 3200 BP that coincided with the collapse of the Mycenaean civilization in Greece and the eastern Mediterranean and the Hittite empire in Asia Minor.

Much of the increase in food supply that has averted a global food crisis arises from plant breeding that has dramatically increased yields. These increases in yields have been called the *"green revolution."* Further and on-going improvements in yields and productivity are required if the world's population is to increase, as predicted. The pessimists believe that increasing soil erosion, and other land use problems such as salinity, will reduce yields in the future; while the optimists believe that negative feedbacks and human ingenuity will resolve, or more than offset, factors that may reduce yields and production. Overlaying these issues are uncertainties associated with global change due to human activities, such as climate change, that might result in environmental shocks that exceed our ability to mitigate or resolve them in sufficient time so as to prevent population decline.

To help understand the factors that may contribute to population overshoot and collapse, several authors have examined the evidence from various populations, and at different points in time. One of the most spectacular collapses that occurred in the past 1,000 years is that of the eastern Pacific island of Rapa Nui, better known as Easter Island. Rapa Nui was uninhabited until a wayward canoe of some fifty or so Polynesians arrived from the west at around the year 400. They found a heavily forested island untouched by human exploitation with plenty of resources. An important part of the diet of the early Rapa Nuians was fish and porpoises harvested a considerable distance offshore. Increasing population and a food surplus encouraged technical innovation in the use of stone and culminated in the carving and erecting of the famous stone heads by around 1100 and that continued for 400 years.

The cultural and technical development represented by the "big heads" was, unfortunately, not reflected in the Islanders' attention to their environment. Unlike most other Polynesian Islands, Rapa Nui has a much more temperate climate and is located south of the tropics. This distinction is shared by the island's flora. The only native palm tree (*Jubea Chilensis*) may have taken up to 60 years or longer to reach maturity and bear fruit on the island (Brander and Taylor, 1998). By contrast, in tropical Polynesia the two most common palm trees can bear fruit in as little as 10 years or less. The Rapa Nui palms were used to build canoes for fishing that provided the fish and the bulk of the protein for the islanders, and for hauling and erecting the "big heads." By about the year 800, archaeological evidence exists for a noticeable decline in forest cover and the "seeds of destruction" (Devlin and Grafton, 1998) were laid with further deforestation. By about 1400, the last palm tree on the island was cut down thus preventing the regeneration of a key resource upon which they depended for their protein and cultural needs. As the last tree was felled the population may already have been in decline from a peak estimated at between 10,000 and 20,000. The population collapse was contemporaneous with evidence of warfare and cannibalism. By the time of Rapa Nui's "discovery" by Europeans in 1722 the population was estimated to be as little as 2,000–3,000.

Brander and Taylor (1998) have modeled the resource–population dynamics of Rapa Nui to understand its population overshoot and collapse. In their model, they assume only one resource ($S(t)$) that exhibits logistic growth (see chapter 2) over time t such that it has it highest rates of growth at an intermediate level of abundance ($K/2$) and has a maximum carrying capacity of K, beyond which growth cannot occur.

Assuming a linear harvesting function for the resource and omitting time subscripts for convenience, the change in the resource stock at any time is given by:

$$dS/dt = rS(1 - S/K) - \alpha\beta LS$$

where r is defined as the intrinsic growth rate of 0.04 that determines the rate of regeneration for given level of S, α is the labor harvesting productivity parameter set equal to 0.00001, β is the share of labor devoted to resource harvesting and is set equal to 0.4 and L is the level of population. The change in the island's population at any point in time is assumed to be:

$$dL/dt = L(b - d + \phi\alpha\beta S)$$

where b is the birth rate and d is the death rate in the *absence* of the resource stock and $b - d = -0.1$, ϕ is a positive constant set equal to 4 and $\alpha\beta S$ is the per capita consumption of the resource.

In the model, each individual is endowed with one unit of labor and is assumed to maximize (subject to a budget constraint) the following instantaneous utility function:

$$u = h^\beta m^{(1 - \beta)}$$

where h is individual consumption of the resource and m is individual consumption of manufactures. Starting from an initial population of 40 in the year 400 and a resource stock of 12,000 that coincides with its carrying capacity, the model simulates a peak population of about 10,000 at around 1200 that is followed by a collapse.

In a more plausible extension of the Brander–Taylor model, Pezzey and Anderies (2003) allow people to allocate the time spent on harvesting and manufactures to vary depending on the resource scarcity by including a desired minimum and positive level of consumption of the resource, defined as $\bar{h}$. Thus in the Pezzey–Anderies model individuals are assumed to maximize the following instantaneous utility function,

$$u = (h - \bar{h})^\beta m^{(1 - \beta)}$$

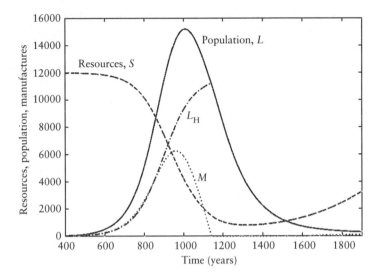

Figure 11.10   Overshoot and collapse in the Pezzey–Anderies model

Source: Pezzey and Anderies (2003)

The total labor spent on harvesting is defined by $L_H = L - L_M$ and the total manufactures is defined as $M = L_M$. The time paths of the resource, population, manufactures, and the labor spent on harvesting are given in figure 11.10 where $\bar{h}$ is set equal to 0.015.

The utility subsistence requirement in the Pezzey–Anderies model leads to a higher level of population and thus a greater overshoot and collapse of population. By contrast, the Brander–Taylor model has an in-built "conservation" factor in the sense that the proportion of time spent on manufactures $(1 - \beta)$, which is fixed, means less time spent on harvesting. No such limiting factor exists in the Pezzey–Anderies model where falling harvests are compensated by a greater time spent on harvesting which feeds into a higher per capita consumption of the resource stock for a longer period. Consequently, it leads to an increase in population growth that would otherwise not occur without utility subsistence. Another, and perhaps less intuitive result, is that the subsistence requirements lead to greater oscillations in the resource–population system.

These resource–population models provide a number of interesting observations. First, environment–economy interactions need to be modeled so as to understand human population dynamics. Second, the reliance on a single or limited number of resources with low intrinsic growth rates (such as slow to mature palms on Rapa Nui or megafauna hunted by upper Palaeolithic hunters) increases the chances of population overshoot and collapse. Third, negative feedbacks (such as negative population growth in absence of resource consumption) and positive feedbacks (such as from utility subsistence) are important in population dynamics. Fourth, technical change is critically important as a means to avoid resource constraints and population overshoot. Technical change probably has a positive relationship with initial population size in geographically isolated regions (Kremer, 1993). Fifth, as Rapa Nui's demise has not been universally repeated, it suggests that people are able to develop institutions to promote sustainable resource use. Thus, perhaps, *the* lesson of Rapa Nui is the importance of institutions and technical change as the means to prevent overexploitation of the environment that, in turn, can lead to population overshoot and collapse.

11.7 A WAY FORWARD

It would seem that our planet should prepare itself for significant increase in both population and per capita income for the foreseeable future. Best estimates suggest that the human population will peak at a level about 50 percent higher than its current level while, on current trends, most of the world's population should enjoy at least a doubling of their real per capita income before the end of the century. In the *absence* of offsetting effects on the environment and assuming no threshold effects, this will lead to close to a three-fold increase in overall environmental degradation within the next hundred or so years. Whether or not our environment can sustain both higher levels of population and income, such a large decline in environmental quality would be undesirable under reasonable assumptions about individual preferences and abatement costs.

The way forward to ensure rising per capita incomes while maintaining critically important natural capital stocks is to manage our economy differently. This requires, among other things, getting incentives right by fully internalizing the costs associated with depleting natural resources or reducing the assimilative capacity of the environment. It also requires appropriate incentives for innovation and technological progress to improve both technical and abatement efficiency and to reduce the material throughput and waste associated with consumption. Such approaches require a radical departure from the common macroeconomic management focus on increasing GDP per capita and short-term planning and decision-making.

A change in economic incentives to give a greater value to the environment involves trade-offs and costs. This does not mean that such trade-offs are not worth making, but it does mean that when it comes to reducing environmental degradation, or even improving environmental quality, there is "no free lunch." For example, in one of the earlier studies of the costs of environmental regulation, Jorgenson and Wilcoxen (1990) estimated that environmental regulations over the period 1973–85 were a measurable and significant opportunity cost in terms of the US economy. Indeed, Palmer et al. (1995) have estimated that annual expenditures for environmental protection in the US are over $100 billion.

A key to reducing costs associated with preventing environmental degradation is to create incentives to develop technologies that reduce energy intensity, material throughput, and wastes associated with the output of goods and services.

The so-called Porter hypothesis goes so far as to suggest that environmental regulations may actually create incentives for innovation that may more than off-set the costs associated with meeting the regulations (Porter and van der Linde, 1995). While such a desirable outcome may occur for an individual firm, or possibly even an industry, it is difficult to comprehend how such a result can occur on a global scale. Nevertheless, even in the absence of such a "win–win" situation, incentives to promote innovation in abatement and demateralization are required if the earth's critically important natural capital stocks are to be maintained in the face of an increasing world population and per capita income.

FURTHER READING

The literature on growth and the environment is rather fragmented because authors focus on particular aspects of the relationship, rather than the big picture. Three useful, but somewhat dated, surveys are chapter 1 of the World Development Report (1992) published by the World Bank, chapter 5 of Daly (1992), and Ayres (1993). The World Development Report argues that growth is beneficial to the environment, while Daly and Ayres take the opposite view. Daly's chapter on "growth fallacies," in particular, is an intriguing and provocative challenge to the mainstream economics profession. Lomborg (2001) and Bailey (1995) provide a much rosier and highly controversial picture of the state of the environment. A useful compendium on various aspects of the environment and environmental trends is Simon (1995).

A wide-ranging and a detailed review of sustainability issues is provided by Pezzey and Toman (2002). Ekins (1994) provides an informative review of the Limits to Growth debate and its relationship to our understanding of sustainable development. Pezzey (1992) is the classic reference on sustainable development from an economic perspective and Rao (2000) is highly recommended as an accessible but comprehensive text. Details on the environmental sustainability index and its updates are available at http://www.ciesin.org/.

Useful summaries of EKC results are provided by de Bruyn and Heintz (table 46.1, 2000), Ekins (table 7.A1, 2000), de Bruyn (table 5.1, 2000) and Stern (table 1, p. 188, 1998). Insightful reviews of the EKC literature and the EKC hypothesis are provided by Stern (1998), de Bruyn and Heintz (2000), Ekins (2000), Rothman and de Bruyn (1998), and Arrow et al. (1995), among others. Harbaugh et al. (2002) re-examine the empirical evidence for an EKC and De Bruyn (2000) provides a good review of the issues of non-stationarity and co-integration for EKC models.

The classic work of Thomas Malthus goes back to his *Essay on Population* first published in 1798 and updated in 1803. His final view on the subject appeared in 1830. Dasgupta (1995) provides a thorough analysis of the interrelationship between development and population growth and Baldwin (1995) provides an interesting discussion of the links between environment, growth, and fertility. Kremer (1993) and Anderies (2002) both provide useful insights from dynamic models of population and focus on the issues of population growth and technological change. Renner (1996) provides a modern perspective on population and environmental degradation and examines the population–conflict–resource use relationships in Chiapas, Mexico, and Rwanda.

REFERENCES

Anderies, J. M. (2003). Economic Development, Demographics, and Renewable Resources: A Dynamical Systems Approach, *Environment and Development Economics*, 8 (2): 219–46.

Arrow, K., Bolin, B., Costanza, R., Dasgupta, P., Folke, C., Holling, C. S., Jansson, B.-O., Levin, S., Mäler, K.-G., Perrings, C., and Pimental, D. (1995). Economic Growth, Carrying Capacity and the Environment, *Science*, 268: 520–1.

Ayres, R. U. (1993). Cowboys, Cornucopians and Long-Run Sustainability, *Ecological Economics*, 8: 189–207.

Bailey, R. ed. (1995). *The True State of the Planet*, Free Press: New York.

Baldwin, R. (1995). Does Sustainability Require Growth?, in I. Goldin and L. A. Winters, eds, *The Economics of Sustainable Development*, OECD and Center for Economic Policy Research, Cambridge University Press, pp. 51–78.

Beede, D. N. and Bloom, D. E. (1995). The Economics of Municipal Solid Waste, *World Bank Research Observer*, 10 (2): 113–50.

Brander, J. A. and Taylor, M. S. (1998). The Simple Economics of Easter Island: A Ricardo-Malthus Model of Renewable Resource Use, *American Economic Review*, 88 (1): 119–38.

Ciriacy-Wantrup, S. V. (1952). *Resource Conservation, Economics and Policies*, University of California Press: Berkeley, CA.

Colborn, T., Dumanoski, D., and Myers, J. P. (1997). *Our Stolen Future*, Plume/Penguin: New York.

Common, M. (1995). *Sustainability and Policy: Limits to Economics*, Cambridge University Press: Sydney.

Daly, H. E. (1992). *Steady-State Economics*, second edition, Earthscan Publications: London.

Dasgupta, P. (1995). The Population Problem: Theory and Evidence, *Journal of Economic Literature*, 33: 1879–1902.

Day, K. and Grafton, R. Q. (2001). Economic Growth and Environmental Degradation in Canada, in K. Banting, A. Sharpe, and F. St-Hilaire, eds, *The Review of Economic Performance and Social Progress, The Longest Decade: Canada in the 1990s*, Institute for Research on Public Policy and the Center for the Study of Living Standards: Montreal, pp. 293–309.

Day, K. and Grafton, R. Q. (2002). Growth and the Environment in Canada: An Empirical Analysis, *Canadian Journal of Agricultural Economics*, 51: 197–216.

de Bruyn, S. M. (2000). *Economic Growth and the Environment: An Empirical Analysis*, Kluwer: Dordrecht.

de Bruyn, S. M. and Heintz, R. J. (2000). The Environmental Kuznets Curve Hypothesis, in J. C. J. M. van den Bergh, ed., *Handbook of Environmental and Resource Economics*, Edward Elgar: Cheltenham, pp. 656–77.

Devlin, R. A. and Grafton, R. Q. (1998). *Economic Rights and Environmental Wrongs: Property Rights for the Common Good*, Edward Elgar: Cheltenham.

Ehrlich, P. (1968). *The Population Bomb*, Ballantine: New York.

Ekins, P. (1994). "Limits to Growth" and "Sustainable Development": Grappling with Ecological Realities, *Ecological Economics*, 8 (3): 269–88.

Ekins, P. (2000). *Economic Growth and Environmental Sustainability: The Prospects for Growth*, Routledge: London.

Fogel, R. W. (1994). Economic Growth, Population Theory, and Physiology: The Bearing of Long-term Processes on the Making of Economic Policy, *American Economic Review*, 84 (3): 369–95.

Global Leaders of Tomorrow Environment Task Force (Chair Kim Samuel-Johnson) (2001). *2001 Environmental Sustainability Index*. Prepared in collaboration with Yale Center for Environmental Law and Policy and the Center for International Earth Science Information Network of Columbia University for the World Economic Forum in Davos, Switzerland, January.

Grafton, R. Q. and Silva-Echenique, J. (1997). How to Manage Nature? Strategies, Predator–Prey Models, and Chaos, *Marine Resource Economics*, 12: 127–43.

Grossman, G. M. and Krueger, A. B. (1995). Economic Growth and the Environment, *Quarterly Journal of Economics*, 112: 353–78.

Hamilton, C. and Turton, H. (2002). Determinants of Emissions Growth in OECD Countries, *Energy Policy*, 30: 63–71.

Harbaugh, W. T., Levinson, A., and Wilson, D. M. (2002). Reexamining the Empirical Evidence for an Environmental Kuznets Curve, *Review of Economics and Statistics*, 84(3): 541–51.

Holdren, J. P. and Ehrlich, P. R. (1974). Human Population and the Global Environment, *American Scientist*, 62 (May–June): 282–92.

Houghton, J. (1997). *Global Warming: The Complete Briefing*, Cambridge University Press: Cambridge.

Intergovernmental Panel on Climate Change (IPCC) (1997). *An Introduction to Simple Climate Models Used in the IPCC Second Assessment Report*, IPCC Technical Paper II (D. Harvey, J. Gregory, M. Hoffert, A. Jain, M. Lal, R. Leemans, S. Raper, T. Wigley, and J. de Wolde, Lead Authors).

Intergovernmental Panel on Climate Change (IPCC) (2001), *Climate Change 2001: Synthesis Report*: www.ipcc.ch/pubtar/syr/005.htm

Jorgenson, D. W. and Wilcoxen, P. J. (1990). Environmental Regulation and U.S. Economic Growth, *Rand Journal of Economics*, 21 (2): 314–40.

Kremer, M. (1993). Population Growth and Technological Change: One Million B.C. to 1990, *Quarterly Journal of Economics*, 108 (3): 681–716.

Kuznets, S. (1955). Economic Growth and Income Inequality, *American Economic Review*, 45 (1): 1–28.

Lomborg, B. (2001). *The Skeptical Environmentalist: Measuring the Real State of the World*, Cambridge University Press: Cambridge, England.

Meadows, D., Meadows, D. L., Randers, J., and Behrens, III, W. W. (1972). *The Limits to Growth: A Report for the Club of Rome's Project on the Predicament of Mankind*, Universe Books: New York.

Moore, S. and Simon, J. L. (2000). *It's Getting Better All the Time: Greatest Trends of the Last 100 Years*, Cato Institute: Washington, DC.

Naidoo, R. and Adamowicz, W. L. (2001). Effects of Economic Prosperity on Numbers of Threatened Species, *Conservation Biology*, 15 (4): 1021–9.

Nordhaus, W. D. (1992). An Optimal Transition Path for Controlling Greenhouse Gases, *Science*, 258 (November): 1315–19.

Nordhaus, W. D. (1999). *Warming the World: Economics Models of Global Warming*, MIT Press: Cambridge, MA.

Palmer, K., Oates, W. E., and Portney, P. R. (1995). Tightening Environmental Standards: The Benefit–Cost or the No-Cost Paradigm?, *Journal of Economics Perspectives*, 9 (4): 119–32.

Pezzey, J. C. V. (1992). Sustainable Development Concepts: An Economic Analysis, World Bank Environment Paper Number 2.

Pezzey, J. C. V. and Anderies, J. M. (2003). The Effect of Subsistence on Collapse and Institutional Adaptation in Population-resource Societies, *Journal of Development Economics* 72: 299–30.

Pezzey, J. C. V. and Toman, M. A. (2002). Progress and Problems in the Economics of Sustainability, in T. Tietenberg and H. Folmer, eds, *International Yearbook of Environmental and Resource Economics 2002/3*, Edward Elgar: Cheltenham, pp. 169–232.

Ponting, C. (1991). *A Green History of the World: The Environment and the Collapse of Great Civilizations*, Penguin Books: New York.

Porter, M. E. and van der Linde C. (1995). Toward a New Conception of the Environment–Competitiveness Relationship, *Journal of Economic Perspectives*, 9: 97–118.

Rao, P. K. (2000). *Sustainable Development: Economics and Policy*, Basil Blackwell: Malden, MA.

Renner, M. (1996). *Fighting for Survival: Environmental Decline, Social Conflict and the New Age of Insecurity*, W. W. Norton & Company: New York.

Rothman, D. S. and de Bruyn, S. M. (1998). Probing into the Environmental Kuznets Curve Hypothesis, *Ecological Economics*, 25: 143–5.

Simon, J. L. (1980). Resources, Population, Environment: An Oversupply of False Bad News, *Science*, 208: 1431–7.

Somerville, R. C. J. (1996). *The Forgiving Air: Understanding Environmental Change*, Berkeley: University of California Press.

Stern, D. I. (1998). Progress on the Environmental Kuznets Curve?, *Environmental and Development Economics*, 3: 173–96.

Stern, D. I. and Common, M. S. (2001). Is There an Environmental Kuznets Curve for Sulfur?, *Journal of Environmental Economics and Management*, 41: 162–78.

Stern, D. I., Common, M. S., and Barbier, E. B. (1996). Economic Growth and Environmental Degradation: The Environmental Kuznets Curve and Sustainable Development, *World Development*, 24 (7): 1151–60.

Svejnar, J. (2002). Transition Economies: Performance and Challenges, *Journal of Economic Perspectives*, 16 (1): 3–28.

Walters, C. W. and Hilborn, R. (1976). Adaptive Control of Fishing Systems, *Journal of Fisheries Research Board of Canada*, 33: 145–59.

World Commission on Environment and Development (1987). *Our Common Future*, Oxford University Press: Oxford.

Williams, J. D. and Nowak, R. M. (1993). Vanishing Species in Our Own Backyard: Extinct Fish and Wildlife of the United States and Canada, in L. Kaufman and K. Mallory, eds, *The Last Extinction*, MIT Press: Cambridge, MA, pp. 115–48.

World Development Report (1992). *Development and the Environment*, International Bank for Reconstruction and Development, World Bank, Oxford University Press.

Worldwatch Institute (2000). *Worldwatch Database Disk*, Worldwatch Institute, Washington, DC.

CHAPTER TWELVE

ENVIRONMENTAL ACCOUNTING

Cut off even in the blossoms of my sin,
Unhouseled, disappointed, unaneled,
No reckoning made, but sent to my account.
(William Shakespeare, *Hamlet*, Act 1, Scene V, line 74)

12.1 AN INTRODUCTION TO NATIONAL ACCOUNTS

The system of national accounts provides a statistical framework and database for summarizing and analyzing economic activity, and the wealth of an economy. The main purpose of national accounts is to provide information that is useful in economic analysis and the formulation of macroeconomic policy. The first international System of National Accounts (SNA), building on the pioneering work of Kuznets (1946), was produced by the United Nations in 1953. The SNA was updated in 1968 and again in 1993. The 1993 SNA was published jointly by the United Nations, World Bank, IMF, OECD, and the European Community. It has been adopted by all the major countries in the world, including China, Russia, and the USA, and provides the conceptual framework for all macroeconomic data used for analytic and policy purposes.[1] The 1993 SNA integrates national income, expenditure, and product accounts, input–output tables, financial flow accounts and national balance sheets, as well as introducing satellite accounts to cover areas such as tourism, health, and the environment. The importance of national accounts is highlighted by the following quote from Robert Repetto:

> Whatever their shortcomings and however little their construction is understood by the general public, the national income accounts are undoubtedly one of the most significant social inventions of the 20th century. It is no coincidence that since these measures have become available governments in all major countries have taken responsibility for the growth and stability of their economies, and enormous investments of talent and energy have been made to understand how economies can be better managed. Their political and economic impact can scarcely be overestimated. (Repetto, 1992, p. 64)

The national accounts aggregate that attracts the most attention is Gross Domestic Product (GDP). GDP measures the total value of market-based productive activity in an economy in a year. Another important aggregate is Net Domestic Product (NDP). NDP is obtained by deducting the depreciation of the capital stock, denoted here by D, from GDP. Hence GDP, NDP, and D in period t are related as follows:

$$NDP_t = GDP_t - D_t.$$

12.2   GDP, NDP, AND SUSTAINABLE DEVELOPMENT

Suppose the level of consumption in an economy each year equals its GDP. What would we expect to happen to consumption and GDP over time? Although such an economy would only be consuming exactly what it produces each year, it does not follow that the economy would be able to sustain its original level of consumption. This is because each year the size of the capital stock would decrease as a result of depreciation due to wear and tear, general ageing, and obsolescence. In the short run the level of GDP in an economy can be increased by running down the capital stock, for example through deforestation or extraction of crude oil. However, in the longer term, the level of GDP that an economy is capable of producing is determined by the size of its capital stock (broadly defined to include all types of capital). As the size of the capital stock falls, the level of output an economy is capable of producing on a sustained basis also falls. In other words, an economy in which consumption always equals GDP would experience falling GDP year after year. A level of consumption equal to current GDP, therefore, is not sustainable over time. To maintain the capital stock and hence GDP at its original level a certain fraction of GDP must be reinvested in the capital stock to counteract the effects of depreciation.

What then is the maximum level of consumption that can be maintained indefinitely? Clearly, for the reasons outlined above, the maximum sustainable level of consumption must be less than GDP. In fact, all that is required is to reinvest an amount equal to the value of total depreciation in that year. Such a level of consumption corresponds exactly with NDP. In other words, NDP can be interpreted as the maximum sustainable level of consumption.[2] By setting consumption equal to NDP, an economy's capital stock and hence GDP will remain constant over time. Such a consumption strategy is sustainable. However, any attempt to increase consumption above this level is not sustainable since it will cause both the capital stock and GDP to decrease over time.

There has been a huge upsurge of interest in the concept of sustainable development since the late 1980s. Unfortunately, sustainable development has been defined in so many different ways that discussion on this important issue has become somewhat confused. Admittedly, most definitions are variations on a theme. Perhaps the most widely quoted definition is the one provided by the

World Commission on Environment and Development (1987), otherwise known as the Brundtland Commission. The Brundtland Commission defines sustainable development as "development that meets the needs of present generations without compromising the ability of future generations to meet their needs." The problem with this definition is that it is so vague and fuzzy as to be of little use in practice. This is why it makes more sense to link the concept of sustainable development directly to the national accounts concepts of consumption and NDP. If a country's aggregate consumption is less than or equal to its NDP, then it must be following a sustainable path of development since its total capital stock will be increasing or at least nondecreasing over time.[3] By implication, it is not necessarily inconsistent with the concept of sustainable development for a country to deplete its stocks of natural resources, so long as it compensates by building up its stocks of produced and human capital. The concern here is that the substitution possibilities between different types of capital are hard to quantify and may be limited. This is particularly the case for natural capital. There must exist some threshold for natural capital below which life on earth becomes infeasible, and hence it may be dangerous to focus exclusively on a single aggregate measure of wealth. For this reason, Pezzey (1989) draws a distinction between a "weak" and "strong" notion of sustainable development. According to the "strong" definition, an economy is following a sustainable path of economic activity only if its per capita produced, natural and human capital stock are all nondecreasing over time. The "weak" definition only requires that the aggregate capital stock be nondecreasing. Pezzey's reasoning could be taken a stage further. It could be argued that "natural capital" itself is too broad an aggregate, since the substitution possibilities between different types of natural capital are also hard to quantify and may also be limited. Therefore, to accurately assess the sustainability of economic activity in an economy it may be necessary to observe a whole series of capital stock aggregates. However, this line of reasoning has limits. For example, it would be counterproductive to argue that sustainable development requires the stocks of all nonrenewable natural assets to be nondecreasing over time. Abandoning the use of nonrenewable assets, such as oil and coal, would entail a catastrophic fall in living standards. Hence if defined this way, sustainable development would become a decidedly unattractive proposition.

12.3   THE TREATMENT OF DEFENSIVE EXPENDITURE AND CLEAN-UP COSTS

The treatment of defensive expenditure and clean-up costs is a continuing source of controversy in the national and environmental accounting literature. Defensive expenditure refers to costs incurred to reduce environmental damage and its effect on people. A distinction can be drawn between costs incurred to reduce the damage done to the environment by economic activity, and the costs incurred to reduce the impact of environmental damage on welfare. Examples of the former include the installation of flue gas desulfurization units in power stations and catalytic converters in cars. An example of the latter is the purchase of face masks by commuters in polluted cities. Considerable sums of money are also spent on cleaning up the environment. Examples include Superfund in the US, which coordinates the clean-up of toxic waste dumps, and the clean-up after an oil slick such as occurred after the *Exxon Valdez* ran aground off the Alaskan coast.

Both defensive expenditure and clean-up costs are included in GDP. One interesting consequence of this is that an environmental disaster can increase GDP (at least in the short run) due to the cost of the clean-up. Clearly this is somewhat problematic if GDP is being used as a proxy for changes in aggregate welfare. As a result it has been suggested by Juster (1973) and numerous others that defensive expenditures and clean-up costs should be excluded from GDP.[4] To do so would be a mistake. The notion of "defensive expenditure" is a slippery concept. It could be argued that most forms of expenditure are defensive at some level, as the following quote from Jaszi (1973) demonstrates:

> I believe that "defensive expenditures" is a disabled veteran among output concepts which cannot be relied upon to provide effective support in output measurement. It suggests that food expenditures defend against hunger, that clothing and housing expenditures defend against cold and rain, that medical expenditures defend against sickness, and religious outlays against the fires of hell. The concept then demands that these expenditures be left out altogether, or that they be recognized only to the extent that they are not offset by a change in needs. For instance, an increase in bread production should be counted only to the extent that it is not offset by healthier appetites; an increase in the output of galoshes, to the extent it is not offset by increased rain; increase in the number of aspirin tablets, to the extent it is not offset by an increase in the number of headaches ... I am stopping at the gates of hell. I think it is a basic mistake to try to construct a measure of national output that attempts to exclude items on the basis of the indefensible distinction that they are "defensive," and to roll into one "needs" and "production," two concepts that should be kept apart. (Jaszi, 1973, p. 91)

Furthermore, it must be remembered that defensive expenditure and clean-up are productive activities. Consider again the example of an oil slick. To argue that the cost of the clean-up operation should be deducted from GDP amounts to confusing the concept of a stock with that of a flow. GDP is a measure of production and hence is a flow while welfare is essentially a stock (see Samuelson, 1961). The oil slick reduces welfare by causing an unexpected capital loss.[5] However, it may well stimulate productive activity in much the same way as war does.

12.4   DEFICIENCIES OF THE SYSTEM OF NATIONAL ACCOUNTS

Almost all the productive activities included in the SNA are geared to the market.[6] Except for subsistence agriculture and the services provided by owner occupied housing, non-market productive activities are systematically omitted, including the production of services within the home and volunteer services.[7] The services provided by consumer durables and environmental assets (e.g., air, water, forests, and ecosystems) are also excluded. Furthermore, although the capital account in the SNA records the depreciation of produced capital, such as plant and machinery, it neglects the depletion of most forms of natural capital, including stocks of water, soil, air, minerals, forests, and biodiversity.[8] By implication both total production and depreciation are underestimated by the SNA. However, from the perspective of sustainable development it is mismeasurement of the latter rather than of the former that matters. This is because most nonmarket production is immediately consumed.[9] Hence if it was included in GDP, NDP and consumption would both rise by a similar amount. Therefore, it would have little effect on the perceived sustainability of current economic activity. In contrast, as discussed below, the exclusion of natural capital from the capital account in the SNA may be seriously misleading, particularly for countries with large endowments of natural resource assets.

An unfortunate consequence of using GDP as the main measure of welfare is that it may encourage countries to follow unsustainable paths of development. This is because GDP makes no deduction for the depreciation of the capital stock. In other words, a country can increase its GDP in the short run by simply running down its capital stock. In fact, Repetto (1992) argues that many developing countries have achieved high levels of GDP and consumption by rapidly depleting their stocks of natural capital. This is why NDP is a much better yardstick for evaluating the performance of countries. However, since NDP, as defined in the SNA, makes no deduction for the depletion of natural capital, its use would not by itself solve this problem.

The solution advocated by Repetto (1992) and Pearce and Atkinson (1995) is to include natural capital in the capital account of the SNA. In consequence the depletion of natural capital as well as the depreciation of produced capital would be deducted from GDP to arrive at NDP.[10] Defined this way, NDP as noted above can be interpreted as the maximum sustainable level of consumption.[11]

12.5   WHY IS NATURAL CAPITAL EXCLUDED FROM THE CAPITAL ACCOUNT OF THE SNA?

Data Problems

The depreciation of produced assets such as machines or buildings is very difficult to measure because the changes in the values of the assets concerned cannot usually be observed and have to be estimated. This largely explains why attention is still focused primarily on GDP, in spite of its conceptual inadequacies. However, the problems encountered when trying to measure the depreciation of produced assets pale into insignificance when compared with the problems that arise in attempts to measure the depletion of natural capital assets. Natural assets were excluded from the capital account of the SNA largely for this reason, and not because national accountants thought they were not important enough. The concern was that the inclusion of natural assets might undermine the integrity of the rest of the system, (see for example Thage (1991)). Instead, separate "satellite" environmental accounts have been proposed (see for example Bartelmus, Stahmer, and van Tongeren (1993)).

Why then is the depletion of the natural capital stock so hard to measure? There are a number of reasons. Part of the problem is a lack of data. No markets exist for some kinds of assets such as the ozone layer or the biosphere. Hence it is not clear how these assets can be valued or their depletion over time estimated. Even when natural assets are traded, the market price may not adequately reflect its social marginal benefit. Hence valuation based on market prices, of a natural asset, may provide estimates that differ markedly from its actual social value (see Dasgupta (2001)).

In principle, the value of any asset is given by the present value of its discounted stream of future benefits. Depletion is the decrease in the present value of these streams of future benefits from one period to the next. Unfortunately, in the case of the ozone layer the benefits provided each period are hard if not impossible to quantify. Alternatively, one could try and measure changes in the value of an asset such as the ozone layer directly from surveys of household preferences or through revealed preference. However, even putting aside the dubious reliability of household surveys, this approach has its own problems. Should one be trying to value the maximum amount society would have been willing to pay to avoid a given amount of damage to the ozone layer, the minimum amount of compensation members of society would have to be paid to accept this damage, or the cost of reversing the damage? These three approaches could generate dramatically different answers. These issues arise in any attempt to place a monetary value on the damage done to natural assets by pollution of one form or another (see chapters 8–10).[12] By implication it is doubtful whether natural assets that never enter the market can be incorporated into the national accounts in a meaningful way.

Even the inclusion of traded natural assets in the capital account would create serious problems since it is exceedingly difficult to value these assets with any degree of confidence. A distinction can be drawn between renewable assets such as a fishery or a forest and nonrenewable assets such as minerals and fossil fuels. Consider first the case of a renewable resource such as a fishery. There is typically a huge amount of uncertainty as to its biomass. And even if the biomass is known, determining its value is far from straightforward (see chapter 4). In general, one cannot even be sure that the biomass and value of a fishery will move over time in the same direction. There is likewise a huge amount of uncertainty about the stocks of minerals and fossil fuels. Furthermore, as Adelman (1990) notes, it is not even clear that the total stock is the appropriate starting point.

The total mineral in the earth is an irrelevant, non-binding constraint. If expected finding-development costs exceed the expected net revenues, investment dries up, and the industry disappears. Whatever is left in the ground is unknown, probably unknowable, but surely unimportant; a geological fact of no economic interest. We cannot save the principle of a fixed stock by defining it as the economic portion, estimated under uncertainty about quality and cost ... What actually exist are flows from unknown resources into a reserve inventory. (Adelman, 1990, pp. 1–2)

From a national accounts perspective, what is important is not so much the level of the stock (or reserve inventory) itself as changes in the stock due to new discoveries and depletion.

Exploration and capital gains

The treatment of exploration is a tricky issue. Exploration is a scientific activity with an expected outcome over the longer term. It counts as production. However, it is not clear how much of the value of a newly discovered oil field should be treated as the output of the exploration activity and how much as an unexpected capital gain. The output is part of GDP and NDP but an unexpected gain is not (see below). If discoveries are not handled correctly and all new discoveries are treated as output produced in the period in which they happen to be found, both GDP and NDP could become extremely volatile. For example, the exceptional oil finds in Alaska in 1970 augmented US oil reserves by nearly 50 per cent, or almost $100 billion at 1987 prices. As Nordhaus and Kokkelenberg (1999, p. 81) observe, if all new discoveries are treated as part of production "the trend in real non-minerals GDP growth would have been seriously distorted, wiping out the 1970 recession and causing an apparent recession in 1971" (see also Hill and Hill, 2003).

Another source of controversy is the treatment of capital gains in NDP. It is important to draw a distinction between expected and unexpected capital gains. Most of the discussion in the environmental accounting literature on the treatment of capital gains has been couched in a perfect foresight setting (see Mäler (1991); Asheim (1996); and Vincent, Panayotou, and Hartwick (1997)). In this context, the general consensus is that capital gains arising from changes in the price or stock of a natural asset should be included in NDP. The treatment of capital gains arising from changes in the interest rate is more controversial. By assuming perfect fore-sight, however, these authors completely ignore the main issue which is the treat-ment of unexpected capital gains. When uncertainty is considered, it is often argued (see for example McElroy (1976) and Eisner (1988)) that unexpected capital gains should be included in NDP. This would be a mistake, since it would break the link between NDP and sustainable consumption. The maximum sustainable level of consumption is a forward looking concept. It is the maximum level of consumption that could be maintained indefinitely without reducing the capital stock. If unex-pected capital gains are included in NDP, then it will measure the maximum level of consumption that will return the capital stock to its original level at the beginning of the period. However, this level of consumption will not, in general, be sustainable

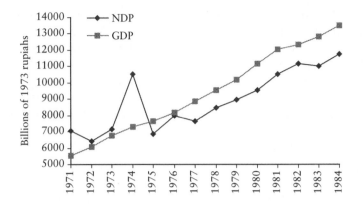

Figure 12.1   GDP and NDP for Indonesia

indefinitely. This point is best clarified with an example. Consider a household that wins a lottery. The household could consume all these lottery winnings in the current period and be as well off at the end of the period as at the beginning. However, it cannot maintain this level of consumption in future periods unless it wins the lottery every single period. The only part of the lottery winnings that can be consumed sustainably (i.e., period after period) is the interest earned on it. Similarly, an oil rich country wins the lottery when a large new oil field is discovered. However, NDP does not rise by the full amount of the increase in the value of the country's stock of oil, but only by the interest earned on the increase in value.[13]

It must be emphasized that discoveries of new mineral stocks are not the only source of unexpected capital gains. Fluctuations in commodity prices can generate huge unexpected capital gains or losses on mineral and fossil fuel stocks. The implications for NDP of the treatment of unexpected capital gains on natural assets is considered in Hill (2003) and Hill and Hill (2003). In addition to breaking the link between NDP and sustainable consumption, the inclusion of unexpected capital gains in NDP can also generate large spurious fluctuations (see for example Repetto et al. (1989) for Indonesia and Young (1993) for Australia). Repetto et al. consider the impact of depletion of petroleum, forestry, and soil on Indonesia's NDP. Figure 12.1 replicates Repetto et al.'s results, focusing exclusively on petroleum (a similar graph appears in Repetto et al. (1989) and Repetto (1992)). The most striking feature of figure 12.1 is the huge upward spike in Indonesia's NDP in 1974 (by means of comparison, Indonesia's GDP is also shown). Repetto et al. attribute the spike in NDP to changes in US tax laws and Indonesian contracts favorable to exploration activities which led to a sharp increase in reported reserves. The large increase in the price of oil that occurred about the same time probably also contributed to the dramatic upward revision in the value of reported oil reserves. Irrespective of the exact cause, Indonesia clearly experienced a very large unexpected capital gain on its stock of oil. By including the full value of unexpected capital gains in NDP, the resulting series can become highly volatile and of dubious use for policy purposes. The NDP series in figure 12.1

suggests that Indonesia performed spectacularly in 1974, and disastrously in 1975. Such a conclusion would be very misleading.

Continuing on this theme, an even more dramatic example is provided by the case of Norway. In some years, changes in the total value of Norway's stock of oil, due to price changes, have exceeded its GDP (see Aaheim and Nyborg, 1995). By implication, in the mid-1980s when the price of oil collapsed, Norway's NDP would have gone negative if all capital gains (losses) on natural capital were included in depletion. Clearly, failure to separate unexpected capital gains from depletion may introduce spurious volatility into measured NDP, particularly for resource-rich countries, thereby undermining its credibility as an indicator of economic performance.

It should now be apparent why the SNA currently excludes both new discoveries and the depletion of natural assets from its capital account. It is unlikely that natural assets that are not traded on the market can ever be included in national accounts, since if there is no way of placing a dollar value on an asset then it cannot be made commensurate with other assets. Even traded natural assets such as crude oil should not be included in the capital account of the SNA until consensus is reached on the treatment of exploration and unexpected capital gains. Otherwise, the integrity of the whole SNA risks being compromised.

12.6   OPERATIONALIZING THE CONCEPT OF DEPLETION

Defining depletion

All prices and values in this chapter are measured in constant dollars. Let V_t denote the value of an asset at the beginning of period t, and R_t the receipts (or profit) earned on the asset in period t. It is assumed that receipts are paid at the end of the period. The real interest rate is assumed constant and is denoted by r.[14] Under perfect foresight, the value of an asset is related to its stream of future receipts and the interest rate as follows:

$$V_t = \left(\frac{1}{1+r}\right)R_t + \left(\frac{1}{1+r}\right)^2 R_{t+1} + \left(\frac{1}{1+r}\right)^3 R_{t+2} + \cdots. \tag{1}$$

Similarly, assuming there is no net investment in the asset during period t, its value in period $t+1$ is given by

$$V_{t+1} = \left(\frac{1}{1+r}\right)R_{t+1} + \left(\frac{1}{1+r}\right)^2 R_{t+2} + \left(\frac{1}{1+r}\right)^3 R_{t+3} + \cdots. \tag{2}$$

Multiplying both sides of (1) by $(1+r)$ yields

$$(1+r)V_t = R_t + \left(\frac{1}{1+r}\right)R_{t+1} + \left(\frac{1}{1+r}\right)^2 R_{t+2} + \cdots. \tag{3}$$

Now, by deducting R_t from both sides of (3) and comparing with (2) it can be seen that

$$V_{t+1} = (1+r)V_t - R_t. \tag{4}$$

This equation plays a key role in the measurement of depletion.

Following Hotelling (1925), depletion is defined as a decrease in the value of an asset between the beginning and end of the period. Under perfect foresight, depletion in period t, D_t, is calculated as follows:

$$D_t = V_t - V_{t+1}. \tag{5}$$

In practice, the path of future receipts is rarely known with certainty. Hence determining the value of the asset at the beginning of periods t and $t+1$ is not straightforward. A number of approaches have been suggested in the environmental accounting literature for operationalizing the concept of depletion.

The simplest case: El Serafy's depletion formula

Exploiting the fact that a finite stream of receipts can be converted into an annuity, El Serafy (1989) argues that depletion should be defined as the difference between receipts in the current period and the annuity. This definition of depletion is exactly equivalent to the one used here. In a perfect foresight setting, if V_t denotes the present value of future receipts, then this can be used to generate an annuity of rV_t. Inspection of (4) reveals that the difference between receipts and the annuity, $R_t - rV_t$, equals $V_t - V_{t+1}$.

In the context of this more general discussion of the link between income and depletion, El Serafy (1989) also proposes a simple formula for measuring the depletion of a nonrenewable natural asset that is easy to implement. It makes the following restrictive assumptions:

(a) perfect foresight;
(b) the asset pays a receipt R for T periods and nothing thereafter;
(c) the interest rate r is constant.

Given assumptions (a)–(c), it follows from (1) that, for $1 \leq t \leq T$, the value of the asset reduces to a geometric progression:

$$V_t = \left(\frac{1}{1+r}\right)R + \left(\frac{1}{1+r}\right)^2 R + \cdots + \left(\frac{1}{1+r}\right)^{T+1-t} R = \frac{R}{r}\left[1 - \left(\frac{1}{1+r}\right)^{T+1-t}\right]. \tag{6}$$

Now it follows from (4) and (5) that

$$D_t = R - rV_t. \tag{7}$$

Combining (6) and (7) we obtain El Serafy's depletion formula:[15]

$$D_t = \frac{R}{(1+r)^{T+1-t}}.$$ (8)

The main attraction of El Serafy's formula is that it is relatively easy to compute. All that is required are estimates of receipts per period, the interest rate and the number of periods until the asset is exhausted. The problem with it is that the underlying assumptions are extremely restrictive and in many cases unrealistic. Although the assumption of constant receipts for a given number of periods may be acceptable for a nuclear power station, it is rather less appropriate for subsoil assets or renewable natural resources.

Despite its simplicity, the El Serafy formula can be easily modified to account for unexpected capital gains. The discovery of new stock should be viewed as simply increasing T, the number of periods until the resource is exhausted. This solution is attractive in that some depletion will still be registered even in the period of a discovery, and hence discoveries will not create large negative spikes in the depletion time series. For example, suppose enough barrels of oil are discovered in period t to allow the current rate of extraction to be maintained for X more periods than previously anticipated. Then recorded depletion in period t will be $R/(1+r)^{T+X+1-t}$ which is still positive, but less than $R/(1+r)^{T+1-t}$. Unexpected price shocks, meanwhile, can be viewed as changing R. For example, suppose the price of oil rises in period t. For an oil-rich country, this means $R_{t-1} < R_t$, and hence depletion in period t will be $R_t/(1+r)^{T+1-t}$ which is greater than $R_{t-1}/(1+r)^{T+1-t}$. In other words, rather than observing a large negative spike, recorded depletion actually rises in an oil rich country when the price of oil rises. This is because the extracted oil is now more valuable.

Allowing for variable receipts

If we relax assumption (b) and allow receipts to vary over time it follows from (4) that

$$D_t = R_t - rV_t.$$ (9)

This formula is also quite simple. In addition to current receipts and the interest rate, all that is required is an estimate of the present value of the natural asset. Again, however, by assuming perfect foresight it bypasses unexpected capital gains. Also, obtaining a reliable estimate of V_t may be extremely problematic. In principle, it may be possible to infer the value of a particular natural resource asset from stock market valuations of all the firms active in that particular market (see for example, Miller and Upton (1985)). Unfortunately, focusing on the case of subsoil assets, most mining firms are large vertically integrated multinationals.

Hence changes in the values of such firms may not correlate very well with changes in the value of their underlying mineral stocks. Furthermore, it must be remembered that the depletion formula in (9) assumes perfect foresight and a constant interest rate. Hence even if the present value of a natural asset could be estimated with reasonable accuracy, equation (9) would still not necessarily provide good estimates of depletion.

An alternative approach which is easier to use and can handle unexpected shocks was proposed by Hartwick (1989). He showed that, given the assumption that marginal receipts rise at the rate of interest over time as predicted by the Hotelling (1931) rule (see chapter 7), depletion equals the product of marginal receipts and the quantity extracted:

$$V_t - V_{t+1} = Q_t(MR_t - MC_t), \tag{10}$$

where Q_t is the quantity extracted, MR_t the marginal revenue and MC_t the marginal cost of extraction.[16] $MR_t - MC_t$ is the rent earned on the marginal unit extracted (marginal receipts). Hartwick refers to $Q_t(MR_t - MC_t)$ as the total Hotelling rent (THR).[17] Normally a profit maximizing firm produces to a level of output where $MR = MC$. However, because the resource is exhaustible, a firm extracting a nonrenewable resource produces less than this amount (i.e., $MR > MC$). Hence, by assuming the Hotelling rule, it is possible to determine the depletion of an asset without ever valuing the asset itself. All that is required are estimates of Q_t, MR_t, and MC_t.

Hartwick (1990) shows how the total Hotelling rent formula can be extended to allow for discoveries of new stock. Let Z_t denote quantity of new stock discovered in period t. In this case, under the assumption of perfect competition (i.e., $P_t = MR_t$), the analog to total Hotelling rent is $[P_t - MC(Q_t)]Q_t - MC(Z_t)Z_t$, where $MC(Z_t)$ denotes the cost of discovering the marginal ton. As long as $MC(Z)$ is significantly less than $MC(Q)$, as it is in the example in Hartwick and Hageman (1993, p. 226), then measured depletion will not be that sensitive to new discoveries. With regard to price shocks, Hartwick and Hageman advocate the following approach:

> If one is analyzing data from the past that feature a structural break because of a then-unanticipated shock, one might use post-discovery prices in the pre-discovery periods near the date of the unanticipated discovery or shock to smooth out calculations of true economic depreciation or to obtain more accurate benefit–cost estimates. (Hartwick and Hageman, 1993, p. 228)

Modeling uncertainty explicitly

One approach to dealing with uncertainty explicitly is to specify a path for expected future receipts, which is revised each period as new information becomes available. Expectations in most cases are likely to be quite vague, and may amount to little more than a belief that the price will rise, fall or remain constant in the future. These beliefs can be modeled as a geometric path. Assuming this structure, the expected receipt in period τ, based on information available at the beginning of period $t + 1$, is given as follows:

$$E_{t+1}R_\tau = \alpha^{\tau - t}R_t, \quad \forall \tau \geq t. \tag{11}$$

If $\alpha < 1$, then the path of future receipts is expected to decline over time, while conversely, if $\alpha > 1$ then it is expected to increase. Allowing for uncertainty, but assuming that the interest rate is fixed, the expected present value of an asset is defined as follows:[18]

$$E_{t+1}V_t = \left(\frac{1}{1+r}\right)R_t + \left(\frac{1}{1+r}\right)^2 E_{t+1}R_{t+1} + \left(\frac{1}{1+r}\right)^3 E_{t+1}R_{t+2} + \cdots. \tag{12}$$

Now, Hill (2003) shows that by assuming a geometric path for expected future receipts we can substitute (11) into (12). As a result, $E_{t+1}V_t$ reduces to a geometric progression which converges as long as $0 < \alpha < 1 + r$.

$$E_{t+1}V_t = \left(\frac{1}{1+r}\right)R_t + \left(\frac{1}{1+r}\right)^2 \alpha R_t + \left(\frac{1}{1+r}\right)^3 \alpha^2 R_t + \cdots$$

$$= \left(\frac{R_t}{1+r}\right)\left(\frac{1}{1 - \alpha/(1+r)}\right) = \frac{R_t}{1+r-\alpha} \tag{13}$$

Now, allowing for uncertainty, with expectations formed at the beginning of period $t + 1$, the formula for depletion given in (9) generalizes as follows:

$$E_{t+1}D_t = R_t - rE_{t+1}V_t. \tag{14}$$

Substituting (13) into (14), we obtain that

$$E_{t+1}D_t = \frac{(1 - \alpha)}{(1 + r - \alpha)}R_t. \tag{15}$$

If this depletion formula is used, unexpected capital gains and losses will not lead to large changes in estimates of depletion, and hence NDP will be reasonably stable over time.[19] Furthermore, this depletion formula is as simple to use as El Serafy's, but has the advantage of being more flexible. It is likely to be applicable to a wider range of situations. As noted earlier, expectations about future receipts in most cases are not held with much conviction and hence are quite vague. Receipts depend on the amount extracted, the cost of extraction and the market price. Even in a perfect foresight setting, the interactions between these variables can be quite complex, as is shown in chapter 7. The main problem, however, is the huge degree of uncertainty over future prices. Hence a complicated projection for the future path of receipts rarely makes much sense. For this reason, the geometric path for expected future receipts is not that unreasonable.

Thus far it has been assumed that r does not vary over time. If future values of r are treated as uncertain, then (9) generalizes as follows:

$$E_{t+1}D_t = R_t - r_t E_{t+1} V_t, \tag{16}$$

where

$$E_{t+1} V_t = E_{t+1} \left\{ \sum_{i=0}^{\infty} \left[\prod_{j=0}^{i} \left(\frac{1}{1 + r_{t+j}} \right) R_{t+i} \right] \right\}. \tag{17}$$

To compute depletion in this case, it is necessary to specify an expected path for future receipts and future interest rates. However, once this is done, depletion is straightforward to compute. The fact that current expectations are unlikely to be fulfilled is not necessarily a problem. The critical thing is that expectations should be revised each period as new information becomes available.

12.7 MEASURING THE WEALTH OF NATIONS

The World Bank in recent years has undertaken an ambitious study to measure the wealth of 92 countries.[20] By wealth, in this context, we mean the dollar value of the total capital stock (i.e., produced, natural, and human capital). This is a much broader definition of wealth than that usually used by economists. A study was undertaken for the year 1994. With just a single cross-section of results it is not possible to draw any conclusions regarding the sustainability of economic activity in a country. However, if this exercise were repeated for a number of cross-sections it could provide extremely useful insights with regard to sustainability.[21] According to the "weak" definition of sustainable development, an economy is following a sustainable path of economic activity if its per capita wealth (broadly defined) is nondecreasing over time. According to the "strong" definition, the per capita produced, natural, and human capital stock must all be nondecreasing over time. With this in mind, the World Bank study constructs separate estimates of the per capita produced, natural, and human capital for each country in the comparison.

Before discussing the findings of the World Bank study, we will consider the methodology used. Given the scale of the exercise, it was necessary to make a number of simplifying assumptions. It is important to bear these in mind when interpreting the results. The least controversial part of the project is the valuation of the produced capital stock, since produced assets are already included in national accounts and for the most part are traded in the market. Produced capital is decomposed into three subaggregates: structures, machinery and equipment, and urban land. The estimates for these subaggregates are derived from the database constructed by Nehru and Dhareshwar (1993), supplemented with some other sources listed in Kunte, Hamilton, Dixon, and Clemens (1998).

The World Bank attempted to value the following components of natural capital: agricultural cropland, sub-soil assets (metals, minerals, oil, coal, and gas), pastures, protected areas, timber, and nontimber forest benefits. Clearly, as the World Bank fully acknowledges, this is a far from exhaustive list of categories of natural capital that provide useful services to an economy. The reason for focusing on these assets is that the services they provide are traded in the market, and hence they can be valued in terms of their projected stream of future benefits (suitably discounted). The choice of discount rate is important and can significantly affect the results. The higher the discount rate, in general, the lower the present value of an asset. Pearce and Ulph (1999) estimate the social rate of return on investment (SRRI) for developed countries to be in the range of 2–4 percent per year. For faster growing developing countries, the SRRI is probably slightly higher. Hence, a discount rate of 4 percent was chosen for the World Bank study. Following El Serafy (1989), it is assumed that natural capital assets yield a constant stream of receipts for T periods, where T is the time to exhaustion, which may be infinite for renewable natural assets if they are not overused. The methodology used to determine the level of per period receipts is quite complicated (see Kunte, Hamilton, Dixon, and Clemens (1998)).

The valuation of human capital is probably even more contentious than the valuation of natural capital. Human resources are decomposed into the following three components: returns to education, raw labor, and social capital. Social capital refers to institutions and other social structures (see Woolcock and Narayan (2000) and World Bank (2002)). The return on human resources is obtained residually as that part of the total return (NDP) that cannot be attributed to natural or produced assets. Separating human capital from produced and natural capital, is not as straightforward as it might seem since the perceived value of a produced or natural asset may depend critically on how it is used, which in turn depends on the amount of human capital applied to it. When valuing assets in the environmental accounting literature, it is often assumed that natural assets will be used optimally. In cases where this is clearly not the case (in practice all too often) it is not clear that such an assumption is appropriate. Also, optimal usage is not independent of the level of human capital in an economy. In other words optimal usage of a coal mine in China may mean something quite different from optimal usage in the United States.

The complete results of the World Bank study are provided in Kunte, Hamilton, Dixon, and Clemens (1998). Less detailed results are provided in World Bank (1995, 1997). The comparison is for the year 1994, and wealth is measured in 1994 US dollars. The United States emerges as the richest country with per capita wealth of $401,000, 77 percent of which is human capital, and only 19 and 4 percent, respectively, takes the form of produced and natural capital. This, in fact, is one of the key findings of the study: namely, that the vast majority of total wealth is of the human variety. For the ten richest countries, the share of produced capital in total wealth never exceeds 33 percent (Norway) and the share of natural capital never exceeds 12 percent (Australia). For some poorer countries, the share of natural capital is much higher. In particular, natural capital constitutes 54 percent of Niger's total wealth. However, this high figure reflects rather the very low levels of produced and human capital in Niger, than an unusually high level of natural capital. The country with by far the highest level of natural capital, per capita, is Saudi Arabia. Its stock of natural capital (primarily oil reserves) is valued at $72,000 per capita, which translates to 42 percent of its total wealth.

Given the magnitude of the undertaking, and the huge measurement problems encountered along the way, there are likely to be systematic biases in the results. In particular, it is probable that the value of natural capital has been underestimated. For example, natural assets such as the barrier reef in Australia, and the Alps in Switzerland attract a considerable amount of tourism revenue, which should be attributed primarily to the natural capital stock, rather than to human capital as at present.

Nevertheless, in spite of these drawbacks, the World Bank study provides useful benchmark estimates. The study is well researched, interesting, and generates reasonably plausible results. It is hoped that the World Bank will repeat the exercise in a few years, so that then it will be possible to address the issue of sustainability.

Another important issue ignored by the World Bank study is the role of ecosystem services such as watershed protection, nutrient cycling, and services provided by the biosphere. This is an issue that has recently attracted media scrutiny as a result of the work of Daily (1997) and Costanza et al. (1997). Daily's edited book provides a range of perspectives on the valuation of ecosystem services. Costanza et al. are more ambitious and try to value the global benefits provided by ecosystem services. They arrive at an estimate of $33 trillion per year, almost double the total GDP of the world (around $18 trillion). If true, this implies that the World Bank study dramatically underestimates the total value of the world's natural capital stock. However, to arrive at this estimate, Costanza et al. had to make a series of heroic assumptions that have attracted criticism in the environmental accounting literature (see for example El Serafy (1998), Turner, Adger, and Brouwer (1998) and Howarth and Farber (2002)). At the same time, these authors acknowledge that Costanza et al. deserve credit for stimulating interest in this topic and, like the World Bank, providing preliminary benchmark estimates.

12.8 MEASURING WELFARE

Repetto (1992, p. 64) observes that "Throughout the world the rate of GDP growth is the primary measure of economic progress." For reasons discussed above, NDP in principle is a better measure of welfare than GDP, since at least it is closely linked with the concept of sustainable consumption. However, given how difficult it is to measure depreciation of the capital stock, it is understandable why GDP is still the main focus of attention. Nevertheless, it is misleading to interpret GDP or NDP as measures of welfare. GDP and NDP are measures of total production in an economy. In contrast, welfare is a much broader concept that should take account of factors such as inequality, unemployment, stress, life expectancy, leisure time, crime, etc. that do not belong in the national accounts.

A number of attempts have been made in recent years to develop indicators of welfare. Two indicators in particular have attracted considerable attention in the media. One is the Index of Sustainable Economic Welfare (ISEW) proposed by Cobb and Cobb, Jr (1994).[22] The ISEW is very ambitious in its objectives. It builds on the Measure of Economic Welfare (MEW) proposed by Nordhaus and Tobin (1972, 1973). Nordhaus and Tobin set out to modify GDP by adding imputations for government and household capital services, nonmarket production and leisure, and then deducting the costs of crime prevention, sanitation, road maintenance, and national defense. Cobb and Cobb, Jr take matters a step further. The ISEW is constructed from the following elements: personal consumption (from the national accounts), equality of income, services of household labor, services of consumer durables, services of streets and highways, public expenditure on health and education, net capital growth, and changes in net international position. Increases in any of these factors are assumed to add to welfare. In addition, the following factors reduce the ISEW: expenditure on consumer durables, defensive private expenditure on health and education, costs of commuting, personal expenditure on pollution control, costs of auto accidents, costs of water pollution, costs of air pollution, costs of noise pollution, loss of wetlands, loss of farmland, depletion of nonrenewable resources, long-term environmental damage, costs of ozone depletion. Cobb and Cobb, Jr proceed to estimate the ISEW for the United States for the period 1950–90. To do this, it is necessary to place a dollar value on each of the headings mentioned above (except for equality of income which is constructed as an index which is then used to adjust the dollar value of personal consumption). Clearly, as Cobb and Cobb, Jr acknowledge, this is a mammoth undertaking, bigger in scope even than that undertaken by the World Bank, although admittedly it is only undertaken for a single country. Their view is that a number, even if inaccurate, is better than no number or for that matter GDP (as a measure of welfare). However, the measurement problems encountered when attempting to construct the ISEW are so severe that it is difficult to have any confidence at all in the resulting aggregate.

Nevertheless, this has not stopped researchers from comparing the ISEW to GDP for various countries and drawing strong conclusions. Most studies find that the ISEW hardly rises and sometimes falls from the late 1970s onwards, while GDP continues to rise. These findings prompted Max-Neef (1995) to propose the "threshold hypothesis," which claims that beyond a certain point, further economic growth reduces welfare. However, the threshold hypothesis has been severely criticized by Neumayer (2000). He argues that the growing gap observed between ISEW and GDP is an "artefact of highly contestable methodological assumptions." More specifically, he attributes it to "the assumption of a cost escalation factor in the valuation of nonrenewable resource depletion and the assumption of cumulative long-term environmental damage."

Although the ISEW has attracted quite a bit of interest in the environmental accounting and development literature, it has received nowhere near as much attention as the second measure of welfare that we consider here. This is the Human Development Index (HDI) which is produced by the United Nations Development Programme (UNDP).[23] The UNDP, in fact, now publishes five different human development indexes. In addition to the flagship HDI discussed here, the UNDP produces two human poverty indexes (HPI-1 and HPI-2 for developing and OECD countries respectively), a gender-related development index (GDI), and a gender empowerment measure (GEM).

The HDI is far less ambitious than the ISEW in its objectives. The HDI is an average of three different indicators: longevity, as measured by life expectancy at birth; educational attainment, as measured by a combination of adult literacy and combined gross primary, secondary, and tertiary enrollment; and standard of living as measured by real per capita GDP. The indexes for longevity and educational attainment are computed relative to fixed minimum and maximum values.

$$\text{Index} = \frac{\text{Actual value of } x_i - \text{Minimum value of } x_i}{\text{Maximum value of } x_i - \text{Minimum value of } x_i}$$

The minimum and maximum values for life expectancy in the HDI are 25 years and 85 years. If life expectancy in a country is 70 years, then the index for longevity is given by $(70 - 25)/(85 - 25) = 0.75$. For literacy the minimum and maximum are 0 percent and 100 percent. If the literacy rate is 60 percent, then the educational attainment index is given by $(60 - 0)/(100 - 0) = 0.6$. The computation of the index for standard of living is more complicated. Until recently, higher levels of per capita GDP were discounted so heavily in the HDI formula that increases in per capita GDP above the world average were virtually ignored. However, a more sensible approach to discounting higher levels of GDP, advocated by Anand and Sen (1994), has now been adopted. All three indexes are bounded between 0 and 1. The overall HDI is constructed by simply taking an average of the three indexes. It, therefore, also is bounded between 0 and 1. One important implication of the extreme form of discounting of real per capita GDP currently used in the HDI is that it will not necessarily correlate that well with real per capita GDP, even though this is one of its three components.

In 2001, the top-ranked countries in the world, according to the HDI, were Norway, Australia, Canada, Sweden, and Belgium. The United States, which usually tops most rankings of income, wealth, or welfare had to settle for sixth place. The reason why the United States is only ranked sixth is because it has a lower life expectancy index than the countries above it. The rankings correlate reasonably well with the World Bank's rankings of wealth. For example, the top 6 countries in the HDI ranking are all among the top-10 richest countries according to the World Bank.

The HDI has two important advantages over the ISEW. The first is its simplicity, which makes it easier for users to understand what it means. Second, unlike the ISEW, it has been computed for a large sample of countries, thus allowing comparisons to be made across countries as well as over time. There are three main criticisms of the HDI. The first is the extreme way in which it discounts GDP (as noted above, the UNDP is in the process of correcting this problem). The second is that it has only three arguments. Although, as noted above, the extreme simplicity of the HDI can be viewed as an advantage, it is at the same time also a disadvantage. The HDI is hardly a comprehensive measure of welfare. Also, it could be argued that there is a certain arbitrariness about the way its three components were selected. The third criticism is the way it combines the three subindexes. It is not clear why equal weight should be given to each of the subindexes. Also, the averaging procedure amounts to adding apples and oranges, since there are no common units. In contrast, all the elements of GDP and the ISEW are measured in dollars (or some other currency) and hence they can be legitimately summed.

12.9 CONCLUSION

There is broad agreement that the current System of National Accounts (SNA) does not take sufficient account of the contribution of natural capital to the economy, nor of the impact of economic activity on the environment. However, rectifying these weaknesses of the SNA is far from easy. Environmental accounting is hampered by a lack of data. It is hard, sometimes verging on impossible, to place a monetary value on natural capital assets that are not traded in the market, and in many cases we cannot even be sure what is happening to the stock of a natural asset over time or exactly how it interacts with the economy. Even when a market price is available, it will not necessarily accurately reflect the marginal benefit of a natural asset to society. The field of environmental accounting also raises a number of difficult conceptual issues, such as the treatment of defensive expenditures, clean-up costs, exploration, and capital gains, all of which are discussed in this chapter. Nevertheless, in recent years, a huge amount of progress has been made. For example, the World Bank has produced estimates of the total value of the produced, natural, and human capital stocks of 92 countries. Such studies have helped to clarify the role of the environment in economic activity. Although the World Bank study had to make a number of assumptions that undermine the credibility of the results, this study should be viewed as a benchmark from which others can build.

NOTES

1   The 1995 European System of National Accounts (ESA), the EU's version of the 1993 SNA, used by all countries in Europe is conceptually identical with the SNA.

2   Strictly speaking this is only true if the relative price of consumption and investment goods is independent of the level of consumption, an assumption that is not that unreasonable for small open economies, and the real interest rate is nondecreasing over time (see Weitzman (1976) and Asheim (1997)).

3   It could be argued that an adjustment should be made for population growth and that what really matters is whether the *per capita* total capital stock is rising or falling over time.

4   According to Peskin and Lutz (1993), this idea, or variants on it, is frequently raised at conferences and workshops on national accounting.

5   The appropriate treatment of unexpected capital gains and losses is discussed later in the chapter.

6   The black economy is included, in principle, even illegal production, although it is obviously difficult to find the relevant data.

7   Eisner (1988) considers how national accounts can be extended to take account of nonmarket productive activities.

8   Natural assets are recognized and recorded in the SNA. The problem is that the depletion of natural assets is not recorded in either the production or capital account, but is relegated to the unfortunately named "other changes in volume of assets account" which is supposed to measure changes in asset values not attributable to transactions. This means that depletion is treated as if it were entirely an unexpected capital loss.

9   One important exception is activities that are educational in nature, such as a parent reading to her children or volunteer literacy programs.

10 This environmentally adjusted version of NDP is sometimes referred to as EDP in the environmental accounting literature (see for example Bartelmus, Stahmer, and van Tongeren (1993)).

11 It should be noted that in principle an adjustment should also be made for depletion or appreciation of the human capital stock. A recent World Bank study discussed later in the chapter attempts to do exactly this.

12 See Aaheim and Nyborg (1995) for a more detailed discussion of these issues, in the context of a polluted river.

13 The confusion on this point can be traced back to misinterpretations of the following quote from Hicks (1946, p. 172): "[D]efine a man's income as the maximum value that he can consume during a week, and still expect to be as well off at the end of the week as he was at the beginning." This statement is ambiguous as to the treatment of unexpected capital gains. Seven pages later Hicks clarifies his position by noting that: "The income which is relevant to conduct must always exclude windfall gains."

14 The case of a variable interest rate is considered in Hill and Hill (2003).

15 It is worth noting that depletion tends to zero as T tends to infinity.

16 See Hartwick (1989) or Hartwick and Hageman (1993) for a proof of this result.

17 THR equals receipts if MR_t and MC_t are both constant. However, in general receipts exceed THR.

18 It should be noted that in general V_t is never known for certain, because it depends on a stream of receipts that may extend indefinitely into the future. Hence $E_{t+1}V_t \neq V_t$.

19 It is important that α should be updated as new information becomes available. In other words the value of α used to computed $E_{t+2}D_{t+1}$ will not necessarily be the same as that used to compute $E_{t+1}D_t$.

20 See World Bank (1995, 1997), Dixon and Hamilton (1996), and Kunte, Hamilton, Dixon, and Clemens (1998).

21 Such a study is undertaken on a smaller scale by Pearce and Atkinson (1995).
22 See also Cobb, Halstead, and Rowe (1995). The Genuine Progress Indicator (GPI) discussed here is closely related to the ISEW.
23 See the Human Development Report published annually by the UNDP. For a critical review of the HDI and how it is constructed, see Anand and Sen (1994) and Gormley (1995).

FURTHER READING

A useful starting point is the "World Bank: Environmental Economics and Indicators" website at http://www-esd.worldbank.org/eei. A number of papers and data relating to sustainability and the valuation of natural capital can be downloaded from this website.

Good surveys of the state of the art in research on environmental accounting are E. Lutz, ed. (1993), *Towards Improved Accounting for the Environment*, Washington, DC: World Bank, and Nordhaus, W. D., and E. C. Kokkelenberg, eds (1999), "Nature's Numbers: Expanding the National Income Accounts to Include the Environment," Washington, DC: National Academy Press. The book by Nordhaus and Kokkelenberg can be downloaded from the website http://www.nap.edu. At a more theoretical level, two useful references are K. A. Brekke (1997), *Economic Growth and the Environment: On the Measurement of Income and Welfare*, Cheltenham, UK and Lyme, US: Edward Elgar, and J. M. Hartwick (2000), *National Accounting and Capital*, Cheltenham, UK and Lyme, US: Edward Elgar.

To find out more about the Human Development Index (HDI), visit the UNDP's website at http://www.undp.org/hdr2001. The Human Development Report and associated research background papers can be downloaded from this website.

The Index of Sustainable Economic Welfare (ISEW) is discussed in Cobb, C. W., and J. B. Cobb, Jr (1994), *The Green National Product: A Proposed Index of Sustainable Economic Welfare*, New York: University Press of America. This book also contains a number of reviews of the ISEW by prominent economists and statisticians.

Daily's (1997) edited book is a useful source on the valuation of ecosystem services. Ecosystem services are also the focus of special issues of the journal *Ecological Economics* in 1998 (25) and 2002 (41), prompted by Costanza et al.'s (1997) controversial paper in the journal *Nature*. An archive of discussion and comments on this paper can be found at http://csf.Colorado.edu/seminars/ecovalue

REFERENCES

Aaheim, A., and Nyborg, K. (1995). On the Interpretation and Applicability of a Green National Product, *Review of Income and Wealth*, 41 (1): 57–71.

Adelman, M. A. (1990). Mineral Depletion, with Special Reference to Petroleum, *Review of Economics and Statistics*, 72 (1): 1–10.

Anand, S., and Sen, A. (1994). Human Development Index: Methodology and Measurement, Occasional Paper 12, New York: United Nations Development Programme.

Asheim, G. B. (1996). Capital Gains and Net National Product in Open Economies, *Journal of Public Economics*, 59: 419–34.

Asheim, G. B. (1997). Adjusting Green NNP to Measure Sustainability, *Scandinavian Journal of Economics*, 99 (3): 355–70.

Bartelmus, P., Stahmer, C., and van Tongeren, J. (1993). Integrated Environmental and Economic Accounting: A Framework for an SNA Satellite System, in E. Lutz, ed., *Towards Improved Accounting for the Environment*, World Bank: Washington, DC, pp. 45–65.

Brekke, K. A. (1997). *Economic Growth and the Environment: On the Measurement of Income and Welfare*, Edward Elgar: Cheltenham, UK and Lyme, US.

Cobb, C. W., and Cobb, J. B., Jr (1994). *The Green National Product: A Proposed Index of Sustainable Economic Welfare*, University Press of America: New York.

Cobb, C., Halstead, T., and Rowe, J. (1995). *The Genuine Progress Indicator: Summary of Data and Methodology*, Redefining Progress: San Francisco.

Costanza, R., d'Arge, R., deGroot, R., Farber, S., Grasso, M., Hannon, B., Limburg, K., Naeem, S., O'Neill, R. V., Paruelo, J., Raskin, R. G., Sutton, P., and van den Belt, M. (1997). The Value of the World's Ecosystem Services and Natural Capital, *Nature*, 387: 253–60.

Daily, G. (1997). *Nature's Services: Societal Dependence on Natural Ecosystems*, Island Press: Washington, DC.

Dasgupta, P. (2001). Valuing Objects and Evaluating Policies in Imperfect Economies, *Economic Journal*, 111 (471): 1–29.

Dixon, J., and Hamilton, K. (1996). Expanding the Measure of Wealth, *Finance and Development*, December: 15–18.

Eisner, R. (1988). Extended Accounts for National Income and Product, *Journal of Economic Literature*, 26: 1611–84.

El Serafy, S. (1989). The Proper Calculation of Income from Depletable Natural Resources, in Y. J. Ahmad, S. El Serafy, and P. Lutz, ed., *Environmental Accounting for Sustainable Development*, World Bank: Washington, DC.

El Serafy, S. (1998). Pricing the Invaluable: The Value of the World's Ecosystem Services and Natural Capital, *Ecological Economics*, 25: 25–7.

Gormley, P. J. (1995). The Human Development Index in 1994: Impact of Income on Country Rank, *Journal of Economic and Social Measurement*, 21: 253–67.

Hartwick, J. M. (2000). *National Accounting and Capital*, Edward Elgar: Cheltenham, UK and Lyme, US.

Hartwick, J. M. (1990). Natural Resources, National Accounting and Economic Depreciation, *Journal of Public Economics*, 43: 291–304.

Hartwick, J. M. (1989). *Non-renewable Resources, Extraction Programs and Markets*, Harwood Academic: Chur, Switzerland.

Hartwick, J. M., and Hageman, A. (1993). Economic Depreciation of Mineral Stocks and the Contribution of El Serafy, in E. Lutz, ed., *Towards Improved Accounting for the Environment*, World Bank: Washington, DC, pp. 211–35.

Hicks, J. R. (1946). *Value and Capital*, second edition, Oxford University Press: Oxford.

Hill, R. J. (2003). Accounting for Unexpected Capital Gains on Natural Assets in Net National Product, Mimeo.

Hill, R. J., and Hill, T. P. (2003). Expectations, Capital Gains and Income, *Economic Inquiry*, 41 (4).

Hotelling, H. (1925). A General Mathematical Theory of Depreciation, *Journal of the American Statistical Association*, September: 340–53.

Hotelling, H. (1931). The Economics of Exhaustible Resources, *Journal of Political Economy* 39 (2), 137–75.

Howarth, R. B., and Farber, S. (2002). Accounting for the Value of Ecosystem Services, *Ecological Economics*, 41: 421–9.

Jaszi, G. (1973). Comment on F. T. Juster, A Framework for the Measurement of Economic and Social Performance, in M. Moss, ed., *The Measurement of Economic and Social Performance*, Columbia University Press: National Bureau of Economic Research, New York, pp. 84–99.

Kunte, A., Hamilton, K., Dixon, J., and Clemens, M. (1998). *Estimating National Wealth: Methodology and Results*, World Bank: Environment Department, Washington, DC.

Kuznets, S. (1946). *National Income: A Summary of Findings*, National Bureau of Economic Research: New York.

Mäler, K.-G. (1991). National Accounts and Environmental Resources, *Environmental and Resource Economics*, 1: 1–15.

Max-Neef, M. (1995). Economic Growth and Quality of Life: A Threshold Hypothesis, *Ecological Economics*, 15: 115–18.

McElroy, M. B. (1976). Capital Gains and Social Income, *Economic Inquiry*, 221–40.

Miller, M. H., and Upton, C. W. (1985). A Test of the Hotelling Valuation Principle, *Journal of Political Economy*, 93: 1–25.

Nehru, V., and Dhareshwar, A. (1993). A New Database on Physical Capital Stock: Sources, Methodology and Results, *Revista de Analisis Economico*, 8 (1), 37–59.

Neumayer, E. (2000). On the Methodology of ISEW, GPI and Related Measures: Some Constructive Suggestions and Some Doubt on the "Threshold" Hypothesis, *Ecological Economics*, 34: 347–61.

Nordhaus, W. D., and Kokkelenberg, E. C. (eds) (1999). *Nature's Numbers: Expanding the National Income Accounts to Include the Environment*, National Academy Press: Washington, DC.

Nordhaus, W. D., and Tobin, J. (1973). Is Growth Obsolete? in M. Moss, ed., *The Measurement of Economic and Social Performance*, National Bureau of Economic Research, Columbia University Press: New York, pp. 509–32.

Nordhaus, W. D., and Tobin, J. (1972). *Economic Growth*, National Bureau of Economic Research, Columbia University Press: New York.

Pearce, D. W., and Atkinson, G. (1995). Measuring Sustainable Development, in D. W. Bromley, ed., *The Handbook of Environmental Economics*, Blackwell: Oxford, UK and Cambridge, USA, pp. 166–81.

Pearce, D. W., and Ulph, D. (1999). A Social Discount Rate for the United Kingdom, in D. W. Pearce, ed., *Economics and Environment: Essays on Ecological Economics and Sustainable Development*, Edward Elgar: Cheltenham, pp. 268–85.

Peskin, H. M., and Lutz, E. (1993). A Survey of Resource and Environmental Accounting Approaches in Industrialized Countries, in E. Lutz, ed., *Toward Improved Accounting for the Environment*, World Bank: Washington, DC, pp. 144–76.

Pezzey, J. (1989). Economic Analysis of Sustainable Growth and Sustainable Development, Environment Department Working Paper No. 15, World Bank.

Repetto, R., McGrath, W., Wells, M., Beer, C., and Rossini F. (1989). *Wasting Assets: Natural Resources in the National Income Accounts*. World Resources Institute: Washington, DC.

Repetto, R. (1992). Accounting for Environmental Assets, *Scientific American*, June: 64–70.

Samuelson, P. A. (1961). The Evaluation of Social Income: Capital Formation and Wealth, in F. A. Lutz and D. C. Hague, eds, *The Theory of Capital*, Proceedings of an IEA Conference, St. Martin's Press: New York.

System of National Accounts (1993). Commission of the European Communities, International Monetary Fund, Organisation for Economic Cooperation and Development, United Nations, World Bank: Brussels/Luxembourg, New York, Paris, Washington, DC.

Thage, B. (1991). The National Accounts and the Environment, Paper presented at the International Association for Research in Income and Wealth IARIW Special Conference on Environmental Accounting, Baden, Austria, May.

Turner, R. K., Adger, W. N., and Brouwer, R. (1998). Ecosystem Services Value, Research Needs, and Policy Relevance: A Commentary, *Ecological Economics*, 25: 61–5.

United Nations Development Programme (2001). *Human Development Report*, Oxford University Press: New York.

United Nations Development Programme (1997). *Human Development Report*, Oxford University Press: New York.

Vincent, J. R., Panayotou, T., and Hartwick, J. M. (1997). Resource Depletion and Sustainability in Small Open Economies, *Journal of Environmental Economics and Management*, 33, 274–86.

Weitzman, M. L. (1976). On the Welfare Significance of National Product in a Dynamic Economy, *Quarterly Journal of Economics* 90, 156–62.

Woolcock, M., and Narayan, D. (2000). Social Capital: Implications for Development Theory, Research and Policy, *The World Bank Research Observer*, 15 (2): 225–49.

World Bank (2002). *World Development Report 2002: Building Institutions for Markets*, Oxford University Press: New York.

World Bank (1997). *Expanding the Measure of Wealth: Indicators of Environmentally Sustainable Development*, World Bank: Environment Department, Washington, DC.

World Bank (1995). *Monitoring Environmental Progress: A Report on Work in Progress*, World Bank: Environmentally Sustainable Development Series, Washington, DC.

World Commission on Environment and Development (1987). *Our Common Future*, Oxford University Press: New York.

Young, M. (1993). Natural Resource Accounting: Some Australian Experiences and Observations, in E. Lutz, ed., *Toward Improved Accounting for the Environment*, World Bank: Washington, DC, pp. 177–83.

CHAPTER THIRTEEN

TRADE AND ENVIRONMENT

The need to ensure that trade and environment policies are mutually supportive is more pressing today than ever before. However, successful integration of these policies can only be achieved through a constructive dialogue based on far broader awareness and understanding of the complex inter-linkages between trade and our environment. (Dr. Klaus Töpfer, Executive Director, UNEP, 2000)

13.1 INTRODUCTION

Over the last fifty years or so, successive rounds of negotiations under the *General Agreement on Tariffs and Trade (GATT)* have meant that *trade liberalization* has proceeded at a rapid pace, bringing with it economic growth. At the same time as the global economy has grown fourfold, world trade has grown by a factor of fourteen (UNEP, 2000). The value of international trade now measures over $6 trillion (US$) per year (UNEP, 2000). In this chapter we will look at the implications for the environment of increased international trade. In particular, the issue of concern is whether free (or freer) trade causes a deterioration of the natural environment. On the one hand, trade may increase world pollution and make people worse off by raising the scale of economic activity and altering the *composition* of commodity production in such as way as to provide incentives for polluting industries to locate in developing countries with low environmental standards (Daly and Goodland, 1994). On the other hand, income gains associated with freer trade may increase both an individual country's well-being, as well as global utility, and, in this way, lead to an increasing demand for environmental quality (see chapter 11).

In the face of these apparently conflicting influences of international trade, an important question to ask is whether traditional gains from *trade liberalization* may be outweighed by damages to the environment from increased pollution. To do this we need to look at the linkages between the environment and trade. Three key types of linkages are:

1 International trade affects the level and pattern of production and consumption of goods in different countries. If these production/consumption activities result in externalities that harm the local environment of the countries where this production and consumption take place, then trade will adversely affect the environment. Thus, trade can cause a change in the amount of *local pollution*, that is, pollution that is contained within a given country or location.
2 Externalities related to production and consumption activities in one country can affect the environment of other countries, leading to an increase in the amount of *global pollution*. While this could arise in the absence of trade, local efforts to employ environmental policies may have trade implications. Alternatively, trade policies can be used in retaliation to reduce exposure to harmful pollution. This linkage may encourage governments to distort their environmental policies as a surrogate for trade policies. That is, they may face pressure to reduce tough environmental policies for fear of losing market share.
3 International trade policies may be used to enforce international environmental agreements and provide a multilateral approach to solving *global pollution* problems. The *World Health Organization (WHO)* and *GATT* along with the *Kyoto protocol* are examples of this. A stumbling block is the issue of the role of ethics and equality (particularly of poor and rich nations).

This chapter examines the role of international trade in affecting the amount of pollution and ultimately the quality of the environment. The chapter is structured as follows. First, a simple non-feedback model of trade and environment will be examined in order to fix ideas and present the results of the early literature. This model tells only a portion of the story, however, since it concentrates upon the effects of trade upon a single country and has no feedback from the rest of the world. In addition, this model is concerned solely with *local pollution* effects. Second, an extended model is presented which allows us to examine in a more general way the issue of whether *trade liberalization* is good for the environment. This model permits us to look at the impact of trade upon two small countries[1] and to examine the *composition effect* of trade, whereby free trade encourages the shifting of commodity production (along with attendant pollution) to the country with lower environmental standards. We will see the implications for pollution levels in the two countries of free trade. Third, by modifying this extended model we can identify two further effects upon pollution associated with a movement from *autarky* to free trade. The scale effect works to increase *local pollution* through expansion of the economy while the technique effect arises from a greater desire to have a cleaner environment at higher income levels. Fourth, the implications of these three effects are examined in the case of *global pollution*. Fifth, we turn to look at the imperfect competition model of trade and the environment to obtain some new insights into policy options. This model incorporates game theory tools to examine issues about strategic government policy towards the environment. Finally, the chapter concludes with some empirical evidence about the role of international trade and the environment and the efforts to combat *global pollution* with *multilateral agreements*.

13.2 A SIMPLE COMPARATIVE ADVANTAGE MODEL OF TRADE AND THE ENVIRONMENT

As early as 1972 worries about potential adverse environmental impacts resulting from *trade liberalization* were expressed at the United Nations Conference on Development and Environment (Stockholm Conference). This spurred many economists to examine these issues within the context of standard trade theory models. In these models, the drivers behind trade were the presence of either differential labor productivities (according to the Ricardian view of the world) or differences in relative factor abundance (according to the Hecksher–Ohlin view). In either case, any such differences would ultimately lead to *comparative advantages* in different products and potential gains from trade through the exploitation of free trade. It was natural to incorporate the environment into these standard trade models as a factor of production and observe how free trade altered the *composition* of goods production (and environmental effects) from some initial *autarky* position.[2]

Model components

We first examine the impact of trade upon the environment with a simple model that describes how a small country – which we call Home – produces two goods using a single resource. It is assumed that the rest of the world does not respond strategically to domestic environmental regulation or trade policy reform and that the world price is taken as given by producers and consumers. In addition, it is assumed that there is a single local – that is, specific to the Home country – environmental externality such that emissions are proportional to output. A number of authors including Siebert (1977), Pethig (1978), Baumol and Oates (1988), Krutilla (1991), Anderson (1992) have used variants of this model to describe either a *small open economy* case or a large open economy case. We concentrate upon the former in this exposition and note at the end the implications of the large open economy situation in which a country must be mindful of the impact of additional production upon the world price of its export commodity.

We begin our discussion with a description of the production side of our small country.[3] We assume that two commodities (x and y) are produced using a single resource (k). Each production function is subject to diminishing marginal returns, where F' indicates the first derivative of the function with respect to its argument and F'' represents the second derivative.

$$x = F(k); \quad F' > 0 \text{ and } F'' < 0$$
$$y = G(k); \quad G' > 0 \text{ and } G'' < 0$$
(1)

Production of either commodity results in the emission of a single pollutant (pe), although in differing amounts, according to the following pollution emissions functions.

$$pe^x = H(x); \quad H' > 0 \text{ and } H'' \geq 0$$
$$pe^y = J(y); \quad J' > 0 \text{ and } J'' \geq 0$$
(2)

In addition to producing the two goods, the resource (k) can be diverted away from commodity production and used to reduce the amount of emissions according to an abatement technology function specific to each commodity. However, the country is constrained by the overall amount of k available for use in four different activities: production of commodities x and y, abatement of pollution in the x industry, and abatement of pollution in the y industry. It is useful to define a^x as the amount of pollution abated when k is used to reduce pollution associated with the production of commodity x, while a^y is the amount of pollution abated when k is used to reduce pollution associated with the production of commodity y.

$$a^x = R(k_x^a); \quad R' > 0 \text{ and } R'' > 0$$
$$a^y = S(k_y^a); \quad S' > 0 \text{ and } S'' > 0$$
(3)

Net emissions associated with the production of x (n^x) are defined as the difference between pollution emissions from x production (pe^x) and emissions abated in x production (a^x). Net emissions associated with the production of y (n^y) are defined similarly.

$$n^x = pe^x - a^x$$
$$n^y = pe^y - a^y$$
(4)

The total ambient level of pollution (z) in the local environment is the sum of pollutants associated with the net emissions from the production of the two goods.

$$z = n^x + n^y$$
(5)

Finally, we need to add a relationship describing the linkage between the total ambient level of pollutant in the country and environmental quality (q). We assume, in particular, that increasing pollution lowers environmental quality at a decreasing rate.

$$q = N(z); \quad N' < 0, \ N'' < 0$$
(6)

In order to complete the production side of the model we assume the existence of representative firms that produce either x or y. These firms are assumed to maximize profits subject to given commodity and factor prices.

We turn our attention next to the consumers in the small country. They are assumed to be identical. The representative demand functions for x and y are given as follows.

$$c^x = C^x(p, I) \quad \text{where} \quad p = \frac{p^x}{p^y} \quad \text{and} \quad I = px + y$$
$$c^y = C^y(p, I) \tag{7}$$

To simplify the model it is assumed that I is both gross national income (under the assumption that the government simply transfers any tax revenue earned from trade or pollution taxes to consumers) and personal disposable income. Consumers are assumed to maximize utility subject to their budget constraints.

With the producer and consumer parts of the model defined we now analyze the impact of *trade liberalization* upon both welfare and pollution for the small country called Home. We assume the small country has a *comparative advantage* in commodity x, but make no assumptions yet about the relative degree of pollution created by either commodity. However, we do assume to start that the government of the home country does not impose an emissions or pollution tax to deal with the externality associated with the production of either commodity.

We begin from a no-trade position and then allow trade to take place between the small country and the rest of the world. We know that this requires specialization in the production of x, thereby requiring a reduction in y production as dictated by the overall resource constraint, k. Our goal is to examine the overall welfare impact upon the country of this *trade liberalization*. We assume that welfare in the small country is determined by level of the service flows from environmental quality, q, and from consumption of the two commodities x and y.[4]

$$W = W(x, y, q) \tag{8}$$

Assuming profit maximization for firms and utility maximization for consumers, then prior to any trade between countries, the Home country must produce all of the x and y which domestic consumers wish to purchase at the *autarky* price. In these circumstances, the relative price of x represents the domestic opportunity cost. Exports and imports are zero by definition.

Once trade takes place between the small country and the rest of the world, the balance of payments must be in equilibrium with the country exporting one commodity and importing another at the fixed world relative trading price $\tilde{p}$. Comparison of the domestic opportunity cost of production with the world relative trading price determines the commodity in which the country has a *comparative advantage*. For the purposes of this analysis, we have assumed this to be commodity x. So, the Home country will import commodity y with the introduction of free trade. The equilibrium condition establishing the post-trade situation is expressed below where e^x is the amount of x exported and m^y is the amount of y imported by the Home country.

$$\tilde{p}e^x + m^y = 0; \quad \text{where } e^x = c^x - x < 0 \text{ and } m^y = c^y - y > 0 \tag{9}$$

Welfare impacts of free trade

We are now in a position to determine the impact upon the Home country's welfare when it moves to a free trade situation from an *autarky* position. We totally differentiate the welfare function identified earlier in equation (8). After making substitutions from the equations described above, the following expression gives the change in welfare.

$$dW = \left[\frac{\partial W}{\partial y} \left(\tilde{p} \frac{dx}{dy} + 1 \right) + \frac{\partial W}{\partial q} N' \left(H' \frac{dx}{dy} + J' \right) \right] dy \tag{10}$$

Since we assume that the country has a *comparative advantage* in x, then, dy will be less than zero. Thus, the expression above tells us what happens to welfare when y decreases. The first part of the right-hand side will be positive as long as the world relative trading price for x is greater than the home price (or the marginal rate of transformation between x and y). This is the standard trade result which asserts that the country gains from trade relative to an *autarky* position by exploiting its *comparative advantage*.

Now, we must consider the impact of additional pollution arising from greater x production upon environmental quality and whether losses here offset trade gains. This impact is considered in the second part of the right-hand side. We can rewrite the term in round brackets as follows, using the functions already defined:

$$H'F' < J'G' \tag{11}$$

The term on the left-hand side of equation (11) describes the marginal increase in pollution in the Home country arising from a marginal increment of the resource (k) devoted to the production of x, while the right-hand side measures the same for y. There are now two cases to be considered.

For case 1 we assume that y is the more pollution-intensive commodity, so fortuitously the country specializes in the production of the less pollution-intensively produced commodity, x. In this case, the right-hand side element that is in brackets is greater than zero. Taken with the earlier trade result, the Home country unequivocally gains from trade since *local pollution* is reduced.

For case 2 we assume that x is the more pollution-intensive commodity. Now, as the country specializes in the production of the "dirtier" good, the gains to welfare from trade are offset by a reduction in environmental quality since the second part of the RHS from equation (10) is negative. This outcome has a policy implication first suggested by D'Arge and Kneese (1972). Suppose we interpret k (the single resource) as a measure of the *assimilative capacity* of a country. Furthermore, assume that the greater the *endowment* of k a country has, then the greater the likelihood that it has a *comparative advantage* in the production of a pollution-intensive commodity. Then, D'Arge and Kneese argue that countries with relatively large environmental assimilative capacities should specialize in and export goods that are relatively pollution-intensive in their production.

One additional outcome can arise. While trade gains are expected in general to be larger than pollution losses, it is possible for trade to reduce welfare when environmental quality losses swamp the trade gains. This can occur when the consumers of the Home country have strong environmental quality preferences and are faced with a steep marginal damage function associated with the production of x.

Environmental policy

As we know from chapter 2, in the absence of well defined and complete property rights to environmental resources, the production of the commodity x (or y) ignores the opportunity cost associated with the degradation of the environment through pollution emissions. The interesting implication of this from a trade perspective is that it may give an inappropriate *comparative advantage* to the small country in the production of a relatively pollution-intensive commodity if the Home country does not try to correct the externality.

In our earlier model we assumed that the Home country did not attempt to solve its environmental problem through the use of some type of economic instrument. In contrast, we will now assume that the small country (Home) uses a pollution tax to correct for the presence of the externality that leads to pollution from the production of commodity x. This may change the extent of its comparative advantage and alter welfare. Assuming that the rest of the world does not adopt any environmental policies, we can examine how the Home country's welfare will change with the adoption of a pollution tax.

Let us assume that the Home country imposes a pollution tax upon the producers of commodity x at the rate of t per unit of emissions. We want to compare the impact of this tax upon welfare relative to a status quo in which free trade takes place. It is instructive to identify the changes that are induced by the introduction of such a pollution tax. First, the tax causes a reduction in the production of commodity x and, along with this, a reduction in the amount of resource k used for production in that sector, and finally a reduction in pollution emitted. Second, exports will fall, along with national income since resources are transferred either to abatement activities in x or to the production of y. Third, environmental quality increases. Therefore, there is a trade-off between improvements in environmental quality and a loss of gains from trade.

While we have identified the presence of a trade-off, the impact upon overall welfare must still be determined. The following expression shows how overall welfare is affected by the introduction of the environmental tax. Note that dI/dt is less than zero as discussed above.

$$\frac{dW}{dt} = \left(\frac{\partial W}{\partial c^y} + \frac{\partial W}{\partial q}\frac{N'}{t}\right)\frac{dI}{dt} \tag{12}$$

In looking at equation (12) we see that the sign of dW/dt depends upon the relative strengths of the two elements in the brackets. It is useful to rewrite these elements in the following way.

$$t\frac{\partial W}{\partial c^y} \quad \text{and} \quad -\frac{\partial W}{\partial q}N' \tag{13}$$

The term on the right-hand side is the marginal environmental damage prevented by imposition of the tax. The term on the left-hand side is the value of the emissions tax in real terms (actual units of good y) evaluated with respect to the marginal utility of commodity y. If the small country employs an environmental tax policy such that the tax is set equal to the marginal damage cost, then welfare is unchanged relative to the free trade position level of welfare. Whether the country is closed or open, it should still follow the well-known rule whereby the emission tax is set according to marginal damage prevented. Thus, the *first-best solution* in the case of *local pollution* is to encourage free trade by reducing *tariff* and other barriers and to pursue local environmental externalities with *Pigouvian taxes*. Provided that environmental policies truly internalize environmental damages, then free trade can benefit all countries.[5]

It is interesting to note, however, the potential impact upon the small Home country's welfare when it does not choose the optimal Pigouvian tax. Note that we can rewrite equation (13) as follows:

$$\frac{dW}{dt} \gtreqqless 0: \quad t\frac{\partial W}{\partial c^y} \lesseqqgtr -\frac{\partial W}{\partial q}N' \tag{14}$$

As equation (14) shows welfare will increase with the introduction of a pollution tax that at the initial free trade situation is less than optimal (in this situation the marginal social costs of producing a commodity (private plus external costs) are higher than the value of the commodity). We might well ask whether this can give rise to a situation in which countries may deliberately choose dirty policies and keep environmental taxes too low. Countries may become *pollution havens* when they use weak environmental policies in order to keep their *comparative advantages* (Daly and Goodland, 1994). This issue will be discussed later in the section that evaluates the extant empirical work on the linkages between trade and the environment.

Krutilla (1991) extended this simple model in order to examine the situation in which a large country with *local pollution* moves from an *autarky* to a free trade outcome. In doing so he was faced with an additional complication, namely, the world relative trading price can no longer be assumed to be fixed. The large country has an additional *terms-of-trade effect* that is irrelevant in the small open country case. The *first-best* outcome from the point of view of the large country is to use optimal Pigouvian taxes to deal with local pollution and to use a *tariff* that is inversely proportional to the elasticity of the demand for the country's net imports. The *second-best outcome* is somewhat different (Markusen, 1975; Krutilla, 1991). In this case, pollution taxes should differ from marginal damage costs. The government should set its pollution tax at a rate that is greater than the marginal social damage cost for the good in which it is a net exporter. By doing this the country is exerting its market power and earning a higher price by forcing producers to pass their higher environmental costs on to foreign purchasers. The opposite policy works best for the case in which the large country is a net importer of a good.

13.3   AN EXTENDED MODEL OF TRADE AND THE ENVIRONMENT

Model components

While the simple model described in the previous section can be used to explore some aspects of the relationship between trade and the environment, it effectively ignores the foreign trading partner of the Home country. Furthermore, it does not lend itself easily to modifications that permit a more complex set of relationships to be described. In this section and the next, a series of models developed by Copeland and Taylor (1994, 1995) and Copeland (2000) are examined. These models exploit duality relationships and employ specific functional forms to produce a more flexible and detailed model. The advantage of these extended models is that they are capable of exploring the separate impacts upon the environment of three particular effects arising from trade, and in particular, freer trade. These three effects are the ones noted in the introductory remarks. In particular, we will look at the separate impacts of the *composition*, technique, and scale effects. The basic model is presented first which allows the *composition effect* to be highlighted. Following this the extensions to the model necessary to obtain the *technique* and *scale effects* are presented.

To begin our discussion of this extended model, we again consider the production of two commodities, x and y and look first at a small country called Home. We assume that Home has an initial *endowment* of two *non-mobile factors*, labor (l) and capital (k). Commodity y is produced only with labor at a one-to-one rate,[6] while x is produced using a constant returns to scale technology employing both capital and environmental services. This model differs from the earlier one in section 10.2 in that, rather than focusing upon pollution as output, we shift our focus to consider environmental resources as inputs in the form of *assimilative capacity*.[7] It is assumed that one unit of environmental services employed in producing x is equal to one unit of pollution (z). To simplify the discussion, particular functional forms are chosen for the production functions. They are shown below.

$$x = F(k, z) = \min (\lambda k, k^{1 - \beta} z^{\beta}); \lambda > 0$$

$$y = G(l) = l$$

(15)

If we concentrate upon the production function for x, we see that there is an implicit trade-off between the level of emissions and the level of output x. Since k is fixed at some initial *endowment* level, then the maximum output of commodity x that Home could make would occur if no effort was made to abate pollution. Output of x would be λk and pollution would be $z = \lambda^{1/\beta} k$. As in the earlier model, in order to reduce pollution, some amount of k must be diverted to abatement, thereby reducing the production of x.

We will also assume that the technologies are the same in the foreign country, just as we did with the earlier model. Moreover, the price of commodity x is assumed to be p, since it is possible to make commodity y the numeraire good and to set its price equal to one. Finally, both the home country and the foreign country are assumed to produce some positive amount of commodity y.[8]

Turning to consumers in the home country, we assume that they get negative utility from the level of pollution, but gain positive utility from consuming both goods, x and y. Assuming *homothetic preferences* and that utility is strongly separable with respect to consumption of x and y and pollution, we have the utility function for a representative consumer:

$$U = U(x, y, z) = \ln(x^{\alpha} y^{1 - \alpha}) - \frac{\eta z^{\gamma}}{\gamma}$$

(16)

In this specification, environmental quality is a normal good and demand functions are linear in income.[9] When γ is greater than one, then the marginal willingness-to-pay for pollution reduction is a non-decreasing function of pollution levels.

In subsequent analysis it is useful to have an alternative formulation of the demand function. This is provided by the dual *indirect utility function* (see chapter 8) shown below. An implicit assumption in this formulation is that the elasticity of marginal damage from additional pollution with respect to income is one.

$$V = \ln \left(\frac{I}{p^{\alpha}} \right) - \frac{\eta z^{\gamma}}{\gamma} \quad \text{with} \quad \gamma \geq 1 \text{ and } \eta > 0$$

(17)

Autarky in the extended model

We begin by observing the Home country in *autarky* producing the quantities of x and y that are demanded by the population. Since relative production is what matters, it assists us to express the relative supply (*RS*) of x to y as shown below on the left-hand side of equation (18). The relative demand (*RD*) of x to y is shown on the right-hand side.

$$RS = \frac{F(k, z)}{l} = \frac{\alpha}{(1 - \alpha)p} = RD \tag{18}$$

Rather than assume a particular price to start as we did in the earlier model, we solve for the autarky price by equating the relative supply of x to y to the relative demand for x to y. These equations solve for the relative price of commodity x (namely, p) which is

$$p = \frac{\alpha l}{(1 - \alpha)F(k, z)} \tag{19}$$

It is now a straightforward matter to define national income as the value of domestic output. We are implicitly assuming that any revenue earned by the government either through pollution taxes or *tariffs* is transferred in lump sum form to consumers.

$$I = px + y = \frac{l}{(1 - \alpha)} \tag{20}$$

It is now possible to establish the conditions for optimal environmental policy for the Home country in autarky. From chapter 3 we know that, in the absence of trade, the government should choose a pollution tax that will internalize the external damage associated with the production of x. From the *indirect utility function* we can easily find the marginal damage associated with the production of one more unit of x. The optimal tax level (t) will be the one that is equal to the marginal damage. As equation (21) shows, the optimal tax is dependent upon the income level and increases as national income rises. Thus, as the Home country becomes wealthier the optimal pollution tax should increase.

$$t = \eta z^{\gamma - 1} I \tag{21}$$

Suppose the government imposes such a pollution tax upon the production of commodity x. Firms in this industry respond by setting their marginal benefit from polluting (that is, the marginal profit earned by producing one more unit of pollution-creating output, x) equal to the tax t. As a result, the efficient level of domestic pollution in an autarky situation occurs simply where the firm's marginal benefit from pollution is equated to the marginal damage to consumers. The resulting efficient level of pollution in autarky is given by:

$$z^A = \left(\frac{\alpha\beta}{\eta}\right)^{1/\gamma} \tag{22}$$

As equation (22) shows, under the particular assumptions described above for this model, the optimal level of pollution is independent of the level of income and also the amount of resources, k and l.[10] In this model, growth (which can be thought of as an increase in the country's *endowment* of resources leading to higher national income) has no effect on pollution. What growth does do, however, is increase the marginal damage and marginal benefit curves in proportion, thereby leading to higher optimal environmental taxes as growth occurs. The important prediction from this model is that higher income countries are expected to adopt more stringent environmental policies leading to higher pollution taxes. In essence, the environment is a relatively more scarce resource as the economy grows. It thereby follows that it is a more highly valued resource in higher income countries. This means that, if the Home country is assumed to be the higher income country because it has more resources or more productive resources, it will have a *comparative advantage* in the production of the clean good, y.

Free trade in the extended model: the composition effect

We can now look at what happens when free trade takes place between the Home country and its trading partner, the Foreign country. As in the earlier model, we will assume that the pollution produced by commodity x production is local, although this assumption is relaxed later in the chapter to allow for *global pollution*. In addition, we will assume that the Home country continues to internalize its environmental externality optimally as discussed above. In particular, this means that it does not use environmental policy to pursue trade goals.

When the Home country begins to trade with the Foreign country, the combination of the *comparative advantages* of the two countries will dictate changes to the *composition* of Home's domestic output (that is, the relative amounts of the polluting commodity, x, and the clean commodity, y) and direct the flow of trade. For simplicity, we will assume that the countries are identical in terms of their production functions. Therefore, any comparative advantage that exists will be determined by relative *endowments* of resources. As mentioned above, it is useful to think about such endowments as being tantamount to the wealth or income of the country.

Using the superscript H to designate variables relating to the Home country and F to designate variables relating to the Foreign country, we again work with relative production levels. In particular, we have the following relationship showing the ratio of Home relative supply to Foreign relative supply:[11]

$$\frac{x^H/y^H}{x^F/y^F} = \left(\frac{k^\sigma/l}{(k^F)^\sigma/l^F}\right)\left(\frac{I^F}{I}\right)^{\beta/(\gamma-\beta)} \tag{24}$$

In this equation σ is defined as being equal to $\gamma(1-\beta)/(\gamma-\beta)$ and this must be greater than zero. Recall that we assume that gamma γ is greater than or equal to one, thereby ensuring that the marginal willingness-to-pay for reductions in pollution levels is a non-decreasing function of those same levels.

Examination of equation (24) shows that, for the situation in which the two countries have identical production functions, the ratio of Home supply of commodities relative to Foreign supply is determined by the ratio of Foreign to Home income alone. In particular, if we assume the Home country to have more income, then it will have a relatively smaller supply of the pollution creating commodity x since the environment will be a relatively scarce factor. Thus, the Home country will have a *comparative advantage* in the clean good y, while the Foreign country will have a *comparative advantage* in the dirty good (x).[12]

After free trade has taken place, the relative price of good x will rise in the Foreign country and, because of its *comparative advantage*, the Foreign country will produce more of this commodity. This will increase *local pollution* in the Foreign country. However, the relative price of good x will fall in the Home country, thereby leading to reduced production and Home pollution. As was mentioned earlier, this model rules out the possibility of growth through free trade as having an impact upon pollution in either country. The only impact that the introduction of free trade may have upon pollution in either the Home or Foreign country is by altering a country's relative production of so-called clean to so-called *dirty goods*, where the latter produce more pollution per unit than do the former. This is called a *composition effect*, which describes changes in the importance of polluting industries in a country once free trade is introduced. When such a shifting of polluting activity from the home country to the foreign country arises from differences in the degree of stringency of pollution regulation, it is known as the *Pollution Haven Hypothesis*.[13] Thus, free trade would result in welfare gains for the Home country consisting of gains from trade and gains from better environmental quality. The Foreign country would have its gains from trade tempered by losses from worse environmental quality.[14]

Free trade in the extended model: composition, scale and technique effects

We now need to address how free trade affects a country's growth and income and, via changes in these key components, its level of pollution. Thus, in addition to the *composition effect*, free trade may give rise to two additional avenues through which pollution is affected. The first may result from income growth induced by free trade. This is called the *scale effect*. It is associated with the increase in overall pollution created by an increase in the level of economic activity.[15] The second effect may reduce the impact of the first, however. It is called the *technique effect*. It comes into play since it is assumed that consumers view environmental quality as a normal good. Accordingly, increases in income will result in an increased willingness to pay higher abatement costs. The government will be able to increase pollution taxes which will, in turn, encourage firms to undertake more abatement. In this way, pollution per unit of output will decline.

While the concept of these three separate effects first found voice in empirical work by Grossman and Krueger (1991), it was not until the 1994 model, and its companion model (1995), that Copeland and Taylor developed an approach capable of encompassing all three effects. The model is essentially an extension of the previous one, but it allows for a continuum of goods to be produced by both a Home country and a Foreign country. The continuum of goods is ordered according to the degree of pollution created during their production. Thus, assuming that a possible I different goods called x can be produced, each good is produced according to the following production function:

$$x_i = x(z, k, i) = \begin{cases} k^{1-\alpha(i)} z^{\alpha(i)} & \text{if } z \leq \lambda k \\ 0 & \text{if } z > \lambda k \end{cases} \qquad (25)$$

This differs from the earlier production function for the single good x in the following two ways. First, the degree of dirtiness in production is no longer a constant (β) since it can now take on different values according to the particular good in the set of I different goods. β is assumed to be greater than zero and less than one and the higher the value of β, the more pollution-intensive the production of a good. Second, the existence of a single, *non-mobile*, resource k is assumed. It is simplest to think of this as the effective labor of a country. For the purposes of what follows next, we will assume that the Home country has relatively more effective labor than the Foreign country.[16]

Given the assumption above, it will be assumed that two countries differ only in their incomes according to the amount of effective labor available in the two countries. As before, the country with the higher income will choose a higher pollution tax. Prior to trade both countries will produce some amounts of both goods if there is local demand for them. However, after free trade, relative production of the goods, x_i, will adjust to the point that the relatively *dirty goods* (high β values) will be produced in the low-income, low-pollution tax country, while the relatively clean goods will be produced in the high-income, high-pollution tax country. As a consequence, pollution will fall in the high-income country and increase in the low-income country. Furthermore, given the relative changes in production after specialization of production has taken place, overall pollution will increase.

It is then possible to show (Copeland and Taylor, 1994) that each country's change in overall pollution arising from the adjustment from autarky to free trade can be decomposed into the three effects: *composition, technique, and scale.*

$$dZ = \frac{\partial Z}{\partial I}dI + \frac{\partial Z}{\partial t}dt + \frac{\partial Z}{\partial \bar{i}}d\bar{i} \tag{26}$$

The first term represents the *scale effect*, namely, the increase in pollution that arises from increased economic activity because of free trade, holding constant the abating technologies and the composition of a country's final output. This effect is positive and described by:

$$\frac{\partial Z}{\partial I} = \frac{\theta(\bar{i})}{t\varphi(\bar{i})} \tag{27}$$

In this equation, θ $(\bar{i})$ represents the share of the Home country's pollution taxes in world income; i overbar represents the pollution-intensity which represents the cross-over point of production for the two countries, Home and Foreign. Namely, all goods with a pollution intensity less than i overbar will be produced in the high-income, low-pollution Home environment. Thus, this represents the status quo *composition* of world production after free trade. The symbol t represents the optimal pollution tax in the Home country and $\varphi(\bar{i})$ is the share of world spending on Home's goods.

The second term represents the *technique effect*. This shows what happens to pollution in the Home country when firms adopt more effective abatement technologies, while holding constant income and the composition of goods produced in the Home country. This effect is negative and its magnitude depends upon the elasticities of substitution in production and consumption. Larger elasticities (greater than one) are expected to lead to larger technique effects.

$$\frac{\partial Z}{\partial \tau} = -\frac{I\theta(\bar{i})}{t^2\varphi(\bar{i})} \tag{28}$$

The third term indicates the impact of the *composition effect* that we discussed earlier in the context of the two-goods production model. In the case of multiple goods, this effect describes the relationship between changes in a country's *local pollution* level and changes in the range of goods produced by that country.

$$\frac{\partial Z}{\partial \bar{i}} = Z\left[\frac{\theta'(\bar{i})}{\theta(\bar{i})} - \frac{\varphi'(\bar{i})}{\varphi(\bar{i})}\right] = \frac{Is(\bar{i})}{t\varphi(\bar{i})^2}\int_0^{\bar{i}}[\beta(\bar{i}) - \beta(i)]s(\bar{i})di \tag{29}$$

In this equation $s(\bar{i})$ represents the share of domestically produced goods to total consumption for the Home country. The sign on equation (29) is positive and indicates that, holding constant income and pollution taxes, if the Home country were to produce a greater range of goods, this would lead to an increase in pollution in the Home country. This arises because the production of marginal goods leads the Home country into those goods that are more polluting.

In order to determine what happens to pollution in the Home country with the advent of free trade, it is necessary to consider the overall impact of the three effects. The *composition effect* will always dominate the *technique* and *scale effects* and, so, free trade will increase pollution. In effect, the *technique effect* will offset the *scale effect* since the marginal willingness-to-pay for pollution is equal to one.[17] However, the country will still enjoy gains from trade from selling commodities to the Foreign country. Hence, free trade unequivocally increases welfare.

It is instructive to look at the impact of growth in the model presented above. Symmetric growth (equi-proportional growth in resources) does not affect world pollution because the *scale effect* is offset by the *technique effect*. Furthermore, equi-proportional growth in both the Home and Foreign country mean that there is no reallocation of goods production and, hence, no *composition effect*. All that happens is that pollution taxes are higher in response to higher incomes.

A more interesting situation is one in which the Home and Foreign countries grow at different rates, perhaps because of the stock effects associated with different levels of human capital at the outset or perhaps through a country's efforts to attract more human capital. In the event that the Home country initially has the higher level of income and this grows more quickly than income in the Foreign country, then the Home country's pollution will increase. This occurs because, in the face of faster income growth, the Home country encourages out-migration of Foreign industries to the Home country. The composition effect requires a wider range of goods to be produced in the Home country, thereby increasing its pollution through the composition effect. Pollution also increases in the Foreign country since it is the cleanest industries that leave that country. Thus, the average pollution intensity increases in the Foreign country.[18] Overall, then, world pollution increases.

13.4 GLOBAL POLLUTION AND FREE TRADE

The results from the previous model are dependent upon a key assumption; namely, that pollution is local to each of the countries and, hence, world pollution is simply the sum of *local pollution* levels. In this case, each country need only take account of its domestic circumstances in the setting of optimal pollution taxes. Free trade works side-by-side with environmental policy to make consumers in all countries better off. However, many of the world's most pressing environmental problems such as climate change and greenhouse gas emissions are global in nature (see chapter 14). Global externalities raise the possibility of strategic or gaming behavior on the part of countries involved in trading. A model that captures the key elements of such concerns will now be presented and discussed.

Following Copeland and Taylor (1995), it is useful to cast the actors in this model in terms of a number of countries (c) in the so-called Northern Region (who have greater *endowments* of human capital or effective labor) and a number of different countries (c^*) in the so-called Southern Region. With the exception of human capital endowments, all other factors are assumed to be identical across the regions. Furthermore, assume that there are a number of countries in each of the two regions so that the case of a large number of countries can be observed.[19] As in the previous model allowance is made for each country in each region to produce a range of different goods, which can be ordered in terms of their degree of pollution emissions.

Consumers in each of the countries are assumed to have identical consumption functions that depend upon goods consumed and aggregate world pollution. This differs from the assumption made in the previous model where only *local pollution* entered the utility function for a particular country. World pollution is considered to be a *public bad*. The *indirect utility function* counterpart to equation (17) for this new situation of multiple consumer goods and an aggregate bad is given as follows. This is for a representative consumer in one country, j.

$$V = \int_0^1 s(i)\ln[s(i)]di - \int_0^1 s(i)\ln[p(i)]di + \ln(I_j) - \frac{\eta\left(\sum_{k=1}^{c+c^*} Z_k\right)^\gamma}{\gamma} \tag{30}$$

As before $s(i)$ represents a budget share function which determines the relative shares of the "*I*" goods in total expenditures, while $p(i)$ is the schedule of prices for the *I* goods. I_j is the national income of country *j* and, as before, this is equal to factor income plus revenue earned from implementing pollution taxes or permits. The final term represents the disutility associated with *global pollution* produced by summing pollution from all countries where $(c + c^*)$ is the sum of all countries in the two regions.

Given the existence of a global bad that gives disutility to consumers of all regions, we need to put some structure on the manner in which a country's regulators might respond. The simplest way to model their behavior is as a *non-cooperative Nash equilibrium*. Thus, the regulators in each country are assumed to treat pollution in the rest of the world as given when they determine the optimal amount of locally produced goods and, hence, pollution. In this case, the most straightforward form of regulation for a country is to introduce a system of fixed, but *transferable, pollution permits* that define the optimal local pollution level. Thus, the goal of a country will be to maximize consumer utility through its choice of local pollution level, holding constant the pollution levels of all other countries. This results in the setting of the number of pollution permits to ensure that the equilibrium permit price is equal to the marginal damage.

In autarky the optimal pollution level for a representative country k in the Northern region results from equating local pollution supply with derived pollution demand.[20] The inverse pollution supply function is obtained by first solving for the optimal pollution permit price (τ_k). For this model this is given in equation (31).

$$\tau_k = \eta\left(\sum_{l=1}^{c+c^*} E_l\right)^{\gamma-1} I_k \tag{31}$$

It is worthwhile noting that the optimal permit price is increasing in the country's income, thereby confirming that environmental quality is a normal good. On the other hand, it is non-decreasing in the global quantity of pollution.

The second step to solving for the inverse supply function for pollution is to recognize that income is the sum of factor earnings and pollution permit revenues. After incorporating this identity into (31), we obtain the required function as follows where the "price of pollution" is in fact the optimal permit price relative to effective labor's per unit factor return.

$$\frac{\tau_k}{r_k} = \frac{\eta K_k \left(\sum_{l=1}^{c+c^*} Z_l \right)^{\gamma - 1}}{1 - \eta Z_k \left(\sum_{l=1}^{c+c^*} Z_l \right)^{\gamma - 1}} \tag{32}$$

An outcome of this model is that, with the assumption of identical technologies and preferences for all countries within a region (north or south), then each country's pollution supply function is identical. Thus, each country within a region will emit the same amount of pollution in equilibrium.

The derived demand for pollution comes from the demand for goods. This is given by (33).

$$\frac{\tau_k}{r_k} = \frac{\bar{\theta} K_k}{Z_k [1 - \bar{\theta}]} \tag{33}$$

In this equation $\bar{\theta}$ is the share of pollution-permit revenue in national income.

When we solve for the *autarky* solution, we obtain each country's level of pollution as the following:

$$Z_k = \left(\frac{\bar{\theta}}{\eta (c + c^*)^{\gamma - 1}} \right)^{1/\gamma} \tag{34}$$

And, adding up pollution across all countries in both regions we obtain *global pollution* in the *autarky* situation.

$$Z_W^A = \left(\frac{(c + c^*)\bar{\theta}}{\eta} \right)^{1/\gamma} \tag{35}$$

As was the case in the first model looked at earlier, world pollution does not depend upon a country's *endowments*. Rather, the *scale* and *technique effects* offset one another. However, an increase in the number of countries will increase world pollution. As world pollution increases, each country faces a higher marginal damage cost and lowers its own pollution. However, the reduction in pollution per country is not enough to offset the increase in pollution from additional countries. Again, the cost of pollution permits differs according to income levels.

Northern countries have higher pollution permit prices because they have higher income levels.

The outcome in the model is similar to the one in the previous model when pollution was merely local. Namely, northern countries will specialize in human capital-intensive but not pollution-intensive goods and their pollution permit prices will be higher than in southern countries. There will be a shifting of pollution-intensive industries to southern countries. While pollution produced by the north will fall it will be more than offset by an increase in pollution by the south. Ultimately, global pollution will increase with free trade relative to an autarky position.

A second outcome is possible in this model if a different assumption is made about the nature of the equilibrium. In order to generate the previous results it was assumed that the relative factor endowments of the countries in the two regions were so unequal that factor prices would not equalize with free trade. In the event that these differences are, in fact, not so great, then free trade will result in an *equalization of relative factor prices*. Thus, pollution permits will be the same for all countries in both regions, as will national income. What will differ is the pollution produced by the two regions. Northern countries will produce less pollution, while southern countries will produce more pollution. They will do so since they export relatively pollution-intensive goods for which they have a *comparative advantage*. However, the two will exactly offset one another and keep global pollution unchanged from the autarky level. This arises since the *scale* and *technique effects* offset one another. Thus, only the *composition effect* comes into play by causing a shift in the regional locations where goods are produced. However, given *factor price equalization* all countries will use the same production techniques, so the total amount of pollution is not affected by the location of production.[21]

As a result of the adjustments made after free trade, southern countries are net gainers from free trade and northern countries are net losers. This arises from the external nature of global pollution and because northern countries cannot prevent southern countries from accepting higher levels of pollution given their lower incomes. Instead, northern countries are forced to reduce their pollution in response to increased pollution coming from southern countries. If northern countries could prevent increased pollution from arising in the south by keeping pollution at pre-free trade levels, through international environmental agreements, then free trade would benefit the north.[22]

While free trade may benefit one region at the expense of the other, the *Nash equilibrium* does not necessarily lead to the optimal amount of global pollution. If we assume that global pollution is a *public bad*, then the efficient amount of pollution is found by equating permit prices (marginal control costs in each country) in all countries and setting this equal to the sum of global marginal damages. This yields an optimal amount of global pollution as follows:

$$Z_W^* = \left(\frac{\overline{\theta}}{\eta}\right)^{1/\gamma} \tag{36}$$

A comparison of this with equation (35) shows that free trade leads to a higher level of global pollution than would be Pareto-efficient. If all countries could agree to equi-proportional reductions in pollution after free trade has taken place, then they could be made better off.

13.5 IMPERFECT COMPETITION, TRADE, AND ENVIRONMENT

One important class of models remains to be examined in this review of the relationship between international trade and the environment. This class of models relaxes the assumption of perfectly competitive market behavior on the part of firms within a country (Brander and Spencer, 1985; Conrad, 1993; Barrett, 1994a, 1994b; Kennedy, 1994; and Ulph 1996a, 1996b). In this realm of imperfect competition, strategic decisions of various actors must be modeled explicitly using game theory tools. These actors include the producers of commodities in two trading countries and government policy-makers in the two countries.

The simplest model assumes that there are two identical firms in two identical countries and that one firm is located in the Home country, while the other firm produces in the Foreign country. Only domestic ownership of the firms is allowed, so profits flow only to the country in which a firm is located. A further simplifying assumption is made so that we can ignore welfare impacts upon residents of either the Home or Foreign country. This assumption is that the output of the two firms is sold to a third country.

The nature of the two-stage game that reveals the relationship between international trade, the environment and policy begins at the end with stage 2. In this stage the firms in the Home country and the Foreign country choose output and abatement to maximize their profits. In stage 1 of the game, the governments of the two countries choose the level, but not the type, of chosen policy instrument.[23]

The stage 2 component of the gaming model shows how each firm chooses its optimal output (x) and abatement levels (a) through maximization of its profits, assuming that the government has set the emissions tax rate at t and that the output of the rival firm is assumed to be fixed. Thus, for the Home firm, the goal is to maximize the following profit function, where the H subscript refers to the home choice of output x and the F subscript refers to foreign output of x and a is the Home choice of abatement:

$$\pi = R(x_H, x_F) - C(x_H) - A(a) - t(x_H - a_H)$$

where
$$\frac{\partial R}{\partial x_H} > 0; \quad \frac{\partial^2 R}{\partial x_H^2} < 0; \quad \frac{\partial R}{\partial x_F} < 0; \quad \frac{\partial R^2}{\partial x_2^F} < 0 \tag{37}$$

and
$$\frac{\partial C}{\partial x_H} > 0; \quad \frac{\partial^2 C}{\partial x_H^2} > 0; \quad \frac{\partial A}{\partial x_H} > 0; \quad \frac{\partial^2 A}{\partial x_H^2} > 0$$

In this equation $R(\cdot)$ is the Home firm's total revenue function, while $C(\cdot)$ is the total production cost function and $A(\cdot)$ is the abatement cost function. For simplicity, it is assumed that one unit of output produces one unit of *local pollution* only, however, this can be abated. So, as in the first model of this chapter, we have net emissions that are the difference between gross output and abatement. Finally, damage to the local environment is expressed as a total damage cost function $D(\cdot)$ that depends upon net emissions and has strictly positive first and second derivatives.

The optimality conditions for the problem above are the following:

$$\frac{\partial R}{\partial x_H} - \frac{\partial C}{\partial x_H} - t = 0$$

$$\frac{\partial A}{\partial a} - t = 0 \tag{38}$$

These familiar optimality conditions require that the firm's marginal revenue equals its marginal cost plus the emissions tax, so the firm abates up to the point at which the marginal abatement cost is equal to the level of the emissions tax.

From the above we can derive the Home firm's *reaction function* that depends upon the output level of the Foreign firm and the domestic emissions tax. In order to examine how the Home firm would react either to changes in the Foreign firm's output level or to the emissions tax, it is useful to look at the derivatives of the reaction function. The first shows how the firm will alter its output level in reaction to an increase in the Foreign firm's output. As we see, the response is to reduce Home output. The second shows how the Home firm will respond to an increase in the emissions tax. Again, the response is to reduce output.

$$\frac{\partial r}{\partial x_F} = \frac{-\partial^2 R / \partial x_H x_F}{\left(\frac{\partial^2 R}{\partial x_H^2} - \frac{\partial^2 C}{\partial x^2} \right)}$$

$$\frac{\partial r}{\partial t} = \frac{1}{\left(\frac{\partial^2 R}{\partial x_H^2} - \frac{\partial^2 C}{\partial x_H^2} \right)} \tag{39}$$

It is assumed that the Foreign firm has the same reaction function and responses. The Nash equilibrium for this model is found by solving the two reaction functions for the equilibrium levels of Home and Foreign output. This will depend upon specific parameters in the underlying functions, however, as we see above the Home firm will reduce its output in the face of an increase in the emissions tax of its Home government. In response, the Foreign firm will increase its output.[24]

We turn next to the first stage of the game. The decision-makers here are the governments of the two countries. Again, we will focus upon the Home country's problem. The Home government is assumed to maximize Home welfare through the choice of the level of the pollution emissions tax (t). In doing so, the Home government takes the emissions tax rate (τ) of the Foreign country as given. Welfare is defined below where $D(\cdot)$ is the total damage cost function described earlier.

$$W(t,\tau) = R(x_H, x_F) - C(x_H) - A(a) - D(x_H - a) \tag{40}$$

When the optimal decisions of the Home firm are incorporated into the function above, we can look at the first-order conditions for optimization in the Home country. These conditions contain the reaction of the Home firm to the Home government's decisions about the level of the emissions tax. In particular, it is useful to define the Home country's equilibrium output level as being dependent upon the two different emissions taxes: t (Home emissions tax) and τ (Foreign emissions tax):

$$x_H = \sigma(t, \tau)$$

where

$$\frac{\partial \sigma}{\partial t} = \frac{\partial r / \partial t}{1 - (\partial r / \partial x_H)^2} < 0$$

and

$$\frac{\partial \sigma}{\partial \tau} = \frac{\partial r}{\partial x_H} \cdot \frac{\partial r}{\partial t} \left(1 - (\partial r / \partial x_H)^2 \right) > 0 \tag{41}$$

This gives the following first-order condition for the Home country with respect to its choice of domestic pollution tax. In (42) B' is the matrix of second derivatives of the inverted function that shows optimal abatement levels according to the level of emissions tax set by the government.

$$\frac{\partial W}{\partial t} = \left(\frac{\partial R}{\partial x_H} - \frac{\partial C}{\partial x_H} - \frac{\partial D}{\partial (x_H - a)} \right) \cdot \frac{\partial \sigma}{\partial t} + \frac{\partial R}{\partial x_F} \cdot \frac{\partial \sigma}{\partial \tau} - \left(\frac{\partial A}{\partial a} - \frac{\partial D}{\partial (x_H - a)} \right) B' = 0 \tag{42}$$

Equation (42) can be rewritten in a way that illuminates the environmental policy implications of this gaming model.

$$t - \frac{\partial D}{\partial (x_H - a)} = \frac{\partial A}{\partial a} - \frac{\partial D}{\partial (x_H - a)} = \frac{(\partial R / \partial x_H)\sigma}{B' - \rho} < 0 \tag{43}$$

Equation (43) shows that the Home government has an incentive to pursue an environmental policy that is less stringent than what we have seen in the early models that do not feature gaming behavior. Here, the Home government sees the possibility of altering the Foreign firm's output through use of domestic pollution taxes. Thus, by keeping the pollution tax on the Home firm at a level that is less than the marginal damage cost imposed by production of x_H, the Home government keeps the output level of the Home firm higher than it would otherwise be. From the reaction function of the Foreign firm, we have seen that its response is to lower its output, thereby leading to higher profits and welfare for the Home firm and country.[25]

Unfortunately, in the *non-cooperative* form of this game, the Foreign country has the same incentive since we have assumed identical functions for the two firms in the two countries. Thus, the outcome is the one identified by name, the Prisoner's dilemma; namely, both countries try to relax their emissions taxes below the Pareto optimal levels. As they do so the two firms expand output until they share the market equally. Profits fall for both firms and local pollution increases in both countries.[26] They are both made worse off than in a situation of cooperation.

In order to examine whether the theoretical models discussed in this chapter can be validated by observing the real world, we turn next to an examination of the empirical evidence relating to the impact of international trade upon the environment.

13.6   EMPIRICAL EVIDENCE

In this section we will explore the empirical evidence linking trade and *trade liberalization* with changes in pollution or environmental quality. There are two questions that can be examined. The first asks whether trade has altered where in the world industrial pollution is created. The second issue is whether such an alteration leads to more or less pollution (either *local* or *global*).[27]

As we saw from the theoretical models, as compared with autarky, a world with free trade means a change in the composition of world production of goods. The reasons for such a change are two-fold. On the one hand, the so-called *pollution haven hypothesis* holds that free trade will encourage polluting activities to relocate from countries with more stringent environmental regulations (e.g., developed countries with relatively higher incomes) to less developed and low income countries. Thus, local pollution will rise in low income countries and fall in high income countries. So, an important question to answer is whether *dirty goods* production has moved to less developed countries away from developed countries.

While evidence for such an adjustment is scarce,[28] it is weakly supportive of the argument that industrial activity has moved to developing countries in response to less stringent environmental policies. Low and Yeats (1992), in a widely cited paper, look at actual trade flows under the assumption that "a country's revealed *comparative advantage* in a specific industry has been measured by the share of the industry in the country's total exports relative to the industry's share in total world exports of manufactures." If the ratio is greater than one, then this suggests that the country has a revealed comparative advantage in a particular sector. Using data from some 109 countries on the share of dirty goods[29] in trade over 1965–88, the authors conclude that the share of dirty industries grew rapidly for developing countries over the period. In particular, they note that the value of shipments from developed countries in dirty goods exports fell by about 6 percent over the period, while the share coming from south-east Asia doubled.

Lucas, Wheeler, and Hettige (1992) employ similar techniques to trace changes in manufacturing output's pollution intensity for 80 countries over the period 1960–88. In particular, they look at the toxic intensity of exports. They find that the growth in toxic intensity has been much more rapid in developing countries and that this is mostly the case in the poorest countries. However, an interesting result from their work suggests that this growth in dirty industries has occurred mostly in those countries that have been closed to trade, not those open to trade. Birdsall and Wheeler (1992) have a similar finding in their examination of the impacts of opening of trade upon Latin American countries. They argue that by opening to trade these less developed countries also import the (higher) pollution standards of more developed countries.

More recently, Mani and Wheeler (1997) looked at international information on industrial production, trade and environmental regulation for the period 1960–95. They examined the five dirtiest sectors: iron and steel, non-ferrous metals, industrial chemicals, pulp and paper, and non-metallic mineral products and the five cleanest sectors: textiles, non-electrical machinery, electrical machinery, transport equipment, and instruments over the period. Their important findings include the observation that pollution-intensive output as a percentage of total manufacturing has fallen in developed countries and increased in developing countries. In addition, the periods in which developed countries saw big increases in pollution control costs coincided with the periods of most rapid increases in net exports of dirty goods from developing countries.

Mani and Wheeler's work produced a second important finding. They found that environmental regulations became more stringent at higher income levels. Thus, they suggested that the *pollution haven* phenomenon is necessarily self-limiting. That is, at the outset developing countries may become pollution havens. However, the growth in income experienced with trade liberalization leads to pressures at home to impose more stringent pollution regulations. These actions ultimately reduce the pollution haven advantage of developing countries.

Finally, Mani and Wheeler sounded a cautionary note about the ability of researchers to prove the existence of pollution havens solely related to income differences, and, hence, regulatory differences between countries. They found that the dirty industries tended to use relatively more capital, energy, and land than did the clean industries. Clearly, information about the relative abundance of these factors, as well as changes in their prices, might also explain locational shifts in pollution-intensive production.

This is, in fact, the underlying view for the second explanation used to support the notion that trade alters the locations where dirty goods are produced. Instead of focusing upon income-related regulatory differences, this second view takes a broader approach. It simply says that *comparative advantage* determines the impacts of trade upon environmental quality.[30] In order to evaluate the strength of this effect we need to compare the variations in trade flows across countries on the basis of a number of different characteristics including: factor costs, the presence of trade barriers, technological differences, pollution abatement costs, and factor abundance.

The best-known empirical analysis of the comparative advantage hypothesis is that of Tobey (1990). Using cross-sectional data for 23 countries on the net exports of five dirty goods, he estimates the empirical relationship between cross-country variation in such exports and a number of regressors that measure different factor endowments, along with an index of the strictness of environmental regulation. He finds that conventional determinants of comparative advantage tend to be significant in the explanation of cross-country trade flows. He also finds that the regulatory stringency measures pertaining to the environment tend to be insignificant explanatory variables.

In some senses these two competing hypotheses provide an incomplete picture. On the one hand, the *pollution haven hypothesis* says that income differences determine environmental regulatory stringency and this determines trade flows and, hence, the impacts upon the environment of *trade liberalization*. On the other hand, the *comparative advantage hypothesis* says that a number of factors affect a country's comparative advantage and ultimately trade flows and environmental changes. However, from the previous discussion of the theoretical models, it is clear that both factors come into play and are likely to be related to economic growth. One important area of empirical research has been the investigation of the relationship between economic growth broadly defined and its impact upon the local environmental pollution. This literature has tried to find empirical evidence of the so-called *environmental Kuznets curve* (EKC). This work (see chapter 11) estimates the relationship between per capita income levels in a cross-section of countries to particular types of pollution. The hypothesis is that pollution initially rises as income increases; however, further income increases result in lower per capita pollution once some threshold level of income is achieved. This work was popularized by Grossman and Krueger (1993) in their study about the potential environmental impacts of the *North American Free Trade Agreement* (NAFTA). They found, in particular, that sulfur dioxide and smoke pollution tended to peak when the level of per capita income was approximately $5,500. Using better data this threshold level of income was subsequently found to be $8,000 in a more recent study.[31] Grossman and Krueger attribute the "hump-shaped" environmental Kuznets curve to the ultimate predominance of what was earlier defined as the *technique effect* over the *scale effect*.

Unfortunately, the Grossman and Krueger results which suggest that economic growth does not necessarily increase pollution do not directly measure the impacts of international trade upon economic growth. It would seem, then, that the EKC measures a number of different impacts as related to environmental quality. In particular, to tie this discussion to the theoretical literature, the EKC probably measures all three effects: *composition, technique,* and *scale*. The question is whether these can be separated empirically into their individual impacts. This has been accomplished recently by Antweiler, Copeland, and Taylor (2001).

Antweiler, Copeland, and Taylor employ a modified version of Copeland and Taylor's model (1994) that was described in previous sections of this chapter. The extension that they look at is the incorporation of different types of consumers (Greens and Browns)[32] into the analysis. They are then able to isolate conceptually a trade-induced *composition effect*, a *scale effect*, and a *technique effect*. These are then employed individually in the empirical model in order to obtain separate estimates of the three different impacts.

The authors employ the *GEMS (Global Environmental Monitoring System)* data to measure pollution intensity (for sulfur dioxide only) of economic activity in particular geographical areas. They have panel data from 43 countries, both developed and developing over the period 1971 to 1997. Moreover, they have data on 108 cities in total within those countries, so are able to investigate at a more disaggregated level than previous empirical work.[33] In their estimation model they hypothesize that emissions levels for a site i at time t are predicated to depend upon city-specific GDP per km^2, a national capital to labor ratio, per capita income, a measure of trade intensity, a measure of a country's real income relative to world income and a number of weather and other site-specific variables. They find positive and significant relationships between the scale of economic activity and pollution concentrations. They also find a strong and significantly negative relationship between per capita income levels and concentrations. Overall, the implication of their findings is that freer trade tends to increase pollution concentration through a *composition* type of effect. However, when estimates of the scale and technique effects are included, then pollution concentrations may actually fall. In particular, using the estimates from the paper, the authors suggest that if trade liberalization raises GDP per person by 1 percent, then the concentration of sulfur dioxide falls by about 1 percent. They conclude the paper by stating that free trade may actually be good for the environment. Clearly, more work can and will be done in this area in the next few years as better data, including panel data on environmental indicators, become available.

NOTES

1 A small country takes the world trading prices for goods as given.

2 This chapter follows the majority of trade and environment literature in its focus upon production-related environmental externalities. Clearly, there are other ways by which pollution can be produced. Two important means are consumers and the transportation of goods across borders. However, these causes are not discussed in this chapter, other than in the section at the end given over to a brief review of further readings in the literature.

3 This model follows Siebert (1977) closely. Details of derivations can be found in the article.

4 This type of pollution is what Ulph (1997) calls eyesore pollution; that is, the country's productive capability remains unaffected by the level of pollution.

5 We can ask what a country might choose to do in the event that the first-best solution is not attainable. Suppose, for example, that the country has imposed a tariff barrier that

cannot be removed. Then, if the tariff barrier encourages too much production of polluting goods, the second-best environmental policy would be to set higher pollution taxes to offset the trade distortion. However, the country would be worse off than if it had pursued the first-best option of using the appropriate tools to achieve each of the targets (environmental policy to deal with pollution and trade policy of no tariffs to achieve free trade gains). Alternatively, suppose a second-best outcome can only be achieved in the face of transactions costs that prohibit the use of the optimal environmental tax. In this case, a country may wish to alter or restrict trade in order to be better off (Anderson, 1992).

6   This is not a crucial assumption and a more general production function is illustrated later in the chapter.

7   As Rauscher (1997) points out, although we are used to thinking about pollution as a joint output of production, these emissions reflect the fact that the environmental resources that have entered the production process as inputs have been used up. So, we take the quantity of emissions as a measure of the consumption of environmental resources.

8   Given these assumptions, then once we assume a zero profit condition for this commodity, we have the simplifying situation that wages are equal to one.

9   The assumption of homothetic preferences is a useful simplification since it allows for the relative demand for commodities to be independent of income levels. This means that the two countries can have an identical pattern of spending on goods, so that this is not a complicating factor for looking at trade flows. Thus, we can ignore the role of income differences in free trade and focus solely upon relative endowment differences to provide the motivation for trade.

10 This is an artifact of the assumption that the elasticity of marginal damage of one more unit of pollution with respect to income is one.

11 See Copeland (2000) for the details of this derivation.

12 Copeland (2000) uses the model of this section to discuss the nature of trade negotiations and the nature of trade agreements upon environmental quality.

13 This will be taken up later in a discussion of the empirical work that has attempted to validate the impact of freer trade upon environmental quality.

14 This result is the same as we obtained with the comparative advantage model. One way to think about this is that a relatively less stringent pollution regulation (because of a lower relative income) in the Foreign country gives it a comparative advantage in the dirty good because abatement costs must be relatively lower.

15 If we allow for differences not only in income, but also capital abundance, then two conflicting factors will determine the pattern of trade. First, if the wealthier country is abundant in capital, then its strict pollution policy will make the autarky price of the dirty good high, while its relative capital abundance will tend to work in the opposite direction and make the price low. The eventual pattern of trade will then depend upon the strength of the two opposing effects. See Copeland and Taylor (1997) and Antweiler, Copeland, and Taylor (1998).

16 Copeland and Taylor (1994, 1995) suggest that we think of effective labor as the product of the size of the labor force and an efficiency index whose value depends upon the level of human capital in a country.

17 In the event that this is greater than one, then the technique effect will offset the scale effect and also offset some part of the composition effect.

18 When growth occurs more quickly in the low-income Foreign country, on the other hand, pollution falls in both countries. The Foreign country attracts new less-polluting industries. This time the composition effect works to reduce pollution in both countries.

19 In this way, we can ignore terms of trade effects present when there are a few large countries.

20 This is a derived demand since it results from consumption of locally produced goods.

21 This differs from the previous model since the dirtiest of the relatively clean goods produced in the northern region produces relatively less pollution on average than the cleanest of the relatively dirty goods produced in the southern region. Hence, the composition effect leads to an increase in global pollution as industries relocate to the South in pursuit of lower permit prices.

22 Barrett (1990, 1994b) explores the potential gains to cooperation through international environmental agreements and points out that benefits from such cooperation may be small and, hence, unlikely to be pursued.

23 Thus, this game assumes that the governments have already chosen to employ emissions taxes. Ulph (1996a, 1996b) looks at a three-stage game in which the third stage describes the decisions of the firms, the second stage describes the levels of a given policy instrument, and the first stage involves the choice of which particular instrument.

24 See Ulph (1997) for details.

25 This is akin to the pollution haven hypothesis discussed earlier. This is also known as "ecological dumping."

26 Interestingly, as Barrett (1994a) discusses, a cooperative equilibrium in this type of model would result in the two countries setting emissions taxes that are greater than the marginal damage costs associated with production. By acting in this way the governments are trying to correct for a sub-optimal Cournot equilibrium in which total output is greater than the profit-maximizing monopoly output level.

27 While not the explicit focus of this chapter, one can look at this issue from the opposite side. Namely, we could ask whether environmental regulation has had much of an impact upon international trade. In a survey of the field of environmental economics, Cropper and Oates (1992) argued that previous government efforts to deal with pollution had little impact upon the nature and significance of international trade. However, as we shall see recent evidence suggests that this has not been so much the case in the last decade.

28 In order to examine the differential impacts of trade upon environmental quality we would ideally need a panel data set consisting of a time series of cross-sections of industrial activity linked directly to pollution outcomes. While the OECD publishes much data on developed countries, there is very little known about less developed countries, particularly with respect to environmental quality indicators.

29 Dirty goods are consistently produced by such industries as: iron and steel, non-ferrous metals, refined petroleum, metal manufactures, and pulp and paper manufactures.

30 Clearly, these two hypotheses may be linked in the sense that environmental regulations themselves may alter some pre-existing comparative advantage held by a country.

31 The particular dataset employed by Grossman and Krueger was the global environmental monitoring system (GEMS) which has recorded sulfur dioxide concentrations in major urban areas in developed and developing countries alike since the 1970s. Their study directly measures pollution levels as related to per capital income levels.

In this, their study differs from the previous empirical literature cited since it does not use actual pollution measures directly.

32   Greens are in favor of more stringent environmental policies than Browns.

33   Such a disaggregated approach may be very important when it comes to analyzing how governments make environmental policy decisions. Markusen, Morey, and Olewiler (1993) develop a model that examines whether plant location and market structure are important factors for government environmental decision-making and competition for business. Hoel (1997) also looks at the issue of mobility of firms across locations.

FURTHER READING

A good starting point for interested readers is the collected chapters written for the *Handbook of Environmental and Resource Economics* edited by J. van den Bergh (1999).

The early work looking at the nexus between international trade and environmental impacts uses partial equilibrium models to explain how a country's welfare could be affected by free trade in the presence of externalities (Baumol and Oates, 1988). Anderson (1992) analyzes the small country case of perfect competition in trade markets and provides diagrams to illustrate the impacts. Krutilla (1991) uses a similar framework to investigate the implications for a large country able to affect world prices and, thereby, alter its terms of trade. In this situation, the terms of trade effects generally mean smaller welfare gains from *trade liberalization*. Furthermore, the *Pigouvian taxes* needed to deal with a *local pollution* externality need to reflect these terms of trade effects. A final class of partial equilibrium models allows for imperfect competition (Dixit and Stiglitz, 1977) in domestic production. Assuming the existence of a domestic monopolist (that operates perfectly competitively in the world market arena), if the world market price is higher than the *autarky* price but lower than the domestic monopoly price, then we have the monopolist exporting its pollution-producing good. If the government adopts an emissions tax to deal with *local pollution*, then the domestic price will increase and encourage the monopolist to cut production in the export market. This means a reduction in pollution. Ulph (1997) provides a succinct survey of more recent developments in the literature.

While the focus in this chapter has been upon production-related pollution externalities when there are *non-mobile factors*, this does not exhaust the conceptual literature. Rauscher (1997) reviews and integrates much of his early work in the area of the impact of international trade on pollution. This book is worthwhile reading for two reasons. First, he allows for factor mobility, unlike in the models discussed in this chapter. Second, he examines pollution that originates from consumption and transportation sources and allows for productivity decreases from pollution.

Chichilnisky (1994) provides a separate and thought-provoking direction in her work. She argues that the lack of well-defined property rights to environmental resources in developing countries adds a layer of complexity to the simple notion that they may gain from exporting their pollution-intensive commodities. In particular, there may be an incentive for developing countries to export more of their *environmental capital* at too low a price. Developed countries, on the other hand, gain from such a state of affairs. Developing countries lose further when they pay higher prices for goods exported from developed countries where these higher prices arise from enhanced pollution abatement regulation. This work also has implications for trade in environmental goods, e.g., *biodiversity*, and may even reach into the realm of ethical considerations surrounding trade and differential environmental quality impacts upon developed versus developing countries.

Ugelow (1982), Dean (1992), WTO , 1999, and Jayadevappa and Chhatre (2000) provide surveys of the extant empirical literature on trade on the environment. A strand of the empirical literature that is interesting but was not explored in this chapter relates to the relationship between environmental regulation and competitiveness of enterprises (Robison, 1988). Other work in the area is reviewed in Jaffe, Peterson, Portney, and Stavins (1995). Aside from regression analysis, simulation analysis has also been used to examine the impact of environmental policies upon economy-wide effects and international trade. *Computable general equilibrium (CGE) models* examine the nature of the relationships at a very highly aggregate level and are capable of providing some broad policy direction. Bergman (1991), Boyd and Krutilla (1992) are examples of this. In addition, the *OECD* has developed a model containing 12 regions in the world. This model has been used to examine unilateral as opposed to co-ordinated policies towards greenhouse gas emissions (Burniaux, Martin, Nicoletti, Oliveira-Martins, 1991).

UNEP (2000) provides an overview of the policy environment that dictates the rules governing international trade and explains the nature of the World Trade Organization and its role. Esty (1994) surveys the issues surrounding the role of international trade agreements in causing changes to the environment. In particular, the question has been asked whether there should there be separate environmental agreements outside of trade agreements such the *General Agreement on Tariffs and Trade (GATT)* or the *North American Free Trade Agreement (NAFTA)*. The latter is the most recent major trade agreement and has been heavily influenced by environmental concerns (Anderson, 1993). For example, it allows for countries to pursue green barriers to trade and signals that the signatories should lower their standards in order to attract firms. This begs the question of whether such agreements ought to encourage the harmonization of environmental standards. The short answer is no (Ulph, 1996). However, international cooperation is necessary for externalities that are global in nature. For this reason there are a number of separate environmental agreements such as the *Convention on International Trade in Endangered Species (CITES)* and the *Montreal Protocol on Substances that Deplete the Ozone Layer*. *UNEP* (2000) discusses the nature of these agreements and whether they, in fact, contradict provisions in *GATT*.

REFERENCES

Anderson, K. (1992). Economics of Environmental Policies in Open Economies, in K. Anderson and R. Blackhurst, eds, *The Greening of World Trade Issues*, Harvester Wheatsheaf: New York, pp. 23–48.

Anderson, T. L. (ed.) (1993). NAFTA and the Environment, Pacific Research Institute for Public Policy: San Francisco.

Antweiler, W., Copeland, B., and Taylor, M. S. (2001). Is Free Trade Good for the Environment?, *American Economic Review*, 91 (4): 877–908.

Barrett, S. (1990). The Problem of Global Environmental Protection, *Oxford Review of Economic Policy*, 6 (1): 68–79.

Barrett, S. (1994a). Strategic Environmental Policy and International Trade, *Journal of Public Economics*, 54 (3): 325–38.

Barrett, S. (1994b). Self-enforcing International Environmental Agreements, *Oxford Economic Papers*, 46: 878–94.

Baumol, W. J. and Oates, W. E. (1988). *The Theory of Environmental Policy*, second edition, Cambridge: Cambridge University Press.

Bergman, L. (1991). General Equilibrium Effects of Environmental Policy: A CGE-Modeling Approach, *Environmental and Resource Economics*, 1: 43–61.

Bhagwati, J. (1993). The Case for Free Trade, *Scientific American*, 269 (5): 42–9.

Bierman, F. (2001). The Rising Tide of Green Unilateralism in World Trade Law: Options for Reconciling the Emerging North-South Conflict, *Journal of World Trade Law*, 53 (3): 421–48.

Birdsall, N. and Wheeler, D. (1992). Trade Policy and Industrial Pollution in Latin America: Where Are the Pollution Havens?, in P. Low, ed., *International Trade and the Environment* World Bank Discussion Paper No. 159, World Bank, Washington, DC, pp. 159–67.

Boyd, R. and Krutilla, K. (1992). Controlling Acid Rain Deposition: A General Equilibrium Assessment, *Environmental and Resource Economics*, 2: 307–22.

Brander, J. and Spencer, B. (1985). Export Subsidies and International Market Share Rivalry, *Journal of International Economics*, 18: 83–100.

Burniaux, J. Martin, J., Nicoletti, G., and Oliveira-Martins, J. (1991). *GREEN – a Multi-region Dynamic General Equilibrium Model for Quantifying the Costs of Curbing CO_2 Emissions: A Technical Manual*, Working Paper 89, OECD, Department of Economics and Statistics: Paris.

Chichilnisky, G. (1994). North-South Trade and the Global Environment, *American Economic Review*, 84: 851–74.

Conrad, K. (1993). Trade Policy under Taxes and Subsidies for Pollution Intensive Industries, *Journal of Environmental Economics and Management*, 25: 121–5.

Copeland, B. R. (2000). Trade and Environment: Policy Linkages, *Environment and Development*, 5: 405–32.

Copeland, B. R. and Taylor, M. S. (1994). North-South Trade and the Environment, *Quarterly Journal of Economics*, 109: 755–87.

Copeland, B. R. and Taylor, M. S. (1995). Trade and Trans-boundary Pollution, *American Economic Review*, 85: 716–37.

Copeland, B. R. and Taylor, M. S. (1997). A Simple Model of Trade, Capital Mobility and the Environment. National Bureau of Economic Research Working Paper 5898. Cambridge, MA. January.

Cropper, M. and Oates, W. (1992). Environmental Economics: A Survey, *Journal of Economic Literature*, 30: 675–740.

Daly, H. (1993). The Perils of Free Trade, *Scientific American*, 269 (5): 50–7.

Daly, H. and Goodland, R. (1994). An Ecological-economic Assessment of Deregulation of International Commerce Under GATT, *Ecological Economics*, 9: 73–92.

D'Arge, R. C. and Kneese, A. V. (1972). Environmental Quality and International Trade, *International Organization*, 26: 419–65.

Dean, J. (1992). Trade and the Environment: A Survey of the Literature, in P. Low, ed., *International Trade and the Environment*, World Bank: Washington, DC., pp. 15–28.

Dixit, A. K. (1987). Strategic Aspects of Trade Policy, in T. Bewley, ed., *Advances in Economic Theory*, Cambridge University Press: New York. Fifth World Congress.

Dixit, A. K. and Stiglitz, J. (1977). Monopolistic Competition and Optimum Product Diversity, *American Economic Review*, 67 (3): 297–308.

Esty, D. (1994). *Greening the GATT: Trade, Environment and the Future*, Institute for International Economics: Washington, DC.

Grossman, G. and Krueger, A. (1991). Environmental Impacts of a North American Free Trade Agreement, Working Paper No. 3914, National Bureau of Economic Research.

Grossman, G. M. and Krueger, A. B. (1993). Environmental Impacts of a North American Free Trade Agreement, in P. Garber, ed., *The US–Mexico Free Trade Agreement*, MIT Press: Cambridge, MA.

Hoel, M. (1997). Environmental Policy with Endogenous Plant Locations, *Scandinavian Journal of Economics*, 99 (2): 241–59.

Jaffe, A., Peterson, S., Portney, P., and Stavins, R. (1995). Environmental Regulation and Competitiveness of US Manufacturing: What Does the Evidence Tell Us?, *Journal of Economic Literature*, 33: 132–63.

Jayadevappa, R. and Chhatre, S. (2000). International Trade and Environmental Quality: A Survey, *Ecological Economics*, 32: 175–94.

Kennedy, P. (1994). Equilibrium Pollution Taxes in Open Economies with Imperfect Competition, *Journal of Environmental Economics and Management*, 27: 49–63.

Krutilla, K. (1991). Environmental Regulation in an Open Economy, *Journal of Environmental Economics and Management*, 20: 127–42.

Low, P. and Yeats, A. (1992). Do "Dirty Industries" Migrate?, in P. Low, ed., *International Trade and the Environment*, World Bank Discussion Paper No. 159, World Bank, Washington, DC, pp. 89–103.

Lucas, R., Wheeler, D., and Hettige, H. (1992). Economic Development, Environmental Regulation, and the International Migration of Toxic Industrial Pollution, 1960–1988, Background Paper for the World Development Report, World Bank WPS-1062.

Mani, M. and Wheeler, D. (1997). *In Search of Pollution Havens? Dirty Industry in the World Economy, 1960–1995*, World Bank Working Paper No. 16, April.

Markusen, J. (1975). International Externalities and Optimal Tax Structures, *Journal of International Economics*, 5: 15–29.

Markusen, J., Morey, E., and Olewiler, N. (1993). Environmental Policy When Market Structure and Plant Locations Are Endogenous, *Journal of Environmental Economics and Management*, 24: 69–86.

Pethig, R. (1976). Pollution, Welfare, and Environmental Policy in the Theory of Competitive Advantage, *Journal of Environmental Economics and Management*, 2: 160–9.

Rauscher, M. (1997). *International Trade, Factor Movements, and the Environment*, Oxford University Press: New York.

Robison, D. (1988). Industrial Pollution Abatement: The Impact on the Balance of Trade, *Canadian Journal of Economics*, 21 (1): 187–99.

Siebert, H. (1977). Environmental Quality and the Gains from Trade, *Kyklos*, 4: 657–73.

Tobey, J. (1990). The Effects of Domestic Environmental Policies on Patterns of World Trade: An Empirical Test, *Kyklos*, 43 (2): 191–209.

Ugelow, J. (1982). A Survey of Recent Studies on Costs of Pollution Control and the Effects on Trade, in S. Rubin (ed.), *Environment and Trade*, Allanheld, Osmun, and Co.: New Jersey.

Ulph, A. (1996a). Environmental Policy and International Trade When Governments and Producers Act Strategically, *Journal of Environmental Economics and Management*, 30: 265–81.

Ulph, A. (1996b). Environmental Policy Instruments and Imperfectly Competitive International Trade, *Environmental and Resource Economics*, 7 (4): 333–5.

Ulph, A. (1997). International Trade and the Environment: A Survey of Recent Economic Analysis, in H. Folmer and T. Tietenberg, eds., *The International Yearbook of Environmental and Resource Economics 1997/1998*, Edward Elgar: Cheltenham.

UNEP (2000). *Environment and Trade: A Handbook,* United Nations and Environment Program, International Institute for Sustainable Development.

Van den Bergh, J. (ed.) (1999). *Handbook of Environmental and Resource Economics,* Edward Elgar: Cheltenham.

World Trade Organization (1999). *Trade and Environment: Special Study No. 4,* WTO: Geneva.

CHAPTER FOURTEEN

THE GLOBAL COMMONS

*And from this followeth another law: that such things as cannot
be divided be enjoyed in common, if it can be; and if the quantity
of the thing permit, without stint; otherwise proportionably to the
number of them that have right.* (The Twelfth Law of Nature
according to Thomas Hobbes, *Leviathan*, 1651)

14.1 WHAT ARE THE GLOBAL COMMONS?

Humans use and manage many environmental resources under collective
arrangements: examples include community fields and forests; water rights to
the local river, near-shore fisheries; and even national parks. We refer to these
shared resources as common property, taking the name from the tradition of the
village commons where local villagers would pasture their animals together
(the terms community property or *res communes* are also used). Economists use
the term global commons to refer to those resources shared internationally. These
resources may involve resources that span national boundaries, such as watersheds and airsheds shared by two or more neighboring countries, to truly
global resources such as the earth's oceans and atmosphere, as well as unique
flora and fauna that may be found only within a small region but hold value for
the global community.

  Resources (or the rights to use the resource) may be held in common for a
number of reasons: they may be an efficient means of sharing risk; have been
devised as a way to overcome problems of unequal access; or reflect the outcome
of historical patterns of ownership or customary traditions developed over time.
Whether or not these resources will be over-exploited depends upon the institutional framework that governs their management and the externalities involved in
their use. The critical difference for the global commons is that either the resources
or the externalities associated with their use cross national boundaries, and
countries must rely on voluntary arrangements among themselves to address
problems of overexploitation.

In this chapter, we first examine why resources (or access to them) may be held collectively, the implications of collective ownership, and what institutional arrangements can help achieve successful outcomes. We look at how the global commons differ from the local commons. We review what economic theory, principally game theory, has to say about what motivates countries to voluntarily address the problems of the global commons and how institutional arrangements can modify their incentives to participate in these arrangements. We then conclude with a description of the major issues involving the global commons: transboundary pollution, biodiversity, and the earth's atmosphere, and assess the performance of international efforts to address these issues.

14.2   WHAT MAKES RESOURCES COMMON PROPERTY?

Human societies have developed a variety of different institutional structures under which resources are utilized. Economists use the idea of property rights to describe the set and system of rules governing the use of goods and resources (see chapter 2). These rights may have a number of dimensions, ranging from the exclusive right to use and dispose of the resource as one sees fit to more limited bundles of rights, in which the user may enjoy limited use of the resource for a fixed period of time. Ownership and use of the resource might be vested in individuals as in the case of private property; alternatively, the resource may be state-owned; communally owned, or not fall under any ownership, as in the case of open-access resources.

Common property resources have been used to refer to both publicly owned resources and to open access resources. Publicly owned resources are where the users share rights and duties exercised under some collective framework (a village, guild, or state). Public ownership may reflect historical patterns of ownership or customary tradition. Communal ownership may also reflect an efficient sharing of risk, where villages would share herding grounds or agricultural fields where variations in the annual yield may have meant that some regions did better than others. It also offers a way to overcome problems of unequal access, as in the case of rivers where users situated on the riverbank could potentially exploit their location to the detriment of more distant users, including those downstream. *Open access resources* are those where there is no effective regulation of resource use.

Economists argue that resources or goods will be suitable for management under a private property regime if they meet two essential criteria: (1) is the resource (or use of it) excludable (can others be prevented from using the resource); and (2) is it rival (does a person's use of the resource diminish the amount available for others)? If a resource meets these criteria, then assigning private property rights to the resource can yield economically desirable outcomes. If, however, there are externalities associated with use of the resource, then such a regime will not necessarily lead to satisfactory outcomes. In the case of negative externalities, the resource will be over-exploited; in the case of positive externalities (such as environmental values associated with a unique ecosystem), the public goods problem means that individual agents have limited incentives to supply the good since they cannot capture the benefits. *Common-pool resources* refer to those resources that are collectively exploited, such as in-shore fisheries, and where users impose reciprocal externalities upon one another through their actions.

The exclusivity of the resource may be a function of how difficult or expensive it is to exclude people from using the resource. This can be an inherent characteristic of the resource (e.g. migratory wildlife and fish stocks). Alternatively, the exclusivity may depend on the institutional arrangements governing the use of the resource. If the institutional structure does not exclude any users, or is ineffective, it can turn the resource into an open access resource. In some cases, a change in the institutional framework can transform the nature of the resource. This happened to several international fisheries through the establishment of the 200-mile Exclusive Economic Zones (EEZ) along countries' coastlines, spurred by the Law of the Sea Conferences. The EEZ transformed what had been an open access resource into common-pool resources through the extension of national jurisdiction over previously open ocean. Regulators have also used private property rights to internalize externalities; this realigns the incentives such that users bear the costs of their actions. This has been suggested for a number of different common-pool resources; examples include the use of quotas in fisheries (see chapter 4) and the use of permit systems in emissions trading for pollution control (see chapter 3). Implicit in these approaches, however, is the idea that an external authority can evaluate the costs and benefits of various actions and has the authority to impose those measures that will maximize net social benefits.

Sources of failure

Research suggests that communities can successfully hold and manage common property resources where they can effectively monitor, enforce, and bargain within the collective entity (Gibson et al., 2000). However, common-pool resources are often subject to overexploitation. Individual users face the incentive to increase their use or share of the resource since the benefit they capture outweighs any increase in cost they incur. If all act accordingly, there can be a significant diminishment in the quality of the resource, either in a reduction in resource abundance or degradation in the environment itself. This problem is especially acute for open access resources, where the lack of restraints often creates a race for the resource since the first to exploit the resource gains most of the benefits. Public goods are subject to the free-rider problem; individuals have no incentive to contribute since it is impossible to exclude them from enjoying the benefit; conversely, exercising restraint brings no benefit (such as voluntarily reducing emissions) unless all engage in similar behavior.

Institutions may fail to overcome this tendency towards overexploitation. As communities get larger and the number of users grows, it becomes more difficult to monitor and enforce adherence to rules on resource use. It also becomes easier to form coalitions that can operate against the interests of the community (Hackett, Schlager, and Walker, 1994). Increased population pressure or techno-logical change may increase the incentive to "cheat"; increased cheating may also lead to a breakdown in communitarian norms, further exacerbating the prob-lem (Dasgupta, 1998). Externalities may link resource use together in a manner not recognized under the property rights regimes. Internalizing those externalities may not be feasible because of the transaction costs associated with bargaining, monitoring, and enforcement. Institutional failures may also occur where property rights are absent or poorly enforced, or government policies directly or indirectly encourage overexploitation or environmental degradation. Finally, the lack of an arbiter can also frustrate the use of market systems; in the absence of enforcement or meaningful sanctions, resources may become open-access goods.

There are three principal ways to enforce rights. The first is to rely on an external authority that can resolve disputes and ensure compliance with the rules. This requires an established structure of authority and power; examples include the use of formal legal systems but could also be customary systems of justice. The second way compliance can be assured is through social norms; if participants know that violations of rights will be met though sanctions of inappropriate behav-ior it becomes individually rational for them to adhere to norms and conventions governing the use of resources and interaction. This behavior contributes to the establishment of trust – the idea of social capital as an institutional component of society and an informal means of monitoring and enforcing acceptable resource uses. The third way in which rights can be enforced is through institutional enforcement; the design and establishment of an institutional structure to monitor performance, adjudicate disputes, and enforce those rights.

What makes the global commons

It is this lack of an external authority that distinguishes the global commons from other common property resources. Without an external authority to establish rights and ensure compliance through enforcement whenever resources cross national boundaries (two or more countries share a river, migratory animal species, or an airshed), or where the externalities cross international boundaries (air pollution transported over long distances) such resources will be vulnerable to overexploitation and degradation. Countries have been reluctant to yield any of their sovereignty over their domestic affairs to the various international insti-tutions that have been developed over the years. Different cultural and social norms, as well as political systems, contribute to a lack of consensus about the nature and scope of many of these problems and how they should be addressed (although these norms may provide a starting point for discussions). Therefore, it is through the development of cooperative agreements such as international treaties, and the use of international institutions, that countries attempt to solve the problems of the global commons.

14.3   MODELING INTERACTION BETWEEN COUNTRIES

To fully understand why countries voluntarily enter into international agreements would require a complex and lengthy analysis of a wide range of factors: political imperatives and domestic constituencies, past history, and cultural norms can all be used to explain why countries may pursue particular sets of actions. Economic models focus on the benefits and costs that accrue to countries as the motivation for them to cooperate. These models often use game theory to analyze the inter-action between different players (countries) in which not only do they evaluate the costs and benefits from taking action, but also consider the strategic implica-tions of their decision. Will countries abide by their commitments? How should countries share the burden and benefits from cooperation? Will a country's par-ticipation be contingent on the expected benefits from cooperation?

In these games, the players face different payoffs according to the various actions they undertake (or fail to undertake). Depending upon the game, it can be shown that under certain circumstances countries will willingly choose to volun-tarily commit to an agreement, while under other circumstances they will refuse to take action. In general, these models highlight several well-known features of game theory models; first, we often end up with outcomes that are not Pareto-optimal; and second, we may be able to escape these sub-optimal outcomes if we allow for repeated interaction or design institutional mechanisms that help overcome myopic behavior on the part of actors.

The modeling procedure consists of several parts: identifying the players; the possible actions they can take at various points in the game; the information they act on at those points; the strategies they may choose (which are a particular set of actions); payoffs for those various strategies; and outcomes determined by the interaction of all the players' strategies. Because the number of potential out-comes can be quite large, there have been a number of different criteria used to identify an equilibrium outcome. There are two important solution concepts. The first, *Nash Equilibrium*, is one in which given every other player's actions, there is no other strategy for the player that makes him or her better off than the strategy they have chosen. The equilibrium chosen under these strategies are self-enforcing but often sub-optimal. The second, *Dominant Strategy*, is one where there is a single strategy for a player that yields the highest payoffs regardless of the other player's strategies.

We can also distinguish between two major types of games. In *cooperative games*, the players can make binding commitments and allows for the possibility of side-payments – the transfer of resources or money from one player to another to ensure different outcomes. Cooperative games are typically used to model bargaining. In *noncooperative games*, in contrast, players cannot make binding commitments, and hence will maximize their own welfare subject to the constraints of the game. Perhaps the best-known example of a noncooperative game is the *Prisoner's dilemma*, which has been used to model the use of common pool resources under open access regimes. In the game, although all resource users recognize everybody will be better off if all collectively restrain their use of the resource; rational individual self-interest leads to overexploitation of the resource. The text box 14.1 illustrates how the Prisoner's dilemma works.

Analyzing problems of the global commons using game theory involves understanding how equilibrium is reached in a particular game. The equilibrium may depend upon the actions open to players, the sequence of those actions, or even how often they may interact. We can then examine this equilibrium relative to the optimal case, and if it is sub-optimal what might be required to move to the Pareto-optimal outcome (or failing that to a feasible outcome that is an improvement upon the existing equilibrium). Below we examine the interaction between players' strategies, the choices they face, and the outcome of games.

The outcome of a game can differ depending upon whether players may move simultaneously or one player may move first. This may create a *first mover advantage* – the player that moves first can credibly commit to a particular strategy or action that then changes the dominant strategy for the other player. The outcome of a game can also depend upon whether it is a one-shot game – the players interact only once – or whether it is a repeated game. In the Prisoner's dilemma, it is possible to show that repeated interaction allows a cooperative equilibrium to emerge (see box 14.1). This happens because the benefits of cooperation can be offset against the punishment from not cooperating and this can serve as sufficient deterrence.

If both players have a dominant strategy there will be a unique equilibrium. In the absence of this, games may have multiple equilibria or even no equilibrium. For example, cooperation can be sustained under the repeated Prisoner's dilemma game – but so can a number of other strategies. It is possible to have several Nash equilibriums, all self-reinforcing, such that for a particular set of actions no players will diverge from their strategy, and the particular Nash equilibrium chosen may not be the one that offers the highest payoff to the players. For example, one can construct a repeated Prisoner's dilemma game in which the equilibrium is one in which players alternately cheat and cooperate ad infinitum, even though the payoffs to sustained cooperation are higher. Where there are more than two players, equilibriums are determined by whether they may be in the *core* – a set of payoffs to a coalition of the players that cannot be bettered outside of the agreement. The core may be empty if there are more than three players. Game theorists have spent considerable time and effort in developing solution concepts that winnow out multiple equilibria so that a unique equilibrium can be identified.

One way in which players can choose a particular equilibrium is through coordination, which can happen through communication. This is modeled in the game through permitting players to talk to one another before they choose their actions; they may be able to identify a *focal point* (a distinguishing characteristic of

BOX 14.1   MODELING INTERNATIONAL FISHERIES AS A PRISONER'S DILEMMA GAME

In this noncooperative game, each country has the choice of setting fishing quotas (effort) cooperatively or choosing individually how much effort to expend fishing. Table 14.1 shows the payoffs to two countries, A and B, depending upon the combination of actions they each undertake. The actions each can choose are whether they set fishing levels cooperatively or fish individually; the payoffs are expressed as ordinal numbers with the first entry the payoff to country A. Each of the cells corresponds to one of the four possible outcomes depending upon the action each country chooses.

Table 14.1   Payoffs to countries A and B, under different actions

| | | Country A | |
		Set fishing quotas cooperatively	Fish individually
Country B	Set fishing quotas cooperatively	3, 3	4, 1
	Fish individually	1, 4	2, 2

Payoffs to (country A, country B)

If country A chooses to fish cooperatively, the payoff to country A will be 3 if country B cooperates as well; if country B chooses to act individually, the payoff to country A falls to 1. From country B's perspective, its payoff increases from 3 to 4 if it chooses to fish individually when country A is cooperating. In this case, both countries have a dominant strategy – fish individually – and the outcome is the payoff 2,2, lower than the payoffs they would receive if they cooperate. This game is also known as the Prisoner's dilemma; it describes games in which players would be better off if they cooperated but individually it is rational for them to choose actions that lead to a sub-optimal outcome.

We noted earlier that the EEZ transformed what had been open access resources into common-pool goods for those fisheries that fell within the 200-mile limit. However, it did nothing to address the problem of fisheries on the open oceans. It is estimated that $124 billion was spent catching $70 billion worth of fish subsidized through government payments in the early 1990s (Safina, 1995). One component of the current negotiations on trade at the WTO involves an effort to find a way to reduce government subsidies and end overharvesting of international fisheries stocks.

a particular set of payoffs) that enables them to choose a mutually preferable equilibrium from among multiple possible outcomes. However, to be feasible this also has to be a Nash equilibrium – identifying a mutually preferable outcome prior to the game starting may not work if players can increase their individual payoffs by deviating from what they say they will do. For example, under the Prisoner's dilemma, both parties could agree to choose the cooperative outcome – but then each has the incentive to deviate from the agreement. This raises the issue of whether or not players can credibly commit themselves to a particular course of action. Allowing side payments turns the game into a cooperative one; if players can make binding commitments, linking side payments to desired actions can help them achieve the Pareto-optimal outcome.

A key element of these models (and the problems in general) depends upon whether the externalities are reciprocal or unilateral. In the Prisoner's dilemma example (and common-pool resources in general) the externalities are reciprocal – all users of the resource bear the costs borne when one user increases their use. Increased greenhouse gas emissions from one country will affect all other countries equally, as will overfishing by one country's fleet raise the cost for all other countries as well. Unilateral externalities exist where the cost (or benefit) is borne largely outside of the country engaging in the activity or behavior causing the externality. Examples include international river basins, in which upstream practices in one country can lead to sedimentation, flooding, or reduced water flows in downstream countries. Prevailing weather patterns may mean that the pollution is transported from one country downwind to others. The example in box 14.2 shows how these kinds of externalities can be modeled in which the benefits and costs of controlling pollution vary across different countries.

Research in experimental economics suggests that norms are important in explaining outcomes. Despite the economic logic that suggests people will free ride if given the opportunity to voluntarily provide a public good, or overuse a resource in the case of a common property resource, experimental games often show surprisingly strong results in which people voluntarily choose more cooperative outcomes than those predicted by economic theory. There is also empirical evidence to support the idea that voluntary efforts and moral suasion can be powerful organizing forces in the provision of public goods (Klein, 2002). At the same time, however, such outcomes can be reached only where there is a well-established system of rights and responsibilities and some authors have taken the view that such systems require the effective enforcement of rights (Dasgupta, 1998). Other authors have examined how this can influence people's valuation of environmental issues; their willingness to pay or engage in voluntary actions will increase if they adopt a more altruistic viewpoint encompassing a shared responsibility rather than simply regarding the problem from the narrow perspective of economic self-interest (Nyborg, 2000). The issue of how we collectively overcome self-interest is a fundamental one, as seen in box 14.3.

14.4   ISSUES IN MODELING

Criticism of using economic models to illustrate the problems of the global commons falls into three general areas. First, we are often dealing with unknown relationships, especially in the case of environmental and ecological interactions,

BOX 14.2   MODELING THE BENEFITS OF COOPERATION

One way in which we can model the willingness of countries to enter into cooperative agreements to address environmental problems is to measure the benefits and costs of cooperation. Using the example of acid rain, we can construct marginal benefit (marginal damage forgone) and marginal cost functions for individual countries. Each country will choose the level of abatement where the marginal costs just equal the marginal damage within each country when they act alone, not taking into account the damage caused to other countries. If we construct an aggregate damage curve, we can determine the optimal abatement effort if all countries that cooperated come up with an estimate of the benefits to be gained through cooperation. Hutton and Halkos (1995) use this approach to model the effect of acid rain deposition in Europe. They construct marginal damage and marginal abatement costs for European countries party to an international agreement to reduce sulfur emissions and construct a model in which countries can either act individually in determining their own level of abatement or act jointly. In this case, noncooperative behavior involves each country choosing the level of abatement that takes into account the deposition from other countries and their own emissions (but only looking at damage within their own country). Cooperative behavior is modeled by having them act as a unified decision-maker and maximize social welfare, setting the marginal abatement cost equal across all countries.

Hutton and Halkos find that, using 1990 data, the gain from cooperation in 2000 would be $44.5 million, while the reduction in sulfur emissions would be an additional 1.7 million tonnes or 120 percent of abatement levels compared to the noncooperative case. They also find that the solution would require side payments (or some other means of compensation) for those countries whose expenditures would exceed the benefits those countries received individually from the higher level of abatement.

and models may therefore be criticized on the grounds that they do not either adequately incorporate all of the costs and benefits associated with different activities, the interaction between all the variables, or do not value the environmental outputs appropriately. This criticism is, of course, equally applicable to environmental economics in general. Second, if we are using game theory to model the problem, the complexity of the problem increases significantly in multi-player games and it may be difficult if not impossible to identify an equilibrium. Therefore, it will be necessary to identify particular strategies or rule out certain behavior to identify equilibrium. This simplification can again be a source of dissatisfaction. Third, there is also the criticism that models which portray countries as unitary actors are somehow less than satisfying, when we know there will be rich and varied forces at work – social and cultural dynamics, the political impact on domestic constituencies, and strategic considerations – in explaining why a country may choose a particular set of actions.

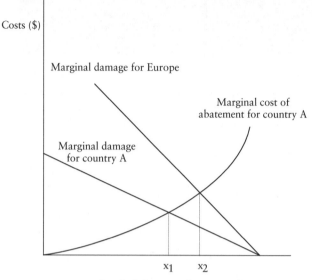

Figure 14.1   Marginal abatement cost and marginal damage curves for country A and regional damage curves

BOX 14.3   IS THERE A NEED FOR A LEVIATHAN?

Thomas Hobbes was concerned with the Laws of Nature that prevented man's life, in his immortal phrase, from being "nasty, brutish, and short." He believed it was our ability to make contracts (covenants in the following quote) and to keep them that formed the basis for the commonwealth (society). In the laws he enunciates, which govern how human society operates, he notes that there is an incentive to break contracts and speaks of the need for a political sovereign that can punish those who violate those contracts in order to ensure people perform their duty. His twelfth law, which prefaces this chapter, describes one possible way of allocating rights to a common property resource. This then raises the question that we will consider in the second half of the chapter – how do we create such a system in the absence of an international sovereign?

"From that law of nature by which we are obliged to transfer to another such rights as, being retained, hinder the peace of mankind, there followeth a third, which is this; that men perform their covenants made; without which, covenants are in vain and but empty words ... there must be some coercive power to compel men equally to the performance of their covenants by the terror of some punishment greater than the benefit they expect by the breach of their covenant, and to make good that propriety which by mutual contract men acquire in recompense of the universal right they abandon; and such power there is none before the erection of the commonwealth" (Chapter XV, Of Other Laws of Nature).

Despite these criticisms, however, this approach does offer insight into the difficulties that need to be overcome in addressing international environmental problems and the importance of institutional design in achieving satisfactory outcomes. Game theory shows the importance of the costs and benefits that players assess in evaluating what voluntary actions they take (e.g. will they participate, what level of effort they may choose), whether or not commitments to take particular actions will be credible (will they comply or deviate), and how those choices can often lead to sub-optimal outcomes. These models show how designing appropriate institutional arrangements – such as providing for side payments or developing credible enforcement mechanisms – can modify the "rules of the game" and countries' behavior and lead to improved outcomes. In the final section, we explore how this economic perspective can shed light on the approaches taken to date and the relative success of efforts to resolve three problems of the global commons: transboundary pollution, biodiversity, and the earth's atmosphere.

14.5   TACKLING THE PROBLEMS OF THE GLOBAL COMMONS

There have been a number of efforts in recent years to address international environmental issues. That international effort has gone into the development of Multilateral Environmental Agreements (MEAs) to address specific issues, as well as capacity building at the international level through organizations such as the United Nations. Some of these efforts have met with partial success. The Law of the Sea conferences established national jurisdiction over near-shore fisheries that reduced over harvesting for some resource stocks, although countries were unable to establish rules governing access to open ocean fisheries and sub-sea deposits, whose status is still unresolved. The Earth Summit at Rio in 1992 was an ambitious effort to develop an international consensus on a number of environmental issues; while it did provide the framework for two major agreements, one involving global warming and the other on protecting biodiversity (the UN Framework Convention on Climate Change and Convention on Biological Diversity respectively), participants were unable to achieve a consensus on how to manage the world's forests (one of the major goals of the summit). Eliciting participation can be problematic; while many countries may sign the initial agreement they may not implement it: for example, despite participating in the negotiations, the US has refused to ratify several of these agreements (such as the Law of the Sea and the UNFCCC) that have been reached.

At the same time, measurable progress has been made in addressing some environmental problems. Below, we examine efforts to address transboundary pollution, and then look at how the international community has approached issues relating to the preservation of biodiversity and protection of the earth's atmosphere. We assess the motives for cooperation among countries, incentives to participate, and how questions of enforcement have been addressed. We look at how multilateral institutions, in particular the UN, have played a role in these MEAs as well. We will also consider the use of trade measures (see also chapter 13), as they have increasingly become seen as one of the ways in which MEAs can accomplish their objectives.

Reducing transboundary pollution

Acid rain and LRTAP

The problem of transboundary acid deposition was first noticed in Scandinavia in the 1950s when acidification of freshwater lakes and streams led to the death of freshwater fishes. It was subsequently identified in Eastern North America and other parts of Europe. Combustion of fossil fuels leads to the release of sulfur dioxide and nitrogen oxide. The main source is power plants but there are secondary contributions from vehicle emissions. These pollutants can be transported up to 600 miles, with the patterns of deposition dependent upon the location of the sources and prevailing weather patterns. The deposition may take the form of wet deposition (precipitated through rainfall) or dry deposition. In many areas, large-scale emitters have significant effects outside of the region. Examples include the power plants of the Ohio Valley in the US, the principal source of air pollution and acid rain in the north-eastern US and neighboring parts of Canada. UK emissions are carried predominantly to neighboring parts of Europe. Weather patterns often mean that the externalities may be largely unilateral. In Sweden, it is estimated that transboundary air pollution may contribute up to 90 percent of all the sulfur deposition in the country (OECD, 1997). The largest negative impact is on human health and premature mortality. Acid deposition can also cause increased acidity of lakes and streams, degrade soils, reduce plant health, and damage building materials. The damage is dependent upon the susceptibility of the receiving material.

In 1979 concerns over pollution levels led the UN Economic Commission for Europe to initiate the Convention on Long-Range Transboundary Air Pollution (LRTAP). The purpose of the Convention is to protect human health and the "environment against air pollution and to endeavor to limit and, as far as possible, gradually reduce and prevent air pollution, including long-range transboundary air pollution." The Convention entered into force in 1983. Although many of its programs are centered on Europe, the Convention has been the basis of regional agreements such as the US – Canada Air Quality Agreement (1991). Areas covered by Convention include North America, Western Europe, most of Eastern Europe and the Russian Federation. The Convention outlines general principles for countries to cooperate in setting pollution level ceiling limits, air pollution abatement efforts, and establishes an institutional framework (monitoring programs) for assessing and monitoring the effects of air pollution. Individual countries develop their own domestic policies to reduce emissions; examples include emission taxes in France and Sweden, mandatory pollution control equipment in the UK, and the use of marketable permits in the US.

The Convention has been subsequently modified by a number of protocols that have extended the Convention, reducing initial sulfur emission limits further and establishing nitrogen oxide limits. These efforts have had some success. Sulfur dioxide emissions in Europe fell by over 20 percent between 1980 and 1988. Levy (1993) argues that while some countries did not change their level of effort from what they would have done in the absence of an agreement, the agreement did influence a set of countries to undertake positive action and that the agreement had the positive effect of placing additional pressure on the US to limit emissions that were affecting Canada.

Toxic chemicals and the Stockholm Convention on POPs

A new concern has emerged in recent years over the accumulation of toxic organic compounds in the environment. Some of these compounds are long-lived in the environment, and can also bio-accumulate, increasing in concentration as they move up through the food chain. Otherwise known as persistent organic pollutants (POPs), they include substances such as PCB, DDT, and are either produced directly as pesticides or for other uses or emitted as part of manufacturing processes (such as dioxins and furans). They can be transported long distances through air and water; substances in the Arctic have been identified as originating from manufacturing plants in the US and Mexico. POPs are a source of particular concern for indigenous peoples living in northern regions that rely on wild fish and game for their diet as the levels of accumulation in human tissue can be enough to cause illness; in some regions, public health authorities have encouraged them to seek alternative sources of food.

The Stockholm Convention on Persistent Organic Pollutants was adopted in 2001 to eliminate or restrict the production of chemicals and pesticides identified as POPs. The Convention imposes different degrees of stringency upon the compounds; some are slated for elimination while others face varying degrees of control including trade restrictions and phased reductions. The Protocol is fairly recent; of the 151 signatories, 12 parties had signed by mid-2002. It parallels other conventions designed to deal with toxic compounds in creating a framework for monitoring production and trade of toxic pollutants, including preparation of information on inventories and the development of procedures for environmentally sound handling and disposal of toxic wastes, and requires countries to certify their production, export, import, and use of these substances.

Preserving biodiversity

Biodiversity describes generally the variety of living organisms found around the world. It can refer to different levels: genetic diversity, species diversity, or eco-system diversity (see chapter 15). Much of these resources are distributed unequally around the world. Tropical forests are thought to hold most of the globe's biodiversity, over half of the earth's 10–30 million species (Lovejoy, 1997). Concerns have centered on the genetic information that is lost when species go extinct or ecosystems are sufficiently disrupted to the point they may no longer function (which may in turn engender extinctions). The international community has made two major efforts to address these issues. The first agreement, the Convention on International Trade in Endangered Species of Wild Fauna and Flora (CITES), is strictly concerned with regulating trade to protect endangered species, while the second is a more ambitious effort to develop a framework to protect and sustain biodiversity around the globe, the Convention on Biological Diversity (CBD). Below we briefly review these two international agreements and their relative success to date.

Endangered species and CITES

The objective of the Convention on International Trade in Endangered Species of Wild Fauna and Flora (CITES) is to use trade restrictions to prevent the over-exploitation of internationally traded species. CITES was signed in 1973 and 154 countries are members. Trade in species and products derived from species are covered by the convention, which works through a licensing system intended to regulate species import, export, and re-export. Countries are responsible for administering licenses and evaluating the effects of trade on the conservation status of species. Species are listed according to three categories set out in the Convention's appendices. Appendix I species are considered most threatened with extinction and can only be commercially traded under exceptional circumstances. Species that are threatened to become endangered as the result of international trade are listed under appendix II. Commercial trade in appendix II species is possible if an export permit is issued and the exporting country can provide assurances that trade is not detrimental to the survival of the species. Appendix III species can be voluntarily submitted by any party wishing to control trade of its own native species. Commercial trade can be carried out if importing parties obtain an export permit from the listing party or a certificate of origin, when species are traded through a third party. Around 800 species are listed in appendix I and about 35,000 are on appendix II.

In force since 1975, the Convention legally binds countries to adhere to its provisions and requires them to use dispute resolution mechanisms prescribed in the agreement. CITES sanctions have proved effective in several instances;

for example, in 1992 the Standing Committee successfully urged parties not to accept CITES documentation from a then non-compliant Italy (British House of Commons, 1999). The result was that legal trade of endangered species in Italy was halted until compliance to CITES provisions subsequently improved. In this case incentives tied to threatened Italian trade were sufficient to convince Italy to comply with CITES provisions as opposed to Italy's international legal obligations as a signatory to the Convention. CITES listings have been credited towards halting declines in several species of concern such as alligators and crocodiles. Widespread public perception that any species under CITES should not be traded has invoked significant political pressures to halt trade in environmentally sensitive species (a current example is environmental campaigns against trade in tropical mahoganies).

Biodiversity and the Convention on Biological Diversity (CBD)

The other major effort to protect the world's flora and fauna began with work by the World Conservation Union (IUCN) that was taken up by the UN Environmental Program (UNEP) in 1990 and became one of the two main accomplishments of the Rio Summit in 1992, the Convention on Biological Diversity (CBD). The mandate of the Convention consists of three interrelated objectives: the conservation of biological diversity; the sustainable use of its components; and the fair and equitable sharing of the benefits arising out of the utilization of genetic resources. There are 181 member countries. The Convention is organized around major themes: agriculture, dry and sub-humid lands, forest, inland waters, marine and coastal, and issues that cut across these different areas. Member countries are called on to conserve and sustainably use biodiversity by developing and adopting national strategies and integrating Convention objectives into sectoral and cross-sectoral policies and minimizing the impact on biodiversity from domestic policies. Some funding is available through the Global Environmental Fund (GEF), a World Bank administered fund available for environmental projects.

The Convention calls for technology transfer to developing countries, to provide financial assistance to developing countries, and technical and resource assistance. The Convention also calls for the development of national biological inventories and members' responsibilities for identifying and monitoring components of biodiversity, as well as determining processes and activities that are threats to biodiversity. Countries are also required to conduct Environmental Impact Assessments (EIAs) on major projects that might impact biodiversity.

In force since 1993, the Convention binds countries to these provisions and requires them to observe the use of Convention dispute resolution mechanisms and/or the International Court of Law to resolve differences. To date no members have invoked dispute resolution mechanisms. Ensuring compliance is a topic of on-going work within the CBD. Recent table propositions include international sharing of information and examining case studies of compliance issues under international laws that pertain to damage caused by marine disasters. It is most members' view that compliance should be achieved through incentives as opposed to punitive measures (CBD Secretariat, 2001).

To date, most efforts of the CBD and its parties have focused on technical aspects such as inventory and classifications of biodiversity, with UNEP publishing global assessments of biodiversity. Recommendations have been made to develop proposals for implementation activities at national and sub-regional levels. In practice, the substantial costs and resources required for implementation are a major barrier to the realization of CBD provisions. Some estimates have placed the cost to developing countries of meeting these requirements as high as $20 billion per year (UNEP, 1993), and species loss and deforestation continue to be a concern, especially in tropical countries.

Protecting the earth's atmosphere

The earth's atmosphere is perhaps the purest form of global commons all countries share. Emissions from one country (aside from the transboundary pollution discussed earlier) impact all other countries. This is especially true for two of the major efforts to address problems of pollutants with potentially damaging effects – ozone and greenhouse gases.

Ozone and the Montreal Protocol

Ozone is produced in the upper atmosphere when ultraviolet light breaks down oxygen. It helps absorb UV radiation as well as infrared radiation. Measurements of naturally occurring ozone levels in the earth's atmosphere have found a great deal of variability, but in the mid-1980s a "hole" was discovered in the ozone layer over the Antarctic where concentration levels had fallen 60–95 percent relative to 1975 levels (Everest, 1988). This led to concerns that further thinning might contribute to increased cancer rates, reduction in crop yields, and the disruption of ecosystems. Although the complete process is not well understood, it is known that several chemicals can act as catalysts to spur the breakdown of ozone. Attention focused on a class of compounds that appeared to be the principal causes of ozone depletion, CFC gases. These were compounds that had been discovered several decades earlier and had been valued for their use as aerosol propellants and cooling liquid.

In 1988 24 countries signed the Montreal Protocol under which emission limits were set for all countries. Developing countries were given a grace period to comply with their limits and industrialized countries assumed the incremental cost of meeting those targets (Benedick, 1998). The Protocol involved the threat of trade restrictions on ozone-depleting substances for countries that did not ratify; in addition, countries that did ratify and not comply with the provisions of the convention were ineligible to receive funding from either the GEF or the financial fund established under the Protocol. The Montreal Protocol has been considered as an international environmental success since there was a rapid decline in global emissions of CFC gases, and the Protocol has been used as a model for other agreements. The success has been attributed in part to the availability of substitutes that could take the place of CFC gases; others have argued that the threat of trade restrictions (even though they were not used) had the effect of ensuring participation (Barrett, 1997). The relatively small number of manufacturers made it feasible to develop a system that could effectively monitor and enforce phased reductions in production (Parson, 1993).

Climate change and the UNFCC

The combustion of fossil fuels not only releases sulfur dioxide and other pollutants; it also releases carbon dioxide, a naturally occurring gas in the atmosphere that is responsible in part for regulating the earth's climate by trapping reflected solar radiation from the earth's surface and retaining heat. Estimates are that carbon dioxide levels have increased by over half of preindustrial carbon dioxide levels, from 270 ppm to 370 ppm today (see chapter 11). Concerns are that the current trend, if continued, could lead to a doubling of carbon dioxide levels to 550 ppm within the next century. It is anticipated that if this happens the earth's temperature could rise by 1.4 to 5.8 degrees Celsius (IPCC); it is expected that the increase in temperature in turn could lead to changes in sea level and weather patterns with the resulting disruption to the natural environment and human societies.

The United Nations Framework Convention on Climate Change (UNFCCC) was adopted in 1992, with the objective of reducing atmospheric concentrations of greenhouse gases (GHGs) to a level that would prevent dangerous interference with the climate system. GHGs include not only carbon dioxide, but also other compounds such as methane, ozone-depleting substances such as CFCs, and nitrous oxides (although carbon dioxide in terms of volume and effect has the largest impact upon climate). As a first step to achieve this objective, the FCCC contained a commitment that industrialized countries would reduce their GHG emissions to the 1990 level by 2000. Recognizing that this voluntary commitment would not be achieved, the parties to the UNFCCC adopted the Kyoto Protocol to the Convention in 1997, laying out a framework for legally binding emission limitations by industrialized countries amounting to 5 percent below the 1990 level by the commitment period of 2008–12. Following four subsequent years of negotiations the rulebook for the Protocol, known as the Marrakesh Accords, was adopted in late 2001 (UNFCCC, 2002).

Table 14.2 shows the variability in emission intensity (CO_2 emissions per unit of GDP), total industrial emissions, and CO_2 emissions per capita for several countries. Total GHG emissions are a function of GDP and population; for developing countries increases in their GDP will be associated with substantial increases in their emissions even if their emission intensity declines. Emissions are also a function of

Table 14.2   Population, GDP, and CO_2 emissions by country, 2000

Country	Population (millions)	GDP per capita ($)	CO_2 emissions per unit of GDP (kg per PP$ of GDP)	Total industrial CO_2 emissions (000 kt)	CO_2 emissions per capita (mt)
Australia*	19	20,640	0.8	306.6	16.7
Brazil*	166	4,630	0.3	273.4	1.7
Canada	30	19,170	0.6	409.4	13.8
China*	1,239	750	1.0	3,363.5	2.5
France	59	24,210	0.3	361.8	6.2
Germany	82	26,570	0.5	861.2	10.5
India*	960	440	0.5	997.4	1.1
Japan	126	32,350	0.4	1,167.7	9.3
Mexico*	96	3,840	0.5	348.1	3.8
UK	59	21,410	0.5	557.0	9.5
US*	270	29,240	0.7	5,301.0	20.0
World Total/ Average	5,897	4,890	0.6	22,653.9	4.0

* Signifies countries that did not pledge emissions reductions under the Kyoto Protocol or have indicated they will not ratify.

Source: World Bank (2000)

the energy mix; countries reliant on coal (which is the greatest contributor of emissions per unit of energy output) will have higher emissions than those relying on natural gas or nuclear power.

The Kyoto Protocol is unique among Multilateral Environment Agreements (MEAs) in that it seeks to impose legally binding targets and explicitly provides for the use of economic instruments to help achieve its environmental objectives. It is also significant because of its long-term and large scope – achieving the UNFCCC goal will require efforts over decades affecting all countries. Thus the likely long-term impacts of the Protocol are wider reaching and more profound than perhaps any other international treaty, environmental or otherwise.

Reductions in 2008–12 in GHG emissions due to the Protocol will have little appreciable impact on climate change given the long-lived nature of GHG in the earth's atmosphere. However, 2008–12 is meant to be the first of many commitment periods, with developing countries asked to take part in efforts to reduce GHGs and further emission limitation targets to be negotiated in subsequent commitment periods. It is this effort over the long term that will serve to achieve the objective of the UNFCCC. Nevertheless, the targets in 2008–12 are difficult and will require substantial effort to change how energy is produced and used if countries are to meet their commitments.

The Protocol established GHG emission limitation or reduction commitments for 38 industrialized countries for 2008–12 and will enter into effect when at least

55 countries including those accounting for at least 55 percent of industrialized country emissions have ratified the Protocol. By October 2002 close to 100 countries had ratified the Protocol, including Canada, Japan, the European Union, and other European countries accounting for close to 44 percent of industrialized country emissions. The current government of the United States has said it will not ratify the Protocol, as has Australia. The Protocol will enter into force when Russia ratifies (as it accounts for approximately 17 percent of 1990 emissions), as it is expected to do (Baker and McKenzie, 2002). It is expected that the Protocol will enter into force by mid-2003. Developing countries do not have targets for 2008–12, but the future negotiations will include consideration of how they can best contribute to global efforts to reduce emissions.

Table 14.3 shows the Kyoto Target, projected emissions for 2010, and the gap between the target and projected emissions. Only two OECD countries – Sweden and the UK – are projected to meet their target, while other countries show that they will need to reduce emissions anywhere between 2 to 25 percent, excluding the US. The US has currently indicated that they will not ratify the Kyoto Protocol, as it would be too costly; instead, they will pursue a variety of measures that would reduce emissions intensity while not compromising economic growth.

To decrease the cost of meeting targets the Protocol established three market-based "flexibility" mechanisms under the principle that the flexibility to seek low-cost contributions anywhere in the world to climate change mitigation will facilitate achieving the UNFCCC objective. International emissions trading (IET) allows trading of emission reductions among industrialized countries that have ratified the Protocol. Countries may allow entities within their countries to also buy and sell in the IET system. Joint implementation (JI) involves investment by an industrialized country, or entities in the country, in projects in another industrialized country to reduce emissions or sequester carbon, resulting in Emission Reduction Units (ERUs). The Clean Development Mechanism (CDM) involves investment by an industrialized country, or entities in the country, in projects in a developed country to reduce emissions or sequester carbon, resulting in Certified Emission Reductions (CERs). The Marrakesh Accords established detailed rules for the operation of each of these mechanisms with further technical details to be established, especially for the CDM. Specific measures for ensuring compliance are still under deliberation. The current focus is on making participation in any international emissions trading systems subject to being in compliance with the agreement; in addition, members that fail to achieve their targets within the first commitment period may find their targets in the second commitment period more stringent.

The costs of climate change: combat or adapt?

Concerns over the cost of climate change have been expressed; both in what the impact might be if no action is taken, as well as what the cost might be to address the problem. Nordhaus (1993) provides a range of estimates for the costs associated with a doubling of carbon dioxide levels for the US, ranging from 1 to 1.3 percent

Table 14.3 Kyoto Protocol targets, projected 2010 emissions, and emission gaps for selected industrialized countries

Country	Kyoto annual target for 2008–12 (% of 1990 emissions)[b]	(Mt CO$_2$-eqivalent)[c]	Projected 2010 emissions (Mt CO$_2$-eq)[d]	Gap between target and projected 2010 emissions (Mt CO$_2$-eq)	Required reduction to reach target (% reduction)
Canada	94	570.8	760.0	189.2	25
Finland	100	77.1	89.9	12.8	14
France	100	545.7	577.0	31.3	5
Germany	79	953.9	978.0	24.1	2
Japan	94	1,155.3	1,320.0	164.7	12
New Zealand	100	72.4	88.1	15.7	18
Norway	101	52.5	63.2	10.7	17
Russian Federation	100	2,372.3	2,200	−172.3	−8
Sweden	104	73.3	71.0	−2.3	−3
United Kingdom	87.5	649.1	632.1	−17.1	−3
United States – Kyoto	93	5,615.5	8,116.0	2,500.5	31
United States – Bush[a]	—	7,761.0	8,116.0	355	4

[a] The Bush administration has stated it will not ratify the Protocol. The target shown corresponds to the target implicit in the Administration's plan to address climate change, and the gap is calculated on that basis.

[b] Emission reduction targets are as specified in the Kyoto Protocol, and adjusted by the EU for its member states according to its internal burden-sharing arrangement. The target for the EU as a whole is 92 percent of the 1990 emission level.

[c] The annual emissions targets for 2008–12 are calculated by multiplying the percent emission commitment times 1990 emissions. Emission estimates for 1990 are from UNFCCC (2002) except for France, Japan and Sweden for which more recent information in these countries' Third National Communications to the UNFCCC are used, as found on the UNFCCC website.

[d] Projected emissions for each country for 2010 are extracted from or calculated using the most recent publications available. Third National Communications, published in 2001 or 2002, are used for each country except Germany. The projected emissions take into account any measures that affect emissions implemented up to around 2000–2001, depending on the country.

Source: Nelson and Vertinsky (2002)

of GDP. Fankhauser (1993) provides estimates of 1.4 percent for OECD countries and 1.5 percent for the developing world of GDP. It should be noted that these estimates are fraught with uncertainty, especially with regards to the impact upon smaller developing countries that have not received as much analysis.

Jaccard and Montgomery (1996) survey a number of different models that estimate the cost to reduce GHG emissions in Canada and the US. They note that "bottom-up" models, which are based on improvements in energy efficiency and changes in energy use, predict that a significant amount of emission reduction can be achieved at a net savings, while "top-down" macro-economic models suggests that there can be significant economic costs associated with meeting stricter environmental regulations. There have been a number of efforts to estimate the costs involved in addressing climate change. Boero et al. (1991) survey the costs of controlling greenhouse gas emissions and find estimates ranging from a 1.0 percent to 5.7 percent reduction in world GDP from 2020 to 2100 (measured relative to a world where there is no attempt to limit emissions). In general, the reduction is due to forgone output through either reducing energy use or the higher costs associated with switching to fuels or investing in technologies that emit less GHG (e.g. switching from coal to natural gas). The discussion in box 14.4 provides a perspective on the technological prospects for reducing GHG and suggests that

BOX 14.4   IS CLEAN ENERGY FEASIBLE?

Hoffert et al. (2002) survey the feasibility of alternative technologies in stabilizing GHG given current energy requirements. They note that in the twentieth century, human population quadrupled while energy consumption increased 16-fold. Current power consumption today is approximately 12 Terawatts, of which 85 percent comes from fossil fuels. Many of the scenarios that look at stabilizing GHG envisage the use of technology and alternative fuels to achieve those objectives, and Hoffert et al. estimate that based on current trends, we would require anywhere from 15 to more than 30 Terawatts of power derived from emission-free energy sources by mid-century. They then investigate a range of technologies that have been suggested. Hydrogen has been proposed as an alternative clean fuel; however, more CO_2 is currently produced by using fossil fuels to create H_2 from natural gas than would be released from burning the fossil fuel for power. Greater use of renewable resources such as solar and bio-fuels are limited by the low power generated per unit of area; they estimate that over 10 percent of the world's landmass (the area currently used for agriculture) would be needed to supply 10 Terawatts of power. In terms of nuclear power, they argue that commercially available uranium resources could supply 6 to 30 years of power between 10 and 30 Terawatts-a temporary and not lasting solution. Finally, they look at other more speculative technologies such as fusion, superconducting electrical grids, and geo-engineering, all of which hold promise, but find that current technology and research efforts today all fall far short of what will be needed in fifty years time. They also consider the use of existing fossil fuel and carbon sequestration to provide a bridge; however, they estimate that it would require sequestration rates of 5-6 GtC/yr to offset 10 Terawatts of power if we use natural gas, doubling to rates of 10 GtC/yr if we use coal (the one fossil fuel resource we do have in plentiful abundance that also emits the most GHG). Currently, it is estimated that temperate forests supply 1 to 3 GtC/yr (implying a significant expansion of forest area to increase sequestration). At the same time, they note that there are concerns about how long-term such storage might be; other carbon sequestration technologies (deepsea) might be possible but again, current research is unequipped to deal with the magnitude of effort and rates that would be required.

there would need to be significant expenditures in R&D if we hope to achieve substantial reductions in the absence of a change in current trends in energy use.

Several NGO groups argue that the environmental benefits associated with reducing fossil fuel emissions mean that society will be better off from implementing measures to reduce GHG and that a strict economic cost–benefit analysis should not be the only test for whether we pursue such measures (see, for example, Tellus et al., 2002). They also argue that the idea of sustainable development, in which future economic growth should not compromise environmental quality nor the ability of ecosystems to function, requires a fundamental change in ethos and how we conduct human affairs. Others argue that any efforts undertaken will not have an impact for at least a century, given current levels of GHG, and that given the uncertainty associated with the degree and effects of climate change, it is more cost effective to wait and adapt.

Is Kyoto the right approach?

The Kyoto Protocol has been criticized on several grounds. First, emissions targets are too ambitious and unrealistic and are only short-term; in the long run even if countries do meet them their effect on climate change will be insignificant. Second, only industrialized countries are covered; any reduction in their emissions will be swamped by rising emissions in countries that aren't covered by the agreement. Third, there is an absence of effective compliance mechanisms (Stavins and Barrett, 2002). In addition, some have criticized the use of market-based mechanisms (such as CDM) that may contribute to "leakage" – shifting GHG emissions from participants to countries not covered by the agreement with no net reduction in emissions. Some countries, such as the US, are advocating the use of R&D to reduce emissions intensity, with the hope that it will permit economic growth at the same time as emissions decline. A number of authors have suggested that an increased reliance on market mechanisms could lower the cost of emissions reductions, which, coupled with technological innovation, may make such reductions politically more feasible. More recently, Kyoto negotiations are now including an emphasis on adaptation, reflecting the concern that the reduction in emissions may not be as much as originally anticipated or required (Baker and Mackenzie, 2002).

14.6 FUTURE ISSUES

Our discussion suggests that an understanding of the costs and benefits involved for parties is an important determinant of the relative success of international efforts to address environmental problems. The success of the Montreal

Protocol and CITES reflect their focus on specific measures in which the costs are limited and the benefits well defined and understood. Efforts to control transboundary pollution have worked, but effort appears to be conditioned by the cost and benefits of individual participation. The UK was originally not party to LRTAP (the Long Range Transport of Air Pollutants), the agreement covering sulfur dioxide emissions in Europe, which is not surprising since much of their emissions were borne by countries downwind. They were brought into the agreement when they became part of the EU; however, their emissions had been substantially reduced by that time through the conversion from coal to natural gas and cleaner fuels. While it is too soon to assess the effectiveness of the Stockholm Convention on reducing POPs, it is noteworthy that just under half the parties that have ratified to date – Canada, Sweden, Norway, Finland, and Iceland – are all countries with populations and ecosystems especially susceptible to the problem. One area of transboundary resources not discussed in the text is that of international river basins; attempts to reach agreements by countries sharing the same resource have been much more difficult and elusive, probably because it takes on the dynamics of a zero-sum game in which one country's diversion of water is another country's loss, and competition for water has been suggested as a potential source of future international conflict (de Villiers, 1999).

The problem of achieving successful international cooperation becomes more apparent in the two most ambitious efforts to date, the CBD and UNFCCC. The number of countries involved, and substantial disparities in costs across countries, distinguishes both of these agreements. In the CBD, the burden falls upon developing countries because of the higher levels of biodiversity found within many of their countries. The UNFCCC would impose more stringent targets on some industrialized countries than others, reflecting the time period chosen in developing targets (principally because several of those countries with less stringent targets switched from coal to other fuels in the intervening time period). Those countries with more stringent targets can be expected to face significant costs in reducing emissions relative to others; table 14.3 shows that Canada, New Zealand, and Norway would have to reduce emissions by 25, 18, and 17 percent respectively. In addition, developing countries have been unwilling to consider joining the UNFCCC, arguing that assuming a cap on their emissions will impose a disproportionate burden upon them since they will be unable to industrialize. The free-rider problem associated with the public good nature is evident in both agreements. Industrialized countries have been unwilling to provide significant funds to the developing countries, despite the acknowledgement of the necessity of it in both agreements, and all countries have been reluctant to adopt domestic measures that are any more stringent than those called for in the agreements. The problem of climate change is only made more difficult by the fact that addressing it now imposes costs on current generations, while the benefit will accrue to future generations.

Incentives for compliance

The ability to enforce compliance with agreements also plays a role in their relative success. Both CITES and the Montreal Protocol utilize trade restrictions, and the removal of trade privileges (or threat) if a member doesn't comply with the agreement, and the public scrutiny that can accompany such a violation, appear to have been effective in eliciting compliance. Trade restrictions have been suggested as a compliance mechanism for other international environmental agreements such as the UNFCCC (Stavins and Barrett, 2002; Barrett, 1997). In this case, environmental considerations enter into international trade, not because such measures are taken to reduce environmental harm (see chapter 13), but because it is hoped that they will promote actions by countries to take action to protect the environment. However, this approach assumes that countries will be willing to voluntarily establish measures that may penalize them, and the idea of environmental-linked trade measures has been resisted by a number of developing countries that feel that such restrictions will simply become another mechanism by which developed countries can establish new trade barriers to their exports. Even industrialized countries appear reluctant to adopt measures that could potentially penalize them for noncompliance and that could reduce their sovereignty over how they manage their domestic resources. An example of such concerns is found in the debate over proposals to list commercial fish species that are considered at risk under CITES. Countries that have fishing fleets argue that such matters are better dealt with by specific multilateral agreements dealing with the particular fish stock. Some NGOs argue that there should be no trade whatsoever in any animal species, regardless of whether they are endangered or not, an idea resisted by developing countries who argue that trade, if properly monitored, can contribute to their development and that such attitudes represent the imposition of Western values (Anonymous, 2002).

At the same time, this debate suggests that the importance of these efforts is not in seeking negative incentives to induce compliance (since countries are unlikely to voluntarily commit themselves), but rather in positive incentives that can be created by paying attention to these issues. The provision of information and public scrutiny can be a source of compliance. Even if the initial agreement is not immediately effective, raising the prominence of the issue and mobilizing political support helps create a framework in which the issue matters. International NGOs both help disseminate information and articulate norms that help advance the global debate. This raises the possibility that the second means of enforcement – the reliance on social norms to sanction inappropriate or unacceptable behavior – may start to play a greater role in establishing and enforcing agreement on how to address these environmental issues. As an example, consider sustainable development, an idea that generates widespread public support although there is yet to be a commonly agreed operable definition. Other concepts that have entered the debate over environmental problems include the *polluter pays principle* – the now widely accepted idea that the party engaged in the activity causing the pollution should pay the full cost associated with it – and the recent introduction of the *precautionary principle*. Originally phrased as the idea that uncertainty about whether or not efforts to resolve an environmental problem would be successful should not preclude one from taking action, it is now also being used to mean that one should not proceed if one is uncertain as to whether a project or economic activity will have a detrimental effect on the environment. Perhaps it is through the development of these ideas that we will be able to develop a consensus on how to deal with these more difficult and currently intractable problems. Ultimately, it is the only way in which we can ever successfully hope to incorporate the impact of our actions today on future generations by internalizing that long-term perspective.

FURTHER READING

Ostrom (1990) reviews the success and failures of common property resources and the importance of institutional arrangements. There is an extensive literature on game theory; some of the more approachable volumes include Gintis (2000) and Rasmussen (1989). Schelling (1984) provides an excellent introduction to how strategic choices can influence decision-making. The idea of trust, social capital, and norms is explored in Ben-Ner and Putternam (1998). Dasgupta et al. (1997) provides an example of game theoretic approaches to a number of different international environmental issues including shared watersheds, biodiversity, and transboundary pollution.

There is substantial literature on all the environmental problems discussed in the text. Victor et al. (1998) is a useful survey of several MEAs. They discuss the issue of compliance (do countries meet their commitments?) and effectiveness (are those commitments meaningful?) and suggest the two are not necessarily the same and that the focus should be on the latter. Alberty and VanDeveer (1996) investigate the characteristics of the Montreal Protocol and question whether the specialized circumstances that contributed to its success make its approach generally applicable to other international environmental problems such as climate change. Benedick (1998) reviews the general politics that shaped the fashioning of the agreement. Schelling (1997) argues that focusing narrowly on how to share the costs and benefits among participants may not be the best way to negotiate a successful climate change agreement; instead, developed countries should recognize that it is in their larger self-interest to assist developing countries in finding clean energy technologies.

There are a number of different studies modeling climate change that range from models that attempt to predict changes in temperatures to models that assess the economic impact of climate change that are reviewed in Boero (1991) and Darmstadter (1991). Weyant (2000) provides an introductory overview of the current models investigating climate change and the issues raised in modeling the costs of adapting to climate change. A list and description of the world's major environmental treaties and conventions is given in Appendix 7 of Grafton et al. (2001).

In addition, all of the MEAs mentioned in the text have their own websites.

LRTAP: http://www.unece.org/env/lrtap/
POPs: http://www.pops.int/
Montreal Protocol: http://www.unep.org/ozone/montreal.shtml
UNFCCC: http://www.unfccc.int
CITES: www.cites.org
CPB: http://www.biodiv.org

REFERENCES

Alberty, M. and VanDeveer, S. (1996). Modeling the Global Environment: Is the Montreal Protocol a Useful Precedent?, in D. Pirages, ed., *Building Sustainable Societies*, M.E. Sharpe: Armonk, New York.

Anonymous (2002). Out of the Blue, *The Economist*, October 31.

Baker and McKenzie (2002). Climate Change Negotiations: COP 8 Outcomes. Available at www.ieta.org. May 12.

Barrett, S. (1997). The Strategy of Trade Sanctions in International Environmental Agreements, *Resource and Energy Economics*, 19: 345–61.

Ben-Ner, A., and Putternam, L. (eds) (1998). *Economics, Values, and Organizations*, Cambridge University Press: Cambridge, UK.

Benedick, R. (1998). *Ozone Diplomacy*. Cambridge: Harvard University Press.

Boero, G., Clarke, R., and Winters, L. (1991). *The Macroeconomic Costs of Controlling Greenhouse Gases: A Survey*, HMSO: London.

CBD Secretariat (2001). Report of the Workshop on Liability and Redress in the Context of the CBD (UNEP/CBD/WS-L&R/3). [Online] Available: http://www.biodiv.org/doc/meetings/wslr/wslr-01/wslr-01-03-en.pdf

Darmstadter, J. (1991). The Economic Cost of CO_2 Mitigation: A Review of Estimates for Selected World Regions. Discussion Paper ENR91-06. Resources for the Future: Washington, DC.

Dasgupta, P., Maler, K., and A. Vercelli (1997). *The Economics of Transnational Commons*. Clarendon Press: Oxford.

Dasgupta, P. (1998). The Economics of Poverty in Poor Countries, *Scandinavian Journal of Economics*, 100 (1): 41–68.

de Villiers, M. (1999). *Water*, Stoddart: Toronto.

Everest, D. (1988). *The Greenhouse Effect: Issues for Policy-Makers*. Joint Energy Programme, Royal Institute of International Affairs, London.

Fankhauser, S. (1993). The Economic Costs of Global Warming: Some Monetary Estimates, in Y. Kaya, N. Nakicenovic, W. Nordhaus, and F. Toth, eds, *Costs, Impacts, and Benefits of CO2 Mitigation*. IIASA CP-93-2: 85–105. Laxenburg, Austria.

Gibson, C., McKean, M., and Ostrom, E. (eds) (2000). *People and Forests: Communities, Institutions, and Governance*. MIT Press: Cambridge, MA.

Gintis, H. (2000). *Game Theory Evolving*. Princeton University Press: Princeton, NJ.

Grafton, R. Q., Pendleton, L. H., and Nelson, H. W. (2001). *A Dictionary of Environmental Economics, Science and Policy*. Edward Elgar: Cheltenham.

Hackett, S., Schlager, E., and Walker, J. (1994). The Role of Communication in Resolving Commons Dilemmas: Experimental Evidence with Heterogeneous Appropriators. *Journal of Environmental Economics and Management*, 27 (2): 99–126.

Hutton, J., and Halkos, G. (1995). Optimal Acid Rain Abatement Policy for Europe: An Analysis for the Year 2000. *Energy Economics*, 17 (4): 259–75.

Hobbes, T. and Martinich, A. P. (ed.) (2002). *Leviathan*. Broadview Press: Ontario.

Hoffert, M., et al. (2002). Advanced Technology Paths to Global Climate Stability: Energy for a Greenhouse Planet, *Science*, 298 (November 1): 981–7.

IPCC, Intergovernmental Panel on Climate Change (1990). *Climate Change: The IPCC Scientific Assessment*. Cambridge University Press: Cambridge.

Jaccard, M., and Montgomery, W. D. (1996). Costs of Reducing Greenhouse Gas Emissions in the USA and Canada, *Energy Policy*, 24 (10/11): 889–98.

Klein, D. (2002). In Spulber, ed., *Famous Fables of Economics: Myths of Market Failures*. Blackwell Publishers: Oxford.

Levy, M. (1993). European Acid Rain: The Power of Tote-Board Diplomacy, in P. Haas, R. Keohane, and Levy M. eds, *Institutions for the Earth: Sources of Effective Environmental Protection*. MIT Press: Cambridge, MA.

Lovejoy, T. E. (1997). Biodiversity: What Is It?, in M. L. Reaka-Kudla et al., eds, *Biodiversity II: Understanding and protecting our natural resources*. Joseph Henry Press: Washington, DC.

Nelson, H. and Vertinsky, I. (2002). The Kyoto Protocol and Climate Change Mitigation: Implications for Canada's Forest Industry. FEPA Working Paper 2002-1. University of British Columbia: Vancouver.

Nordhaus, W. (1993). *Managing the Global Commons: The Economics of Climate Change*. MIT Press: Cambridge, MA.

Nyborg, K. (2000). Homo Economicus and Homo Politicus: Interpretation and Aggregation of Environmental Values, *Journal of Economic Behavior and Organization*, 42: 305–22.

OECD (1997). *Environmental Taxes and Green Tax Reform*, OECD: Paris.

Ostrom, E. (1990). *Governing the Commons: The Evolution of Institutions for Collective Action*. Cambridge University Press: New York.

Parson, E. (1993). Protecting the Ozone Layer in P. Haas, R. Keohane, and M. Levy, eds, *Institutions for the Earth: Sources of Effective Environmental Protection*, MIT Press: Cambridge, MA.

Rasmussen, E. (1989). *Games and Information: An Introduction to Game Theory*, Basil Blackwell: Oxford.

Safina, C. (1995). The World's Imperiled Fish, *Scientific American*, 273 (5): 46–53.

Schelling, T. (1984). *Choice and Consequence*. Harvard University Press: Cambridge, MA.

Schelling, T. (1997). The Costs of Combating Global Warming: Facing the "Tradeoffs", *Foreign Affairs*, 76 (6): 8–14.

Stavins, R. and Barrett, S. (2002). Increasing Participation and Compliance in International Climate Change Agreements, Kennedy School of Government Working Paper RWP-02-031.

Tellus Institute and MRG and Associates (2002). *The Bottom Line on Kyoto: Economic Benefits of Canadian Action*. Prepared for the David Suzuki Foundation and the World Wildlife Fund. April, Vancouver.

UNEP (1993). *Global Biodiversity*. UNEP: Nairobi.

UNFCCC (2002). Report of the Conference of the Parties on its Seventh Session Held at Marrakesh. Part Two: Action Taken by the Conference of the Parties. UNFCCC/CP/2001/13/Add.1

Victor, D., Rautsiala, K., and Skolnikoff, A. (eds) (1998). *The Implementation and Effectiveness of International Environmental Commitments*. MIT Press: Cambridge, MA.

Weyant, J. (2000). An Introduction to the Economics of Climate Change Policy. Prepared for the Pew Center on Global Climate Change: www.pew.org

World Bank (2000). *The Little Green Data Book*, World Bank: Washington, DC.

CHAPTER FIFTEEN

BIODIVERSITY

Human society has a choice in regard to the amount of diversity that will be retained along its development path, and ... this choice has thus far been made in a haphazard fashion, resulting in unmanaged diversity depletion. (Swanson, 1995)

15.1 INTRODUCTION

Since the 1980s there has been an increased awareness about the potential loss of biological diversity (or *biodiversity* as it is commonly known). As current biodiversity is the result of more than three billion years of evolution, some degree of evolution with respect to the number, variety, and variability of living organisms or species extinction is to be expected in any period. Leakey and Lewin (1995) point out that, back in the earth's distant past, five mass extinctions took place and during each one at least 65 percent of species became extinct. Furthermore, they estimate that 99.9 percent of all species that have ever lived are extinct. While the catalyst for these previous extinctions is believed to be meteorite collisions, it is widely accepted that the human species is responsible for a dramatic and unprecedented increase in the current extinction rate. In fact, Leakey and Lewin (1995) predict a sixth human-caused extinction. In this they are supported by other evidence. Tuxhill and Bright (1998) argue that the background rate of extinction prior to the appearance of human populations was about 1 to 3 species a year. It is now believed that the current rate of species extinction is in excess of 1,000 species a year, thereby resulting in an extinction rate that has been estimated at over 1,000 times the natural rate of extinction (Wilson, 1988). Concerns over such a dramatic increase in the extinction rate have resulted in forecasts about the detrimental consequences of biodiversity losses for the current level of economic activity and future growth possibilities (Perrings, Mäler, Folke, Holling, and Jansson, 1995; Tuxhill and Bright, 1998; Commission for Environmental Cooperation, 2002).

Since biodiversity refers to a number of different concepts, it is useful to define this term more precisely. The Convention on Biodiversity (an international treaty adopted at the United Nations Conference on Environment and Development commonly called the Earth Summit held in Rio de Janeiro in 1992) used the following working definition:

> Biodiversity refers to the number, variety, and variability of all living organisms in terrestrial, marine and other aquatic ecosystems and the ecological complexes of which they are part. (UNCED, CBD, Article 2)

Given this definition, it is important to note that concern for biodiversity has not focused solely upon the endangerment and possible extinction of individual species. Growth at the extensive margin in tropical forest zones has led to a reduction in the sizes of these *ecosystems*. Since ecosystems such as tropical forests and wetlands have been identified as important repositories of biological diversity, many scientists now fear not just species losses, but losses of gene pools and even of large-scale ecosystems.[1] Holling, a prominent scientist, fears that this means that an important characteristic of biological systems, namely *resilience*, is currently in the process of being lost (Holling, 1973; Holling, Schindler, Walker, and Roughgarden, 1995). The resilience of a system is its ability to cope with changes in environmental circumstances, such as global climate change. Once a particular threshold has been passed with respect to variability, some concern has been expressed that there may be an unstoppable destabilization effect (Perrings et al., 1995). Since extinction is *irreversible*, the consequences of current rates of extinction may be the imposition of enormous costs, not only upon current generations, but also upon future generations. Thus, at issue is the efficient use of biodiversity by human populations.

Why is the efficient use of biodiversity such an important goal? For economists an appealing way to think about biodiversity is as a means of providing the *natural capital* (Pearce and Moran, 1994; Perrings, 1994; Costanza et al., 1997) that underpins our economic activity and well-being. If we are interested in the issue of the *sustainability* of economic activity on the planet, then a necessary condition for continued development is that the opportunities associated with the stock of *natural capital* should be increasing (or at least non-decreasing) over time. A second, and related, role played by biodiversity may be as the stock of information upon which research and development processes intended for the betterment of humankind are built. In either case, the loss of biological diversity will make it difficult, or perhaps even impossible, to promote sustainable economic activity on the planet. Some researchers believe that the depletion of the aggregate stock of natural capital through an increasing rate of extinction may pose the greatest threat to sustainability, in spite of positive technical changes intended to counteract losses (Perrings and Pearce, 1994).[2]

This chapter examines issues relating to biological diversity. In previous chapters we have looked at the role played by individual resources such as minerals, fisheries, water, and forests in supporting economic activity. In each of those cases the focus has been upon the linkage between the value of the resource or asset base and the employment of that asset in providing secondary products for the market. When it comes to analyzing biological diversity there are other considerations. In particular, it is no longer sufficient to concentrate merely upon the size of the asset base. In order to examine how best to use our stock of biodiversity, we must also look at the composition of the asset base and its variability in relation to economic decision-making. What makes biodiversity such a complicated issue is the following. Not only does biodiversity represent a number of different components of the stock of natural capital, it also represents the thousands of ecological processes that are crucial to the proper functioning of our environment. In many cases, these processes are not understood in great detail and do not provide easily recognizable output that can be valued by human beings. These characteristics make it difficult to measure both the quantity and value of biodiversity. Since the science underlying biodiversity and its processes is still not well understood, it follows that economic, legal, and policy analyses are even less well developed. Biodiversity is a topic that can best be described as evolving.

The next section of this chapter presents more precise definitions of biological diversity and is followed by a section that examines the range of goods and services obtained from the various components of biodiversity. The section following this looks at methods used to obtain economic values relating to biodiversity. The chapter concludes with a brief review of the causes for biodiversity loss and a discussion of regulatory methods that might be employed to stem losses from excessive exploitation of biological resources.

15.2   DEFINITIONS OF BIOLOGICAL DIVERSITY

There are three fundamental levels of biological organization: genes, species, and ecosystems, where genes are found within species and species exist within ecosystems (Pearce and Moran, 1994; National Academy of Science, 1999). When we talk about biodiversity this masks what is meant with respect to each of the three levels.

Genetic diversity means the variations in the genetic information that is found in the genes of living organisms (e.g., the Human Genome Project which is attempting to describe DNA sequences). The number of genes varies according to the complexity of the organism. In addition to the degree of variability in the number of genes within a population of a given species, there is also variability of genes between populations of species. Greater diversity means that evolutionary processes can proceed more freely and implies a more resilient system.

The simplest measure of species diversity is the number of species, currently thought to number between 10 and 50 million globally (McNeely, Miller, Reid, Mittermeier, and Warner, 1990; Pimm, Russell, Tittleman, and Brooks, 1995). It is a difficult exercise to define a species. This makes it difficult to count the current number of species. In addition to number of species as a measure of diversity, the variability of species in a given area is also important. A common unit of measurement is a statistical index of species diversity (incorporating both the total number of species and the relative abundance of all species (evenness) (National Academy of Science, 1999). However, this suffers from being non-monotonic,[3] so a higher number does not necessarily imply more diversity and, hence, *resilience*.

An ecosystem is a distinct assemblage of plants and animals. Ecosystem diversity is used to describe both the number of different habitats or biomes (tundra, coniferous forest, desert, tropical rain forest, wetland, etc.), as well as the variety of biotic communities and ecological processes within a given ecosystem. It has not been demonstrated that there needs to be a relationship between species diversity and the stability of an ecosystem (Johnson, Vogt, Clark, Schmitz, and Vogt, 1996). However, it is now believed that it is the prevalence of certain *keystone species* (either individual organisms or groups of organisms) which ultimately determine the robustness of a particular ecosystem (Folke, Holling, and Perrings, 1996).

15.3 IMPORTANCE OF BIODIVERSITY TO HUMANS

Biodiversity was earlier referred to as an asset, part of the natural capital that provides services to human beings. Before discussing methods of how to value a reduction in biodiversity arising from a depletion of such natural capital, it is useful to categorize the various service flows arising from it. In this discussion we shall hold to the economic view that value is anthropocentric in nature; that is, it is derived from the benefits flowing to human populations from the goods and services provided by biodiversity. However, a counter-position has been made that there are intrinsic values in the natural capital stock, that is, species are of value in themselves, and not just as filtered through a human lens.[4]

Total economic value is comprised of use (active) and non-use values (see chapter 8). Within use value are three categories: direct, indirect, and future. Direct use values flow to human beings when they benefit from being able to use the products of biodiversity in the form of harvested or extracted species (e.g., timber, fish, plants) either directly or incorporated into other consumer goods. A second type of direct use value is non-consumption benefits such as aesthetic services provided by eco-tourism types of activities. Indirect use values are provided by biodiversity in the form of ecosystem services such as recycling of organic materials, watershed protection, *carbon sequestration*, and water filtering. Future values arise from the value of the option to make use of an asset in the future (Weisbrod, 1964), in other words, the amount of money that individuals would be willing to pay to conserve biodiversity for future, as yet undefined, use.[5] Indirect and future values are sometimes referred to as passive use values. Finally, non-use values are typically viewed as so-called pure *existence values* (Krutilla, 1967), namely, values that are not associated with actual or planned use of the resource. It should be noted that, while some services provided by biodiversity are private, many others are public. It is the latter that serve as the focus of the following discussion about the means by which economists have conceptualized the value of biodiversity.

In order to examine how we might value a reduction in biodiversity according to a change in total economic value we begin by considering the utility function of a representative individual. The level of utility is assumed to depend upon quantities of n private or market goods (symbolized by a vector X comprised of elements: $x_1, x_2, ..., x_n$) and fixed levels of m environmental and resource service flows (symbolized by a vector Q comprised of elements: $q_1, q_2, ..., q_m$). For the purposes of this discussion, it is assumed that these levels are fixed to the individual. The prices of market goods are also assumed fixed to an individual and are symbolized by the vector P comprising the following elements: $p_1, p_2, ..., p_n$. For simplicity we assume that environmental services flows are unpriced. The individual is assumed to maximize utility subject to a budget constraint, where M is taken as income. The individual's budget constraint is $PX \leq M$. Maximization of utility yields the set of demand functions for the market goods, conditioned upon the levels of environmental services. From the optimization exercise we obtain the dual *expenditure function*. This describes the minimum expenditure necessary to produce a given level of utility (say U^0), conditional upon market prices and the level of environmental services (see chapter 8).

$$E = e(P; Q; U^0)$$ (1)

Let us assume that Q consists of a single element of q. We can now examine the *welfare* change associated with a reduction in the level of q (e.g., some form of biodiversity loss). We will be interested in obtaining the value of a marginal reduction in q. This is found by partially differentiating the expenditure function with respect to q to obtain the value (W_q) associated with the marginal reduction.

$$W_q = -\frac{\partial E}{\partial q}$$ (2)

At least two competing measures can be defined that measure this value. The first measure, *equivalent surplus*, uses the new (lower) utility level as the reference point and determines how much income an individual would be willing to forgo in order to prevent a loss in biodiversity from occurring.[6] This is called the *willingness-to-pay* (WTP) income measure.

$$ES = e(P, q^0, U^1) - e(P, q^1, U^1) = e(P, q^0, U^1) - M$$ (3)

The second measure, *compensating surplus*, is a *willingness-to-accept* (WTA) income measure. It poses the question of how much income would be necessary to compensate an individual for a reduction in biodiversity (that is, put the individual back to his/her original utility level).

$$CS = e(P, q^0, U^0) - e(P, q^1, U^0) = M - e(P, q^1, U^0)$$ (4)

Using the *household production function* framework first proposed by Bockstael and McConnell (1983) as the basis for valuation, Freeman (1993) shows how the compensating (or equivalent) surplus measure above can be decomposed into three parts: use value (pertaining to the values associated with an individual's actual use of the environment), non-use value (pertaining to current non-use of the environment but with the potential for passive or future use) and *existence value* (pertaining to the value placed upon the environment without any active or passive use aspect). To see this, let us define q^{min} as the threshold or minimum viable level of a resource (or biodiversity). Define, as well, the *choke price* for use of the resource as $P*$ (this is the price at which demand for the services of the resource falls to zero). Finally, define the current price of the resource as p^1. Then, Freeman shows the following:

$$CS = CS_U + CS_N + CS_E$$

$$= e(P, q^0, U^0) - e(P*, q^0, U^0) + e(P*, q^0, U^0) - e(P*, q^{min}, U^0)$$

$$+ e(P*, q^{min}, U^0) - e(P, q^1, U^0)$$

$$= e(P, q^0, U^0) - e(P, q^1, U^0) \tag{5}$$

In this equation, when there is a threshold value for q, the total value of a reduction in q that causes the threshold to be crossed is the sum of three components.[7] These are a loss of use value, a loss of a user's non-use value and the loss of the pure existence value. The first component is clearly a measure of the active use values discussed earlier, while the latter two components measure non-use or passive use values.

As it stands, these equations apply to a static, timeless, and certain framework. Suppose there is the potential for an irreversible destruction of a unique natural asset. In this context, the proper measure of welfare loss is the compensating increase in wealth required to maintain lifetime utility at its original level. This is approximated by the present value of the *compensating surpluses* for all future years and could in principle reflect both use and non-use values.[8]

Given the two alternative measures that an economist could use to measure the value of biodiversity loss, which should she choose? Early work by Randall and Stoll (1980) implied that, in practice, there would not be a big difference between the equivalent surplus and compensating surplus measures. However, more recent work by Hanemann (1991) shows that, when income is held constant in the case of valuing a single environmental good (q), then there is a potentially large difference between the two measures that is dependent upon the shape of the indifference curve and the degree of substitution as viewed by the individual. In particular, the compensating surplus measure (which is the amount of income necessary to compensate for a loss of biodiversity) can be substantially higher than the equivalent surplus measure (which is the income one is willing to pay to avoid the loss). In practice, as we shall see, it is most common to use the equivalent or willingness-to-pay approach.[9]

15.4   VALUING BIODIVERSITY LOSS

In this section we will explore a number of the various avenues that have been pursued by economists in their attempts to obtain both direct and indirect values relating to biodiversity. In order to illustrate the breadth of material we will look separately at the three different types of biodiversity: genetic, species, and ecosystem.

Valuing genetic material

One of the most important services that flows from genetic material pertains to the medicinal use of unique gene properties in the development of drugs. Modern pharmaceutical research has relied heavily upon plant-based genetic material to develop life-saving and health-improving medications. In the developed world some 25 percent of all medical drugs are based on plants or their derivatives; however, this number is three times higher in developing countries (Principe, 1991). Thus, an important component of the value of genetic material is related to health benefits or potential health benefits.

For plant-based drugs already on the market, three approaches have been used to obtain the value of the genetic material contained within. Firstly, one can look at the values arising from market-traded plant material on the assumption that market values represent true willingness-to-pay values. However, this tends to yield a fairly low value since it simply represents the direct or active use of the material as an input into a production process and, presumably, only measures the value added of the input to firms. In addition, it may be subject to *market failures* in the form of non-competitive behavior, thereby leading to market prices that are not true willingness-to-pay values. A second approach is to look at the market value of plant-based drugs. The argument is that these drugs might not exist save for the unique genetic properties of the plants upon which they are based. On the one hand, these market values will tend to overstate the values of the underlying plants if there is monopoly power such as arises from the presence of patents. On the other hand, it may also understate the true willingness-to-pay by human beings for the medical properties of the drugs. Finally, the third approach looks at values of plant-based drugs in terms of their life-saving properties. This latter tends to provide the highest value of the three approaches since it represents the willingness-to-pay for health or life-saving properties of drugs and contains a number of individual components of value (including option values).

Some empirical estimates of the values of genetic material using each of these three approaches are available. A cautionary note is in order, however, with regard to the usefulness of these estimates. It must be noted that, as values observed for existing drugs, these values are not necessarily relevant to assessing the value of preventing the existence of species not presently known to be sources of potentially valuable drugs. Amongst others, Principe (1989, 1991) has produced estimates for the value of the top 40 plant species that account for the plant-based drugs produced in developed countries. He has estimated that the market value of trade in medicinal plants for the United States is $US 5.7 billion, while the equivalent amount for OECD countries is about $US 15.2 billion. The market values of prescription and over-the-counter plant-based drugs are estimated to be $US 15.5 billion and $US 59.4 billion, respectively. Finally, assuming the value of a *statistical life* to be $US 4 million and the number of lives saved to be 30,000, an estimate of the value associated with avoided deaths from these top 40 plant species is about $US 240 billion for the US and $US 720 billion for OECD countries. All values are for 1990.

Given the uncertainty inherent in the usefulness of any particular plant or genetic material, the methods described above may not be appropriate if we want to obtain values for as yet undiscovered genetic material. One approach is simply to look at the sums of money already committed by companies for the exclusive rights to *bioprospect*. The best known example of such a transaction occurred in 1991 when Merck and Co., the world's largest pharmaceutical company, paid Costa Rica about $US 1 million, as well as the promise to pay royalties associated with new commercial products, for the private rights to examine 2,000 samples of the gene pool. More recently, Glaxo Wellcome, the world's second largest pharmaceutical company, signed an agreement with a Brazilian company for the right to screen 30,000 samples of compounds of plant, fungus, and bacterial origin. The value of the transaction was $US 3.2 million, in 1999 dollars (Nunes and van den Bergh, 2001).

There are at least two reasons to believe that the values emerging from the exercise described above are lower bounds values. Firstly, since there is a *public goods* nature to genetic material from plants, these markets are just beginning to emerge. Hence, the "market" values would tend to underestimate the value to society. Secondly, these observed prices for genetic material also include compensation for collection and processing effort, rather than for the genetic material itself. In some cases, the "implicit" value of the latter may be very small. Simpson, Sedjo, and Reid (1996) cite documents indicating that of the $US 1 million deal with Costa Rica, less than 10 percent was for the genetic material with the bulk of the money going to equipment and expenses of Cost Rica's Instituto Nacional de Biodiversidad (INBio).

A second approach used to value as yet undiscovered genetic resources also relies upon the notion that they are important to pharmaceutical companies. In this context the value of preserving a species, typically a plant species, is essentially the potential value of an unknown species for the production of new drug therapies. As mentioned earlier, one can think of biodiversity as a stock of information upon which research and development processes are built (Swanson, 1996). While one might believe that the market values of already discovered drugs might provide information about the value of potential drugs, these numbers ignore the costs associated with testing plants for new genetic material to be used in drugs and associated development costs of such new drugs. As such they cannot be used as they are. Instead a number of researchers have developed a number of techniques to modify these numbers so as to take account of research and development costs. These efforts have greatly advanced the state of knowledge in this area within the last decade.

Aylward (1993) is representative of the class of models that estimate net returns to biodiversity prospecting before calculating an average value per species. His model assumes that a genetic prospector is able to examine a wild area that contains over 10,000 different plant species. Over the course of one year it is assumed that 10,000 species are screened in an attempt to find one potential pharmaceutical product. If a 1 in 10,000 success rate is assumed, then, on average, one new drug source will be found by the end of one year. The gross return of the new drug is calculated as a revenue stream and private costs associated with prospecting and development are subtracted from gross return to obtain net return. The costs are attributed to different components: research and development costs and the costs of biotic samples. In order to apportion the net return across the different factors associated with bio-prospecting, the expected net return to each factor is assumed to be equal to its proportional share in the total cost of the prospecting process.

The expected net return attributable to a biotic sample subjected to a screening process is equal to the species success rate (assumed to be 1 in 10,000) multiplied by the net private return to biotic samples, adjusted for the number of samples per species that are screened. If two samples from each species are screened, then the success rate for biotic samples (as opposed to species) is 1 in 20,000. Finally, the average net return per biotic sample is estimated to be $21.23. This is an average because it involves the calculation of the net value of a new plant-based commercial drug multiplied by a success probability rate. The outcome is the average value for the individual species being screened.

Simpson, Sedjo, and Reid (1996) argue that it is inappropriate to measure the average value of a species as is done by Aylward. Instead, they argue that the marginal value of a species is the correct economic approach and, that by examining the marginal value, researchers can take account of redundancy (substitutability) among natural compounds. The marginal value is the incremental contribution of a species to the probability of making a commercial discovery.

The Simpson, Sedjo, and Reid model assumes that the return (R) to pharmaceutical companies of plant-based drug discoveries is the revenue net of the production, advertising, marketing costs but gross of the research and development costs (C). They assume that n species are to be sampled and p is the probability of any species sampled at random resulting in a successful commercial drug product. Then, each new sampling is described by independent *Bernouilli trials* with equal probabilities of success. Finally, given redundancy of compounds, it is assumed that testing for a particular outcome will end with the first successful finding.

Simpson, Sedjo, and Reid define $V(n)$ to be the value of an entire collection of species. This is described as follows:

$$V(n) = \frac{(pR - C)}{p}[1 - (1 - p)^n] \tag{6}$$

Thus, the value of a marginal species is simply $V(n + 1) - V(n) = (pR - C)(1 - p)^n$. The authors then show that the upper bound (or optimal) value of the marginal species can be written as follows, where they assume the probability of success is the one that maximizes the value of the marginal species.

$$V(n + 1) - V(n) \approx \left(\frac{R - C}{(n + 1)e}\right)\left(\frac{R - C}{R}\right)^n \tag{7}$$

In equation (7), e is the base of the natural logarithm (2.718). In this equation, it is important to note that as n (the number of species in a collection) gets large, the value of the marginal species goes to zero, regardless of the costs associated with research and development. This finding reflects an underlying belief in the inherent substitutability of individual species.

Using estimates from previously published data on research and development costs and success rates, Simpson, Sedjo, and Reid employ their model to estimate the maximum possible value of a marginal species. The highest value they obtain is \$US 9,431. However, the results are very sensitive to the choice of parameter values. In particular, the estimates given in the paper arise from the assumption of a very large expected return rate of 50 percent and a success rate of 10 in 250,000 or 1 in 25,000 species. It should also be noted that values arising from this type of exercise are not estimates of the value of a gene *per se*. Rather, they are estimates of the expected value of an untested species in situ that could be used for the purposes of discovering a commercially valuable substance.

While output based upon the value of a marginal species is interesting, it is not particularly helpful for undertaking policy analysis such as whether a particular piece of land should be conserved in order to maintain biodiversity options. Thus, the authors go one step further and apply these estimates of the value of a marginal species to estimate the maximum willingness to pay to preserve a hectare of land in a number of biodiversity hotspots. To do this they assume a given relationship between the number of species in an area of size A is given by the following relationship:

$$n = \alpha A^Z \tag{8}$$

In equation (8) n is the number of species, α is a measure of species richness in an area and Z is a constant obtained from biological work (Simpson, Sedjo, and Reid, 1996).

Then, to infer the maximum value for the marginal hectare of land for biodiversity prospecting, the value function from equation (6) is differentiated with respect to the size of the area (A).

$$\frac{\partial V}{\partial A} = \frac{\partial V}{\partial n} \frac{\partial n}{\partial A} \tag{9}$$

In this equation the second term on the right-hand side ($\partial n/\partial A$) is simply found as ZD, where D is the number of species per unit of area (species density).

Simpson, Sedjo, and Reid perform this exercise using data from 18 biodiversity hotspots to yield the following results. Western Ecuador obtains the highest maximum willingness-to-pay of $US 20.63 per hectare, since it has the greatest number of *endemic* plant species per hectare. The area with the second highest willingness-to-pay per hectare is southwestern Sri Lanka with a value of $US 16.84 per hectare. However, most other biodiversity hotspots have very low marginal values per hectare that are under $US 2 per hectare. For an area such as central Chile, with a much lower ratio of endemic plant species per hectare than western Ecuador, the estimate of the maximum willingness to pay to preserve one more hectare of land is only $US 0.74.

It must be recalled that these values represent only private values on the part of pharmaceutical companies hoping to use plant species as inputs into their production processes. It may be that the social incentives for biodiversity preservation are much larger since the consumer surplus from the development of new plant-based drugs is likely to be much larger than the returns to drug companies. However, the point of this work is that, if there are a large number of potential species, there is likely to be substitutability amongst them, so that the value of the marginal species is likely to be very low.

Rausser and Small (2000) have criticized Simpson, Sedjo, and Reid on a number of fronts. Of particular importance is the argument that the Simpson, Sedjo, and Reid model assumes sampling without replacement from a large set of research leads, incurring fixed costs per draw. Thus, the finding of very low marginal values for species arises because the authors make unrealistic assumptions about the nature of scientific inquiry. Rausser and Small modify the Simpson, Sedjo, and Reid model by allowing for sequential search. The insight that they provide is that efficient search techniques will make the number of potential leads (actual species tested) smaller, thereby reducing research and development costs. In particular, with scientific data describing the nature of leads, it is possible to order them in such a way as to examine high-hit probabilities first and low-hit probabilities last. Testing is then done sequentially. If a particular test is successful, the company obtains a return and, once a discovery is made, testing stops for the particular project. This implies that testing will be done first on the most promising leads and may never be done on leads for which the ratio of expected costs to returns is less than the probability of success.

In this framework the incremental value of a given lead, say the nth lead, can be thought of as the maximum amount that a firm would be willing to pay at the start of a search project for a call option[10] on the nth lead. The option ensures that the lead will be available if it should be needed. With probability of a_n the first $n-1$ tests do not provide a hit and so the nth lead is tested. This will cost c and has a probability p_n of being successful, at which point the firm gains R and stops searching. But, the effective payoff is net of the continuation value of V_{n+1} that would have applied if the search had been forced to skip the nth lead. Since multiple discoveries are redundant, a success at the nth stage means that further searching is without value. Further, as a result of this redundancy, the expected value of a project is not the sum of the value of the leads. Rather, it is the sum of *scarcity rents* that arise from limits on the number of leads and *information rents* that arise because certain leads yield a very high chance of success which means an avoidance of expensive search costs.

The value of an undiscovered natural resource is called its scarcity rent (see chapter 7). This reflects how scarce the resource is and how unique. In this context it can be interpreted as the expected amount that any particular lead would contribute to the value of the project if it were a perfect substitute for any other marginal lead, ex ante. Given the sequential nature of scientific discovery, however, a further type of rent can be defined. This is information rent. This captures the degree to which a change in one's prior information about where to search for leads increases a subsequent lead's expected incremental value. Thus, since information is in short supply it has an additional "scarcity" value that arises from its ability to reduce the costs of searching for a firm. Thus, a firm should be willing to pay a premium to access more likely and promising leads rather than spend time and money on less likely prospects, even if the latter can be purchased cheaply.

Thus, the incremental value of the nth lead (V_n) can be written as the sum of the scarcity and information rents as in equation (10) below. N is the total number of possible leads.

$$v_n = \left\{ \left(\frac{a_n}{1-p_n}(p_n - p_N)R + \left[\sum_{i=n+1}^{N-1} \frac{a_i}{1-p_n}(p_n - p_i) \right]c \right) \right\} + a_N(p_N R - c) \qquad (10)$$

In equation (10), the last term is the scarcity rent of a lead. This is, in fact, the value of the marginal lead since it is the expected amount that it would contribute to the value of a project if all leads were substitutes for one another, ex ante. As long as the number of leads is finite and we expect that random screening is profitable, then the scarcity rent will be positive.

The first term in brackets is the information rent. The first component of this term represents the increase in expected benefits associated with a higher probability of obtaining a hit before exhausting all leads. The second component in square brackets represents the drop in expected costs of search that will no longer be needed if a hit is made earlier. Thus, information rent will depend upon a particular lead's success probability compared to the success probabilities of other leads. So, the issue is whether information rents can be large enough to encourage firms to undertake conservation on their own.

Using the same parameters as Simpson, Sedjo, and Reid (1996), Rausser and Small calculate the incremental values ($ per hectare) for the same 18 biological hotspots as mentioned earlier. They calculate, for example, an incremental value of $9,177 per hectare for western Ecuador. This should be compared to the Simpson estimate of $20.63 which is essentially merely scarcity rent. For central Chile, the gap between the two estimates is much smaller. The incremental rent is $231 while the scarcity rent is $0.74. The difference between western Ecuador and central Chile is largely due to a much higher hit probability in the former, along with a much higher density of endemic species and a much smaller forest area. These are the features that contribute to incremental information rent.

These results serve to reinforce the earlier argument that measurement of the average value of a species is not appropriate when we are looking at obtaining values that represent losses associated with a reduction in biodiversity. In particular, if we see genetic material as inputs into innovation, it is clear that each species or gene is not equally marginal. This argues against the use of *benefit transfer* mechanisms to obtain values for genes that have yet been discovered.[11]

Valuing endangered species

Over the last twenty years or so a number of researchers have tried to obtain economic values of rare, threatened, and endangered species to US citizens (mostly) using survey methodology, particularly the contingent valuation approach. (See chapter 9 for a discussion of this method.) Much of this work has focused upon the values that humans attach to large or charismatic animal populations. Loomis and White have undertaken a meta-analysis to summarize the results from 20 studies. Using meta-analysis (Smith and Kaoru, 1990) the researchers collect a variety of information from the original studies and use this information as data in a regression function to explain the average willingness-to-pay (equivalent surplus) for endangered species. This is total economic value as was defined earlier in this chapter; however, not all motivations may be present since they are not explored or valued separately.

In their paper, Loomis and White calculate the mean WTP from 20 different studies in constant $US 1993. However, it should be noted that these studies were conducted as early as 1983 and as late as 1994. The subjects of these studies ranged from whales of various species to sea turtles, from bald eagles, spotted owls to red-cockaded woodpeckers and cranes. By and large they are for what Loomis and White call "charismatic megavertebrates" but argue that the total value expressed probably includes value for components of the ecosystem that support these animals, including plant material and other lesser species that provide food for these megavertebrates.

The highest annual willingness-to-pay values in the 20 studies are for the northern spotted owl (average of $70 with a low value of $44 and a high value of $95). The lowest values are for striped shiners (a fish species) of $6. While these previous studies have been couched in terms of amounts that an individual would be willing to pay annually on an on-going basis, other studies ask respondents for their single lump-sum willingness-to-pay values. Here the highest value is for bald eagles – $216 – with a low of $178 and a high of $254. The lowest lump-sum value is for cutthroat trout – $15 lump sum – with a low of $13 and a high of $17.

The WTP values are then regressed on a number of variables chosen to represent differences across the 20 studies and other factors that economic theory would suggest explain variations in WTP. Thus, the regressors in the model include: the size of species population described in the survey, whether a one-time or annual payment was requested, whether the contingent valuation approach is open-ended or dichotomous choice, the type of species (fish, marine mammal, bird) and the response rate to the survey, as well as whether only local residents or non-residents were questioned.

Loomis and White find that the estimated model explains about 68 percent of the variation in WTP. In addition, the signs of the regressors in general conform to economic theory. Namely, the larger the population cited, the larger the WTP. One-time or lump-sum payments are found to be larger than annual payments. Visitors have higher WTP values (this may be the result of having a larger recreation component to total economic value and being better informed about the species). On the other hand, the actual cvm format (open ended versus dichotomous choice) is found to have no significant effect upon the WTP, nor were the response rate and year of study important. The implication of the latter is that results appear robust over time and study approach, thereby giving greater confidence to the valuing of unstudied endangered species via a benefit transfer approach.

What are some of the shortcomings of this approach to valuing individual species? It misses ecological complementarities among species (for example, owls, salmon, etc. all depend upon an old growth forest ecosystem). It also misses out on substitution effects, both in terms of budgetary concerns and in terms of utility. Some work has focused upon the valuation of multiple species within the same contingent valuation survey and, therefore, moved closer to valuing biodiversity. The estimates of WTP are larger than those obtained when a single species is valued, however, not substantially larger as we would expect to be the case given that species may be seen as substitutable in the minds of respondents. It has been shown theoretically and empirically that the value for a single item in a CVM survey may be different from the value it obtains if presented as part of a package of items (Hoehn and Loomis, 1993; Hoehn, 1991). The role of context in valuation has been a widely debated issue (Kahneman and Knetsch, 1992; Smith, 1992). The important aspect to be considered from this discussion is: which species should be included in a given survey and how should they be ordered?

However, we must realize that, since these estimates are human-centered, they are based upon a respondent's current understanding of the role and value that a species has in a particular ecosystem. Even for scientists and other researchers this information is not complete. Thus, these values may be underestimates of the overall value to society from their preservation.

Ecosystem valuation

The components included in an ecosystem for valuation purposes are its role in providing habitat for plant and animal species, as well as its role in providing what de Groot (1994) calls ecosystem functions or ecological services such as the provision of flood control, climate regulation and water purification. Daily (1997) provides an even more compelling reason for valuing the entirety of ecosystem services. She defines them as "the conditions and processes through which natural ecosystems, and the species that make them up, sustain and fulfill human life. They maintain biodiversity and the production of ecosystem goods, such as seafood, forage, timber, biomass fuels, natural fiber, and many pharmaceuticals, industrial products and their precursors. The harvest and trade of these goods represent an important and familiar part of the human economy. In addition to the production of goods, ecosystem services are the actual life-support functions, such as cleansing, recycling, and renewal, and they confer many intangible aesthetic and cultural benefits as well" (page 3). It can be argued that, in valuing individual species, individuals also provide an implicit value of the habitat services provided by the ecosystem in which the species is living. We might think of this as a top–down approach to valuation. However, some would argue that human beings may not be well enough informed of the ecological services or understand the complex roles to be prepared to answer a top–down type of contingent valuation question about their willingness-to-pay for preventing loss of ecosystems leading to endangered species.[12]

As an alternative a number of researchers have adopted a bottom–up approach to measuring the value of particular ecosystems. Rain forests are of particular interest (Pearce and Moran, 1994; Carson, 1998; Torras, 2000), in part, because tropical forests are home to more than 50 percent of all known species on a surface area that is less than 7 percent of the entire land surface of the earth. Wetland, range, and coastal regions have also been valued (Folke, 1991; Pearce and Moran, 1994; Barbier, 1994; Turner, Folke, Gren, and Bateman, 1995).

Valuing rain forest ecosystems

One recent example of a bottom–up approach to the valuation of a rain forest is Torras (2000). He attempts to determine the loss of total economic value, as defined earlier in this chapter, of Brazilian Amazonian deforestation over the period 1978–93. It may well be one of the world's most valuable rain forests since its vegetation is believed to play an important role in regulating global temperatures. In addition, it has approximately 10 percent of the world's plant and animal species, along with much of the world's fresh surface water. Deforestation may mean the losses of such goods and services. Using previously published estimates for the values of a number of component goods and services from the rain forest, Torras calculates the economic loss per hectare and for the total area attributable to deforestation.

For direct values (such as timber and food) market estimates are used. Direct benefits such as recreational (ecotourism) values are captured using travel cost methods (see chapter 10). For many of the ecosystem services[13] such as the value of nutrient losses resulting from soil erosion, the replacement cost method is employed. In this approach, widely used in the valuing of these types of services, the benefit lost from deforestation is measured by the cost of replacing or restoring the environmental asset. This is used to obtain estimates of the benefits of flood control, erosion control and water regulation from the forest. On the other hand, the climate regulating functions associated with the rain forest are valued using the damage costs associated with the release of carbon into the atmosphere as trees are cut down.[14] Option benefits are obtained as the expected future benefits from plants. *Existence values* are obtained using CVM and some revealed preference methods such as the observed charitable contributions made to conservancy organizations.

After assembling the empirical estimates from much of the extant literature, Torras then calculates the per hectare per year value of the Brazilian Amazonian rain forest over the period 1978–93 as being $1,175 (with total direct values being $549, total indirect values being $414, option values being $18 and existence values being $194). All values are for 1993. He acknowledges that this value is probably conservative in the sense that the Amazonian ecosystem may be subject to threshold effects that result in non-linear impacts. Thus, a sudden decrease in rain forest would imply greater scarcity and hence a larger marginal value than the one he has calculated based upon previous forest area data.

An example of the top–down type of analysis is that undertaken by Kramer and Mercer (1997). The authors employed contingent valuation methodology to obtain willingness-to-pay values – containing all three components identified earlier – for the protection of tropical rain forests. In their work, they found that respondents, through lack of information, were unable to say exactly how much they would allocate to the protection of specific rain forests. Rather, the estimated willingness of between $US 21 and $US 31 per household (1992 dollars) could be attributed to a generic 5 percent overall increase in rain forest protection. Thus, they conclude that CV may only be appropriate in the context of the determination of the global value of rain forests, not the relative importance of individual rain forests.

Examples of valuing wetlands

Folke (1991) uses the replacement cost method to obtain the value of a Swedish wetland (Martebo Mire on the island of Gotland in the Baltic Sea). He focuses upon evaluating the life-support functions of the wetland to society such as irrigation, water purification, sewage transport, and fish habitat. He then compares the loss of the wetland's functions with the costs of replacing them, where feasible, with human-made technology. He employs a unique approach; namely, by looking at the amount of energy captured via photosynthesis as a common measure of the ecosystem's potential to generate environmental goods and services. The loss of life support or primary value (glue) can be approximated via an analysis of how much of the capacity of the wetland plants to capture the sun's energy has been lost. The lost components are then evaluated with reference to estimates of the costs of human-made replacement technology.[15] The author concludes that the annual monetary cost of the loss of wetland services for this region is between $US 0.4 million and $US 1.2 million in 1991 dollars. However, he goes on to argue that this value deals mainly with measuring the values of output or the secondary values provided by ecosystems and then only some of them.

Bateman, Willis, Garrod, Doktor, Langford, and Turner (1992) use a top–down contingent valuation methodology approach to value wetlands (the Broads) in England. Survey respondents were asked how much they would be willing to pay in order to preserve the Broads in their current state. The authors obtained a mean willingness-to-pay per household per year of £77 (1991 prices) using an open-ended question format with on-site visitors and a mean willingness-to-pay per household per year of £244 using a dichotomous choice approach. These values presumably include all three components of use values. Interestingly, subsequent work using a mail survey of the general population produced smaller willingness-to-pay values for individuals located further from the Broads. This might be attributable to a zero direct use value which would suggest that values for individuals in the general population might include existence values alone; however, this was not examined *per se*.

Valuing the entire world's ecosystem services

Perhaps the best known effort to put a value upon the entirety of ecosystem services for the earth was published in 1997 by a group of 13 individuals from 4 countries. Amongst these individuals were economists, ecologists, and geographers (Costanza et al., 1997). The authors identified 17 different categories of ecosystem services including food production, raw materials, recreation and water supply, climate regulation, the hydrological cycle, erosion control, nutrient cycling and waste purification. They calculated the values for each of these items from already published data for a number of land and ocean environments on the earth. Their estimates of the total value of the ecosystem services provided by the earth come to between $US 16 and $US 54 trillion per year with an average value of $US 33 trillion. In order to put this into perspective the authors point out that the total value of world GNP is about $US 18 trillion which measures, of course, the value of market transactions. By contrast, most of the ecosystem services are obtained outside any market transactions.

Debt-for-nature swaps

Recently some researchers have attempted to discover a type of global existence value pertaining to biodiversity using a revealed preference type of approach. This involves an examination of "market-type" transactions that take place between a developing country that is rich in biodiversity but debt-poor and developed countries or non-governmental organizations (NGO). Such transactions are termed "debt-for-nature swaps" since they entail the purchase of a developing country's secondary debt. In exchange for the purchaser's offer to accept less than the face value of the debt, the developing country must agree to undertake certain activities to prevent biodiversity loss. If we assume that the payment made to purchase the debt by the NGO or developed countries represents willingness-to-pay for biodiversity, then the value of such market transactions may represent a global existence value for biodiversity. Some recent examples include debt-for-nature swaps pursued by the US Government with El Salvador ($US 14 million), Belize ($US 9 million), and Thailand ($US 9.5 million). The main impetus for all of these agreements is the maintenance of forested areas. Previous work by Pearce and Moran (1994) summarizing past debt-for-nature swaps has suggested that $US 5.00 per hectare is a rough approximation to existence values associated with biodiversity.

Nunes and van den Bergh (2001) provide a summary of recent valuation work pertaining to biodiversity.[16] In particular, their article contains several tables of interest to the researcher involved in the ranges of values for the various components of biodiversity. However, they argue that the available economic valuation estimates should generally be regarded as providing an incomplete (lower bound) perspective on unknown value of biodiversity losses. It bears repeating that, since the science surrounding biodiversity is not yet finalized, economic valuation of biodiversity losses is still very much in its infancy. A second caveat must be applied to these types of valuation exercises, as well. Authors typically value "static" adjustments to current biodiversity states; they do not value diversity *per se*, nor do they touch upon the irreversibility issue.

15.5 CAUSES OF BIODIVERSITY LOSS AND POLICY RESPONSES

Chapter 4 presented a model of fish population dynamics in which a particular growth function (the logistic growth function) was adopted. In order to allow for loss of biodiversity through the extinction of individual species, we must modify the logistic growth function to incorporate irreversibility of outcomes. This involves identifying a minimum viable stock level greater than zero at which population growth is zero and below which the growth rate is negative. Should fishing effort increase to a supercritical level, then the species population may be reduced below its minimum viable level. At this point, extinction of the population is ultimately inevitable, regardless of future effort levels. Clark (1990) terms this a case of critical depensation. Continuing with this extended fisheries model,[17] we can identify the economic conditions under which species extinction is most likely to occur. These include the following: high market prices for species hunted, low costs of harvesting, low natural growth rates of stock, high discount rates, and a critical minimum threshold population size that is relatively large.[18]

While this type of analysis assists us in understanding the circumstances under which a single species may be susceptible to extinction, other factors are at play that help to explain the mass extinction of species and ecosystem losses. As was discussed in the introduction to this chapter, human population growth has been cited as the major cause leading to a loss of biodiversity. The role of human population growth is traced by observing that increasing population levels appear to require a greater conversion of land from natural vegetation to agriculture and other uses than has previously been the case.[19] It may also lead to habitat fragmentation. Moreover, these uses frequently have secondary impacts that are far reaching and non-conserving in their nature. For example, pollution is created, harmful chemicals are employed, exotic species are introduced into existing ecosystems[20] and water courses are rerouted. Over the last few decades, habitat loss or degradation has become the primary threat to the maintenance of the current level of biodiversity.[21] This is made even more serious by the fact that population growth is occurring more rapidly in environmentally sensitive areas unable to support an ever-increasing density of human settlements. However, simple population growth and its location do not provide a complete answer for the current extent of biodiversity loss. Two other broad factors come into play. They have exacerbated the impacts of population growth. These two factors are the existence of market failures that prevent the emergence of conservation values for biodiversity that would compete against development values and inefficient or contradictory government policies.

Markets are the means by which individuals can express their values for goods and/or services. With increasing population levels, continued development of scarce land becomes a rational and efficient outcome for private decision-makers. However, there are reasons for believing that such decisions are not socially optimal in the case of biodiversity because of the presence of market failure. The leading cause of market failure in this case is the public goods nature of many of biodiversity's services both at a local and a global level. The presence of public goods prevents complete property rights from being enjoyed and this, in turn, either prevents the emergence of markets that would provide owners with values for many of biodiversity's services or does not allow the market to express all relevant values. For example, farmers often drain wetlands in order to further their agricultural activities. These wetlands, however, support migratory bird populations and their draining can lead to endangerment for wildlife populations. The resultant outcome is inefficient in the sense that society does not devote enough of its scarce resources to the preservation of biodiversity. A lack of complete information about the role played by wildlife, as well as other fauna and flora, in supporting biodiversity exacerbates this situation.

While governments could mitigate the danger of such an outcome through policies that either create or improve property rights and encourage recognition of social benefits, they have more often than not employed policies that make the situation worse. In some cases, government policies such as subsidies in support of the draining of wetlands exaggerate the rate of return to agriculture's or development's use of land and, in this way, lead to a type of government intervention failure.

Part of the difficulty with achieving a socially optimal level of biodiversity is that there is not a global consensus for setting biodiversity preservation priorities according to the criterion of efficiency. To do this requires the development of a biodiversity or diversity function to be optimized (Solow, Polasky, and Broadus, 1993; Weitzman, 1992). These authors suggest that one approach is to assume that, when species become extinct, then a reduction in biodiversity is said to have occurred. They then propose two competing measures of biodiversity based solely upon genetic differences between species. In their model, they suggest that one possible conservation goal might be the preservation of the status quo species, while a second might be the conservation of as much diversity in species as possible. This latter is motivated by the observation that closely related species have similar characteristics and, thus, are somewhat redundant. A key feature of both biodiversity indices is that they use the degree of substitution between individual species. This is important when we think about the option value associated with a particular species and its role in preserving biodiversity. In either case, they suggest that the optimization problem be one which minimizes the expected loss in diversity. One shortcoming of their model is that the values of individual species are not incorporated, so that the relative importance of particular species to the satisfaction of human wants does not play a role.

Weitzman (1992) uses a similar approach to that of Solow, Polasky, and Broadus (1993) in his proposal for a diversity function that measures biological differences between species. However, he takes the analysis one step further by integrating this function into a cost–benefit framework. In this context the benefits arise from a greater probability of more diversity in the long term, while the cost is represented by conservation program expenditures. However, to put this model into practice requires both valuation information, as well as scientific information about the unique and substitutable characteristics of individual species.

In the absence of such information it may be efficient for governments to consider the implications of irreversible decisions and act cautiously.[22] At a minimum, some degree of attenuation of the open access nature of exploitation of biodiversity should be adopted. This is, in fact, what was done in 1992 at the United Nations Earth Summit when many nations signed the Convention on Biological Diversity. The Convention has now been ratified by over 130 countries and came into force in December 1993.[23] The goals of the Convention include: "conservation of biological diversity, the sustainable use of its components, and the fair and equitable sharing of the benefits arising out of the utilization of genetic resources." Unlike other international treaties, this Convention clearly gives some degree of sovereign property rights to biodiversity to individual nations when it is made clear that other nations have an obligation to pay for benefits received (OECD, 1996).

In addition to providing a blueprint for relationships between individual nations with regard to biodiversity, the Convention comes out in favor of a number of policy tools that can be used within an individual country to encourage biodiversity. Economic incentive measures, in particular, are identified as the means of achieving the three goals identified in the Convention. In a general way, then, incentives are intended to make biodiversity an asset. And, to further this view, the convention appears in favor of the creation of property rights within a nation so as to encourage private decisions that are in keeping with socially optimal outcomes.

In this context, four different types of incentive policy measures can be identified. The first is positive incentives. These are monetary inducements to encourage conservation of biodiversity. Voluntary management agreements, whereby payments are made to landowners to reimburse them for the incremental cost of providing non-marketable biodiversity services, have been employed in Sweden, Austria, Switzerland, and the United Kingdom (OECD, 1996). Alternatively, Conservation Reserve programs employed in countries such as the United States and the United Kingdom encourage farmers in environmentally sensitive areas to retire land from agricultural production. This type of policy suffers from potential non-compliance problems and may also be a drain on a country's financial resources from the point of view both of monitoring and payouts.

The second type of policy relies upon disincentives to adjust economic decisions. This is very much in accordance with the *polluter pays principle* and relies upon costs imposed upon users and those who damage resources to discourage activities that reduce biodiversity. User or access fees are imposed upon hunters, fishers, etc. A type of *double dividend* benefit may arise when revenues from user groups can be turned over to farmers and other land-owners to encourage biodiversity-enhancing measures.

A third type of policy involves the introduction of indirect incentives. These are mechanisms that create or improve market signals to encourage conservation, thereby allowing a means by which values from biodiversity may be realized. Examples of such policies include the widespread adoption by most maritime nations of *individual transferable quotas* for fisheries, the increasing reliance in the United States upon air emissions trading rights schemes, and the encouragement of tree-planting to obtain benefits from *carbon sequestration*.

The final policy direction is the removal of perverse incentives as a means of curtailing unsustainable policies towards conservation and biodiversity maintenance. Reform of agricultural polices, in particular, the removal of production subsidies that have encouraged inefficient farming practices, has been promoted in a number of countries, including the United States. A second broad policy effort involves the removal of implicit subsidies to water users that have encouraged profligate use of fresh water throughout the world.

In addition to these policies that aim to alter the behavior of private decision-makers, a number of governments have also been proactive in terms of pursuing direct activities that are aimed at preserving the public goods aspects of biodiversity.

Most developed countries have policies relating to government investment in conserving genetic stocks diversity through programs to encourage plant breeding and selective breeding of species. In addition, species conservation policies such as are embodied in the United States Endangered Species Act provide rules regarding danger to certain identified species subject to potential extinction. Finally, there have also been efforts to encourage conservation at the ecosystem level in the form of the creation of statutory protected areas.

The biodiversity policy arena continues to evolve and the jury is yet out as to the relative effectiveness of policies aimed at reducing biodiversity loss.[24] It is clear, however, that the issue of property rights will play a central role in determining the efficient and sustainable use of biodiversity resources. Governments who wish to manage their biodiversity resources in an efficient and sustainable fashion will need to continue to be pro-active in the developing of such rights for the consequences of continuing on in the same old haphazard fashion are indeed sobering.

NOTES

1 The recent report on the state of the environment under the North American Free Trade Agreement (NAFTA) expresses particular concern for the biodiversity loss in Mexico. This is one of the twelve countries in the warmer regions of the world (others include Ecuador and Costa Rica) that can be described as "megadiverse." Together these twelve countries contain between 60 and 70 percent of current total biodiversity on earth (Commission for Environmental Cooperation, 2001).

2 One has only to read Brander and Taylor's (1998) explanation of how resource depredation might explain the decline of a civilized world on Easter Island to be persuaded by this view.

3 That is, a higher number can be obtained either through more evenness or more species but more of either one alone does not necessarily mean more diversity.

4 In this context, there are a number of different components that are used by ecologists to describe biological "value." These include: richness (the number of species or habitats in a given area), endemism (the narrowness of species distribution within a given area), rarity (of species or habitats in region), and ecosystem services (the importance of the natural habitat or a resident single species capable of influencing ecosystem function for various services valuable to humans).

5 Obtaining such a value requires adopting a framework that incorporates uncertainty such as described in chapter 8.

6 If the services of biodiversity are private, then we would talk about the equivalent variation that arises when the price of such services rises or the compensating variation should the price fall. These measures are also obtained as differences in expenditure function values. In the event of individuals purchasing these services through a market, the market price would in many instances serve as a measure of value for the purposes of valuing biodiversity loss.

7 This allows for the analyst to make a distinction between the loss of non-use values associated with degradation of a resource that continues to exist and the loss associated with the destruction of the resource.

8   Chapter 8 discusses valuation when there is uncertainty.
9   This is also the approach that was officially sanctioned by the NOAA (National Oceanic and Atmospheric Administration) "Blue Ribbon" panel of experts that reported on the use of contingent valuation methods for the valuing of resource damages (Arrow et al., 1993).
10   A call option is the right to purchase stock at a specified (exercise) price within a specified time period.
11   Benefit transfer is the means by which an economic value (or function describing how value is determined) obtained for a particular object from one site can be used as a surrogate for the value at a different site.
12   At this point in time, scientific understanding of the role played by various flora and fauna is simply not well documented nor understood. For this reason, some authors argue that it is not possible to obtain meaningful values for some of the life-support functions of ecosystems because individuals being asked to value these services are not aware of the complexity and specifics (the so-called glue of life-support value). Some go so far as to say there are two kinds of value to biodiversity – primary or glue value and secondary or economic value (Holling, Schindler, Walker, and Roughgarden, 1995).
13   Barbier (1994) is another example of an effort to value environmental functions available in ecosystems.
14   Torras cites a number of studies that have attempted to value the carbon sequestration values of tropical forests. These include the well-known Nordhaus (1991a) estimates of the damage costs associated with carbon release: from a low of $1.80 per ton of carbon released to $66 per ton. In his work, Torras adopts a middle-ground value of $7.30 which is closely matched by more recent estimates of $10 per ton (Brown and Pearce, 1994). Nordhaus (1991b) surveys the alternative approaches that have been adopted to obtain damage cost estimates per ton of carbon released. These include: determining the additional cost of alternative low-carbon emissions technologies that can replace the cheaper high-carbon emissions technologies currently in use. Two such examples are CO_2 scrubbing and substitution of methane for oil and coal. A second option is quite different since it involves the use of trees as a carbon sink. The costs of a slowing of the deforestation of tropical forests can be obtained, along with the cost of reforesting open land.
15   Bockstael et al. (2000) caution against the indiscriminate use of the replacement cost approach. They argue that three conditions must be met in order for the replacement cost measures to be equivalent to economic values. First, the human made replacement technologies must provide functions that are equivalent in quality and magnitude to the natural function. Second, these human made replacement technologies must be the least cost way of obtaining these services. Third, if the natural ecosystem functions were no longer available, it would have to be the case that society would be willing in aggregate to bear the costs of these human made replacement technologies. In general, we would not expect these three conditions to be met. Thus, these numbers must be used with care.
16   Pearce and Moran (1994) perform a similar service in their review of the early valuation work.
17   The economic part of the model assumes that the harvest price and the per unit harvest cost are constant and do not depend upon the biomass. Clearly, adjustments in these factors that would account for increasing relative scarcity might be sufficient to prevent optimal extinction.

18   Thus, the economic intuition behind the optimal extinction result is that the value of biomass in the sea is relatively low when compared to the value of fish on the quay (with thanks to Phil Neher). This can be caused by too slow a growth rate of the biomass for investment purposes when compared to the interest rate on alternative investments (namely, harvesting the fish and putting the proceeds into a bank account) or by too high a current price when compared to the harvesting costs. Overriding all of these individual circumstances is the general lack of well-defined property rights that circumscribe the manner in which fish stocks are exploited. The most notorious outcome that results from incomplete property rights is, of course, that of open access by which any individual may commence fishing without regard for the externality imposed upon fellow fishers and future generations. It should be noted, however, that while open access provides only weak incentives to conserve stocks, it does not automatically result in extinction.

19   An upcoming issue is ocean biodiversity and the potentially detrimental presence of human population and development at the interface between land and ocean.

20   One interesting example of the impacts of the introduction of exotic species is one associated with the arrival of the Maori people in New Zealand, long before the Europeans ever set foot there. The Maoris brought rats with them. Extinction of a number of species is attributed to the arrival of this exotic species (Diamond, 1990).

21   Ecologists would argue that our "ecological footprint" upon the earth, with its emphasis upon ever increasing consumption, is growing so large as to be unsustainable (Rees and Wackernagel, 1994).

22   Indeed, the Convention has embraced two such principles: that of the *precautionary approach* and the *safe minimum standard*. In the case of the former, unless there is certainty that there will be no harmful effects, actions should not be taken that might threaten habitats used by an endangered species (OECD, 1996). The second principle, that of a *safe minimum standard*, requires that there be a presumption in favor of not harming the environment unless the opportunity costs of that action are very high.

23   The United States of America continues to be one the few countries that have not yet signed this convention.

24   The OECD (1996) summarizes recent efforts of member countries to adopt policies aimed at preventing biodiversity loss. It is interesting to note that many policies are in fact not primarily directed at conservation goals, but have in fact helped to promote them.

FURTHER READING

Economists initially became interested in biodiversity because of concerns about whether the current pace of economic development was sustainable. Interested readers are directed to *Blueprint for a Green Economy* by Pearce, Markandya, and Barbier (1989). These authors note the existence and potential finiteness of natural capital, which they argue is fundamentally different from man-made or human capital, and can have a limiting impact upon sustainable rates of gross domestic product growth. They also focus upon the lack of completely defined property right systems as one particular problem area for sustainability and, hence, biodiversity.

Subsequent work by economists in the area of biodiversity shines much light upon the measurement and valuation of biodiversity; in particular, considerable effort has been made to assess the loss in value to humans due to actions that lead to species extinction. Pearce and Moran (1994) in *The Economic Value of Biodiversity* provide a seminal book that presents appropriate methodologies, along with selected case studies.

The valuation area has grown tremendously since the 1990s. A number of years ago, Steve Polasky, currently the Fesler–Lampert Professor of Ecological/Environmental Economics at the University of Minnesota, began a website devoted to biodiversity. It has now grown to a searchable data base available at http://www.apec.umn.edu/faculty/spolasky/Biobib.html. Interested readers can obtain values for different types of ecosystems (rainforest, wetland, etc.) and for different countries. This database also provides an exhaustive list of references for other aspects of the biodiversity issue including the relationship between climate change and biodiversity, landscape ecology, and investment and decision-making under uncertainty.

More recently, some economists have turned their attention to the issue of how best to devise regulations, particularly at the international level, to encourage species preservation in developing countries. Timothy Swanson (1997) has long been interested in the role that property rights play to discourage behavior that leads to extinction. He has published a critical analysis of the Framework for Implementing the Convention on Biological Diversity in which he proposes specific actions to attain the goal of the preservation of species diversity.

Finally, the issue of biodiversity goes beyond economic considerations. Mark Sagoff's (1980, 1988) work on the ethical aspects of species preservation presents a perspective other than the anthropocentric viewpoint adopted in economics. In the 1988 book, he focuses upon the intrinsic value of species. He also provides criticism of the use of cost–benefit analysis for environmental decision-making. In addition, the scientific community has long been concerned with the extent and consequences of biodiversity loss. E. O. Wilson's book entitled *The Diversity of Life* published in 1992 by Harvard University Press is considered a classic analysis of the rationale for preservation of ecosystems from the scientific viewpoint.

REFERENCES

Arrow, K., Solow, R., Portney, P., Leamer, E., Radner, R., and Schuman, H. (1993). Report of the NOAA Panel on Contingent Valuation, *Federal Register*, US Department of Commerce, 58 (10): 4602–14.

Aylward, B. (1993). A Case Study of Pharmaceutical Prospecting, in *The Economic Value of Species Information and Its Role in Biodiversity Conservation: Case Studies of Costa Rica's National Biodiversity Institute and Pharmaceutical Prospecting*. Report to the Swedish International Development Authority. London, Environmental Economics Center.

Barbier, E. (1994). Valuing Environmental Functions: Tropical Wetlands, *Land Economics*, 70 (2): 155–73.

Bateman, I., Willis, Garrod, Doktor, Langford, and Turner (1992). *Recreation and Environmental Preservation Value of the Norfolk Broads: A Contingent Valuation Study*. Report to the National Rivers Authority, Environmental Appraisal Group, University of East Anglia.

Bockstael, N. and McConnell, K. (1983). Welfare Measurement in the Household Production Function Framework, *American Economic Review*, 73 (4): 806–14.

Bockstael, N., Freeman, A. M., Kopp, R., Portney, P., and Smith, V. K. (2000). On Measuring Economic Values for Nature, *Environmental Science and Technology*, 34: 1384–9.

Brander, J. and Taylor, M. S. (1998). The Simple Economics of Easter Island: A Ricardo-Malthus Model of Renewable Resource Use, *American Economic Review*, 88 (1): 119–38.

Brown, K. and Pearce, D. (1994). The Economic Value of Non-marketed Benefits of Tropical Forests: Carbon Storage, in J. Weiss, ed., *The Economics of Project Appraisal and the Environment*, Edward Elgar: London, pp. 102–23.

Carson, R. (1998). Valuation of Tropical Rainforests: Philosophical and Practical Issues in the Use of Contingent Valuation, *Ecological Economics*, 24: 15–29.

Clark, C. W. (1990). *Mathematical Bioeconomics: The Optimal Management of Renewable Resources*, second edition, John Wiley and Sons: New York.

Commission for Environmental Co-operation (2001). *The North American Mosaic: State of the Environment Report*: http://www.cec.org/files/PDF/PUBLICATIONS/soe_en.pdf

Conference on Environment and Development, United Nations (UNCED) (1992) Convention on Biological Diversity: http://www.cec.org/pubs_docs/documents/index.cfm?varlan=english&ID=629; Legal Deposit-Bibliothèque nationale du Canada, 2001.

Costanza, R., d'Arge, R., de Groot, R., Farber, S., Grasso, M., Hannon, B., Naeem, S., Limburg, K., Paruelo, J., O'Neill, R., Raskin, R., Sutton, P., and van den Belt, M. (1997). The Value of the World's Ecosystem Services and Natural Capital, *Nature*, 387: 253–60.

Daily, G. (1997). Introduction: What Are Ecosystem Services?, in G. Daily, J. Reichert, and J. Myers, eds, *Nature's Services: Societal Dependence on Natural Ecosystems*, Island Press: Washington, DC, pp. 1–10.

De Groot, R. (1994) Environmental Functions and the Economic Value of Natural Ecosystems, in A.-M. Jansson, M. Hammer, C. Folke, and R. Costanza, eds, *Investing in Natural Capital*, Island Press: Washington, DC., pp. 151–67.

Diamond, J. (1990). New Zealand as an Archipelago: An International Perspective, in D. R. Towns, C. H. Daugherty, and I. A. E. Atkinson, eds, *Ecological Restoration of New Zealand Islands*, Conservation Sciences Publications No. 2, Department of Conservation: Wellington, pp. 3–8.

Folke, C. (1991). The Societal Value of Wetland Life Support, in C. Folke and T. Kaberger, eds, *Linking the Natural Environment and the Economy: Essays from the Eco-eco Group*, Kluwer Academic Publishers: Dordrecht, pp. 141–71.

Folke, C., Holling, C. S., and Perrings, C. (1996). Biological Diversity, Ecosystems, and the Human Scale, *Ecological Applications*, 6: 1018–24.

Freeman, A. M. III (1993). *The Measurement of Environmental and Resource Value: Theory and Methods*. Resources for the Future: New York.

Hanemann, W. M. (1991). Willingness to Pay and Willingness to Accept: How Much Can They Differ?, *American Economic Review*, 81 (3): 635–47.

Hoehn, J. P. (1991). Valuing the Multidimensional Impacts of Environmental Policy: Theory and Methods, *American Journal of Agricultural Economics*, 73: 289–99.

Hoehn, J. and Loomis, J. (1993). Substitution Effects in the Valuation of Multiple Environmental Programs, *Journal of Environmental Economics and Management*, 25: 56–75.

Holling, C. S. (1973). Resilience and Stability of Ecological Systems, *Annual Review of Ecology and Systematics*, 4: 1–23.

Holling, C. S., Schindler, D. W., Walker, B. W., and Roughgarden, J. (1995). Biodiversity in the Functioning of Ecosystems: An Ecological Synthesis, in C. Perrings, K.-G. Mäler,

C. Folke, C. Holling, and B.-O. Jansson, eds, *Biodiversity Loss: Economic and Ecological Issues*, Cambridge University Press: Cambridge, chapter 2.

Johnson, K. H., Vogt, K. A., Clark, O. J., Schmitz, and Vogt, D. J. (1996). Biodiversity and the Productivity and Stability of Ecosystems, *Trends in Ecology and Evolution*, 11: 372–7.

Kahneman, D. and Knetsch, J. L. (1992). Valuing Public Goods: The Purchase of Moral Satisfaction, *Journal of Environmental Economics and Management*, 22: 57–70.

Kramer, R. and Mercer, E. (1997). Valuing a Global Environmental Good: US Residents' *Willingness-to-pay* to Protect Tropical Rain Forests, *Land Economics*, 73 (2): 196–210.

Krutilla, J. V. (1967). Conservation Reconsidered, *American Economic Review*, 57 (4): 778–86.

Leakey, R. and Lewin, R. (1995). *The Sixth Extinction: Biodiversity and Its Survival*, Weidenfeld and Nicolson: London.

Loomis, J. and White, D. (1996). Economic Benefits of Rare and Endangered Species: Summary and Meta-analysis, *Ecological Economics*, 18: 197–206.

McNeely, J., Miller, K., Reid, W., Mittermeier, R., and Werner, T. (1990). *Conserving the World's Biological Diversity*, World Bank: Washington, DC.

Moran, D. and Pearce, D. (1997). The Economics of Biodiversity, in H. Folmer and T. Tietenberg, eds, *The International Yearbook of Environmental and Resource Economics 1997/1998*, Edward Elgar: Cheltenham, New Horizons in Environmental Economics Series, pp. 82–113

National Academy of Sciences (1999) *Perspectives on Biodiversity: Valuing Its Role in an Everchanging World*, Committee on Noneconomic and Economic Value of Biodiversity, National Research Council: New York.

Nordhaus, W. (1991a). A Sketch of the Economics of the Greenhouse Effect, *American Economic Review*, 81: 146–50.

Nordhaus, W. (1991b). The Cost of Slowing Climate Change: A Survey, *Energy Journal*, 12 (1): 37–65.

Nunes, P. and van den Bergh, J. (2001). Economic Valuation of Biodiversity: Sense or Nonsense?, *Ecological Economics*, 39: 203–22.

Organization for Economic Co-operation and Development (1996). *Saving Biological Diversity: Economic Incentives*, OECD: Paris.

Pearce, D. and Moran, D. (1994). *The Economic Value of Biodiversity*, The World Conservation Union, Earthscan Publications Ltd: London.

Pearce, D., Markandya, A., and Barbier, E. (1989). *Blueprint for a Green Economy*, Earthscan Publications: London.

Perrings, C. (1994). Biotic Diversity, Sustainable Development and Natural Capital, in A.-M. Jansson, M. Hammer, C. Folke, and R. Costanza, eds, *Investing in Natural Capital*, Island Press: Washington, DC, pp. 92–112.

Perrings, C. and Pearce, D. (1994). Threshold Effects and Incentives for the Conservation of Biodiversity, *Environmental and Resource Economics*, 4 (1): 13–28.

Perrings, C., Mäler, K.-G., Folke, C., Holling, C., and Jansson, B.-O. (1995). Introduction: Framing the Problem of Biodiversity Loss, in C. Perrings, K.-G. Mäler, C. Folke, C. Holling, and B.-O. Jansson, eds, *Biodiversity Loss: Economic and Ecological Issues*, Cambridge University Press: Cambridge.

Pimm, S., Russell, G., Tittleman, J., and Brooks, T. (1995) The Future of Biodiversity, *Science*, 269: 347–50.

Principe, P. (1989). The Economic Significance of Plants and Their Constituents as Drugs, in H. Wagner, H. Hikino, and N. Farnsworth, eds, *Economic and Medicinal Plant Research*, Vol. 3, Academic Press: London, pp. 1–17.

Principe, P. (1991). *Monetizing the Pharmacological Benefits of Plants*, United States Environmental Protection Agency: Washington, DC.

Randall, A. (1991). Total and Non-use Values, in J. B. Braden and C. D. Kolstad, eds, *Measuring the Demand for Environmental Quality*, North-Holland: Amsterdam.

Randall, A. and Stoll, J. (1980). Consumer's Surplus in Commodity Space, *American Economic Review*, 70 (3): 449–55.

Rausser, G. and Small, A. (2000). Valuing Research Leads: Bioprospecting and the Conservation of Genetic Resources, *Journal of Political Economy*, 108 (1): 173–206.

Rees, W. and Wackernagel, M. (1994). Ecological Footprints and Appropriated Carrying Capacity: Measuring the Natural Capital Requirements of the Human Economy, in A.-M. Jansson, M. Hammer, C. Folke, and R. Costanza, eds, *Investing in Natural Capital*, Island Press: Washington, DC., pp. 362–90.

Sagoff, M. (1980). On the Preservation of Species, *Columbia Journal of Environmental Law*, 7(1): 33–67.

Sagoff, M. (1988). *The Economy of the Earth: Philosophy, Law, and the Environment*, Cambridge Community Press: New York.

Simpson, R. D., Sedjo, R. and Reid, J. (1996). Valuing Biodiversity for Use in Pharmaceutical Research, *Journal of Political Economy*, 104 (1): 163–85.

Smith, V. K. and Kaoru, Y. (1990). Signals Or Noise: Explaining the Variation in Recreation Benefit Estimates, *American Journal of Agricultural Economics*, 72: 419–33.

Smith, V. K. (1992). Arbitrary Values, Good Causes, and Premature Verdicts, *Journal of Environmental Economics and Management*, 22 (1): 71–89.

Solow, A., Polasky, S., and Broadus, J. (1993). On the Measurement of Biological Diversity, *Journal of Environmental Economics and Management*, 24 (1): 60–8.

Swanson, T. M. (1995). *The Economics and Ecology of Biodiversity Decline*, Cambridge University Press: Cambridge.

Swanson, T. M. (1996). The Appropriation of Evolution's Values: An Institutional Analysis of Intellectual Property Regimes and Biodiversity Conservation, in T. M. Swanson, ed., *Intellectual Property Rights and Biodiversity Conservation*, Cambridge University Press: Cambridge, pp. 141–75.

Swanson, T. (1997). *Global Action for Biodiversity: An International Framework for Implementing the Convention on Biological Diversity*, Earthscan Publications: London.

Torras, M. (2000). The Total Economic Value of Amazonian Deforestation, *Ecological Economics*, 33: 283–97.

Turner, R. K., Folke, C., Gren, I., and Bateman, I. (1995). Wetland Valuation: Three Case Studies, in C. Perrings, K.-G. Mäler, C. Folke, C. Holling, and B.-O. Jansson, eds, *Biodiversity Loss: Economic and Ecological Issues*, Cambridge University Press: Cambridge.

Tuxhill, J. and Bright, C. (1998). Losing Strands in the Web of Life, in *State of the World 1998*, World Watch Institute, W.W. Norton: New York, chapter 3.

United Nations Conference on Environment and Development (UNCED) CBD (Convention on Biological Diversity) United Nations Environment Program. Signed June 5, 1992. Depository is Secretary-General of the United Nations.

Weitzman, M. (1992) On Diversity, *Quarterly Journal of Economics*, 107: 363–406.

Weisbrod, B. (1964). Collective Consumption Services of Individual Consumption Goods, *Quarterly Journal of Economics*, 77: 189–210.

Wilson, E. (1988). *Biodiversity*, National Academy Press: Washington, DC.

Wilson, E. O. (1992). *The Diversity of Life*, Harvard University Press, Harvard, MA.

CHAPTER SIXTEEN

SUSTAINING THE ENVIRONMENT

We take a more optimistic view that sustainability is possible, contingent on the resilience of nature, flexibility of societies, and creativity of people. (Stephen Carpenter, William A. Brock, and Donald Ludwig, *Collapse, Learning, and Renewal* (2002), p. 173)

16.1 THE BIG PICTURE

This book is structured around a series of lectures that cover fifteen topics divided into four main themes: general theoretical approaches to understanding human behavior and environmental problems, natural resources, environmental valuation, and global links between human activity and the environment. By necessity, each topic is "reductionist" in the sense that it is selective and focuses on a particular domain or sub-discipline. Nevertheless, as you will know from reading this book, such an approach can be enormously helpful at understanding, measuring and helping to resolve environmental problems.

Common themes of the book are efficiency – doing the best we can with what we have – and the linking of environmental problems and outcomes with individual behavior and incentives. The next step in "putting it all together," and which is the focus of chapters 11–15, is an awareness of the myriad of interactions, feedbacks and causal loops that exist between economic/social systems and environmental systems. These interactions form a *complex system*, or rather a series of nested complex systems, so-called because the interaction of many parts of a system can lead to system behavior called *self-organizing criticality*, whereby small changes in one part of the system can result in very large changes or phase transitions in the overall system.

Complex systems theory emerged from physics and mathematics as explanations of phase-transitions, or shifts to fundamentally different states in physical structures (Kadanoff, 1966), and also in ecology as a basis for explaining population dynamics (Levins 1970, May 1973). A fundamental insight from both the physics and ecological models of complex systems is that a comprehension of

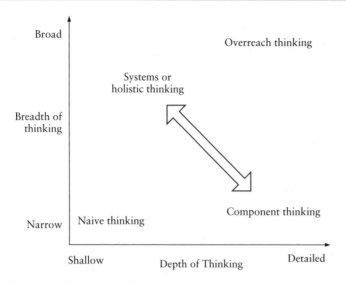

Figure 16.1   Systems or holistic thinking

Adapted from Figure 8–4 (Richmond, 2001, p. 114)

the subcomponents or parts of a system, no matter how refined or detailed, fails to give an understanding of the overall system behavior given a sufficient enough time scale. For example, a careful and detailed analysis of a particular fish species and the effects of harvesting may prove practically useless for management purposes if interactions from other species (such as predator–prey relationships), climatic factors (such as El Niño events), or other human interactions (such as marine pollution) are not modeled or properly understood.

Partial equilibrium analysis and understanding the dynamics of sub-components of a system reveal many critical insights and are important approaches used throughout this book. Although very helpful, we argue that such approaches are incomplete and that environmental and resource economists also need a tool-kit that features both a "microscope" and a "telescope" to obtain a broad and, where appropriate, a detailed perspective of the environment and our place within it. The "microscope" requires many of the tools used throughout this book and may be called "component thinking" as they help us to better understand key components of socioeconomic-environmental systems. The "telescope" requires that we have sufficient breadth to understand key feedbacks across systems but only a level of detail that is necessary to understand the underlying *system* (rather than component) dynamics. This may be called holistic or systems thinking.

Component and systems thinking are complementary ways of understanding and modeling the human–environmental interactions or systems, and can be visualized in figure 16.1. Both approaches are needed to obtain the "big picture" of human–environmental interactions. The double-sided arrow in the figure indicates that both can inform each other in our understanding of the environment and economic systems. Indeed, the two approaches are used in global models of climate change that require detailed parameters (such as elasticities of substitution between fuel sources) and broad understanding of the feedbacks from emissions to climate variability and temperature. Alternative ways of thinking in the figure include approaches that are both narrow in breadth and shallow in depth of thinking (naïve thinking) that is likely to yield only the most obvious insights, and thinking that is both broad and highly detailed (overreach thinking) which may reveal little as it lies beyond our capacities to either model or understand phenomena.

16.2   ENVIRONMENTAL MANAGEMENT

If we wish to improve the human condition, knowledge and understanding should have a purpose. Our goal in writing this book thus was not simply to inform you, the reader, but to result in better understanding and thinking to improve environmental management. Although it is possible to effectively manage a system without fully understanding the underlying dynamics or feedbacks, a greater understanding does enable managers to anticipate and plan for unexpected events.

Adaptive management

A framework for managing human interactions within the environment is presented in figure 16.2. Any system that is "managed" requires as a *minimum* three components: goals to know where we should be going, "control levers" to affect outcomes, and methods of evaluation or monitoring to know whether we have achieved what we wanted. The management "control levers" include strategies that represent the overall ways of controlling the system (such as whether a fishery is regulated by output controls or by input controls on fishers) and tactics that are the specific means to implement the strategies (such as regulations as to the maximum vessel size that are often used with input controls in fisheries). *Adaptive management* also requires data collection, responses to evaluate performance and, where necessary, feedback learning and improved understanding into revised goals, strategies, and tactics.

Economics plays a role in each of these steps. It provides objectives, such as efficiency, that enable us to do the best we can with the resources available to us. An understanding of incentives and the value of the environment (see chapter 8) under different scenarios also help in developing effective strategies and tactics (see chapters 2 and 3). Finally, economics plays an important role in monitoring performance such as measuring of rents in resource industries (see chapter 7) or the estimation of marginal external costs associated with pollution (see chapter 3). It also provides a framework for assessing costs and benefits in terms of alternative methods of implementation and evaluation.

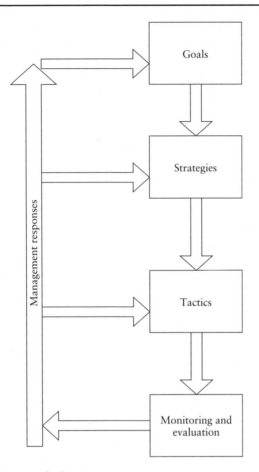

Figure 16.2   Flow diagram of adaptive management

Unfortunately, many environmental systems and natural resources are not adaptively managed. This may be because the managers lack the means or resources to apply the necessary control levers, as is the case in many poor countries, or because the goals have never been explicitly stated or have been subverted. Also, some environmental goals may be in conflict with social or economic goals. In many cases, managers lack the will, time, or resources to monitor or evaluate their strategies. Further, where monitoring and evaluation does occur, managers may be prevented from change by institutional inertia, or by vested interests that may be disadvantaged by proposed changes.

Overlying these management problems is the inherent uncertainty associated with the environment where disturbances and shocks can disrupt the best-laid management plans. To help address uncertainty, so-called *active adaptive management* (Walters and Hilborn, 1976) has been proposed. It requires that managers build models of the system they manage, collect information and experiment to distinguish between the models, and to use these models to assess the effects of different strategies and tactics under a range of scenarios. Thus for each chosen management action or strategy a process exists to assess different strategies under various scenarios and models, and to feed back any learning from outcomes into subsequent actions. Active adaptive management can be characterized as a "systems thinking" approach to management in the sense that it tries to both model and assess the interconnections across systems. Although no approach can ever fully understand or address the complexity of ecological-economic systems, it does offer a framework to manage as effectively as possible given the socioeconomic-environmental constraints.

Risk and uncertainty

Risk and uncertainty are intimately related to environmental management where disturbances, shocks, and surprises are frequent occurrences. In general parlance, risk is synonym for a dangerous chance or hazard while uncertainty is associated with the unpredictable, indeterminate, or unknown. In risk analysis, risk is sometimes defined as the probability of a hazard or undesirable event occurring multiplied by the costs associated should the event occur. Risk has also been interpreted as referring to situations in which the possible outcomes are insurable. For most economists, however, risk is defined differently and includes events that are undesirable (being struck by lightning) and desirable events (winning a lottery). Specifically, *risk* in economics refers to future events that can be assigned objective probabilities (based on past events and statistical analysis). By contrast, in economics *uncertainty* refers to future events for which we can, at best, assign subjective probabilities (and for which we have very little objective basis for predicting their likelihood). Thus, choosing to gamble at a casino where there are defined probabilities of winning and losing represents risk while determining what the average world temperature will be 100 years hence represents uncertainty. In other words, the essential difference is that gambling at a casino results in predictable events (the probabilities of winning are given) while the average temperature in 2105 is inherently unpredictable.

The distinction between risk and uncertainty can sometimes become blurred because some objective probabilities may be used to help determine future and unknowable events. For example, we can use palaeoclimate data to analyze the relationship between world average surface temperatures and atmospheric carbon dioxide concentration. In turn, this analysis can be used to develop a probability that increased atmospheric carbon dioxide concentration will raise the earth's future temperature. However, because many other factors determine temperature (incoming solar radiation or water vapor in the atmosphere, etc.) the outcome of increased atmospheric carbon dioxide concentration is inherently uncertain. Thus, even with probabilistic data, when predicting future world surface temperatures we face an inherent uncertainty.

Managing risk and uncertainty

A well-developed set of methods for addressing risk exists in economics and statistics. The most common approach to managing risk is to pool or share it whereby the hazard associated with a risky event that has a very high cost (such as a supertanker going aground) is shared. For example, an insurance company selling a policy that covers against a very costly (for both the insurance company and policy holder) and risky event may choose to reinsure some of the risk in return for a premium payment to the reinsuring company. Thus, in the event of the insured outcome occurring, part of the costs of the claim is shared.

In financial management, risk can be reduced by diversification. For instance, the risk associated with a portfolio of n shares is often defined by the variance in the return, as given by (1).

$$\text{Variance in expected portfolio return} = \sum_{i=1}^{n} \sum_{j=1}^{n} x_i \, x_j \, \sigma_i \, \sigma_j \, \rho_{ij} \qquad (1)$$

where x_i is the proportion of the portfolio in asset i, σ_i is the standard deviation of the rate of return of asset i and ρ_{ij} is the coefficient of correlation between the returns of asset i and j. As the number of assets in the portfolio increases, the variation in return declines provided the additional asset is not perfectly correlated with the overall portfolio. However, no matter how many assets are added to the portfolio, risk (variance in expected return) cannot be eliminated because assets are correlated to some extent. Thus as n approaches the total number of shares in the market, the level of risk of the portfolio converges to the variation in the expected market return, called the market or nondiversifiable risk. This is illustrated in figure 16.3.

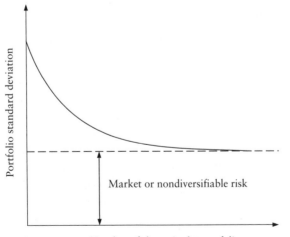

Figure 16.3   Benefits of risk diversification

In general, most investors are only prepared to hold riskier assets (with higher variance of expected returns) if they are compensated by a higher *expected* rate of return. Thus, risk is not necessarily something to be avoided as zero risk is often associated with a low expected return. Indeed, depending on people's preferences, some individuals may actively seek a high level of risk (with the accompanying expected benefits or returns) in their investments, leisure activities, or other areas of their lives.

The risk–return trade-off has parallels in terms of decisions over uncertainty. For instance, in terms of climate change, choosing to do nothing (business as usual) generates initially higher payoffs in terms of per capita income as no resources are devoted to mitigation, but this is at the cost of an increase in the subjective probability of higher climate variability in the future. Consequently, the decision of what to do in terms of mitigating emissions of greenhouse gases will depend on the perceived or subjective probability of climate change and the immediate trade-off or loss in short-run output or income from mitigation. Thus, even if individuals or countries have the same subjective probabilities about future climate change, their decisions about mitigation may be very different depending on their marginal utility of income.

In environmental management a common misconception is that more or better information automatically reduces risk or uncertainty. For instance, an increased sample size or a greater number of observations will, in general, reduce the standard error of the estimated parameters of models thus increasing a model's *precision*. However, this does not necessarily increase the *accuracy* of predictions because the estimated model may be incorrect or subject to bias. In other words, more and better quality data do *not* necessarily result in better understanding or ability to predict the future if they simply reinforce our acceptance of models that are poor or unreliable representations of the environment. Moreover, if increased precision encourages managers to have a misplaced confidence in their models and decisions, it may even result in worse outcomes than if managers were more careful, and thus more responsive and willing, to learn from additional information.

The key to "managing" uncertainty, therefore, is not information or knowledge *per se*, but how the information is used. In other words, what approaches can be used to utilize information and to learn to make better decisions in the face of uncertainty? A first step in answering this question is to separate decisions that depend on uncertain outcomes into those that are *adaptive* (decisions that do not change whether the event occurs or its severity, but do reduce the costs associated with the event) and those that are *corrective* (decisions that change the likelihood of the event or its severity). These decisions are not necessarily mutually exclusive. For example, in the case of climate change it is possible to simultaneously mitigate (reduce anthropogenic emissions of greenhouse gases) and adapt (build dykes and barriers against the possibility of rising sea levels).

The next step in managing uncertainty is to establish a set of decision rules for what action should take place given uncertain events. For example, such rules could include a rule that ensures decisions maximize the present value of net returns, the *minimax rule* (see chapter 11 for a discussion and a description of other decision rules such as the safe minimum standard) that minimizes the maximum possible damage associated with a decision or a *satisficing rule* that ensures a minimum set of criteria are satisfied given the decision. The choice of the decision rule and approaches, such as the precautionary principle (see chapter 15), is important as different decision rules may result in different decisions for the same subjective probabilities. In other words, implicit in a decision rule are the goals of management. The third step requires an active adaptive approach to management whereby the possible effects of the decision under different scenarios and models are compared using both "systems thinking" and "component thinking." This requires modeling of different scenarios and an approach to model building outlined in chapter 1. This could include, for example, sensitivity analysis of different parameters or Monte Carlo approaches and simulations to evaluate models and to compare across different models. In addition, it could include a comparison of the outcomes for the various models under different decisions. The fourth and last step continues the process by which additional information and insights are used to learn and to improve decision-making by testing the assumptions and models used to make the decisions. The four-step approach to managing uncertainty does not prevent unforeseen and undesired events, but it does provide a framework for better decision-making, and ultimately better management in an uncertain world.

Incentives and ingenuity

Surprising as it may be to economists, many environmental systems are managed with little or no regard to human behavior or incentives. Many examples exist where the feedback from human behavior to the environmental system is ignored, and sometimes with disastrous results. In a notorious example, Nepal in 1957 nationalized its forests ostensibly to reduce deforestation by putting them under state control. Unfortunately, the effects were the opposite to what was intended as initially landowners denuded their land of trees to prevent it being nationalized. The change of control of forests in remote areas from communities to the state also undermined centuries-old community management and responsibilities, further contributing to deforestation (Bromley and Chapagain, 1984). Other "quick fix" solutions that ignore the response of people, such as the banning of ivory sales from elephants to increase elephant populations or the banning of imports of tropical timber to prevent deforestation, may result in unintended consequences. For example, a ban on ivory sales may actually *reduce* the elephant population in some countries, depending on the discount rate and the size of the existing elephant population (Bulte and Van Kooten, 1996).

A "systems thinking" approach to environmental management recognizes the inherent feedbacks between people's behavior, incentives, and environmental outcomes. The examples found throughout this book suggest that management is improved if the rights and responsibilities of the individuals that extract a flow of benefits from the environment match collective or societal interests (Grafton, 2000). For example, this may involve an emissions charge on a polluting firm (see chapter 3) or the creation of individual harvesting rights for fishers that can promote resource conservation (see chapter 4).

For time scales of a few years or more, human ingenuity and innovation also plays an important role in determining environmental outcomes. For example, the problem of stratospheric ozone depletion caused by CFCs has been addressed effectively, in part, because of the development of substitute chemicals in response to changes in regulations. Air pollution in the United States and most developed countries is much lower today than a generation ago because of technologies developed to reduce car emissions (see chapters 3 and 11). Since the first oil shock (see chapter 7), a whole range of renewable energy sources have been developed and improved including wind power, photovoltaic cells, and fuel cells that recombine hydrogen and oxygen to produce electricity and water. Such technologies will play an increasingly important role in reducing environmental impacts in the future.

Innovation, be it institutional or technical, provides a critical part in ensuring a sustainable environment. Thus a key to successful long-run environmental management is harnessing human ingenuity for the collective good. In part, this requires an economic system where innovation and research and development are rewarded. It also requires appropriate incentives to "induce" innovations, such as those that reduce material throughput and waste and increase energy efficiency.

16.3   MANAGING OUR FUTURE

In the past twenty years or so we have become much more aware of the effects of pollution and resource depletion on a global scale. Part of this understanding has grown from an appreciation of the long time scales that arise between causes and their effects. The most obvious examples are climate change, where time scales of centuries are relevant, and stratospheric ozone depletion where time scales measured by the decade are appropriate. Long time scales may also be required for other aspects of the environment such as the link between habitat fragmentation and species extinction or extirpation (see chapter 15).

Longer time scales of cause and effect pose particular difficulties for the environment. First, the potential problem may go undetected or be misunderstood for long periods of time thus hindering effective policies to address the problem. Second, time scales measured over generations may reduce incentives for the present generation to confront environmental problems today. Third, threshold effects at particular levels of accumulation or depletion (see chapter 1) and non-linearities between "dose and response" may lead to irreversible consequences with very high costs.

Resilience

A factor that has contributed to an understanding of global environmental issues is the interconnectedness of systems, problems, and causes. Increasingly, decision makers are realizing that a "systems approach" is important to managing our future. For example, in fisheries management the question is not simply how many fish are caught, but the breakdown by species, size, gender, and age are also critically important to ensure the long-term viability of the industry. Systems approaches to management help reduce the chance of catastrophic collapse of natural populations on which people depend for their livelihood.

To capture the concept of vulnerability of ecosystems or environments, ecologists have coined the word *resilience*. The term is defined as the ability of a system to return to its former state following a shock or disturbance and can be measured by the relative size of the disturbance (Holling, 1973), or by the time it takes (Pimm, 1984) for the system to return to its former state. Both ways of looking at resilience are insightful and imply that successful long-term management requires a broad understanding of environmental systems (see chapter 15).

Adaptive cycles

An approach that incorporates the concept of resilience in a general framework is called the "adaptive cycle," whereby natural systems are hypothesized to cycle between one of four phases or states (Holling and Gunderson, 2002). At the very end or at the "top" of the cycle or conservation phase, often characterized by so-called "climax communities," the environmental system is at its most connected, but is also the least resilient to shocks or disturbances. Paradoxically, in this phase of the cycle the system may seem the most stable because the system may have existed for a long period of time.

An illustration of the adaptive cycle is given in figure 16.4. In the figure, the length of the black arrows is *inversely* proportional to the time it takes to move from one phase to another. Thus, the transition from the conservation to release phase may be very rapid compared to the transition from the exploitation to conservation phase. The two "axes" are the system's potential energy and connectivity, both of which are hypothesized to peak at the end of the conservation phase and then rapidly decline in the release phase. In this perspective, a system with the greatest potential energy and connectivity is the most vulnerable to a shock or disturbance that can shift the system into a fundamentally different state.

An example of an adaptive cycle is a well-established forest community. Mature stands of trees illustrate the conservation phase of the cycle and are more vulnerable to disruption due to fire, because of the build-up of flammable materials, than mixed-aged stands. The effects of fire also show that the shift from the conservation to a release phase can be both rapid and unpredictable in terms of its timing. After

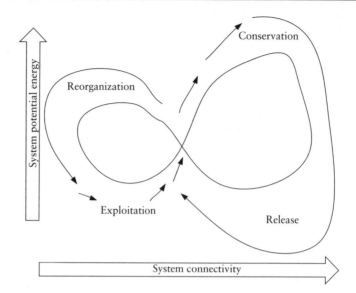

Figure 16.4   The "adaptive cycle"

Adapted from Figure 2.1 (Holling and Gunderson, p. 34, 2002)

the release or phase transition, the forest is hypothesized to reorganize, but many possible paths may occur as opportunities are created for competition, colonization and migration into the environmental system. Eventually, certain trees and animal species, or components of the system, are hypothesized to begin to dominate in the exploitation phase and a long transition begins again towards another conservation phase.

Adaptive cycles have been found for a number of environmental systems (rangelands, lakes, forests) and have been hypothesized to exist for political and economic systems. The value of the concept, however, is not so much in whether the adaptive cycle is ubiquitous, but whether it gives insights into how to manage the environment under uncertainty. Its principal implications are important for managing the future. The adaptive cycle suggests, first and foremost, that uncertainties, surprises and change are inherent in environmental systems and that the goal of long-term stable targets or goals (such as maximum sustainable yield in a fishery) is unachievable, and costly, if it reduces system resilience. The framework also implies that human disturbances interact in complex ways within the environment and that managing the future is about managing human or socio-economic systems and their connections to the environment (such as avoiding placing residential communities next to mature plantation forests because of the dangers of forest fires). The adaptive cycle also implies that approaches that give managers the opportunity to experiment, to learn, and to be flexible to shocks and changes, such as active adaptive management, provide the greatest long-term options to environmental managers in an uncertain world.

Role of economics

Explicitly recognizing the connections and time scales of environmental systems will contribute little to better management unless the linkages to socioeconomic systems are also made. As we have shown throughout this book, economics has an important contribution to make to help achieve this worthy goal. In part 1 (chapters 1–3) we showed there is a well-developed framework for both understanding and modeling the causes and possible remedies for resource degradation and pollution. Part II (chapters 4–7) provides a detailed treatment of the particular set of problems, market failures and solutions for the most important natural resources – fisheries, forests, water and non-renewable resources. Part III (chapters 8–10) emphasizes the preeminent role economics plays in valuing the environment and which is a *sine qua non* for better environmental and resource management. Part IV (chapters 11–16) shows that economic analysis provides a powerful analytical framework for understanding and helping to resolve the world's global environmental challenges, such as population growth, biodiversity, and climate change. Thus, our book provides a firm foundation for understanding economic-environmental problems and trade-offs, and a framework for helping to make our world a better place to live.

FURTHER READING

A good introduction to "systems thinking" and the environment is Ford (1999) while an easily accessible introduction to complexity theory is Ward (2001). A multitude of texts exist on risk and uncertainty. Moore (1983) provides a comprehensive survey of risk management in business while Kay and Regier provide an ecological perspective. Diamond and Rothschild (1989) is an authoritative reference on uncertainty in economics and Kolb (1995) is a highly accessible text on financial management and investment theory. LeRoy and Singell (1987) provide an informative historical perspective on risk and uncertainty in Economics.

Hilborn and Walters (1992) is a definitive reference on active adaptive management and Ludwig et al. (1993) is a sobering review of the past mistakes in the exploitation of renewable resources. A useful reference on the benefits of anti-poaching activities for elephant ivory, and the dynamics of poacher behavior, is Kremer and Morcom (2000).

The classic reference on resilience is Holling (1973). The insights of an interdisciplinary group of researchers on resilience and complex systems are presented in a volume edited by Gunderson and Holling (2002) that forms the basis for much of this chapter's discussion on adaptive cycles. Another insightful multi-authored presentation that distills the wisdom of various scientists (including a couple of economists) in terms of resource management is Mangel et al. (1997).

For readers seeking overviews of environmental and resource economics, we recommend a review by Cropper and Oates (1992) and another by Dasgupta (1996). A recent survey of the global state of the environment is provided in the July 6, 2002, issue of *The Economist*.

REFERENCES

Bromley, D. W. and Chapagain, D. P. (1984). The Village against the Center: Resource Depletion in South Asia, *American Journal of Agricultural Economics*, 66: 868–73.

Bulte, E. and Van Kooten, G. C. (1996). A Note on Ivory Trade and Elephant Conservation, *Environment and Development Economics*, 1: 433–43.

Carpenter, S. R., Brock, W. A. and Ludwig, D. (2002). Collapse, Learning, and Renewal, in L. H. Gunderson and C. S. Holling, eds, *Panarchy: Understanding Transformations in Human and Natural Systems*, Island Press: Washington, DC.

Cropper, M. L. and Oates, W. E. (1992). Environmental Economics: A Survey, *Journal of Economic Literature*, 30: 700–21.

Dasgupta, P. (1996). The Economics of the Environment, *Environment and Development Economics*, 1 (4): 387–428.

Diamond, P. and Rothschild, M. (1989). *Uncertainty in Economics: Readings and Exercises*, revised edition, Academic Press: San Diego.

Ford, A. (1999). *Modeling the Environment: An Introduction to System Dynamics Modeling of Environmental Systems*, Island Press: Washington, DC.

Grafton, R. Q. (2000). Governance of the Commons: A Role for the State?, *Land Economics*, 76: 504–17.

Gunderson, L. H. and Holling, C. S. (eds) 2002. *Panarchy: Understanding Transformations in Human and Natural Systems*. Island Press: Washington.

Hilborn, R. and Walters, C. J. (1992). *Quantitative Fisheries Stock Assessment: Choice, Dynamics and Uncertainty*, Chapman and Hall: London.

Holling, C. S. (1973). Resilience and Stability of Ecological Systems, *Annual Review of Ecology and Systematics*, 4: 1–24.

Holling, C. S. and Gunderson, L. H. (2002). Resilience and Adaptive Cycles, in L. H. Gunderson and C. S. Holling, eds, *Panarchy: Understanding Transformations in Human and Natural Systems*, Island Press: Washington.

Kadanoff, L. P. (1966). Scaling Laws for Ising Models near T_c. *Physics*, 2 (6): 263–72.

Kay, J. J. and Regier, H. A. (2000). Uncertainty, Complexity, and Ecological Integrity: Insights from an Ecosystem Approach, in P. Crabbé, A. Holland, L. Ryszkowski, and L. Westra, eds, *Implementing Ecological Integrity*, Kluwer Academic Publishers: London.

Kolb, R. W. (1995). *Investments*, fourth edition, Kolb Publishing: Boulder, CO.

Kremer, M. and Morcom, C. (2000). Elephants. *The American Economic Review*, 90 (1): 212–34.

Leroy, S. F. and Singell, Jr, L. G. (1987). Knight on Risk and Uncertainty, *Journal of Political Economy*, 95 (2): 394–406.

Levins, R. (1970). Complex Systems, in C. H. Waddington, ed., *Towards a Theoretical Biology*, Edinburgh: Edinburgh University Press.

Ludwig, D., Hilborn, R. and Walters, C. (1993). Uncertainty, Resource Exploitation, and Conservation: Lessons from History, *Science*, 260 (7): 36.

Mangel, M., L. M. Talbot, G. K. Meffe, M. T. Agardy, D. L. Alverson, J. Barlow, D. B. Botkin, G. Budowski, T. Clark, J. Cooke, R. H. Crozier, P. K. Dayton, D. L. Elder, C. W. Fowler, S. Funtowicz, J. Giske, R. J. Hofman, S. J. Holt, S. R. Kellert, L. A. Kimball, D. Ludwig, K. Magnusson, B. S. Malayang III, C. Mann, E. A. Norse, S. P. Northridge, W. F. Perrin, C. Perrings, R. M. Peterman. G. B. Rabb, H. A. Regier, J. E. Reynolds III, K. Sherman, M. P. Sissenwine, T. D. Smith, A. Starfield, R. J. Taylor, M. F. Tillman, C. Toft, J. R. Twiss Jr., J. Wilen, and T. P. Young (1997). Principles for the Conservation of Wild Living Resources, *Environment and Development Economics*, 2 (1): 40–72.

May, R. M. (1973). *Stability and Complexity in Model Ecosystems*. Princeton University Press: Princeton, New Jersey.

Moore, P. G. (1983). *The Business of Risk*, Cambridge University Press: Cambridge, England.

Pimm, S. L. (1984). The Complexity and Stability of Ecosystems, *Nature*, 307: 321–6.

Richmond, B. (2001). *An Introduction to Systems Thinking*. High Performance Systems, Inc: Hanover, NH.

The Economist (2002). How many planets? A survey of the global environment, July 6.

Walters, C. J. and Hilborn, R. (1976). Adaptive Control of Fishing Systems, *Journal of the Fisheries Research Board of Canada*, 33: 145–59.

Ward, M. (2001). *Universality: The Underlying Theory Behind Life, the Universe and Everything*. Macmillan: London.

GLOSSARY

A

Absolute scarcity: The notion that the absolute level or amount of non-renewable resources must decline with use.

Active adaptive management: An approach that requires managers to build models of the system they manage, collect information and experiment to distinguish between the models, and to use these models to assess the effects of different strategies and tactics under a range of scenarios.

Adaptive cycle: Notion that systems cycle between one of four phases or states that includes a conservation, release, reorganization, and exploitation phase, each of which has different levels of potential energy and system connectivity.

Adaptive decisions: Decisions that do not reduce the likelihood or severity of an event, but reduce the costs associated with the event.

Adaptive management: An approach whereby managers specify measurable objectives, strategies to achieve the goals, tactics to implement the strategies, and methods of evaluation to check if goals have been reached and to improve overall management.

Adjoint variable: Also known as the co-state variable, is the shadow or imputed price of the state variable at a given instant in time

Allocative efficiency: Cost minimization of inputs for any given level of output.

Ambient permits: Marketable pollution permits defined in terms of the ambient levels of environmental quality at defined locations or receptor sites.

Anadromous fish: Fish species that spend their adult life in the ocean but spawn in fresh water, such as salmon.

Annual allowable cut: The maximum level of timber that can be harvested on public forest lands, typically determined on the basis of the area available for harvest and the annual increase in timber volumes associated with growth in the forest.

Annuity: A fixed payment made at regular intervals for a fixed number of years, for life, or forever.

Anthropocentric: The belief that humans hold a special place in nature; being centered primarily on humans and human affairs. Understanding the non-human world through human values and experiences.

Asset test: A test that must be satisfied if a non-renewable resource is being extracted optimally. It requires that the product of the current value of the shadow price of the resource and the remaining reserves be zero at the end of the optimization period. This can be satisfied if either the current value of the shadow price is zero, or if the mineral has been completely exhausted. In the first case, it is no longer worthwhile to extract the mineral, and in the second, the mine has been exhausted and there is no more mineral left to extract.

Assimilative capacity: Assimilative capacity is the capacity of natural assets such as atmosphere, bodies of water, forests to absorbs pollutants within certain limits without detrimental effects.

Attractors: The points to which a dynamic system is attracted, or moves towards, over time.

Attribute based stated choice methods (ABSCM): See *Stated preference methods*. Measures respondent preferences for different attributes of the good in question.

Autarky: Situation where a country has no trade with any other country(ies), such that all goods and services are produced and consumed domestically.

Aquifer: An underground body of water.

B

Back-stop technology: A technology that is able to supply an input (such as energy), but is currently uneconomic to employ.

Benefit transfer: An approach to valuation that obtains estimates of economic values by transferring existing benefit estimates from studies already completed for another location or issue.

Bernouilli trials: A Bernouilli trial has one of two outcomes: success or failure.

Best available technology: A form of environmental regulation that dictates the type of abatement technology that is to be employed by a polluting firm.

Best management practice: A government or industry program that assists firms and farms to reduce pollution by identifying pollution-reducing production processes.

Bifurcation: A point where a marginal change in a parameter of a system results in a fundamentally different system behavior and oscillation between two attractors.

Biodiversity: The number, variety, and variability of all living organisms in all ecosystems and the ecological complexes of which they are part.

Biomass: The total weight of a population. Biomass is a commonly used measure of abundance where the number of individuals may be very large, such as in fisheries.

Bioprospect: Payment of a sum of money for the exclusive rights to own/use the biological fruits of scientific research.

Block rate price structure: A form of pricing commonly used by public utilities. The marginal price rises/falls at discrete intervals in the case of increasing/decreasing rate structures.

Boundary condition: A constraint on the value of a state variable at the beginning or end of a dynamic optimization problem.

Boundary Waters Treaty: A treaty signed in 1909 by Canada and the United States that sets out the procedures for managing water bodies that are shared or that form part of their international boundary.

Budget constraint: The limit on the consumption bundles that a consumer can afford.

C

Cap-and-trade program: Emission permit trading program where an overall cap or total level of emissions is set by a regulator and permits are allocated to polluters who are allowed to trade permits among themselves.

Capital gain: An increase in the value of an asset.

Capital stuffing: The overuse (from a societal perspective) of capital to harvest a resource that arises from improperly specified property rights.

Capture fisheries: Fisheries where the fish are hunted and caught rather than farmed.

Carbon sequestration: The net removal of CO_2 from the atmosphere into long-lived pools of carbon, e.g. trees.

Carrying capacity: The hypothetical maximum number or size of a population that cannot be exceeded due to environmental constraints.

Catchability coefficient: A parameter in a harvesting function that is often used to proxy differences in technology, efficiency, or fishing gear.

Catch per unit of effort: The total catch of fish per unit of fishing effort. The measure is sometimes used as an indicator of stock abundance in fisheries.

Chaos: Deterministic dynamic systems that exhibit apparent random behavior and are characterized by extreme sensitivity to initial conditions.

Cheap talk: A statement that explains to a survey respondent that they are being asked a hypothetical question, and that individuals often do not treat hypothetical as they would in actual transactions. This serves to improve the accuracy of elicited responses.

Choice experiments: A stated preference research technique used to elicit respondents' trade-offs and preferences given a set of choices.

Choke price: Price at which demand is "choked" off or goes to zero.

CINCS: Critically important natural capital stocks such as a stable global climate.

Clean Development Mechanism: Under the Kyoto Protocol, countries and designated parties are permitted to invest in projects in developing countries that lead to emissions reductions so long as they meet certain criteria.

Club goods: Goods or resources characterized by ease of exclusion and congestibility.

Coase theorem: If property rights exist then, under certain conditions, irrespective of the assignment of property rights, liability or legal entitlements, the parties affected by a technological externality who negotiate or bargain among themselves will achieve an efficient outcome. The conditions to ensure this result are that parties negotiate or bargain at zero cost, there is no strategic behavior in the bargaining, all parties have complete and full information, and the initial distribution of rights does not affect the marginal valuation of resources or assets.

Command-and-control regulation: A form of environmental regulation in which polluters are ordered to abate by specific amounts or through the use of prescribed technologies.

Common law: Law based on judicial precedent and that forms the basis of many of the *de jure* property rights in the English-speaking world.

Common-pool resource: A resource characterized by rivalry in use and difficulty in excluding others from its use.

Comparative advantage: Term for when one country is able to produce a good at lower opportunity cost than another country.

Compensating variation: Given a change in prices, CV is the welfare measure of the amount an individual would need to be compensated to maintain the original level of utility. This measure is the change in income needed to make a person as well off as they were before the change.

Compensating surplus: A measure of how welfare changes for an individual when the quantity of a public good is increased or decreased. The reference point is the level of utility prior to the change.

Compensation principle: If those that stand to benefit from a policy can hypothetically compensate those who are harmed, to a point where those harmed are indifferent between the old and new situation, then the policy is said to satisfy the compensation principle.

Complex system: Systems that have the characteristic of self-organizing criticality.

Component thinking: Thinking and modeling that help us to better understand key components of socioeconomic-environmental systems.

Composition effect (of trade): International trade encourages the shifting of commodity production (along with attendant pollution) to the country with lower environmental standards.

Computable general equilibrium (CGE) models: Economic models that describe economic behavior in a number of markets for one or more economies. These models are solved computationally for equilibrium aggregate values or changes due to specified policies. The equations are calibrated with data from the countries being modeled. Parameters needed to make the models run are either assumed or adapted from estimates elsewhere.

Congestibility: The notion that increased use or exploitation of a good or asset beyond a certain point reduces the benefits to existing users.

Congestion externality: A particular type of a technological externality in fishing that arises from the close proximity and simultaneous use of fishing gear or vessels that increases harvesting costs.

Consumer surplus: A measure of the benefits to consumers from the consumption of a good or service, measured by the difference between the price actually paid for a good, and the maximum amount that an individual is willing to pay for it. Defined as the area below the demand curve up to the total quantity consumed, minus total expenditures on the good or service.

Contingent valuation: A survey based technique for valuing non-market uses of a natural resources based on stated preferences of consumers. The value of the good is elicited from survey respondents' trade-offs in a hypothetical market.

Control variable: Variable in dynamic optimization problems which is under the "control" or can be directly determined in the program.

Convention on Biological Diversity (CBD): International treaty signed by over 130 nations to guide decisions about biodiversity.

Convention on International Trade in Endangered Species (CITES): An international voluntary agreement between countries whose goal is to ensure that international trade in specimens of wild animals and plants does not threaten their survival. It came into force on July 1, 1975.

Cooperative games: Games in which the players can make binding commitments and engage in side-payments, or the transfer of resources or money from one player to another. This can lead to different outcomes than where the same game is modelled as a non-cooperative game.

Corrective decisions: Decisions that affect the likelihood or severity of future events.

Co-state variable: See *Adjoint variable*.

Cost-effective pollution control: Method of pollution control that ensures the marginal cost of abatement is equalized across sources.

Credit programs: Emission permit program where polluters receive tradable emission credits for any reductions in their emissions below an admissible standard.

Critical depensation: A situation where below a critical stock or population size, the population will become extinct.

Cultivars: The genetically identical offspring that have been propagated from a particular plant that has been selected for desirable characteristics (such as rapid growth).

D

De facto **rights:** Property rights that are recognized by norms of behavior, but are not necessarily enforceable by law.

Defensive expenditure: Expenses incurred to prevent damage and its effects on people, such as the installation of flue gas desulfurization units in coal-fired power stations and the building of dykes to prevent flooding.

De jure **rights:** Property rights that are recognized by the appropriate legal authorities.

Demersal fish: Fish caught in mid-water or near the sea floor and that include such species as haddock, hake, cod, and pollock.

Depensation: When the proportional growth rate of the population is increasing in the size of the population. Depensation potentially poses major problems for fishery managers because small changes in the stock can lead to large changes in recruitment.

Depletion: The decrease in the value of the stock of natural assets attributable to economic activity.

Depletion effect: See *Stock effect*.

Depreciation: The decrease in the value of the stock of produced assets attributable to economic activity.

Differential rent: See *Ricardian rent*.

Dirty goods: Commodities whose production processes generate a relatively large amount of pollution.

Discount rate: The adjustment that allows receipts paid in different periods to be compared. Receipts paid in earlier periods are valued more highly since they can be invested in bonds that pay interest and because agents are assumed to be impatient.

Discrete choice: A form of analysis that identifies preference information from discrete choices made by consumers. The simplest form of discrete choice response is a single presented offer and a request for a Yes or No response. See *Random utility model*.

Doctrine of prior appropriation: A legal rule specifying that the priority for water withdrawals is determined by the date at which users laid claim to the water.

Dominant strategy: The single strategy (or set of actions) for a player that yields the highest payoffs regardless of the other players' strategies.

Double dividend: The notion that environmental quality can improve while at the same time increasing incentives to work (by reducing marginal income tax rates or payroll taxes) and raising productivity. The term is most frequently applied to the possibility of switching taxes away from "goods" (such as labor) to "bads" (such as pollution). This is said to occur if the revenue from green taxes is used to cut distortionary taxes in an economy.

Dredging: Method of catching certain fish species, especially for scallops and oysters, that involves running a heavy steel frame across the sea floor.

Duality theory: Economic theory which states that maximizing utility and minimizing expenditure embody the same essential information on preferences. Duality identifies the connection between Marshallian demand, expenditure, indirect utility function, and Hicksian demand functions.

Dynamic constraint: A constraint on the state variable in a dynamic optimization problem.

Dynamic efficiency: A circumstance where economic agents have on-going incentives over time to continuously improve efficiency and current practices.

Dynamic pool models: Population models that are able to separate a population into distinct age groups or size groups.

E

Earth Summit: The international meeting held by developed and developing countries in Rio de Janeiro in 1992 to discuss environmental concerns. It led to two international agreements (the Framework Convention on Climate Change) and the CBD, as well as issuing two non-binding statements, one on general principles of sustainable forest management and the other on general principles of sustainable development and the creation at the UN of the Commission on Sustainable Development.

Econometrics: The application of statistical methods to the empirical estimation of economic relationships. Econometric models reveal the relationships between the dependent and explanatory variables under question.

Economic efficiency: Maximum output is produced for the inputs used, and inputs are allocated to minimize costs for any output level.

Economic rent: Returns that exceed those required to ensure the supply of a factor of production.

Ecosystem: A distinct assemblage of plants and animals and the interrelationships among them.

Ecosystem services: Services provided by ecosystems such as watershed protection, nutrient cycling and filtering of harmful radiation by the biosphere. Ecosystem services are usually nonrivalrous and nonexcludable. Hence they are hard to value and are often omitted from environmental accounts.

EDP: The environmentally adjusted version of NDP. It equals GDP minus depreciation on the produced capital stock and depletion of the natural capital stock.

Endemic: Plants and animals that are indigenous to in a specific area.

Endowment: The amount of something that a person or country simply has, rather than their having acquired it. In trade models, endowments refer to primary factors of production.

Environmental accounting: A statistical framework for analyzing the impact of economic activity on the environment.

Environmental bond: A bond that must be paid prior to undertaking an action that poses an environmental risk. Should the individual or firm's action result in a defined deterioration in environmental quality, the bond is forfeit.

Environmental capital: Natural assets such as land, air, minerals, etc.

Environmental Kuznets curve: An inverted U relationship as represented between certain measures of environmental degradation or pollution (on vertical axis) and per capita income (on horizontal axis).

Environmental valuation: The estimation of economic values of services provided by the natural environment. Commonly used to construct measures (usually monetary measures, but not always) of welfare arising from changes in the environment.

Equalization of relative factor prices: The tendency for trade to cause factor prices in different countries to become identical.

Equivalent surplus: A measure of how welfare changes for an individual when the quantity of a public good is increased or decreased. The reference point is the level of utility after the change.

Equivalent variation: The change in income needed to place an individual at the utility level that would be realized with a change in prices, without that change actually occurring.

Ex ante: Before the fact. Valuation is most often conducted in an *"ex ante"* fashion. For example, values may be identified as the individual's willingness to pay to reduce health risks, given that they currently do not have the illness.

Expenditure function: The minimum amount of money than an individual needs to spend at given current prices in order to obtain a specified level of utility.

Existence value: See *Passive use value*: A non-use value associated with the importance placed on knowing that the resource in question exists.

Exploitation ratio: Proportion of fish removed from a fishery due to fishing.

Exploration: The search for new stocks of natural resource assets.

Expenditure function: The amount of income devoted to consumption of goods dependent on demand and the price of goods.

Ex post: After the fact. For example, *ex post* valuation would assess willingness to pay to reduce the health risks given that an individual currently suffers from the illness.

Externality: The result of an activity that causes incidental benefits or damages to others with no corresponding compensation provided to or paid by those who generate the externality.

F

Fall-down effect: The transition between higher harvest levels to lower harvest levels as a forest with mature timber is transformed into an even-aged forest.

Faustmann rotation: The optimal age at which to harvest trees when the forest is being managed for timber production on a perpetual basis, and that will yield the highest economic return.

Feedback effects: Effects that can be either positive or negative and that represent responses to a disturbance, shock, or perturbation. Positive feedbacks reinforce while negative feedbacks tend to counteract the initial disturbance.

First-best solution: Is where the marginal cost (including all external costs) is equal to the marginal benefit (including all external benefits).

Fishing effort: A single or a composite measure of the fishing inputs applied in harvesting fish.

Fixed point: Point or value of a variable from which there is no tendency to move.

Flow pollutant: Pollutants whose effects are only felt at the time of discharge and can be readily assimilated by the environment.

Fundamental equation of non-renewable resources: A portfolio balance condition that ensures the present value of rents from a mine are maximized. It requires that any rise in the resource price, lower marginal costs of extraction in the future from having marginally greater remaining reserves, and lower marginal costs in the future associated with technological progress equal the instantaneous return from extracting a marginal amount of the resource and placing the returns in a bank to receive a rate of return equal to the discount rate.

Fundamental equation of renewable resources: A rate of harvesting of a renewable resource that maximizes the present value of the rents. It requires that the instantaneous rate of return from investing in the resource exactly equal the instantaneous return from disinvesting (harvesting) in the resource.

G

GDP: Gross Domestic Product measures the market value of total production in an economy over a specified period of time (usually a year).

Gear selectivity: The ability of fishing gear to discriminate between different fish species or fish of different sizes within a species.

GEMS (Global Environmental Monitoring System): International dataset that has recorded sulfur dioxide concentrations in major urban areas in developed and developing countries alike since the 1970s.

General Agreement on Tariffs and Trade (GATT): The General Agreement on Tariffs and Trade (GATT) was first signed in 1947. The agreement was designed to provide an international forum that encouraged free trade between member states by regulating and reducing tariffs on traded goods and by providing a common mechanism for resolving trade disputes.

Geometric progression: A series of numbers where each term in the series is obtained by multiplying the previous term by a common scalar.

Gillnets: Method of fishing that involves the laying of nets in which fish become entrapped.

Global pollution: Pollution that originates in one country but whose impacts are felt in other countries.

Gordon–Schaefer model: The static economic optimization model of a fishery that combines a logistic growth function of the population and a linear aggregate harvesting function.

Greenhouse gases (GHGs): The atmospheric gases that contribute to global warming by trapping heat is the earth's atmosphere. The most significant in terms of impact is carbon dioxide (CO_2). The other major gases are methane (CH4), chlorofluorocarbons (CFCs – the same gases that deplete ozone), and nitrous oxides (NO_x–the same gases that are a component of acid deposition).

Green revolution: Name given to the development and adoption of high-yielding grain varieties (especially wheat and rice) that significantly increased yields per hectare in many countries, especially in Asia.

H

Hardwood species: Typically broad leaved and in temperate climates deciduous species such as maple and oak that produce commercial timber valued for its durability and appearance.

Hartman rotation: The optimal age at which to harvest trees when the environmental amenities associated with the trees along with the economic benefits are taken into account.

Hartwick's rule: A rule that the rents from the extraction of non-renewable resources be invested in reproducible capital so as to ensure a sustainable level of consumption over time.

Human Development Index (HDI): An index constructed by the United Nations Development Program (UNDP), is an average of indicators of life expectancy, educational attainment and per capita GDP. The UNDP computes the HDI for a wide range of countries.

Hedonic price methods: The examination of market prices to assess the contribution of various attributes to the price of the good. The objective of hedonic price analysis in environmental valuation is to "untangle" the contribution of environmental attributes from other components of price.

Hedonic wage analysis: See *Hedonic price analysis*. Used to evaluate the response of wage rates to changes in employment characteristics as well as environmental/health characteristics of the employment.

Highgrading: The dumping of less desirable fish at sea with the intent of catching more desirable and higher priced fish before returning to port.

Holdren–Ehrlich decomposition: Stated as $ED = P \cdot Y \cdot I$ where ED is overall environmental impact, P is total population, Y is per capita consumption or income and I is an overall environmental impact coefficient. It implies that a rising total consumption or income ($P \cdot Y$) must be more than offset by a declining I to prevent further environmental degradation.

Homeostasis: The tendency of natural systems to maintain an equilibrium through the interaction of positive and negative feedback effects.

Homothetic preferences: Preference structure that ensures that consumers with different incomes but facing the same prices will demand goods in the same proportions.

Hotelling rule: A market equilibrium condition for non-renewable resources that is satisfied only under strict conditions. If the marginal cost of extracting ore is zero the rule states that the growth rate of the resource price of a nonrenewable resource equals the discount rate. If the marginal cost of extraction is positive and a constant, the rule states that the growth rate of the net price (price of ore less marginal cost of extraction) of a non-renewable resource equals the discount rate.

Household production function: A framework for analyzing decision-making which assumes that a household purchases market goods and combines these with a time input to produce commodities that are valued by members of the household.

Human capital: The value of the knowledge embodied in the workers of firms. One measure of it is the discounted stream of future wages generated by the total sum of workers in an economy.

Hydrologic cycle: The set of physical processes whereby water moves and changes form around the planet.

I

Incentive compatible: A mechanism designed with incentives reveal true values. A valuation task is incentive compatible if the respondent faces incentives to answer truthfully.

Indicated resource: A mineral resource whose quality can be estimated with a reasonable level of confidence.

Indirect utility function: A function which identifies an individual's preferences given limited income and the price of goods.

Individual transferable quotas: Harvesting rights allocated to individual fishers that sum to the total allowable catch. Quota holders may trade their rights and must not harvest more than they have quota, plus any permitted overages.

Inferred resource: A mineral resource whose quality and quantity can be estimated with a low level of confidence.

In situ value: See *User cost.*

International emissions trading (IET): Countries that ratify the Kyoto Protocol are permitted to trade emissions reductions allowances under the framework established by the Protocol.

Intrinsic growth rate: A parameter, usually defined by r, in the logistic growth function.

Irreversible: Once a decision is undertaken, it is not possible to reverse the effects of that decision.

ISEW: The Index of Sustainable Economic Welfare is a broad measure of welfare, proposed by Cobb and Cobb Jr (1994) that takes GDP as its starting point, and then extends it to factor in services of household labor, consumer durables and roads, and makes deductions for defensive expenditure on health, education, costs of commuting, inequality, costs of air, water and noise pollution, amongst other variables.

Isopleth plots: Graphical representation of different yield-per-recruit relationships as a function of the age their enter the fishery and overall fishing mortality.

J

K

Keystone species: Either individual organisms or groups of organisms that ultimately determine the robustness or resilience (ability to cope with change) of a particular ecosystem.

Knife-edge selection: The notion that fish become immediately vulnerable to fishing as soon as they reach a particular size.

Kyoto Protocol: The United Nations Framework Convention on Climate Change (UNFCCC) was adopted on May 9, 1992. By June 19, 1993 the Convention had received 166 signatures. The Convention entered into force on March 21, 1994. The text of the (Kyoto) Protocol to the UNFCCC was adopted at the third session of the Conference of the Parties to the UNFCCC in Kyoto, Japan, on December 11, 1997. It is a multilateral effort to reduce greenhouse gas emissions by having signatories commit to legally binding targets. Moreover, under the Protocol, an international "emissions trading" regime will allow developed countries that reduce emissions beyond their agreed target to sell the excess emissions credits to others.

L

Local pollution: Pollution that is contained within a given country or location.

Logistic growth: Populations that are characterized by density dependence such that the growth in the population is determined by the size of the population.

Longlines: Method of fishing whereby baited hooks and lines and left to "soak," and then recovered.

M

Marginal abatement cost: The incremental cost to a polluter of reducing its pollution level by one unit.

Marginal rate of substitution: The amount of one good that you would be willing to trade away for an additional unit of another.

Marginal utility of income: The change in the value of utility derived from income. Individuals with different marginal utility of incomes will, for example, not all hold the same value of an extra dollar.

Market failures: Set of circumstances under which a market fails to allocate scarce resources efficiently so as to achieve the greatest surplus to society. The four sources of market failures are: (1) the existence of public goods; (2) the presence of market power; (3) the existence of externalities; and (4) lack of perfect information.

Market risk: Risk that is unavoidable and cannot be reduced by risk diversification.

Marshallian demand: Demand for a good or service that is determined by prices and income.

Materials balance condition: The sum of material taken from the environment must equal the mass of residuals returned to the environment plus the mass converted into energy and the net investment in capital goods and durable goods.

Maximum economic yield (MEY): The hypothetical yield or harvest from a renewable resource that maximizes the current rent, but leaves the size of the current population or biomass unchanged.

Maximum likelihood (ML): Mathematical estimation of parameters from a statistical model. The method maximizes the likelihood that the observed data could have generated the parameters.

Maximum principle: A principle used in the solution to optimal control problems that specifies the necessary conditions that must be satisfied for optimal paths of the control and state variables.

Maximum sustainable yield (MSY): The hypothetical maximum yield or harvest from a renewable resource, but leaves the current size of the population or biomass unchanged.

Measured resource: A mineral resource whose quality and quantity can be estimated with a high level of confidence.

Megafauna: Large, often mammalian animals, that are often highly vulnerable to both hunting and habitat loss.

Meta-analysis: Statistical procedure designed to accumulate experimental and correlational results across independent studies that address a related set of research questions.

Mineral resource: A concentration of material of intrinsic economic interest where there exists a reasonable prospect for eventual economic extraction.

Mineral reserve: The economically extractable part of a measured or indicated mineral resource.

Mineralogical barrier: A threshold where it is technically possible to extract a mineral but it is of several orders of magnitude times greater in cost than current methods of mining.

Minmax strategy: Decision rule to minimize the maximum possible damage associated with a decision.

Modified Hotelling rule: A market equilibrium result that arises from the costly extraction of a non-renewable resource. It states that the growth rate in the net price of the resource plus the ratio of the stock effect (change in cost from a marginal depletion of the resource) and the net price equals the discount rate. See *Hotelling rule.*

Montreal Protocol on Substances that Deplete the Ozone Layer: A multilateral agreement signed on September 16, 1987 whose goal was the "elimination" of ozone-depleting substances.

Morbidity: Illness or lack of health. Morbidity can be described in terms of the incidence and/or prevalence of certain diseases or disabilities. It is usually expressed as a rate: the number of cases of disease per 1,000 persons at risk.

Most rapid approach path: An optimal path that moves the state variable(s) as rapidly as possible to the optimal steady state.

Multicollinearity: The tendency of associated variables to change together, complicating the identification of one effect from another.

Multilateral Environmental Agreement (MEA): An international environmental agreement signed by two or more countries, usually addressing a specific environmental concern or issue. See, for example, CBD, CITES, Kyoto Protocol, and Montreal Protocol.

N

Naive thinking: Thinking or modeling that is both simplistic in its scope and narrow in its depth.

Nash equilibrium: The outcome(s) of a game, determined by the fact that for each player, given every other player's actions, there is no other strategy for the player that makes him or her better off than the strategy they have chosen. There may be one, none, or multiple Nash equilibria in a game.

National accounts: A statistical framework for analyzing economic activity and its impact on the wealth of an economy.

Natural capital: Naturally occurring assets that are either used in production or provide nonmarket services. Refers to the earth's natural resources and the ecological systems that provide vital life-support services to society and all living things.

NDP: Net Domestic Product equals GDP minus depreciation on the produced capital stock. Sometimes it is defined more broadly as GDP minus depreciation of the produced capital stock and depletion of the natural capital stock (see *EDP*).

Negligence-based liability: Liability for actions that arises only if it can be proven that the persons responsible were negligent by contravening accepted practice or existing regulations or standards.

Net investment: The difference between the total receipts generated by a stock of assets and the amount consumed.

Non-cooperative Nash equilibrium: Equilibrium concept in which actors operate independently under the assumption that the actions (choices) of other actors are fixed.

Non-mobile factors: Factor inputs that cannot move to another country.

Non-point source pollution: A form of pollution whose source and quantity are very difficult to identify. An example is nitrogen run-off from a farm.

North American Free Trade Agreement (NAFTA): An agreement signed by the United States, Canada, and Mexico to form a free trade area. It went into effect on January 1, 1994.

O

Obsolescence: A decrease in the value of successive vintages of an asset over time attributable either to changes in tastes or technological progress.

Occam's razor: Maxim that the simplest logical model that addresses the research problem is preferred over alternative models.

Opportunity cost of time: The value of time spent engaged in activities that do not contribute to an individual's income.

Optimal paths: Trajectories for the control and state variables in dynamic optimization problems.

Option price: A state-independent measure of value, arising from the incorporation of uncertainty into a model of welfare calculation. Option price measures the willingness to pay for a given project, regardless of the state of nature that is eventually realized.

Option value: Often referred to as an additional measure of value associated with demand uncertainty. However, option value is actually the difference between the expected value of consumer surplus and option price. This is not an independent measure of value and is also often confused with *Quasi option value* (see below).

Organization for Economic Cooperation and Development (OECD): An international organization that helps governments tackle the economic, social and governance challenges of a globalized economy.

Overreach thinking: Thinking that tries to be both broad in scope and detailed, but is beyond our mental capacities.

P

Pareto criterion: A criterion or decision rule used to compare different states of the world. By this criterion, unanimity is needed to move to one state of the world from another.

Pareto efficiency: An outcome is Pareto efficient if it is not possible to make someone better off without making someone else worse off.

Pareto principle: In an endowment economy, an allocation of goods to agents is Pareto optimal if no other allocation of the same goods would be preferred by every agent.

Particulate matter: Microscopic matter found in the air that has a deleterious effect on human health.

Passive use value: An economic value attached to an environmental or natural resource that is not based on the tangible human use of the resource. It may include existence values, bequest values, altruistic values, and option values.

Path dependence: A situation occurring where the order of the evaluation may affect the outcome. Path dependence of price and income variables may affect the welfare measure estimated.

Pecuniary externality: An outcome that arises whenever an individual, agent or firm undertakes an action that has an external effect that is transmitted through the price system.

Pelagic fish: Species, such as sardines and herring, commonly caught near the ocean surface and that typically congregate or school in large numbers.

Perfect foresight: A model format in which it is assumed that the time paths of all variables are known.

Performance test: A test at the final optimization period in the optimal extraction of a non-renewable resource that must be satisfied if the resource is being extracted optimally.

Period doubling: Term used to describe behavior of dynamic systems whereby a small change in a parameter doubles the period of time it takes for the system to travel between attractors.

Persistent organic pollutants: Chlorinated organic compounds, such as DDT, dioxin and PCBs, that persist for a long time in the environment and bioaccumulate in the food chain.

Pigouvian taxes: A tax on firms based on the external costs they impose upon others. Ideally the tax is set equal to the marginal external cost.

Point source pollution: A form of pollution whose source and flow is straightforward to identify. An example is phosphorus emissions from a sewage treatment plant.

Polluter pays principle: Concept that those who pollute should bear the costs of abatement and remedial actions associated with pollution.

Pollution abatement: Efforts to reduce the amount of pollution produced.

Pollution haven: Countries with relatively less stringent environmental regulations than other countries.

Pollution haven hypothesis: An argument that free trade will encourage polluting activities to relocate from countries with more stringent environmental regulations (e.g. developed countries with relatively higher incomes) to less developed and low income countries. Thus, over time, local pollution will rise in low income countries and fall in high income countries.

Porter hypothesis: The notion that stricter environmental regulations and standards can lead to unanticipated technological innovations that may reduce overall production costs, thereby reducing both environmental degradation and total production costs.

Potential Pareto improvement: A decision rule whereby one state of the world is preferred to another when those who gain from the change are sufficiently better off to compensate the losers, even if such transfers are not undertaken.

Precautionary principle: A principle that states that a lack of scientific consensus about undesirable uncertain events (such as climate change) is not a justification for inaction to prevent or reduce the likelihood of the events.

Principle of optimality: The fundamental basis of dynamic programming that permits us to solve a set of smaller problems for each decision stage, such that the value of the state variable in the next period depends only on the value of the state variable in the current period, and the decision in the current period.

Prisoner's dilemma: This is a "zero-sum" or win-lose game. If players do not cooperate, then both end up being worse off than if they had cooperated. In other words each player's dominant strategy yields the lowest possible joint payoffs of the game (and where all players would have been better off playing cooperatively).

Private good: Goods or resources that are rival in use (one person's use precludes someone else from using it) and have the characteristic that it is relatively easy to exclude others from using them.

Probable reserve: The economically extractable part of an indicated (and in some cases, measured) mineral resource.

Produced capital: Assets that have been produced such as roads, factories, and machines.

Proved reserve: The economically extractable part of a measured resource.

Public bad: The opposite of a public good. An example is pollution. Once it is produced it is hard to exclude any one from being harmed by it (non-excludability) and harm to one individual does not impinge upon harm to another individual (non-rivalry).

Public good: A good that is both non-exclusive and non-rival. A good is non-exclusive if it is not possible to prevent use by others. A good is non-rival if benefits enjoyed by one individual do not impinge upon benefits enjoyed by another individual.

Q

Quasi option value: The value of forthcoming information conditional on choosing a reversible option. It is a value premium associated with avoiding the irreversibility or maintaining flexibility while learning about the situation. At times referred to as *Option value* (see above).

Quasi-rent: Traditionally defined as earnings to a factor of production temporarily fixed in supply. Redefined as the short-run rents that arise from the judicious use of labor and capital (physical, human, and social).

Quota busting: The deliberate harvesting and selling of fish in excess of the amount of individual transferable quotas owned, purchased or leased.

R

Random utility model: A theory of choice that assumes that an individual's utility over options is characterized by a systematic component and a random component. The random component arises from the researcher's inability to observe all elements of the individual's utility function. Given assumptions of the structure of the random component this theory can be used to estimate preference parameters from observed individual choices.

Reaction function: A relationship where one firm's optimum (best) output is a function of the output of a second firm.

Receipt: A payment made to the owner of an asset for services provided by the asset in that period.

Recruitment: The number or weight of a species that enters a population. In fisheries, recruitment frequently refers to the weight of fish that become vulnerable to harvesting at a given point in time.

Relative scarcity: Physical and price measures of the scarcity of non-renewable resources which may increase or decrease over time.

Reserve-to-use ratio: Ratio of total reserves of a mineral to annual amount of use or depletion.

Resilience: The ability of a system to return to its former state following a shock or disturbance. It can be measured by the relative size of the disturbance, or by the time it takes for the system to return to its former state.

Resource rent tax: A tax or charge on non-renewable resource extraction equal to a fixed proportion of rents in excess of extraction and exploration costs, including a return on the capital employed.

Reversal paradox: A potential problem that may arise when using the Pareto criterion to compare two inefficient (second-best) states of the world A and B. The paradox arises because it is possible under certain preferences for A to be preferred to B, but also for B to be preferred to A.

Ricardian rent: Returns from the sale of units of an output that exceed both the variable costs of production and the return to the fixed factor in an alternative use.

Riparian rights: A legal doctrine that provides property owners limited rights to use water flowing past their property.

Risk: Future events that can be assigned objective probabilities (based on past events and statistical analysis).

Risk aversion: Desire to avoid uncertainty. Risk aversion is usually quantified by the mathematical expected value that one is willing to forego in order to get greater certainty.

Risk diversification: A strategy for reducing risk whereby the net returns of assets, projects or actions are chosen so as to reduce the overall variance of the aggregate net returns.

Risk pooling: The sharing of risk between economic agents. Risk pooling is a useful strategy when faced by risky events with very high costs.

Roy's identity: Mathematical theorem identifying the connection between Hicksian demand and the indirect utility function.

S

Safe minimum standard: When undertaking actions in the face of uncertainty, this standard requires that there be a presumption in favor of not harming the environment unless the opportunity costs of that action are very high. The notion that by acting today, with appropriate management tools, society can guard against the potential of very high costs in the future.

Satisficing rule: Decision rule that ensures a minimum set of criteria are met or satisfied.

Scale effect: It is associated with the increase in overall pollution created by an increase in the level of economic activity.

Scarcity rent: Return to the owner of the resource that arises from its limited supply. For a mine owner, it equals the user cost multiplied by the amount of mineral extracted.

Scientific method: An approach or method of inquiry whereby propositions or models are formulated and are then tested to see whether they conform to empirical observations.

Schaefer model: Name given to a logistic growth function commonly used in population models in fisheries.

Scoping and sequencing: Two elements often identified in stated preference surveys. Scoping examines whether respondents' values are sensitive to the scope of the public good being valued. Sequencing refers to the fact that the order of the valuation questions may affect the valuation level.

Second best: An allocation of resources which is efficient subject to the presence of some constraint (such as a tax) that prevents a first-best allocation.

Self-organizing criticality: Term used to describe the behavior found in complex systems, where at certain points or thresholds, small changes in one part of the system can result in very large changes or phase transitions in the overall system.

Severance tax: A tax payable equal to a fixed proportion of the value of mineral extracted.

Shadow price: The marginal value of an asset or resource that is determined from an optimization problem. In general, the shadow price does not equal its market price.

Shephard's lemma: Mathematical theorem identifying the connection between Marshallian demand and the expenditure function.

Shut-down point: The point at which the user cost of a non-renewable resource is zero and it is no longer profitable to extract it.

Simultaneity bias: A violation of the classical linear regression model due to correlation between the dependent variable and the error term.

Site quality: A measure of the potential productivity of a site typically expressed by the height of trees at different ages.

Small open economy: Open economy refers to a country that trades commodities with other countries. Small refers to the fact that the country's volume of trade relative to world trade is so small as to have no effect upon the market prices of commodities.

SNA: The official system of national accounts used by most countries in the world.

Social discount rate: The rate at which society discounts future costs and benefits.

Softwood species: The mainly cone-bearing coniferous species that have historically provided the majority of commercial forest products such as lumber and plywood for building materials, and pulp for paper, cardboard, and newsprint.

State dependence: A measurement that is conditional on different states of the world, and may change depending on which state is realized.

Stated preference methods: Survey based techniques which elicit respondent preferences for different states of the world or attributes of alternatives.

State variable: Variable that helps describe the "state" of a dynamic system and that can only be indirectly determined by control variables.

Statutory protected areas: Areas (typically landmasses) that are protected from encroachment by legal statute.

Stock effect: Term given to the circumstance where, for a given level of extraction of a non-renewable resource, costs will be higher the lower are the remaining reserves.

Stock pollutant: Pollutants whose effects accumulate over time and dissipate slowly.

Stock externality: A negative technological externality in the harvesting of resources whereby an increased harvest or yield reduces the yield of others and may also increase their harvesting costs.

Stock-recruitment models: Population models that relate future recruitment to the current population or biomass.

Strategic behavior: Behavior that seeks to maximize the outcome benefits depending on expected behavior of other firms or individuals.

Strict liability: Liability where persons are liable for all damages associated with their actions whether or not they were negligent, or in violation of the existing standards and practices.

Strong sustainability: The view that economic activity in an economy is sustainable only if the produced, natural and human capital stocks are all nondecreasing over time. This is a strong concept of sustainability since it does not allow for produced or human capital to be substituted for natural capital.

Subsidies: Payment by government to individual/firm without expectation of the production of a good.

Surplus yield models: Population models that consider only the interaction between the total population and the growth in the population.

Sustainability: The notion whether a pattern of resource use can be continued indefinitely.

Sustainable development: According to most definitions, an economy is following a path of sustainable development if it allows the present generation to meet its needs without reducing the ability of future generations to meet their needs. Sometimes it is defined more precisely as a situation where an economy's capital stock is not decreasing over time (see weak and strong sustainability).

System: A collection of interconnected and interrelated components where overall behavior or function cannot be understood without comprehending the causal loops and feedbacks between the components.

System thinking: A holistic approach to thinking and modeling where there is sufficient breadth to understand key feedbacks across systems, but only at a level of detail that is necessary to understand the underlying system (rather than component) dynamics.

T

Takings: Changes in regulations that materially damage people's property rights.

Tariff: A tax on trade, usually an import tariff but sometimes used to denote an export tax. Tariffs may be ad valorem (tax depends upon market price) or unit (specific amount).

Technical efficiency: The maximum possible output for any level of input.

Technique effect: When consumers view environmental quality as a normal good, then increases in income will result in an increased willingness to pay higher abatement costs. The government will be able to increase pollution taxes which will, in turn, encourage firms to undertake more abatement. In this way, pollution per unit of output will decline.

Technological externality: An inefficient outcome that arises whenever an individual, agent or firm undertakes an action that has an external affect, other than through the price system, on the utility function of consumers or production function of producers. A technology externality may be either positive or negative depending on whether it benefits or harms other parties.

Terms of trade: The relative price of a country's exports compared to its imports.

Terms-of-trade effect: When a country is large, then it is able to alter its terms of trade.

Territorial user rights in fisheries: Property rights that assign a given area of the sea or ocean to a community or individual or company.

Trade liberalization: The actions taken to reduce the barriers to international trade, e.g., reduction in tariffs on traded goods and relaxation of non-tariff barriers.

Tragedy of the commons: Term given to the overexploitation or overuse (in an economic sense) of common-pool resources due to the absence of property rights.

Transactions costs: The costs associated with the negotiation, exchange and enforcement of property rights.

Transferable pollution permits: Rights to pollute that can be traded among polluters.

Transboundary water: A body of water that is shared by or forms the boundary between two political jurisdictions.

Transition equation: The equation that determines the dynamic behavior of a state variable in a dynamic programming problem.

Transversality condition: A terminal time condition in an optimal control problem.

Travel cost model: A revealed preference technique that uses costs of gaining access to a non-market resource as a proxy for its market price. From this the Hicksian demand and consumer surplus, representing the value of the resource, can be defined.

Trawl gear: Fish harvesting gear that consists of cone-shaped nets that are dragged through the water near the sea bottom or in mid-water.

Troll gear: Fish harvesting gear that employs lines and hooks with lures and bait that are set to lines and rods.

U

Uncertainty: Future events for which we can, at best, assign subjective probabilities and for which there is very little objective basis for predicting their likelihood.

United Nations Environment Programme (UNEP): A global non-governmental organization whose goal is to provides leadership and encourage partnership to achieve sustainable development (use of the environment so that human beings can improve their quality of life without compromising that of future generations).

User cost: The current value of the shadow price of a non-renewable resource which represents its marginal value in situ, or in the ground.

Use value: Value derived from actual use of a good or service, including consumptive, non-consumptive, and indirect uses. This is a potential source of bias in valuation of the environment.

Usufructory rights: A legal principle that allows someone to use a natural resource without owning it.

Utilitarianism: A moral theory that argues that decision-making should attempt to maximize the greatest good for the greatest number of individuals.

V

Value of information: The value associated with forthcoming information in light of current uncertainty.

Value of statistical life (VSL): The value of reducing the risk of death. Reducing mortality risks by 1 in 10,000 for a population of 10,000 people is statistically equivalent to reducing 1 mortality or 1 statistical life.

W

Warm glow: The tendency to alter behavior because of the general "cause" associated with the program, rather than the specifics of the program itself.

Water market: A legal institution where agents may buy and sell (or lease) the rights to specified quantities of water.

Weak complementarity: The notion that an environmental service or attribute (such as the quantity and size of fish in a lake) is an exogenous characteristic that determines the utility from consuming a marketed good or service (such as a fishing rod and gear). More precisely, weak complementarity implies that the marginal utility of the environmental service is zero when the amount demanded of the marketed good or service is zero.

Weak sustainability: The view that economic activity in an economy is sustainable if the total capital stock broadly defined to include all produced, natural and human capital is nondecreasing over time. This is a weak concept of sustainability in the sense that it allows produced and human capital to be substituted for natural capital.

Welfare economics: The framework for undertaking normative judgments about different patterns of economic activity.

Willingness to pay / accept: The acceptable bid amount that an individual is prepared to pay/receive for acquiring/giving up the good in question.

World Health Organization (WHO): The World Health Organization, the United Nations specialized agency for health, was established on April 7, 1948. WHO's objective, as set out in its Constitution, is the attainment by all peoples of the highest possible level of health.

X

Y

Yield-per-recruit: The total yield or catch of fish from the time an age class enters a fishery until it completely disappears due to fishing and natural mortality, divided by the total number or weight of recruits.

Z

INDEX